CATALOGUE OF
THE GRAHAM BROWN
AND LLOYD COLLECTIONS

Professor Thomas Graham Brown.
Photograph by Basil R. Goodfellow. By permission of Peter Lloyd Esq CBE.

MOUNTAINEERING

CATALOGUE OF THE GRAHAM BROWN
AND LLOYD COLLECTIONS
IN THE
NATIONAL LIBRARY OF SCOTLAND

NATIONAL LIBRARY OF SCOTLAND
EDINBURGH
1994

© **NATIONAL LIBRARY OF SCOTLAND**

First published 1994

**A Cataloguing in Publication record is available
from the British Library.**

Designed and typeset direct from word processor diskette by
Thameslink Desktop Publishing Ltd
99-101, St. Leonard's Road, Windsor, Berkshire SL4 3BZ
Tel (0753) 863356

Printed by
Bell & Bain Limited
303 Burnfield Road, Thornliebank, Glasgow G46 7UQ
Tel 041 649 5697

Printed on Archive Text 90gsm

Cover illustration
The region of Seracs, from Edward T. Coleman,
Scenes from the Snow-fields of Mont Blanc. London, 1859.

ISBN 0 902220 98 5

CONTENTS

PREFACE

Like many great research libraries the National Library of Scotland has been fortunate in the generosity of a great number of private donors, many of whom have given, bequeathed or assisted in the purchase of special collections, whose wide range of books and other materials has greatly enriched the quality of the Library's resources.

Among the fields in which the Library's holdings of books deposited in terms of successive Copyright Acts have been greatly enhanced by gifts, pride of place goes to Alpine and mountaineering literature. Two major collections bequeathed in the 1960s, together with British material deposited via legal deposit, have made the National Library of Scotland one of the principal European centres for the study of Alpinism and of mountaineering in general. The two benefactors to whom the Library owes these outstanding collections are Professor Thomas Graham Brown, who bequeathed his collection (some 20,000 items) to the Library in 1965, along with the residue of his estate to provide for additions to it; and Robert Wylie Lloyd, who had earlier bequeathed his collection of 1,659 volumes in 1958. It is, therefore, appropriate that the present volume should comprise a catalogue of these two exceptional collections.

Thanks are due to Dr Alex Cain and Miss Alison Harvey Wood, Assistant Keepers in the Department of Printed Books, who compiled the catalogue and prepared it for the press; to Mr John Bowles, Senior Research Assistant in the Department of Printed Books, who contributed substantially to the latter stages of the Catalogue's preparation; and to Monica McCluskey, Kenneth Maclennon, Judith Miller, Ian Scott, Michael Staley and John Woods for their assistance in preparing the data for the Catalogue. The costs of publishing the catalogue have been met from the Graham Brown Trust Fund, and thanks are due to the Trustees of the Fund for offering their encouragement to the proposal to produce the present work.

Ann Matheson
Keeper
Department of Printed Books

August 1993

R.W. Lloyd (centre) with his favourite guide Josef Pollinger and son Adolf.
Alpine Journal, vol. 54 no. 208 (1944).

INTRODUCTION

The National Library of Scotland is fortunate in having strong collections in the fields of mountaineering, and of Arctic and Antarctic exploration - very appropriately for a country that has produced mountaineers like Norman Collie, Harold Raeburn, Dougal Haston and Hamish MacInnes as well as Polar explorers like Sir John Ross and his nephew Sir James Clark Ross.

The present Catalogue lists mountaineering collections from the two important bequests by Thomas Graham Brown (1882-1965) and by Robert Wylie Lloyd (1868-1958) housed in the Department of Printed Books, together with additions to these collections purchased from the fund bequeathed to the Library by Graham Brown. The Catalogue does not, however, include the many books on mountaineering received by the Library under successive Copyright Acts. Maps and manuscripts associated with the Graham Brown collection have not been included in the present Catalogue[1], but it does include Polar material, which has been purchased over the last two decades from the Graham Brown Fund. A shelf-catalogue has already been published of the Wordie collection, given to the Library by Sir James Mann Wordie (1889-1962), the geologist and explorer.[2]

ROBERT WYLIE LLOYD

Robert Wylie Lloyd was born in Lancashire. He appears to have had an unhappy and impoverished childhood, a fact that may have influenced his ruthless determination to succeed in business. This he managed to do admirably, and he devoted much time and money to compiling an extensive range of collections on subjects as diverse as oriental art, European paintings, Turner drawings, Alpine books and illustrations, and entomology - his bookplate incorporates a beetle and a climber's ice-axe. His collection of over five thousand coloured aquatints and drawings of Swiss scenes, reputedly comparable even with those in Swiss public institutions, is now in the British Museum. The Alpine books were left to the National Library of Scotland.[3]

Lloyd first visited the Alps in 1896, and was elected to the Alpine Club in December 1901, having been rejected for membership on a previous application on the grounds of too little experience. He was later elected one of its Vice-Presidents, and was continuously active in the Club until his death. His main climbing grounds were the Valais and Mont Blanc, though in later life he spent much time in the Dolomites. However, it is said that it was never safe to assume that he was unacquainted with any district, even Lapland. He regretted very much that he had not visited the Himalayas in his climbing days which, unfortunately, came to an end after a serious operation in 1937. He financed several mountaineering expeditions and, as Treasurer of the Mount Everest Committee, he was energetic in raising money for the expedition of 1953. It was said that 'his assiduity in raising funds for Everest was only matched by his extreme reluctance to part with them'. 'To the outside world', wrote his obituarist in *The Times*, 'Lloyd was reticent and a hard man, but in the small inner circle of his friends he was kindness itself, well read and knowledgeable and a delightful companion.'[4]

His book collection is idiosyncratic in several respects. One is the existence of numerous multiple copies, sometimes as many as five of a particular book. Another is the quantity of material which relates not strictly to mountaineering, but to Switzerland in general - travels, history, and even religious history. This makes the

Graham Brown on the Tour Ronde prospecting his future route
on the Pear buttress, Brenva, Mont Blanc, July 1931.
Photograph by Basil R. Goodfellow. By permission of C.L. Jones Esq.

collection an important source for many aspects of Swiss studies and, indeed, for the history of European travel in general, as Lloyd acquired many books in which Switzerland represented only part of a more extensive tour. There are books of all kinds in the collection, serious and chatty, technical and popular, early and modern, common and rare. The browser of the catalogue may have the impression that it was essentially a *collector's* library rather than a *user's* library. The copies are in good condition, and many are unopened.

THOMAS GRAHAM BROWN

Thomas Graham Brown was born in Edinburgh, and he became as distinguished a physiologist as he was a mountaineer. He was Professor of Physiology in the University of Wales from 1920 to 1947, and was elected a Fellow of the Royal Society in 1927. He was over thirty when he started climbing, and his first Alpine climb took place when he was 42. Thereafter, he made a major ascent every summer from 1924 to 1938 in the Alps, the Himalayas or Alaska, and as late as 1952 he climbed the Matterhorn, thinking that in his seventieth year, he should seize the opportunity which might not occur again. He was a prolific writer, contributing numerous articles to climbing periodicals, and his book *Brenva*[5], which describes his ascent of Mont Blanc by the Brenva face, is a mountaineering classic. As Charles Evans wrote in the *Dictionary of National Biography*, 'in the thirties he was one of the few British mountaineers whose Alpine reputation was internationally recognised as outstanding.'[6]

His collection of books is remarkable in that it was essentially a practical mountaineer's library, and the books bear signs of having been much used. His house in Manor Place in Edinburgh was a centre where young mountaineers could enjoy his generosity in giving advice, and in lending them his books.[7] His library contained vast quantities of extracts from periodicals and volumes of press cuttings, and of particular value are the many volumes of extracts, especially from the *Alpine Journal*, arranged by geographical area. His collection reflects his personal activities more than Lloyd's, containing, for example, his own working proofs of *Brenva*, and of the *Alpine Journal*, of which he was editor from 1949 to 1953.

Thomas Graham Brown was also a distinguished photographer. He was one of the first to see the scope of miniature photography, and bought one of the first Leica cameras. It was his habit to record his climbs in meticulous detail, firing off a dozen or so shots in all directions at every halt. These would all be carefully written up in his notebook, and properly catalogued.[8] This huge collection of negatives, prints and slides, together with the documentation, are also in the Library.

Graham Brown also had the foresight to leave a generous sum of money to the Library along with his books[9], the income from which is used to add material from all periods to the collection, so that it remains a *current* collection, rather than a static one which would increasingly be of historical importance only.

CURRENT COLLECTING POLICY

As the Library is privileged to receive, by legal deposit, copies of all current British publications[10], the income from the Graham Brown Fund is devoted almost entirely to the purchase of non-British publications. These purchases continue to reflect Graham Brown's keen interest in the Alps and, to a lesser extent, the Himalayas. In addition, books in all languages, covering all the world's mountainous regions from Alaska to Antarctica, are bought. Material of a historical nature - biographies of climbers, histories of climbs and climbing - is bought substantially, in all languages, as are climbing guides relating to all parts of the world. Mountain photography, much of it produced in Japan and of superb quality, is acquired. The great explosion of interest in mountain recreation is reflected in the purchase of material on such topics as backpacking, hill-walking and mountain-biking, and the environmental issues which accompany them. Manuscripts and maps which shed light on any aspect of mountains and mountaineering are also bought.

Polar material is actively purchased. While the emphasis on discovery and exploration has been maintained, other topics such as the oceanography of Polar seas, the history of Polar whaling and international relations in Polar regions are also covered to a lesser extent.

The Graham Brown Fund also enables the Library to purchase substantial collections of mountaineering and Polar materials such as the photographic archive of Fanny Bullock Workman, the intrepid Himalayan explorer and mountaineer (subsequently, Mrs Workman's manuscripts have been placed on deposit in the Library). Another substantial recent acquisition is a large collection of glass lantern slides of Scotland and other mountain areas taken by Arthur Gardner and his brother Hugh during the years 1920 to 1935. The Fund also enables the Library to purchase important bibliographic rarities, including recently one of the only three copies printed of a 1909 de luxe edition of Sir Ernest Shackleton's *Heart of the Antarctic*.

The existence of these fine collections has made the National Library of Scotland a prime centre for mountaineering and Polar studies, and has already attracted a number of major gifts. The Library is particularly anxious further to enhance its strengths by the acquisition of personal accounts of climbing expeditions, climbing diaries, and correspondence relating to mountaineering. The Keeper of Printed Books and the Keeper of Manuscripts would be glad to be informed of private papers or collections of books that ought to be preserved.

John R. Bowles
Alex M. Cain
Alison E. Harvey Wood
August 1993

REFERENCES

[1]. An inventory of the manuscript material and a shelf-list of the maps are available for consultation in the Library's Department of Manuscripts and Map Library respectively. The manuscripts from the Lloyd collection are described and indexed in v.IV of the Library's *Catalogue of Manuscripts*.

[2]. *Shelf-catalogue of the Wordie collection of Polar exploration* (Boston, Mass., 1964.) The Wordie collection contained his set of *Meddelelser om Grønland*. The Library makes it a matter of policy to acquire continuously this essential tool for Arctic research in all its dimensions.

[3]. 'In memoriam: Robert Wylie Lloyd', *Alpine Journal 63* (1958), 232-8.

[4]. *The Times*, 30 April 1958.

[5]. T. Graham Brown, *Brenva* (London, 1944).

[6]. *Dictionary of National Biography, 1961-1970*, 151-2.

[7]. 'In memoriam: T. Graham Brown', *Scottish Mountaineering Club Journal 28* (1966), 246-8.

[8]. 'In memoriam: Thomas Graham Brown', *Alpine Journal 71* (1966), 193-4.

[9]. *Thomas Graham Brown 1882-1965* (Edinburgh: National Library of Scotland, 1982). Exhibition catalogue.

[10]. All books received in this way are listed in the Library's General Catalogue of Printed Books, and can be consulted in the Reading Rooms. The Library's on-line catalogue, which currently contains material catalogued since 1978, can also be consulted on the JANET network.

CONTENT AND ARRANGEMENT OF THE CATALOGUE

The present Catalogue contains everything received in the Library up to 30 June 1987. It was compiled from entries in the National Library's General Catalogue of Printed Books. As there are three sequences in the General Catalogue, each employing different rules and containing various amounts of information, a certain amount of editing had to be undertaken to produce conformity, and this also led to the choice of entry by title as the main approach. There is, however, an index of names of persons and corporate bodies, as authors, editors, publishers, and also as subjects. There are also indexes of series, and of non-book material which, being untitled, does not fit easily into a title catalogue. It is intended that additions to the Catalogue will be issued in microfiche, for which a pocket has been provided on the reverse endpaper.

The structure of the title entry is:

> Title / author.   Edition.   Place, date.   [Series.]   Notes.
> Shelfmark.   Record number.

Names are given in the form used in the *Alpine Club Library Catalogue* (1982), if they exist there; otherwise according to the *Anglo-American Cataloguing Rules*, 2nd ed. (1978).

MICROFICHE SUPPLEMENT

As has already been mentioned in the Introduction to this Catalogue, additions to the Graham Brown collection are regularly acquired. In order that the Catalogue should remain up-to-date, a first microfiche supplement has been produced, which includes all Graham Brown acquisitions catalogued between 30 June 1987 and 31 December 1992. This supplement is placed in a special pocket in the inside of the back cover of this catalogue. Future cumulated supplements will be published at 3-yearly intervals, and purchasers of the Catalogue are invited to request them by sending in the form in the microfiche pocket.

CATALOGUE

'View of the precipitous rocks which dominate Port Leopold'.
J.R. Bellot. *Voyage aux mers polaires*. Paris, 1880.

-A-

A chacun sa montagne / Giuseppe Mazzotti; traduit par E. Gaillard. Chambéry, 1945. Ill. Translated from *La montagna presa in giro*.
GB/A.1210.   a001.

A fil di cielo: impressioni di vita e ambiente alpini / Attilio Viriglio. Torino, 1929. Ill. [La piccozza e la penna.]
GB/B.290(15) (impf.).   a002.

A Formazza: edizione critica degli statuti concessi alla valle da Gian Galeazzo Sforza nell'anno 1487 / compilata da Alberto Alessi Anghini. [Omegna], 1971.
GB/B.366(8).   a003.

A l'assaut du Kangchenjunga, 8580 m. / Paul Bauer. Paris, 1932. Ill. [Collection d'études, de documents et de témoignages pour servir à l'histoire de notre temps.] Translated from *Kampf um den Himalaja*.
GB.1312(29); GB.1333(27).   a004.

A l'ombre des clochers du val d'Aosta / Robert Berton. Genova, 1970. Ill.
GB/C.22(14).   a005.

A la conquête du Mont Everest / C.K. Howard-Bury; traduction française par G. Moreau. Paris, 1923. Ill., map. Translated from *Mount Everest*.
GB.805.   a006.

A la découverte des bêtes de l'Alpe / René Pierre Bille. Paris, 1968. Ill. [Visages de la nature.]
GB/A.433.   a007.

A la veillée: récits divers, contes et croquis vaudois pour jeunes et vieux / Alfred Cérésole. Lausanne, [1889?].
GB/A.1340.   a008.

A mes montagnes / Walter Bonatti; [traduit de l'italien par F. Germain]. [Paris], 1972. Ill., maps. [Sempervivum; 38.]
GB/A.988(2).   a009.

A scuola di roccia / Cesare Maestri. 2a ed. Rocca San Casciano, 1966. Ill.
GB/A.141.   a010.

A scuola di roccia / Cesare Maestri. [Milan], 1981. Ill., ports. [Le guide Vallardi.]
GB/A.2021(7).   a011.

A te, Alpe … : liriche / Carlo Pelosi. Bergamo, 1933.
GB/B.377(37).   a012.

A travers l'Engadine, la Valteline, le Tyrol du Sud et les lacs d'Italie supérieure / Stephen Liégeard. Paris, 1877.
GB/A.711.   a013.

A travers l'Oberland bernois / A. Muller. Mulhouse, 1891.
GB/A.1441.   a014.

A travers le Tyrol / Jules Gourdault. Tours, 1884. Ill., map.
GB/A.2127.   a015.

A travers les Alpes / Edouard Gachot. Paris, [1900?]. Ill.
GB/A.1083.   a016.

A travers les Alpes autrichiennes / Maurice Grandjean. Tours, [1896?]. Ill.
GB/B.417.   a017.

A travers les Alpes françaises: carnet d'un touriste. Paris, [n.d.]. Ill., ports., music.
Lloyd.1622(2).   a018.

A travers les Alpes françaises: onze jours chez les grands guides / Georges Barbarin. Paris, [1950]. Ill., map, ports.
GB/A.1081.   a019.

A travers les Pyrénées / Emile Labroue. Paris, [1900]. Ill.
GB/B.112.   a020.

A travers les Vosges / Fritz Ehrenberg. Zürich, [1890]. Ill., maps. [L'Europe illustrée; 146-9.] Translated from *In die Vogesen*.
GB/A.835(6).   a021.

A tu per tu con Indios delle Ande / Mario Fantin. Rovereto, 1968. Ill., map. [Alle soglie della civiltà.]
GB/B.297.   a022.

A tu per tu con Jivaros e Colorados / Mario Fantin. Rovereto, 1967. Ill., map. [Alle soglie della civiltà.]
GB/B.295.   a023.

A tu per tu con le Alpi / Tita Piaz. [Bologna], 1966. Ill.
GB/A.1372.   a024.

A tu per tu con Senufo e Baule / Mario Fantin. Rovereto, 1968. Ill., map. [Alle soglie della civiltà.]
GB/B.296.   a025.

A.E. Nordenskiölds polarfärder, och A.E. Nordenskiöld såsom geolog / A.G. Nathorst. Stockholm, 1902. Ill., maps, port. Pp.[141]-224 of *Ymer*, 1902, h.2.
GB.1335(53).   a026.

Aasivissuit — the great summer camp: archaeological, ethnographical and zoo-archaeological studies of a caribou-hunting site in West Greenland / Bjarne Grønnow, Morton Meldgaard and Jørn Berglund Nielsen. Copenhagen, 1983. Ill., map. [Meddelelser om Grønland. Man & society; 5.]
GB/A.1820/5.   a027.

L'**abate** Amato Gorret / Lino Vaccari. Torino, 1909. Ports. Pp.[3]-21 of the *Bollettino del Club Alpino Italiano*, vol.39, no.72.
GB.1881(14).   a028.

L'**ABC** per la montagna / Dieter Seibert. Milano, 1974. Ill., maps.
GB/A.2032(3).   a029.

The **Abendberg**: an Alpine retreat founded by Dr. Güggenbuhl for the treatment of infant cretins / L.G., Geneva. Edinburgh, 1848.
Lloyd.182.   a030.

Abenteuer Eiger / Toni Hiebeler. Rüschlikon-Zürich, 1973. Ill.
GB/A.1135.   a031.

Abenteuer Everest: durchs Sherpaland zur Chomolongma / Toni Hiebeler. Rüschlikon-Zürich, 1974. Ill., maps.
GB/A.1918.   a032.

L'**Abetone** e dintorni: itinerari naturalistici e sci-alpinistici / Giordano Mazzolini. Nuova ed. aggiornata. Pisa, [1985].
GB/A.2193.   a033.

Abode of snow: a history of Himalayan exploration and mountaineering / Kenneth Mason. London, 1955. Ill., maps, ports.
GB.712.   a034.

The **abode** of snow: observations on a journey from Chinese Tibet to the Indian Caucasus, through the upper valleys of the Himalaya / Andrew Wilson. Edinburgh, 1875.
GB.925; Lloyd.1124; Lloyd.1157.   a035.

The **abominable** snow-women / Dorothy Braxton. Wellington, 1969. Ill., maps, ports.
GB/A.1599.   a036.

Above the snow line: mountaineering sketches between 1870 and 1880 / Clinton Dent. London, 1885. Ill.
GB.368; GB.369; GB.411; Lloyd.473; Lloyd 473A,B.
                                                    a037.

Abseits der Piste: 100 stille Skitouren in den Alpen / Walter Pause. 7., neubearb. Aufl. München, [1967]. Ill., maps.
GB/A.170.   a038.

Abstracts of the Proceedings / Geological Society. No.550-743. London, 1890-1901.
Lloyd.1605(15) (impf.).   a039.

L'**Académie** de Genève: esquisse d'une histoire abrégée de l'Académie fondée par Calvin en 1559 / J. E. Cellerier; [edited by Auguste Bouvier]. Genève, 1872.
Lloyd.1615(9).   a040.

Accanto a me la montagna / Spiro Dalla Porta Xidias. Bologna, [1963]. Ill. [Voci dai monti; 1.]
GB/A.845.   a041.

Access to mountains / J. Parker Smith. [Edinburgh], 1891. Pp.259-72 of *Blackwood's Magazine*, Aug.1891.
GB.1313(5).   a042.

Accidents in North American mountaineering, including Canada and the United States. No.30-33, 1977-80. Banff, Alta, 1977-80.
GB/B.525(11).   a043.

Account of a botanical excursion in the Alps of the Canton of Valais, Switzerland, in August, 1835; and catalogue of the plants collected, with occasional remarks / R. J. Shuttleworth. Edinburgh, [1835?]. From the *Magazine of Zoology and Botany*, no.7,12.
Lloyd.863.   a044.

An **account** of an ascent to the summit of Mont Blanc, in August, 1819 / J. Undrell. [London, 1821.]
GB.672; Lloyd.861.   a045.

An **account** of an ascent to the summit of Mont Blanc, in August, 1819 / J. Undrell. [London, 1821.] Pp.373-82 of *Annals of Philosophy*, May 1821. Lloyd.860. a046.

Account of Colonel Beaufoy's journey to the summit of Mount Blanc. [Edinburgh, 1817.] Pp.59-61 of *Blackwood's Edinburgh Magazine*, April 1817. GB.662(2). a047.

An **account** of Corsica, the journal of a tour to that island: and memoirs of Pascal Paoli / James Boswell. 2nd ed. London, 1768. Map. GB.569. a048.

Account of Koonawur, in the Himalaya, etc. / Alexander Gerard; edited by George Lloyd. London, 1841. Map. GB.1001. a049.

An **account** of several voyages to the South and North / John Narborough [et al.]. Amsterdam, 1969. GB/A.1862. a050.

An **account** of Shelley's visits to France, Switzerland and Savoy, in the years 1814 and 1816: with extracts from *The history of a six weeks' tour* / Charles I. Elton. London, 1894. Ill. Lloyd.508; Lloyd.1185. a051.

An **account** of some German volcanos, and their productions with a new hypothesis of the prismatical basaltes, established upon facts: being an essay of physical geography for philosophers and miners: published as supplementary to Sir William Hamilton's *Observations on the Italian volcanos* / R.E. Raspe. London, 1776. Ill. Lloyd.504. a052.

An **account** of Switzerland, and the Grisons: as also of the Valesians, Geneva, the forest-towns, and their other allies / Vendramino Bianchi. London, 1710. Translated from *Relazione del paese de' Svizzeri*. GB/A.1322. a053.

An **account** of Switzerland, written in the year 1714 / [Temple Stanyan]. London, 1714. GB.416; Lloyd.574. a054.

An **account** of Switzerland: written in the year 1714 / [Temple Stanyan]. Edinburgh, 1756. Lloyd.218. a055.

An **account** of the Arctic region with a history and description of the northern whale-fishery / W. Scoresby. Edinburgh, 1820. 2v; ill., maps. GB.670-1. a056.

An **account** of the attempts that have been made to attain the summit of Mont Blanc, written in the year 1786 / Horace Bénédict de Saussure. [London], 1809. Pp.677-722 of Pinkerton's *A general collection of the best and most interesting voyages and travels*, vol.4. GB.1241. a057.

Account of the discovery of the White Hill, or Mont Blanc, in the Alps. Edinburgh, 1785. A review of the book by Marc Théodore Bourrit. Pp.29-32 of the *Scots Magazine*, vol.47, 1785. GB.1735. a058.

An **account** of the glacieres or ice alps, in Savoy. Ipswich, 1747. GB.431; Lloyd.729. a059.

An **account** of the glacieres, or ice alps, in Savoy, in two letters / one from an English gentleman [i.e. William Windham, assisted by Robert Price and Benjamin Stillingfleet], the other from Peter Martel. London, 1744. Ill., map. GB.1183; Lloyd.1225. a060.

An **account** of the islands of Orkney / James Wallace. To which is added, An essay concerning the Thule of the ancients [by Sir Robert Sibbald]. London, 1700. Originally published as *A description of the isles of Orkney*. GB.329. a061.

An **account** of the late persecution of the Protestants in the vallys of Piemont; by the Duke of Savoy and the French King, in the year 1686. Never before publisht. Oxford, 1688. GB.622. a062.

An **account** of the present state of the Hebrides and western coasts of Scotland / James Anderson. Edinburgh, 1785. Map. GB.716. a063.

Account of the reptiles and batrachians collected by Mr Edward Whymper in Ecuador in 1879-80 / G.A. Boulenger. [London, 1882.] From *Annals and Magazine of Natural History*, June 1882. GB.612(2). a064.

Account of the success of a young man belonging to Chamouni, who acts as a guide to travellers

passing Mount Blanc. Edinburgh, 1786. Pp.526-8 of the *Scots Magazine*, vol.48, 1786.
GB.730. a065.

An **account** of the Vallais, and of the goitres and idiots of that country: account of the glaciers of Savoy, and of Mont Blanc / from Coxe's *Letters from Switzerland*. London, 1780. Pp.89-93,94-7 of the *Annual Register*, 1779.
GB.1739. a066.

Accounts / Alpine Club. 1944, 1954, 1956, 1958. [London], 1945-59.
GB.1321(40-3); GB.1321(44) (another copy of the 1944 issue). a067.

[**Accounts** of climbs by C.D. Frankland from the *Yorkshire Ramblers' Club Journal*, including an obituary.] [Leeds, 1922-29.]
GB.1875. a068.

Achttausend drüber und drunter / Hermann Buhl. München, 1955. Ill., ports.
GB.878. a069.

Aconcagua and Tierra del Fuego: a book of climbing, travel and exploration / Martin Conway. London, 1902. Ill., map.
GB.745; Lloyd.847. a070.

Across country from Thonon to Trent: rambles and scrambles in Switzerland and the Tyrol / Douglas W. Freshfield. London, 1865.
GB.867; Lloyd.1041; Lloyd.1041A,B,C,D,E. a071.

Across East African glaciers: an account of the first ascent of Kilimanjaro / Hans Meyer; translated by E.H.S. Calder. London, 1891. Ill., maps, port. Translated from *Ostafrikanische Gletscherfahrten*.
Lloyd.1292. a072.

Across Spitsbergen / R.E. Peary. [New York, 1897.] Ill. A review of Martin Conway's book *The first crossing of Spitsbergen*. Pp.24-9 of the *Book Buyer*, 1897.
GB.1880(56). a073.

Die **Adamello** Gruppe / Karl Schulz. [Berlin, 1893?] Ill. Pp.[177]-244 of *Erschliessung der Ostalpen*, Bd.2.
GB.1374. a074.

Adamello ieri — oggi / Vittorio Martinelli. Brescia, 1971-73. 3v; ill.
GB/A.1067. a075.

Additional notes on the glacial phenomena of Spitsbergen / E.J. Garwood. [London, 1899.] Ill., map. From the *Quarterly Journal of the Geological Society* for November 1899, vol.55.
GB.1335(46). a076.

Additions and amendments to the 1959 *List of Members* / Alpine Club. London, [1960].
GB.1321(32). a077.

Address list / Royal Air Force Mountaineering Association. Dec.1958, Feb.1962. [London, 1958-62.]
GB.1331(26-7). a078.

Address to Section E, Geography and Ethnology, at the meeting of the British Association at Norwich, August 20th, 1868 / by the President of the Section [i.e. Sir George Henry Richards]. [N.p., 1868.]
Lloyd.1583(12). a079.

Adelboden, Bernese Oberland: 1st class Alpine health-resort 1400 meter above the sea. [Adelboden, ca 1930.] Ill., maps. Published by the Verkehrsverein Adelboden.
GB/A.1589(7). a080.

Adrift in the ice-fields / Charles W. Hall. Boston, 1877. Ill.
GB/A.1621. a081.

The **Adula** Alps / W.A.B. Coolidge. London, 1893. [Conway and Coolidge's climbers' guides; 6.]
GB.1324(11); Lloyd.22. a082.

Adventure in the Alps: extracted from *Days of fresh air* / L.S. Amery. London, 1940. Pp.19-23 of *World Digest*, vol.2 no.11.
GB.1339(20). a083.

Adventures in Alaska and along the trail / Wendell Endicott. New York, 1928. Ill., maps.
GB/A.1768. a084.

Adventures in the Arctic / Richard G. Montgomery. New York, 1932. Ill., map, ports. Originally published as *Pechuck*.
GB/A.1774. a085.

Adventures in Tibet / Sven Hedin. London, 1904.
GB.783. a086.

The **adventures** of a mountaineer / Frank S. Smythe. London, 1940. Ill., ports. [Travellers' tales.]
GB.700; GB.720 (impf.). a087.

Adventures of an Alpine guide / Christian Klucker; translated from the 3rd German ed. by Erwin and Pleasaunce von Gaisberg; edited and with additional chapters by H.E.G. Tyndale. London, 1932. Ill., map, ports. Translated from *Erinnerungen eines Bergführers*.
GB.843; Lloyd.951. a088.

The **adventures** of Mr. John Timothy Homespun in Switzerland / [Fanny Kemble?]; stolen from the French of *Tartaron de Tareascon* [sic] *aux Alpes* [by Alphonse Daudet]. London, 1889.
Lloyd.888. a089.

The **adventures** of the Economical Family. London, 1873. Ill., ports.
GB/A.1931. a090.

Adventures with my alpen-stock and carpet-bag, or A three weeks' trip to France and Switzerland / William Smith. London, 1864. Port.
Lloyd.192. a091.

Adventures with my alpenstock and knapsack, or A five weeks' tour in Switzerland, in 1874, with some notes on Paris, Strasbourg, and other places / Alfred Carr. York, 1875.
Lloyd.298. a092.

Adventurous alliance: the story of the Agassiz family of Boston / Louise Tharp. Boston, [1959]. Ill.
GB/A.959. a093.

Afghanistan / Eric Darmon. Paris, 1978. Ill. [Les grands voyages.]
GB/A.2020(1). a094.

Afghanistan / G. Graham Brown. Edinburgh, 1941. A review of Sir Percy Sykes's *A history of Afghanistan*. Reprinted from the *Scottish Geographical Magazine*, vol.57, Nov.1941.
GB.1329(21). a095.

After Everest: the experiences of a mountaineer and medical missionary / T. Howard Somervell. London, 1936. Ill., maps, port.
GB.1014. a096.

Agassiz' und seiner Freunde geologische Alpenreisen in der Schweiz, Savoyen und Piemont; unter Agassiz', Studer's und Carl Vogt's Mitwirkung verfasst von E. Desor; herausgegeben von Carl Vogt. 2. verm. Aufl. Frankfurt am Main, 1847. Maps.
GB.223. a097.

[**Agenda** of the Annual Meeting of the Geographical Club, 1947.] [London], 1947.
GB.1334(37). a098.

Agno e Chiampo: notizie raccolte dalla Sezione Vicentina del C.A.I. per l'elettrificazione della tramvia Vicenza — Recoaro — Chiampo. [Vicenza], 1929. [Valli dell'Alto Vicentino.]
GB/B.403(7). a099.

El **Aguinaldo**. 1830. [Philadelphia], 1829. Ill. Containing an article *Aventura en los Alpes*.
GB.16. a100.

L'**Aiguille** de Bionnassay / Emile Gaillard. Chambéry, 1929. Ill., map. Extrait de la *Revue alpine*, 3e trimestre 1928, avec corrections et addenda.
Lloyd.890. a101.

Aiguille du Géant ou Dent du Géant / Emile Fontaine. Lyon, 1911. Ill. Extrait de la *Revue alpine* de janvier-février 1911.
Lloyd.1624(6). a102.

Aiguille du Midi, Vallée Blanche: par l'image / Georges et Pierre Tairraz. [Paris], 1967. [Le monde en images.]
GB/A.409. a103.

Aiguille Joseph Croux, m.3221, catena del M. Bianco, versante italiano: prima ascensione / Maria Mazzuchi. Torino, 1901. Ill. Estratto dalla *Rivista mensile del Club Alpino Italiano*, anno 1900, vol.19 no.12.
GB.1333(37); GB.1333(38). a104.

Aiguille Noire de Pétéret, m.3780 – catena del Monte Bianco / Adolfo Hess. [Turin, 1909.] Ill. Pp.[179]-202 of the *Bollettino del Club Alpino Italiano*, vol.40 no.73.
GB.1880(49). a105.

Aiguille Verte — Dolent — Argentière — Trient / Lucien Devies, Pierre Henry. Grenoble, [1949]. Ill. [Guide Vallot. La chaîne du Mont Blanc; 3.].
GB.94; GB/A.1815. a106.

Aiguille Verte — Triolet — Dolent — Argentière — Trient / Lucien Devies, Pierre Henry. 4e éd. Paris, 1975. Ill. [Guide Vallot. La chaîne du Mont Blanc; 3.]
GB/A.1495; GB/A.2013(3). a106.1.

L'**Aiguille** Verte, m.4127, nella catena del Monte Bianco: note topografiche ed alpinistiche: prima ascensione pel versante ovest / E. Canzio, G.B. e G.F. Gugliermina, G. Lampugnani. Torino, 1905. Ill. Published by the Club Alpino Italiano.
GB.1188(2). a107.

Aiguilles: ein Bergbüchlein / C. Egger. Zürich, [1924]. Ill.
GB/A.1922. a108.

The **Aiguilles** d'Arves, Dauphiné / W.A.B. Coolidge. Samaden, 1889. Reprinted from *Sleigh Bells 1869*, the Christmas number of the *St. Moritz Post and Davos News*.
Lloyd.1594(1). a109.

Les **Aiguilles** d'Arves et le col de Petit Jean / Ettore Canzio. Lyon, 1901. Extrait du numéro 7, 1er juillet 1901, de la *Revue alpine*.
Lloyd.1594(2). a110.

Les **Aiguilles** de Chamonix / Henri Isselin. [Paris], 1961. Ill. [Sempervivum; 37.]
GB/A.190. a111.

Les **Aiguilles** de Chamonix / Jacques de Lépiney, E. de Gigord, A. Migot. Paris, 1925. Ill. [Guide Vallot. Description de la haute montagne dans le massif du Mont-Blanc; 1.]
Lloyd.357. a112.

Les **Aiguilles** de Chamonix / Jacques de Lépiney, E. de Gigord, A. Migot. 2e éd. Paris, 1926. Ill. [Guide Vallot. Description de la haute montagne dans le massif du Mont-Blanc; 1.]
GB.90; GB.91. a113.

Aiguilles de Chamonix. Grandes Jorasses / Lucien Devies. Grenoble, 1947. Ill. [Guide Vallot. La chaîne du Mont Blanc; 2.]
GB.93. a114.

Aiguilles de Chamonix. Grandes Jorasses / Lucien Devies. Addendum. Grenoble, [1948]. Ill. [Guide Vallot. La chaîne du Mont Blanc; 2.]
GB.93A. a115.

Aiguilles de Chamonix, Grandes Jorasses / Lucien Devies. 2e éd. Grenoble, 1951. Ill., maps. [Guide Vallot. La chaîne du Mont Blanc; 2.]
GB/A.1814. a115.1.

Les **Aiguilles** de Chamonix / Lucien Devies, Pierre Henry. 3e éd. Paris, 1977. Ill. [Guide Vallot. La chaîne du Mont Blanc; 2.]
GB/A.2013/2. a115.2.

Les **Aiguilles** Rouges: Perrons-Fis, massifs de Colonné et de Platé / Pierre Bossus. [Paris], 1974. Ill.
GB/A.1328. a116.

Al castello d'Osilio: gita inaugurale della Sezione di Sassari del C.A.I., 18 maggio 1879 / D. Lovisato. Sassari, 1879. Ill.
GB/A.1349(6). a117.

Al di là della storia: i grandi capitoli della ricerca archeologica nella regione tridentina / Adolfo Gorfer. Trento, 1980. Ill., maps.
GB/B.555. a118.

Al Mont Rouge de Pétéret / G. Paul Preuss. Torino, 1912. Pp.284-6 of the *Rivista del Club Alpino Italiano*, vol.31 no.9.
GB.1318(24). a119.

Al sole delle Dolomiti / Severino Casara. Milano, 1947. Ill.
GB/B.252(4). a120.

Alaska / Robert Reynolds; text by John J. Morris. [Portland, Or., 1971.] Ill.
GB/B.508. a121.

Alaska: a profile, with pictures / Merle Colby. New York, 1940. Ill., map.
GB/A.1725. a122.

Alaska: handbook no.86, Aug. 1897. Washington, [1897]. Map.
GB/A.1675(9). a123.

Alaska: its southern coast and the Sitkan Archipelago / E. Ruhamah Scidmore. Boston, 1885.
GB/A.2171. a124.

Alaska: the Great Bear's cub / Mary Lee Davis. Boston, 1930. Ill., map.
GB/A.1700. a125.

Alaska: the land of yesterday, today and tomorrow. Chicago, 1934. Ill., maps. Published by the U.S. Department of the Interior.
GB.1336(38). a126.

Alaska, 1899: Copper River exploring expedition / [report by] Captain W.R. Abercrombie, Second U.S. Infantry, commanding [et al.]. Washington, 1900.
GB/A.1744. a127.

Alaska and the Klondike gold fields: containing a full account of the discovery of gold / A.C. Harris. [N.p., 1897.] Ill., maps.
GB/A.1586.   a128.

The **Alaska** frontier / Thomas Willing Balch. Philadelphia, 1903. Maps.
GB/A.1716.   a129.

Alaska holiday / Barrett Willoughby. Boston, 1940. Ill., ports.
GB/A.1769.   a130.

Alaska, U.S.A. / Herb and Miriam Hilscher. Boston, 1959. Ill., map, port.
GB/A.1658.   a131.

Alaskan Eskimo words / compiled by Knud Rasmussen; edited by H. Ostermann. New York, 1976. Map. [Thule expedition, 5th, 1921-1924. Report; vol.3 no.4.]
GB/A.1828.   a132.

The **Alaskan** Eskimos: as described in the posthumous notes of Knud Rasmussen / [edited by] H. Ostermann; edited after the latter's death with the assistance of E. Holtved; translated by W.E. Calvert. New York, 1976. Ill. [Thule expedition, 5th, 1921-1924. Report; vol.10 no.3.]
GB/A.1839.   a133.

Alaskan glacier studies of the National Geographic Society in the Yakutat Bay, Prince William Sound and Lower Copper River regions / Ralph Stockman Tarr, Lawrence Martin. Washington, 1914. Ill., maps.
GB.1215.   a134.

Alaskan oil: costs and supply / M.A. Adelman, Paul G. Bradley, Charles A. Norman. New York, 1971.
GB/A.1780.   a135.

The **Alaskan** ten-footed bear, and other legends / Ruth McCorkle. Seattle, 1958. Ill.
GB/A.1791(4).   a136.

Alba alpina e altri scritti / Guido Rey; un saggio di Ugo De Amicis; biografia di Adolfo Balliano. Torino, 1954. Ill. [Montes.]
GB/B.399.   a137.

Albin Indergand: Roman / Ernst Zahn. Frauenfeld, 1904.
GB/A.30.   a138.

Albrecht von Hallers Leben / Adolf Haller. Basel, 1954. Port.
GB/A.2027.   a139.

[**Album** of engraved views of Switzerland.] [Constance, n.d.] 2v; ill.
GB/A.818-9.   a140.

[**Album** of mountaineering photographs.] [N.p., n.d.]
GB.1928.   a141.

[**Album** of photographs, mainly of the meteorological station on Ben Nevis, and of views from the station.] [N.p., ca 1900.]
GB/A.1897.   a142.

[**Album** of photographs of scenes in France, Switzerland, Italy and Belgium.] [N.p., ca 1895.]
GB/C.81.   a143.

[**Album** of photographs of Switzerland, Germany and France, including Swiss mountaineering views.] [N.p., ca 1900.]
GB/C.89.   a144.

[**Album** of photographs of winter sports in Switzerland, Norway and Scotland.] [N.p.], 1894-1907. Probably compiled by a member of the Strutt or Scott of Buccleuch family.
GB/B.420.   a145.

Album pittoresque d'un voyage en Suisse: le Léman. Paris, [ca 1890]. Ill.
GB/B.331.   a146.

Album von Combe-Varin: zur Erinnerung an Theodor Parker und Hans Lorenz Küchler. Zürich, 1861. Ill.
GB/A.679.   a147.

Album von Salzburger-Alpenlande / nach d. Natur gez. v. Gg. Pezolt, Lith. v. Leop. Rottmann. Salzburg, [n.d.].
GB/C.1.   a148.

Alessandro Volta alpinista: con un poemetto fin qui inedito / Mario Cermenati. [Turin, 1899.] Ports. Pp.[213]-88 of the *Bollettino del Club Alpino Italiano*, no.65.
GB.1333(28[2]).   a149.

Alexander Burgener, König der Bergführer: ein Tatsachenroman / Adolf Fux. 3. Aufl. Bern, [1961]. Ill.
GB/A.372.   a150.

Alla scoperta delle Alpi / Massimo Cappon. Milano, 1982. Ill., maps. [Libri illustrati Mondadori.]
GB/B.631.   a151.

Alle porte d'Italia / Edmondo De Amicis. 10a. impressione della nuova ed. del 1888 riveduta dall'autore con l'aggiunta di due capitoli. Milano, 1919.
GB/A.1034(15).   a152.

Le **allegre** vacanze di Basilio in montagna: romanzo / Aldo Depoli. [Lecco], 1971. Ill.
GB/A.1281(2).   a153.

Die **Allgäuer** Alpen / Anton Spiehler. [Berlin, 1893.] Ill. Pp.[38]-94 of *Erschliessung der Ostalpen*, Bd.1.
GB.1367(1).   a154.

Allgäuer Alpen: ein Führer für Täler, Hütten und Bergfahrten / Ernst Zettler. München, 1925. Ill., map.
GB/A.2018(3).   a155.

Die **Allgäuer** Alpen: Land und Leute / Max Förderreuther. Kempten, 1907. Ill., maps.
GB/B.136.   a156.

Allgemeine Bergsteiger-Zeitung: Nachrichtenblatt für Touristik u. Wintersport. No.699-703. Wien, 1936.
GB.1341(1-5).   a157.

L'**Allobroge**: revue scientifique et littéraire des Alpes françaises et de la Savoie / rédigé par un homme de lettres [Eugène Bonnefous]. Année 1-2, 1840/41-1842. Grenoble, [1841-42]. Ill.
GB/B.373-4.   a158.

The **allotetraploid** *Saxifraga Nathorsti* and its probable progenitors *S. aizoides* and *S. oppositifolia* / Tyge W. Böcher. Copenhagen, 1983. [Meddelelser om Grønland. Bioscience; 11.]
GB/A.1819(11).   a159.

Alltagszauber: Novellen / Wilhelm Fischer. 2. Aufl. München, 1913.
GB/A.50.   a160.

Almanach historique nommé Le messager boiteux pour l'an 1823: avec une relation des choses les plus remarquables arrivées en Europe dans l'année précédente / Antoine Souci. Basle, [1822].
Lloyd.1591(5); Lloyd.1591(7); Lloyd.1592(2).   a161.

Almanach historique, nommé Le postillon de la paix et de la guerre, pour l'an de grâce 1823: avec une relation des choses les plus remarquables arrivées en Europe dans l'année précédente / Antoine Souci. Basle, [1822].
Lloyd.1591(6).   a162.

Almanach historique nommé Messager boiteux pour l'an de grâce 1823: avec un recueil d'anecdotes curieuses tirées du Grand livre du monde / Antoine Souci. Vevey, [1822].
Lloyd.1591(1).   a163.

Alone / Richard E. Byrd. New York, 1938.
GB/A.1584.   a164.

Along Hadrian's British wall / H.F. Abell. [London, 1892.] Pp.812-23 of the *National Review*, vol.19 no.114.
GB.1336(19).   a165.

L'**Alpe** d'Engstligen dans l'histoire / W.A.B. Coolidge. Bern, [1910]. Separatabdruck aus den *Blättern für bernische Geschichte, Kunst und Altertumskunde*.
GB.1340(21).   a166.

L'**Alpe** Dévero / Luciano Rainoldi. 2a ed. riveduta e ampliata. [Vigevano], 1976. Ill. Published by the Club Alpino Italiano, Sezione di Vigevano.
GB/A.2023(11).   a167.

L'**Alpe** enchanteresse: Salzbourg, le Salzkammergut, les Hauts Tauern / comte J. du Plessis. Paris, 1913. Ill., maps. [Collection de voyages illustrés.]
GB/A.1295(9).   a168.

Alpe Friulana: Carnia, Tarvisiano: un mondo da scoprire / coordinamento editoriale: Cesare Russo. Udine, 1979. Ill., maps.
GB/A.2020(14).   a169.

Alpe, neige, roc: revue alpine internationale. No.1-12, juin 1951-déc.1956, 1959-61. Lausanne, 1951-61. Ill. Wanting no.3 (juin 1952), no.11 (juin 1956).
GB/B.603(1951-56); GB/B.617(1959-61).   a170.

Alpe Veglia / Luciano Rainoldi. Vigevano, 1972. Ill., maps. Published by the Club Alpino Italiano, Sezione di Vigevano.
GB/A.1281(4).   a171.

Alpeggi Biellesi: tecniche casearie tradizionali, terminologia, arte pastorale / Giacomo Calleri; Piero Foddanu sull'abitazione alpina. Torino, [1966]. Ill. [Centro Studi Biellesi. Pubblicazione; 6.]
GB/B.272.   a172.

Die **Alpen** — Les Alpes — Le Alpi — Las Alps: Monatsschrift des Schweizer Alpenclub. Vol.1 no.1-vol.29 no.10, Jan.1925-Oct.1953. Bern, 1925-53. Wanting Aug., Oct.1941, Jan., Mar.1942, Dec.1945, May-Dec.1950, May 1952-Sept.1953.
GB.1503-28; GB/A.343 (another copy of vol.9, 1933); Lloyd.1350-53 (another copy of v.24, 26-28).   a173.

Die **Alpen** — Les Alpes — Le Alpi — Las Alps: Zeitschrift des Schweizer Alpenclub. Vol.32, 1956. Bern, 1956.
GB/A.344.   a174.

Die **Alpen**: le Alpi: las Alps: les Alpes / herausgegeben vom Schweizer Alpen-Club. Vol.43-1967-   . Bern, 1967-   .
GB/A.750.   a175.

Die **Alpen**: le Alpi: las Alps: les Alpes: Monatsbulletin / herausgegeben vom Schweizer Alpen-Club. Vol.43-   , 1967-   . Bern, 1967-   .
GB/A.751.   a176.

Les **Alpes** — Le Alpi — Las Alps — Die Alpen: bulletin mensuel du Club alpin suisse. Vol.32-42, 1957-66. Berne, 1957-66.
GB/A.345-54.   a177.

Les **Alpes** — Le Alpi — Las Alps — Die Alpen: revue du Club alpin suisse. 1957-66. Berne, 1957-66. Wanting the 3rd trimestre of 1963.
GB/A.355-64.   a178.

Die **Alpen** / Albrecht von Haller. Erlenbach-Zürich, 1968. Ill.
GB/B.288(18).   a179.

Die **Alpen** / Bernhard Cotta. 2. Ausg. Leipzig, 1851. Ill.
GB/A.1327.   a180.

Die **Alpen** / herausgegeben von Hans Schmithals. [2nd ed.]. Zürich, [1927]. Ill., map.
GB.1284.   a181.

Die **Alpen** / R.H. Francé. Leipzig, [n.d.]. Ill., maps. Published by the Deutsche Naturwissenschaftliche Gesellschaft.
GB/B.124.   a182.

Die **Alpen** / Robert Sieger. Leipzig, 1902. Ill., map. [Sammlung Goschen.]
GB/A.182.   a183.

Die **Alpen**: Handbuch der gesammten Alpenkunde / Friedrich Umlauft. Wien, 1887. Ill., maps.
GB/A.89.   a184.

Die **Alpen**. Les Alpes / Albrecht von Haller; die französische Uebersetzung von V.B. Tscharner. Bern, 1795.
Lloyd.1249.   a185.

Die **Alpen** in der englischen Literatur und Kunst / Robert Spindler. New York, 1967. Ill. [Beiträge zur englischen Philologie; 32.] A reprint of the Leipzig, 1932 ed.
GB/A.181(3).   a186.

Die **Alpen** in der europäischen Geschichte des Mittelalters: Reichenau-Vorträge, 1961-62 / Theodor Mayer, Rudolf Egger, Hermann Vetters [et al.]. Stuttgart, [1965]. Ill. [Vorträge und Forschungen; 10.]
GB/A.467.   a187.

Die **Alpen** in der schweizer Malerei: the Alps in Swiss painting. Zürich, 1977. Ill. Catalogue of an exhibition, Tokyo and Chur, 1977.
GB/A.1644.   a188.

Die **Alpen** in Farben / Kurt Peter Karfeld; bearbeitet von Jos. Jul. Schätz. 2. Aufl. München, 1940. Ill.
GB/B.573.   a189.

Die **Alpen** in Farben / Kurt Peter Karfeld; bearbeitet von Jos. Jul. Schätz. 3. Aufl. München, 1941. Ill.
GB/B.118.   a190.

Die **Alpen** in Frühzeit und Mittelalter: die archäologische Entdeckung einer Kulturlandschaft / Ludwig Pauli. 2. durchgesehene und erg. Aufl. München, 1981. Ill., maps.
GB/A.1933.   a191.

Die **Alpen** in Natur- und Lebensbildern / H.A. Berlepsch. Leipzig, 1861. Ill.
GB/A.194.   a192.

Die **Alpen** mit Adleraugen / Walter Pause, Franz Thorbeke. Seebruck am Chiemsee, 1967. Ill.
GB/B.325.   a193.

Alpen rozen / G.H. van Senden; met aanteekeningen vermeerderd en nagezien door B.T. Lublink Weddick en P.H. Witkamp. 2e druk. Amsterdam, [1857?]. Ill., map.
GB/A.1800.   a194.

Die **Alpen** rufen! / Carl D. Koch. Berlin, [1937]. Ill.
GB/B.129.   a195.

Die **Alpen** rufen! / Carl D. Koch. Berlin, [ca 1940]. Ill.
GB/A.1486.   a196.

Die **Alpen** und ihre Maler / E.W. Bredt. Leipzig, [n.d.]. Ill.
GB/B.115.   a197.

Die **Alpen** vom Mont Ventoux bis zum Wienerwald / Karl Lukan. Neubearb. Aufl. Wien, 1963. Ill.
GB/B.574.   a198.

Alpen-Lieder für Männer-Stimmen / herausgegeben von Johannes Wepf. 3. verm. und verb. Aufl. Schaffhausen, 1858.
GB/A.733.   a199.

Die **Alpen-Passe** / Kurt Mair. 4. unveränderte Aufl. Berlin, [1938]. 2v; ill., maps.
GB/A.86-7.   a200.

Die **Alpen-Pflanzen** Deutschlands und der Schweiz in colorirten Abbildungen nach der Natur und in natürlicher Grösse / J.C. Weber; mit systematisch geordnetem Text von C.A. Kranz. 2. Aufl. München, [ca 1870]. 4v.
GB/A.130-3.   a201.

Die **Alpen-Pflanzen** Deutschlands und der Schweiz in colorirten Abbildungen nach der Natur und in natürlicher Grösse / J.C. Weber; mit systematisch geordnetem Text von C.A. Kranz. 3. Aufl. München, 1872. 4v.
Lloyd.7-10.   a202.

Die **Alpen-** und Italienpolitik der Merowinger im VI. Jahrhundert / Georg Löhlein. Erlangen, 1932. [Erlanger Abhandlungen zur mittleren und neueren Geschichte; 17.]
GB/B.403(14).   a203.

Das **Alpenbuch** / unsere Mitarbeiter: W. Adrian, Hans Bloesch [et al.]. Bern, [ca 1930]. Ill., map. Published by the Direction générale des postes suisses.
GB/B.289(21).   a204.

Alpenfestung: ein Dokumentarbericht / Heinz Weibel-Altmeyer. München, [1966].
GB/A.142.   a205.

Alpenflug / Walter Mittelholzer; unter Mitarbeit von H. Kempf. Zürich, [1928]. Ill.
GB.971.   a206.

Alpenflüsse: Kajakflüsse: Technik, Taktik, Training, Touren / Robert Steidle, Walter Pause. München, 1969. Ill., maps.
GB/A.456.   a207.

Der **Alpenföhn** in seinem Einfluss auf Natur- und Menschenleben / Gustav Berndt. Gotha, 1886. Map. [A. Petermanns Mitteilungen aus Justus Perthes' geographischer Anstalt. Ergänzungsheft; 83.]
GB/B.390(1).   a208.

Der **Alpenfreund**: Monatshefte für Verbreitung von Alpenkunde unter Jung und Alt / herausgegeben von Ed. Amthor. Bd.1-11. Gera, 1870-74. Ill., maps.
GB/A.1093-7 (Bd.1,3-4,6-7); GB/A.1447-56 (Bd.2-11).   a209.

Alpenglühen: Naturansichten und Wanderbilder: ein Hausbuch für das deutsche Volk / Freiherr von Schweiger-Lerchenfeld. Stuttgart, [1893]. Ill.
GB/B.522.   a210.

Die **Alpenkunde** im Altertum / Franz Ramsauer. [Munich], 1901. Pp.[46]-68 of the *Zeitschrift des Deutschen und Osterreichischen Alpenvereins*, Bd.32.
GB.1322(17[2]).   a211.

Alpenreise vom Jahre 1781 / G.K.Ch. Storr. Leipzig, 1784-86. 2v; ill.
GB.440-1.   a212.

Alpenreisen / J.G. Kohl. Dresden, 1849-51. 3v.
GB/A.645-7.   a213.

The **alpenstock**, or Sketches of Swiss scenery and manners, 1825-1826 / Charles Joseph Latrobe. London, 1829. Ill.
GB.1046.   a214.

The **alpenstock**, or Sketches of Swiss scenery and manners, 1825-1826 / Charles Joseph Latrobe. 2nd ed. London, 1839. Ill.
GB.145; Lloyd.268.   a215.

Alpenvereinsjahrbuch / Schriftleitung: Werner Heissel; herausgegeben vom Osterreichischen

und vom Deutschen Alpenverein. 1971-   .
Innsbruck, 1971-   . Ill.
GB/A.920.   a216.

Alpenwanderungen: Fahrten auf hohe und
höchste Alpenspitzen / A.W. Grube. Oberhausen,
1873. 2v (in 1); ill.
GB/A.1129.   a217.

Alpenwanderungen: Fahrten auf hohe und
höchste Alpenspitzen / nach den Original-
berichten ausgewählt, bearbeitet und gruppiert
von A.W. Grube; neu bearb. und erg. von C.
Benda. 3. Aufl. Leipzig, 1886. Ill.
GB.963.   a218.

Die **Alpenwirthschaft** in ihrem ganzen Umfange
und drauf bezügliche Urkunden und Sagen / H.
Gusset. Bern, 1869.
GB/A.2026.   a219.

Les **Alpes** – Le Alpi – Las Alps – Die Alpen. See
nos. a177 and a188.

Les **Alpes**. Paris, 1969. Ill., maps, ports.
GB/B.601.   a220.

Les **Alpes** / Paul Veyret. Paris, 1972. Maps. [Que
sais-je?; 1463.]
GB/A.1050(8).   a221.

Les **Alpes**: description pittoresque de la nature et
de la faune alpestre / Friedrich von Tschudi;
[translated by Albert Vouga and A.F.W.
Schimper]. Berne, 1859. Ill. Translated from *Das
Thierleben Alpenwelt*.
GB.851; Lloyd.1227.   a222.

Les **Alpes**: descriptions et récits / H.A. Berlepsch.
Bâle, 1869. Ill.
GB/A.1415.   a223.

Les **Alpes**: du Grossglockner au parc des Ecrins /
René Mannent. Paris, 1978. Ill. [Connaissance du
monde.]
GB/B.500.   a224.

Les **Alpes**: études et souvenirs / Emile Talbert. 8e
éd. Paris, 1900. Ill. [Bibliothèque des écoles et des
familles.]
GB/A.75.   a225.

Les **Alpes**: histoire et souvenirs / Xavier Roux.
Paris, [1877]. [Bibliothèque historique et littéraire.]
GB/A.942(1).   a226.

Alpes: Léman, Savoie, Dauphiné, Provence, Corse
/ [edited by Robert Doré]. Paris, 1938. Maps.
[Guides diamant.]
GB/A.1459(4).   a227.

Les **Alpes**: Lyon, Dauphiné, Savoie, Genève.
Nouv. éd. Paris, [1931]. Ill., maps. [Guides Bricet.]
GB/A.1468(1).   a228.

Alpes (Savoie et Dauphiné) / J. Debelmas, avec la
collaboration de H. Arnaud [et al.]. Paris, 1970. Ill.,
maps. [Guides géologiques régionaux.]
GB/B.290(3).   a229.

Les **Alpes** au point de vue de la géographie
physique et de la géologie: voyages photo-
graphiques dans le Dauphiné, la Savoie, le nord
d'Italie, la Suisse et le Tyrol / A. Civiale. Paris,
1882. Ill., maps.
GB/A.838.   a230.

Les **Alpes** bernoises / Eugène de La Harpe avec la
collaboration du dr. H. Dübi. Lausanne, 1915. Ill.
GB/C.3.   a231.

Les **Alpes** dans la nature et dans l'histoire /
W.A.B. Coolidge; édition française par Edouard
Combe. Paris, 1913.
GB/A.2182.   a232.

Les **Alpes** de la haute Engadine / J.L. Binet-
Hentsch. Genève, 1859.
GB/A.801(10).   a233.

Alpes de Provence, Tinée, Ubaye: randonnées et
escalades faciles / Vincent Paschetta. Grenoble,
1979. Ill., maps. [Guides Paschetta des Alpes-
Maritimes.]
GB/A.1911(1).   a234.

Les **Alpes** de Savoie. Vol.1: Les massifs entre l'Arc
et l'Isère / Emile Gaillard. Mâcon, [1912]. Maps.
Lloyd.267.   a235.

Les **Alpes** de Savoie. Vol.6 pt.1: Le massif du Mont
Blanc: entre les cols de la Seigne, d'Enclave, du
Midi et du Géant: guide pour l'alpiniste / Emile
Gaillard. Mâcon, [1925]. Maps.
GB.62.   a236.

Les **Alpes** du Dauphiné / E. Debriges. Paris, 1885.
Ill.
GB.1335(2).   a237.

Les **Alpes** du Dauphiné. Vol.2 pt.1: Le Haut Dauphiné: le Meije et les Ecrins, du signal de Pied-Montet au col de la Temple: guide pour l'alpiniste / Emile Gaillard. Mâcon, 1929. Maps.
GB.80.   a238.

Les **Alpes** du soleil: Haut-Var, Vésubie, Tinée, Roya, Saint-Jeannet, Ubaye, Queyras, Viso / Jean Marie Morisset. Paris, 1979. Ill. [Les cent plus belles courses et randonnées.]
GB/B.586.   a239.

Alpes enchantées / François Cali. [Paris], 1966. Ill., map. [Le monde en images.]
GB/A.126.   a240.

Alpes et Danube, ou Voyage en Suisse, Styrie, Hongrie et Transylvanie / baron Charles d'Haussez. Paris, 1837. 2v.
GB/A.72-3.   a241.

Alpes et Danube, ou Voyage en Suisse, Styrie, Hongrie et Transylvanie / baron Charles d'Haussez. 2e éd. Paris, 1837. 2v.
GB/A.978 (wanting v.2).   a242.

Alpes et glaciers de la Suisse / Ed. Osenbrüggen; traduit par C.F. Girard. Bâle, [1870]. Ill.
GB/B.20.   a243.

Les **Alpes** et la Suisse: oeuvres choisies / ouvrage publié par la Section des Diablerets du Club alpin suisse à l'occasion du centenaire d'Eugène Rambert. Lausanne, 1930. Ill.
GB/A.380.   a244.

Les **Alpes** et les états alpins / Pierre Gabert, Paul Guichonnet. Paris, 1965. Ill. [Magellan. La géographie et ses problèmes; 14.]
GB/A.38.   a245.

Les **Alpes** et les grandes ascensions / E. Levasseur avec la collaboration de membres des clubs alpins. Paris, 1889. Maps.
Lloyd.1622(4).   a246.

Alpes et neige: 101 sommets à ski / Philippe et Claude Traynard. [Grenoble], 1965. Ill.
GB/A.140.   a247.

Alpes et Pyrénées: arabesques littéraires composées de nouvelles historiques, anecdotes, descriptions, chroniques et récits divers / Amable Tastu, Julie Delafaye-Bréhier, Eugénie Foa. Paris, 1842. Ill.
GB/A.466.   a248.

Les **Alpes** françaises: la flore et la faune, le rôle de l'homme dans les Alpes, la transhumance / Albert Falsan avec la collaboration de G. de Saporta. Paris, 1893. Ill. [Bibliothèque scientifique contemporaine.]
GB/A.1082.   a249.

Les **Alpes** françaises: les montagnes, les eaux, les glaciers, les phénomènes de l'atmosphère / Albert Falsan. Paris, 1893. Ill. [Bibliothèque scientifique contemporaine.]
GB/A.42.   a250.

Les **Alpes** françaises à vol d'oiseau / Raoul Blanchard, Fleury Seive. Grenoble, 1928. Ill.
GB/A.1214.   a251.

Les **Alpes** Pennines dans un jour: soit panorama boréal de la Becca de Nona depuis le Mont-Blanc jusqu'au Mont-Rose / G. Carrel. Aoste, 1855.
GB.248; Lloyd.1615(15); Lloyd.1659(6).   a252.

Alpes pittoresques: description de la Suisse / MM. le mis. de Chateauvieux, Dubochet [et al.]; publié sous la direction de M. le vte. Alcide de Forestier. Paris, 1837-38. 2v; ill., maps.
GB/C.19-20.   a253.

Les **Alpes** que j'aime / présentées par Maurice Herzog; légendées par Max Aldebert; racontées par Guillaume Hanoteau. Paris, 1964. Ill.
GB/B.266.   a254.

Les **Alpes** suisses / Eugène Rambert. 2e éd. Bâle, 1869. 4v (in 2).
GB/A.173-4.   a255.

Les **Alpes** suisses / Eugène Rambert. 5e sér. Bâle, 1875.
GB/A.367.   a256.

Les **Alpes** suisses: ascensions et flâneries / Eugène Rambert. Lausanne, 1888. 2v.
GB.366-7.   a257.

Les **Alpes** suisses dans la littérature et dans l'art / Gustave Bettex, Edouard Guillon. Montreux, 1913. Ill.
GB/A.505.   a258.

Les **Alpes** valaisannes / Eugène de La Harpe; avec la collaboration d'Henry Correvon [et al.]. Genève, 1979. Ill. Facsimile reprint of the Lausanne, 1911 ed.
GB/B.521.   a259.

Les **Alpes** vaudoises / Aug. Vautier. Lausanne, [1907?]. Ill.
GB/C.6.   a260.

Alpes vaudoises / Louis Seylaz. Lausanne, 1948. Ill.
GB/B.333.   a261.

Le **Alpi** / Giotto Dainelli. Torino, 1963. 2v; maps.
GB/B.16-7.   a262.

Le **Alpi** / Michele Maza. Milano, 1981. Ill., maps. [Per terra e mare.]
GB/A.1917.   a263.

Le **Alpi** / Shiro Shirahata. Milano, 1983. Ill. Translated from the Japanese.
GB/B.643.   a264.

Le **Alpi**: rivista mensile del Centro Alpinistico Italiano [of the Club Alpino Italiano]. Vol.58-59. Roma, [1939-40].
Lloyd.1260-1; GB.1645(1-3) (other copies of odd issues).   a265.

Le **Alpi** al popolo / Mario Tedeschi; con un profilo di Mario Tedeschi di Camillo Giussani. Milano, 1945. Ill. Published by the Centro Alpinistico Italiano, Sezione di Milano and the Consociazione Turistica Italiana.
GB/B.254.   a266.

Alpi Apuane / Angelo Nerli, Attilio Sabbadini. Milano, 1958. Ill., maps. [Guida dei monti d'Italia.] Published by the Club Alpino Italiano and the Touring Club Italiano.
GB/A.468.   a267.

Alpi Apuane: escursionismo e alpinismo / M. De Bertoldi, A. Nerli, V. Sarperi. Bologna, 1976. Ill. [Itinerari alpini; 36.]
GB/A.1589(17).   a268.

Alpi Cozie centrali: dal colle delle Traversette al colle del Monginevro / Eugenio Ferreri; a cura di Pietro Losana [et al.]. Milano, 1982. Ill., maps. [Guida dei monti d'Italia.]
GB/A.1953.   a269.

Alpi Cozie settentrionali / per cura di Eugenio Ferreri. Pt. 1: Sotto-gruppi: Granero – Frioland; Boucier – Cournour; Queyron – Albergian – Sestières; Assietta – Rocciavrè. Torino, 1923. Ill., maps. [Guida dei monti d'Italia. Alpi occidentali; 3.]
GB/A.1166.   a270.

Le **Alpi** di Val Grosina: guida alpina / Alfredo Corti, Walther Laeng. Brescia, 1909. Ill.
GB/A.1.   a271.

Le **Alpi** e l'Europa / P. Bassetti [et al.]. Roma, 1974-75. 4v; maps.
GB/A.1968.   a272.

Alpi e Prealpi: mito e realtà / Aurelio Garobbio. 1: Brianza, Sottoceneri, Lario, valli dell'Adda, Engadina, valli bergamasche, Valcaminica. Bologna, 1967. Ill.
GB/A.1272.   a273.

Alpi e Prealpi: mito e realtà / Aurelio Garobbio. 2: Val Trompia e Val Sabbia, lago di Garda, Monte Baldo, Valli Giudicarie, Val di Non e Val di Sole. Bologna, 1969. Ill.
GB/A.1273.   a274.

Alpi e Prealpi: mito e realtà / Aurelio Garobbio. 3: Lessinia, Val Lagarina, valli della Fersina, Valsugana, Valle del Vanoi, valli dolomitiche del bacino dell'Adige. Bologna, [1973.] Ill.
GB/A.1274.   a275.

Le **Alpi** Feltrine: Vette – Cimonega – Pizzocco / E. Bertoldin, G. De Bortoli, S. Claut. Feltre, 1972. Ill., maps. Published by the Club Alpino Italiano, Sezione di Feltre.
GB/A.1050(16).   a276.

Le **Alpi** Feltrine: Vette – Cimonega – Pizzocco / E. Bertoldin, G. De Bortoli, S. Claut. Cortina, 1977. Ill., maps, ports.
GB/A.1957.   a277.

Alpi Giulie / Gino Buscaini. Milano, 1974. Ill., maps. [Guida dei monti d'Italia.]
GB/A.1947.   a278.

Le **Alpi** Giulie attraverso le immagini / Giulio Kugy; traduzione di Ervino Pocar. Bologna, 1970. Ill. Translated from *Die Julischen Alpen im Bilde*.
GB/B.268.   a279.

Alpi Graie e Pennine ovvero lato settentrionale della Marca d'Ivrea / Iacopo Durandi. Bologna, 1973. Facsimile reprint of the Torino, 1804 ed.
GB/B.377(15).   a280.

Alpi Graie meridionali / Giulio Berutto, Lino Fornelli. Milano, 1980. Ill., maps. [Guida dei monti d'Italia.]
GB/A.1954.   a281.

Alpi Liguri: dal colle di Cadibona al colle di Tenda / Euro Montagna, Lorenzo Montaldo. Milano, 1981. Ill., maps. [Guida dei monti d'Italia.]
GB/A.1951.   a282.

Alpi Marittime / Giovanni Bobba. Torino, 1908. Ill. [Guida dei monti d'Italia.]
GB/A.8.   a283.

Le **Alpi** nostre e il Monferrato: libro di lettura per le scuole elementari superiori / Giuseppe Cesare Abba. Bergamo, 1901. Published by the Istituto Italiano d'Arti Grafiche.
GB/A.942(9).   a284.

Le **Alpi** nostre e la Lombardia montana tra l'Adda e il Mincio / Giuseppe Cesare Abba. Bergamo, 1901. Ill. Published by the Istituto Italiano d'Arti Grafiche.
GB/A.434(4).   a285.

Le **Alpi** nostre e le regioni ai loro piedi / Giuseppe Cesare Abba. Bergamo, 1916. Ill., map. Published by the Istituto Italiano d'Arti Grafiche.
GB/A.918.   a286.

Le **Alpi** orientali / Roberto Barbetta; per gli allievi ufficiali della scuola di Caserta. Caserta, [1916]. Ill.
GB/A.803(1).   a287.

Le **Alpi** orientali in epoca classica: problemi di orografia storica / Mario Bagnara. Firenze, 1969. [Università di Padova. Pubblicazione della Facoltà di Lettere e Filosofia; 47.]
GB/B.255.   a288.

Alpi Pennine / Gino Buscaini. Milano, 1970-71. 2v; ill., maps. [Guida dei monti d'Italia.]
GB/A.831-2.   a289.

Le **Alpi** Pennine: le 100 più belle ascensioni fra il Gran San Bernardo e il Sempione / Michel Vaucher; traduzione di Rosalba Donvito Gossi. Bologna, 1980. Ill., maps. Translated from *Les Alpes valaisannes*.
GB/B.575.   a290.

Alpi Retiche occidentali / Luigi Brasca [et al.]. Brescia, 1911. [Guida dei monti d'Italia. Alpi centrali; 1.] Published by the Club Alpino Italiano.
GB/A.1145; GB/A.1964(14).   a292.

Alpi ticinesi e mesolcinesi / Ermes Borioli. 3a ed. [Zurich], 1973. Ill., maps. [Guide del Club Alpino Svizzero.]
GB/A.1963.   a293.

Alpi Venoste, Passirie, Breonie: giogaia di Tessa – monti Sarentini dal passo di Resia al passo del Brénnero / Silvio Saglio. Roma, 1939. Ill., maps. [Guida dei monti d'Italia.]
GB/A.1998.   a294.

Alpina: eine Schrift der genauern Kenntniss der Alpen gewiedmet. Bd.1-4. Winterthur, 1806-9.
GB/A.534-7.   a295.

Alpine adventure, or Narratives of travel and research in the Alps / by the author of *The Mediterranean illustrated* [i.e. William H.D. Adams]. London, 1878.
Lloyd.323.   a296.

Alpine adventures / A. Carson Roberts. London, 1936. 3v. Pp.317-22, 472-81, 583-9 of vol.153 no.915-917 of the *Cornhill Magazine*.
GB.1338(18-20).   a297.

Alpine adventures / Stanley Snaith. London, 1946. Ill.
GB.351; GB.352.   a298.

The **Alpine** Annual 1950: adapted from the 1949 numbers of the *Alpine Journal* / edited by T. Graham Brown. London, 1950. Ill.
GB.854.   a299.

The **Alpine** Annual 1950: adapted from the 1949 numbers of the *Alpine Journal* / edited by T. Graham Brown. London, 1950. A prospectus.
GB.1333(29).   a300.

Alpine Architektur / Bruno Taut. Hagen, 1919. 5v (in 1).
GB/C.121.   a301.

Alpine ascents and adventures, or Rock and snow sketches / H. Schütz Wilson. London, 1878.
Lloyd.452; Lloyd.519.   a302.

Alpine ascents and adventures / H. Schütz Wilson. 2nd ed. London, 1878.
GB.308; Lloyd.520.   a303.

Alpine beginner / Elizabeth S. Cowles. [N.p., 1933?] Ill., ports.
Lloyd.1620(23).   a304.

Alpine byways, or Light leaves gathered in 1859 and 1860 / by a lady [i.e. Mrs Henry Freshfield]. London, 1861. Ill., maps.
GB.438; Lloyd.601; Lloyd.601A (impf.).   a305.

The **Alpine** career, 1868-1914, of Frederick Gardiner / W.A.B. Coolidge. [N.p.], 1920. Port.
GB.1306(14); Lloyd.1603(3). a306.

Alpine Chronik des Oesterreichischen Touristen-Club. Jahrg.1 Nr.1-Jahrg.2 Nr.3, 1880-1881. Wien, 1880-81. Continues as *Chronik des Oesterreichischen Touristen-Club*. Jahrg.1882-85.
GB/A.1582. a307.

Alpine climbers / Charles H. Chase. London, [1888].
Lloyd.112; Lloyd.112A. a308.

Alpine climbing: narratives of recent ascents of Mont Blanc, the Matterhorn, the Jungfrau, and other lofty summits of the Alps / by the author of *The Mediterranean illustrated* [i.e. William H.D. Adams]. London, 1881. Ill.
GB.135; GB.136; Lloyd.168. a309.

Alpine climbing: narratives of recent ascents of Mont Blanc, the Matterhorn, the Jungfrau, and other lofty summits of the Alps / by the author of *The Mediterranean illustrated* [i.e. William H.D. Adams]. London, 1882. Ill.
GB.137. a310.

The **Alpine** Club: 1920-1932 / T. Graham Brown. [London], 1933. Reprinted from the *Alpine Journal*, May 1933.
GB.1305(21); Lloyd.1612(2). a311.

Alpine Club – Club Alpino Inglese. [Turin, 1893.] Pp.326-8 of the *Bollettino del Club Alpino Italiano*, vol.27 no.60.
GB.1881(9). a312.

The **Alpine** Club and the British Mountaineering Council: correspondence. [London, 1945.]
GB.1319(17). a313.

The **Alpine** Club centenary: retrospect and prospect / Tom Longstaff. London, 1957. Ill. Pp.294-6 of the *Geographical Magazine*, vol.30 no.6.
GB.1318(10). a314.

Alpine Club exhibition: catalogue of a collection of mountain paintings and photographs exhibited at the XIXth Century Art Gallery. London, 1894.
GB.1315(5); Lloyd.802. a315.

Alpine Club exhibition: exhibition of Alpine paintings at 23 Savile Row, London, May 5 to May 31, 1913. London, 1913. A catalogue.
Lloyd.1608(1). a316.

The **Alpine** Club exhibition (December 9-29, 1909): a loan collection of Alpine prints, engravings & black & white drawings. London, [1909]. A catalogue.
Lloyd.1617(20). a317.

The **Alpine** Club jubilee dinner. [London], 1907. Menu card.
GB.1334(42). a318.

The **Alpine** Club register, 1857-1863, 1864-1876, 1877-1890 / A. L. Mumm. London, 1923-28. 3v.
GB.702-4; Lloyd.967-8 (wanting v.3). a319.

Alpine days and nights / W.T. Kirkpatrick. With a paper by the late R. Philip Hope. London, 1932. Ill., ports.
GB.486; Lloyd.616. a320.

The **Alpine** 'distress signal' scheme / C.T. Dent. [London, 1895.] Ill. Pp.[109]-19 of the *Badminton Magazine*, Aug.1895.
GB.1880(53); GB.1880(54). a321.

Alpine flowers for English gardens / William Robinson. New ed., rev. London, 1875. Ill.
Lloyd.646. a322.

Alpine Gefahren / Fritz Schmitt. Innsbruck, 1968. Ill. [Lehrschriften für die Jugendgruppen and Jungmannschaften des O.A.V.].
GB/A.434(2). a323.

Alpine glaciers / A.E. Lockington Vial. London, 1952. Ill.
GB.1199. a324.

Alpine guide to southwestern British Columbia / Dick Culbert. Vancouver, 1974. Ill., maps.
GB/A.1883(7). a326.

The **Alpine** Journal. Vol.1-69, 1863/64-1964. London, 1864-1964.
GB.1391-1459; Lloyd.1045-1104 (other copies of v.1-61); Lloyd.1046A-B, Lloyd.1063A-D, Lloyd.1067A, Lloyd.1068A, Lloyd.1070A, Lloyd.1078A-B (other copies of odd issues). a328.

The **Alpine** Journal. Vol.26 no.197-vol.63 no.297. [London, 1912-58.] Proofs and first revise copies of extracts including photographs. Incomplete.
GB.1882-1910. a329.

The **Alpine** Journal. Index, vols.1-15 / edited by F.A. Wallroth. London, 1892. Map.
GB.1460; Lloyd.1105. a330.

The **Alpine** Journal. Index, vols.16-38. London, 1929.
GB.1461; Lloyd.1106.   a331.

The **Alpine** Journal. Index, vols.39-58 (1927-1952). London, 1954.
GB.1462.   a332.

An **Alpine** journal / W. Martin Conway. London, 1894. Pp.[210]-24 of the *Contemporary Review*, no.344, August 1894.
GB.1336(15).   a333.

An **Alpine** journey / Frank S. Smythe. London, 1934. Ill.
GB.1101.   a334.

An **Alpine** journey / Frank S. Smythe. London, 1941. Ill. [Black jacket books.]
GB.222.   a335.

Alpine lyrics / [William Bainbridge]. London, 1854.
Lloyd.160.   a336.

Alpine Majestäten: alpine Ansichten aus aller Welt. Hft.1-7. München, [ca 1900]. Ill.
GB/B.595(1).   a337.

Alpine Majestäten: bayerische Alpen. München, [ca 1900]. Ill.
GB/B.595(2).   a338.

Alpine Majestäten und ihr Gefolge: die Gebirgwelt der Erde in Bildern / August Rothpletz, Ernst Platz. München, 1901-02. 2v; ill.
GB/C.8-9.   a339.

Alpine memories / Emile Javelle; translated and with an introduction by W.H. Chesson. London, 1899. Ill., ports. Translated from *Souvenirs d'un alpiniste*.
GB.581; Lloyd.763; Lloyd.763A.   a340.

Alpine notes. London, [1952]. Reprinted from the *Alpine Journal*, vol.58, Nov.1952.
GB.1307(2).   a341.

Alpine notes & The climbing foot / George Wherry. Cambridge, 1896. Ill., ports. Reprinted, with additions, from the *Cambridge Chronicle*.
GB.417; Lloyd.494; Lloyd.494A,B,C.   a342.

[**Alpine** panoramas from the *Jahrbuch des Schweizer Alpenclub*, vol.32.] [Bern, 1896.] 4pt.
GB.1333(19-22).   a343.

[**Alpine** papers collected by Thomas N. Brushfield.] [N.p., n.d.] 8v.
Lloyd.1233-40.   a344.

The **Alpine** pass of Hannibal / Douglas W. Freshfield. [London], 1886. Map. Pp.638-44 of the *Proceedings of the Royal Geographical Society* for 1886.
GB.1156.   a345.

An **Alpine** pass on 'Ski' / A. Conan Doyle. [London, 1894.] Ill., ports. Pp.[657]-61 of the *Strand Magazine*, vol.8.
GB.1336(13).   a346.

The **Alpine** pass route: a walking guide across the Swiss Alps / Jonathan Hurdle. Sheffield, 1983. Ill., maps.
GB/A.2165(1).   a347.

The **Alpine** passes: the Middle Ages, 962-1250 / J.E. Tyler. Oxford, 1930.
GB.844.   a348.

Alpine photography / Olaf Bloch. Ilford, [1937?]. Ill.
GB/A.1597(8).   a349.

Alpine pilgrimage / Julius Kugy; translated by H.E.G. Tyndale. London, 1934. Ill., ports. Translated from *Aus dem Leben eines Bergsteigers*.
GB.865.   a350.

Alpine plants: figures and descriptions of some of the most striking and beautiful Alpine flowers / edited by David Wooster. Ser.1. 2nd ed. London, 1874. Ill.
Lloyd.1307.   a351.

Alpine plants: figures and descriptions of some of the most striking and beautiful Alpine flowers / edited by David Wooster. Ser.2. London, 1874. Ill.
Lloyd.1306.   a352.

Alpine poems / Edward Henry Blakeney. Winchester, 1929.
GB.1318(17).   a353.

The **Alpine** portfolio: the Pennine Alps, from the Simplon to the Great St. Bernard / edited by Oscar Eckenstein, August Lorria. London, [1899]. Ill.
Lloyd.1540.   a354.

The **Alpine** Post. Vol.11-vol.18 no.2, summer season 1892 – winter season 1895/96. St. Moritz, 1892-96.
Lloyd.1533-6 (impf.); GB.1334(30-31) (another copy of v.13 no.19-20).   a355.

The **Alpine** regions of Switzerland and the neighbouring countries: a pedestrian's notes on their physical features, scenery, and natural history / T.G. Bonney. Cambridge, 1868. Ill.
GB.1000; Lloyd.1127; Lloyd.1127A,B.   a356.

Das **alpine** Relief: nach zwei Vorträgen, gehalten im Dezember 1904 im Bernoullianum, Basel / S. Blumer. [N.p., 1904.]
GB/A.1052(7).   a357.

Alpine rescue / Ashenden [i.e. Sidney Nowill]. Edinburgh, 1958. Pp.[97]-110 of *Blackwood's Magazine*, vol. 283 no.1709, February 1958.
GB.1333(11).   a358.

Alpine resting places: a story above the clouds / 'Shirley'. [London, 1883.] Pp.17-25 of *Good Words*, vol.24.
GB.1336(25) (impf.).   a359.

The **Alpine** root-grubber. [London, 1892.] Pp.611-7 of the *Cornhill Magazine*, 1892.
GB.1881(19).   a360.

Alpine roundabout / Anthony M. Robinson. London, 1947. Ill.
GB.833.   a361.

Alpine sketches / Henry George Willink. [N.p., n.d.] Ill., port.
Lloyd.1241.   a362.

Alpine sketches, comprised in a short tour through parts of Holland, Flanders, France, Savoy, Switzerland and Germany, during the summer of 1814 / by a member of the University of Oxford [i.e. George Wilson Bridges]. London, 1814.
GB.585; Lloyd.1161; Lloyd.1161A.   a363.

The **Alpine** Ski Club Annual. No.2. London, [1909].
Lloyd.1604(7).   a363.1.

Alpine Skitouren: eine Auswahl. Bd.1: Zentralschweiz, Bedrettotal / bearbeitet von Fritz Ineichen und Mitarbeitern aus S.A.C.-Kreisen. Wallisellen, 1973. Ill., maps.
GB/A.1334.   a364.

Alpine Skitouren: eine Auswahl. Bd.2: Graubünden / bearbeitet von Christian Caduff und Mitarbeitern aus S.A.C.-Kreisen. [Zurich], 1962. Ill.
GB/A.1346.   a365.

Alpine sports. 1932/33-1933/34. Cambridge, [1933-34].
Lloyd.1614(9-10).   a365.1.

Alpine studies / W.A.B. Coolidge. London, 1912. Ill.
GB.1060; Lloyd.1163.   a366.

Alpine tit-bits / F.T. Wethered. London, 1892. Pp.390-407 of the *Gentleman's Magazine*, vol.273 no.1942.
GB.1880(9).   a367.

An **Alpine** touring guide to the West Kootenays / T. Van Alstine, D. Houghton. [Castlegar, B.C., 1977?] Ill., maps.
GB/B.525(13).   a368.

An **Alpine** valley, and other poems / Lawrence Pilkington. London, 1924. Ill.
Lloyd.1603(1).   a369.

Alpine Welt: ein Sammelbuch für Bergfreunde / bearbeitet von Max Rohrer. 2. veränderte und verm. Aufl. München, 1923. Ill., map, ports., facsims.
GB/B.488.   a370.

Alpine wonderland: a collection of photographs / Jos. Jul. Schätz. London, 1936. Translated from *Wunder der Alpen*.
Lloyd.1488.   a371.

The **Alpine** world of Mount Cook National Park / [Andy Dennis, Craig Potton]. Wellington, [1985?].
GB/B.653.   a372.

Alpiner Hochleistungstest: eine interdisziplinare Studie / herausgegeben von G. Hartmann mit Beiträgen von P. Astrup [et al.]; unter dem Patronat der Schweizerischen Stiftung für Alpine Forschungen. Bern, 1973. Ill.
GB/A.1252.   a373.

Ein **alpiner** Ritter von der traurigen Gestalt: Prof. Dr. Karl Schulz in Leipzig / Guido Eugen Lammer. 2. durchgesehene und verm. Aufl. Wien, 1888.
Lloyd.1147.   a374.

Alpines Bücherverzeichnis enthaltend: Reiseführer, landschaftliche Schilderungen usw., Karten, Pläne, Panoramen. Mit einem Anhang: Gebirgsreliefs. 4. Aufl. München, 1913. Maps.
GB/A.184.   a375.

Alpines Handbuch / herausgegeben von Deutschen und Osterreichischen Alpenverein. Leipzig, 1931. 2v; ill., maps.
GB/B.407-8. a376.

Alpineum helveticum / Max Oechslin. Luzern, 1948. 2v; ill.
GB/C.10-11. a377.

Alpini della Julia: storia della 'divisione miracolo' / Aldo Rasero. 2a ed. Milano, 1972. Ill., maps. [Uomini e armi; 1.]
GB/A.1055. a378.

Alpinisches und Transalpinisches: neun Vorträge / Karl Witte. Berlin, 1858. Ill.
GB/A.178. a379.

Alpinisme / Club alpin français, Groupe de haute montagne. Année 1 no.1-année 29 no.109, jan.1926-automne 1954. Paris, 1926-54.
GB/B.244-5(23); GB.1644(1-17) (other copies of odd issues); Lloyd.1444-8 (no.22-110, 1931-54 (impf.)); Lloyd.1667a (another copy of no.94). a380.

L'**alpinisme** / Paul Bessière. Paris, 1967. Ill. [Que sais-je?; 1255.]
GB/A.175. a381.

L'**alpinisme**: performance physique et spirituelle: conférences faites lors de l'Assemblée internationale professionnelle d'alpinisme de l'Union touristique 'Les Amis de la nature', du 27 au 29 octobre 1967 à Bochum, Allemagne. Zürich, 1968.
GB/B.119(10). a382.

L'**alpinisme** à Saint-Martin-Vésubie, Madone de Fenestre, Boreon, Adus, Colmiane, Lac Negre, Argentera, Matto / Vincent Paschetta. 3e éd. Nice, 1949. Ill., map. Published by the Club alpin français, Section des Alpes-Maritimes.
GB/A.2020(9). a383.

Alpinisme acrobatique / Guido Rey; traduit par Emile Gaillard. Chambéry, 1919. Translated from *Alpinismo acrobatico*.
GB/A.2124. a384.

Alpinisme anecdotique / Charles Gos. Neuchâtel, [1934]. [Montagne.]
GB.1323(8); Lloyd.1616(7). a385.

L'**alpinisme** en Suisse / texte de A. Flückiger et de Walter Lesch pour le chapitre *Les cristalliers*. Zürich, [ca 1960]. Ill. Published by the Schweizerische Zentrale für Verkehrsförderung.
GB/A.799(7); GB/A.1351(2). a386.

Alpinisme et compétition / Pierre Allain. Nouv.éd. Genève, 1978. Ill. [Les Alpes et les hommes; 6.]
GB/A.1615. a387.

Alpinisme et randonnée. No.1-42, nov.1978-avril 1982. Paris, 1978-82.
GB/B.637. a388.

Alpinisme et volcanisme: l'éruption du Vésuve en 1906 / Emile Fontaine. Tours, 1928. Ill.
Lloyd.1608(6). a389.

Alpinisme hivernal: le skieur dans les Alpes / Marcel Kurz. Paris, 1925. Ill.
GB/A.1218. a390.

Alpinisme moderne / collaborateurs: Mario Bisaccia [et al.]; sous la direction de Giancarlo Del Zotto; traduction et adaptation par Félix Germain. Paris, 1971. Ill. [Sempervivum; 51.] Translated from *Alpinismo moderno*.
GB/A.836(1). a391.

L'**alpinismo** / Aurelio Garobbio, Giovanni Rusconi. Firenze, 1974. Ill. [Enciclopedie pratiche Sansoni.]
GB/A.2020(5). a392.

L'**alpinismo** / Carlo Guaraldo. Padova, 1969. Ill. [I radar: enciclopedia del tempo libero; ser.10 n.10.]
GB/B.245(30). a393.

Alpinismo / Club Alpino Italiano, Sezione di Torino. Anno 4-9, 1932-7. Torino, [1932-37]. Incomplete.
Lloyd.1470-4. a393.1.

Alpinismo / G. Albani, G. Scotti. 2a ed. Roma, 1930. Ill. [Manuali SUCAI.] At head of title: Gruppi Universitari Fascisti. Published by the Sezione Universitaria, Club Alpino Italiano.
GB/A.2020(6). a394.

Alpinismo / Giovanni Pizzi. Milano, 1926. Ill. [Manuali Hoepli.]
GB/A.1562. a395.

L'**alpinismo** / Massimo Cappon. Milano, 1981. Ill.
GB/B.580. a396.

L'**alpinismo** / sotto la direzione di Bernard Amy; traduzione di Marina Antonioli Cerruti. [Milan],

1978. Ill. [Exploits.] Translated from *Technique de l'alpinisme*.
GB/A.2014. a397.

Alpinismo: tecnica moderna su roccia e ghiaccio / Carlo Negri. Milano, 1943. Ill.
GB/A.2023(5). a398.

Alpinismo: discorso letto all'Università Popolare di Venezia / Giovanni Chiggiato. Roma, 1910. [Biblioteca della Rivista di Roma; 3.]
GB/B.440(15). a399.

Alpinismo: manuale pratico / Rolando Perzalghi. Milano, 1957. Ill. [Olimpia.]
GB/A.2018(7). a400.

Alpinismo a quattro mani / Giovanni Saragat, Guido Rey. Torino, 1898.
GB/A.1556. a401.

Alpinismo acrobatico / Guido Rey. Nuova ed. sotto gli auspici della Sezione di Torino del C.A.I. Torino, 1932. Ill. [La piccozza e la penna.]
GB/A.839. a402.

L'**alpinismo** d'altri tempi / Erminio Piantanida. Pisa, 1971. Ill. [Biblioteca dell'Ussero. Nuova ser.]
GB/A.860(6). a403.

Un **alpinismo** di ricerca / Alessandro Gogna. [Milan], 1975. Ill. [Exploits.]
GB/A.1381(1). a404.

Alpinismo e alimentazione / Carlo Losito. 2a ed. Alta Brianza, 1972.
GB/A.1580(1). a405.

Alpinismo e non alpinismo / Giuseppe Mazzotti. Treviso, 1946. Ill. [Biblioteca alpina; 2.]
GB.1327(10). a406.

Alpinismo e sci / Renato Tedeschi. Roma, 1930. Ill.
GB/A.799(14). a407.

Alpinismo eroico / a cura del Comitato Nazionale del C.A.I. per le Onoranze ad Emilio Comici. Milan, 1942. Ill.
GB/A.796. a408.

Alpinismo español en el mundo / José María Azpiazu Aldalur. Vol.1. [Madrid?], 1980. Ill., maps.
GB/B.535. a409.

Alpinismo italiano extraeuropeo, al 112° anno: saggio di cronologia ed analisi critica:

elaborazione dall'Archivio del CISDAE in Bologna / Mario Fantin. Bologna, 1967. Ill. Publication of the Centro Italiano Studio Documentazione Alpinismo Extraeuropeo.
GB/B.338(5). a410.

Alpinismo italiano nel mondo / a cura del Comitato Scientifico del Club Alpino Italiano. Milano, 1953. Ill.
GB/B.279. a411.

Alpinismo italiano nel mondo: antologia ad opera di Mario Fantin / comitato di redazione: Giovanni Bertoglio, Toni Ortelli. Milano, 1972. 2v; ill., maps.
GB/B.339-40. a412.

Alpinismo mexicano / Armando Altamira G. México, 1972. Ill., maps.
GB/B.366(10). a413.

Un **alpinismo** possibile: un'esperienza e una proposta / Bepi Pellegrinon. Bologna, 1969. Ill. [Voci dai monti; 18.]
GB/A.474. a414.

Alpinismo romantico / Sandro Prada. Bologna, 1972. [Voci dai monti; 22.]
GB/A.951. a415.

Alpinismo senza chiodi: cronache di montagna del principio del secolo / Bartolomeo Figari. Bologna, 1966. Ill.
GB/B.119(3); GB/B.290(8). a416.

L'**alpinismo** su ghiaccio / Mirko Minuzzo. Milano, 1973. Ill.
GB/A.1115(8). a417.

Alpinismo su roccia e su ghiaccio / a cura di Guido Oddo. Novara, 1970. Ill. [I documentari; 30.] Published by the Istituto Geografico De Agostini.
GB/B.393. a418.

L'**alpinismo** su roccia in 12 lezioni / Mirko Minuzzo. Milano, 1973. Ill.
GB/A.1115(6). a419.

Der **Alpinismus** in Bildern / Alfred Steinitzer. München, 1913. Ill.
GB/B.330. a420.

Der **Alpinismus** in Bildern / Alfred Steinitzer. 2. erg. Aufl. München, 1924. Ill.
GB/B.121. a421.

Alpinismus in Bildern: Geschichte und Gegenwart / herausgegeben von Karl Lukan mit Beiträgen von Willi End [et al.]. Wien, [1967]. GB/B.111. a422.

Der **Alpinist** und Geograph Eduard Richter / Johannes Frischauf. Laibach, 1905. GB/A.181(14). a423.

Alpiniste, est-ce toi? / A. de Chatellus. Genève, 1980. Ill., ports. [Les Alpes et les hommes; 19.] GB/A.1792. a424.

Die **Alpinisten**: Roman / Franz Wichmann. Berlin, [n.d.]. 2v (in 1). GB/A.32. a425.

Alpinisti ciabattoni / A.G. Cagna. Milan, [1934]. GB/A.1159. a426.

Alpinus, conteur dauphinois: nouveaux récits précédés d'une vie d'Alpinus / Raymond Coche. [Paris, 1946.] Ill. [La vie en montagne.] GB/A.202. a427.

The **Alps** / Arnold Lunn. London, 1914. [Home university library.] GB.142. a428.

The **Alps** / Friedrich Umlauft; translated by Louisa Brough. London, 1889. Ill., map. Translated from *Die Alpen*. Lloyd.1293; Lloyd.1293A. a429.

The **Alps** / Shiro Shirahata. New York, 1980. Ill. Translated from the Japanese. GB/B.545. a430.

The **Alps** / W. Martin Conway. London, 1904. Ill. GB/A.146. a431.

The **Alps**: a poem / George Keate. London, 1763. GB.1182; Lloyd.1297; Lloyd.1621(9). a432.

Alps across the footlights / J. Monroe Thorington. [New York, 1940.] Ill., facsims. Reprinted from the *American Alpine Journal*, vol.4 no.1, 1940. GB.1333(45). a433.

Alps and men: pages from forgotten diaries of travellers and tourists in Switzerland / Sir Gavin de Beer. London, 1932. Ill., ports. GB.809; GB.810. a434.

The **Alps** and Pyrenees / Victor Hugo; translated from the French by John Manson. London, 1898. Translated from *Alpes et Pyrénées*. GB/A.1019. a435.

Alps and sanctuaries of Piedmont and the Canton Ticino / Samuel Butler. London, 1882. Ill. Lloyd.925. a436.

Alps and sanctuaries of Piedmont and the Canton Ticino. Op. 6 / Samuel Butler. 2nd ed. London, 1882. Ill. GB.633. a437.

Alps and sanctuaries of Piedmont & the Canton Ticino / Samuel Butler. London, 1923. Ill. GB/A.430. a438.

The **Alps** and the eastern mails / Sir Cusack Patrick Roney. London, 1867. Map. Lloyd.910; Lloyd.1583(6). a439.

The **Alps** and the Rhine: a series of sketches / J.T. Headley. London, 1846. [Wiley and Putnam's library of American books.] GB.365; GB.439; GB/A.1387; Lloyd.561. a440.

The **Alps** from end to end / W. Martin Conway. [London], 1895. Ill. GB.1154; Lloyd.1270; Lloyd.1271; Lloyd. 1271A. a441.

The **Alps** from end to end / W. Martin Conway; with a chapter by W.A.B. Coolidge. [London], 1900. Ill. Lloyd.827. a442.

The **Alps** in 1864: a private journal / A.W. Moore; [edited by Alex. B.W. Kennedy]. London, 1867. GB.976; GB.977; Lloyd.969; Lloyd.969A,B,C,D. a443.

The **Alps** in 1864: a private journal / A.W. Moore; edited by Alex. B.W. Kennedy. Edinburgh, 1902. GB.1190; Lloyd.1359; Lloyd.1359A,B. a444.

The **Alps** in 1864 / A.W. Moore; edited by E.H. Stevens. Oxford, 1939. 2v; ill., maps. [Blackwell's mountaineering library; 5.] GB.546-7; GB.548-9 (impf.). a445.

The **Alps** of Hannibal / William John Law. London, 1866. 2v (in 1); map. GB.818. a446.

The **Alps** of the Bernina, W. of the Bernina Pass / E.L. Strutt. London, 1910. 2v; map. [Conway and Coolidge's climbers' guides; 15-16.] GB.1324(9-10); Lloyd.30-31. a447.

The **Alps** of the Dauphiné / E. Debriges. London, 1887. Ill. A series of letters published in the *Siècle* in September 1884.
Lloyd.897. a448.

The **Alps**, or Sketches of life and nature in the mountains / H. von Berlepsch; translated by Leslie Stephen. London, 1861. Ill.
GB.847; Lloyd.1014; Lloyd.1029. a449.

The **Alps**, or Sketches of life and nature in the mountains / H. von Berlepsch; translated by Leslie Stephen. London, 1861. Ill. With a note by the translator on the explorations of 1861.
Lloyd.928. a449.1.

The **Alps**, Switzerland, and the north of Italy / Charles Williams. London, 1854. Ill., map, ports.
GB.1273; Lloyd.1468. a450.

Als Letzter am Seil: zwölf Erstbesteigungen in den schweizer und in den französischen Alpen / E.R. Blanchet; Ubertragung aus dem Französischen von Heinrich Erler. Berlin, [1938]. Ill. Translated from *Au bout d'un fil.*
GB/A.420. a451.

Alta Badia: guida per l'escursionista / Albino Frenademez. [Corvara], 1971. Ill., map.
GB/A.1295(6). a452.

Alta montagna. La fontana dei sospiri. La damigella di Bard / Salvator Gotta. Rocco San Casciano, [1958]. Port. [Teatro italiano contemporaneo; 17.]
GB/A.835(8). a453.

Alta via degli eroi da Feltre a Bassano del Grappa / Italo Zandonella. Bologna, 1975. Ill., maps. [Itinerari alpini; 22.]
GB/A.1351(16). a454.

Alta via dei silenzi: dalle sorgenti del Piave a Vittorio Veneto / Toni Sanmarchi. Bologna, 1972. Ill. [Itinerari alpini; 8.]
GB/A.942(15). a455.

L'**alta** via del Brenta / Giorgio Armani. Trento, 1979. Ill., map, port. Col patrocinio della Società Alpinisti Tridentini.
GB/A.1965(5). a456.

Alta via delle Alpi / Mario Fantin. Bologna, 1957. Ill.
GB/B.362. a457.

Alta via delle Alpi Carniche: dal Monte Peralba a Moggio Udinese / Manlio De Cillia, Angelo De Ferrari. Bologna, 1976. Ill. [Itinerari alpini; 32.]
GB/A.1589(15). a458.

Alta via delle Dolomiti / Piero Rossi. 2a ed. Bologna, 1971. Ill; maps. [Itinerari alpini; 3.]
GB/A.867(7). a459.

Alta via delle Dolomiti. 3: Alta via dei Camosci: da Villabassa a Longarone attraverso i monti (Picco di Vallandro, Monte Piana, Cristallo, Sorapis, Pelmo, Bosconero) / Mario Brovelli, Bruno Tolot. Cortina, [1979?].
GB/A.1911(15). a460.

Alta via delle leggende: da Bressanone a Feltre (Plose, Odle, Puez, Sella, Marmolada, pale di San Martino, Alpi Feltrine) / Mario Brovelli, Sigi Lechner. Bologna, 1973. Ill., maps. [Itinerari alpini; 14.]
GB/A.1270(1). a461.

Alta via di Grohmann: da San Candido a Pieve di Cadore (Lavaredo, Cadini, Sorapiss, Antelao) / Toni Sanmarchi. Bologna, 1973. Ill., maps. [Itinerari alpini; 12.]
GB/A.1199(16). a462.

Alta via di Tiziano: da Sesto a Pieve di Cadore (Croda dei Toni, Popera, Marmarole, Antelao) / Toni Sanmarchi. Bologna, 1973. Ill., maps. [Itinerari alpini; 13.]
GB/A.1199(17). a463.

Alta via 'Dino Buzzati': i principali sentieri, le vie ferrate, i bivacchi ed i rifugi delle pale di S. Martino / Gabriele Franceschini, Lalla Morassutti. Cortina d'Ampezzo, 1979. Ill., map, port. [Sentieri e vie ferrate; 1.]
GB/A.2018(11). a464.

Alta via ladina: Catinaccio – Sella – Marmolada / Paolo Cavagna, Tony Rizzi. Trento, [1972]. Ill., map. [L'uomo e le Dolomiti.]
GB/A.1050(19). a465.

Alta via n.7 / Piero Fain, Toni Sanmarchi. Bologna, 1976. Ill. [Itinerari alpini; 31.]
GB/A.1589(3). a466.

Das **Alter** des schweizerischen diluvialen Lösses / Heinrich Brockmann-Jerosch. Zürich, [1909]. *Vierteljahrsschrift der Naturforschenden Gesellschaft in Zürich.* Sonderabdruck aus Jahrgang 54, 1909.
GB/A.1052(16). a467.

Die **älteste** Schutzhütte im Berner Oberland: ein Beitrag zur Geschichte der bernischen Touristik / Jubiläumschrift von W.A.B. Coolidge. Bern, 1915. Published by the Schweizer Alpenclub, Sektion Grindelwald.
GB.1335(60). a468.

Die **ältesten** Karten der West-Alpen / Eugen Oberhummer. [Munich], 1909. Facsims. Pp.1-20 of the *Zeitschrift des Deutschen und Osterreichischen Alpenvereins*, Bd.40.
GB.1331(58); GB.1331(59). a469.

Alti sentieri attorno al Monte Bianco / Cosimo Zappelli. Bologna, 1969. Ill., maps. [Itinerari alpini; 2.]
GB/A.473. a470.

Alti sentieri attorno al Monte Bianco / Cosimo Zappelli. 2a ed. Bologna, 1972. Ill., maps. [Itinerari alpini; 2.]
GB/A.942(14). a471.

Alti sentieri attorno al Monte Rosa / Piero Carlesi. Bologna, 1980. Ill., maps. [Itinerari alpini; 50.]
GB/A.1589(22). a472.

[**Altitudes** of the principal snow peaks visible from Kumaon reported at the Nov.23 1816 meeting of the Wernerian Natural History Society.] [London], 1817. Pp.231-4 of *Annals of Philosophy*, vol.9, 1817.
GB.1880(43). a473.

Alto Adige, Dolomiti: guida per il turista / Marcello Caminiti. Novara, 1961. Ill., map. Published by the Istituto Geografico De Agostini.
GB/B.377(3). a474.

L'**Alto** Adige nella storia / Mario Ferrandi. Calliano, 1972. Ill.
GB/A.1216. a475.

Altopiano di Siusi, Sciliar: itinerari escursionistici e naturalistici, arrampicate / Dante Colli. Bologna, [1986]. [Itinerari alpini; 62.]
GB/A.1589(36). a476.

Am Lugenbankl: lustige tiroler Bauern-geschichten / Karl Deutsch. München, 1912.
GB/A.33. a477.

Am Seil vom Stabeler Much / erzählt von Karl Springenschmid. 8.Aufl. München, [ca 1925]. Ill.
GB/A.1499. a478.

L'**amateur** d'abîmes: récit / Samivel. Paris, 1969.
GB/A.1295(4). a479.

Ame et visage du Valais / Ignace Marietan. Lausanne, 1949. Ill. [Collection alpine.]
GB/A.1646. a480.

Amendments to bye-laws adopted at the special general meeting, Royal Geographical Society, 13th October 1952. [London, 1952.]
GB.1333(2). a481.

America in the Antarctic to 1840 / Philip I. Mitterling. Urbana, 1959. Maps.
GB/A.1600. a482.

The **American** Alpine Club's handbook of American mountaineering / Kenneth A. Henderson. Boston, 1942. Ill.
GB/A.1894. a483.

The **American** Alpine Journal. Vol.1 no.2-3. New York, 1930-31. Published by the American Alpine Club.
GB.1332(4-5). a484.

The **American** Alpine Journal: index, 1929-1976 / Earlyn Church, editor and chief indexer. New York, 1979.
GB/A.2052(3). a485.

American entries in the travellers' book of the Grands Mulets, 1861-75 / J. Monroe Thorington. [New York, 1952.] Reprinted from the *American Alpine Journal*, vol.8 no.2, 1952.
GB.1333(23). a486.

The **American** Journal of Science and Arts. Vol.2 no.2, Nov.1820. New-Haven, 1820.
Lloyd.1001. a486.1.

American whalers in the Western Arctic: the final epoch of the great American sailing whaling fleet: a portfolio of watercolour drawings / William Gilkerson; introduced and related in text by John R. Bockstoce. Fairhaven, 1983. Ill.
GB/C.112. a487.

Americans in Antarctica, 1775-1948 / Kenneth J. Bertrand. New York, 1971. Ill. [Special publication / American Geographical Society; 39.]
GB/A.2118. a488.

Americans on Everest: the official account of the ascent led by Norman G. Dyhrenfurth / James Ramsey Ullman and other members of the

expedition. Philadelphia, [1964]. Ill., maps.
GB/A.2061.   a489.

Among the Alps: a narrative of personal experiences / Samuel Aitken. [London, 1900.] Ill.
Lloyd.1532.   a490.

Among the Esquimaux, or Adventures under the Arctic Circle / Edward S. Ellis. Philadelphia, 1918. Ill.
GB/A.1727.   a491.

Among the Himalayas / L. Austine Waddell. Westminster, 1899. Ill.
GB.1057.   a492.

Among the Himalayas / L. Austine Waddell. 2nd impr. Westminster, 1900.
GB.649.   a493.

Among the Kara-Korum glaciers in 1925 / Jenny Visser-Hooft; with contributions by Ph. C. Visser. London, 1926.
GB.997.   a494.

Among the mountains / F. Harrisson. [N.p., n.d.]
GB.1326(35).   a495.

Among the Selkirk glaciers: being the account of a rough survey in the Rocky Mountains regions of British Columbia / William Spotswood Green. London, 1890. Ill., map.
Lloyd.527.   a496.

Among the snow-mountains of the Tyrol / A.E.W. Mason. [London, 1895.] Pp.411-8 of *Temple Bar*, vol.104 no.412.
GB.1880(6).   a497.

Die **Ampezzaner** Alpen / Otto Zsigmondy. Die Sextener Gruppe / Carl Diener. [Berlin, 1894.] Ill. Pp.[442]-538 of *Erschliessung der Ostalpen*, Bd.3.
GB.1380.   a498.

Amphipoda (crustacea) of the Thule area, Northwest Greenland: faunistics and taxonomy / Jean Just. Copenhagen, 1980. Ill., maps. [Meddelelser om Grønland. Bioscience; 2.]
GB/A.1819(2).   a499.

The **Amulet**, or Christian and literary remembrancer. 1828. London, 1828. Ill.
GB.33.   a500.

Amundsen's expedition and the Northwest passage / A.W. Greely. [New York, n.d.] Map,

port. Pp.625-32 of the *Century Magazine*, vol.73.
GB.1341(13).   a501.

L'**anabaptiste**, ou Le cultivateur par expérience: almanach nouveau pour l'an de grâce 1823 / Jacques Klopfenstein. Belfort, [1822].
Lloyd.1591(3).   a502.

L'**ancienne** Genève, 1535-1798: fragments historiques / Louis Dufour-Vernes. Genève, 1909.
Lloyd.1617(4).   a503.

Andare in montagna / Fulvio Campiotti. Milano, 1969. Ill. [Manuali del turismo.] Published by the Touring Club Italiano.
GB/A.1270(2).   a504.

Le **Ande** / José Miguel Cei. Milano, 1974. Ill., maps. [Natura.]
GB/B.431.   a505.

Le **Ande**: monografia geografico-alpinistica / Pietro Meciani. Bologna, [1965?]. Ill., maps.
GB/A.2022(3).   a506.

Die **Anderungen** des Klimas seit der grössten Ausdehnung der letzten Eiszeit in der Schweiz / Heinrich Brockmann-Jerosch. [Stockholm, 1910.] Sonderabdruck aus *Postglaziale Klimaveränderungen*.
GB/A.1052(17).   a507.

Los **Andes** de Patagonia / Lucien Gallois. Paris, [1901]. Ill., maps. Traducido de los *Annales de géographie*, tomo 10, 15 de mayo de 1901.
GB/B.137.   a508.

Andorra: 'Prinzessin des Glücks' / Werner Lengemann. Eisenach, [1961]. Ill.
GB/B.324.   a509.

Andreas Fischer: Hochbirgswanderungen in den Alpen und im Kaukasus / R. Wyss. [Bern, 1920.] A review. Pp.238-40 of the *Jahrbuch des Schweizer Alpenclub*, Jahrg.54.
GB.1318(21).   a510.

Andrées Polarfærd, 1897 / S.A. Andrée, Nils Strindberg, og Knut Frænkel; udgivet paa Grundlag af S.A. Andrées, Nils Strindbergs og Knut Frænkels Sommeren 1930 paa Hvideøen fundne Optegnelser af Svenska sällskapet för antropologi och geografi. København, 1930. Ill., maps, ports., facsims.
GB/B.515.   a511.

Anello Alta Pusteria / Italo De Candido. Bologna, [1979]. Ill. [Itinerari alpini; 44.]
GB/A.1589(20). a512.

L'**Anello** Bianco: sci-alpinismo in Comelico e Sappada / Italo De Candido. Bologna, 1976. Ill. [Itinerari alpini; 33.]
GB/A.1589(16). a513.

L'**anello** del Cadore / Italo De Candido. Bologna, 1978. Ill., map. [Itinerari alpini; 41.]
GB/A.1589(8). a514.

L'**anello** del Comelico / Italo De Candido. Bologna, 1974. Ill. [Itinerari alpini; 18.]
GB/A.1349(2). a515.

Anello delle Alpi Giulie occidentali / Società Alpina delle Giulie, Sezione di Trieste del C.A.I., Gruppo Alpinisti Rocciatori Sciatori. Trieste, 1978. Ill., map.
GB/A.1967(1). a516.

Anello di Cortina / Italo De Candido. Bologna, 1981. Ill. [Itinerari alpini; 54.]
GB/A.1589(30). a517.

L'**anello** di Sappada / Italo De Candido. Bologna, 1975. Ill. [Itinerari alpini; 25.]
GB/A.1351(18). a518.

Anello Zoldano: itinerari in sei tappe fra le Dolomiti di Zoldo / Paolo Bonetti, Paolo Lazzarin. Bologna, [1986]. Ill., maps. [Itinerari alpini; 60.]
GB/A.1589(39). a519.

Les **Anglais** dans les Pyrénées et les débuts du tourisme pyrénéen (1739-1896) / Joseph Duloum. Lourdes, 1970. Ill.
GB/A.1225. a520.

L'**anima** della montagna / L.A. Garibaldi. Torino, 1933. Ill. [La piccozza e la penna; 9.] Published by the Club Alpino Italiano, Sezione di Torino.
GB/A.1033. a521.

L'**anima** delle Dolomiti / Carlo Felice Wolff; [translated by Clara Ciraolo et al.]. Bologna, 1971. Ill. [Le Alpi.]
GB/A.1307. a522.

Animadversions on the reflections [by Antoine Varillas] upon Dr. B's travels / [Gilbert Burnet]. [Amsterdam?], 1688.
GB.74. a523.

Ankogel- und Goldberggruppe: einschliesslich Hafner- und Hochalmspitze / Liselotte Buchenauer. München, 1975. Ill., map. [Alpenvereinsführer. Reihe, Zentralalpen.]
GB/A.1676(2). a524.

Anleitung, auf die nützlichste und genussvollste Art die Schweitz zu bereisen / J.G. Ebel. 2. verm. Aufl. Zürich, 1805. 4v. Wanting v.1-2; v.3-4 bound in 1.
GB.240. a525.

Anleitung auf die nützlichste und genussvollste Art die Schweitz zu bereisen / J.G. Ebel. 3. sehr verm. Aufl. Zürich, 1809-10. 4v; ill., maps.
GB.457-60. a526.

Anleitung auf die nützlichste und genussvollste Art die Schweiz zu bereisen / J.G. Ebel; im Auszuge ganz neu bearbeitet von G. v. Escher. 7. Original-Aufl. Zürich, 1840. Ill., map.
GB/A.1324. a527.

Anleitung zu wissenschaftlichen Beobachtungen auf Alpenreisen / herausgegeben vom Deutschen und Oesterreichischen Alpenverein; bearbeitet von C. v. Sonklar, C.W. Gümbel [et al.]. Wien, 1882. 2v (in 1); ill., map.
GB/A.379. a528.

Anleitung zum Kartenlesen im Hochgebirge mit besonderer Berücksichtigung der vom D. u. O. Alpenverein herausgegeben Spezialkarten / Joseph Moriggl. München, 1909. Ill., maps.
GB/A.458. a529.

Anleitung zur Ausübung des Bergführer-Berufes / J. Buchheister, Johannes Emmer, Eduard Richter, Moriz Zeppezauer; herausgegeben von Deutschen und Oesterreichischen Alpenverein. 2. Aufl. Wien, 1891. Ill., maps.
GB/A.185. a530.

Annales / Groupe de haute montagne, Club alpin français. 1966- . Paris, [1967-]. Ill.
GB/B.370. a531.

Annales des Alpes: recueil périodique des Archives des Hautes-Alpes. Année 1897-1913. Gap, 1897[-1913].
GB/A.1106-13. a532.

Annales des Alpes: table alphabétique et table chronologique. Gap, 1914.
GB/A.1114. a533.

Annales oder grundliche Beschreibung der fur-
nembsten Geschichten unnd Thaten, welche sich
in gantzer Helvetia bis auff das 1627 Jahr ver-
lauffen / Michael Stettler. Bern, 1626-27. 2v (in 1).
GB/B.309.   a534.

The **annals** of Mont Blanc: a monograph / Charles
Edward Mathews; with a chapter on the geology
of the mountain, by T.G. Bonney. London, 1898.
Ill., maps, ports., facsims.
GB.953; GB/A.1217; Lloyd.989; Lloyd.989A.
                                                            a535.

Annals of some remarkable aerial and Alpine
voyages, including those of the author / T.
Forster. London, 1832. Ill.
GB.697(5).   a536.

Annapurna: conquest of the first 8000-metre peak
— 26,493 feet / Maurice Herzog; translated by
Nea Morin and Janet Adam Smith. London, 1952.
Ill., ports. Translated from *Annapurna premier
8.000*.
GB.544; Lloyd.713.   a537.

Annapurna II '81: note geo-topografiche: sulla
spedizione / A. Luigi Rampini. [N.p.], 1981.
GB/B.570(15).   a538.

Annapurna face sud / Chris Bonington; traduit
par Jeanne et Félix Germain. [Paris], 1972. Ill.,
maps. [Sempervivum; 54.] Translated from
Annapurna south face.
GB/A.987(4).   a539.

Annapurna premier 8.000 / Maurice Herzog.
Paris, 1952. Ill., maps, ports. [Sempervivum; 16.]
GB/A.1598.   a540.

Annuaire / Club alpin français. Année 1-17, 21-30,
1874-90,1894-1903. Paris, 1874-1904. Wanting
année 22, 1895.
Lloyd.1128-44 (année 1-17); GB/A.1485 (année 21,
1894); GB/A.1304 (année 23, 1896); GB/A.78-82
(année 24-30, 1897-1903); Lloyd.1128A (another
copy of 1875); Lloyd.1129A (another copy of 1876);
GB/A.1944 (another copy of 1902).
                                                            a541.

Annuaire / Groupe de haute montagne, Club
alpin français. No.1-5, 1926-31; 1955. Paris, 1926-
55.
Lloyd.1610 (no.1-4, 1926-30); GB/B.245(24) (no.5,
1931); GB/B.366(2) (1955); Lloyd.1659(4-5)
(another copy of no.1-2).   a542.

Annuaire / Société des touristes du Dauphiné.
Année 27-38, 1901-12. Grenoble, 1901-12. Ill.
GB/A.2069.   a543.

Annuaire de poche / Club alpin français. 1950/
51. Paris, [1950]. Ill., maps.
GB/A.1468(18).   a544.

The **annual** cycle of phytoplankton primary
production and hydrography in the Disko Bugt
area, West Greenland / Ole G. Norden Andersen.
Copenhagen, 1981. Ill., maps. [Meddelelser om
Grønland. Bioscience; 6.]
GB/A.1819(6).   a545.

The **annual** cycle of temperature, salinity, currents
and water masses in Disko Bugt and adjacent
waters, West Greenland / Ole G. Norden
Andersen. Copenhagen, 1981. Ill., maps.
[Meddelelser om Grønland. Bioscience; 5.]
GB/A.1819(5).   a546.

Annual cycles of primary production and of
zooplankton at Southwest Greenland, with
figures of some bottom invertebrate larvae / Erik
L.B. Smidt. Copenhagen, 1979. Ill., map.
[Meddelelser om Grønland. Bioscience; 1.]
GB/A.1819(1).   a547.

The **annual** of the Mountain Club of South Africa.
No.13-33, 1910-30. Cape Town, 1910-30. Ill.
Continues *The Mountain Club Annual*. Continued
by *Journal of the Mountain Club of South Africa*.
GB/A.2160 (wanting no.14-17,21-22,24,32); GB/
B.440(10) (another copy of no.25).   a548.

Annual report of the Geologists Association
together with list of members, catalogue of the
library, laws of the Association. 1872, 1879.
London, 1873-80.
Lloyd.1605(19).   a549.

Annual reports; accounts / Fell and Rock
Climbing Club of the English Lake District. 1953/
54, 1961. Kendal, [1954]-61.
GB.1330(2-3).   a550.

Annuario/ClubAlpinoAccademicoItaliano. 1927-
31. [Torino, 1978.] Ill. A reprint of the 1932 ed.
GB/A.1581.   a551.

Annuario / Club Alpino Italiano, Sezione
Antonio Locatelli. 1957-61. [Bergamo, 1957-61.]
Ill., maps.
GB/B.440(2-6); GB/B.312(1-2) (another copy of
1958-59).   a552.

Annuario / Club Alpino Italiano, Sezione di Biella. 1946-48, 1955, 1962-67, 1972. Biella, 1946-73. Ill.
GB/A.1580(9-13); GB/A.805(1) (1955). a553.

Annuario / Club Alpino Italiano, Sezione di Como. 1955. [Como], 1955.
GB/B.390(9). a554.

Annuario / Club Alpino Italiano, Sezione di Lecco. 1958. [Lecco, 1959.]
GB/B.289(10). a555.

Annuario / Club Alpino Italiano, Sezione di Milano. Anno 6-21/22, 1893-1909/10. Milano, 1894-1910. Wanting parts for 1903 and 1908.
GB/A.828(8-19); GB/A.1468(17) (1907). a556.

Annuario / Club Alpino Italiano, Sezione di Piacenza. 1953-56. Piacenza, [1953-56]. Wanting the issue for 1955.
GB/B.289(7-9). a557.

Annuario / Club Alpino Italiano. Sezione Ligure. 1906, 1914, 1915, 1925, 1957. Genova, 1906-57. Ill., ports.
GB/A.844 (1906, 1914 and 1915); GB/A.799(2) (1925); GB/A.906 (1957). a558.

Annuario generale: comuni e frazioni d'Italia / Touring Club Italiano. 1968. Milano, 1968. Maps.
GB/A.1971. a559.

Another ascent of the world's highest peak, Qomolangma. Peking, 1975. Ill.
GB/B.595(4). a560.

Ansichten der Kronprinz Rudolf-Bahn längs der Strecke von Kastenreith durch's Gesäuse bis Selzthal-Liezen / Franz Hölzlhuber. Vienna, [1876].
GB/A.2094. a561.

Ansichten und Panoramen der Schweiz / Hans Conrad Escher; die Ansichten 1780-1822 herausgegeben von Gustav Solar; Text von Gustav Solar und Jost Hösli. Zürich, 1974.
GB/B.415. a562.

Ansichten und Panoramen der Schweiz / Hans Conrad Escher. Zürich, 1976. Ill.
GB/C.61. a563.

Antarctic Australia / Jutta Hosel. Melbourne, 1981.
GB/B.616. 564.

The **Antarctic** book: winter quarters, 1907-1909. London, 1909. Ill., ports.
GB/B.625. a565.

Antarctic icebreakers / Lorene K. Fox. New York, 1937. Ill., maps, ports.
GB/A.1925. a566.

The **Antarctic** problem: an historical and political study / E.W. Hunter Christie. London, 1951. Ill., maps.
Lloyd.1172. a567.

Antarctica: a traveller's tale / Jean Bailey. London, 1980. Ill.
GB/A.2112. a568.

Antarctica: the last horizon / John Béchervaise. Rev. and expanded ed. Stanmore, N.S.W., 1979.
GB/B.614. a569.

Antarctica: the story of the New Zealand party of the Trans-Antarctic Expedition / A. S. Helm, J.H. Miller. Wellington, 1964.
GB/A.2114. a570.

Antarctica and international law: a collection of inter-state and national documents / W.M. Bush. London, 1982.
GB/A.2132. a571.

Antarctica's forgotten men / L.B. Quartermain. Wellington, 1981.
GB/A.2106. a572.

Antartide / Carlo Mauri [et al.]; [traduzioni: Marcello Manzoni]. Bologna, 1968. Ill.
GB/B.267. a573.

Anthologie romande de la littérature alpestre / préface, choix de textes et notes de Edmond Pidoux. Lausanne, 1972.
GB/A.1290. a574.

Anthropological observations on the Central Eskimos / Kaj Birket-Smith; [translated by W.E. Calvert]. New York, 1976. Ill. [Thule expedition, 5th, 1921-1924. Report; vol.3 no.2.]
GB/A.1827. a575.

Antichi viaggi di scoperta in Islanda, Groenlandia e America / Gwyn Jones; traduzione di Giorgio Romano. Milano, 1966. Ill. Translated from *The Norse Atlantic saga*.
GB/A.497. a576.

Anton Oitzinger: ein Bergführerleben / Julius Kugy. Graz, 1935. Ill., ports.
GB.707. a577.

Antrona – Bognanco – Sempione / Luciano Rainoldi. Vigevano, 1976. Ill., map. Published by the Club Alpino Italiano, Sezione di Vigevano.
GB/A.2033(7). a578.

Anuario / Club Alpino Español. 1929/30. [Madrid?], 1930. Ill.
GB/B.403(24). a579.

Aosta e la Grande Vallée / Angiolo Biancotti. Torino, 1956. Ill.
GB/A.496. a580.

Aosta e la sua valle. Torino, 1924. [Guide illustrate Reynaudi.]
GB/A.67. a581.

Aosta et sa vallée / aux soins de la Section d'Aoste du Club alpin italien. Turin, [1904]. Ill., maps. [Guides illustrés Reynaud; 6.]
GB.723. a582.

Aoste: histoire, antiquités, objets d'art / André Zanotto. Aoste, 1967. Ill., map.
GB/A.1373. a583.

Apôtres inconnus / le R.P. Duchaussois. Paris, [1924]. Ill.
GB/A.1631. a584.

Appalachia. Vol.7 no.4-vol.39 no.4, 1895-1973. Boston, 1895-1973. The numbers from vol.15 no.4 to vol.18 no.3 are described as parts of *Bulletin / Appalachian Mountain Club* and have separate numbering for the *Bulletin* and *Appalachia*.
GB.1536-54 (impf.) (v.7-34); GB/B.604 (v.35-39).
a585.

Appalachia. Bulletin. Vol.17 no.3-6, 8; vol.18 no.5, 6, 9; vol.19 no.2-4; vol.20 no.9; vol.22 no.4, 11; vol.23 no.6; vol.26 no.7; vol.28 no.1, 5, 6. Boston, 1951-62.
GB.1556-74. a587.

Appalachia. Index to vol.1-10, 1876-1904. Boston, 1906.
GB.1555. a588.

Appalachia. Annual reports. 1950, 1956. Boston, [1951-57].
GB.1575-6. a589.

Appalachia. Register. 1951, 1953, 1955. Boston, [1951-55].
GB.1577-9. a590.

Appalachian Mountain Club membership register. Sept.1961. Boston, [1961].
GB.1306(22). a591.

An **appendix** to the *Gentleman's guide through Italy*, containing catalogues of the paintings, statues, busts, &c. / by the author of the *Guide* [i.e. Thomas Martyn]. [London], 1787.
GB.139(2); GB.234(2); Lloyd.1569(2). a592.

L'**Appennino** bolognese: descrizioni e itinerari / Club Alpino Italiano, Sezione di Bologna. Bologna, 1881.
GB/A.1749. a593.

L'**Appennino** bolognese: descrizione e itinerari (1881). Bologna, 1972. Ill., maps. Facsimile reprint of the Bologna, 1881 ed.
GB/A.1289. a594.

L'**Appennino** modenese descritto ed illustrato / Dante Pantanelli; [edited by D. Pantanelli, V. Santi]. [Bologna], 1972. Ill., maps. Facsimile reprint of the Rocca San Casciano, 1895 ed.
GB/A.1053. a595.

L'**Appennino** tosco-emiliano. Milano, 1982. Ill., maps. [Viaggio in Italia; 6.]
GB/B.635(6). a596.

Appenzellerland: schweizerische Alpenposten, Poststrassen im Appenzellerland / herausgegeben von der Generaldirektion der Post-, Telegraphen- und Telephonverwaltung. Bern, 1952. Ill., map.
GB/A.1034(9). a597.

Application to the Prime Minister from the Committee of the Scottish National Antarctic Expedition for a grant of £6,800 to cover publication and other expenses. Edinburgh, 1909.
GB/A.2139(6). a598.

L'**apprenti** montagnard: les plus belles courses graduées du massif du Mont-Blanc / Gaston Rébuffat. Paris, 1946. Ill. [Grands vents.]
GB.1341(20). a599.

Approach to the hills / C.F. Meade. London, 1941. Ill., maps.
GB.814. a600.

Aquatic sport on Ben Nevis / Willy Rickmer Rickmers. [Edinburgh, 1905.] Ill. Reprinted from the *Scottish Mountaineering Club Journal*, vol.8, 1905.
Lloyd.1605(1). a601.

Ararat / Giulio Leclercq. Milano, 1899. Ill. [Biblioteca illustrata dei viaggi intorno al mondo per terra e per mare; 21.]
GB/A.836(3). a602.

Archaeological collections from the Western Eskimos / Therkel Mathiassen; [translated by W.E. Calvert]. New York, 1976. Ill. [Thule expedition, 5th, 1921-1924. Report; vol.10 no.1.]
GB/A.1837. a603.

Archives d'Hauteville: journaux de voyage 1808-1820. Lausanne, [ca 1925]. 2v.
GB/A.865-6. a604.

Arctic / Finn Schultz-Lorentzen. Toronto, 1976.
GB/A.1760. a605.

The **Arctic** / Fred Bruemmer. Montreal, 1974. Ill.
GB/B.630. a606.

Arctic: journal of the Arctic Institute of North America. Vol.1-19(1), 1948-66. Montreal, 1948-66. Ill., maps.
GB/A.2166. a607.

The **Arctic** 1927 / A.Y. Jackson. Moonbeam, Ont., 1982.
GB/A.2093. a608.

Arctic adventure: my life in the frozen North / Peter Freuchen. New York, 1935. Ill., maps, ports.
GB/A.1934. a609.

Arctic and sub-arctic life / John Rae. [London?], 1877. Published by the Royal Institution of Great Britain.
GB/A.1965(13). a610.

Arctic area: indigenous period / Henry B. Collins. México, 1954. Published by the Instituto Panamericano de Geografía e Historia.
GB/A.2207. a611.

An **Arctic** boat journey, in the autumn of 1854 / Isaac I. Hayes; edited, with an introduction and notes, by Dr. Morton Shaw. London, 1860. Maps.
GB.270. a612.

An **Arctic** boat journey in the autumn of 1854 / Isaac I. Hayes. New ed., enl. Boston, 1867. Ill., map.
GB/A.2163. a613.

Arctic bush mission: the experiences of a missionary bush pilot in the Far North / John R. Chambers. Seattle, [1970]. Ill., ports.
GB/B.519. a614.

Arctic command: the story of Smellie of the Nascopie / Roland Wild. Toronto, 1955. Ill., map, ports.
GB/A.1937. a615.

The **Arctic** diary of Russell Williams Porter / edited by Herman Friis. Charlottesville, 1976. Ill.
GB/B.533. a616.

Arctic Eldorado: a dramatic report on Canada's Northland – the greatest unexploited region in the world — with a workable four year plan / Raymond Arthur Davies. Toronto, 1944.
GB/A.1790. a617.

Arctic explorations. Edinburgh, 1850. No.17 of *Chambers's Papers for the people*, vol.3.
GB.1341(15). a618.

Arctic explorations / Elisha Kent Kane. Philadelphia, 1856. 2v.
GB.1017-8. a619.

Arctic explorations: the second Grinnell expedition in search of Sir John Franklin, 1853, '54, '55 / Elisha Kent Kane. London, 1861. Ill., map, port.
GB.514. a620.

Arctic explorations: the second Grinnell expedition in search of Sir John Franklin / Elisha Kent Kane. London, 1864. Ill.
GB/A.1611. a621.

Arctic explorations: the second and last United States Grinnell expedition in search of Sir John Franklin / Elisha Kent Kane. Hartford, Conn., 1868. Ill.
GB/A.1647. a622.

Arctic laboratory / John C. Reed, Andreas G. Ronhovde; a history (1947-1966) of the Naval Arctic Research Laboratory at Point Barrow, Alaska. Washington, 1971.
GB/A.1614. a623.

Arctic mood: a narrative of Arctic adventures / Eva Alvey Richards. Caldwell, Idaho, 1949. Ill., map.
GB/A.1959. a624.

Arctic odyssey: the life of Rear Admiral Donald B. MacMillan / Everett S. Allen. New York, 1962. Ill., maps, ports.
GB/A.1875.   a625.

Arctic passage: the turbulent history of the land and people of the Bering Sea, 1697-1975 / William R. Hunt. New York, 1975. Ill.
GB/A.1763.   a626.

Arctic patrols: stories of the Royal Canadian Mounted Police / William Campbell. Milwaukee, 1936.
GB/A.1702.   a627.

The **Arctic** regions: a narrative of discovery and adventure. London, 1852.
GB/A.1690.   a628.

Arctic researches and life among the Esquimaux: being the narrative of an expedition in search of Sir John Franklin in the years 1860, 1861 and 1862 / Charles Francis Hall. New York, 1865. Ill., maps.
GB/A.1892.   a629.

Arctic Riviera: a book about the beauty of North-East Greenland / Ernst Hofer. Berne, 1957.
GB/B.512.   a630.

Arctic sunbeams, or From Broadway to the Bosphorus by way of the North Cape / Samuel S. Cox. New York, 1882.
GB/A.2178.   a631.

Arctic systems / edited by P.J. Amaria, A.A. Bruneau and P.A. Lapp. New York, 1977. Ill.
GB/A.1654.   a632.

Arctic trader: the account of twenty years with the Hudson's Bay Company / Philip H. Godsell. Toronto, 1943. Ill., ports.
GB/A.1721.   a633.

The **Arctic** whaleman, or Winter in the Arctic Ocean, being a narrative of the wreck of the whale ship *Citizen* / Lewis Holmes. Boston, 1861. Ill.
GB/A.1840.   a634.

An **Arctic** whaling diary: the journal of Captain George Comer in Hudson Bay 1903-1905 / edited by W. Gillies Ross. Toronto, 1984. Ill., maps.
GB/A.2184.   a635.

An **Arctic** whaling sketchbook / William Gilkerson. Fairhaven, Mass., 1983. Ill.
GB/C.117.   a636.

Arctic wings / William A. Leising. Garden City, N.Y., 1959. Ill., ports.
GB/A.1872.   a637.

The **Arctic** world / Fred Bruemmer, principal writer & photographer; William E. Taylor, general editor; contributors: Ernest S. Burch [et al.]. San Francisco, 1985.
GB/B.652.   a638.

Arctica 1978 / 7th Northern Libraries Colloquy, 19-23 septembre 1978 / publié sous la direction de Jean Malaurie; volume préparé par Sylvie Devers. Paris, 1982.
GB/B.612.   a639.

Arktis Antarktis: Northern Lights segling / Rolf Bjelke, Deborah Shapiro. Stockholm, 1985.
GB/B.655.   a640.

Der **Arlberg** und die Klostertaler Alpen mit den Grenzgebieten des südlichen Bregenzer Waldes: ein Hochgebirgsführer / Walther Flaig. Innsbruck, 1929. Ill., maps. [Wagner's Alpine Spezialführer; 1.]
Lloyd.68.   a641.

Armonie montane: poesie della montagna / Paolo Ghiringhelli. Milano, 1911.
GB/A.1349(16).   a642.

Army organization: our infantry forces and infantry reserves: a paper read at the Royal United Service Institution / Arthur Leahy. [London, 1868.]
Lloyd.1583(20).   a643.

Arnold of Winkelried: a drama / [M.L.]. London, 1834.
Lloyd.1602(22).   a644.

Arosa: ein Führer für die Fremden / herausgegeben von Kurverein Arosa. 2., neu bearb. Aufl. Chur, 1891. Map.
GB/A.1381(4).   a645.

Arrampicare è il mio mestiere / Cesare Maestri. 4a ed. Milano, 1972. Ill.
GB/A.1047.   a646.

Arrampicate sui colli Euganei: guida alpinistica dei monti Pendice e Pirio / Club Alpino Italiano, Sezione di Padova. Padova, [1980].
GB/A.2119.   a647.

Arrampicate sui sassi di Cimaganda / Antonio Boscacci. [N.p., 1983?] Ill.
GB/A.2076(7). a648.

Arrangements / Association of British Members of the Swiss Alpine Club. 1943, 1946, 1952. [London, 1943-52.]
GB.1322(10-11). a649.

The **art** and sport of Alpine photography / Arthur Gardner. London, 1927. Ill.
GB.858. a650.

L'**art** de l'alpinisme / Pierre Allain. Paris, 1956. Ill. [Bibliothèque de l'alpinisme.]
GB/A.916. a651.

The **art** of travel, or Shifts and contrivances available in wild countries / Francis Galton. 4th ed., entirely recast and much enlarged. London, 1867. Ill.
Lloyd.172. a652.

L'**art** rustique en Suisse / Daniel Baud-Bovy. Londres, 1924. Ill., facsims. [Studio Special Number. 1924.]
Lloyd.1502. a653.

Art und Unart in deutschen Bergen: Volkshumor in Reimen und Inschriften / gesammelt von Rob. Falck. Berlin, [n.d.].
GB/A.48. a654.

L'**arte** di arrampicare di Emilio Comici / Severino Casara. Milano, [1957]. Ill.
GB/B.252(5). a655.

Arte e civiltà nell'Italia antica / Amedeo Maiuri. Milano, 1960. Ill., maps. [Conosci l'Italia; 4.]
GB/B.562. a656.

L'**arte** moderna dal neoclassico agli ultimi decenni / a cura di Angela Ottino Della Chiesa. Milano, 1968. Ill. [Conosci l'Italia; 12.]
GB/B.568. a657.

L'**arte** nel medioevo: il Duecento e il Trecento. Milano, 1965. Ill. [Conosci l'Italia; 9.]
GB/B.566b. a658.

L'**arte** nel medioevo dalle catacombe alle cattedrali romaniche. Milano, 1964. Ill. [Conosci l'Italia; 8.]
GB/B.566a. a659.

L'**arte** nel Rinascimento. Milano, 1962. Ill. [Conosci l'Italia; 6.]
GB/B.564. a660.

L'**arte** nel Seicento e Settecento: il periodo del barocco e del rococo. Milano, 1966. Ill. [Conosci l'Italia; 10.]
GB/B.567. a661.

The **Arth-Rigi** Railway / translated from the original German. Zürich, [1895?]. [Swiss scenes.]
GB/A.1817(1). a662.

Arthur W. Wakefield. [London, 1949.] An obituary notice. Pp.99-103 of the *Climbers' Club Journal*, N.S. vol.9 no.1.
GB.1338(13). a663.

[**Articles** on Alpine subjects extracted from various sources.] [N.p., 1807-1928.] 52v.
GB.1649-1700. a664.

[**Articles** on Alpine travel extracted from various journals.] [N.p., 1820-81.]
GB.1648. a665.

[**Articles** on the Alps, mainly of mountaineering interest, with a few maps.] [N.p., n.d.] 33v; maps.
Lloyd.1626-58. a666.

An **artist** in the Himalayas / A.D. MacCormick. London, 1895. Ill., map, ports.
Lloyd.1107. a668.

Arvendel, or Sketches in Italy and Switzerland / Gerard T. Noel. London, 1826.
GB.679; Lloyd.1176. a669.

Ascendo al Monto-Blanka en 1787 / Horace Bénédict de Saussure; eltirajo el *Voyage dans les Alpes*, tradukita de René de Saussure en Esperanto. Bern, 1918. Ill., port.
GB.895. a670.

Une **ascension** au Mont-Blanc / G. Pfeiffer. Vevey, [1898?]. Ill.
Lloyd.234. a671.

Une **ascension** au Mont-Blanc en 1843 / Jacques Carelli de Rocca Castello. Varallo, 1843.
Lloyd.866. a672.

Ascension au Mont-Blanc faite en 1843, de compagnie avec M. Nicolson et M. Ordinaire: contenant quelques détails sur une précédente tentative d'ascension par l'auteur seul / G.C. Savoisien. Bonneville, 1844.
Lloyd.1039. a673.

Une **ascension** au Mont-Blanc en 1864 / Piachaud. Genève, 1865. Tiré de la *Bibliothèque universelle et revue suisse*, livr. de mai 1865.
GB.882; Lloyd.718.   a674.

Une **ascension** au Mont-Blanc, le 14 juillet 1846 / comte Fernand de Bouillé. Nantes, 1846.
Lloyd.1603(2); Lloyd.1603(2)A.   a675.

Une **ascension** au Mont-Blanc et études scientifiques sur cette montagne / Jean Falconnet. Annecy, 1887. Extrait des *Documents de l'Académie salésienne*, tome 9.
GB.1185; Lloyd.1268.   a676.

Ascension au sommet du Mont-Blanc, le 22 et le 23 août 1837 / Henry Martin Atkins; traduit de l'anglais [by Jourdan]. Genève, 1838. Translated from *Ascent to the summit of Mont Blanc*.
Lloyd.1606(17).   a677.

Ascension de la Jungfrau / F. Thioly. Genève, 1865.
GB.1332(28); GB.1332(29); Lloyd.1620(30).   a678.

Ascension de la Jungfrau et du Schreckhorn: extrait des *Excursions et séjours dans les glaciers* / E. Desor. Neuchâtel, 1844.
GB/A.2074.   a679.

Ascension de la Meije, 16-17 juillet 1900 / Edmond Abdou, Louis Borelli. [Marseille, 1900.] Pp.[39]-42 of the *Bulletin annuel de la Société des excursionnistes marseillais*, année 4.
GB.1313(3).   a680.

Ascension des Dents-d'Oche et du Midi / par F.T. [i.e. F. Thioly]. Genève, 1863. Ill.
GB.1332(25); Lloyd.1588(2); Lloyd.1588(2)A,B,C.
                                                     a681.

Ascension du docteur Edmund Clark et du capitaine Markham Sherwill à la première sommité du Mont Blanc, les 25, 26 et 27 août 1825 / Markham Sherwill; traduit par Alexandre [Pelletier]. [Paris], 1827. Translated from *Ascent of Captain Markham Sherwill*.
GB.736; Lloyd.674; Lloyd.674A.   a682.

Ascension du Finsteraarhorn / F. Thioly. Genève, 1865.
GB.1332(26); GB.1332(27); Lloyd.1515.   a683.

Ascension du Mont-Cervin, Matterhorn / F. Thioly. Géologie du Mont-Cervin, d'après Giordano. Genève, 1871.
Lloyd.1602(29).   a684.

Ascension du Mont-Combin ou Graffeneire, le 8 juillet 1865 / L. Maquelin. Genève, 1866.
Lloyd.1612(7).
a685.

Ascensioni del duca degli Abruzzi, 1894: Aiguille du Moine – traversata dell'Aiguille des Charmoz / F. Gonella. Torino, 1895. Ill., ports. Estratto dal *Bollettino del C.A.I.* per l'anno 1894, vol.28 n.61.
Lloyd.1467.   a686.

Ascensioni scelte della Svizzera centrale e zone limitrofe / Franco Malnati; edito a cura del Club Alpino Italiano, Sezione di Varese, Gruppo Roccia. [N.p.], 1981. Ill., maps.
GB/A.1999.   a687.

Ascensions aux cimes de l'Etna et du Mont-Blanc / Henri de Tilly. Genève, 1835. Ill.
GB.678; Lloyd.764; Lloyd.906.   a688.

Les **ascensions** célèbres aux plus hautes montagnes du globe: fragments de voyages / recueillis, traduits et mis en ordre par Zurcher et Margollé. Paris, 1867. Ill. [Bibliothèque des merveilles.]
GB.244; Lloyd.358.   a689.

Les **ascensions** célèbres aux plus hautes montagnes du globe: fragments de voyages / recueillis, traduits et mis en ordre par Zurcher et Margollé. 2e éd. Paris, 1869. Ill. [Bibliothèque des merveilles.]
Lloyd.300.   a690.

Les **ascensions** célèbres aux plus hautes montagnes du globe / Frédéric Zurcher et Elie Margollé. 4e éd. rev. et augm. Paris, 1879. [Bibliothèque des merveilles.]
GB.189.   a691.

Ascensions du Mont-Cervin en 1868 / Giovanni Giorgio Carrel. Aoste, 1868. Extrait de la *Feuille d'Aoste*, no.49.
Lloyd.1574(3).   a692.

Ascensions du Mont-Rose et du Mont-Blanc en juillet 1863 / Moise Briquet, L. Maquelin. Genève, 1864. Extrait du *Journal de Genève*.
Lloyd.1616(10).   a693.

Ascensions et passages nouveaux dans la chaîne du Mont-Blanc: le Caiman / Emile Fontaine. Genève, 1911. Ill. Extrait de l'*Echo des Alpes*, septembre 1911.
Lloyd.1620(12).   a694.

Ascent: the mountaineering experience in word and image / edited by Allen Stick and Steve Roper. San Francisco, 1980. Ill., map, ports.
GB/B.602(2). a695.

Ascent and tour of Mont Blanc and passage of the Col du Géant, between Sept. 2nd and 7th 1860 [i.e. 1850] / J.D. Gardner. Chiswick, 1851.
GB.26; Lloyd.61; Lloyd.61A,B,C. a696.

An **ascent** of Ararat. [London, 1878.] Pp.364-6 of *Chambers's Journal*, 1878.
GB.1880(34). a697.

The **ascent** of Cameroons Peak and travels in French Congo / M.H. Kingsley; paper read at a meeting of the [Liverpool Geographical] Society on the 19th March, 1896. Liverpool, 1896.
Lloyd.1602(15). a698.

Ascent of Captain Markham Sherwill, accompanied by Dr. E. Clark, to the summit of Mont Blanc, 25th, 26th, and 27th of August 1825: in letters addressed to a friend. London, 1826.
Lloyd.1582(1). a699.

The **ascent** of Chimborazo. [London, 1881.] 2v; ill. From the *Leisure Hour*, 1881.
GB.1646(27). a700.

The **ascent** of Denali – Mount McKinley / Hudson Stuck. New York, 1913. Ill., ports. Pp.531-2 of *Scribner's Magazine*, vol.54 no.5, Nov. 1913.
GB.1333(41). a701.

The **ascent** of Denali – Mount McKinley: a narrative of the first complete ascent of the highest peak in North America / Hudson Stuck. London, 1914. Ill., map, ports.
GB.607. a702.

The **ascent** of Everest / Sir John Hunt. London, 1953. Ill.
GB.924; Lloyd.1044; Lloyd.1044A. a703.

The **ascent** of Everest / Sir John Hunt; edited and abridged for schools, with the assistance of the author, under the direction of Leonard Brooks. London, [1954]. Ill., maps, ports.
Lloyd.523. a704.

The **ascent** of Everest / Sir John Hunt; retold for younger readers under the direction of Leonard Brooks. London, 1954.
Lloyd.524. a705.

The **ascent** of Illimani / Sir Martin Conway. [New York], 1899. Ill. Pp.[657-72] of *Harper's New Monthly Magazine*, Oct. 1899.
GB.1880(39). a706.

The **ascent** of Mont-Blanc: a series of four views printed in oil colours by George Baxter, the original sketches, and the description by John Macgregor. [N.p., 1853?] Ill.
Lloyd.1621(18). a707.

Ascent of Mont Blanc by Mademoiselle d'Angeville / Chr. Muller. [London, 1841.] Pp.387-91 of the *New Monthly Magazine*, Nov. 1841.
GB.1738(1). a708.

The **ascent** of Mont Blanc, together with some remarks on glaciers / Alfred Wills. London, 1858.
GB.60(2); GB.1326(21). a709.

The **ascent** of Mount Everest / based on the illustrated lectures delivered by Brigadier Sir John Hunt, Sir Edmund Hillary and other members of the British Mount Everest Expedition 1953. London, 1953. Ill. Pp.[385]-99 of the *Geographical Journal*, December 1953.
GB.1332(2). a710.

The **ascent** of Mount St. Elias, Alaska, by Prince Luigi Amedeo di Savoia Duke of the Abruzzi / Filippo De Filippi; translated by Linda Villari. [London], 1900. Ill., maps, ports.
GB.1275. a711.

The **ascent** of Nanda Devi / H.W. Tilman. Cambridge, 1937. Ill., maps, ports.
GB.892. a712.

The **ascent** of Scawfell Pike, or A day in the mountains / by the author of *The Picts or Romano-British Wall* [i.e. Richard Abbatt]. London, 1851. Ill.
Lloyd.132. a713.

An **ascent** of the Grivola / T.G. Bonney. [Cambridge, 1864.] Extracted from the *Eagle*, no.19 vol.55, March 1864.
Lloyd.1581(4). a714.

The **ascent** of the Matterhorn. [London, 1880.] Pp.24-6 of *Chambers's Journal*, Jan.10, 1880.
GB.1318(5). a715.

The **ascent** of the Matterhorn / Edward Whymper. London, 1880. Ill., maps, ports., facsims.
GB.1028; Lloyd.1119. a716.

An **ascent** of the Matterhorn / H. Schütz Wilson. [London, 1876.] Pp.550-60 of the *Gentleman's Magazine*, July 1876.
Lloyd.1610(7). a717.

An **ascent** of the Matterhorn from the south side / C.E. Mathews. London, [1871]. Reprinted from the *Alpine Journal*, November 1871.
Lloyd.1581(7). a718.

Ascent of the Wetterhorn. [Edinburgh, 1846.] Pp.59-61 of *Chambers's Edinburgh Journal*, N.S., no.108.
GB.1772. a719.

The **ascent** of Yerupaja / John Sack. London, 1954. Ill., map, ports.
GB.350; GB.432. a720.

Ascent to the summit of Mont Blanc, on the 22nd and 23rd of August, 1837 / Henry Martin Atkins. London, 1838. Ill.
GB.611; GB.733; GB.734; Lloyd.955; Lloyd.955A,B; Lloyd.1012; Lloyd.1013. a721.

Ascent to the summit of Mont Blanc, 16th-18th of 9th month, September, 1834 / Martin Barry. London, [1835]. Ill.
GB.936; Lloyd.1051; Lloyd.1051a. a722.

Ascent to the summit of Mont Blanc, 16th-18th of 9th month, September, 1834 / Martin Barry. London, 1835. A different issue from a722.
GB.935(1); GB.937; GB.938. a723.

Ascent to the summit of Mont Blanc, 16th-18th of 9th month, September, 1834 / Martin Barry. London, 1835. From the *Edinburgh Philosophical Journal* for January 1835.
Lloyd.1020. a723.1.

Ascent to the summit of Mont Blanc, 16th-18th of 9th month, September, 1834 / Martin Barry. [Edinburgh], 1836.
GB.933; GB.986; Lloyd.1022; Lloyd.1022A. a724.

Ascent to the summit of Mont Blanc / Martin Barry. Edinburgh, 1836. A different issue from a724.
Lloyd.1625. a725.

Ascent to the summit of Mont Blanc, 16th-18th of 9th month, September, 1834 / Martin Barry. Edinburgh, 1836. Ill. A different issue from a724 and a725.
Lloyd.1212. a725.1.

Ascent to the summit of the Cock's Comb Mountain. [N.p., n.d.] Pp.363-8 of an unidentified work.
Lloyd.1608(3). a726.

Ascents and adventures: a record of hardy mountaineering in every quarter of the globe / Henry Frith. London, 1884. Ill.
GB.273; Lloyd.394; Lloyd.394A. a727.

Ascents and passes in the Lake District of England: being a new pedestrian and general guide to the district / Herman Prior. London, [1865]. Map.
Lloyd.127. a728.

Assault on eternity: Richard E. Byrd and the exploration of Antarctica, 1946-47 / Lisle A. Rose. Annapolis, [1980]. Ill.
GB/A.2111. a729.

The **assault** on Mount Everest, 1922 / Hon. C.G. Bruce and other members of the expedition. London, 1923. Ill., maps.
GB.1161. a730.

L'**assaut** des Aiguilles du Diable: une arête, une ascension, un film / Marcel Ichac. Paris, 1946. Ill.
GB/A.1648. a731.

L'**assaut** du Mont Everest, 1922 / Hon. C.G. Bruce; traduction française par A. de Gruchy et E. Gaillard. Chambéry, [1923]. Ill., maps. Translated from *The assault on Mount Everest, 1922*.
GB.1317(5). a732.

At grips with Everest / Stanley Snaith. London, 1937. Ill., map.
GB.511. a733.

At the Oybin. [London, 1886.] Pp.204-13 of the *Cornhill Magazine*, Aug. 1886.
GB.1880(4). a734.

Atala. René. Le dernier des Abencérages. Les quatre Stuarts. Voyages / François René de Chateaubriand. Paris, [1827?].
GB.1061. a735.

Atlas de la flore alpine / Henry Correvon. Paris, 1901. 6v; ill. Published by the Deutscher Alpenverein.
GB/A.212-7. a736.

Atlas der Alpenflora / herausgegeben vom Deutschen und Oesterreichischen Alpenverein. Wissenschaftlicher Redactuer: Dr. Palla. 2. neubearb. Aufl. Graz, 1897. 5v; ill.
GB/A.609-13. a737.

Atlas pittoresque de Genève, ou Collection des vues les plus intéressantes de cette ville, avec des notices historiques sur son état ancien et moderne / dessinées et gravées par Pierre Escuyer. Genève, 1822. Ill.
Lloyd.439. a738.

An **atlas** to Ebel's *Traveller's guide through Switzerland*. London, 1818.
Lloyd.336. a739.

An **atlas** to Ebel's *Traveller's guide through Switzerland*. London, [1819].
GB.290; Lloyd.337. a740.

An **atlas** to Ebel's *Traveller's guide through Switzerland*. London, 1835.
Lloyd.338. a741.

Attack on Everest / Neil Macintyre. London, 1936.
GB.336. a742.

Atti del 1° Congresso Nazionale della Montagna, Sondrio, 13-14 dicembre 1931. Roma, 1932. Published by the Confederazione Nazionale Sindacati Fascisti dell'Agricoltura.
GB/B.289(23). a743.

Atti del LXX Congresso Nazionale del Club Alpino Italiano, 31 agosto al 6 settembre 1958. Lucca, 1959. Ill.
GB/B.312(24). a744.

Le **attività** del trapper / Andrea Mercanti. Milano, 1979. Ill. [I manuali del trapper.]
GB/A.1987. a745.

Attraverso i ghiacciai del Monte Bianco: prima traversata del col de l'Aiguille Verte: ascensione del Mont Dolent per il versante svizzero / G.F. e G.B. Gugliermina. Torino, 1904. Ill. Published by the Club Alpino Italiano.
GB.1188(3). a746.

Attraverso le Alpi: storia aneddotica delle guerre in montagna a difesa d'Italia, 1742-1748 / Vittorio Turletti. Torino, [1935?]. Ill.
GB/A.622. a747.

Au bout d'un fil: douze ascensions nouvelles dans les Alpes suisses et françaises / E.R. Blanchet. Paris, [1937]. Ill.
GB.1321(49). a748.

Au bout d'un fil: seize ascensions nouvelles dans les Alpes suisses et françaises / E.-R. Blanchet. Nouv. éd. Paris, 1950. Ill. [Montagne.]
GB/A.2165(2). a749.

Au coeur de l'Antarctique: expédition du *Nimrod* au pôle Sud / E.H. Shackleton; la traduction et l'adaptation par Charles Rabot. Paris, 1910.
GB/B.642. a750.

Au coeur de l'Europe: les Alpes / Paul et Germaine Veyret. Paris, 1967. Ill., maps.
GB/B.135. a751.

Au coeur de notre Pilat: promenades, excursions, randonnées / Roger Bargeton. 3e éd. St. Etienne, 1973. Ill., maps.
GB/A.1270(4). a752.

Au delà de la verticale / Georges Livanos. [Paris], 1958. Ill. [Sempervivum; 35.]
GB/A.188. a753.

Au delà des cimes / Edouard Wyss. Neuchâtel, 1933. Ill. [Appel des sommets; 11.]
GB/A.1034(17). a754.

Au Mont-Blanc: aiguilles – sommets – vallées et glaciers, ascensions et excursions, sports d'hiver / Roger Tissot. Grenoble, [1924]. Ill., map.
GB/A.862. a755.

Au pays alpin (d'Aix à Aix) / Armand Grebauval. Paris, [1902]. Ill. [Voyages en tous pays.]
GB/A.1594. a756.

Au pays des Alpins / Henry Duhamel. Grenoble, 1899. Ill.
GB/B.130. a757.

Au pays des glaciers: récits pittoresques, scènes & aventures: souvenirs personnels des touristes et des géologues. Lille, [1900?]. Ill.
GB/B.571. a758.

Au pays des isards / un des cinq frères Cadier (George Cadier). Pau, 1968. Ill.
GB/B.119(5). a759.

Au pays des isards / les cinq frères Cadier. Pau, 1969. Ill., map, ports.
GB/B.119(7).   a760.

Au pays des manchots: récit du voyage de la *Belgica* / Georges Lecointe. Bruxelles, 1904. Ill., maps. At head of title: Expédition Antarctique Belge.
GB/A.1602.   a761.

Au pied des volcans polaires: notes d'un voyage aux Faeroë, à Jan Mayen et en Islande / Raymond Chevallier. Paris, [1927]. Ill., map.
GB/A.1887.   a762.

Au royaume du Mont-Blanc / Paul Payot. Bonneville, 1950. Ill., ports., facsims., music.
Lloyd.1624(13).   a763.

Au royaume du Mont-Blanc / Paul Payot. 2e éd. Chamonix, [1950]. Ill., ports., facsims., music.
GB.587.   a764.

Auction of surplus books from the S.M.C. [Scottish Mountaineering Club] library, 7th Dec., 1961. [Edinburgh, 1961.]
GB.1331(35).   a765.

Auf Bergen zu Gast: Erinnerungen aus meinen Wanderungen in den Alpen / Karl Horneck. Salzburg, 1968. Ill.
GB/A.207.   a766.

Auf Kundfahrt im Himalaja: Siniolchu und Nanga Parbat: Tat und Schicksal deutscher Bergsteiger / herausgegeben von Paul Bauer. München, [1937]. Ill., map, ports.
GB.1255.   a767.

Auf schweizer Alpenstrassen / offizielle Publikation der Gesellschaftswagengruppe. Sur les routes alpestres suisses / publication officielle de l'Association suisse des propriétaires d'autocamions. Jahrg.8. Bern, [ca 1935]. Ill.
GB/B.288(14).   a768.

Auf wolkigen Höhen / Hans Fritz von Tscharner. Bern, [1936]. Ill., ports.
GB.683.   a769.

Augusta Praetoria: revue valdôtaine de culture régionale. Année 2 no.1, janv.-mars 1949. Aoste, 1949.
GB.1333(13).   a770.

Aurora australis, 1908-1909 / edited by Sir E. Shackleton. Antarctica, 1908. Ill.
GB/B.422.   a771.

The **Aurora** Borealis: a literary annual / edited by members of the Society of Friends. Newcastle-upon-Tyne, 1833.
GB.118.   a772.

Aus dem Kanton Graubünden / gesammelt und herausgegeben von O. Sutermeister. Hft.1. Zürich, [ca 1900]. [Sammlung deutsch-schweizerischer Mundart-Literatur.]
GB/A.1199(2).   a773.

Aus dem Leben eines Bergsteigers / Julius Kugy. München, 1925. Ill., port.
GB.1227.   a774.

Aus dem nordalbanischen Hochgebirge / Erich Liebert. Sarajevo, 1909. Ill. [Zur Kunde der Balkanhalbinsel. Reisen und Beobachtungen; 10.]
GB/C.22(12).   a775.

Aus dem oesterreich. Hochgebirge: Ersteigung der hohen Wildspitze im Oetzthale / Anton von Ruthner. Wien, 1863. Separat-Abdruck aus den *Mittheilungen der k.k. geographischen Gesellschaft*, Jahrg.6.
GB.1130(7).   a776.

Aus dem Saas- und Monte Rosa-Gebiet / Carl Schulz. [Bern, 1883?] Reprint from the *Schweizer Alpenclub Jahrbuch*, v.18, 1883?.
GB.285.   a777.

Aus dem westlichen Himalaja: Erlebnisse und Forschungen / Károly Jenö Ujfalvy. Leipzig, 1884. Ill., maps.
GB/A.76.   a778.

Aus den Alpen / Robert von Lendenfeld. I. Band: Die Westalpen. Wien, 1896. Ill.
GB/B.11; Lloyd.1466.   a779.

Aus den Bergen der Maurienne und der Tarentaise / Karl Blodig, Ludwig Purtscheller. [Munich, 1895-96.] Ill. Pp.[68]-119 of the *Zeitschrift des Deutschen und Oesterreichischen Alpenvereins* for 1895, and pp.[173]-211 of the issue for 1896.
GB.1385.   a780.

Aus den Bergen der Sernftales: alpine Erlebnisse und Erinnerungen, 1896-1904 / Karl Frey. Zürich, [1904?]. Ill.
GB/A.34.   a781.

Aus den Hochregionen des Kaukasus: Wanderungen, Erlebnisse, Beobachtungen / Gottfried Merzbacher. Leipzig, 1901. 2v; ill., maps.
GB/A.1481-2.   a782.

Aus den schweizer Bergen: Land und Leute / E. Rambert; deutsche Ausgabe von G. Roux. Basel, 1874. Ill.
GB/B.256.   783.

Aus den tessiner Bergen / C. Täuber. Zürich, [ca 1910]. Ill.
GB/A.1034(18).   a784.

Aus der Berninagruppe: Notiz über die erste Besteigung der Ringelspitze und des Tristelhorns / A. Ludwig. [Geneva, 1899.] Ill. Pp.1-24, 339-348 of the *Jahrbuch des Schweizer Alpenclub*, Jahrg.33.
GB.1333(36).   a785.

Aus der Firnenwelt: gesammelte Schriften / J. Jacob Weilenmann. Leipzig, 1872. 3v; ill., map.
GB.183-5.   a786.

Aus der Firnenwelt: gesammelte Schriften: eine Auswahl / J.J. Weilenmann. 1: Rhätikon, Silvretta, Ferwall. München, 1923. Ill. [Grosse Bergsteiger.]
GB/A.1503.   a787.

Aus der Firnwelt des Mont-Blanc / Karl Blodig. München, 1908. Ill. Pp.[210]-33 of the *Zeitschrift des Deutschen und Österreichischen Alpenvereins*, Bd.39.
GB.1331(51[1]).   a788.

Aus der Firnwelt des Mont-Blanc / Karl Blodig. München, 1909. Ill. Pp.145-76 of the *Zeitschrift des Deutschen und Österreichischen Alpenvereins*, Bd.40.
GB.1331(51[2]).   a789.

Aus der Geschichte der Erde / Aug. Aeppli. [N.p., 1900?] 3v.
GB/A.1052(9-11).   a790.

Aus der Sommerfrische: kleine Geschichten / Hans Hoffmann. Berlin, 1898.
GB/A.41.   a791.

Aus Deutschösterreichs Gauen / Friedrich Morton. Vol.1. Wien, 1921. Ill., map.
GB/A.432.   a792.

Aus goldener Ferienzeit: ein Strauss fröhlicher Berglieder / Theodor Schmidt. Breslau, 1908.
GB/A.54.   a793.

Aus meinem Bergerleben / Hans Pfann. Stuttgart, [ca 1950]. Ill.
GB/A.421.   a794.

Aus Sibirien: lose Blätter aus meinem Tagebuch / Wilhelm Radloff. 2. Ausg. Oosterhout, 1968. 2v (in 1); ill., map. Facsimile reprint of the Leipzig, 1893 ed.
GB/A.1671.   a795.

Aus Tirol: Berg- und Gletscher-Reisen in den österreichischen Hochalpen / Anton von Ruthner. Neue Folge. Wien, 1869. Ill., map.
GB.583.   a796.

Ausflug nach Frankreich, England und Belgien zur Beobachtung der dortigen Eisenbahnen / L. de Negrelli. Frauenfeld, 1838.
GB/A.800(7).   a797.

Ein **Ausflug** zu den Himalayas / Max von Kübeck. Wien, 1881.
GB/A.63.   a798.

Ausführliche und wahrhafte Nachricht vom Anfange und Fortgange der grönländischen Mission / Hans Egede. Hamburg, 1740. Translated from *Omstændelig og udforlig relation*.
GB/A.1881.   a799.

Ausstellung alter Berner Meister aus der Sammlung Dr. Engelmann: illustrierter Katalog / C. von Mandach. Bern, 1920. Ill., ports. In the Kunstmuseum, Bern.
Lloyd.1608(2).   a800.

Ausstellung-S. Freudenberger, F.N. König, Mai-Juni 1923: illustrierter Katalog. Bern, [1923]. In the Kunstmuseum, Bern.
Lloyd.1602(3); Lloyd.1659(2).   a801.

Australia and Antarctica / John Béchervaise. Cove, N.S.W., 1967.
GB/A.2048(8).   a802.

Autour de deux lacs: voyage des écoles industrielles de Neuchâtel, La Chaux-de-Fonds et La Sagne, dans les cantons de Neuchâtel, Vaud et Fribourg, les 3.4.5 et 6 juillet, 1865 / Guillaume dr., A. Bachelin, A. de Mandrot [et al.]. Neuchâtel, 1864 [1865?]. Ill. [Courses scolaires; année 2.]
GB/C.45.   a803.

Autour de Panestrel / W.A.B. Coolidge. Lyon, 1906. Extrait de la *Revue alpine* de juin 1906.
GB.1340(15).   a804.

Autour de Sainte-Croix, Jura suisse / Henry Cuenot. 3e éd. Yverdon, 1901. Ill.
GB/A.177. a805.

Autour du Mont-Viso / H. Gentil. [France], 1976. Ill., maps. [Guide skieur; 2.] [Alpes et Midi-ski.]
GB/A.2017(7). a806.

Autour du pôle Sud / Jean Charcot. [Vol 2]: Expédition du *Pourquoi Pas?* 1908-1910. Paris, 1929. Ill.
GB/A.2138. a807.

Autumn chamois-hunting / A.S. Marshall-Hall. [London, 1887.] Pp.270-84 of the *Gentleman's Magazine*, Sept. 1887.
GB.1332(32). a808.

An **autumn** holiday: a three week's journey through Germany into Switzerland, and returning home by way of France / Frances Harrisson. [N.p., 1888.]
Lloyd.1615(2). a809.

An **autumn** in Italy, being a personal narrative of a tour in the Austrian, Tuscan, Roman and Sardinian states, in 1827 / J.D. Sinclair. Edinburgh, 1829. [Constable's miscellany; 46.]
Lloyd.43. a810.

Autumn rambles, or Fireside recollections of Belgium, the Rhine, the Moselle, German spas, Switzerland, the Italian lakes, Mont Blanc, and Paris / written by a lady [i.e. Mrs Staley]. Rochdale, 1863.
GB.291; GB.292; Lloyd.400. a811.

Autumnal rambles among the Scottish mountains, or Pedestrian tourist's friend / Thomas Grierson. Edinburgh, 1850.
GB.211. a812.

Auvergne, Piedmont, and Savoy: a summer ramble / Charles Richard Weld. London, 1850.
Lloyd.707. a813.

Aux glaces polaires: Indiens et Esquimaux / le R.P. Duchaussois. Lyon, [1920]. Ill., maps, ports.
GB/A.1736. a814.

Aux Pyrénées et aux Alpes: voyages de vacances / Victor Martin. Tours, 1897. Ill.
GB/A.1389. a815.

Av Jotunheimens saga / Theodor Caspari. Oslo, [n.d.]. Ill.
GB/B.139. a816.

The **avalanche**, or The old man of the Alps: a tale / translated from the French. Clapham, 1829.
GB.345; Lloyd.254; Lloyd.254A. a817.

Avalanche handbook / Ronald I. Perla, M. Martinelli. Washington, D.C., 1978. Ill. [Agriculture handbook / U.S. Department of Agriculture Forest Service; 489.]
GB/B.520(2). a818.

The **avalanche** hunters / Montgomery M. Atwater. Philadelphia, 1968. Ill.
GB/A.1973. a819.

Avant-premières à l'Everest / Gabriel Chevalley, René Dittert, Raymond Lambert. Paris, 1953. Ill., maps, ports. [Sempervivum; 21.]
GB/A.1559. a820.

Aventures en montagne / Henry Bordeaux. Neuchâtel, 1946. [Montagne.]
GB/A.1295(15). a821.

Avventure dell'alpinismo / Karl Lukan; [traduzione di Francesco Saba Sardi]. Milano, 1972. Ill., map, ports. [International library.] Translated from *Die grossen Bergabenteuer*.
GB/B.433. a822.

-B-

The **B.S.** counter: life in Alaska / Marian Glenz. New York, 1971.
GB/A.1729. b001.

Bacchus in Graubünden / J.A.S. [N.p., 1883.] Pp.50-61 of vol.47 no.277 of an unidentified periodical.
GB.1336(28). b002.

Backpacking in Chile and Argentina plus the Falkland Islands / Hilary Bradt, John Pilkington; with contributions by Krieger Conradt, David Greenman, Ladislaw Reday; edited by John Pilkington. Boston, 1980. Ill., maps. [The Backpacking guide series.]
GB/A.2032(4). b003.

Bad weather on Mont Maudit / Frank S. Smythe. London, 1929. Pp.687-712 of *Blackwood's Magazine*, vol.226 no.1369, Nov.1929.
GB.1880(57). b004.

Die **Badenfahrt** / David Hess. [Zurich], 1818. Ill., map.
GB/A.1335. b005.

Badile, north-east face: Cassin route: second ascent, 27th-29th August 1948 / Bernard Pierre. [London, 1949.] Ill. Pp.49-56 of the *Climbers' Club Journal*, N.S. vol.9 no.1.
GB.1337(11). b006.

Bagnères de Luchon et ses environs / Victor Petit. Bagnères-de-Luchon, [n.d.]. Ill.
Lloyd.1451. b007.

Les **bains** de Saint-Gervais, près du Mont-Blanc, en Savoie / André Matthey. Paris, 1818.
GB.1315(19). b008.

Balloting list for the election of Council and officers at the Annual General Meeting of the Royal Geographical Society. June 1947, 1950, 1951. [London, 1947-51.]
GB.1329(23-5). b010.

Balmat oder Paccard?: ein Mont-Blanc-Roman / Karl Ziak. Wien, 1930.
GB.169. b011.

Bardonecchia e le sue valli / G. Paolo Di Pascale. 2a ed. Como, 1970. Ill., map.
GB/A.867(2). b012.

Bàrnabo delle montagne. Il segreto del bosco vecchio: romanzi / Dino Buzzati. 3a ed. Milano, 1973. [I Garzanti; 442.]
GB/A.1270(16). b013.

Barometer manual / compiled by Rear-Admiral Fitzroy. 5th ed. London, 1861. Published by the Board of Trade, Great Britain.
Lloyd.1583(22). b014.

La **Barre** des Ecrins — 4100m. / Henri Isselin. [Paris], 1960. Ill.
GB/A.191. b015.

La **Barre** des Ecrins, 4,103 mètres / H. Duhamel. Paris, 1881. Ill. Extrait de l'*Annuaire du Club alpin français*, vol.7, 1880.
GB.1306(9). b016.

La **Barre** des Ecrins en 1882 / Felix Perrin. Paris, 1883. Ill., map. Extrait de l'*Annuaire du Club alpin français*, vol.9, 1882.
Lloyd.1624(8). b017.

Barry vom Grossen St. Bernhard: die Geschichte eines berühmten Hundes / Adolf Fux. 3. Aufl. Bern, 1968. Ill.
GB/A.389. b018.

Les **batailles** pour l'Himalaya, 1783-1936 / Claire Eliane Engel. [Paris, 1936.] Ill. [Vie en montagne.]
GB.1315(14). b019.

Batailles pour le Mont-Blanc / Henri Baud. Vesoul, 1961. Ill., map, port.
GB.1308(3). b020.

La **battaglia** del sesto grado, 1929-1938 / Vittorio Varale. Milano, [1965]. Ill. [La vostra via sportiva; 8.]
GB/A.1003. b021.

The **battle** of Königgrätz: a lecture delivered at the Royal United Service Institution / Colonel Walker. [London, 1868.] Maps.
Lloyd.1583(19). b022.

Der **Bau** der Schweizeralpen / Joos Cadisch. Zürich, 1926. Ill., map.
GB/A.93. b023.

Der **Bau** der Schweizeralpen: sechs Vorträge / P. Arbenz. [N.p., 1909.] Ill.
GB/A.1052(12). b024.

Bau und Entstehung der Alpen / Leopold Kober. Berlin, 1923. Ill.
GB/B.227.   b025.

Bavaria, Tirol and the Dolomites: June-July 1880 / R.G. [i.e. Robert Gwynne]. [N.p., 1880.] Ill.
GB/C.21.   b026.

Beaten tracks, or Pen and pencil sketches in Italy / by the author of *A voyage en zigzag* [i.e. Elizabeth Tuckett]. London, 1866.
Lloyd.1121.   b027.

The **Beaufort** Sea, MacKenzie Delta, MacKenzie Valley, and northern Yukon: a bibliographical review / edited by C. Ross Goodwin, Lynda M. Howard. [Ottawa?],1984.
GB/B.602(8).   b028.

Beautés et merveilles de la nature en Suisse / H.N. Hemann. Paris, 1837. Ill.
GB/A.729.   b029.

The **beauties** & wonders of nature and science: a collection of curious, interesting & valuable information / edited by Linney Gilbert, assisted by his literary friends. London, [n.d.]. Ill.
Lloyd.957.   b030.

Beautiful mountains: in the Jugoslav Alps / F.S. Copeland. Split, [1930]. Ill.
GB.1187.   b031.

Beauty spots of the Continent / H. Baden Pritchard. London, 1875.
Lloyd.575.   b032.

Beeren Eiland. [New York], 1899. Pp.976-7 of *Science*, N.S. vol.10 no.261.
GB.1880(14).   b033.

Behring Sea seizures, 1886-87: correspondence. [Ottawa? 1888?]
GB/A.1891.   b034.

Belgium, the Rhine, Switzerland and Holland: an autumnal tour / J.S. Buckingham. London, [1845]. 2v.
GB.726-7; Lloyd.1111-2.   b035.

Belle insegne della Svizzera / René Creux; versione italiana di Claudio Bernasconi. Zurigo, 1962. Published by the Schweizerische Zentrale für Verkehrsforderung.
GB/A.516(3).   b036.

Below the snow line / Douglas W. Freshfield. London, 1923.
GB.787; Lloyd.918; Lloyd.918A.   b037.

Il **Belvedere** di Lanzo d'Intelvi: stazione climatica a metri 950 sul mare / A. Rolando. Milano, 1883.
GB/A.1468(12).   b038.

Bemerkungen auf einer Alpen-Reise über den Brünig, Bragel, Kirenzenberg, und über die Flüela, den Maloya und Splugen / Karl Kasthofer. Bern, 1825.
GB/A.991.   b039.

Bemerkungen auf einer Alpen-Reise über den Susten, Gotthard, Bernardin, und über die Oberalp, Furka und Grimsel: mit Erfahrungen über die Kultur der Alpen und einer Vergleichung des wirthschaftlichen Ertrags der udenschen und bernischen Alpen / Karl Kasthofer. Aarau, 1822.
GB/A.488.   b040.

Bemerkungen auf einer Reise durch das südliche Deutschland, den Elsass und die Schweiz in den Jahren 1789 und 1799 / C.U.D. von Eggers. Kopenhagen, 1801. 2v.
GB/A.649-50.   b041.

Bemerkungen auf einer Reise durch einen Theil der Schweiz und einige ihrer naechsten Umgebungen / Albrecht Erbach. Heidelberg, [1809].
GB/A.1794.   b042.

Bemerkungen eines reisenden Weltmanns auf einer Reise durch Frankreich, Sardinien, Malta, Sicilien, Italien und die Schweiz / nach dem Französischen. Bresslau, 1791.
GB/A.757.   b043.

Bemerkungen über die Wälder und Alpen des bernerischen Hochgebirgs: ein Beitrag zur Bestimmung der Vegetationsgrenze schweizerischen Holzarten / Karl Kasthofer. 2. verm. und verb. Aufl. Aarau, 1818.
GB/A.1261.   b044.

Ben Nevis / edited by H. Macrobert. Edinburgh, 1920. Ill. [Scottish Mountaineering Club guide; 1, sect. E.]
GB.1313(24).   b045.

Beobachtungen ueber das Gebirge bey Koenigshayn in der Oberlausitz / [Carl A. von Schachmann]. Dresden, 1780. Ill.
Lloyd.1284.   b046.

Beobachtungen und Anmerkungen auf einer im J. 1775 u. 76 gethanen Reise, aus Deutschland nach der Schweiz und Oberitalien: als Fragment aus seinem Tagebuch gezogen / Joh. Ge. Sulzer. Bern, 1780.
GB/A.726. b047.

Der **Berg** in der Malerei: der Schweizer Alpen-Club zur Hundertjahrfeier 1963 an seine Mitglieder / Ulrich Christoffel. Bern, 1963.
GB/B.119(8). b048.

Berg und Mensch: ein Buch der Andacht / Oskar Erich Meyer. Berlin, [1941?]. Ill.
GB/A.443. b049.

Berg-, Land- und Seereise / Ulrich Hegner. Zürich, 1818.
GB.1326(36). b050.

Berg- und Gletscher-Fahrten in den Hochalpen der Schweiz / G. Studer, M. Ulrich, J.J. Weilenmann [and Georg Hoffmann]. Zürich, 1859. Ill.
GB.179; GB.180; Lloyd.301. b051.

Berg- und Gletscher-Fahrten in den Hochalpen der Schweiz / G. Studer, M. Ulrich, J.J. Weilenmann, H. Zeller. 2. Sammlung. Zürich, 1863. Ill.
GB.181; Lloyd.302. b052.

Berg- und Gletscherfahrten in den Alpen in den Jahren 1860 bis 1869 / Edward Whymper; autorisirte deutsche Bearbeitung von Friedrich Steger. Braunschweig, 1872. Ill., map.
GB.1024. b053.

Berg- und Gletscher-Reisen in den österreichischen Hochalpen / Anton von Ruthner. Wien, 1864. Ill., map.
GB.663. b054.

Bergakrobaten: Kletterfahrten an Montblanc-Nadeln und Dolomiten-Türmen / Guido Rey; die deutsche Ubertragung von Heinrich Erler besorgt und unter Mitarbeit von Walter Schmidkunz neu durchgesehen. Erfurt, [ca 1941]. Ill. Translated from *Alpinismo acrobatico*.
GB/A.442. b055.

Bergamo e le sue valli / a cura di R. Petrali Cicognara. Roma, 1939. Ill., map. Published by the Ente Provinciale per il Turismo, Bergamo.
GB/A.1020. b056.

Bergbauern: lustige tiroler Geschichten / Rudolf Greinz. Leipzig, 1906.
GB/A.25. b057.

Bergbleamln: Gedichte in oberbairischer Mundart / Karl Stieler. 5.Aufl. München, [n.d.].
GB/A.69. b058.

Das **Bergbuch**; eine Sammlung der schönsten Aussätze und Bilder, die in der Monatschrift *Der Bergsteiger* erschienen sind / herausgegeben von Julius Gallhuber. Wien, [1934?]. Ill.
GB/A.2140. b059.

Berge — ewiges Abenteuer / Kurt Maix. München, [1966]. Ill.
GB/A.204. b060.

Berge: eine Bildfolge / Karl Jud; mit ausgewählten Texten und einem Vorwort von Hans Walter. Zürich, [1967].
GB/A.457. b061.

Berge als Schicksal / Wilhelm Paulcke. München, [1936]. Ill., ports.
GB.643. b062.

Berge der Heimat, Gipfel der Welt / Dölf Reist. Frauenfeld, [1965]. Ill.
GB/B.13. b063.

Die **Berge** der Schweiz: das Erlebnis der Hochalpen / Herbert Maeder. Olten, [1967]. Ill.
GB/B.128. b064.

Berge der Welt: Schriftenreihe für Alpinismus Expeditionen Wissenschaft / herausgegeben von der Schweizerischen Stiftung für Alpine Forschungen. Bd. 4-5,7, 1949-50,1952. Bern, 1949-52. Ill., maps.
GB/B.538; GB.1155. b065.

Berge einer Jugend / Hans Hofmann-Montanus. Wien, [1948]. Ill.
GB/A.437. b066.

Berge im Schnee: das Winterbuch / Luis Trenker. Berlin, [1932]. Ill.
GB/B.235. b067.

Berge über uns: ein kleines Alpenbuch / Herbert Cysarz. München, 1935.
GB/A.1364. b068.

Berge und Heimat: das Buch von den Bergen und ihren Menschen / Luis Trenker, Walter

Schmidkunz. Berlin, 1939. Ill.
GB/A.1487.   b069.

Berge und Heimat: das Buch von den Bergen und ihren Menschen / Luis Trenker, Walter Schmidkunz. Berlin, 1940. Ill.
GB/B.243.   b070.

Berge unserer Alpen / Toni Hiebeler. München, 1976. Ill., maps.
GB/B.483.   b071.

Berge unter fremden Sternen / Ernst Schmied. Bern, [1965]. Ill., map.
GB/A.375.   b072.

Eine **Bergfahrt** von Courmayeur nach Chamonix / Carl Bosshard. [N.p., 1930?]
GB.1314(4).   b073.

Bergfahrten: Erchliessungsfahrten in den Ortler-Adamello- und Presanella-Alpen (1864-1868) / Julius Payer; herausgegeben von Wilhelm Lehner. Regensburg, 1920. Ill.
GB/B.424.   b074.

Bergfahrten im Pamir / Ph. Borchers und K. Wien; mit Beiträgen von Dr. Allwein und E. Schneider. Innsbruck, 1929. Ill., map, ports. Sonderabdruck aus der *Zeitschrift des Deutschen und Osterreichischen Alpenvereins*, Bd.60, 1929.
GB.1173.   b075.

Bergfahrten in Bolivia / Henry Hoek. Innsbruck, 1905-07. 2v; ill. Sonderabdruck aus der *Zeitschrift des Deutschen und Osterreichischen Alpenvereins*, Bd.36, 1905, Bd.38, 1907.
GB.1317(13-4).   b076.

Bergfahrten in den Grödner Dolomiten / Fritz Benesch. München, 1899. Ill.
GB/C.29.   b077.

Bergfahrten von Norman-Neruda / herausgegeben von May Norman-Neruda. München, [1901]. Port.
GB/A.68.   b078.

Die **Bergführerdynastie** der Innerkofler im südtirolischen Sexten und die Geschichte ihres Heimattales / Josef Rampold. Wien, 1975. Sonderabdruck aus dem *Anzeiger der phil.-hist. Klasse der Osterreichischen Akademie der Wissenschaften*, Jahrg.112 Nr.5, 1975.
GB/A.1675(1).   b079.

Bergheimat: Jahresschrift des Liechtensteiner Alpenvereins. 1971-   . Schaan, [1971-   ]. Ill.
GB/A.1313.   b080.

Der **Bergkamerad**: Wochenschrift für Bergsteiger, Skilaufer und Wanderer. Jahrg. 12-22, 1950/51-1960/61. München, [1950-60]. Ill., maps. Wanting Jahrg.17, 1955/56.
GB/A.1469-78.   b081.

Bergkristall: Roman / Gustav Friedrich Renker. Basel, [n.d.].
GB/A.49.   b082.

Bergland Graubünden / Gottlieb Heinrich Heer. 2. Aufl. Bern, [1960]. Ill.
GB/A.376.   b083.

Berglieder / Ernst Altenberger. Wien, 1924.
GB/A.56.   b084.

Bergluft: Sonntagsstreifereien eines alten Clubisten / Arnold Halder. Bern, [1869].
GB/A.987(2).   b085.

Bergreisen / herausgegeben von Christian August Fischer. Leipzig, 1804-05. 2v (in 1); maps.
GB.176.   b086.

Bergsteigen / Ernst Enzensperger, unter Mitwirkung von Eugen Roeckl, Wilhelm Welzenbach und Anton Ziegler. Berlin, [ca 1924]. Ill. [Handbuch der Leibesübungen; 6.] Published by the Deutsche Hochschule für Leibesübungen.
GB.731.   b087.

Bergsteigen: Festschrift des Osterreichischen Alpen-Klubs zur Feier seines fünfundsiebzigjährigen Bestandes 1878-1953 / S. Walcheren-Wien. [Vienna, 1954.] Ill. Sonderfolge der *Osterreichischen Alpenzeitung*, Jahrg.72 Folge 1273, Jan.-Feb.1954.
GB.1319(6).   b088.

Bergsteigen — richtig, sicher und mit Freude / Karl Lukan. Wien, 1969. Ill.
GB/A.435.   b089.

Der **Bergsteiger** / Deutscher Alpenverein. Wien, 1930. Extracted from *Der Bergsteiger*, Jahrg.8 no.5, Mai 1930.
GB.1318(15).   b090.

Der **Bergsteiger** / Deutscher Alpenverein. Feb., Okt.1935, Nov.1941, Okt.1951. München, 1935-51.
GB.1643(2-5).   b091.

Der **Bergsteiger** / geleitet von Jos. Jul. Schätz. München, 1949. Ill.
GB/B.250; GB/B.441. b092.

Der **Bergsteiger**: Berge und Heimat: Organ des Österreichischen Alpenvereins. Jahrg.37,39- , 1970, 1972-   . München, 1970-   .
GB/B.425 (1970); GB/A.2070 (1972-). b093.

Bergsteiger-Biwak / Fritz Schmitt. München, [n.d.]. Ill.
GB.1326(22). b094.

Bergsteigerbrevier: ein Blütenlese aus den Werken alpiner Dichtkunst und Erfahrungs-weisheit / gesammelt und herausgegeben von A. Dreyer. München, [ca 1920]. Ill.
GB/A.1484. b095.

Ein **Bergsteigerleben**: alpine Aufsätze und Vorträge, Reisebriefe und Kerguelen-Tagebuch / Josef Enzensperger; herausgegeben vom Akademischen Alpenverein, München. 2., verm. und veränderte Ausg. München, 1924. Ill.
GB/B.132. b096.

Bergtage: Gewalt und Glück der Höhen / Otto Ampferer. München, 1930. Ill.
GB/A.195. b097.

Bergvagabunden: ein Hans-Ertl-Buch / Walter Schmidkunz. Erfurt, 1937. Ill.
GB/A.1501. b098.

Bergwanderungen in den Ostalpen / Alfred Dessauer. München, 1912. Ill.
GB.904. b099.

Bergwelt Korsika: ein Führer für Wanderer und Bergsteiger / Hans Schymik. Stuttgart, 1973. Ill. [Wanderbücher für jede Jahreszeit.]
GB/A.1270(14). b100.

Bergwelt Rumäniens: ein Führer für Wanderer und Bergsteiger / Michael Berker. Stuttgart, 1972. Ill., maps. [Wanderbücher für jede Jahreszeit.]
GB/A.1295(5). b101.

Bergwelt, Wunderwelt: eine alpine Welt-geschichte / herausgegeben von Luis Trenker unter Mitwirkung von Walter Schmidkunz. Leipzig, 1935. Ill.
GB/B.419. b102.

Bericht der Sektion Mark Brandenburg des D. u. Oe. Alpenvereins über das Gründungsjahr 1899 und die sechs Sektionsjahre 1900-1905. Berlin, [n.d.].
GB/A.181(5). b103.

Bericht des Akademischen Alpinen Vereines Innsbruck. 1930/31 und 1931/32, 1932/33. Innsbruck, [1932-33].
GB.1647(4-5). b104.

Die **Berner** Hochalpen / C. Täuber. 2. Aufl. Zürich, [1910?]. Ill.
GB/A.942(13). b105.

Das **Berner** Oberland im Lichte der deutschen Dichtung / ausgewählt und eingeleitet von Otto Zürcher. Leipzig, 1923. [Die Schweiz im deutschen Geistesleben; 18.]
GB/A.582. b106.

Bernese Alps including the Oberland / John Ball. London, 1873. Ill., maps. [Ball's Alpine guides.]
GB/A.708. b106.1.

Bernese Alps including the Oberland / John Ball. New ed. London, 1875. Ill., maps. [Ball's Alpine guides.]
Lloyd.319. b106.2.

The **Bernese** Oberland / G. Hasler, W.A.B. Coolidge, H. Dübi. London, 1902-08. 4v (in 5). [Conway and Coolidge's climbers' guides; 9-13.]
GB.1324(14-8); Lloyd.25-29; Lloyd.25A,B (other copies of v.1); GB.1324(19) (another copy of v.4 pt.1). b107.

The **Bernese** Oberland. Vol.1 / W.A.B. Coolidge. New ed. London, 1909-10. 2v. [Conway and Coolidge's climbers' guides; 9.]
GB.1324(12-3). b108.

The **Bernese** Oberland / T.G. Bonney. London, 1878. 2v; ill. [Picturesque Europe; 34-5.]
GB.1334(38-9). b110.

The **Bernese** Oberland in summer and winter: a guide / Julian Grande. London, 1911. Ill., maps.
GB/A.511. b111.

La **Bernina** / Pierre Blanc. [N.p.], 1972. Ill.
GB/B.570(8). b112.

Die **Bernina**, 1786 / Johann Baptist von Tscharner. 2. Aufl. besorgt von Heinrich F.S. Bachmair und Walter Schmidkunz. München, 1933. [Jahresgabe der Gesellschaft alpiner Bücherfreunde; 12.]
GB.166. b113.

Bernina-Gruppe / Marcel Kurz. Chur, 1932. Ill. [Clubführer durch die Bündner Alpen; 5.] Published by the Schweizer Alpenclub.
GB/A.1026. b114.

Bernt Balchen / Gunnar Lorentz, Sigge Hommerberg; oversatt og bearbeidet av E. Omholt-Jensen. Oslo, 1946. Ill., maps, ports., facsims.
GB/B.524(9). b115.

Die **Berriasschichten** an der Axenstrasse / August Tobler. Lausanne, 1895. [Eclogae geologicae helveticae; 4.]
GB/A.514(13). b116.

Berühmte Kletterziele in den Dolomiten: die Brentagruppe / Remo Pedrotti; herausgegeben vom Regionalassessorat für Fremdenverkehr der Region Trentino-Tiroler Etschland. Trento, 1956. Ill., map.
GB/B.119(11). b117.

Beschreibung der Merkwurdigkeiten, welche er in einer Ao. 1742. gemachten Reise durch einige Orte des Schweitzerlandes beobachtet hat / Johann Georg Sulzer. Zürich, 1743.
Lloyd.676. b118.

Beschreibung der Natur-Geschichten des Schweizerlands / Johann Jacob Scheuchzer. Zürich, 1706-08. 3v; ill., maps.
GB.563-4 (wanting v.3); Lloyd.761 (bound in 1v.). b119.

Beschreibung der savoyischen Eisgebürge: Fortsetzung der Beschreibung der penninischen und rhätischen Alpen / Marc Théodore Bourrit. Zürich, 1786. Translated from *Description des glacières, glaciers et amas de glace du duché de Savoye*.
GB.206. b120.

Beschreibung der schweizerischen Alpen und Landwirthschaft, nach den verschiedenen Abweichungen einzelner Kantone / Johann Rudolf Steinmüller. Winterthur, 1802-04. 2v.
GB/A.639-40. b121.

Beschreibung des lobl. Orths und Lands Glarus: samt einem Anhang von dem Toggenburger-Geschäfft / Johann Heinrich Tschudi. Zürich, 1714. Maps.
Lloyd.188. b122.

Beschreibung des Quecksilber-Bergwerks zu Idria in Mittel-Crayn / Johann Jacob Ferber. Berlin, 1774. Ill., plans.
GB.579(2). b123.

Beschreibung des Zürich Sees / Hans Erhard Escher. Zürich, 1692.
Lloyd.122. b124.

Beschreibung dess berühmbten Lucerner- oder 4. Waldstätten Sees und dessen fürtrefflichen Qualiteten und sonderbaaren Eygenschafften / Johann Leopold Cysat. Lucern, 1661.
Lloyd.585. b125.

Beschreibung einer Reise, die im Jahr 1776 durch einem Theil der bernischen Alpen gemacht worden von Iac. Sam. Wyttenbach. [Bern, 1777?] Ill.
GB/C.42. b126.

Der **beste** Kenner des Mont-Blanc, T. Graham Brown. Lausanne, 1936. A portrait from the calendar *Pickel und Ski* for 1936.
GB.1341(14). b127.

Eine **Besteigung** der Cima de Jazi / Roemer. [N.p., 1863.]
GB.1335(59). b128.

Die **Besteigung** des Jungfrauhorns durch Agassiz und seine Gefährten / E. Desor; aus dem Französischen von C. Vogt. Solothurn, 1842. Ill., map.
Lloyd.484. b129.

Besteigung des Piz Bernina, 4052m., nebst vergleichenden Betrachtungen über das Reisen in der Schweiz und in den Ostalpen / Julius Meurer. [Munich], 1884. Ill. Pp.[75]-98 of the *Zeitschrift des Deutschen und Osterreichischen Alpenvereins*, 1884.
GB.1881(56). b130.

Die **Besteigungen** des Kilimandscharo: ein historischer Uberblick / Wilhelm Methner. Innsbruck, 1930. Ill. Pp.[82]-96 of the *Zeitschrift des Deutschen und Osterreichischen Alpenvereins*, Bd.61.
GB.1322(18[3]). b131.

Better built by Burns / (R. Burns Ltd.). Manchester, [n.d.]. A catalogue of camping equipment.
GB.1313(29). b132.

Between heaven and earth / Gaston Rébuffat, Pierre Tairraz; translated by Eleanor Brockett. London, 1965. Ill. Translated from *Entre terre et ciel*.
GB/A.125. b133.

Between the Oxus and the Indus / R.C.F. Schomberg. London, 1935. Ill.
GB.836.   b134.

Beyond Cape Horn: travels in the Antarctic / Charles Neider. San Francisco, 1980. Ill.
GB/A.2115.   b135.

Beyond the Pir Panjal: life among the mountains and valleys of Kashmir / Ernest F. Neve. London, 1912.
GB.952.   b136.

Beyträge für allgemeine Naturlehre und Geologie / Johann Georg Tralles. Bern, 1790. Ill. [Bestimmung der Höhen der bekanntern Berge des Canton Bern; 1.]
GB/A.799(10).   b137.

Beyträge zu der Naturgeschichte des Schweizerlandes / Jacob Samuel Wyttenbach. Bern, 1773. 2v (in 1).
GB.382.   b138.

Beyträge zur nähern Kenntniss des Schweizerlandes / Hs. Rudolf Schinz. Zürich, 1783-91. 5v (in 2); maps.
GB/A.697-8(1).   b139.

Bezwinger der Titanen: im Kampf um die Berge der Welt / Hans Albert Förster. Leipzig, [1949]. Ill., maps.
GB/A.453.   b140.

Bhoutan, royaume d'Asie inconnu / Michel Peissel. Paris, 1971. Ill., maps. [Clefs de l'aventure.]
GB/A.1035(10).   b141.

Bhutan, a kingdom in the Himalayas: a study of the land, its people and their government / Nagendra Singh. New Delhi, 1972. Ill., maps.
GB/A.1332.   b142.

Bibliografia alpinistica-storica e scientifica del gruppo del Monte Rosa, dal colle del Théodule al passo del Monte Moro, 1527-1924. Novara, 1925. Published by the Istituto Geografico De Agostini.
GB.1329(43).   b143.

Bibliografia del gruppo del Monte Rosa / Alberto Durio. [Turin], 1927. Estratto dalla *Rivista mensile del Club Alpino Italiano*, vol.46, maggio-giugno 1927.
GB.1318(9).   b144.

Bibliografia di Umberto Nobile / Gertrude Nobile Stolp. Firenze, 1984. Ill.
GB/A.2189.   b145.

Bibliographia caucasica et transcaucasica / M.M. Miansarov. Tom.1 sect. 1-2. Amsterdam, 1967. A facsimile reprint of the St. Petersburg, 1874-76 ed.
GB/A.1071.   b146.

Bibliographie de la littérature du Nord d'après les matériaux recueillis par la Société d'Archangel: Novaia Zemla. Pt.1: Bibliographie des livres, des articles et des notices, publiés par les savants russes, les voyageurs et les écrivains / par A. Th. Schidlowsky. [St. Petersburg], 1910.
GB.1319(3).   b147.

Bibliographie sommaire: les Alpes françaises, le Dauphiné et Grenoble, économie et géographie humaine / Gilbert Nigay. [N.p., 1967.]
GB/A.181(4).   b148.

A **bibliography** of Alaskan literature, 1724-1924 / James Wickersham. Fairbanks, Alaska, 1927. [Miscellaneous publications of the Alaska Agricultural College and School of Mines; 1.]
GB/A.2191.   b149.

A **bibliography** of the ascents of Mont Blanc from 1786-1853 / Henry F. Montagnier. London, 1911. Reprinted from the *Alpine Journal*, Aug. 1911.
GB.1741(1).   b150.

Bibliography of the Himalayas / R.K. Gupta. Gurgaon, 1981.
GB/A.2029.   b151.

Bibliography of the Naval Arctic Research Laboratory / compiled and edited by Wade W. Gunn. [Washington], 1973. [Arctic Institute of North America technical paper; 24.]
GB/B.440(14).   b152.

Bibliotheca Fageliana: a catalogue of the library of Greffier Fagel, of the Hague / digested by Sam. Paterson. [London, 1802.]
Lloyd.709.   b153.

Bibliothek Hans Steinwachs: Versteigerung in Bern in der Kunsthalle am Helvetia-Platz den 11. und 12. Juni 1934. Bern, 1934. 2v; facsims.
Lloyd.1621(10-1).   b154.

Bidrag till Kung Karls Lands geologi / A.G. Nathorst. [Stockholm, 1902?] Ill., map. [Reprinted from] *Geol. fören. förhandl.* n:o.208 bd.23 hft.5.
GB.1335(55).   b155.

Bietschhorn- , Lötschentaler Breithorn- , Nest-horn- und Aletschhorngrupppen / Daniel Bodmer, Toni Labhart, Christoph Blum. 4., neubearb. Aufl. des *Hochgebirgsführers durch die Berner Alpen* von W.A.B. Coolidge und H. Dübi. Bern, 1972. Ill., maps. [Hochgebirgsführer durch die Berner Alpen; 3.] Published by the Schweizer Alpenclub, Sektion Bern.
GB/A.989(3). b155.1.

Bietschhorn- , Lötschentaler Breithorn- , Nest-horn- und Aletschhorngruppen / Daniel Bodmer, Toni Labhart, Christoph Blum. 5., ergänzte Aufl. des *Hochgebirgsführers durch die Berner Alpen* von W.A.B. Coolidge und H. Dübi. Zürich, 1976. Ill., maps. [Hochgebirgsführer durch die Berner Alpen; 3.] Published by the Schweizer Alpenclub, Sektion Bern.
GB/A.989(4). b155.2.

Bietschhorn- und Aletschhorngruppen / F. Triner, W. von Bergen. 2., neubearb. Aufl. des *Hochgebirgsführer durch die Berner Alpen* von W.A.B. Coolidge und H. Dübi. Bern, 1931. Ill., maps. [Hochgebirgsführer durch die Berner Alpen; 3.] Published by the Schweizer Alpenclub, Sektion Bern.
GB.162. b156.

Bild und Bau der Schweizeralpen / Carl Schmidt. Basel, 1907. Ill., maps. Beilage zum *Jahrbuch S.A.C.*, Jahrg.42, 1906/7.
GB/B.403(19). b157.

Bilder aus der schweizer Bergen: eine Sammlung von Blättern berühmter Fleister. [N.p., ca 1890.]
GB/C.32(1-20). b158.

Biographical conversations, on celebrated travellers; comprehending distinct narratives of their personal adventures / William Bingley. 2nd ed. London, 1819.
Lloyd.318. b159.

The **Biographical** Magazine: containing portraits of eminent and ingenious persons of every age and nation, with their lives and characters. Vol.1-2. London, 1819-20.
GB.1078-9. b160.

Biographical notice of Jean Payot of Chamonix: issued with the fourth edition of Whymper's *Guide to Chamonix and Mont Blanc*, 1899. Edin-burgh, 1899. Port.
Lloyd.1616(2). b161.

Biographical notice of Johann zum Taugwald of Zermatt / Edward Whymper. Edinburgh, [1899]. Port.
GB.1335(10); Lloyd.1614(4); Lloyd.1616(1).
b162.

Biologiia Belago moria. Biology of the White Sea / [redaktsionnaia kollegiia; N.A. Pertsov et al.]. Tom.3. Moskva, 1970. Ill., port. [Trudy Belo-morskoi biologicheskoi stantsii MGU.]
GB/A.1783. b163.

Biology of the peregrine and gyrfalcon in Greenland / William A. Burnham, William G. Mattox. Copenhagen, 1984. Ill.,map. [Meddelelser om Grønland. Bioscience; 14.]
GB/A.1819(14). b164.

Biology of the squid, Gonatus Fabriccii (Lichtenstein, 1818) from West Greenland waters / Thomas K. Kristensen. Copenhagen, 1984. [Meddelelser om Grønland. Bioscience; 13.]
GB/A.1819(13). b165.

Bis zum Gipfel der Welt vom Mont Blanc zum Mount Everest / Hans Albert Forster, Franz Grassler. Leipzig, 1959. Ill.
GB/A.2063. b166.

Bis zur Spitze des Mount Everest: die Besteigung, 1924 / Edward Felix Norton und andern Teil-nehmern; Deutsch von W. Rickmer Rickmers. Basel, 1926. Ill., maps. Translated from *The fight for Everest, 1924*.
GB.1141. b167.

Bishop George Francis Graham Brown memorial appeal. London, [1943].
GB.1313(25); GB.1313(26). b168.

I **bivacchi** italiani delle Alpi e degli Appennini: le stazioni del Corpo Nazionale di Soccorso Alpino / Carlo Arzani. Milano, 1971. Ill., maps. Estratto da *Rassegna alpina*.
GB/A.836(9). b169.

A **bivouac** on the Aiguille du Plan / Frank S. Smythe. London, 1928. Pp.229-39 of the *Cornhill Magazine*, Aug. 1928.
GB.1335(63). b170.

Biwak auf dem Dach der Welt: auf Bergpfaden durch Tadshikistan / Georg Renner. Leipzig, 1975. Ill., maps.
GB/A.1994. b171.

Blandt danske og norske fangstmænd i Nordøst-grønland / Elmar Drastrup. København, 1932.
GB/A.2086. b172.

Blaxland-Lawson-Wentworth 1813 / edited by Joanna Armour Richards. Hobart, 1979. Ill., maps.
GB/A.2087. b173.

Blicke in die östlichen Alpen und in das Land um die Nordküste des adriatischen Meeres / Philipp Baron von Canstein. Berlin, 1837. Map.
GB/A.423. b174.

Bognanco: il paese delle cento cascate: guida-zibaldone per il turista, il curioso, il valligiano / Paolo Bologna. Bognanco, 1976. Ill., map.
GB/A.1966(8). b175.

The **Bolivian** Andes: a record of climbing exploration in the Cordillera Real in 1898 and 1900 / Sir Martin Conway. London, 1901. Ill., maps, port.
Lloyd.1002. b176.

Bollettino / Club Alpino Italiano. No.15-16, 21-79. Torino, 1869-1967. Ill., maps.
Lloyd.1620(19-19a) (no.15-6); GB/A.1504-43 (no.21-79); GB/B.273-5 (other copies of no.61,62,75); GB/B.302 (another copy of no.64); GB/B.321 (another copy of no.75). b177.

Bollettino / Club Alpino Italiano. Indice generale dei cinquanta primi numeri (dal 1865 al 1884) / compilato da Luigi Vaccarone. Torino, 1885.
GB/A.1544. b178.

Bollettino / Club Alpino Italiano, Sezione Fiorentina. Anno 4 no.2, marzo 1913. Firenze, 1913.
GB.1329(40). b179.

Bollettino / Comitato Glaciologico Italiano e Commissione Glaciologica del Club Alpino Italiano. No.16, 1936. Torino, 1936. Ill.
GB/B.313(2). b180.

Bollettino mensile / Club Alpino Italiano, Sezione Ligure. Anno 2 no.1-anno 9 no.5, genn. 1921-maggio 1930. Genova, [1921-30]. Wanting 1924-26.
GB/A.981-5. b181.

Bollettino trimestrale / Società Alpina Meridionale. Anno 1,4, 1893,1896. Napoli, 1893-96.
GB/A.1123-4. b182.

Bolzano: incontro con il centro antico / Hermann Frass; [versione italiana a cura di Carlo Galasso].
Bolzano, 1968. Ill.
GB/C.5(10). b183.

Bolzano ed i suoi dintorni: guida turistico-alpinistica / a cura del prof. Mario Martinelli e del primo ispettore scolastico Lucillo Merci. 2a ed. Bolzano, 1954. Ill., maps. Published by the Club Alpino Italiano, Sezione di Bolzano.
GB/A.1349(10). b184.

[A **book** of children's scraps.] [N.p., n.d.]
Lloyd.1463. b185.

The **book** of curiosities, or Wonders of the great world / John Platts. London, [1822].
Lloyd.826 (impf.). b186.

The **book** of shells; containing the classes Mollusca, Conchifera, Cirrhipeda, Annulata and Crustacea. 3rd ed. London, 1841.
GB.32. b187.

Books on the Alps. [London], 1871. A review from *The Times*, 22/8/1871, of Sir Leslie Stephen's book *The playground of Europe* and two others.
GB.1341(18). b188.

[**Booksellers**' catalogues, with special reference to books on mountaineering and exploration.] [N.p., 1872-1960.]
GB.1911. b189.

Border lands of Spain and France: with an account of a visit to the Republic of Andorre. London, 1856.
GB.494. b190.

Bormio antica e medioevale e le sue relazioni con le potenze finitime / Enrico Besta. Milano, 1945. [Raccolta di studi storici sulla Valtellina; 5.]
GB/A.1408. b191.

Il **bosco** contro il torrente: la redenzione delle terre povere / G. Di Tella. [Milano, 1910?] Ill. Published by the Touring Club Italiano, Commissione di Propaganda 'Per il bosco e per il pascolo'.
GB/B.289(12). b192.

Bosconero / Giovanni Angelini. [Bologna], 1964. Ill. [Le Alpi Venete.] Published by the Club Alpino Italiano, Sezione di Belluno.
GB/B.312(22). b193.

Botany. New York, 1976. [Thule expedition, 5th, 1921-1924. Report; vol.2, no.1-3.] Contents: Vascular plants / Johs. Grøntved. — Mosses / A.

Hesselbo. — Lichens / B. Lynge.
GB/A.1823(1-3). b194.

A **boy**'s ascent of Mont Blanc / Albert Smith.
London, [1860]. Originally published as *The story of Mont Blanc*.
GB.132; Lloyd.167. b195.

A **boy**'s ascent of Mont Blanc / Albert Smith.
London, [1871]. Originally published as *The story of Mont Blanc*.
GB.107. b196.

The **boy**'s birthday book: a collection of tales, essays, and narratives of adventure / Mrs. S.C. Hall, William Houtt [et al.]. London, 1864. Ill.
Lloyd.411. b197.

Bradshaw's illustrated hand-book to Switzerland and the Tyrol. London, [1862]. Ill., maps.
Lloyd.139. b198.

Bradshaw's illustrated hand-book to Switzerland and the Tyrol. London, [1866]. Ill., maps.
GB/A.731. b199.

Bradshaw's illustrated hand-book to Switzerland and the Tyrol. London, [1867]. Ill., maps.
Lloyd.140. b200.

Bradshaw's pedestrian route-book for Switzerland, Chamouni, and the Italian lakes / edited by J.R. Morell. London, [1868]. Maps.
Lloyd.121. b201.

The **brave** Swiss boy. [London], 1897. From *Chambers's Journal*.
GB.1319(10) (impf.). b202.

Brennerbuch: Naturansichten und Lebensbilder aus Tirol, insbesondere aus der Umgebung der Brennerbahn / Heinrich Noe. München, 1869.
GB/A.721. b203.

The **Brenta** Dolomites / [Remo Pedrotti]; [translated by Bryn Brooks]. Rovereto, 1966. Ill, map. Translated from *Le Dolomiti di Brenta*.
GB/B.390(8). b204.

Die **Brenta** Gruppe / Karl Schulz. [Berlin, 1894.] Ill. Pp.[297]-348 of *Erschliessung der Ostalpen*, Bd.3.
GB.1381. b205.

Brenta-Gruppe / Horst Wels. 2. Aufl. München, 1969. Ill., map. [Dolomiten-Klettenführer; 3.]
GB/A.1050(15). b206.

Brenta-Presanella: escursioni e passeggiate / a cura dell'Azienda Autonoma di Soggiorno Madonna di Campiglio e Pinzolo. Bolzano, 1977.
GB/A.1964(9). b207.

Brenva / T. Graham Brown. London, 1944. Ill., map.
GB.753-8 (6 copies); Lloyd.844; Lloyd.844A.
b208.

Brenva / T. Graham Brown. [London, 1944.] The dustjacket.
GB.1334(25). b209.

Brenva / T. Graham Brown. [London, 1944.] Photographs and proofs of plates.
GB.1912(9-11). b210.

Brenva / T. Graham Brown. [London, 1944.] Proofs of various stages.
GB.1647(16-23). b211.

Brenva / T. Graham Brown. London, 1945.
Lloyd.845. b211.1.

Brenva / T. Graham Brown; traduit par Bernard Lemoine. Paris, 1955. Ill.
GB.1311(1); GB.1311(2). b212.

The **Brenva** face / T. Graham Brown. [London], 1939. Ill. Reprinted from the *Alpine Journal*, Nov.1939.
GB.1305(23); Lloyd.1612(5). b213.

The **Brenva** face / T. Graham Brown. [London, 1939.] Corrected proof sheets.
GB.1341(6). b214.

Bressanone / testi ed impaginazione a cura di Valerio Dejaco; traduzione dal tedesco del prof. Giuseppe Giudiceandrea. Bolzano, 1968. Ill.
GB/A.1287. b215.

Bressanone e dintorni: storia, monumenti artistici, passeggiate / a cura della Libreria Athesia, Bressanone. Bolzano, 1976. Ill., maps.
GB/A.1964(6). b216.

Breve fra vidderne: jagtskildringer og andre beretninger fra Grønland / Johannes Sangtoft. København, 1946. Ill.
GB/A.1855. b217.

Breve storia dell'alpinismo dolomitico / Paolo Melucci. Firenze, 1960. [Collana di studi alpini; 1.]
GB/A.995(10). b218.

Breve vocabolario di termini topografici: italiano-inglese, inglese-italiano / Santi Monaco. Firenze, 1954. Published by the Istituto Geografico Militare.
GB/A.1034(8).   b219.

Breviario di montagna / Sandro Prada. 4a ed. [Milan?], 1950.
GB/A.1034(11).   b220.

Le **Bric** Bouchet et le Pelvas: guide des escalades / H. Gentil. [N.p., 1970.] Ill.
GB/B.377(32).   b221.

A **brief** account of the Vaudois, his Sardinian Majesty's Protestant subjects in the valleys of Piedmont / in a letter from a gentleman on his travels in Italy [i.e. Mr. Goldwin]. London, 1753.
Lloyd.345.   b222.

A **brief** historical sketch of the valley of Chamouni / Markham Sherwill. Paris, 1832.
GB.850; Lloyd.654; Lloyd.1582(2).   b223.

A **brief** relation of a new and unfortunate voyage to the South Seas, undertaken by M. Marion. [Edinburgh, 1785.] Pp.81-2 of the *Scots Magazine*, Feb.1785.
GB.1313(9).   b224.

Briefe / Friedrich von Matthisson. Zürich, 1795. 2v (in 1).
GB/A.1043.   b225.

Briefe an Karl Kraus / Else Lasker-Schüler; herausgegeben von Astrid Gehlhoff-Claes. Köln, [1959].
GB/A.1329.   b226.

Briefe aus den Jahren 1830 bis 1847. 1: Reisebriefe aus den Jahren 1830 bis 1832 / Felix Mendelssohn-Bartholdy; herausgegeben von Paul Mendelssohn Bartholdy. 8. Aufl. Leipzig, 1869.
GB/A.1044.   b226.1.

Briefe aus den Jahren 1830 bis 1847. 2: Briefe aus den Jahren 1833 bis 1847 / Felix Mendelssohn-Bartholdy; herausgegeben von Paul Mendelssohn Bartholdy und Carl Mendelssohn Bartholdy; nebst einem Verzeichnisse der sämmtlichen musikalischen Compositionen von Felix Mendelssohn Bartholdy zusammengestellt von Julius Rietz. 5. Aufl. Leipzig, 1865.
GB/A.1045.   b227.

Briefe aus der Schweiz nach Hannover geschrieben, in dem Jahre 1763 / [J.G.R. Andreae?]. 2. Abdr. Zürich, 1776. Ill.
GB/B.277.   b228.

Briefe aus der Schweiz und Italien / Georg Arnold. Lübeck, 1796-97. 2v.
GB/A.568-9.   b229.

Briefe die Schweiz betreffend / C.C.L. Hirschfeld. Neue und verm. Ausg. Leipzig, 1776.
GB/A.580(1).   b230.

Briefe einer reisenden Dame aus der Schweitz, 1786. Frankfurt, 1787.
GB/A.770.   b231.

Briefe eines reisenden Dänen: geschrieben im Jahr 1791 und 1792 während seiner Reise durch einen Theil Deutschlands, der Schweiz und Frankreichs / Sneedorf. Züllichau, 1793.
GB/A.662.   b232.

Briefe eines Sachsen aus der Schweiz an seinen Freund in Leipzig / [C.G. Küttner]. Leipzig, 1785. 2v.
GB/A.713-4.   b233.

Briefe geschrieben auf einer Reise durch die Schweiz im Jahr 1810 / J.F. Benzenberg. Dusseldorf, 1811-12. 2v; ill.
GB/A.1459(2-3).   b234.

Briefe über die Schweiz / Christoph Meiners. Berlin, 1784-90. 4v. Wanting v.2-4.
GB/A.1152.   b235.

Briefe über Graubünden / J.F. Heigelin. Stuttgard, 1793. Ill.
GB/A.667.   b236.

The **bright** shawl / Joseph Hergesheimer. Leipzig, 1923. [Collection of British authors. Tauchnitz edition; 4593.]
GB/A.915(2).   b237.

The **British** caver: a netherworld journal. Vol.53-72, 1969-79. Crymych, 1969-79. Ill.
GB/A.2072.   b238.

The **British** Highlands with rope & rucksack / Ernest A. Baker. London, 1933. Ill.
GB.838.   b239.

British hills and mountains / J.H.B. Bell, E.F. Bozman, J. Fairfax Blakeborough. London, 1940.

Ill., maps. [British heritage series.]
GB.698. b240.

British manly exercises: in which rowing and sailing are now first described; and riding and driving / Donald Walker. London, 1834. Ill.
GB.125. b241.

British mountaineering / Claude E. Benson. London, 1909. Ill.
GB.343. b242.

The **British** Mountaineering Journal. Vol.3 no.4, vol.5 no.2. Birkenhead, 1935-37.
GB.1319(14-5). b243.

British mountaineers / Frank S. Smythe. London, 1942. Ill., ports. [Britain in pictures.]
GB.881. b244.

British work in Spitsbergen: some historical notes / R.N. Rudmose-Brown. [Edinburgh, 1911.] Reprinted from the *Scottish Geographical Magazine*, vol.27, April 1911.
GB.1335(52). b245.

[**Broadsides** printed during the Arctic expedition undertaken by the *Alert* and the *Discovery*, 1875-76.] Bellot Harbour, [1875-76].
GB/B.501(1-9). b246.

[**Brochure**] / Austrian Alpine Club. Welwyn Garden City, [1972]. Ill.
GB/A.988(6). b247.

Brown's knots and splices, with table of strengths of ropes, etc. and wire rigging / Captain Jutsum. Rev. and enl. Glasgow, 1943. Ill.
GB/A.2165(3). b248.

Bruderklaus, oder Des seligen Nikolaus von der Flue lehrreiche und wundervolle Lebensgeschichte / herausgegeben von Georg Sigrist. Lucern, 1843. Ill.
GB/A.648. b249.

Le **Brunnegghorn** dans l'histoire / W.A.B. Coolidge. [N.p., 1920.] Pp.[365]-7 of *Comptes rendus du Congrès de l'alpinisme à Monaco, 1920*, tom.2.
GB.1340(51). b250.

Le **Brunnegghorn** dans l'histoire / W.A.B. Coolidge. Ed. rev. par l'auteur. [N.p., 1920.] Tirage à part des *Comptes rendus du Congrès de l'alpinisme à Monaco, 1920*, tom.2.
GB.1340(52). b251.

Buch der Reisen: Bilder und Studien aus Italien, der Schweiz und Deutschland / Adolf Ignaz von Tschabuschnigg. Wien, 1842.
GB/A.29. b252.

Le **bûcher**, les grands arbres, le vinaigre: commentaire sur un incident au cours de la marche d'Hannibal / M.A. de Lavis-Trafford. Saint-Jean-de-Maurienne, 1958.
GB/A.1350(9). b253.

Bücherverzeichnis der Zentral-Bibliothek des Deutschen und Oesterreichischen Alpenverein in München. München, 1902.
Lloyd.1606(16). b254.

Buddhists and glaciers of western Tibet / Giotto Dainelli. London, 1933. Ill., map.
GB.1112. b255.

The **builders** of Florence / J. Wood Brown. London, 1907. Ill.
GB.1270. b256.

Bulletin / American Geographical Society. Vol.38 no.3, March 1906. New York, 1906.
GB/A.1791(1). b257.

Bulletin / Climbers' Club. No.1-13, 1911-14. London, 1911-14. Wanting no.11.
Lloyd.1618(3-21). b257.1.

Bulletin / Club alpin français, Section de Paris-Chamonix. Nouv.sér. Année 5 no.23-24, avril 1951. Paris, 1951.
GB.1311(5-6). b258.

Bulletin / Institut national genevois. Tom.39, 1909. Genève, 1909.
Lloyd.787. b258.1.

Bulletin / Midland Association of Mountaineers. No.1-6, March 1933-July 1939. [N.p.], 1933-39. Ill. Continues as *Journal*.
GB/A.1637. b259.

Bulletin / New Zealand Alpine Club. Vol.68 no.1, Feb.-Mar.1981. [Christchurch?], 1981.
GB/A.1974(1). b260.

Bulletin / Schweizer Alpenclub, Section genevoise. Année 1 no.1-9,12; année 2 no.1,3,4; année 3 no.3-5,7,9,10; année 4 no.1,2,5-8,10-12; année 5 no.2-6,9,12; année 7 no.1-5,9; année 10 no.11; année 13 no.8; année 15 no.2; année 25

no.12; année 26 no.9; année 30 no.8. Genève, 1925-54.
GB/B.377(19-31) (année 1-2); GB.1645(25-63) (année 3-30). b261.

Bulletin / Scottish Mountaineering Club. Jan.1949. Edinburgh, 1949.
GB.1331(30). b262.

Bulletin / Scottish Mountaineering Club. Easter Meet notice, separate insert. Jan.1951. [Edinburgh], 1951.
GB.1305(19). b263.

Bulletin / Société d'études des Hautes Alpes. Année 1 (1882)-1969; sér. 1-7. Gap, 1882-1969.
GB/A.880 (impf.). b264.

Bulletin / Société d'études des Hautes-Alpes: table des matières contenues dans les dix premières années, 1882-91. Gap, 1895.
GB/A.881. b265.

Bulletin / Société d'études des Hautes Alpes: table générale des matières du *Bulletin* de 1882 à 1965 / Marcel Faillot. Gap, 1967.
GB/A.973. b266.

Bulletin / Wayfarers' Club, Liverpool. 1942. Liverpool, 1942.
GB/B.542b. b267.

Bulletin pyrénéen: organe de la Fédération des sociétés pyrénéistes. No. 97-207, fév.1911/janv.-fév.-mars 1933. [N.p], 1911-33. Ill., maps.
GB/A.1691. b268.

Bullettino trimestrale / Club Alpino di Torino. Anno 1865 no.1-anno 1866 no.7. Bologna, 1970. Facsimile reprint of the Torino 1865-67 ed.
GB/A.829. b269.

Das **Bündner** Oberland: Itinerarium für das Excursionsgebiet des S.A.C. St. Gallen, 1874.
GB/A.879(2). b270.

Das **Bündner** Oberland, oder Der Vorderrhein mit seinen Seitenthälern / G. Theobald. Chur, 1861. Ill.
GB/A.800(5). b271.

Business in pneumania / Frank S. Smythe. London, 1936. Ill. Pp.191-203 of the *Windsor Magazine*, no.493, Jan. 1936.
GB.1338(17). b272.

By the roaring Reuss: idylls and stories of the Alps / W. Bridges Birtt. London, 1898. Ill.
Lloyd.545; Lloyd.545A,B. b273.

-C-

C.A.I. Sezione Fiorentina 1868-1968 / a cura della Sezione Fiorentina del C.A.I. nel centenario della fondazione. [Florence], 1969. Ill.
GB/B.313(9). c001.

C'è sempre per ognuno una montagna / Giancarlo Bregani. Bologna, 1969. Ill. [Voci dai monti; 17.]
GB/A.479. c002.

Cadore e Ampezzano / [a cura di] Franco Fini; con un saggio di Ugo Fasolo: Il Cadore fino al 1866. Contributi: Eraldo Amadesi [et al.]; traduzioni: Anna Luisa Samoggia [et al.]. Bologna, 1981. Ill.
GB/B.540. c003.

Cadore, or Titian's country / Josiah Gilbert. London, 1869. Ill., map.
Lloyd.1356. c004.

Les **cadrans** solaires du val d'Aoste / texte et mise en pages de Robert Berton. Genova, 1972. Ill.
GB/B.377(6). c005.

Le **caïman**, le crocodile / Emile Fontaine. [Geneva, 1910.] Ill. From *Echo des Alpes*, mai 1910.
Lloyd.1608(7). c006.

Caire di Cougourda (Alpi Marittime) / Bruno e Francesco Salesi. Sanremo, [1973].
GB/A.1199(18). c007.

The **Cairngorm** Club Journal. Vol.1-3, 11-16, 1893-1952. Aberdeen, 1893-1952. Incomplete.
Lloyd.1619(25-41) (v.1-3,13); GB.1645(7-11) (v.11-12,16). c008.

The **Cairngorm** mountains / John Hill Burton. Edinburgh, 1864.
Lloyd.329; Lloyd.329A. c009.

The **Cairngorms** / Henry Alexander. Edinburgh, [1928]. A prospectus.
GB.1313(36). c010.

Calanques: Sainte-Baume, Sainte-Victoire: les 400 plus belles escalades et randonnées / Gaston Rébuffat. Paris, 1980. Ill.
GB/B.583. c011.

Caledonian sketches, or A tour through Scotland in 1807 / Sir John Carr. London, 1809.
GB.658. c012.

[**Calendar** for 1982.] [Switzerland? 1981.]
GB/B.570(16). c013.

Calendrier alpin, avec des notices sur les
éruptions volcaniques, explorations polaires /
Vincent Campanile. 5e éd. Naples, 1902.
GB/A.915(1). c014.

The **call** of the mountains / Colin Wyatt. London,
1952. Ill.
GB.1281. c015.

The **call** of the snow: season 1923-24 / William Le
Queux. [N.p., 1923.] Ill.
GB.1326(12). c016.

Camarade prend ton verre: storia delle guide di
Courmayeur / Renato Chabod. Bologna, 1972. Ill.
GB/B.334. c017.

Cambridge mountaineering, 1925-26 / edited by
L.R. Wager and P. Wyn Harris. Cambridge, [1926].
Published by the University of Cambridge
Mountaineering Club.
GB.1312(24). c018.

Cambridge mountaineering, 1932 / edited by J.C.
Ilhurst. Cambridge, [1932]. Ill. Published by the
University of Cambridge Mountaineering Club.
GB/A.1035(5). c019.

Cambridge mountaineering, 1934 / edited by J.A.
Ramsay. London, [1934]. Ill. Published by the
University of Cambridge Mountaineering Club.
GB/A.1035(6). c020.

Camp Six: an account of the 1933 Mount Everest
expedition / Frank S. Smythe. London, 1937. Ill.,
map, ports.
GB.970. c021.

Camp Six, by F.S. Smythe / [signed: E.G.H.K.].
[London, 1938.] A review. Pp.231-2 of the *Climbers'
Club Journal*, N.S. vol.5 no.3.
GB.1338(26). c022.

Camping in the Canadian Rockies: an account of
camp life in the wilder parts of the Canadian
Rocky Mountains / Walter Dwight Wilcox. New
York, 1896. Ill.
GB/A.144. c023.

Camps and climbs in Arctic Norway / Tom Weir.
London, 1953. Ill., ports., maps.
GB.711; GB.802. c024.

The **Camps** and Tours Union Magazine. Vol.22,
March-April 1949. Chorley Wood, 1949.
GB.1305(17). c025.

Canada north: man and the land / John K.
Naysmith. Ottawa, 1972. Ill., maps. Published by
the Northern Economic Development Branch,
Department of Indian Affairs and Northern
Development.
GB/B.478(6). c026.

Canadian Alpine Journal. Vol.1 no.1, vol.33, 1907,
1950. Banff, 1907-50. Ill., maps. Published by the
Alpine Club of Canada.
GB/A.2139(5) (v.1); GB.1329(49) (v.33). c027.

Canadian Geographical Journal. Vol.15 no.2,4.
London, 1937.
GB.1643(6-7). c028.

The **Canadian** Rockies: early travels and
explorations / Esther Fraser. Edmonton, 1969. Ill.,
map, ports.
GB/A.1962. c029.

The **Canadian** Rockies: twenty specially selected
views of the Rocky Mountains. Montreal, [1920?].
GB/A.2139(8). c030.

The **Canadian** Rockies trail guide: a hiker's
manual to the National Parks / Brian Patton, Bart
Robinson. Rev. ed. Canmore, Alta, 1978. Ill., maps.
GB/B.525(9). c031.

The **Canadian** Rockies — Yellowhead pass route.
Winnipeg, [1911]. Ill., map. Published by the
Grand Trunk Pacific Railway, General Passenger
Department.
Lloyd.1618(22). c032.

The **Canterbury** Mountaineer. No.16-49, 1946/7-
1980/81. Christchurch, 1947-81. Published by the
Canterbury Mountaineering and Tramping Club.
Wanting no.25, 1955/56.
GB/A.2167; GB.1318(12) (another copy of no.18).
c034.

The **Canterbury** Mountaineer: extracts from the
Canterbury Mountaineering Club's journal, no.2,
Aug.1933. [Christchurch, 1933.]
GB.1315(13). c035.

Canzel- und Agend-Büchlein der Kirche zu Bern.
Bern, 1752.
GB.159(1). c036.

Canzuns de Baselczia de Farasp / edidos da A. Decurtins. [N.p., 1920?]
GB/B.337(17). c037.

Cape Breton: ships and men / John P. Parker. Aylesbury, 1967. Ill., ports.
GB/A.1798. c038.

Capodanno sulla nord-est del Badile / Franco Rho. Bologna, 1968. Ill. [Voci dai monti; 13.]
GB/A.948. c039.

Captain J.E. Bernier's contribution to Canadian sovereignty in the Arctic / Yolande Dorion-Robitaille. Ottawa, 1978. Ill., maps, ports., facsims. Under authority of the Minister of Indian and Northern Affairs.
GB/B.501(10). c040.

Captain Musafir's rambles in Alpine lands / G.B. Malleson. London, 1884. Ill.
Lloyd.1294. c041.

La **capture** des glaciers / Stanislas Meunier. Paris, 1897. Maps. Pp.[149]-52 of *Le Naturaliste*, 2e sér. no.248.
GB.1880(10). c042.

Caribou Eskimos: material and social life and their cultural position / Kaj Birket-Smith; [translated by W.E. Calvert]. New York, 1976. Ill. [Thule expedition, 5th, 1921-24. Report; 5.]
GB/A.1829(1-2). c043.

Carnet de l'alpiniste / publié sous les auspices du Club alpin français. Paris, 1911.
GB/A.942(5). c044.

Carnets sahariens: l'appel du Hoggar et autres méharées / Roger Frison-Roche. Paris, 1965. Ill., map. [L'aventure vécue.]
GB/A.201. c045.

La **Carnia**: saggio di geografia regionale / Eugenia Bevilacqua. Firenze, [1960]. Ill., maps. [Università di Padova. Facoltà di Lettere e Filosofia. Pubblicazioni; 35.]
GB/B.312(12). c046.

Le **carovane** scolastiche alpine / Vincenzo Ricci; programma delle escursioni del 1893. Torino, 1893. Published by the Club Alpino Italiano, Sezione di Torino.
GB/B.290(14). c047.

Carte en relief de la Suisse / Ed. Beck. Berne, 1878.
GB/B.485. c048.

La **casa** a torre nell'Appenino reggiano: abitazioni medioevali nella montagna: linee di storia della architettura tra medioevo e l'età moderna / [a cura di Giuliano Cervi]. [Reggio?], 1981. Ill., map.
GB/A.1967(3). c049.

La **casa** rurale nel Trentino / Giuseppe Barbieri; con contributi di Renzo Albertini [et al.]. Firenze, 1962. Ill. [Ricerche sulle dimore rurali in Italia; 22.]
GB/A.1377. c050.

La **casa** rurale nella montagna bellunese / Elio Migliorini, Alessandro Cucagna. Firenze, 1969. Ill. [Ricerche sulle dimore rurali in Italia; 26.]
GB/B.386. c051.

La **casa** su la montagna: novelle, racconti, bozzetti / Federico Tosti. Milano, 1952.
GB/A.1138. c052.

Case contadine in Valle d'Aosta / Luigi Dematteis. Torino, 1984. [Quaderni di cultura alpina.]
GB/B.641. c053.

The **case** for Doctor Cook / Andrew A. Freeman. New York, 1961. Map.
GB/A.1920. c054.

Casso Torre parete ovest / Casimiro Ferrari. [Milan], 1975. Ill., map. [Exploits.]
GB/A.1966(6). c055.

Castelli e torri valtellinesi / Egidio Pedrotti. Milano, 1957. Ill. [Raccolta di studi storici sulla Valtellina; 10.]
GB/B.403(13). c056.

Castelli, rocche e roccie storiche: vedute dell'Appennino e paesaggi alpini del Cadore e de' monti bellunesi: fotografie / Alessandro Cassarini. [Bologna, ca 1880.]
GB/B.337(2). c057.

Castelli valdostani e canavesani / Giuseppe Giacosa. Torino, [ca 1960]. Ill.
GB/A.1229. c058.

Il **Castello** di Sarre: memorie storiche / Giuseppe Corona. Aosta, 1973. Ill. Facsimile reprint of the

Biella, 1881 ed.
GB/B.383. c059.

Castle Rock: a rock climbing guide / Dave Fearnley; edited and published by Ian Whitehouse for the New Zealand Alpine Club. [Christchurch?], 1982. Ill., maps.
GB/A.2165(10). c060.

Catalogo della Biblioteca Nazionale [del] Club Alpino Italiano / a cura di A. Richiello con la collaborazione di D. Mottinelli. Torino, 1968.
GB/B.289(22). c061.

Catalogue / Camera Club: exhibition of Alpine photography with the co-operation of the Alpine Club, March 1931. [London], 1931.
GB.1327(1). c062.

Catalogue: books and periodicals / Alpine Club Library. Vol.1-   . London, 1982-   .
GB/B.520(3). c063.

Catalogue des fougères, prêles et lycopodiacées des environs du Mont-Blanc / Venance Payot. Paris, 1860. Map.
Lloyd.953. c064.

Catalogue des membres: Mitglieder-Verzeichniss des Schweizer Alpen-Club, November, 1898. Neuchâtel, 1898.
Lloyd.1604(1). c065.

Catalogue des plantes suisses, qui se vendent chez Emmanuel Thomas. Lausanne, 1837-[53]. 2v (in 1).
Lloyd.1605(2). c066.

Catalogue of a loan exhibition of Scottish art and antiquities at 27, Grosvenor Square, London, by kind permission of Mr and Mrs Robert Fleming, February 5th-March 1st 1931. London, 1931.
GB/A.2139(4). c067.

Catalogue of books in the Library of the Alpine Club / revised by Sir F. Pollock. London, 1888.
Lloyd.852. c068.

Catalogue of books in the Library of the Alpine Club. Edinburgh, 1899. Editor's preface signed: Henry Cockburn.
GB.907; Lloyd.1000; Lloyd.1000A. c069.

Catalogue of books in the Library of the Alpine Club. Edinburgh, 1899. Editor's preface signed: Henry Cockburn. A proof copy.
Lloyd.1612(1). c070.

Catalogue of books in the [Rucksack] Club's Library located in the 'Special Collections' section of the Manchester Corporation Central Library / Frank Collins. [Manchester], 1954.
GB.1332(8). c071.

Catalogue of books in the Scottish Mountaineering Club Library. Edinburgh, 1962.
GB.1306(20). 072.

Catalogue of equipment for mountaineers: exhibited at the Alpine Club, December, 1899. London, [1899]. Ill.
Lloyd.935. c073.

A **catalogue** of select books from the Ingleton Collection: a library of Antarctica & Australiana, bibliography & cartography, hydrology & nautica, New Zealand & Pacific, voyages and travels / [compiled and annotated by Geoffrey C. Ingleton]. Sydney, [1977]. Ill.
GB/A.1694. c074.

Catalogue of the Alpine library formerly belonging to Mr. F. E. Blackstone, of the British Museum. Birmingham, [n.d.].
GB.1327(4). c075.

A **catalogue** of the books belonging to the Sheffield Library, Surrey-Street. Sheffield, 1846.
GB.338. c076.

Catalogue of the Centenary Exhibition, 1857-1957: in the [Alpine] Club Gallery, London, from November 5th to December 10th, 1957. [London, 1957.]
GB.1313(18). c077.

Catalogue of the exhibition of photographs from the Mount Everest Expedition, 1921 / arranged by the Mount Everest Committee of the Royal Geographical Society and the Alpine Club, January 1922. London, [1921]. Ill.
Lloyd.1606(11). c078.

Catalogue of the Himalayan literature / Yoshimi Yakushi. Kyoto, 1972.
GB/A.1227. c079.

Catalogue of the Himalayan literature / Yoshimi Yakushi. Tokyo, 1984.
GB/B.620. c080.

Catalogue of the library of the Arctic Institute of North America, Calgary. Third supplement. Boston, 1980. 3v.
GB/C.93-95. c080.1.

Catalogue of the splendid collection of antient armour / Gothic Hall, Pall Mall. London, 1818.
Lloyd.1578(1). c081.

Catalogue sommaire des peintures, sculptures, dessins, gravures en médailles et sur pierres fines et objets d'art divers de l'école contemporaine exposés dans les galeries du Musée National du Luxembourg / Léonce Bénédite. Paris, [1900]. Ill.
Lloyd.1613(13). c082.

[**Catalogues** of Alpine photographs by W.F. Donkin and cuttings from *The Times* and *Morning Post* of March 18, 1889 containing reviews of an exhibition of his photographs.] [London, 1889.]
GB.1881(3-5). c083.

Catastrophe du 23 août 1866: un sauvetage au Mont-Blanc: narration par un des acteurs / Charles Depraz. Annecy, 1866.
Lloyd.1574(1). c084.

Catena centrale delle Pale di S. Martino: arrampicate ed escursioni / Gabriele Franceschini. Cortina d'Ampezzo, 1978. Ill., map.
GB/A.2046. c085.

La **catena** del Monte Bianco / Henry Bregeault [et al.]; traduzione di Pinin Lampugnani. Roma, 1931.
GB/B.495. c086.

La **catena** della Levanna — Alpi Graie centrali / W.A.B. Coolidge. Torino, 1901. Ill. Estratto dal *Bollettino del C.A.I.* pel 1901, vol.34 n.67.
GB.1340(8). c087.

La **catena** settentrionale del Gran San Pietro: a proposito della guida *The Mountains of Cogne* di G. Yeld e W.A.B. Coolidge / Giovanni Bobba. [Turin], 1894. Ill. Published by the Club Alpino Italiano, Sezione di Torino.
GB/B.289(25). c088.

Catinaccio: alpinismo per tutti: rifugi, sentieri, vie attrezzate / Mauro Pedrotti, Gildo Venturelli. Trento, 1981. Ill., maps. [Dolomiti di Fassa.]
GB/A.2023(8). c089.

Catinaccio dal passo dell'Alpe di Tires al passo di Castalunga / Dante Colli, Gino Battisti. Bologna, 1984. Ill., maps. [Itinerari alpini; 58.]
GB/A.2165(7). c090.

Catinaccio, Sciliar, Sassolungo: le Dolomiti occidentali, guida geografico-turistica / Carlo Artoni. Calliano, 1973. Ill.
GB/B.378. c091.

The **cause** of an ice age / Sir Robert Ball. London, 1891. [Modern science; 1.]
Lloyd.578. c092.

Cave men new and old / Norbert Casteret; translated by R.L.G. Irving. London, 1951. Ill., ports. Translated from *Exploration*.
GB.751. c093.

Cayre des Erps (m.2501 — Alpi Marittimi) / Bruno e Francesco Salesi. Sanremo, [1970].
GB/A.1295(10). c094.

Ce monde qui n'est pas le nôtre / Robert Tézenas du Montcel. [Paris], 1965.
GB/A.138. c095.

Celui qui va devant / Max Liotier. [Grenoble], 1968. [Sempervivum; 45.]
GB/A.181(15). c096.

Cenni sulla flora ticinese con tavole per riconoscere arbusti e alberi / Mario Jaeggli. 3a ed. Bellinzono, 1953. Ill.
GB/A.836(7). c097.

Centenary celebrations / Alpine Club. London, 1957. A circular.
GB.1319(1). c098.

The **cento**: a selection of interesting approved passages from living authors. London, 1823.
Lloyd.804. c099.

Cento anni di alpinismo dolomitico italiano / Piero Rossi. Bologna, 1936. Ill. Estratto dalla *Rivista Mensile del Club Alpino Italiano*, 1936, n.3/4.
GB/C.22(16). c100.

Cento nuovi mattini: scalate brevi e libere in Piemonte, Val d'Aosta, Lombardia, Liguria, Emilia, Toscana, Lazio, Sardegna / Alessandro Gogna. Bologna, 1981. Ill., maps.
GB/B.541. c101.

Centomila gavette di ghiaccio / Giulio Bedeschi. Milano, 1966. Ill.
GB/A.490. c102.

The **Central** Alps, including the Bernese Oberland / John Ball. New ed. London, 1870. Ill., maps. [The Alpine Guide; 2.]
Lloyd.277; Lloyd.317A. c103.

The **Central** Alps, including the Bernese Oberland / John Ball. New ed. London, 1876. Ill., maps. [The Alpine Guide; 2.]
GB/A.830.   c103.1.

The **Central** Alps, including the Bernese Oberland / John Ball. New ed. London, 1882. Ill., maps. [The Alpine Guide; 2.]
Lloyd.317.   c103.2.

The **Central** Alps, pt.1 / John Ball. New ed., reconstructed and revised on behalf of the Alpine Club under the general editorship of A.V. Valentine-Richards. London, 1907. Ill., maps.
GB.289; Lloyd.382; Lloyd.382A.   c103.3.

The **Central** Alps, pt.2 / John Ball. New ed., reconstructed and revised on behalf of the Alpine Club under the general editorship of George Broke. London, 1907. Ill., maps.
Lloyd.383.   c103.4.

The **Central** Alps of the Dauphiny / W.A.B. Coolidge, H. Duhamel and F. Perrin. London, 1892. [Conway and Coolidge's climbers' guides; 4.]
GB.1324(4); Lloyd.20.   c104.

The **Central** Alps of the Dauphiny / W.A.B. Coolidge, H. Duhamel and F. Perrin. 2nd ed., rev. London, 1905. [Conway and Coolidge's climbers' guides; 4.]
Lloyd.169.   c105.

Centres d'escalades de Sormiou, Sugiton. Marseille, 1967. Ill., map. Published by the Club alpin français, Section de Provence.
GB/A.1350(14).   c106.

Centres d'escalades des Goudes, St. Michel. Marseille, [ca 1969]. Ill., map. Published by the Club alpin français, Section de Provence.
GB/A.1350(13).   c107.

I **centri** abitati più elevati dell'Appennino con particolare riguardo a quelli dell'Abruzzo / Eugenia Bevilacqua. Roma, 1952. Ill., maps. [Memorie di geografia antropica; vol.7 fasc.3.]
GB/B.312(3).   c108.

A **century** of mountaineering, 1857-1957 / Arnold Lunn. London, 1957. Ill. Published by the Swiss Foundation for Alpine Research.
GB.1136.   c109.

A **century** of Swiss alpine postal coaches / [collaborators: Bloesch et al.; Debeer (trans.);

editors: General Post Office (Motor Car Service), Berne]. Geneva, [1932]. Ill.
GB/B.288(16); Lloyd.1622(3).   c110.

Il **Ceresio**: disegni a sanguigna / Franco Belluschi; testo di Giuseppe Ghielmetti. Bellinzona, 1969. Ill. [Acque e terre; 2.]
GB/C.5(6).   c111.

[**Certificate** of T. Graham Brown's election as Fellow of the Royal Society.] London, 1927.
GB.1333(18).   c112.

[The **certificate** which T.W. Hinchliff forced the guide-chef to give to him after the ascent made by him and Walters with only two guides each, in defiance of the Chamonix regulations.] Chamonix, 1857.
GB.1322(3).   c113.

Le **Cervin**. [N.p., 1969?]
GB/B.570(7).   c114.

Le **Cervin** / Charles Gos. Neuchâtel, [1948]. 2v; ill., ports. [Montagne.]
GB.1314(1-2); GB.1314(3) (wanting v.1).   c115.

Le **Cervin** et les hommes / Walter Schmid; traduit par Berthe Medici et Georges Boghossian. 2e éd. Lausanne, [1965]. Ill. Translated from *Menschen am Matterhorn*.
GB/A.525.   c116.

Cervino: cima exemplare / Gaston Rébuffat; traduzione di Rosalba Donvito. Bologna, 1966. Ill. Translated from *Cervin: cime exemplaire*.
GB/A.999.   c117.

Cervino 18/1965: Matterhorn — Mont Cervin / fotografie e testi di Mario Fantin. Bologna, 1965. Ill.
GB/B.308.   c118.

Il **Cervino** e la sua storia / Marziano Bernardi; a cura di Vittorio Zumaglino. Torino, [1944]. Ill.
GB/B.283.   c119.

Il **Cervino** e la sua storia / Teodoro Wundt; dal tedesco, a cura di Antonio Lazzarino. 2a ed. Milano, [1924]. Ill., map.
GB/A.1323(5).   c120.

Il **Cervino** e la sua tavolozza / Ernesto Caballo. Alpignano, 1963. 2v.
GB/C.40-1.   c121.

Il **Cervino** nella storia fino al 1800 / W.A.B. Coolidge. [Turin, 1912.] Pp.6-9 of the *Rivista del*

Club Alpino Italiano, vol.31.
GB.1880(51[1]).   c122.

Il **Cervino** nella storia fino al 1800 / W.A.B.
Coolidge. Torino, 1912. Estratto dalla *Rivista del
Club Alpino Italiano*, vol.31 n.1, anno 1912.
GB.1340(26).   c123.

Ces montagnes qui flottent sur la mer / Charles-
Pierre Péguy, avec la collaboration d'Annik
Moign. [Paris], 1969. [Sempervivum; 47.]
GB/A.434(1).   c124.

Cetology: a systematized exhibition of the whale
in his broad genera: natural history excerpts from
Moby Dick / edited and illustrated by Ronald
Keller. New York, 1973. Ill.
GB/A.2137.   c125.

The **chain** of Mont Blanc / Louis Kurz. London,
1892. [Conway and Coolidge's climbers' guides; 5.]
GB.1324(6); Lloyd.21.   c126.

La **chaîne** de l'Aiguille Verte / Henry de Ségogne
[et al.]. Paris, 1926. Ill., maps. [Guide Vallot.
Description de la haute montagne dans le massif
du Mont Blanc; 2.]
GB.87; GB.88; Lloyd.164.   c127.

La **chaîne** du Mont-Blanc / Henry Bregeault,
Edouard de Gigord [et al.]. Paris, 1928. Ill., map.
Lloyd.1526; Lloyd.1526A.   c128.

La **chaîne** du Mont Blanc à travers les siècles /
W.A.B. Coolidge. [Berne, 1902.] Ill. Extrait de
l'*Annuaire du Club alpin suisse*, année 37.
GB.1329(47).   c137.

La **chaîne** du Mont Blanc avant 1800: notes
supplémentaires / W.A.B. Coolidge. Lyon, 1911.
Extrait de la *Revue alpine* de juillet 1911.
GB.1335(30); GB.1335(31).   c138.

Le **chaînon** de la Madre di Dio: premières
ascensions / Victor de Cessole. Nice, 1904. Extrait
du 24e *Bulletin de la Section des Alpes-Maritimes du
Club alpin français*.
Lloyd.1594(4).   c139.

Lo **chalet** di Cenise / Achille Calosso. Torino,
[1972]. Ill. [Biblioteca della montagna; 1.]
GB/A.1281(1).   c140.

Chambers's Journal of Popular Literature, Science
and Arts. Ser.3. Extracts, no.117-365. London,
1856[-60].
GB.1337(1).   c141.

Chambers's miscellany of useful and entertaining
tracts. Edinburgh, [1844-47]. 12v (in 1).
GB.199(1).   c142.

Chambers's repository of instructive and
amusing tracts. Vol.9. Edinburgh, [1854].
Lloyd.391.   c143.

Chamois hunting in the mountains of Bavaria /
Charles Boner. London, 1853. Ill.
GB/A.1388; Lloyd.1126.   c144.

Chamois hunting in the mountains of Bavaria /
Charles Boner. New ed. London, 1860. Ill.
Lloyd.580; Lloyd.580A.   c145.

Chamonix: album de 43 vues. Zurich, [1910?]. Ill.
[Souvenir-albums édition illustrato.]
GB/A.1675(12).   c146.

Chamonix and the range of Mont Blanc: a guide /
Edward Whymper. London, 1896. Ill., maps.
GB.1321(51); Lloyd.457; Lloyd.457A,B,C,D,E.
                                                   c147.

Chamonix and the range of Mont Blanc: a guide /
Edward Whymper. 2nd ed. London, 1897. Ill., maps.
Lloyd.458.   c148.

Chamonix and the range of Mont Blanc: a guide /
Edward Whymper. 3rd ed. London, 1898. Ill., maps.
Lloyd.459.   c149.

Chamonix and the range of Mont Blanc: a guide /
Edward Whymper. 4th ed. London, 1899. Ill., maps.
Lloyd.460.   c150.

Chamonix and the range of Mont Blanc: a guide /
Edward Whymper. 5th ed. London, 1900. Ill., maps.
Lloyd.461.   c151.

Chamonix and the range of Mont Blanc: a guide /
Edward Whymper. 6th ed. London, 1901. Ill., maps.
Lloyd.462.   c152.

Chamonix and the range of Mont Blanc: a guide /
Edward Whymper. 7th ed. London, 1902. Ill., maps.
Lloyd.463.   c153.

Chamonix and the range of Mont Blanc: a guide /
Edward Whymper. 8th ed. London, 1903. Ill., maps.
Lloyd.464.   c154.

Chamonix and the range of Mont Blanc: a guide /
Edward Whymper. 9th ed. London, 1904. Ill., maps.
Lloyd.465.   c155.

Chamonix and the range of Mont Blanc: a guide / Edward Whymper. 10th ed. London, 1905. Ill., maps. Lloyd.466. c156.

Chamonix and the range of Mont Blanc: a guide / Edward Whymper. 11th ed. London, 1906. Ill., maps. Lloyd.467. c157.

Chamonix and the range of Mont Blanc: a guide / Edward Whymper. 12th ed. London, 1907. Ill., maps. Lloyd.468. c158.

Chamonix and the range of Mont Blanc / Edward Whymper. 13th ed. London, 1908. Lloyd.469. c159.

Chamonix and the range of Mont Blanc / Edward Whymper. 14th ed. London, 1909. Lloyd.470. c160.

Chamonix and the range of Mont Blanc: a guide / Edward Whymper. 15th ed. London, 1910. Ill., maps. GB.342; Lloyd.471. c161.

Chamonix and the range of Mont Blanc: a guide / Edward Whymper. 16th ed. London, 1911. Ill., maps. GB.1321(50); Lloyd.472. c162.

Chamonix and the range of Mont Blanc: a guide / Edward Whymper. Goring, 1974. Ill., maps. [Gaston's Alpine books.] Facsimile reprint of the London, 1896 ed. GB/A.1597(5). c163.

Chamonix et le Mont Blanc / Paul Payot. Grenoble, 1949. Ill., map. Lloyd.1615(18). c164.

Chamonix, le Mont-Blanc, les deux Saint-Bernard, et la vallée de Sixt: nouvel itinéraire descriptif des Alpes centrales et de leurs vallées / J.L. Manget. 4e éd., rev. et augm. Genève, 1852. Ill., maps. GB.1323(12). c165.

Chamonix, Mont-Blanc. Chamonix, 1905. Ill., maps, ports. GB/A.1965(1). c166.

Chamonix, Mont Blanc / Charles Vallot. Paris, 1927. Ill., maps. [Guide Vallot. Description de la moyenne montagne dans le massif du Mont-Blanc; 1.] Lloyd.130. c167.

Chamonix, Mont-Blanc, 1900 / Gaston Rébuffat. [Geneva?], 1981. Ill., ports., facsims. GB/B.570(1). c168.

Chamonix — Mont-Blanc — Saint-Gervais-les-Bains / Charles Vallot. Grenoble, 1950. Ill., maps. [Guide Vallot. Tourisme en montagne dans le massif du Mont-Blanc.] GB/A.1563. c169.

Chamouni and Mont Blanc: a visit to the valley and an ascent of the mountain in the autumn of 1855 / Eustace Anderson. London, 1856. Ill. GB.150; Lloyd.212; Lloyd.212A. c170.

Chamounix, le Mont-Blanc et les deux St-Bernard: nouvel itinéraire descriptif des Alpes centrales et de leurs vallées, conduisant aux eaux thermales de St-Gervais / J.L. Manget. Genève, 1839. Map. GB.1335(34). c171.

Champéry et le Val d'Illiez: histoire et description / Arthur de Claparède. Genève, 1886. GB/A.522. c172.

The **champion** lady mountaineer (Mrs E. Main) / Marcus Tindal. [London, ca 1900.] Ill., ports. Pp.[354]-64 of *Pearson's Magazine*, vol.7. GB.1336(5). c173.

Change of air, or The pursuit of health: an autumnal excursion through France, Switzerland & Italy, in the year 1829 / James Johnson. London, 1831. GB.725. c174.

Change of air, or The pursuit of health: an autumnal excursion through France, Switzerland & Italy, in the year 1829 / James Johnson. 3rd ed. London, 1832. Lloyd.873. c175.

A **chapter** in the life history of an old University: being the introductory lecture of the session 1881-2, delivered to the students of University College, London, on October 4th, 1881 / T.G. Bonney. Cambridge, 1882. Lloyd.1603(6). c176.

Charles the Great's passage of the Alps in 773 / W.A.B. Coolidge. [London, 1906.] Reprinted from the *English Historical Review*, July 1906, pp.[493]-505. GB.1340(46). c177.

Charmoz and Grepon / George H. Morse. London, 1927. Ill. Reprinted from the *Alpine*

Journal, Nov. 1927.
GB.1306(10). c178.

Les **chars** préhistoriques du Val Camonica / Martine van Berg-Osterrieth. Capo di Ponte, 1972. Ill. [Archivi; 3.] Published by the Centro Camuno di Studi Preistorici.
GB/B.391. c179.

Charter and regulations of the Royal Geographical Society. London, 1872.
Lloyd.1602(19). c180.

La **chasse** au chamois / comte Hector Tredicini de Saint-Severin. Paris, 1897. Ill.
Lloyd.1616(23). c181.

Les **chefs** de file de l'alpinisme anglais / L. Spiro. [Geneva], 1916. Pp.[143]-78 of *Echo des Alpes*, no.1, 1916.
GB.1309(2). c182.

Le **chemin** de Clarabide / Jean Château. Paris, 1970. [Sempervivum; 48.]
GB/A.804(7). c183.

Chemin de fer des Houches au sommet du Mont Blanc: projet Saturnin Fabre: études préliminaires et avant-projet / Joseph et Henri Vallot. Paris, 1899. Maps.
GB/C.5(9). c184.

Le **chemineau** de la montagne / Jacques Dieterlen. Paris, 1951. Ill. [La vie en montagne.]
GB/A.1213; GB/A.2033(3). c185.

Chez les Esquimaux: notes de voyage, visite pastorale, ordination, etc. / O. Charlebois. [Ottawa? 1925?] Ill., map.
GB/A.1676(15). c186.

Chiacchiere di un alpinista / Camillo Giussani. Nuova ed. riv. e ampliata. Milano, 1951. Ill.
GB/A.1151. c187.

Le **chiesette** alpine / Giuseppe Bonomini; a cura di L. Zampedri e A. Fappani. Brescia, 1964. Ill. [Brescia.] Published by the Club Alpino Italiano, Sezione Valtrompia (Brescia).
GB/A.516(6). c188.

The **Child**'s Companion and Juvenile Instructor. New series. 1849-1850. London, 1849-50.
GB.31. c189.

Childe Harold's pilgrimage: a romaunt / Lord Byron. London, 1812.
GB.1246. c190.

Childe Harold's pilgrimage: canto the third / Lord Byron. London, 1816.
GB.641. c191.

Childe Harold's pilgrimage: canto the fourth / Lord Byron. London, 1818.
GB.642. c192.

Children of the Arctic / by the snow baby [Marie Ahnighito Peary] and her mother [Josephine Diebitsch Peary]. London, 1903.
GB.1224. c193.

Chillon / Albert Naef. Tom. 1: La Camera Domini, la chambre des comtes et des ducs de Savoie à Chillon. Genève, 1908. Ill.
Lloyd.1623(1). c194.

Chimney-corner stories / William Martin. London, [1861]. Ill.
GB.173. c195.

China to Chitral / H.W. Tilman. Cambridge, 1951. Ill.
GB.1077; Lloyd.1214. c196.

La **chiusa** della Valsassina: guida all'arrampicata sul calcare bianco dello Zucco dell'Angelane e della Rocca di Baiedo / Andrea Savonitto. [Lecco], 1981. Ill., ports.
GB/A.2021(4). c197.

Les **Chouruns** du Dévoluy — Hautes-Alpes / E.A. Martel. [N.p., ca 1901.] Ill., maps.
GB.1335(38). c198.

Christian Almer, 1826-1898 / W.A.B. Coolidge. [N.p., 1899.] Port. Separatabdruck aus dem *Jahrbuch des Schweizer Alpenclub*, Jahrg.34.
GB.1329(18); Lloyd.1592(2); Lloyd.1624(1). c199.

The **Christian** wreath, or Prose, poetry and art. London, [ca 1852]. Ill.
GB.115. c200.

Chronique alpine: courses diverses: Mont Blanc, par le glacier de la Brenva / Jacques Lagarde. Lyon, 1926. Pp.145-7 of the *Revue alpine*, vol.27 no.3.
GB.1881(38[2]). c201.

Chroniques du mont Saint-Bernard / M. Le Gallais. Nouv. éd. Tours, 1861. Ill. [Bibliothèque des écoles chrétiennes.]
GB/A.1497.   c202.

Chronology of events during Operation Deep Freeze (September 1954-March 1958) / prepared by Public Information Office, U.S. Naval Support Force, Antarctica. [Washington, 1958.]
GB/B.520(4).   c203.

Chute de neige précoce dans les Alpes / M.A. de Lavis-Trafford. Saint-Jean-de-Maurienne, [1958]. Ill. Extrait de *L'identification topographique du col alpin franchi par Hannibal, Travaux de la Société d'histoire et d'archéologie de Maurienne, Savoie,* tome 13, 1956.
GB/A.860(5).   c204.

Cima dell'uomo, Costabella, Monzoni, Vallaccia: itinerari e vie di salita in val di Fassa / Bruno Federspiel. Bologna, 1979. Ill., map. [Itinerari alpini; 42.]
GB/A.1589(18).   c205.

La **cima** di Entrelor / Renato Chabod. Bologna, 1969. Ill. [Montagne; 6.]
GB/A.476.   c206.

Le **cime** dell'Auta: sottogruppo della Marmolada / Bepi Pellegrinon; aggiornamento della parte alpinistica della guida *Odle, Sella, Marmolada,* di Ettore Castiglioni. 2a ed. Bologna, 1967. Ill. Estratto dal n.1, 1962 di *Le Alpi Venete.*
GB/B.338(3).   c207.

Le **cime** di Lavaredo nel centenario della prima ascensione 1869-1969 / Antonio Sanmarchi. Bologna, 1969. Ill., maps. Published by the Club Alpino Italiano, Sezione Cadorina.
GB/B.366(1).   c208.

La **cime** du Mont-Blanc / Horace Bénédict de Saussure; pages extraites et annotées à l'usage des écoles du *Quatrième voyage dans les Alpes,* par R.L.G. Irving et R.L.A. du Pontet. London, 1933. Ill., map. [Modern French authors.]
GB/1326(19).   c209.

Cimes d'Oisans: récits de courses en Dauphiné / Jacques Boell. [Paris, 1946.] Ill. [La vie en montagne.]
GB/A.162.   c210.

Cimes et merveilles / Samivel. [Paris], 1952. Ill. [Belles pages — belles couleurs.]
GB/B.439(2).   c211.

Cimes et neige: 102 sommets à ski / Philippe et Claude Traynard. [Paris], 1971. Ill., maps.
GB/A.1001.   c212.

Il **Cimon** della Pala nel centenario della prima ascensione 1870-1970 / a cura di Giuliano Conci, Giovanni Meneguz, Enrico Taufer. [N.p.], 1970.
GB/A.518.   c213.

Cinematografia alpina a colori e suoni / Ugo De Amicis. Milano, 1935.
GB/A.1084.   c214.

Les **cinq** cols de la Dent Blanche / W.A.B. Coolidge. [N.p., 1923.] Pp.[33]-48 of *Annales valaisannes,* 4, 1923.
GB.1340(53).   c215.

Cinquant'anni di vita della Sezione di Milano [Club Alpino Italiano], 1873-1923 / Francesco Mauro [et al.]. Milano, 1923. Ill., map, ports.
GB/B.337(3).   c216.

Cinquant'anni di vita della Società Escursionisti Milanesi, 1891-1941 / a cura di Eugenio Fasana. Milano, [1941]. Ill.
GB/A.1226.   c217.

Cinquanta escursioni in Val del Piave di Peralba a Quero / Italo Zandonella; collaborazione tecnica, fotografica e prefazione di Silvino Tremonti. Bologna, 1977. Ill., maps. [Itinerari alpini; 37.]
GB/A.1589(5).   c218.

Cinquante ans en montagne / Roger Frison-Roche, Pierre Tairraz. [Paris, 1974.] Ill.
GB/A.2141.   c219.

Circular / Royal Air Force Mountaineering Association. Dec. 1950-Mar. 1962. [London, 1950-62.] Incomplete.
GB.1331(1-25).   c220.

Civetta / Oscar Kelemina. Mestre, 1970. Ill., maps. [Dolomiti orientali.]
GB/A.507.   c221.

Civetta- , Monflaconi- und Schiara-Gruppe / Toni Hiebeler. 2.Aufl. München, 1964. Ill., maps. [Dolomiten-Kletterführer; 2.]
GB/A.1061.   c222.

Civetta-Moiazza / Vincenzo Dal Bianco, Giovanni Angelini. Bologna, 1970. Ill, map. [Itinerari alpini; 4.]
GB/A.867(8).   c223.

A **classical** tour through Italy an. 1802 / John Chetwode Eustace. 4th ed. Leghorn, 1818. 4v.
Lloyd.446-9.   c224.

The **classification** of the Tertiary period by means of the mammalia / W. Boyd Dawkins. [N.p., 1880.] From the *Quarterly Journal of the Geological Society* for August 1880.
Lloyd.1611(3).   c225.

Classics in the literature of mountaineering and mountain travel from the Francis P. Farquhar Collection of mountaineering literature: an annotated bibliography / James R. Cox; annotations and introductory essay by Nicholas B. Clinch, James R. Cox, and Muir Dawson. Los Angeles, 1980.
GB/B.537.   c226.

Claudine, or Humility, the basis of all the virtues: a Swiss tale / by the author of *Always happy* [M.E.B.]. London, 1822. Ill.
Lloyd.152.   c227.

Claudine, or Humility, the basis of all the virtues: a Swiss tale / by the author of *Always happy* [M.E.B.]. 2nd ed. London, 1823. Wanting the dedication.
Lloyd.153 (impf.).   c228.

The **climatic** position of Interlaken in the Bernese Oberland: its sanitary advantages and enjoyments / L. Delachaux. Interlaken, 1881. Map.
Lloyd.1602(14).   c229.

A **climb** up the Jungfrau. [London, 1854.] Pp.123-8 of *Leisure Hour*, 1854.
GB.1329(41).   c230.

The **climb** up to Hell / Jack Olsen. London, 1962. Ill., ports.
GB.669.   c231.

A **climber**'s guide to the interior ranges of British Columbia / J. Monroe Thorington. 3rd ed. New York, 1955. Map.
GB/A.2130.   c232.

A **climber**'s guide to the interior ranges of British Columbia north / William Lowell Putnam. 6th ed. [N.p.],1975. Ill., maps. Published by the American Alpine Club and the Alpine Club of Canada.
GB/A.1883(3).   c233.

A **climber**'s guide to the interior ranges of British Columbia south / Robert Kruszyna, William L. Putnam. 6th ed. [New York], 1977. Ill.
GB/A.1883(4).   c234.

Climber's guide to Yosemite Valley / Steve Roper. San Francisco, [1971]. Ill. [A Sierra Club totebook.]
GB/A.2017(9).   c235.

The **climber**'s note-book / [C.W.]. London, 1906.
GB/A.1351(5).   c236.

Climbers' and hikers' guide to the world's mountains / Michael R. Kelsey. 2nd ed. Springville, 1984.
GB/A.2192.   c237.

The **Climbers'** Club Bulletin. No.26, May 1931. [London], 1931.
GB.1329(5).   c238.

The **Climbers'** Club Journal. Vol.1-13; N.S. vol.1-12. London, 1879-1957. The N.S. is incomplete in all vols.
Lloyd.1322-34,1336-47; Lloyd.1322A-1337A (other copies of odd issues); GB.1329(37), GB.1647(25) (other copies of N.S. no.1).   c239.

The **Climbers'** Club Journal. Index. Vol.9, vol.10 pt.1, vol.11-13 pt.2. London, 1908-10.
Lloyd.1135; Lloyd.1135A.   c239.1.

Climbers' Club publications, 1898-1942. [London, 1942.] Pp.75-7 of the *Climbers' Club Journal*, N.S. vol.7 no.1.
GB.1338(12).   c240.

Climbers' guide to Ben Nevis / G. Graham MacPhee. Edinburgh, 1954. Ill. Published by the Scottish Mountaineering Club.
GB.83.   c241.

Climbers' guide to the central Pennine Alps / W. Martin Conway. London, 1890. [Conway and Coolidge's climbers' guides; 1.]
GB.1324(5); Lloyd.17.   c242.

Climbers' guide to the eastern Pennine Alps / W. Martin Conway. London, 1891. [Conway and Coolidge's climbers' guides; 2.]
GB.1324(7); Lloyd.18.   c243.

Climbing and exploration in the Karakoram-Himalayas / Sir Martin Conway. London, 1894. Ill., map.
GB.1148.   c244.

Climbing and exploration in the Karakoram-Himalayas / Sir Martin Conway. London, 1894. 3v; ill., maps, port.
Lloyd.1319-21.   c245.

Climbing and exploration in the Karakoram-Himalayas / Martin Conway. Scientific reports / T.G. Bonney, A.G. Butler [et al.]. London, 1894. 2v; maps.
GB.1149 (wanting pt.1); Lloyd.1312-3; Lloyd. 1316-8.   c246.

Climbing at Wasdale before the First World War / George S. Sansom. Castle Cary, 1982. Ill., map, ports.
GB/B.596.   c247.

Climbing boots and equipment / Robert Lawrie, Ltd. Burnley, 1934. A catalogue.
GB.1326(2).   c248.

Climbing days / Dorothy Pilley. London, 1935. Ill., ports.
GB.920.   c249.

A **climbing** guide to Dartmoor / J.W. Denton. Torquay, [1950?]. Published by the Climbers' Club.
GB/B.501(16).   c250.

Climbing guide to Gibraltar / A.D. Marsden. Yeovil, [1965?]. Maps. Published by the Joint Services Mountaineering Association.
GB/B.635(5).   c251.

Climbing high / Charles S. Houston. [Boston, 1937.] Ill., ports. Pp.301-9 of *Appalachia*, June 1937.
GB.1339(36).   c252.

Climbing high / Charles S. Houston. [Boston, 1937.] Ill., ports. An offprint from *Appalachia*, N.S. vol.4 no.7, June 1937.
GB.1338(25).   c253.

Climbing in Britain / edited by J.E.Q. Barford. Harmondsworth, 1946. Ill. [Pelican books; A160.]
GB.1326(40); Lloyd.1613(1).   c254.

Climbing in the British Isles / W.P. Haskett Smith. London, 1894. 2v; ill.
Lloyd.80-81; GB.52, Lloyd.81A (other copies of v.2).   c255.

Climbing in the Ogwen district / James Merriman Archer Thomson. London, 1910. Ill. Lloyd.131.   c255.1.

Climbing Mont Blanc in a blizzard / Garrett P. Serviss. [New York, 1896.] Ill. Pp.274-83 of *Pearson's Magazine*, Sept. 1896.
GB.1329(32).   c256.

Climbing Mount Sorata / W. Martin Conway. [New York, 1899.] Ill. Pp.[863]-76 of *Harper's New Monthly Magazine*, 1899.
GB.1880(38).   c257.

The **climbing** of high mountains / W. Martin Conway. [London, 1893.] Pp.345-57 of *Fortnightly*, Sept. 1893.
GB.1336(18); GB/A.797(11).   c258.

Climbing on the Himalaya and other mountain ranges / J. Norman Collie. Edinburgh, 1902. Ill., maps.
GB.908; GB.919; Lloyd.959; Lloyd.959A.   c259.

Climbing our northwest glaciers / Bob and Ira Spring. Washington, 1953. Ill., ports. Pp.103-14 of the *National Geographic Magazine*, vol.104 no.1, July 1953.
GB.1333(15).   c260.

Climbing reminiscences of the Dolomites / Leone Sinigaglia; translated by Mary Alice Vialls. London, 1896. Ill., map, port.
Lloyd.1243; Lloyd.1243A,B,C.   c261.

Climbing the Lakeland mountains with J.E.B. Wright, the Keswick guide: programme of climbs for 1926 season. [Keswick? 1926.]
GB.1329(39).   c262.

Climbing the Scotch Alps / Arthur Campbell Gordon. [London, 1901.] Ill. Pp.53-8 of the *Temple Magazine*, 1901.
GB.1881(31).   c263.

Climbs / W. Henry Lewin. [London, 1932.] Ill., port.
GB.828.   c264.

Climbs & exploration in the Canadian Rockies / Hugh E.M. Stutfield, J. Norman Collie. London, 1903. Ill., maps.
GB.959; Lloyd.1026.   c265.

Climbs and ski-runs: mountaineering and ski-ing in the Alps, Great Britain and Corsica / Frank S.

Smythe. London, 1957. Ill., ports.
GB.752; GB.793 (impf.); GB.829; GB.830.   c266.

Climbs and ski runs, by F.S. Smythe: a review / C.E. Benson. Leeds, 1930. P.80 of the *Yorkshire Ramblers' Club Journal*, vol.6 no.19.
GB.1881(27); GB.1881(28).   c267.

Climbs from Courmayeur / Claude Wilson. [N.p.], 1911. Reprinted from the *Alpine Journal*, May 1911.
GB.1335(24).   c268.

Climbs from the Fründen hut / W.D. Macpherson. [London], 1939. Ill. Reprinted from the *Alpine Journal*, May 1939.
GB.1339(25).   c269.

Climbs in the Alps, made in 1865 to 1900 / W.A.B. Coolidge. London, [n.d.].
GB.1335(27); Lloyd.455.   c270.

Climbs in the Alps, made in 1865 to 1900 / W.A.B. Coolidge. 2nd impression. London, [n.d.].
GB.1326(53).   c271.

Climbs in the Horungtinder, Norway / Asbjørn Gunneng, Boye Schlytter. Oslo, 1933. Ill. Published by the Norsk Tindeklub.
GB/A.1597(4).   c272.

Climbs in the New Zealand Alps: being an account of travel and discovery / E.A. Fitzgerald, with contributions by Sir Martin Conway, T.G. Bonney, C.L. Barrow. London, 1896. Ill., map.
Lloyd.1263; Lloyd.1264; Lloyd.1264A.   c273.

Climbs in the New Zealand Alps: being an account of travel and discovery / E.A. Fitzgerald, with contributions by Sir Martin Conway, T.G. Bonney, C.L. Barrow. 2nd ed. London, 1896. Ill., map.
GB.1164.   c274.

The climbs of Norman-Neruda / Louis Norman-Neruda; edited, and with an account of his last climb, by May Norman-Neruda. London, 1899. Ill., ports.
GB.928; Lloyd.1015.   c275.

Climbs on Alpine peaks / Pope Pius XI; translated by J.E.C. Eaton. London, 1923. Ill., map, ports.
GB.870.   c276.

Climbs on Alpine peaks / Pope Pius XI; translated by J.E.C. Eaton. 3rd impr. London, 1929.

[Benn's Essex Library.]
Lloyd.220.   c277.

Climbs on Great Gable / H.S. Gross, and Rock climbing in Borrowdale / A.R. Thomson. Barrow-in-Furness, [1925]. [Climbers' guides to the English Lake District; 4.] Published by the Fell and Rock Climbing Club of the English Lake District.
GB.1328(9).   c277.1.

The **climbs** on Lliwedd / J.M. Archer Thomson, A.W. Andrews. London, 1909-10. 2v; ill. Published by the Climbers' Club.
GB.64 (wanting v.2); Lloyd.135 (wanting v.2).
        c278.

Climbs on Mont Blanc / Jacques and Tom de Lépiney; translated by Sydney Spencer. London, 1930. Ill. Translated from: *Sur les crêtes du Mont-Blanc*.
GB.638.   c279.

Climbs on Mont Blanc / Jacques and Tom de Lépiney. [London, 1930.] A prospectus.
GB.1313(34).   c280.

Climbs on the Scawfell Group: a climbers' guide / C.F. Holland. Barrow-in-Furness, [1924]. [Climbers' guides to the English Lake District; 3.] Published by the Fell and Rock Climbing Club of the English Lake District.
GB.1328(8).   c280.1.

Clogwyn du'r Arddu / J.M. Edwards, J.E.Q. Barford. [London, 1942.] Ill. Pp.38-59 of the *Climbers' Club Journal*, N.S. vol.7 no.1.
GB.1339(14[1]).   c281.

Clogwyn du'r Arddu / J.M. Edwards, J.E.Q. Barford. Manchester, 1942 [1950]. Ill. Reprinted from the *Climbers' Club Journal*.
GB.1309(3).   c282.

Clogwyn du'r Arddu: west buttress climb / A.B. Hargreaves. [London, 1929.] Pp.47-9 of the *Climbers' Club Journal*, N.S. vol.4 no.1, 1929.
GB.1880(31).   c283.

Cloud walkers: six climbs on major Canadian peaks / Paddy Sherman. Toronto, 1965. Maps.
GB/A.1683.   c284.

Club alpin suisse: carte de membre / T. Graham Brown. Sion, 1937. Port.
GB.1327(7).   c285.

Club Alpino Italiano, 1925-1975: 50 anni di attività della Sezione di Conegliano. [Conegliano, 1975.] Ill., ports.
GB/B.403(23). c286.

Club Alpino Italiano, la Sezione di Busto Arsizio nel cinquantenario 1922-1972 / [a cura di Piero Pellegatta]. [Busto-Arsizio, 1972.] Ill., ports.
GB/B.403(22). c287.

Club Alpino Italiano, Sezione di Bassano del Grappa nel 75° della fondazione. [Bassano del Grappo, 1967.] Ill., ports. Bollettino n.4, 1967.
GB/B.403(21). c288.

Club Alpino Italiano, Sez. di Milano: 75° anniversario della fondazione, 1873-1948 / [redazione e testo del dott. Vincenzo Fusco]. Milano, [1948]. Ill.
GB/A.1580(8). c289.

Club Nachrichten / Sektion Bern, Schweizer Alpenclub. Jahrg.7 Nr.12-Jahrg.30 Nr.1, Dez.1929-Jan.1952. Bern, 1929-52. Incomplete.
Lloyd.1624(15-117). c289.1.

Clubführer durch die Glarner-Alpen / im Auftrag des Centralcomités des S.A.C. Ed. Naef-Blumer. [N.p.], 1902.
GB/A.1553. c290.

Clubführer durch die Glarner Alpen / im Auftrag des S.A.C. Ed. Naef-Blumer; Anhang: Skiführer durch die Glarneralpen, im Auftrage des S.A.C. redigiert von P. Tschudi und Mathias Jenni. 6. Aufl. neu überarbeitet von Mathias Jenni-Züblin. [N.p.], 1949. Ill.
GB/A.1561. c291.

Clubführer durch die Graubündner-Alpen / F.W. Sprecher, E. Naef-Blumer [et al.]. Zürich, 1916-18. 2v; ill., maps. Published by the Schweizer Alpenclub.
GB/A.1176-7. c292.

Clubführer durch die Tessiner-Alpen / L. Lisibach, G. End, J. Kutzner; herausgegeben vom Schweizer Alpen-Club. [Zurich, 1908.] 2v; ill.
GB/A.1554-5. c293.

Clubhütten / Schweizer Alpenclub. Lausanne, 1928. Ill., maps.
GB/A.926. c295.

Clubhütten — cabanes — capanne / Schweizer Alpenclub. Aarau, 1967. Ill., map.
GB/A.777. c296.

Clusone: guida illustrata. Clusone, 1930. Ill., maps.
GB/A.1368. c297.

The **coal** region of central Spitzbergen / Gerard de Geer. Stockholm, 1912. Map. Reprinted from *Ymer*, 1912, hft.3.
GB.1335(5). c298.

The **coast** of northeast Greenland with hydrographic studies in the Greenland Sea: the Louise A. Boyd Arctic Expeditions of 1937 and 1938 / Louise A. Boyd; with contributions by Richard Foster Flint [et al.]. New York, 1948. 2v; maps. [Special publication / American Geographical Society; 30.]
GB/A.2090. c299.

Un **coin** des Alpes, ou Une ascension nocturne: suivi de Souvenirs de l'Oberland bernois et de la Suisse centrale et de Un pêcheur vosgien sur une île flottante / F.A. Robischung. Tours, 1881.
GB/A.940. c300.

Coire and its environs / E. Killias. Zürich, [1895?]. Ill. [Swiss scenes.]
GB/A.1817(7). c301.

Le **col** alpin franchi par Hannibal: son identification topographique / M.A. de Lavis-Trafford. Saint-Jean-de-Maurienne, [1956]. Ill., map. Première impression dans le *Bulletin commémorant le centenaire de la Société d'histoire et d'archéologie de Maurienne*, tom.13, 1956.
GB/A.1046. c302.

Il **col** de Collon nella storia / W.A.B. Coolidge; versione italiana di W. Laeng. Torino, 1915. Estratto dalla *Rivista del Club Alpino Italiano*, vol.34 n.2, anno 1915.
GB.1340(44). c303.

Le **col** de Galest et le col de la Galise / W.A.B. Coolidge, H. Duhamel. Lyon, 1905. Extrait de la *Revue alpine*, nov. 1905.
GB.1340(14). c304.

The **Col** de la Brenva / Claude Wilson. London, 1912. Ill. Reprinted from the *Alpine Journal*, Aug. 1912.
GB.1315(3); GB.1315(4). c305.

The **Col** de la Brenva: the Aiguille de Leschaux / R. Ogier Ward. London, 1928. Ill. Reprinted from the *Alpine Journal*, May 1928.
GB.1312(20). c306.

Le **col** de la Leisse et les Quecées de Tignes / W.A.B. Coolidge, H. Duhamel. Lyon, 1905. GB.1340(13).   c307.

Il **col** de Seilon nella storia / W.A.B. Coolidge; versione italiana di W. Laeng. Torino, 1915. Estratto dalla *Rivista del Club Alpino Italiano*, vol.34 n.3, anno 1915. GB.1340(42).   c308.

Le **col** dit Infranchissable: the first crossing from France into Italy, 22 July, 1923 / R.W. Lloyd. [London], 1924. Ill. Reprinted from the *Alpine Journal*, May 1924. Lloyd.1611(6).   c309.

Le **col** Lombard et les passages avoisinants dans l'histoire / W.A.B. Coolidge. Lyon, 1913. Extrait de la *Revue alpine* de mars 1913. GB.1340(30).   c310.

Col Maudit and other climbs / T. Graham Brown. London, 1933. Ill. Reprinted from the *Alpine Journal*, Nov. 1933. GB.1305(22); Lloyd.1612(6).   c311.

Col *Norge* da Roma all'Alaska / Antonio G. Quattrini; con una nota illustrativa di U. Nobile. 2a ed. Firenze, [ca 1930]. GB/A.1847.   c312.

Cold: the record of an Antarctic sledge journey / Laurence McKinley Gould. [Northfield, Minn.], 1984. Ill., maps, ports. GB/B.646.   c313.

Il **colle** Clapier nella storia / W.A.B. Coolidge. Torino, 1911. Estratto dalla *Rivista del Club Alpino Italiano*, vol.30 n.6, anno 1911. GB.1340(24).   c314.

Il **colle** di San Teodulo nella storia / W.A.B. Coolidge. [Turin, 1911.] Pp.292-9 of the *Rivista del Club Alpino Italiano*, vol.30. GB.1880(51[2]).   c315.

Il **colle** di San Teodulo nella storia / W.A.B. Coolidge. Torino, 1911. Estratto dalla *Rivista del Club Alpino Italiano*, vol.30 n.10, anno 1911. GB.1340(25).   c316.

Il **colle** Gnifetti / Guido Rey. Torino, 1894. Ill. Pp.[1]-36 of the *Bollettino del Club Alpino Italiano*, vol.27 no.60. GB.1881(12).   c317.

Il **colle** Zurbriggen: 1a traversata/ G.F.G. [G.F. Gugliermina]. [Turin, 1899.] Pp.303-23 of the *Bollettino del Club Alpino Italiano*, vol.32 no.65. GB.1881(7).   c318.

Collection de dessins, aquarelles, gouaches, miniatures sur ivoire, enluminures sur parchemin, oeuvres d'art du XIIe au XIXe siècle: catalogue / C.A. Mincieux. Genève, [n.d.]. Ill. Lloyd.1605(10).   c319.

[A **collection** of ephemera relating to Captain R.F. Scott's expedition to the South Pole.] [N.p., 1904-67.] GB/C.119(1-35).   c320.

A **collection** of some of the finest prospects in Italy, with short remarks on them / Ridolfino Venuti. London, 1762. Ill. Lloyd.57.   c321.

A **collection** of Swiss costumes, in miniature, designed by Reinhardt. Collection de costumes suisses. London, 1822. Ill. GB/B.329.   c322.

College echoes / Saint Andrews University Students' Representative Council. N.S. vol.27 no.9. St. Andrews, 1932. GB.1318(11).   c323.

College essays delivered in Trinity College, Cambridge, February 22 and December 16, 1862 / William Everett. Cambridge, 1863. GB/B.635(9).   c324.

I **colli** di Fenêtre e di Crête Sèche nella storia / W.A.B. Coolidge. Torino, 1914. Estratto dalla *Rivista del Club Alpino Italiano*, vol.32 n.12, anno 1913. GB.1340(37).   c325.

Colli Euganei: guida alpinistico-turistica. Padova, 1963. Ill., maps. Published by the Club Alpino Italiano, Sezione di Padova. GB/A.1356.   c326.

Les **collines** niçoises, circuits automobiles et promenades à pied / Vincent Paschetta. 7e éd. Grenoble, 1971. Ill., maps. [Guide Paschetta des Alpes-Maritimes. 3: Nice, Riviera-Côte d'Azur; 2.] GB/A.1468(4).   c327.

La **colonia** tedesca di Alagna-Valsesia e il suo dialetto / opera postuma del dottor Giovanni Giordani. 2a ed. Bologna, [1973]. Facsimile reprint

of the Varallo Sesia, 1927 ed.
GB/A.1306.   c328.

Colour in the Canadian Rockies / Walter J. Phillips, Frederick Niven. Toronto, 1937. Ill.
Lloyd.1232.   c329.

Coloured vade-mecum to the Alpine flora / text in English, French and German by L. Schröter and C. Schröter. 18th and 19th ed. Zürich, [ca 1910]. Ill.
GB/A.1367.   c330.

Les **cols** de glaciers des Alpes dauphinoises dans l'histoire / W.A.B. Coolidge. Grenoble, 1912. Extrait de la *Revue des Alpes dauphinoises*, 1911-12.
GB.1340(28).   c331.

Les **cols** de la Chambre et de la Montée du Fond / W.A.B. Coolidge. Lyon, 1911. Extrait de la *Revue alpine* de juin 1911.
GB.1340(23).   c332.

Cols et sommets: ascensions et traversées dans les Alpes de la Valteline, des Grisons et du Tyrol / B. Galli-Valerio. Lausanne, [ca 1913]. Ill.
GB/A.1446.   c333.

Comasine in Val di Peio: appunti e memorie / Giuseppe Gabrielli. [Comasine, 1972.] Ill. Published by the Centro Studi per la Val del Sole.
GB/A.1323(1).   c334.

Combats pour l'Eiger / Toni Hiebeler; traduction de Monique Bittebierre. [Grenoble], 1965. Ill. [Sempervivum; 41.]
GB/A.137.   c335.

Come fotografare in montagna / Emilio Frisia. Milano, [1967]. Ill.
GB/A.835(7).   c336.

Come si va in montagna / Fulvio Campiotti. Milano, [1958]. Ill.
GB/B.289(28).   c337.

The **comforts** of human life, or Smiles and laughter of Charles Chearful and Martin Merryfellow. London, 1807.
GB.144.   c338.

The **Comic** Annual. London, 1832.
GB.128.   c339.

Comicalities of travel / [T. Brooke]. Chester, 1836. Ill.
Lloyd.476.   c340.

Commander Bedford Pim. [N.p., n.d.] Port.
Lloyd.1574(10).   c341.

Commando climber / Mike Banks. London, 1955. Ill.
GB.680 (impf); GB.681.   c342.

Comment on devient alpiniste / George Ingle Finch; traduit par R. de Malherbe et E. Gaillard. Chambéry, 1926. Ill. Translated from *The making of a mountaineer*.
GB/A.1080.   c343.

Le **compagnon** du grand nord / Pierre Duchaussois. Montréal, 1958.
GB/A.1676(11).   c344.

A **companion** to Keller's panorama of Switzerland: comprising a description of Mont Righi. London, [ca 1829]. Ill., map.
GB.1335(3).   c345.

A **comparative** manual of affixes for the Inuit dialects of Greenland, Canada, and Alaska / Michael Fortescue. Copenhagen, 1983. [Meddelelser om Grønland. Man & society; 4.]
GB/A.1820/4.   c346.

Compendio della storia generale de' viaggi / Jean François de La Harpe. Venezia, 1784. Map.
GB/A.512.   c347.

A **compendium** of modern geography / Alexander Stewart. 8th ed., rev. and enl. Edinburgh, 1846. Ill., maps.
GB/A.385.   c348.

The **complete** mountaineer / George D. Abraham. 2nd ed. London, 1908. Ill.
GB/A.483.   c349.

Compte rendu d'une ascension scientifique au Mont Blanc / Jules Janssen. [Paris?], 1890. Pp.[431]-47 of the *Comptes rendus des séances de l'Académie des sciences*, 1890.
GB.1880(27).   c350.

Compte rendu d'une ascension scientifique au Mont Blanc / Jules Janssen. Paris, [1890].
GB/B.260(2).   c351.

Compte rendu des séances de la Société vaudoise des sciences naturelles à Lausanne: séance du 15 mai, 1895. [N.p., 1895.] Extrait des *Archives des sciences physiques et naturelles*, juillet 1895.
GB/A.514(16).   c352.

Comune di Courmayeur: soggiorno degli stranieri / T. Graham Brown. Courmayeur, 1928.
GB.1327(5). c353.

Con gli Alpini all'80° parallelo / Gennaro Sora. 2a ed. Verona, 1930. Ill.
GB/A.445. c354.

Con gli Alpini in A. O. / Franco Garelli. Milano, 1937. Ill.
GB/B.311. c355.

Concentrations of mercury, selenium and lead in blood samples from mothers and their newborn babies in four Greenlandic hunting districts / Jens C. Hansen [et al.]. Copenhagen, 1984. Ill., map. [Meddelelser om Grønland. Man and society; 6.]
GB/A.1820/6. c356.

Concerto grosso: racconti di montagna / Carlo Arzani. Lecco, 1970. Ill.
GB/C.22(21). c357.

Congrès de Monaco, 1er au 10 mai 1920: Congrès de l'alpinisme: comptes rendus des séances. Paris, 1921. 2v.
GB.1307(6-7). c358.

Congrès international de l'alpinisme tenu à Paris du 11 au 15 août 1900: compte rendu. Clermont, 1902.
Lloyd.1620(4). c359.

La **connaissance** de la montagne / Paul Payot. Bonneville, 1944. Ill.
Lloyd.1618(34). c360.

Les **conquérants** de l'inutile, des Alpes à l'Annapurna / Lionel Terray. [Paris], 1961. Ill.
GB.1309(7). c361.

Les **conquérants** de l'inutile, des Alpes à l'Annapurna / Lionel Terray. [Paris], 1970. Ill.
GB/A.1309. c362.

Conquering the Great Rose: an account of the first ascent of the world's longest non-polar glacier / Fanny Workman. [New York, 1914.] Ill. Pp.[44]-55 of *Harper's Monthly Magazine*, 1914.
GB.1880(44). c363.

The **conquest** of Mount McKinley: the story of three expeditions through the Alaskan wilderness to Mount McKinley / Belmore Browne; appendix by Herschel C. Parker. New York, 1913. Ill., maps.
GB.989. c364.

La **conquête** de l'Everest par le Sherpa Tensing / Yves Malartic. Paris, [1953]. Ill., maps, ports.
Lloyd.1608(8). c365.

La **conquête** des pôles / Henry Bidou. 10e éd. [Paris], 1940. Ill., maps, ports. [La découverte du monde.]
GB/A.1707. c366.

La **conquête** du massif alpin et de ses abords par les populations préhistoriques / Marguerite E. Dellenbach. Grenoble, 1935. Maps.
GB/A.472. c367.

La **conquête** du Mont-Blanc / Claude Nisson. Paris, 1930. Ill. [Des fleurs et des fruits.]
GB/A.1139. c368.

La **conquête** souterraine / Pierre Minvielle. [Grenoble], 1967. Ill. [Sempervivum; 43.]
GB/A.938(4). c369.

Les **conquêtes** de ma jeunesse / André Roch. Neuchâtel, [1942]. Ill.
GB.1310(6). c370.

La **conquista** del K2, seconda cima del mondo / Ardito Desio. Milano, 1954. Ill., ports., maps, facsim.
GB.737. c371.

La **conquista** dell'Everest / Sir John Hunt; con un capitolo sull'assalto finale di Sir Edmund Hillary; [traduzione di Donato Barbone, revisione alpinistica di Pietro Mechini]. Bari, 1954. [All'insegna dell'orizzonte; 6.] Translated from *The ascent of Everest*.
GB/A.1571. c372.

I **conquistatori** del K2 / Elio Donati. Torino, 1954. Ill., map.
GB/A.1557. c373.

Le **conservateur** suisse, ou Recueil complet des Etrennes helvétiennes. Ed. augm. Lausanne, 1813-17. 8v
GB/A.570-7. c374.

Le **conservateur** suisse, ou Recueil complet des Etrennes helvétiennes. Ed. augm. 2e éd. Lausanne, 1856-58. Vol.9-14.
GB/A.807-12. c375.

Conservation, tourism & mountaineering in the Himalayas / edited by N.D. Jayal, Mohan Motwani. Dehra Dun, 1986. Ill.
GB/A.2210. c376.

Considérations géologiques sur le mont Salève et sur les terrains des environs de Genève / Alphonse Favre. Genève, 1843.
GB/B.288(20). c377.

Les **constantes** de l'art tessinois / Alexandre Cingria. Lausanne, 1944. Ill.
GB/A.1221. c378.

Constitution and rules of The Scottish Mountaineering Trust. Memorandum by the Honorary Treasurer with reference to the proposed Trust. [Edinburgh, 1958?] 2v.
GB.1331(33-4). c379.

Constitution of the E.U.M.C. [Edinburgh University Mountaineering Club]. [Edinburgh, n.d.]
GB.1331(29). c380.

Constitution of the Harvard Mountaineering Club. [Cambridge, Mass., n.d.]
GB.1331(42). c381.

Constitution, Welsh Mountaineering Club. (Proposals.) [N.p., n.d.]
GB.1331(43). c382.

Contes à pic / Samivel. [Saint-Paul], 1965. Ill. [Sempervivum; 14.]
GB/A.687. c383.

The **Continent** in 1835: sketches in Belgium, Germany, Switzerland, Savoy, and France including historical notices; and statements relative to the existing aspect of the Protestant religion in those countries / John Hoppus. London, 1836. 2v.
Lloyd.697-8. c384.

Continental adventures: a novel / [Charlotte Anne Eaton]. 2nd ed. London, 1827. 3v.
Lloyd.377-9. c385.

Continental excursions, or Tours into France, Switzerland and Germany, in 1782, 1787, and 1789: with a description of Paris, and the glacieres of Savoy / Thomas Pennington. London, 1809. 2v.
Lloyd.931-2. c386.

The **continental** traveller, being the journal of an economical tourist to France, Switzerland and Italy: to which is added, A tour in Spain. London, 1833.
Lloyd.232. c387.

Continental way-side notes: the diary of a seven months' tour in Europe / R.S. Standen. London, 1865.
GB/A.763. c388.

A **continuation** of reflections on Mr Varillas's *History of heresies*: particularly on that which relates to English affairs / Gilbert Burnet. Amsterdam, 1687.
GB.46A(4). c389.

Contributi alla storia della Valsesia / a cura della Società Valsesiana di Cultura. Varallo, 1971. Ill.
GB/B.364. c390.

Contributions to Chipewyan ethnology / Kaj Birket-Smith; [translated by W.E. Calvert]. New York, 1976. Ill. [Thule expedition, 5th, 1921-1924. Report; vol.6 no.3.]
GB/A.1831. c391.

Contributions to the glacial geology of Spitzbergen / E.J. Garwood, J.W. Gregory. [London, 1898.] Ill. From the *Quarterly Journal of the Geological Society* for May 1898, vol.54.
GB.1335(48). c392.

The **conventions** of mountaineering / J.H. Doughty. [Uxbridge, 1928.] Pp.398-408 of the *British Ski Year Book*, vol.4 no.9.
GB.1881(75). c393.

Cook's continental time tables and tourists' hand book. July 1897. London, 1897. Maps.
Lloyd.1615(17). c398.

Cordigliera tra cielo e ghiaccio: impressioni scritte e istanti colti dall'obiettivo nel corso delle nostre spedizioni sulla Cordigliera Andina / Giuseppe Agnolotti, Giorgio Pettigiani. Bologna, [1981?]. Ill., map.
GB/A.2022(8). c399.

The **Corno** Bianco / Claude Wilson. [London, 1895.] Ill., map. Pp.475-92 of the *Alpine Journal*, vol.17, Aug. 1895.
GB.1312(27). c400.

Corno Bianco m.3320 — in seguito ad una ascensione con guida per vecchia via / Luigi Brasca. Torino, 1909. Ill., map. Pp.[189]-212 of the *Bollettino del Club Alpino Italiano*, no.72.
GB.1880(19). c401.

Le **Corno** Stella, Alpes Maritimes: première ascension / Victor de Cessole. Paris, 1904. Extrait de l'*Annuaire du Club alpin français*, vol.30, 1903.
Lloyd.1594(5). c402.

Coro alpino eporediese: una tradizione che unisce / documentazione fotografica di Ferrucio Veisi;

testi di Mario Perrucca e di Ermanno Franchetto. [Ivrea], 1972. Ill., music.
GB/B.388. c403.

[**Correspondence**, 1773-1787] / Marc Théodore Bourrit. [N.p., n.d.] A photocopy.
GB.1328(5). c403.1.

Correspondence with the Hudson's Bay Company on Arctic exploration, 1844-1855 / John Rae; edited by E.E. Rich, assisted by A.M. Johnson. London, 1953. Maps, port. [Hudson's Bay Record Society. Publications; 16.]
GB.1131. c404.

Corse de Calenzana à Conca: 15 jours de marche. 7. éd., rev. et corr. Paris, 1982. Cover title: Sentier de la Corse de Calenzana à Conca. Published by the Fédération française de la randonnée pédestre, Comité national des sentiers de la grande randonnée.
GB/A.2021(1). c405.

Cortina e le sue montagne / Bepi Degregorio. 2a ed. Rocca San Casciano, 1955. Ill.
GB/A.843. c406.

Cortina in winter / W. Rickmer Rickmers. Innsbruck, 1910. Ill., map.
Lloyd.1620(24). c407.

Coryats crudities hastily gobled up in five moneths trauells in France, Sauoy, Italy, Rhetia comonly called the Grisons country, Heluetia alias Switzerland. London, 1611.
GB.774 (impf.). c408.

Cosmographie, containing the chorographie and historie of the whole world / Peter Heylyn. London, 1652. Maps. Translated from *Mikrokosmos*.
GB.1285. c409.

Cosmorama / Jehoshaphat Aspin. [London, 1826.]
GB.11 (impf.). c410.

The **cottages** of the Alps, or Life and manners in Switzerland / by a lady [Anna Cummings Johnson]. London, 1860. 2v (in 1).
GB/A.1262. c411.

Country and travel. Vol.1 no.4, Dec.1950. London, 1950.
GB.1338(1). c412.

Country life in Piedmont / Antonio Gallenga. London, 1858.
Lloyd.536. c413.

The **country** of the Vosges / Henry W. Wolff. London, 1891. Map.
Lloyd.1120. c414.

Coup d'oeil sur la structure géologique des environs de Montreux / Hans Schardt. Vévey, 1893. Ill. Tiré du *Bull. Soc. Vaud. Sc. Nat.*, vol.29 no.112.
GB/A.514(7). c415.

Coup d'oeil sur la structure géologique et minéralogique du groupe des Monts Dores / H. Lecoq, J.B. Bouillet. Paris, 1830. Ill.
GB.1315(7). c416.

Courage / J.M. Barrie. London, [1922].
GB.314. c417.

Courmayeur / Linda Villari. [London, 1887.] Pp.[773]-7 of *Leisure Hour*, 1887.
GB.1336(23). c418.

Courmayeur and Grand Hotel Royal Bertolini. Turin, [n.d.]. Ill., maps.
GB.1339(35). c419.

Courmayeur et Pré-St-Didier, Val d'Aoste: leurs bains, leurs eaux & leurs environs / Auguste Argentier. Aoste, 1864.
GB.1335(1). c420.

Une **course** à Chamounix: conte fantastique / Adolphe Pictet. Genève, 1930. Ill., ports., facsims.
GB/B.293; GB/B.355. c421.

Course à l'éboulement du glacier de Gétroz et au lac de Mauvoisin, au fond de la vallée de Bagnes, 16 mai, 1818 / [Philippe Sirice Bridel]. Vevey, [1818?]. Ill.
GB.389; Lloyd.1576(1); Lloyd.1576(1)A. c422.

Course au Moléson / F. Thioly. Genève, 1865.
GB.1332(30); Lloyd.1148. c423.

Course de Bâle à Bienne par les vallées du Jura / [Philippe Sirice Bridel]. Bâle, 1789. Map.
GB/A.800(10). c424.

The **course** of Hannibal over the Alps ascertained / John Whitaker. London, 1794. 2v (in 1).
Lloyd.583. c425.

Courses alpestres en Suisse et en Savoie. Genève, [1851]. Pièces détachées de *La nouvelle bibliothèque littéraire*.
GB.930; Lloyd.1588(1).   c426.

Courses dans les Pyrénées: la montagne et les eaux / Henri Nicolle. 2e éd. Paris, 1855.
GB/A.1592.   c427.

Courses faites à différentes époques dans le Valais et les montagnes avoisinantes. Lausanne, [1843]. Map.
GB/A.156.   c428.

Coursing at Ashdown Park, painted by Stephen Pearce. London, 1869. Reprinted from the *Sporting Gazette*, October 2, 1869.
Lloyd.1574(7).   c429.

Crag, glacier, and avalanche: narratives of daring and disaster / Achilles Daunt. London, 1889. Ill.
Lloyd.443.   c430.

Crags. No.2-25, May 1976-June/July 1980. Sheffield, 1976-80. Ill., maps.
GB/B.570(3).   c431.

Crags for climbing in and around Great Langdale / George Basterfield, and Rock climbing in Buttermere / A.R. Thomson. Barrow-in-Furness, [1926]. [Climbers' guides to the English Lake District; 5.] Published by the Fell and Rock Climbing Club of the English Lake District.
GB.1328(10).   c431.1.

Craig yr Ysfa memory / A.B. Hargreaves. [London], 1944. Pp.220-4 of the *Climbers' Club Journal*, vol.7 no.3.
GB.1339(5).   c432.

Cresta e torrioni Saragat (Alpi Marittime) / Bruno e Francesco Salesi. Sanremo, [1967]. Ill., map. Published by the Club Alpino Italiano, Sezione Alpi Liguri.
GB/A.1349(12).   c433.

Cristallogruppe und Pomagagnonzug: ein Führer für Täler, Hütten und Berge / Jürgen und Angelika Schmidt. München, 1981. Ill., maps. [Alpenvereinsführer. Reihe: Südliche Kalkalpen.]
GB/A.1965(11).   c434.

Croda Rossa: Becchei, Sénnes, Signore, Croda Rossa: Plan de Corones, Colli Alti: Pico di Vallandro / Danilo Pianetti, Ugo Pomarici, Vito Di Benedetto. Cortina, 1977. Ill. [Sci alpinismo.]
GB/A.2017(5).   c435.

La **croix** du Cervin / Charles Gos. Paris, [1933]. Ill.
GB/A.1148.   c436.

Cronaca alpina della Sezione di Vicenza / Alessandro Cita; In giro pei Sette Comuni, per Melchiori Giacomo. Torino, 1881. Estratto dal *Bollettino del Club Alpino Italiano*, no.44, anno 1880.
GB/B.289(24).   c437.

Cronaca di Ampezzo nel Tirolo dagli antichi tempi fino al XX secolo / Pietro Alverà. Cortina, 1985.
GB/B.650.   c438.

Crossing the Atlantic. Edinburgh, 1845. Pp.29-31 of *Chambers's Edinburgh Journal*, N.S. no.80.
GB.1332(19).   c439.

A **cruise** on the Friesland meres / Ernst R. Suffling. London, 1894. Ill.
Lloyd.1615(20).   c440.

The **crystal** hunters: a boy's adventures in the higher Alps / Geo. Manville Fenn. London, [1892]. Ill.
GB.229.   c441.

The **crystal** hunters: a boy's adventures in the higher Alps / Geo. Manville Fenn. New ed. London, 1897. Ill.
GB.322.   c442.

Igl **cudasch** de la Ruth: suaintar la Bibla spunida an talian / digl Gion Luzzi. Tusan, 1953.
GB/A.1199(12).   c443.

Cultura alpina in Liguria: realdo e verdeggia / Pierleone Massajoli. Genova, 1984. Ill., maps.
GB/B.634.   c444.

Cunard Atlantic News. R.M.S. *Aquitania*. June 7-8, 1934. R.M.S. *Mauretania*. Sept.27-Oct.1, 1934. [N.p.], 1934.
GB.1334(11-17).   c445.

Cuneo e i suoi dintorni: cronistoria, edilizia, arte, paesaggio, ordinamento economico-amministrativo, turismo / Camillo Fresia. Cuneo, 1935. Ill., maps.
GB/A.2019(13).   c446.

Cunturínes fánis (nel regno di Dolasilla) / Danilo Pianetti, Ugo Pomarici, Vito Di Benedetto. Cortina d'Ampezzo, 1976. Ill., map. [Guida sci alpinistica.]
GB/A.2017(2).   c447.

Curiosities of Modern Travel: a year-book of adventure. 1847. London, 1847.
GB.149. c448.

The **curious** traveller, being a choice collection of very remarkable histories, voyages, travels, &c., digested into familar letters and conversations. London, 1742. Ill.
GB.390. c449.

[**Cuttings** from *The Times*, weekly edition, relating to climbs made by W.W. Graham in the Himalayas.] [London, 1883-84.]
GB.1881(66-70). c450.

Der **Cyper**, ein Bergsteigerleben / Norbert Mantl. Innsbruck, 1967. Ill.
GB/A.181(7). c451.

-D-

Da Courmayeur tutta la valle d'Aosta / Renata Pescanti Botti. Savona, 1967. Ill.
GB/C.31. d001.

Da Torino a Chambéry ossia le valli della Dora Riparia e dell'Arc e la Galleria delle Alpi Cozie / Andrea Covino. Torino, 1871. Ill., maps.
GB/A.31. d002.

Dai Monti Pallidi alle sette Montagne di Vetro / Aurelio Garobbio. Milano, 1960. Ill.
GB/B.434. d003.

Dal Caucaso al Himalaya, 1889-1909: Vittorio Sella, fotografo, alpinista, esploratore / a cura di Maria Raffaella, Fiory Ceccopieri; collaborazione alle ricerche ed alla stesura dei testi di Alfonso Bernardi. Milano, 1981. Ill.
GB/B.622. d004.

Dal Monte Rosa al Cervino: ascensioni senza guide / Cesare Fiorio. Torino, 1896. Ill.
Lloyd.1213. d005.

Dal Monte Soglio alla Levanna / Pensiero Acutis. Torino, 1970. Ill.
GB/B.289(18). d006.

Dal Sempione allo Stelvio: centododici itinerari in sci / Maurizio Gnudi, Franco Malnati. Torino, 1977. Ill. [Itinerari; 3.] [Biblioteca della montagna; 6.]
GB/A.2006. d007.

Dall'Artico all'Antartico: viaggi e avventure / Piero Ghiglione. Torino, 1963. Ill. [Piccole storie.]
GB/A.492. d008.

Dall'attendamento S.A.R.I. in Valle d'Ayas-S. Jacques d'Ayas / per cura di Sarino Anziano. Torino, 1923. [Itinerari alpini; 5.] Published by Club Alpino Italiano, Sezione di Torino, Gruppo Studentesco S.A.R.I.
GB/A.516(7). d008.1.

Dalle Alpi alle Ambe / Amilcare Rossi. Roma, [1937]. Ill., facsims.
GB/B.290(10). d009.

Dalle Ande all'Himálaya / Piero Ghiglione. Torino, 1936. Ill. [La piccozza e la penna; 12.]
GB/A.975. d010.

Dallo Stelvio al Tonale: Merano, Bolzano, Dolomiti di Brenta / Manlio Besozzi. Novara, [1928]. Ill. [Visioni italiche.] Published by the Istituto Geografico De Agostini.
GB/B.336.   d011.

Dallo Stelvio al Tonale: Merano, Bolzano, Dolomiti di Brenta / Manlio Besozzi. Roma, 1929. Ill. [Visioni italiche.]
GB/B.516.   d012.

Damographia oder Gemsen-Beschreibung / Adam Lebwald von und zu Lebenwald. München, 1933. [Jahresgabe der Gesellschaft alpiner Bücherfreunde; 13.] Facsimile reprint of the Salzburg, [1693] ed.
GB/A.85.   d013.

Les **dangers** dans la montagne: indications pratiques pour les ascensionnistes / Emil Zsigmondy; traduit par Abel Lemercier. Paris, 1886. Ill. Translated from *Die Gefahren der Alpen*.
GB/A.88; Lloyd.1618(1).   d014.

Les **dangers** des ascensions / H. Baumgartner; traduit par S. Ch. et le dr. E.B. 2e éd. Genève, 1888.
Lloyd.1617(1).   d015.

Dangers of Alpine mountaineering. London, [1878]. Pp.213-24 of *Temple Bar*, 1878.
GB.1881(73).   d016.

Daniæ descriptio noua, insularum ac partium praecipuarum, huius plagæ arcticæ theatrum repræsentans / Jon Jensen Colding. [Frankfurt am Main], 1594.
Lloyd.1570(2).   d017.

Dans l'Alpe ignorée: explorations et souvenirs / Julien Gallet. Lausanne, 1910. Ill.
GB/A.919.   d018.

Dans les Alpes avec Geiger / photos: Yves Debraine; texte: Georges Gygax. Lausanne, 1967. Ill.
GB/A.179.   d019.

Dans les Alpes et le Jura: souvenir d'un alpiniste / Hippolyte Balavoine. Paris, 1911.
GB/A.160.   d020.

Dans les Alpes françaises: une vue d'ensemble, une excursion, un massif: Alpes du sud, du Mont Cénis au Léman, le Mont Blanc, géant des Alpes / F. Gex. Paris, 1929. Ill.
GB/A.1141.   d021.

Dans les Alpes Pennines: histoire topographique de la Haute Valtelline entre 1820 et 1862 et le Lyskamm dans l'histoire entre 1820 et 1861 / W.A.B. Coolidge. Aoste, 1912. Extrait du *Bulletin de la Société de la flore valdôtaine*, no.8.
GB.1340(29).   d022.

Dans les Montagnes Rocheuses / baron Edmond de Mandat-Grancey. Paris, 1884. Ill., map.
GB/A.833.   d023.

Darjiling / comte Goblet d'Alviella. Milano, 1899. Ill. [Biblioteca illustrata dei viaggi intorno al mondo per terra e per mare; 15.]
GB/A.836(2).   d024.

Der **Däumling** im Gosaukamm / Dr. G., Freiherr von Saar. [Vienna, 1914.] Ill. Pp.[177]-84 of the *Osterreichische Alpenzeitung*, no.907.
GB.1319(4).   d025.

Davos-Platz: a new Alpine resort for sick and sound in summer and winter / by one who knows it well [i.e. Mrs Macmorland]. London, 1878. Map.
Lloyd.145.   d026.

A **day** and a night on the Aiguille du Dru / T.A. Nash. [London, 1889.] Pp.497-509 of the *Alpine Journal*, vol.14.
Lloyd.1608(9).   d027.

A **day** on the Alps / A. Gurney. [N.p., 1892.] Pp.[657]-64 of *Newbery House Magazine*, June 1892.
GB/A.797(13).   d028.

A **day** on the glaciers: containing an account of an excursion to the 'Jardin', at Chamounix / Albert. [London], 1841. Pp.196-8 of no.1078 and pp.214-6 of no.1079 of the *Mirror*.
GB.1313(21).   d029.

The **day** the rope broke: the story of a great Victorian tragedy / Ronald W. Clark. London, 1965. Ill., map, port.
GB.916.   d030.

A **day** with the German-Austrian Alpine Club / George C. Ramsay. [London, 1876.] Pp.402-7, 532-6 of *Good Words*, 1876.
GB.1331(56).   d031.

De Alpibus commentarius: die Alpen / Josias Simler; Einleitung, Ubersetzung und Erläuterungen von Alfred Steinitzer. München, 1931. Ill., maps. Published by the Gesellschaft Alpiner Bücherfreunde.
GB/B.123.   d032.

De Genève à Zermatt par la vallée d'Anniviers et le col du Trift / F. Thioly. Genève, 1867.
GB.1332(24); Lloyd.1108.   d033.

De glacier en glacier en Suisse et en Savoie: souvenirs de voyage / César Pascal. Paris, [1884].
Lloyd.1614(2).   d034.

De l'Eiger à l'Iharen / Alain de Chatellus. Paris, 1947. Ill.
GB.1329(3).   d035.

De l'orographie des Alpes dans ses rapports avec la géologie / E. Desor. Neuchâtel, 1862. Map.
GB/B.440(9).   d036.

De l'utilité, et de l'importance des voyages, et des courses dans son propre pays / le chevalier de Robilant. Bologna, 1972. Ill. Facsimile reprint of the Turin, 1790 ed.
GB/B.313(8).   d037.

De la Mer Bleue au Mont Blanc: impressions d'hiver dans les Alpes / P. Lancrenon. Paris, 1906. Ill.
GB/A.925.   d038.

De Paris à Venise: notes au crayon / Charles Blanc. Paris, 1857. Ill.
GB/A.802(2).   d039.

De Pau au pic d'Ossau et à Gavarnie / publié par la section de Pau du Club alpin français. Paris, [1897?]. Ill., map.
GB/A.1351(11).   d040.

De prisca ac uera Alpina Rhætia cum cætero Alpinarum gentium tractu descriptio / Aegidius Tschudi; [translated by Sebastian Münster]. [Basel], 1538.
Lloyd.1624(14).   d041.

De rebus Helvetiorum, siue antiquitatum libri V / Franciscus Guillimannus. [Fribourg], 1598.
Lloyd.917.   d042.

De republica Helvetiorum libri duo / Josias Simler. [Zurich], 1576.
GB.405.   d043.

De republica Helvetiorum libri duo: describitur non tantum communis totius Helvetiæ politia verum etiam fœderum omnium origo & conditiones exponuntur / Josias Simler. [Zurich], 1577.
Lloyd.1570(1).   d044.

De Saussure: sa vie, ses voyages et ses observations dans les Alpes / Louis Bouvier. Genève, 1877. Souvenir du Congrès médical de Genève, 12-17 septembre 1877.
Lloyd.1613(23).   d045.

Death in the barren ground / Edgar Christian; edited by George Whalley. [Toronto], 1980. Ill., map.
GB/A.1888.   d046.

A **defence** of the reflections on the ninth book of the first volum [sic] of Mr. Varillas's *History of heresies*: being a reply to his answer / Gilbert Burnet. Amsterdam, 1687.
GB.46A(3).   d047.

The **delectable** mountains / Douglas Busk. London, [1946]. A prospectus.
GB.1313(31).   d048.

Les **délices** de la Suisse où l'on peut voir tout ce qu'il y a de plus remarquable dans son pays / [Abraham Ruchat]. Leide, 1714. 4v; ill., maps.
GB.54-7.   d049.

Les **délices** de la Suisse (1714) / Abraham Ruchat. Genève, 1978. 4v (in 2); ill., maps. Facsimile reprint of the Leiden, 1714 ed.
GB/A.1641.   d050.

Deliciæ urbis Bernæ: Merckwurdigkeiten der hochlöbl. Stadt Bern: ausmehrentheils ungedruckten authentischen Schrifften zusammen getragen / [edited by J.R. Gruner]. Zürich, 1732.
GB/A.1410.   d051.

Dell'antica condizione del Vercellese, e dell'antico borgo di Santià: dissertazione / Jacopo Durandi. Bologna, 1973. Facsimile reprint of the Torino, 1766 ed.
GB/B.377(13).   d052.

Delle Alpe Scuzie (e non Cozie) e dell'omonimo patrimonio della Chiesa Romana / Raffaele Foglietti. Macerata, 1898.
GB/B.366(7).   d053.

Delle scuole e degli uomini celebri di Belluno. Dell'Agordino: cenni storici, statistici, naturali. Impressioni e desideri dall'Agordino / Pietro Mugna. [N.p.], 1972. Facsimile reprints of the Venezia, 1858, Venezia, 1858, and Padova, 1874 eds.
GB/B.377(35).   d054.

Delta: dal sogno alla realtà / Jean-Bernard Desfayes. Aosta, 1979. Ill. [Gli sport.]
GB/A.2023(6). d055.

Den Bergen verfallen: Alpenfahrten / Eleonore Noll-Hasenclever; mit Geleitwort und Lebensbild versehen und mit Beiträgen von G. Dyhrenfurth, W. Martin, Hermann Trier und Willi Welzenbach; herausgegeben von Heinrich Erler. Berlin, [1932]. Ill.
GB.606. d056.

Denali's wife / Charles S. Houston. [New York, 1935.] Ill. Reprinted from the *American Alpine Journal*, vol.2 no.3, 1935.
GB.1338(15). d057.

Der denkende Wanderer / Henry Hoek. München, 1932. Ill.
GB/A.37. d058.

Denkschriften der Allgemeinen Schweizerischen Gesellschaft für die gesammten Naturwissenschaften. Bd.1 Abt.1-2. Zürich, 1829-33.
GB/A.2095. d059.

La **Dent** Blanche dans l'histoire / W.A.B. Coolidge. Lausanne, [1918]. Extrait du no.1, 1918 des *Annales valaisannes*.
GB.1340(41). d060.

Dent Blanche, the E. arête, reached from the S. / R.W. Lloyd. [London], 1913. Ill. Reprinted from the *Alpine Journal*, February 1911.
Lloyd.1602(28). d061.

Die **Dent** d'Hérens von Breuil nach Praraye / E.F.L. Fankhauser. [Berne, 1901.] Ill. Separatabdruck aus dem *Jahrbuch des Schweizer Alpenclub*, Jahrg. 36, pp.75-85.
Lloyd.1594(9). d062.

Denti della Vecchia e dintorni (Alpi Orobie): itinerari alpinistici ed escursionistici in Val Gerola / Sandro Gandola. Lecco, 1981. Ill., map.
GB/A.2018(15). d063.

Dents du Midi region: an interim guide / translated and edited with new material by the associates of West Col Productions. Reading, 1967. Ill. [West Col Alpine guides.] Translated and adapted from *Escalades choisies du Léman à la Méditerranée*, by Félix Germain.
GB/A.1295(16). d064.

Der skal være så smukt i Grønland / Palle Koch. København, 1968.
GB/B.525(2). d065.

Une **dernière** ascension / Edouard Desor. Neuchâtel, 1854. Extrait de la *Revue suisse* de janvier 1854.
GB/A.1791(7). d066.

Dernières victoires au Cervin / Giuseppe Mazzotti; traduit par E. Gaillard. Neuchâtel, 1934. Ill. [Montagne.]
GB/A.165. d067.

Derniers souvenirs de l'Alpe: suite du volume *Dans l'Alpe ignorée* / Julien Gallet. Lausanne, 1927.
GB/A.956. d068.

Derniers voyages en zigzag, ou Excursions d'un pensionnat en vacances dans les cantons suisses et sur le revers italien des Alpes / Rodolphe Töpffer. 2e éd. Genève, 1911. Ill.
GB/A.799(1); GB/A.800(11). d069.

Des cabanes du C.A.I. en général: rapport présenté à l'Assemblée générale de l'U.I.A.A. / Silvio Saglio. [N.p., ca 1950.] Ill. Published by the Union internationale des associations d'alpinisme.
GB/B.390(4). d070.

Des Calanques aux faces Nord / Sylvia d'Albertas. Neuchâtel, 1948. Ill.
GB/A.515(2). d071.

Des chamois parmi les hommes / Jean Bouvet. Neuchâtel, 1966.
GB/A.1295(12). d072.

Des risques de la montagne / Emile Fontaine. Tours, 1927. Ill.
Lloyd.1608(5). d073.

Des Schweizerlands Geschichten für das Schweizervolk / Heinrich Zschokke. Reutlingen, 1823.
GB/A.753. d074.

The **descent** of the Brenva Face of Mont Blanc / R.W. Lloyd. London, 1913. Ill. Reprinted from the *Alpine Journal*, 1912.
Lloyd.1602(23). d075.

Descriptio de situ Helvetiæ & vicinis gentibus / per Henricum Glareanum. Idem de quatuor Helvetiorum fœdere panegyricon. Cum commentarijs

Osualdi Myconij. Ad Maximilianum Augustum Henrici Glareani panygyricon. [Basel], 1519.
GB/A.1244. d076.

Description de Genève, ancienne et moderne: suivie de la relation de l'ascension de Mr. de Saussure sur la cime du Mont-Blanc / H. Mallet. Genève, 1807.
Lloyd.366; Lloyd.366A (impf.). d077.

Description de la fête des vignerons de Vevey, le 5 aoust 1819. Vevey, [1819].
Lloyd.1615(10). d078.

Description de la ville de Berne, ornée d'un plan et quelques vues intéressantes / N. Koenig. Berne, 1810. 2v (in 1); ill., map.
Lloyd.605; Lloyd.1575(1). d078.1.

Description des Alpes Pennines et Rhétiennes / Marc Théodore Bourrit. Genève, 1781. 2v.
GB.453 (bound in 1v.); GB.538-9; Lloyd.594-5; Lloyd.929-30. d079.

Description des aspects du Mont-Blanc du côté de la Val-d'Aost / Marc Théodore Bourrit. Lausanne, 1776.
GB.524; Lloyd.492. d080.

Description des cols, ou passages des Alpes / Marc Théodore Bourrit. Genève, 1803. 2v (in 1); ill.
GB.371; GB.1311(3) (v.1); GB.1315(1) (v.2); Lloyd.563. d081.

Description des glacières, glaciers & amas de glace du duché de Savoye / Marc Théodore Bourrit. Genève, 1773.
GB.472; Lloyd.581. d082.

Description des montagnes et des vallées qui font partie de la principauté de Neuchâtel et Valangin / [S.F. Osterwald]. 2e éd., rev., corr. et considérablement augm. Neuchâtel, 1766.
GB/A.799(13); Lloyd.181. d083.

Description du département du Simplon, ou de la ci-devant république du Valais / Schiner. Sion, 1812.
GB/A.993. d084.

Description du Mont-Rigi, des chemins qui y conduisent, et de la célèbre perspective dont on jouit sur sa cime, pour servir de texte explicatif au *Panorama* de Henri Keller. [N.p.], 1824. Ill.
GB.1328(3); Lloyd.649. d085.

Description et itinéraire des bords du lac de Genève, ou Manuel du voyageur dans la vallée du Léman / J.L. Manget. Genève, 1822.
GB/A.1381(3). d086.

Description of a painting of Jerusalem and the surrounding country, as it appears at this time, from the Mount of Olives: painted by E. Donovan [exhibited in] the London Museum, Fleet Street. London, [n.d.].
Lloyd.1590(1). d087.

Description of a view of Bern, and the high Alps, with the surrounding country / taken by Henry Ashton Barker; and now exhibiting in the great Rotunda of his Panorama, Leicester Square. London, 1821. Ill.
GB.571; Lloyd.965; Lloyd.1587(1). d088.

Description of a view of Mont Blanc, the valley of Chamounix, and the surrounding mountains, now exhibiting at the Panorama, Leicester Square / painted by Robert Burford from drawings taken by himself in 1835. London, 1837. Ill.
GB.589; GB.1335(33); Lloyd.1587(4). d089.

Description of a view of the Bernese Alps, taken from the Faulhorn Mountain: and part gf [sic] Switzerland, now exhibiting at the Panorama, Leicester Square / painted by Robert Burford, assisted by H.C. Selous. London, [1852]. Ill.
GB.784. d090.

Description of a view of the city and Lake of Geneva, and surrounding country: now exhibiting in the Panorama, Strand: painted by R. Burford. London, 1827. Ill.
Lloyd.1587(3). d091.

Description of Mount Pilate with its legends, popular traditions / [August Heinrich Petermann]; translated from the German by Wna Emma Benziger. Lucerne, 1865.
GB.17. d092.

Description of the monument, erected on the Hill of Hoad, Ulverstone, in memory of Sir John Barrow, Bart., A.D.1850. Ulverstone, [1850]. Ill.
Lloyd.1583(17). d093.

Description of the new Rob Roy canoe, built for a voyage through Norway, Sweden and the Baltic / dedicated to the Canoe Club, by the Captain (J. Macgregor). London, 1866.
Lloyd.1583(21). d094.

A **description** of the scenery of the lakes in the North of England / William Wordsworth. 4th ed. London, 1823.
GB.86. d095.

A **description** of the valley of Chamouni, in Savoy / Samuel Glover. London, 1821.
GB.1225; Lloyd.1383. d096.

A **description** of the Western Islands of Scotland / Martin Martin. London, 1703.
GB.354. d097.

A **description** of the Western Isles of Scotland, called Hybrides / Donald Monro. Edinburgh, 1774.
GB.148. d098.

Description sommaire des Alpes allemandes / [Ch. Schaub]. Genève, 1861. Tiré de la *Bibliothèque universelle*, mai et juin 1861.
GB/A.1350(5). d099.

Description topographique des Alpes / Karl, Erzherzog von Österreich. Londres, [1837]. An extract, translated from *Geschichte des Feldzuges von 1799*.
Lloyd.1617(7). d100.

Descriptions géographiques et récits de voyages et excursions en Suisse / Adolf Wäber. Berne, 1899. 2v. [Bibliographie nationale suisse; 3.]
Lloyd.985 (wanting v.2). d101.

[**Descriptions** of views painted by Henry A. Barker, John Burford and Robert Burford and exhibited at the Panorama, Strand, and the Panorama, Leicester Square.] London, 1814-43.
Lloyd.1590(2-35). d102.

Descriptive synopsis of the Roman Gallery, in the Egyptian Hall, Piccadilly. London, 1818. Ill.
Lloyd.1578(2). d103.

Descrizione della rinomata grotta di Adelsberg in Carniola. Adelsberg, 1891.
GB/A.802(9). d104.

Deserti di ghiaccio, oceani di sabbia: spedizioni in Persia, in Groenlandia, nel medio Atlante, traversata aerea del Sahara / Leonardo Bonzi. Milano, 1936. Ill., maps.
GB/B.437. d105.

The **desolate** Antarctic / Lord Mountevans. 2nd impr. London, 1950. Ill., maps, ports.
Lloyd.896. d106.

The **desperate** people / Farley Mowat. Rev ed. Toronto, 1977. Ill., maps, ports. Vol.2 of his *Death of a people — the Ihalmiut*.
GB/A.1762. d107.

Det gælder Grønland / Mads Lidegaard. København, 1968. Map.
GB/B.525(1). d108.

Det hängde på ett har / Wilfrid Noyce. Klippan, 1963. Ill. Translated from *They survived*.
GB/A.2143. d109.

Deucalion: collected studies of the lapse of waves, and life of stones / John Ruskin. Orpington, 1875-83. 8v.
GB.1880(17-8) (v.7-8). d110.

Deucalion: collected studies of the lapse of waves, and life of stones / John Ruskin. First supplement: The limestone Alps of Savoy: a study in physical geology / W. Gershom Collingwood. Orpington, 1884.
GB.1127. d111.

Deutsche Alpen-Zeitung. Neue Folge. Bd. 1 Nr.1-20, Jän.-Aug. 1881. Wien, 1881.
GB/B.150. d112.

Deutsche Alpenzeitung, zugleich Alpenfreund. Mai 1929, Mai 1932. München, 1929-32.
GB.1334(6-7). d113.

Deutsche am Nanga Parbat: der Angriff 1934 / Fritz Bechtold. München, [1935]. Ill., ports.
GB.1172. d114.

Deutsche am Nanga Parbat: der Angriff, 1934 / Fritz Bechtold. 9. Aufl. München, 1940. Ill., maps, ports.
GB/A.976. d115.

Deutsche Forscher im Südpolarmeer / Ernst Herrmann; Bericht von der Deutschen Antarktischen Expedition, 1938-1939. Berlin, 1941. Ill., maps.
GB/A.504. d116.

Die **deutsche** Himalajafahrt 1929 / Paul Bauer. Innsbruck, 1930. Ill. Pp.[1]-57 of the *Zeitschrift des Deutschen und Osterreichischen Alpenvereins*, Bd.61.
GB.1322(18[1]). d117.

Deutsche Himalaya Expedition, 1973: Besteigung des Dhaulagiri III 7715m.: [August 1973 bis Februar 1974] / herausgegeben von der

Deutschen Himalaya Expedition 1973. München, [1974?]. Ill., ports.
GB/B.366(13). d118.

Deutsche Kaukasus-Rundfahrten. I: In den swanetisch-tartarischen Alpen: die Münchner Fahrt im Jahre 1928 / Paul Bauer. II: Die Erschliessung der Swjetgarkette: die Wiener Fahrt im Jahre 1929 / Hugo Tomaschek. Innsbruck, 1930. Ill. Pp.[58]-81 of the *Zeitschrift des Deutschen und Osterreichischen Alpenvereins*, Bd. 61.
GB.1322(18[2]). d119.

Die **deutschen** Alpen: ein Handbuch für Reisende durch Tyrol, Oesterreich / Adolph Schaubach. Tl.5: Die südöstliche Abdachung vom Grossglockner bis Triest. Jena, 1847.
GB.801. d120.

Die **deutschen** Alpen: eine Wanderung durch Vorarlberg, Tirol, Salzburg und die oberbayrischen Gebirge / Karl Kollbach. 2. unveränderte Aufl. Köln, [ca 1900]. Ill.
GB/A.2145. d121.

Die **deutschredenden** Gemeinden im Grauen oder Oberen Bunde — Rhätien — der Schweiz / W.A.B. Coolidge. [Vienna, 1893.] Separat-Abdruck aus Nr.376 und 377 vom 9. und 23. Juni 1893 der *Oesterr. Alpen-Zeitung*.
GB.1340(3). d122.

Deux ascensions au Mont-Blanc: études de météorologie et d'histoire naturelle / Charles Martins. [Paris, 1865.]
Lloyd.1618(25). d123.

Deux ascensions au Mont-Blanc en 1869: recherches physiologiques sur le mal des montagnes / Louis Lortet. Paris, 1869.
GB.1162. d124.

Deux ascensions dans le massif du Mont Blanc / E.A. Martel. Berne, 1888. Ill. Extrait du *Jahrbuch S.A.C.*, Bd.23, 1887.
GB.1335(66); GB.1335(67). d125.

Deux ascensions scientifiques au Mont Blanc: leurs résultats immédiats pour la météorologie, la physique du globe et des sciences naturelles / Charles Martins. Paris, 1865. Extrait de la *Revue des deux mondes*, livraison du 15 mars 1865.
GB.1130(3); Lloyd.1620(16). d126.

Deux peintres suisses: Gabriel Lory le père, 1763-1840, et Gabriel Lory le fils, 1784-1846 / Conrad von Mandach. Lausanne, 1920. Ill., ports.
Lloyd.1519. d127.

Les **deux** pics Jocelme / W.A.B. Coolidge. Lyon, 1909. Extrait de la *Revue alpine* d'avril 1909.
GB.1340(20); Lloyd.1594(3). d128.

The **development** of mountain exploration / W. Martin Conway. London, 1894. Pp.[736]-45 of the *New Review*, vol.10 no.61, June 1894.
GB.1336(16). d129.

Deviating views on the glacial period especially in Europe / F. Arentz. Christiania, 1910.
GB.1332(1). d130.

Devonian osteolepiform fishes from East Greenland / Erik Jarvik. Copenhagen, 1985. [Meddelelser om Grønland. Geoscience; 13.]
GB/A.1818(13). d131.

Le **diable** des Dolomites / Tita Piaz; traduit par Félix Germain. [Paris], 1963. Ill. [Sempervivum; 39.]
GB/A.187. d132.

Diablerets bis Gemmi / bearbeitet von Hans Baumgartner [et al.]. Nachdruck der 3., neubearb. Aufl. des *Hochgebirgsführer durch die Berner Alpen* von W.A.B. Coolidge und H. Dübi. Bern, 1968. Ill., maps. [Hochgebirgsführer durch die Berner Alpen; 1.] Published by the Schweizer Alpenclub, Sektion Bern.
GB/A.989(1). d132.1.

Il **dialetto** trentino: dizionario trentino-italiano: florilegio di poesie e prose dialettali / Lionello Groff. Trento, 1955.
GB/A.1035(1). d133.

Diamir — kral vrchov: provovýstup Diamírskou stenou na severný vrchol Nanga Parbatu / Marián Sajnoha. Bratislava, 1981. Ill., maps.
GB/A.1992. d134.

Diario dell'alpinista: guida rapida alle capanne e rifugi alpini / Club Alpino Italiano, Sezione di Bergamo. [3a ed.]. Bergamo, 1929. Maps.
GB/A.1751; GB/A.835(2). d135.

Diario dell'alpinista: guida rapida alle capanne e rifugi alpini / Club Alpino Italiano, Sezione di Bergamo. [4a ed.]. Bergamo, 1930. Maps.
GB/A.1752. d135.1.

Diario dell'alpinista: guida rapida alle capanne e rifugi alpini / Club Alpino Italiano, Sezione di

Bergamo. 5a ed. Bergamo, 1931. Maps.
GB/A.1753.   d135.2.

Diario dell'alpinista: guida rapida alle capanne e rifugi alpini / Club Alpino Italiano, Sezione di Bergamo. 10a ed. Bergamo, 1937. Maps.
GB/A.1754.   d135.3.

Diario dell'alpinista: guida rapida alle capanne e rifugi alpini / Club Alpino Italiano, Sezione di Bergamo. 11a ed. Bergamo, 1949. Maps.
GB/A.1755.   d135.4.

Diary of a pedestrian in Cashmere and Thibet / Captain Knight. London, 1863. Ill.
GB.944.   d136.

The **diary** of a solitaire, or Sketch of a pedestrian excursion through part of Switzerland / [Edwin S. Rickman]. London, 1835.
GB.983; GB/A.621; Lloyd.934; Lloyd.934A,B.
                                              d137.

The **diary** of a tour to the Upper Engadine and northern Italy, made in the summer of 1898 / George O. Howell. Plumstead, 1899. Ill.
Lloyd.1605(3).   d138.

The **diary** of a traveller over Alps and Appenines, or Daily minutes of a circuitous excursion / [Murray Forbes]. London, 1824.
GB.1020; GB.1021; Lloyd.806; Lloyd.1114; Lloyd.1182.   d139.

The **diary** of an invalid: being the journal of a tour in pursuit of health in Portugal, Italy, Switzerland and France in 1817, 1818 and 1819 / Henry Matthews. 4th ed. London, 1824. 2v.
Lloyd.511-2.   d140.

Diary of travels and adventures in Upper India, from Bareilly, in Rohilcund, to Hurdwar, and Nahun, in the Himmalaya Mountains / C.J.C. Davidson. London, 1843. 2v.
GB.529-30.   d141.

Dictionnaire biographique des Genevois et des Vaudois / Albert de Montet. Lausanne, 1877-78. 2v.
Lloyd.1609(11-2).   d142.

Dictionnaire biographique des Hautes-Alpes: avec bibliographie, armoiries, sceaux et portraits / F. Allemand. Genève, 1973. Facsimile reprint of the Gap, 1911 ed.
GB/A.1417.   d143.

Dictionnaire de la montagne / Jacques Gautrat. Paris, 1970. [Microcosme.]
GB/A.835(4).   d144.

Dictionnaire géographique, historique et politique de la Suisse / [V.B. de Tscharner]. Nouv. éd., corr. et augm. Genève, 1776. 2v (in 1); map.
GB.556; GB/A.1366.   d145.

Dictionnaire géographique-statistique de la Suisse / Markus Lutz; traduit de l'allemand et revu par J.L.B. Leresche. Lausanne, 1836-37. 2v.
GB/A.617-8.   d146.

Dictionnaire historique, politique et géographique de la Suisse / Vincent Bernhard de Tscharner. Nouv. éd. augm. [by P.H. Mallet and J.S. Wyttenbach]. Genève, 1788. 3v; map.
Lloyd.752-4.   d147.

Dictionnaire savoyard / publié sous les auspices de la Société florimontane par A. Constantin, J. Désormaux. Marseille, 1973. Map. [Etudes philologiques savoisiennes.] Facsimile reprint of the Annecy, 1902 ed.
GB/A.1219.   d148.

Le **difficoltà** alpinistiche / Arturo Tanesini. Milano, 1946. [Montagna; 1.]
GB/A.1032.   d149.

Dinner 7th March: list of guests / Midland Association of Mountaineers. [Birmingham, 1959.]
GB.1322(8).   d150.

Directissime Pumori: sept guides savoyards dans l'Himalaya / récit recueilli par Josette Mélèze. Paris, [1973].
GB/A.2056.   d151.

La **direttissima** invernale alla nord dell'Eiger / Toni Hiebeler; traduzione di Spiro Dalla Porta Xidias e Franca Bearzi. Bologna, 1967. Ill. [Voci dai monti; 9.] Translated from *Die John Harlin-Route*.
GB/A.851.   d152.

Discorsi storici-filosofici sopra il Vesuvio estratti dal libro intitolato *Racconto storico filosofico del Vesuvio* / Giuseppe Maria Mecatti. Napoli, 1754. Ill.
GB/A.1301.   d153.

A **discourse** on the attraction of mountains, delivered at the anniversary meeting of the Royal Society, November 30, 1775 / Sir John Pringle. London, 1775.
GB.872; Lloyd.1621(6).   d154.

The **discovery** of a North-West passage by H.M.S. *Investigator*, Capt. R. M'Clure, during the years 1850-1851-1852-1853-1854 / Sir Robert MacClure; edited by Sherard Osborn. 4th ed. Edinburgh, 1865.
GB.257.   d155.

Disease pattern in Upernavik in relation to housing conditions and social group / Peter Bjerregaard and Beth Bjerregaard. Copenhagen, 1985. [Meddelelser om Grønland. Man & society; 8.]
GB/A.1820(8).   d156.

Dissertatio physica et mathematica de montium altitudine barometro metienda / auctore Christiano Henrico Damen. [The Hague], 1783.
GB/A.2105.   d157.

A **dissertation** on the passage of Hannibal over the Alps / by a member of the University of Oxford [i.e. Henry L. Wickham and John A. Cramer]. Oxford, 1820. Maps, facsim.
Lloyd.1585(2).   d158.

A **dissertation** on the passage of Hannibal over the Alps / Henry L. Wickham, J.A. Cramer. 2nd ed. London, 1818. Maps, facsim.
Lloyd.1027.   d159.

Dissertation sur la glace, ou Explication physique de la formation de la glace, & de ses divers phénomènes / Jean Jacques Dortous de Mairan. Paris, 1749. Ill.
GB.178.   d160.

Dix grandes montagnes: Snowdon — Ben-Nevis — Mount Cook — Cervin — Ushba — Mont-Blanc — Mont-Logan — Nanga-Parbat — Kangchenjunga — Mont-Everest / R.L.G. Irving; traduit par Claire Eliane Engel. Neuchâtel, 1945. Ill. Translated from *Ten great mountains*.
GB.1320(4).   d161.

Dizionarietto dei termini alpinistici e degli sport alpini. Milano, 1934. Published by the Club Alpino Italiano, Comitato Scientifico, Commissione Toponomastica.
GB/A.1050(4).   d162.

Dizionario del dialetto di Cortina d'Ampezzo / Vincenzo Menegus Tamburin. Vicenza, 1973. Ill.
GB/A.1312.   d163.

Dizionario enciclopedico dell'alpinismo e degli sport invernali / Fulvio Campiotti. Milano, 1970.

[I dizionari enciclopedici; 3.]
GB/A.526.   d164.

Dizionario geografico: de montibus, silvis, fontibus, lacubus, fluminibus, stagnis seu paludibus, et de nominibus maris / Giovanni Boccaccio; traduzione di Nicolo Liburnio. Torino, 1978. Ill. Translated from *De montibus*. Facsimile reprint of the Firenze, 1598 ed.
GB/A.1964(3).   d165.

Do glaciers excavate? / T.G. Bonney. [London, 1893.] Pp.[482]-504 of the *Geographical Journal*, June 1893.
GB/A.797(10).   d166.

Dobbiaco: paesaggio e storia fra i Monti Defregger e le Dolomiti: guida a passeggiate, escursioni ed ascensioni dal Corno Fana a Misurina / Walther Schaumann; traduzione di Carlo Milesi. Cortina, 1978. Ill. [Guida dell'escursionista.] Translated from *Toblach, Landschaft und Geschichte*.
GB/A.2017(4).   d167.

Doctor Kane of the Arctic seas / George W. Corner. Philadelphia, [1972]. Ill.
GB/A.1706.   d168.

Doe Crags and climbs round Coniston: a climbers' guide / George S. Bower. Barrow-in-Furness, [1922]. [Climbers' guides to the English Lake District; 1.] Published by the Fell and Rock Climbing Club of the English Lake District.
GB.1328(6).   d168.1.

Does it rest on the rock? London, [1880?]. [Every week; 256.]
GB.1326(52).   d169.

The **Doldenhorn** and Weisse Frau: ascended for the first time / Abraham Roth, Edmund von Fellenberg. Coblenz, 1863. Ill., map.
GB.1317(6); Lloyd.1285; Lloyd.1285A.   d170.

Doldenhorn und Weisse Frau: zum ersten Mal erstiegen / Abraham Roth, Edmund von Fellenberg. Coblenz, 1863. Ill., map.
GB.1130(1).   d171.

The **Dolomite** mountains: excursions through Tyrol, Carinthia, Carniola, & Friuli in 1861, 1862, & 1863: with a geological chapter / Josiah Gilbert, G.C. Churchill. London, 1864. Ill., map.
Lloyd.840; Lloyd.840A.   d172.

Dolomite strongholds: the last untrodden Alpine peaks / Joseph Sanger Davies. London, 1894. Ill., map.
Lloyd.651. d173.

Dolomite strongholds: the last untrodden Alpine peaks / Joseph Sanger Davies. 2nd ed. London, 1896. Ill., map.
Lloyd.401; Lloyd.401A. d174.

Dolomiten: Civettagruppe: ein Führer für Täler, Hütten und Berge / Andreas Kubin. München, 1981. Ill., maps. [Alpenvereinsführer. Reihe: Südliche Kalkalpen.]
GB/A.1965(10). d175.

Dolomiten: ein Führer durch die Täler, Orte und Berge der gesamten Dolomiten / Julius Gallhuber. Wien, 1929. 3v (in 1); ill., maps.
GB/A.1804. d176.

Dolomiten: Sellagruppe: ein Führer für Täler, Hütten und Berge / Egon Pracht. München, 1980. Ill., map. [Alpenvereinsführer. Reihe: Südliche Kalkalpen.]
GB/A.1965(9). d177.

Dolomiten Höhenroute Nr.2: von Brixen auf Bergpfaden nach Feltre / Sigi Lechner, Mario Brovelli. [N.p.], 1969. Maps. Published by the Verkehrsamt der Provinz Belluno.
GB/A.2018(13). d178.

Dolomiten-Kletterführer: die schönsten Berg- und Kletter-Fahrten in den Dolomiten / Gunther Langes. München, 1959-63. 3v; ill., maps.
GB/A.1676(17-9). d179.

The **Dolomites** / Samuel Hield Hamer. 2nd ed. London, 1910. Ill.
Lloyd.1109. d180.

The **Dolomites** / Th. Christomannos, F. Benesch; [translated by Marie Adametz]. 3rd ed. Vienna, [1925?]. Ill., map. Translated from *Die neue Dolomitenstrasse*.
GB/A.1799. d181.

Dolomiti / Dario Scarpa. Trento, 1984.
GB/A.2206. d182.

Dolomiti: [24 photographs]. Merano, [1940].
GB/A.2048(4). d183.

Dolomiti: con escursioni a Merano, al gruppo dell'Ortles e alla Madonna di Campiglio. Novi Ligure, 1935. Maps. [Guide italiane; 11.]
GB/A.1050(2). d184.

Dolomiti: genesi e fascino / Hermann Frass; testo geologico: P. Victor Welponer; [traduzione a cura di Willy Dondio]. [3rd ed.]. Bolzano, 1972. Ill. Translated from *Wunderwelt der Dolomiten*.
GB/B.372. d185.

Dolomiti: gruppo del Catinaccio — Dolomiti di Gardena e di Fassa — Pale di S. Martino — Dolomiti di Sesto / Remo Pedrotti. Calliano, 1970. Ill.
GB/B.337(4); GB/B.347. d186.

Dolomiti di Belluno: le vie 'attrezzate' del gruppo della Schiara, la Gusela del Vescovà / Piero Rossi. Bologna, 1964. Published by the Club Alpino Italiano, Sezione di Belluno.
GB/B.338(17). d187.

Dolomiti di Brenta / E. Castiglioni. Milano, 1949. Ill., maps. [Guida dei monti d'Italia.]
GB/A.2012. d188.

Dolomiti di Brenta / Pino Prati. Trento, 1926. Ill., maps. [Pubblicazione / Società degli Alpinisti Tridentini.]
GB/A.2019(2). d189.

Dolomiti di Cortina d'Ampezzo / Enrico Rossaro. Calliano, 1969. Ill., maps. [Montagne celebri.]
GB/B.346. d190.

Dolomiti di Sesto: escursionismo e vie normali di salita alle principali cime / Luca Visentini. Bolzano, 1983. Ill., maps.
GB/A.2135. d191.

Dolomiti e altri quadri / Francesco Sapori. Milano, 1940. Ill.
GB/A.1215. d192.

Dolomiti, il giardino delle rose: racconti, disegni, fotografie sulle montagne di Vaél, Vaiolet, Larsec, Antermoia, Valbona, Principe e Sciliar / Luca Visentini. Bolzano, 1983. Ill.
GB/B.626. d193.

Dolomiti, le vie ferrate: 60 percorsi attrezzati fra il gruppo di Brenta e le Dolomiti di Sesto / Reinhold Messner; versione italiana di Willy Dondio. 4a ed. italiana. Bolzano, 1981.
GB/A.2037. d194.

Dolomiti occidentali / iniziata dal Touring Club Italiano, in collaborazione col Club Alpino

Italiano. Milano, 1930. Ill., map. [Da rifugio a rifugio; 2.]
GB/A.961.   d195.

Le **Dolomiti** orientali: guida turistico-alpinistica sotto gli auspici della Sezione di Venezia del C.A.I. e della Fondazione Antonio Berti / Antonio Berti. 4a ed., aggiornamento della 3a ed. a cura di Camillo Berti con la collaborazione di Tito Berti e Carlo Gandini. Milano, 1971-73. 2v; ill., maps. [Guida dei monti d'Italia.]
GB/A.1945.   d196.

Domestic residence in Switzerland / Elizabeth Strutt. [London], 1842. 2v; ill.
GB.558-9; Lloyd.703-4.   d197.

The **Dominican** church of Santa Maria Novella at Florence: a historical, architectural, and artistic study / J. Wood Brown. Edinburgh, 1902. Ill.
GB.1274.   d198.

Door de bergwoestijnen van Azië: Karakorum, Aghil en Kuen Lun-gebergte / P.C. Visser. Rotterdam, 1931. Ill., maps.
GB/A.872.   d199.

Dörcherpack: Blätter aus einem bescheidenen Menschensein / Richard Bredenbrücker. Berlin, 1896.
GB/A.24.   d200.

Dove la neve cade d'està / Walter Maestri. 2a ed. Bologna, [1952]. Ill. [Le Alpi; 4.]
GB/A.822.   d201.

Dove nasce la luce — Monte Rosa: fotografie / Gianfranco Bini. Milano, 1981.
GB/B.606.   d202.

Dow Crag, Great Langdale and outlying crags / A.T. Hargreaves [et al.]. Manchester, 1938. [Climbing guides to the English Lake District; 4.] Published by the Fell and Rock Climbing Society of the English Lake District.
GB.48(4).   d203.

Down a crevasse. [London], 1860. Pp.615-7 of *All the Year Round*, Dec.6 1860.
GB.1880(24).   d204.

Down to a sunless sea / J.M. Boon. Edmonton, 1977. Maps.
GB/A.1816.   d205.

Downward bound: a mad guide to rock climbing / Warren 'Batso' Harding. Englewood Cliffs,

[1975]. Ill.
GB/A.1676(3).   d206.

Dr. Paccard's lost narrative: a note: with a facsimile of the prospectus of Dr. Paccard's book / Henry F. Montagnier. London, 1912. Reprinted from the *Alpine Journal*, Feb. 1912.
GB.1133(1); GB.1335(61).   d207.

Dr. Paccard's notebook. [London, 1934-57.] Extracts from and about the notebook from the *Alpine Journal* and from T.G. Brown and Sir G. de Beer's *The first ascent of Mont Blanc*.
GB.1755.   d208.

Il **Dragonet** (Alpi Marittime): vallone del Dragonet, vallone della Vagliotta, vallone di Lourousa / Bruno e Francesco Salesi. Cuneo, [1973]. Ill.
GB/B.377(2).   d209.

Drawing from nature: a series of progressive instructions in sketching, from elementary studies to finished views, with examples from Switzerland and the Pyrenees / George Barnard. London, 1865. Ill.
GB.1252.   d210.

Die **drei** letzten Jahrhunderte der Schweizer-geschichte: mit besondrer Berücksichtigung der geistigen und religiösen Zustände und der Sitten-geschichte / Heinrich Gelzer. Aarau, 1838-40. 3v.
GB/A.681-3.   d211.

Die **drei** letzten Probleme der Alpen: Matterhorn-Nordwand, Grandes Jorasses-Nordwand, Eiger-Nordwand / Anderl Heckmair. München, [1949]. Ill., map.
GB.807.   d212.

Drei und dreissig Jahre verschollen im Packeis: die arktische Freiballon: Expedition des Schweden Salomon August Andrée / Adrian Mohr [et al.]. Leipzig, 1930. Ill., maps.
GB/A.1638.   d213.

Du col Collon au col de Théodule / Marcel Kurz. 2e éd. Lausanne, 1930. [Guide des Alpes valaisannes; 2.] Published by the Schweizer Alpenclub.
GB.119.   d214.

Du col de Collon au col du Théodule / Heinrich Dübi; traduit de l'allemand, révisé et complété par A. Wohnlich; avec utilisation des *Climbers' Guides* et des manuscrits du Dr W.A.B. Coolidge et de Sir

Martin Conway. Genève, 1922. Ill. [Guide des Alpes valaisannes; 2.]
Lloyd.187; Lloyd.187A.   d215.

Du col de Théodule au Monte Moro. Du Strahlhorn au Simplon / Marcel Kurz. 2e éd. Kriens, 1937. 2v; maps. [Guide des Alpes valaisannes; 3a-b.] Published by the Schweizer Alpenclub.
GB.120-1.   d216.

Du côté de l'Aiguille Verte / Henri Isselin. [Grenoble], 1972. Ill. [Sempervivum; 56.]
GB/A.995(2).   d217.

Du lac de Garde aux Dolomites: itinéraires touristiques et de naturalisme / [textes touristiques: Silvio Ducati; textes sur le naturalisme: Benedetto Bonapace, Tullio Largaiolli; traduit par Wanda Quadrini Schir]. [Trento], 1968. Ill., maps.
GB/B.338(14).   d218.

Du Mont Blanc à l'Himalaya / Gaston Rébuffat. [Paris], 1955. Ill.
GB/B.602(5).   d219.

Du retrait et de l'ablation des glaciers de la vallée de Chamonix constatés dans l'automne de 1865. Note sur les traces et les terrains glaciaires aux environs de Baveno sur le Lac Majeur / Charles Martins. [Geneva, 1866.] Tiré des *Archives des sciences de la bibliothèque universelle*, juillet, 1866.
GB.883.   d220.

Du val d'Anniviers à Zermatt par le glacier de Zinal et le col du Trift: course exécutée en août 1868 / A. Wistaz. Genève, 1869.
GB/A.516(9).   d221.

Du vocabulaire des anciens voyageurs / M.A. de Lavis-Trafford. [N.p., 1955.] Extrait de la *Revue de Savoie*, no.4, juillet-août-sept. 1955.
GB/B.289(5).   d222.

Due soldi di alpinismo / Gianni Pieropan. Bologna, 1970. [Voci dai monti.]
GB/A.946.   d223.

Duemila metri della nostra vita / Fernanda e Cesare Maestri. 2a ed. Milano, 1972. Ill. [Vita vissuta.]
GB/A.974.   d224.

Dunkle Wand am Matterhorn: die abenteuerliche Geschichte der Nordwand / Toni Hiebeler. Frankfurt, 1962. Ill.
GB/A.410.   d225.

Durch Asiens Wusten: drei Jahre auf neuen Wegen in Pamir, Lopnor, Tibet und China / Sven Hedin. Leipzig, 1923. 2v; ill., maps.
GB/A.2144.   d226.

Durch das Berner Oberland / Friedrich Ebersold. Zürich, [1890?]. Ill. [Europäische Wanderbilder.]
GB/A.800(1).   d227.

Durch die Alpen: Kreuz- und Quer-Züge / L. Starklof. Leipzig, 1850.
GB/A.515(6).   d228.

Durch die Schweitz, Italien auch einige Oerter Deutschlandes und Franckreichs im 1685. und 86. Jahre gethaner Reise / Gilbert Burnet. Leipzig, 1688. 2v (in 1). Translated from *Some letters*.
GB/A.1403.   d229.

Durchs Schweizerland: Sommerfahrten in Gebirg und Thal / Woldemar Kaden. Gera, 1895. Ill.
GB/A.94.   d230.

The **Dutch** at the North Pole and the Dutch in Maine: a paper read before the New York Historical Society, 3d March, 1857 / J. Watts de Peyster. New York, 1857.
GB/B.440(8).   d231.

-E-

E.A. Martel 1859-1938: bibliographie / C. Chabert, M. de Courval. Autun, 1971. Ill. [Travaux scientifiques du Spéléo-club de Paris, C.A.F.]
GB/B.290(12). e001.

E.T. Compton: Maler und Bergsteiger zwischen Fels und Firn / herausgegeben von Ernst Bernt unter Mitwirkung des Osterreichischen Alpenvereins Museums, Innsbruck. Rosenheim, 1982. [Rosenheimer Raritäten.]
GB/B.623. e002.

E.W. Steeple, 1872-1940 / W.O. Duncan. [London, 1941.] Pp.43-4 of the *Climbers' Club Journal*, N.S. vol.6 no.3.
GB.1339(15[2]). e003.

The **Eagle**: a magazine supported by members of St. John's College. No.4-35, vol.6, April 1859-June 1869. Cambridge, 1859-69.
Lloyd.1619(1-24) (impf.). e004.

'The **Eagle**'s Nest' in the valley of Sixt: a summer home among the Alps: together with some excursions among the great glaciers / Alfred Wills. London, 1860. Ill., maps.
GB.484. e005.

'The **Eagle**'s Nest' in the valley of Sixt / Alfred Wills. 2nd ed. London, 1860.
GB.485; Lloyd.587; Lloyd.587A,B; Lloyd.612; Lloyd.612A,B. e006.

The **early** Alpine guides / Ronald Clark. London, 1949. Maps, ports.
GB.806. e007.

Early American mountaineers / Allen H. Bent. [Boston, 1909.] Ill., ports., facsims. Reprinted from *Appalachia*, vol.13 no.1.
GB.1332(12). e008.

The **early** attempts on Mont Blanc de Courmayeur from the Innominata basin / T. Graham Brown. [London, 1941.] Reprinted from the *Alpine Journal*, no.261-3, Nov. 1940-Nov. 1941.
GB.894; GB.1313(1) (pt.1 only). e009.

Early lady climbers / Claire Eliane Engel. [London, 1943.] Reprinted from the *Alpine Journal*, vol.54 no.266.
GB.1339(34). e010.

The **early** mountaineers / Francis Gribble. London, 1899. Ill., maps, ports., facsim.
GB.996; Lloyd.1009; Lloyd.1009A. e011.

Early records of the Col de St. Théodule, the Weissthor, the Adler, and other passes of the Zermatt district / Henry F. Montagnier. [London], 1918. Reprinted from the *Alpine Journal*, Feb. 1918.
GB.1313(8). e012.

The **early** Swiss pioneers of the Alps / Heinrich Dübi. [London, 1920-23.] Port. Pp.75-99, 224-34, 340-66 of vol.33, and pp.144-52 of vol.35 of the *Alpine Journal*.
GB.1748. e013.

Early travellers in the Alps / Sir Gavin de Beer. London, 1930. Ill., map.
Lloyd.924. e014.

Earth and the great weather: the Brooks Range / Kenneth Brower. San Francisco, [1971]. Ill., map. [The earth's wild places; 3.]
GB/B.510. e015.

East Switzerland including the Engadine and Lombard valleys / John Ball. New ed. London, 1876. Maps. [Ball's Alpine guides.]
GB/A.706. e015.1.

The **eastern** Alps, including the Bavarian Highlands, Tyrol, Salzkammergut, Styria, Carinthia, Carniola and Istria: handbook for travellers / Karl Baedeker. 6th ed. remodelled and augmented. Leipsic, 1888. Maps.
GB.75. e016.

The **eastern** Alps, including the Bavarian Highlands, the Tyrol, Salzkammergut, Styria and Carinthia / Karl Baedeker. 8th ed. Leipsic, 1895.
Lloyd.105. e017.

The **eastern** Alps, including the Bavarian Highlands, the Tyrol, Salzkammergut, Styria and Carinthia / Karl Baedeker. 12th ed. Leipsic, 1911.
Lloyd.106. e018.

Eastern crags / Harold Drasdo. Stockport, 1959. [Rock-climbing guides to the English Lake District; 2.] Published by the Fell and Rock Climbing Society of the English Lake District.
GB.50. e019.

Les **eaux** souterraines / Félix Trombe. 3e éd. [Paris], 1977. Ill. [Que sais-je?; 455.]
GB/A.2019(11). e020.

L'**écho** des Alpes: publication de la Section genevoise du Club alpin suisse. 1865-1924. Genève, 1865-1924. Also described as: publication des sections romandes. Subsequently amalgamated with *Jahrbuch des Schweizer Alpenclub* and *Alpina* to form *Die Alpen*.
GB/A.220-60.   e021.

L'**écho** des Alpes: index, 1865-1889 / Edouard Combe. Genève, 1892. Published by the Schweizer Alpenclub.
GB/A.261.   e022.

Echoes from the north: a collection of legends, yarns and sagas / Willis N. Bugbee. Syracuse, 1946.
GB/A.1663.   e023.

Eclaircissemens sur le projet de réforme pour le Collège de Genève / Horace Bénédict de Saussure. [Geneva], 1774.
GB.1316(14).   e024.

Economie et sociologie de la montagne: Albiez-le-Vieux en Maurienne / Placide Rambaud. Paris, 1962. Ill., maps. [Etudes et mémoires / Ecole pratique des hautes études (VIe section). Centre d'études économiques; 50.]
GB/A.2031(6).   e025.

Les **Ecrins** / Alain Girier. 2e éd. [N.p.], 1973. Ill.
GB/B.570(12).   e026.

Ecuador: all'ombra dei vulcani / P. Basaglia [et al.]. Venice, 1981.
GB/B.578.   e027.

Edelweiss / Francesco M. Parisi. Genova, 1894.
GB/A.938(6).   e028.

Edelweiss: an Alpine rhyme / Mary Lowe Dickinson. New York, 1876.
GB/A.176.   e029.

Edinburgh mountaineering song book / Edinburgh University Mountaineering Club. [Edinburgh], 1955.
GB.1329(27).   e030.

The **Edinburgh** Philosophical Journal. Vol.1-3,8, 1819-20,1823. Edinburgh, 1819-23.
Lloyd.833-6.   e030.1.

Edinburgh University Mountaineering Club song book. New ed. [Edinburgh, n.d.]
GB.1332(15).   e031.

Edward and Alfred's tour in France and Switzerland, in the year 1824. London, 1826. 2v.
GB.24-5.   e032.

Edward Whymper / Frank S. Smythe. London, 1940. Ill., maps, ports., facsims.
GB.999.   e033.

Egyptian Hall, Piccadilly. Mr Albert Smith's Ascent of Mont Blanc. [London, 1855?] A programme.
Lloyd.1609(2).   e034.

Eiger: trente jours de combat pour la 'Directissime' / Jörg Lehne, Peter Haag; traduction de Monique Bittebierre. Paris, 1967. Ill. Translated from *Eiger, Kampf um die Direttissima*.
GB/A.447.   e035.

L'**Eiger** (3975m.) / Paul Keller. [N.p.], 1972.
GB/B.570(13).   e036.

Eiger, parete nord — la morte arrampica accanto / Toni Hiebeler; traduzione di Spiro Dalla Porta Xidias e E. Erich Rieckhoff. Bologna, 1966. Ill. [Voci dai monti; 5.] Translated from *Eigerwand — der Tod klettert mit*.
GB/A.847.   e037.

Eighty years in New Zealand: embracing fifty years of New Zealand fishing / George Edward Mannering. Christchurch, 1943.
Lloyd.899.   e038.

Die **Eisgebirge** des Schweizerlandes / Gottlieb Sigmund Gruner. Bern, 1760. 3v (in 1); ill., maps.
GB.406; GB.479 (v.1 only); Lloyd.551-3.   e039.

Eisleben, or Stormont and Whitemont: an Alpine sketch / H. Schütz Wilson. [N.p., n.d.]
Lloyd.891.   e040.

Die **Eiszeit** in Norddeutschland / Felix Wahnschaffe. Berlin, 1910. Ill.
GB/A.1052(14).   e041.

Elegy for the fallen climbers / Michael Roberts. London, 1936. Pp.578-83 of the *London Mercury*, vol.33 no.198.
GB.1338(22).   e042.

The **elements** of optics: designed for the use of students in the university / James Wood. 5th ed. Cambridge, 1828.
GB/A.2107.   e043.

Elenco soci: 1° supplemento, Catalogo [della] Biblioteca sezionale, Ski Club / Club Alpino Italiano, Sezione di Milano. Milano, 1903.
GB/A.802(13). e044.

Eloge de Charles Bonnet / Jean Simon Lévesque de Pouilly. Lausanne, 1794.
Lloyd.1616(4). e045.

Emilia-Romagna / Umberto Toschi. Torino, 1961. Ill., maps. [Le regioni d'Italia; 7.]
GB/B.551. e046.

Empor! Georg Winklers Tagebuch: in memoriam: ein Reigen von Bergfahrten hervorragender Alpinisten von heute / Mitarbeiter: Otto Ampferer, Otto Bauriedl [et al.]; Herausgeber: Erich König. Leipzig, [1906]. Ill., ports., facsims.
GB.1236. e047.

En altitude / Pierre Scize. Grenoble, [1930]. Ill.
GB/A.1651. e048.

En la cima de las montañas y de la vida / Federico Reichert; [versión castellana de Rubén Dario]. Buenos Aires, 1967. Ill., map, port.
GB/A.2039. e049.

En la lando de la Blanka Monto / Léon Huot-Sordot; el la franca lingvo tradukis Dro. Noël. Paris, 1913. Ill., port. [Kolekto de Lingvo internacia.]
Lloyd.1611(2). e050.

En marche dans le Pilat du matin: randonnées pédestres sur les versants s.e. et s.o. du Pilat / Maison des jeunes et de la culture de Bourg-Argental, Syndicat d'initiative de St.-Genest-Malifaux. St. Etienne, 1972. Ill., maps.
GB/A.1270(10). e051.

En montagne: récits et souvenirs / C. Egmond d'Arcis. Genève, [1936].
GB/A.835(10). e052.

En pays fribourgeois: manuel du voyageur / Charles Cornaz-Vulliet. Fribourg, [1888]. Ill., map. [La Suisse romande en zig-zag; pt.1 sect.3.]
GB/A.962. e053.

En Savoie / Moise Hornung. Genève, 1872.
GB/A.455(5). e054.

En Suisse: le sac au dos / Albert Laporte. Paris, [ca 1870]. Ill.
GB/B.259. e055.

Encordées / Micheline Morin. Neuchâtel, [1936]. Ill. [Montagne.]
GB.1320(3); GB.1320(9). e056.

The **end** of a great mountain climber (Owen Glynne Jones) / Harold Spender. London, 1903. Ill., port. Pp.[81]-9 of the *Strand Magazine*, vol.25 no.145.
GB.1336(6). e057.

The **end** of a holiday, 1914 / Sir Alex. B.W. Kennedy. [N.p.], 1914.
GB.1306(18); Lloyd.1604(4). e058.

L'**enfant** des Alpes / Jeanne Cazin. 7e éd. Paris, 1909. Ill.
GB/A.1459(8). e059.

Engadin: Zeichnungen aus der Natur und dem Volksleben eines unbekannten Alpenlandes / Jakob Papon. St. Gallen, 1857.
GB/A.802(3). e060.

Das **Engadin** und sein Inn und seine Seen / Fr. Brügger, R. Gelpke, F. Frey-Fürst. St. Moritz, 1923. Ill.
GB/A.1115(1). e061.

L'**Engadine** / texte original de Hermann Hilt-brunner adapté de l'allemand par Joh. Widmer. Paris, 1929. Map. [Les Grisons; 3.]
GB/A.923. e062.

Engiadina terra fina / herausgegeben von Walter Amstutz; die Hauptmitarbeiter für Textliche Bearbeitung sind Emma Nater, Walter Schmidkunz [et al.]. 2. Aufl. München, 1937. Ill.
Lloyd.1486. e063.

England's liberty and prosperity under the administration of the Duke of Wellington, based on independence of election: illustrated in a memorial on the contest for Essex / T. Forster. 2nd ed. Colchester, 1830.
GB.697(2). e064.

The **English** moths and butterflies together with the plants, flowers, and fruits whereon they feed, and are usually found / Benjamin Wilkes. London, [1749]. Ill.
Lloyd.1516. e065.

An **English** mountaineer, A.W. Moore / Henry Eberli. Whitby, [1919?]. From the *Whitby Gazette* of Sept.5,12,19,26, 1919.
Lloyd.1616(9). e066.

The **Englishman** in the Alps: being a collection of English prose and poetry relating to the Alps / edited by Arnold Lunn. London, 1913.
GB.143. e067.

Die **Ennsthaler** Alpen / Heinrich Hess. Die Hochschwab Gruppe / Dr. August von Böhm. Schneebert und Raxalpe / Edmund Forster. [Berlin, 1893.] Pp.[366]-414 of *Erschliessung der Ostalpen*, Bd.1.
GB.1372. e068.

An **enquiry** into the ancient routes between Italy and Gaul: with an examination of the theory of Hannibal's passage of the Alps by the Little St. Bernard / Robert Ellis. Cambridge, 1867. Maps.
Lloyd.1118. e069.

Entdeckungen und Abenteuer in den Polar-Seen, nebst Erläuterungen über Clima, geologische Beschaffenheit und Natur-Geschichte dieser Gegenden, so wie auch einem ausführlichen Bericht über den Wallfischfang / von den Professoren Leslje, Jameson und Hugh Murray. Leipzig, 1834. Ill., map. Translated from *Narrative of discovery and adventure*.
GB/A.2073. e070.

Entre Arc et Stura / W.A.B. Coolidge. Lyon, 1908. Extrait de la *Revue alpine* de novembre-décembre 1908.
GB.1340(18). e071.

Entre Isère et Doire / W.A.B. Coolidge. Lyon, 1912. Extrait de la *Revue alpine* de juin, juillet et août 1912.
GB.1340(27). e072.

Entre le col de Collon et le col de Valcournera / W.A.B. Coolidge. Aoste, 1914. Extrait du *Bulletin de la Société de la flore valdôtaine*, no.10.
GB.1340(38). e073.

Entre terre et ciel / Gaston Rébuffat. [Grenoble], 1962. Ill.
GB.1080. e074.

Entre Valloire et Briançonnais / W.A.B. Coolidge. Grenoble, 1914.
GB.1340(36). e075.

Entstehen und Vergehen der Alpen: eine allgemeinverständliche Einführung besonders für Bergsteiger und Freunde der Alpen / Wilfried von Seidlitz. Stuttgart, 1926. Ill., maps.
GB/A.980. e076.

Die **Entstehung** der Alpen / Eduard Süss. Wien, 1875.
GB/B.312(7). e077.

Die **Entstehung** der Alpenkarten / Eugen Oberhummer. [Munich], 1901. Facsims. Pp.[21]-45 of the *Zeitschrift des Deutschen und Osterreichischen Alpenvereins*, Bd. 32.
GB.1322(17[1]). e078.

Die **Entwicklung** und Verstaatlichung der Gotthardbahn: Inaugural-Dissertation / Max Sigmund Wey. Luzern, 1914.
GB/A.1220. e079.

Environmental regeneration in Himalaya: concepts and strategies / edited by J.S. Singh. Naini Tal, 1985. Ill., maps.
GB/A.2205. e080.

Epics of the Alps / C.F. Meade. London, 1937. 2v. Pp.268-81, 417-25 of the *Cornhill Magazine*, vol.156 no.932-3.
GB.1338(23-4). e081.

Episoden aus Reisen durch das südliche Deutschland, die westliche Schweiz, Genf und Italien in den Jahren 1801, 1802, 1803 nebst Anhangen vom Jahr 1805 / Friederike Brun. Zürich, 1806-09. 2v.
GB/A.692-3. e082.

Episodes of two seasons: 1914, 1919: with the first ascent of the French, or north face of the Col de Bionnassay / R.W. Lloyd. London, 1921. Ill. Read before the Alpine Club and reprinted from the *Alpine Journal*, November 1920.
Lloyd.1602(26); Lloyd.1659(1). e083.

An **epitome** of fifty years' climbing / Claude Wilson; edited by H.F. Montagnier. [N.p.], 1933.
GB.1333(6); Lloyd.1618(26). e084.

L'**épopée** alpestre: histoire abrégée de la montagne et de l'alpinisme de l'antiquité à nos jours / Charles Gos. Neuchâtel, [1944].
GB.1327(17); GB.1327(18). e085.

L'**épopée** de l'Everest / Sir Francis Younghusband; traduction de J. et F. Germain. Grenoble, 1947. Ill., maps, ports. Translated from *The epic of Mount Everest*.
Lloyd.1604(6). e086.

La **epopeya** del Everest / Sir Francis Younghusband; traducción por M. Manent. Barcelona, 1946. Ill., maps, ports. Translated from *The epic of*

Mount Everest.
Lloyd.943.   e087.

The **Equatorial** Andes and mountaineering.
[London, 1892.] Pp.348-71 of the *Quarterly Review,*
October 1892.
GB.1880(41).   e088.

Equipment for mountaineers: report of the
Special Committee on Equipment for
Mountaineers, [Alpine Club]. London, 1892.
Lloyd.1609(4).   e089.

Erdkunde der schweizerischen Eidsgenossen-
schaft: ein Handbuch für Einheimische und
Fremde / Gerold Meyer von Knonau. 2., ganz
umgearbeitete, stark vermehrte Aufl. Zürich,
1938-39. 2v.
GB/A.64-5.   e090.

Erfolg am Kantsch 8438m.: die Himalaya-
Expedition des Deutschen und Osterreichischen
Alpenvereins / Günter Sturm. München, 1975. Ill.
GB/A.1597(2).   e091.

Erhvervelse av statshøihet over polarområdet /
Gustav Smedal. Oslo, 1930.
GB/A.1845.   e092.

Erinnerungen / Friedrich von Matthisson;
[edited by J.H. Fuessli]. Zurich, 1810-16. 5v; ill.
GB/A.591-5.   e093.

Erinnerungen an die Rigi / Gerold Meyer von
Knonau. St. Gallen, 1836.
GB/A.801(1).   e094.

Erinnerungen aus meiner dritten Schweizerreise
/ Sophie von La Roche. Offenbach, 1793. Ill.
GB/A.562.   e095.

Erinnerungen eines Bergführers / Christian
Klucker; herausgegeben und mit Lebensbild
versehen von Ernst Jenny. 2. verb. Aufl. Zürich,
[1930]. Ill.
GB.496.   e096.

Die **Erkundung** des Mustaghpasses im Kara-
korum-Himalaya / Aug. C.F. Ferber. Innsbruck,
1905. Ill. Sonderabdruck aus der *Zeitschrift des
Deutschen und Osterreichischen Alpenvereins*, Bd.36,
1905.
GB.1317(12).   e097.

Erläuterungen zur geologischen Übersichtskarten
der nordöstlichen Alpen: ein Entwurf zur vorzu-
nehmenden Bearbeitung der physikalischen

Geographie und Geologie ihres Gebietes / A. von
Morlot. Wien, 1847. Ill., map.
GB/A.71; GB/A.1675(4).   e098.

Erlebnisse und Gedanken eines alten Bergsteigers, 1880-1930 / Charles Simon. Zürich,
[1932]. Ill., ports.
GB.831.   e099.

Erlebte Berge / Willy Furter. Zürich, [1967]. Ill.
GB/B.122.   e100.

Erlebtes und Erdachtes / Franz Nieberl.
München, 1925.
GB/A.84.   e101.

Die **Eroberung** der Alpen / Wilhelm Lehner.
München, [1924]. Ill.
GB.1218.   e102.

Die **Eroberung** der Berge: ein Buch vom
Abenteuer des Bergsteigens / Ludwig Bühnau.
Wien, 1969. Ill., maps.
GB/A.440.   e103.

Die **Eroberung** des Nordpols: Schilderung der
Fahrten und Entdeckungsreisen nach den Polar-
gebieten. Neue, bis zur Auffindung des Nordpols
ergänzte Ausgabe für die Jugend / dargestellt von
D. Haek. Berlin, [ca 1900].
GB/A.2201.   e104.

Gli **eroi** del Chomolungma / Massimo Mila,
Tensing Norkey. [Turin, 1954.] Ill. [Nuova Atlan-
tide; 2.]
GB/A.1228.   e105.

Eroismo e tragedia sul Monte Api / Piero
Ghiglione. Milano, 1954. Ill., map.
GB.687.   e106.

Die **Erschliessung** der Dauphiné-Alpen und
Besteigung der Barre des Ecrins / Karl Schulz.
München, [1886]. Ill. Separat-Abdruck aus der
*Zeitschrift des Deutschen und Oesterreichischen
Alpenvereins.*
GB/A.181(1).   e107.

Die **Erschliessung** der Ostalpen / unter
Redaction von E. Richter; herausgegeben vom
Deutschen und Oesterreichischen Alpenverein.
Berlin, 1893-94. 3v; ill.
GB/B.304-6.   e108.

Die **Erschliessung** des Himalaya: eine Skizze /
Marcel Kurz; übersetzt von Paul Montandon.

Bern, 1935. Ill., maps. Sonderabdruck aus *Die Alpen*, Jahrg.9 Hft.7,9-11, 1933.
GB.1339(1). e109.

Der **erste** bekannte Ubergang über den Allalinpass / Adolf Wäber. [Bern, 1904.] Pp.358-61 of the *Jahrbuch des Schweizer Alpenclub*, Jahrg.39.
GB.1881(48). e110.

Die **erste** deutsche Nordpolar-Expedition im Jahre 1868 / K. Koldewey. Gotha, 1871. Ill., maps. [Petermann's Geographischen Mittheilungen. Ergänzungsheft; 28.]
GB/A.2161. e111.

Die **erste** — direkte — Ersteigung des Montblanc vom Brenvagletscher: route de la Sentinelle, Schildwache-Route, 1. und 2. September 1927 / T. Graham Brown. Wien, 1929. Pp.70-7 of *Osterreichische Alpenzeitung*, April 1929, Folge 1048.
GB.1339(16). e112.

Die **erste** — direkte — Ersteigung des Montblanc vom Brenvagletscher: route de la Sentinelle, Schildwache-Route, 1. und 2. September 1927 / T. Graham Brown. [Vienna, 1929.] Proof sheets.
GB.1339(17-9). e113.

Eine **Ersteigung** der Ortelsspitze / Anton von Ruthner; mitgetheilt in der Versammlung der k.k. Geographischen Gesellschaft in Wien am 15 Juni, 1858. [Vienna, 1858.]
GB.1130(4). e114.

Die **ersten** fünfundzwanzig Jahre des Schweizer Alpenclub: Denkschrift / im Auftrag des Centralcomités verfasst von Ernst Buss. Glarus, 1889.
GB/A.801(11). e115.

Die **ersten** fünfzig Jahre des Schweizer Alpenclub: Denkschrift / im Auftrag des Centralcomitées verfasst von Heinrich Dübi. Bern, 1913. Ill., ports.
GB/B.313(3). e116.

Eryri, the mountains of longing / Amory Lovins; edited by David R. Brower. San Francisco, [1971]. Ill., map. [The earth's wild places; 5.]
GB/B.509. e117.

Escalade dans la Vallée Etroite: Paroi des Militi, Tour Germaine, Croix de Refuge / Syndicat des guides de la Guisane. Villeneuve-la-Salle, [ca 1962]. Ill. Based on *Le palestre torinesi di arrampicamento* by Arturo Rampini.
GB/A.1350(12). e118.

Escalades / Edward Whymper. Neuchâtel, [ca 1946]. Ill. [Montagne.]
GB/A.1297. e119.

Escalades: guide des parois, région de Montréal / Bernard Poisson. Montréal, 1971. Ill., map.
GB/A.1883(2). e120.

Escalades dans le massif de la Sainte-Baume: Bartagne, Beguines / Alexis Lucchesi. Pau, 1976. Ill.
GB/A.1580(6). e121.

Escalades dans le massif des Calanques: Devenson, Gardiole / Alexis Lucchesi. Pau, 1976.
GB/A.1580(5). e122.

Escalades dans le massif des Calanques: en Vau / Alexis Lucchesi. 2e éd. Pau, 1976. Ill.
GB/A.1580(4). e123.

Escalades dans le massif des Calanques: les Goudes, St-Michel / Alexis Lucchesi. Pau, [1977]. Ill.
GB/A.1580(2). e124.

Escalades dans le massif des Calanques: Sormiou / Alexis Lucchesi. Pau, 1977. Ill.
GB/A.1580(3). e125.

Escalades dans le massif du Luberon: falaises de Buoux / Mutuelle Sports, Loisir, Culture, Section alpinisme et escalade. Marseille, [1974].
GB/A.1580(7). e126.

Escalades dans les Calanques: Devenson, Riou, Muraille de Chine, Sainte-Baume / Ph. Hiély. Marseille, [1973]. Maps.
GB/A.1350(4). e127.

Escalades dans les Calanques: en Vau, Vallon des Rampes / Ph. Hiély. Marseille, [1973]. Maps.
GB/A.1350(2). e128.

Escalades dans les Calanques: la Grande Candelle, le Candellon, le Socle, la Muraille du Cap Gros, la Cathédrale / Ph. Hiély. Marseille, [ca 1980]. Ill.
GB/A.1281(5); GB/A.2023(9). e129.

Escalades dans les Calanques: Marseille-Veyre, Vallon des Aiguilles / Ph. Hiély. Marseille, [1973]. Maps.
GB/A.1350(3). e130.

Escalades en Chartreuse et Vercors / Serge Coupé. Tom.1: Chartreuse, Vercors nord. [Paris],

1973. Ill., maps.
GB/A.1201. e131.

Escalades et escapades dans les Alpes / Joseph
Corin. Liége, 1904. Ill.
Lloyd.1606(3). e132.

Escursioni da Pontedilegno e dintorni / Lino
Pogliaghi. Bologna, 1980. Ill., map. [Itinerari
alpini; 52.]
GB/A.1589(27). e133.

Escursioni ed arrampicate nel Canavese /
Alessandro Gogna, Gian Piero Motti. Bologna,
1980. Ill., maps. [Itinerari alpini; 48.]
GB/A.1589(24) (v.1 only). e134.

Escursioni in Val d'Ansiei: le Dolomiti di Auronzo
di Cadore / Gianni Pais Becher. Bologna, 1976. Ill.,
map. [Itinerari alpini; 30.]
GB/A.1589(2). e135.

Escursioni in Val di Fassa / Alessandro Gogna.
Bologna, 1973. Ill., map. [Itinerari alpini; 11.]
GB/A.1199(15). e136.

Escursioni in Valsavarenche / Giovanni Canziani,
Carlo Colnago. Bologna, 1982. [Itinerari alpini;
56.]
GB/A.1589(32). e137.

Escursioni nei parchi alpini: 60 incontri con la
natura protetta dall'Argentera alle Alpi Giulie /
Oscar Casanova. Torino, 1977. Ill. [Biblioteca della
montagna; 5.]
GB/A.1966(1). e138.

Escursioni nelle Alpi Giulie orientali (vzhodne
Julijske Alpe) / Piero Rossi, Stanislav Gilić.
Bologna, 1973. Ill., map. [Itinerari alpini; 10.]
GB/A.1199(14). e139.

Escursioni nelle Grigne / Giancarlo Mauri.
Bologna, 1976. Ill., maps. [Itinerari alpini; 27.]
GB/A.1468(20). e140.

L'**esercito** italiano tra la 1ª e la 2ª guerra mon-
diale, novembre 1918-giugno 1940. Roma, 1954.
GB/A.2043. e141.

Eskimoland speaks / William B. Van Valin.
Caldwell, Idaho, 1941. Ill., ports. At head of title:
Midnight sunlight and nocturnal noon.
GB/A.1782. e142.

The **Eskimos** of Bering Strait, 1650-1898 /
Dorothy Jean Ray. Seattle, 1975. Ill.
GB/A.1649. e143.

Esperienze intorno alla generazione degl'insetti /
Francesco Redi. Firenze, 1668. Ill.
Lloyd.1247. e144.

Esplorazioni polari, 1773-1938 / Nino Bussoli.
Milano, [1942]. Ill., maps, ports.
GB/A.1578. e145.

Essai de recherche d'un déterminisme des
comportements humains dans un environnement
austral (Territoire des Terres Australes et Antarctiques Françaises): travail effectué au cours
d'une mission à l'Ile de la Nouvelle-Amsterdam,
pendant la campagne 1960-1962 / J. Bessuges.
Paris, 1963. Published by the Comité national
français des recherches antarctiques.
GB/B.113. e146.

Essai historique sur la destruction de la Ligue et
de la liberté helvétiques / Jacques Mallet du Pan.
[London, 1798.] Extrait du *Mercure britannique*, oct.
1798.
GB/A.801(5). e147.

Essai statistique sur le canton de Vallais /
Philippe Sirice Bridel. Zurich, 1820. Ill., map.
Lloyd.35. e148.

Essai statistique sur le canton de Vaud / Philippe
Sirice Bridel. Nouv. éd., rev. et augm. Zurich, 1818.
Ill., map.
Lloyd.13. e149.

Essai sur les glaciers et sur le terrain erratique du
bassin du Rhône / Jean de Charpentier. Lausanne,
1841. Ill., map.
GB.826; Lloyd.880. e150.

Essai sur les soulèvemens jurassiques du
Porrentruy: description géognostique de la série
jurassique et théorie orographique du soulève-
ment / J. Thurmann. Paris, 1832-36. 2v (in 1);
maps.
GB/B.406. e151.

Essai sur les usages des montagnes, avec une
lettre sur le Nil / Elie Bertrand. Zuric, 1754.
GB.557; Lloyd.678. e152.

Essais d'autographie / R.T. [i.e. Rodolphe
Töpffer]. Genève, 1849. Ill.
Lloyd.1567(2). e153.

An **essay** on the beneficent distribution of the sense of pain / G.A. Rowell. 2nd ed., with notes. London, 1862.
Lloyd.1583(10). e154.

Essay on the origin, symptoms, and treatment, of cholera morbus, and of other epidemic disorders, with a view to the improvement of sanitary regulations / T. Forster. 2nd ed. London, 1831.
GB.697(4). e155.

An **essay** to direct and extend the inquiries of patriotic travellers: with further observations on the means of preserving the life, health and property of the inexperienced in their journies / Count Leopold von Berchtold. London, 1789. 2v.
Lloyd.398-9. e156.

The **essential** R.B. Cunninghame Graham / selected, with an introduction and preface, by Paul Bloomfield. London, 1952. Map.
GB.497. e157.

Estimates for 1900 and balance sheet for 1899 / Geological Society. [London], 1900.
Lloyd.1605(21). e158.

... **et** la montagne conquit l'homme: histoire du développement de l'alpinisme / [edited by Myrtil Schwartz]. Paris, 1931. Ill.
GB/A.205. e159.

L'**état** de la Suisse, écrit en 1714 / Temple Stanyan; [translated by chevalier Schaub]. Amsterdam, 1714. Translated from *An account of Switzerland*.
GB.160; Lloyd.340. e160.

L'**état** et les délices de la Suisse, en forme de relation critique / par plusieurs auteurs célèbres; [edited by Johann G. Altmann]. Amsterdam, 1730. 4v; ill., map.
GB/A.1689. e161.

L'**état** et les délices de la Suisse, ou Description helvétique historique et géographique / [edited by Johann G. Altmann]. Nouv. éd. corr. & augm. Basle, 1764. 4v; ill., maps.
Lloyd.176-9. e162.

L'**état** et les délices de la Suisse / [edited by Johann G. Altmann]. Nouv. éd. corr. & augm. Basle, 1776. 4v.
Lloyd.116-9. e163.

L'**état** et les délices de la Suisse / [edited by Johann G. Altmann]. Neuchâtel, 1778. 2v.
Lloyd.1279-80. e164.

Eternal Himalaya / H.P.S. Ahluwalia. New Delhi, 1982. Ill., maps.
GB/B.627. e165.

The **eternal** ice / K.T. McNish. [Cape Town, 1971.] Ill.
GB/A.1585. e166.

Ethnological collections from the Northwest Passage / Kaj Birket-Smith. New York, 1976. Ill. [Thule expedition, 5th, 1921-1924. Report; vol.6 no.2.]
GB/A.1830. e167.

Etoiles et tempêtes — six faces nord / Gaston Rébuffat. Paris, 1955. Ill. [Sempervivum; 24.]
GB.1332(7). e168.

Etrennes helvétiennes et patriotiques. No.5-37, 1788-1819. Lausanne, 1788-1819. Wanting no.7, 9-10, 15-6, 19, 22, 27, 32-4, 36.
GB/A.1178-98; Lloyd.180 (another copy of no. 37). e169.

Etrennes sentimentales et champêtres / [François A.A. Gonthier, Louis F. Gautenon, Gabriel Antoine Mieville]. Lausanne, 1795.
GB/A.741. e170.

Etudes administratives sur les Landes, ou Collection de mémoires et d'écrits relatifs à la contrée renfermée entre la Garonne et l'Adour / le bon. d'Haussez. Bordeaux, 1826.
GB/A.2104(1). e171.

Etudes de bibliographie alpine sur les périodiques de 1892 / H. Ferrand. Grenoble, 1893. Extrait de l'*Annuaire de la Société des touristes du Dauphiné*, année 1892.
GB.1333(39). e172.

Etudes de littérature alpestre et La marmotte au collier / Eugène Rambert. Lausanne, 1889.
GB/A.2150. e173.

Etudes glaciaires / F.A. Forel. Genève, 1884-89. 4v; ill. Extrait des *Archives des sciences physiques et naturelles*, tom.12 no.6, tom.17 no.6, tom.18 no.7, tom.21 no.1.
GB/A.793(6), GB/A.514(3), GB/A.793(8,13). e174.

Etudes sur l'orographie et l'hydrographie des Alpes de Savoie / Etienne Ritter; communication faite à la Société de géographie de Genève le 22 mars 1895. Genève, 1895. Extrait du *Globe*, tom.34.
GB/A.514(12). e175.

Etudes sur les glaciers / Louis Agassiz. Neuchâtel, 1840. 2v. Wanting the atlas.
Lloyd.1380.   e176.

Das **Europa-Reisebuch**: die Alpenländer: Schweiz, Osterreich, Oberitalien, Südostfrankreich / Theodor Müller-Alfeld. Berlin, [1958]. Ill.
GB/A.428.   e177.

[**European** Alps] / Shiro Shirahata. [Tokyo], 1985. Ill.
GB/B.648.   e178.

The **eventful** voyage of H.M. Discovery Ship *Resolute* to the Arctic regions in search of Sir John Franklin / George F. MacDougall. London, 1857. Ill., maps.
GB.995.   e179.

Everest: a guide to the climb: chart. London, [1953?].
GB.1326(16).   e180.

Everest: ein Bildbericht der Schweizerischen Stiftung für Alpine Forschungen. Zürich, 1953. Ill., maps, ports.
Lloyd.1450.   e181.

Everest: is it conquered? / S.M. Goswami. Calcutta, [1954].
Lloyd.1616(19).   e182.

Everest: relazione fotografica / pubblicata dalla Fondazione Svizzera per Esplorazioni Alpine; [traduzione di Enrico Rivoire; revisione alpinistica di Pietro Meciani]. Milano, 1953. Ill., map.
GB/B.590.   e183.

Everest: the challenge / Sir Francis Younghusband. London, 1936. Ill.
GB.824.   e184.

Everest: the unfinished adventure / Hugh Ruttledge. London, 1937. Ill., maps, ports.
GB.1210; Lloyd.1354.   e185.

Everest 1933 / Hugh Ruttledge. London, 1934. Ill., maps.
GB/A.1927.   e186.

Everest 1933 / Hugh Ruttledge. London, [1934]. A prospectus.
GB.1318(22).   e187.

Everest 1952 / André Roch; publié sous les auspices de la Fondation suisse pour explorations alpines et du Comité himalayen de Genève. Genève, 1952.
GB.1334(26).   e188.

L'**Everest** (Chomo-Lungma): la più alta montagna del mondo: sua conoscenza e sua conquista / Manfredo Vanni. Torino, 1947. Ill. Sotto gli auspici della Sezione di Torino del Club Alpino Italiano.
GB/A.1976.   e189.

Everest, notre conquête? / Wilfrid Noyce; traduction de J. et F. Germain. [Paris], 1958. Ill. Translated from *South Col*.
GB/A.186.   e190.

The **everlasting** hills / James Waller. Edinburgh, 1939. Ill.
GB.693.   e191.

Evolution de l'alpinisme dans les Alpes françaises: thèse: essai de bibliographie alpine / Arthur Raymann. Grenoble, 1912.
GB/A.1076.   e192.

L'**évolution** de la cartographie de la région du Mont-Cenis et de ses abords aux XVe et XVIe siècles: étude critique des méthodes de travail des grands cartographes du XVIe siècle: Fine, Gastaldi, [et al.] / M.A. de Lavis-Trafford. Chambéry, 1950. Ill., maps.
GB/B.14.   e193.

Ewige Berge: Erlebnisse und Geschichte / Josef Ittlinger. München, 1924.
GB.355.   e194.

An **exalted** horn / [H. Schütz Wilson]. London, 1873. Pp.97-117 of his *Studies and romances*.
GB.1881(41).   e195.

The **Excitement**, or A book to induce young people to read / edited by Robert Jamieson. 1832,1838-41. Edinburgh, 1831-41.
Lloyd.60 (1832); GB.36-9 (1838-41).   e196.

The **Excitement**. N.S. Edinburgh, 1847. Containing an account of the ascent of the Matterhorn by Mr Speer.
Lloyd.59.   e196.1.

Une **excursion** à Chamouny en 1790 / Victor Augerd. Impressions d'une ascensionniste. Un séjour à Retord / Henriette d'Angeville. Souvenirs des fêtes de Sion et de Genève / [Victor Augerd, the Younger]; [edited by Victor Augerd, the Younger.] Villefranche, 1886. Tirage à part du *Bulletin de la Section de l'Ain du Club alpin*, no.1. Lloyd.1624(7). e197.

Excursion A1, Spitzbergen / Gerard de Geer. Stockholm, 1912. Ill., ports. Extrait du *Compte rendu du XIe Congrès géologique international*. GB.1335(6). e198.

Une **excursion** au Mont-Blanc / J.C. Ducommun. Genève, 1858. Ill. GB.637; GB.890(1). e199.

Une **excursion** au Mont-Blanc / J.C. Ducommun. 2e éd. Genève, 1859. Ill. GB.890(2); Lloyd.1581(11); Lloyd.1581(11)A,B,C. e200.

Excursion dans le Val d'Illiers, par Samoëns, le col de Goléze et le col de Couz, du 17 au 19 juillet 1858 / F.T. [i.e. F. Thioly]. [N.p., 1858?] Ill. Lloyd.945. e201.

Excursion dans les mines du Haut Faucigny, et description de deux nouvelles routes pour aller sur le Buet & le Breven, avec une notice sur le Jardin / Berthoud van Berchem. Lausanne, 1787. Lloyd.493. e202.

Excursions et escalades de la Dent du Midi au Buet / Auguste Wagnon. Lausanne, 1895. Ill., map. Lloyd.417. e203.

Excursions et séjour de M. Agassiz sur la mer de Glace du Lauteraar et du Finsteraar, en société de plusieurs naturalistes / E. Desor. [Geneva, 1841.] Ill. Extrait de la *Bibliothèque universelle de Genève*, n.s. tom.32, 1841. GB/A.181(13). e204.

Excursions et séjours dans les glaciers et les hautes régions des Alpes, de M. Agassiz et de ses compagnons de voyage / E. Desor. Neuchâtel, 1844. Ill., map, ports. GB.253; GB.659; Lloyd.376. e205.

Excursions et sensations pyrénéennes: cimes ariégeoises / Jean d'Ussel. Paris, 1901. Ill. GB/A.1645. e206.

Excursions in Dauphiné / R.C. Nichols. London, 1862. Lloyd.1620(9). e207.

Excursions in Dauphiné: being the passage of the Col de la Tempe and the Col de l'Echauda / R.C.

Nichols. London, 1862. Ill., map. From *Peaks, passes and glaciers*, ser.2 vol.2. Lloyd.1618(24). e208.

Excursions in Switzerland / Fenimore Cooper. Paris, 1836. 2v. Originally published as *Sketches of Switzerland*. GB.613 (bound in 1); GB.718 (bound in 1); Lloyd. 610-1. e209.

Excursions in the Graian Alps: the Grand Apparei and the Bec d'Invergnuon / R.C. Nichols. London, 1865. Map. Lloyd.719. e210.

Exhibition of Alpine paintings at the [Alpine] Club rooms, London, December 8 to December 31, 1930: catalogue. London, 1930. GB.1313(11). e211.

Exhibition of Alpine photographs / Alpine Club. Dec. 1927, 1928, 1931. London, 1927-31. GB.1321(45-7). e212.

Exhibition of Swiss coloured prints lent by members of the Alpine Club and their friends: December 1924: catalogue. London, 1924. Ill. GB.1306(3); GB.1306(4); Lloyd.874; Lloyd.874A; Lloyd.1611(9). e213.

Expedición Alpamayo 72, Andes del Perú. [N.p., 1972?] Ill., map. Published by the Club Excursionista de Gracia. GB/B.390(7). e214.

Expedición navarra al Himalaya 79: Dhaulagiri 8.172 / Gregorio Ariz Martinez. Pamplona, 1979. Ill., maps. GB/B.536. e215.

An **expedition** across the Rocky Mountains into British Columbia, by the Yellow Head or Leather Pass: read before the British Association / Viscount Milton, W.B. Cheadle. London, [1866?]. Lloyd.892. e216.

Expedition against the pirates of the Nicobar Islands. [London, 1867.] Lloyd.1583(11). e217.

L'**expédition** au pôle Nord / Gustave Lambert. Paris, 1868. Map. Extrait du *Bulletin de la Société de géographie*. GB/A.2052(1). e218.

L'**expédition** du Tegetthoff: voyage de découvertes aux 80e-83e degrés de latitude nord / J.

Payer; traduit de l'allemand par Jules Gourdault. Paris, 1878. Ill. Translated from *Die österreichisch-ungarische Nordpol-Expedition*.
GB/A.1633. e219.

Die **Expeditionen** zur Rettung von Schröder-Stranz und seinen Begleitern / geschildert von ihren Führern, A. Staxrud und K. Wegener; im Auftrage des Komitees 'Hilfe für deutsche Forscher im Polareis', herausgegeben von A. Miethe. Berlin, 1914. Ill., map.
GB.837. e220.

Expeditions among the Great Andes of Ecuador / Edward Whymper. [London, 1880-82.] 6v. From the *Alpine Journal*, Nov. 1880-May 1882.
GB.612(1). e221.

The **expeditions** of the first International Polar Year, 1882-83 / William Barr. Calgary, 1985. [Technical paper / Arctic Institute of North America; 29.]
GB/A.2186. e222.

Expeditions on the glaciers: including an ascent of Mont Blanc, Monte Rosa, Col de Géant, and Mont Buét / [John Barrow]. London, 1864. Reprinted from *Colburn's New Monthly Magazine*.
GB.286; Lloyd.496; Lloyd.496A,B. e223.

Expeditions to nowhere / Paddy Sherman. Toronto, 1981. Ill., maps.
GB/A.2034. e224.

Experimentelle Tektonik: Nachahmung komplizierter Faltenformen: Inaugural-Dissertation / Arthur Vogt. Freiburg, 1910. Ill.
GB/A.1052(4). e225.

Experiments among the mountains. London, 1897. Pp.95-6 of *Chambers's Journal*, Feb.6, 1897.
GB.1336(9). e226.

Experiments on the generation of insects / Francesco Redi; translated by Mab Bigelow. Chicago, 1909. Ill., port., facsim. Translated from *Esperienze intorno alla generazione degl'insetti*.
Lloyd.912. e227.

An **exploration** in 1897 of some of the glaciers of Spitsbergen / W. Martin Conway. [London, 1898.] Ill., map. From the *Geographical Journal* for August, 1898.
GB.1335(47). e228.

Exploration in the northernmost Andes / Allan Cunningham. [London, 1954.] Ill., maps. Pp.334-55 of the *Geographical Journal*, no.123, Sept. 1954.
GB.1333(16). e229.

The **exploration** of Huagaruncho: a Peruvian journey. I. Travels and climbing of the advance party / G.C. Band. II. The ascent of Huagaruncho / M.H. Westmacott. III. Away from the mountains / John Kempe. [London], 1957. Ill., map. Pp.[437]-8 of the *Geographical Journal*, vol.123 pt 4.
GB.1333(17). e230.

The **exploration** of northern Canada, 500 to 1920: a chronology / Alan Cooke, Clive Holland. Toronto, 1978. Maps.
GB/A.1606. e231.

The **exploration** of the Caucasus / Douglas W. Freshfield. London, 1896. 2v; ill., map.
GB.1287-8; Lloyd.1513-4; Lloyd.1513A-4A. e232.

Explorations dans l'océan glacial Arctique: Islande, Jan Mayen, Spitzberg / Charles Rabot. Paris, 1895. Pp.[5]-69 of the *Bulletin de la Société de géographie*, sér.7 tom.15.
GB.1880(12). e233.

Explorations in the glacier regions of the Selkirk Range, British Columbia, in 1888 / W. Spotswood Green. London, 1889. Pp.153-70 of the *Proceedings of the Royal Geographical Society*, vol.11 no.3, March 1889.
GB.1336(22). e234.

Les **explorations** polaires (pôle Nord, pôle Sud) / E.L. Elias; traduction du commandant Beauvais. Paris, 1930. Ill., maps, ports., facsim. [Bibliothèque historique.]
GB/A.1717. e235.

Explorer's wife / Emma Wotton De Long. New York, 1938.
GB/A.1681. e236.

Explorers of the North / Frank Rasky. Toronto, 1976. 2v; ill., map.
GB/A.2156 (wanting v.2). e237.

Exploring expedition: correspondence between J.N. Reynolds and the Hon. Mahlon Dickerson, touching the South Sea Surveying and Exploring Expedition. [New York? 1838?]
GB/B.440(20). e238.

Exploring the Stein River Valley / Roger D. Freeman, David Thompson. Vancouver, 1979. Ill., maps. [Exploring series.]
GB/B.525(8). e239.

Extract from *An account of two late attempts to ascend Mont-Blanc* / Joseph von Hamel. [London, 1821.] Pp.33-42 of the *Annals of Philosophy*, Jan. 1821.
GB.1736(2). e240.

Extract from *An account of two late attempts to ascend Mont-Blanc* / Joseph von Hamel. London, 1822. Pp.662-71 of the *Annual Register*, 1821.
GB.1737(1). e241.

[An **extract** from the *Alpine Journal*, vol.2 no.12, relating to a climb of the Moming Pass in the Alps.] [London, 1865.]
GB.1647(24). e242.

[An **extract** from the *Alpine Journal*, vol.18 no.134, relating to climbing in the Pyrenees.] [London, 1896.]
GB.1880(16). e243.

[**Extracts** and a reprint from the *Alpine Journal* relating to the climbing of the Täschhorn in the Swiss Alps.] [London, 1876-1931.]
GB.1804. e244.

[**Extracts** and a reprint from the *Alpine Journal* relating to the Matterhorn under the headings: attempts; conquest, 1865; early ascents, to 1876; and various.] [London, 1863-1937.] 3v.
GB.1815-7. e245.

[**Extracts** and a reprint from the *Alpine Journal* relating to various ascents of Monte Rosa.] [London, 1868-1939.] 2v.
GB.1758; GB.1807. e246.

[**Extracts** and reprints from the *Alpine Journal* of articles by E.H. Stevens about Michel Gabriel Paccard.] [London, 1929-35.] 2v.
GB.1746; GB.1863. e248.

Extracts from my journal, 1852: ascent of Mont Blanc / J.R. Bulwer. Norwich, 1853. Ill.
GB.1033; GB.1271; Lloyd.1158; Lloyd.1480; Lloyd.1496. e249.

[**Extracts** from *Once a week*, relating mainly to mountaineering.] [London, 1865-71.]
GB.1338(29). e250.

[**Extracts** from the *Alpine Journal* and other periodicals referring to the mountaineering exploits of H.B. de Saussure.] [London, 1787-1931.]
GB.1879. e251.

[**Extracts** from the *Alpine Journal* and other periodicals relating to the Col des Grandes Jorasses.] [London, 1864-1934.]
GB.1757. e252.

[**Extracts** from the *Alpine Journal* and other periodicals relating to the first ascent of the Matterhorn without guides, 1876.] [N.p., 1871-1931.]
GB.1750. e253.

[**Extracts** from the *Alpine Journal* and other sources relating to various ascents of the Aiguille de Bionnassay in the Mont Blanc range.] [London, 1905-30.]
GB.1866. e254.

[**Extracts** from the *Alpine Journal*, and reprints from the *Revue alpine* and the *Bulletin de la Société de la flore valdôtaine* relating to the Col du Géant in the Alps.] [N.p., 1878-1922.]
GB.1163. e255.

[**Extracts** from the *Alpine Journal* and the *Climbers' Club Journal* relating to the mountaineering exploits of V.J.E. Ryan.] [London, 1915-47.]
GB.1768. e256.

[**Extracts** from the *Alpine Journal* and the *Revue alpine* relating to mountaineering on the Col des Hirondelles in the Alps.] [N.p., 1864-1935.]
GB.1769. e257.

[**Extracts** from the *Alpine Journal* and the *Schweizer Alpen-Club Jahrbuch* relating to mountaineering on the Wetterhorn.] [N.p., 1878-1952.] 2v.
GB.1771, GB.1877. e258.

[**Extracts** from the *Alpine Journal* by and about William Longman.] [London, 1877-78.]
GB.982. e259.

[**Extracts** from the *Alpine Journal* comprising articles by and references to Frank S. Smythe.] [London, 1923-37.]
GB.1874. e260.

[**Extracts** from the *Alpine Journal* comprising articles by and references to Geoffrey Winthrop Young.] [London, 1902-23.]
GB.1861. e261.

[**Extracts** from the *Alpine Journal* comprising articles by R.L.G. Irving.] [London, 1907-31.]
GB.1855. e262.

[**Extracts** from the *Alpine Journal* relating to Alpine dangers.] [London, 1866-1932.]
GB.1846. e263.

[**Extracts** from the *Alpine Journal* relating to ascents of the Bietschhorn.] [London, 1864-1933.]
GB.1851. e264.

[**Extracts** from the *Alpine Journal* relating to ascents of the Breithorn.] [London, 1892-1928.]
GB.1842. e265.

[**Extracts** from the *Alpine Journal* relating to ascents of the Finsteraarhorn in the Bernese Oberland.] [London, 1864-1930.]
GB.1854. e266.

[**Extracts** from the *Alpine Journal* relating to ascents of the Jungfrau under the headings: North face and N.E. arête; primitive route; Rottal, except Silberhorn; and Jungfraujoch.] [London, 1863-1934.]
GB.1813. e267.

[**Extracts** from the *Alpine Journal* relating to climbing in Great Britain.] [London, 1888-1933.]
GB.1794. e268.

[**Extracts** from the *Alpine Journal* relating to climbing in the Eiger area of the Bernese Oberland.] [London, 1888-1935.]
GB.1853. e269.

[**Extracts** from the *Alpine Journal* relating to climbing in the Karakoram Mountains.] [London, 1893-1935.] 2v.
GB.1818-9. e270.

[**Extracts** from the *Alpine Journal* relating to climbing in the Rocky Mountains.] [London, 1895-1934.] 3v.
GB.1828-30. e271.

[**Extracts** from the *Alpine Journal* relating to climbing in the Sesiajoch area of the Alps.] [London, 1863-1916.]
GB.1841. e272.

[**Extracts** from the *Alpine Journal* relating to climbing in the Silberhorn area of the Bernese Oberland.] [London, 1866-1932.]
GB.1857. e273.

[**Extracts** from the *Alpine Journal* relating to Mount Everest, with particular reference to the expeditions of 1921, 1922, 1924 and 1933.] [London, 1903-37.] 2v.
GB.1838-9. e274.

[**Extracts** from the *Alpine Journal* relating to mountaineering expeditions, 1863-1934.] [London, 1863-1934.] 3v.
GB.1784-6. e275.

[**Extracts** from the *Alpine Journal* relating to mountaineering in Africa.] [London, 1872-1935.]
GB.1840. e276.

[**Extracts** from the *Alpine Journal* relating to mountaineering in Alaska, with particular reference to Mounts Foraker, Logan and McKinley.] [London, 1869-1935.] 3v.
GB.1825-7. e276.1.

[**Extracts** from the *Alpine Journal* relating to mountaineering in America, excluding the Rockies and Alaska.] [London, 1867-1906.]
GB.1850. e276.2.

[**Extracts** from the *Alpine Journal* relating to mountaineering in British Columbia.] [London, 1901-37.]
GB.1862. e277.

[**Extracts** from the *Alpine Journal* relating to mountaineering in general, selected by T. Graham Brown.] [London, 1878-1934.] 3v.
GB.1791-3. e278.

[**Extracts** from the *Alpine Journal* relating to mountaineering in Iceland, Greenland and Lapland.] [London, 1873-1933.]
GB.1872. e279.

[**Extracts** from the *Alpine Journal* relating to mountaineering in New Zealand.] [London, 1891-1933.] 2v.
GB.1831-2. e280.

[**Extracts** from the *Alpine Journal* relating to mountaineering in Norway.] [London, 1867-1932.]
GB.1865. e281.

[**Extracts** from the *Alpine Journal* relating to mountaineering in Spitzbergen.] [London, 1895-1923.]
GB.1867. e282.

[**Extracts** from the *Alpine Journal* relating to mountaineering in the Alps under the headings: general; geology; glaciers: historical; various; and

Eastern Alps.] [London, 1866-1937.] 8v.
GB.1795-1802.   e283.

[**Extracts** from the *Alpine Journal* relating to mountaineering in the Andes.] [London, 1878-1934.]
GB.1864.   e284.

[**Extracts** from the *Alpine Journal* relating to mountaineering in the Bernese Oberland under the headings: various; Oberland cols; Lauteraarsattel, Mönch.] [London, 1863-1935.] 2v.
GB.1811-2.   e285.

[**Extracts** from the *Alpine Journal* relating to mountaineering in the Bernina Group of mountains.] [London, 1867-1935.]
GB.1843.   e286.

[**Extracts** from the *Alpine Journal* relating to mountaineering in the Caucasus, with special reference to William F. Donkin.] [London, 1869-1937.] 4v.
GB.1821-4.   e287.

[**Extracts** from the *Alpine Journal* relating to mountaineering in the Dauphiné district of the French Alps.] [London, 1864-1933.]
GB.1803.   e288.

[**Extracts** from the *Alpine Journal* relating to mountaineering in the Dolomites.] [London, 1870-1913.]
GB.1820.   e289.

[**Extracts** from the *Alpine Journal* relating to mountaineering in the Graian Alps.] [London, 1865-1925.]
GB.1814.   e290.

[**Extracts** from the *Alpine Journal* relating to mountaineering in the Himalayas, with special reference to W.W. Graham.] [London, 1867-1937.] 5v.
GB.1833-7.   e291.

[**Extracts** from the *Alpine Journal* relating to mountaineering in the Meije range, Dauphiné.] [London, 1864-1933.]
GB.1873.   e292.

[**Extracts** from the *Alpine Journal* relating to mountaineering in the Monte Viso range of the Alps.] [London, 1882-1904.]
GB.1858.   e294.

[**Extracts** from the *Alpine Journal* relating to mountaineering in the Nanda Devi area of the Himalayas.] [London, 1927-37.]
GB.1859.   e295.

[**Extracts** from the *Alpine Journal* relating to mountaineering in the Zermatt area.] [London, 1863-1933.] 3v.
GB.1808-10.   e296.

[**Extracts** from the *Alpine Journal* relating to mountaineering in various parts of the world, selected by T. Graham Brown.] [London, 1867-1934.] 4v.
GB.1787-90.   e297.

[**Extracts** from the *Alpine Journal* relating to mountaineering on the Aiguille Blanche de Pétéret in the Alps.] [London, 1885-1934.]
GB.1767.   e298.

[**Extracts** from the *Alpine Journal* relating to mountaineering on the Col de Trélatête in the Alps.] [London, 1864-1929.]
GB.1752.   e299.

[**Extracts** from the *Alpine Journal* relating to mountaineering on the Jungfrau from the Rottal.] [London, 1864-76.]
GB.1759.   e300.

[**Extracts** from the *Alpine Journal* relating to mountaineering on the Zinal Rothorn in the Alps.] [London, 1863-1933.]
GB.1756.   e301.

[**Extracts** from the *Alpine Journal* relating to old books on mountaineering in the Alpine Club Library.] [London, 1895-1934.] 2v.
GB.1848-9.   e302.

[**Extracts** from the *Alpine Journal* relating to the 1931 ascent of Mount Kamet.] [London, 1931-33.]
GB.1871.   e303.

[**Extracts** from the *Alpine Journal* relating to the climbing of Mount Ararat.] [London, 1879-1922.]
GB.1869.   e304.

[**Extracts** from the *Alpine Journal* relating to the history of the mountaineering work done by Swiss pioneers in the Alps.] [London, 1881-1928.]
GB.1878.   e305.

[**Extracts** from the *Alpine Journal* relating to the mountaineering exploits and publications of T.

Graham Brown.] [London, 1927-49.] 2v.
GB.1844-5.   e306.

[**Extracts** from the *Alpine Journal* relating to the rival claims of Michel G. Paccard and Jacques Balmat to the discovery of the route to the summit of Mont Blanc.] [London, 1878-1934.] 2v.
GB.1805-6.   e307.

[**Extracts** from the *Alpine Journal* relating to the two German expeditions to Nanga Parbat in the Himalayas in 1932 and 1934.] [London, 1930-37.]
GB.1860.   e308.

[**Extracts** from the *Alpine Journal* relating to various ascents of Nordend in the Alps.] [London, 1894-1933.]
GB.1847.   e309.

[**Extracts** from the *Alpine Journal* relating to various attempts and ascents of Kanchenjunga in the Himalayas.] [London, 1927-33.]
GB.1868.   e310.

[**Extracts** from the *Alpine Journal*, the *Revue alpine* and *Short stalks* relating to mountaineering on the Aiguille de Bionnassay in the Alps.] [N.p., 1865-1928.]
GB.1751.   e311.

[**Extracts** from the *Climbers' Club Journal* relating to the climbing of Clogwyn du'r Arddu. [London, 1938-49.]
GB.1338(3-8).   e314.

[**Extracts** from the *Rivista del Club Alpino Italiano* relating to the expedition of the Duke of the Abruzzi to the Himalayas in 1909.] Torino, [1909-12.] Map.
GB.1852.   e315.

[**Extracts** from the *Rivista mensile del Club Alpino Italiano* relating to the deaths of Guglielmo Bompadre, Antonio Castelnuovo and Pietro Sommaruga on the Nordend, 1909.] [Turin, 1909-10.] Ports.
GB.1881(8).   e316.

[**Extracts** from the *Yorkshire Ramblers' Club Journal* concerning Frank S. Smythe.] [Leeds, 1927-34.]
GB.1876.   e317.

[**Extracts** from the *Zeitschrift des Deutschen und Osterreichischen Alpenvereins* and another unidentified source relating to climbing in the Pétéret Ridge of the Alps.] [Munich, 1901-12.]
GB.1331(53).   e318.

[**Extracts** from various journals relating to the fatal accident on the Matterhorn, 14th July 1865, including Edward Whymper's accounts.] [N.p., 1865-1956.]
GB.1749.   e319.

[**Extracts** from various sources concerning Michel Carrier's biography of Jacques Balmat.] [N.p., 1925-57.]
GB.1753.   e320.

[**Extracts** from various sources, including MS., relating to mountaineering in the Mont Blanc range.] [N.p., 1787-1958.] 34v.
GB.1701-34.   e321.

[**Extracts** from various sources relating to mountaineering on the Barre des Ecrins in the Alps.] [N.p., 1863-1950.] 2v.
GB.1760, GB.1870.   e322.

[**Extracts** from various sources relating to the early Courmayeur guides.] [N.p., 1880-1923.]
GB.1770.   e323.

[**Extracts** from various sources relating to the first ascent of Mont Brouillard by the East Face, 1932.] [N.p., 1932-33.]
GB.1766.   e324.

[**Extracts** mainly from the *Alpine Journal* relating to mountaineering in the Mont Blanc area.] [London, 1817-1949.] 11v.
GB.1773-83.   e324.1..

[**Extracts** mainly from the *Alpine Journal* relating to mountaineering on the Col du Mont Dolent in the Alps.] [N.p., 1865-1933.]
GB.1761.   e325.

[**Extracts** mainly from the *Alpine Journal* relating to mountaineering on the Col du Tour Noir in the Alps.] [London, 1863-1946.]
GB.1763.   e326.

[**Extracts** mainly from the *Alpine Journal* relating to mountaineering on the Täschhorn, South Face, Ryan-Lochmatter route.] [London, 1906-44.]
GB.1754.   e327.

[**Extracts** mainly from the *Alpine Journal* relating to mountaineering on the Weisshorn.] [London, 1861-1933.] 2v.
GB.1764, GB.1856.   e328.

[**Extracts** mainly from the *Climbers' Club Journal* and the *Alpine Journal* relating to mountaineering

on the Grépon from the Mer de Glace Face.]
[London, 1911-49.]
GB.1762.   e329.

Extrait du voyage de M. Bourrit en Piémont par la
mer de Glace de Chamouni du 28 août 1787.
[Geneva, 1787.]
GB.461(4).   e330.

Eye on Everest: a sketch book from the great
Everest expedition / Charles Evans. London,
1955.
GB.1174; GB.1186.   e331.

-F-

F.N. Koenig, 1765-1832 / Conrad von Mandach.
Genève, 1923. Ill., ports.
Lloyd.1621(8).   f001.

La **face** nord des Grandes Jorasses / Edouard
Frendo. Paris, 1947. Ill.
GB.1329(2).   f002.

A **facsimile** of Christian Almer's Führerbuch,
1856-1894 / reproduced under the super-
intendence of C.D. Cunningham and W. de W.
Abney. London, 1896. Ports.
GB.387; Lloyd.557; Lloyd.557A,B,C,D,E.   f003.

Facts and enquiries respecting the source of
epidemia, with an historical catalogue of the
numerous visitations of plague, pestilence, and
famine, from the earliest period of the world to the
present day / T. Forster. 3rd ed. London, 1832.
GB.697(6) (impf.).   f004.

Facts from the world of nature, animate and
inanimate / Jane Loudon. London, 1848. Ill.
GB.171.   f005.

Die **Fahrt** der Wegä über Alpen und Jura am 3.
Oktober 1898 / Alb. Heim, Jul. Maurer, Ed.
Spelterini. Basel, 1899. Ill., maps.
GB/A.1127.   f006.

Fahrt zum Himalaja / Walter Grosspietsch.
Leipzig, 1979. Ill.
GB/A.1995.   f007.

Fahrten im Montblancgebiet / Walter Stoesser. I.
Montblanc. [Munich, 1930.] Pp.[97]-104 of the
*Zeitschrift des Deutschen und Osterreichischen Alpen-
vereins*, Bd.61.
GB.1331(57).   f008.

Faits pour servir à l'histoire des montagnes de
l'Oisans / L. Elie de Beaumont. Paris, 1834. Extrait
des *Annales des mines*, sér.3 tom.5.
Lloyd.822.   f009.

Falcade attraverso i secoli / Bepi Pellegrinon.
[Bologna, 1971.] Ill.
GB/A.1270(13).   f010.

The *Falcon* on the Baltic: a coasting voyage from
Hammersmith to Copenhagen in a three-ton yacht
/ E.F. Knight. London, 1902. Ill., map. [The silver
library.]
GB.313.   f011.

Fall and decline / [F.H.K., i.e. F.H. Keenlyside]. [London, 1943.] P.105 of the *Climbers' Club Journal*, N.S. vol.7 no.2.
GB.1339(11). f012.

Famiglia alpinistica: tipi e paesaggi / G. Saragat, Guido Rey. 2a ed. Torino, 1908. Ill., facsims.
GB/A.867(3). f013.

Familien-Statistik der löblichen Pfarrei von Zermatt, mit Beilagen / Joseph Ruden. Ingenbohl, 1869.
Lloyd.516. f014.

Family name / Arnold Lunn. London, 1931.
GB.341. f015.

Family notes / Frederick A.Y. Brown. Genoa, 1917. Port.
GB.1069. f016.

Famous climbs in the Dolomites / Remo Pedrotti; artistic composition: Hermann Frass. Bolzano, [1954]. Ill., map. Published by the Tourist Department of the Trentino-Alto Adige Region.
Lloyd.1621(5). f017.

Fangstmenn på Ishavet / Alfred Skar. Oslo, 1935. Ill.
GB/B.524(11). f018.

Farlige fjell / Arthur Klæbo. Oslo, 1942. Ill.
GB/A.206. f019.

Farthest North: being the record of a voyage of exploration of the ship *Fram*, 1893-96, and the fifteen months sleigh journey by Dr. Nansen and Lieut. Johansen. [London, 1898?] Ill., ports.
GB/A.1796. f020.

Les **fastes** du Mont Blanc: ascensions célèbres et catastrophes depuis M. de Saussure jusqu'à nos jours / Stéphen d'Arve. Genève, 1876.
GB.1333(35); Lloyd.1040. f021.

Das **Faulhorn** im Grindelwald: ein Topographie- und Panoramgemälde entworfen von mehreren Alpenfreunden / herausgegeben von J.J. Schweizer. Bern, 1832. Ill.
GB/A.800(6); GB/A.1460. f022.

La **fauna**. Milano, 1959. Ill., maps. [Conosci l'Italia; 3.]
GB/B.561. f023.

Fauna e caccia in Valle d'Aosta / Pietro Marguerettaz. Aosta, [1968]. Ill.
GB/C.22(19). f024.

Il **favoloso** mondo delle Dolomiti: guida al mondo naturale delle Dolomiti trentine, con descrizione dei gruppi e delle principali escursioni / B. Bonapace, S. Ducati. Trento, 1972. Ill., maps.
GB/A.1248. f025.

A **feast** of many courses / J. Monroe Thorington. New York, [1962]. Reprinted from the *American Alpine Journal*, 1962.
GB.1333(9). f026.

Features of Karakoram glaciers connected with pressure, especially of affluents / W. Hunter Workman. Berlin, 1913. Ill. Sonderabdruck aus *Zeitschrift für Gletscherkunde*, Bd.8, 1913.
GB.1318(23). f027.

Gli **felici** progressi de Catholici nella Valtellina per estirpatione dell'heresie, cominciando dall'anno del signore 1618 sin'all'anno 1623 / Francesco Ballarino. Milano, 1623.
GB/A.696. f028.

Die **Felsen** Niedersachsens: Kletterführer / Rudolf Behrens; neubearb. und herausgegeben von Holm Uibrig. 2. Aufl. Hannover, 1958. Maps.
GB/B.525(6). f029.

Les **femmes** alpinistes: Miss Brevoort / Mary Paillon. Paris, 1900. Port. Extrait de l'*Annuaire du Club alpin français*, vol.26, 1899.
GB.1306(16); Lloyd.993; Lloyd.1620(11). f030.

Femmes héroiques: les soeurs grises canadiennes aux glaces polaires / le R.P. Duchaussois. Nouv. éd. Paris, 1928. Ill., maps, ports.
GB/A.1719. f031.

[**Ferns** and mosses from the Himalayas / collected by Lady Fitzroy Somerset.] [N.p., 1841.]
GB/C.116. f032.

Fernsicht vom St.Chrischona-Berg bei Basel in die nordlichen Jura-Gegenden und die Hoch-Alpen der Schweiz. Basel, 1845. Ill.
GB/A.1305. f033.

Festschrift zum fünfundzwanzigjährigen Bestehen der Sektion Berlin des Deutschen und Oesterreichischen Alpenvereins am 9. Dezember 1894. Berlin, 1894. Ill.
GB/A.101. f034.

Festschrift zur Hauptversammlung des Oesterreichischen Alpenvereins im Kufstein, 16 und 17 Sept. 1967. Kufstein, 1967. Ill.
GB/C.5(1). f035.

Fiery particles / C.E. Montague. Repr. London, 1936. [Phoenix library.]
GB.194.   f036.

Fifty classic climbs of North America / Steve Roper, Allen Steck. London, 1979. Ill., maps.
GB/B.618.   f037.

Le **Figaro**. Année 124 no.1833-44, 1er-14 août, 1950. Paris, 1950. Containing an account of the French expedition to Annapurna.
Lloyd.1564 (impf.).   f038.

The **fight** for Everest: 1924 / E.F. Norton and other members of the Expedition. London, 1925. Ill., maps, ports.
GB.1189; Lloyd.1348.   f039.

[**Films**, slides, prints and enlargements, relating mainly to mountaineering, taken by T. Graham Brown.] [N.p., 1926-54.]
GB.1921-27.   f040.

La **fin** d'une conquête: photographies prises par avion. Romans-sur-Isère, 1953. Ill.
GB.1319(11).   f041.

La **fine** dell'alpinismo / Guido Rey; a cura di Adolfo Balliano. Torino, 1939. Ill. [La piccozza e la penna; 2a ser. 1.]
GB/B.438.   f042.

Finsteraarhornfahrt / Abraham Roth. Berlin, 1863. Ill., map.
GB.359; Lloyd.1611(4).   f043.

First across the roof of the world: the first-ever traverse of the Himalayas — 5,000 kilometres from Sikkim to Pakistan / Graeme Dingle, Peter Hillary. London, 1984.
GB/A.2185.   f044.

First aid to the injured: with special reference to accidents occuring [sic] in the mountains / Oscar Bernhard; translated by Michael G. Foster. London, 1900. Ill. Translated from *Samariterdienst*.
Lloyd.310.   f045.

The **first** American accident on the Matterhorn / J. Monroe Thorington. New York, [1960]. Ill., port. Reprinted from the *American Alpine Journal*, 1960.
GB.1332(23).   f046.

The **first** ascent of Mont Blanc / Richard J.F. Edgcumbe. London, 1892. Pp.772-82 of the *National Review*, no.114, Aug. 1892.
GB.1331(55).   f047.

The **first** ascent of Mont Blanc / T. Graham Brown, Sir Gavin de Beer. London, 1957. Ill. Pp.89-91 of the *Periodical*, Autumn 1957.
GB.1307(1).   f048.

The **first** ascent of Mont Blanc: published on the occasion of the centenary of the Alpine Club / T. Graham Brown, Sir Gavin de Beer. London, 1957. Ill., maps, facsims.
GB.768; GB.769; GB.770; GB.771.   f049.

The **first** ascent of Mont Blanc / T. Graham Brown, Sir Gavin de Beer. [London, 1956-57.] Proofs at various stages.
GB.1880(22-3); GB.1913-20.   f050.

The **first** ascent of Mont Blanc direct from the Brenva glacier and other climbs in 1927 / Frank S. Smythe. London, 1928. Ill. Pp.58-77 of the *Alpine Journal*, vol.40 no.236.
GB.1881(1).   f051.

The **first** ascent of Mont Blanc direct from the Brenva glacier and other climbs in 1927 / Frank S. Smythe. London, 1928. Ill. Reprinted from the *Alpine Journal*, May 1928.
GB.1881(2).   f052.

The **first** ascent of Mount Everest. London, 1953. Ill. Colour supplement, *The Times*.
GB.1298(2); GB.1298(3); GB.1912(7).   f053.

The **first** ascent of the Finsteraarhorn: a re-examination / J.P. Farrar. [London], 1913. Ill., port. Reprinted from the *Alpine Journal*, Aug. 1913.
GB.1312(28); Lloyd.1609(9), Lloyd.1609(9)A,B.
                                                    f054.

The **first** ascent of the French or north face of the Col de Bionnassay: read before the Alpine Club, June 1, 1920 / R.W. Lloyd. London, 1920. Ill. Reprinted from the *Alpine Journal*, November 1920.
Lloyd.1602(27).   f055.

The **first** crossing of Greenland / Fridtjof Nansen; translated from the Norwegian by Hubert Majendie Gepp. New ed., abridged [by C.J. Longman]. London, 1898. [The silver library.]
GB.361.   f056.

The **first** crossing of Spitsbergen / Sir Martin Conway; with contributions by J.W. Gregory, A. Trevor-Battye, and E.J. Garwood. London, 1897. Ill., maps.
Lloyd.1282.   f057.

The **first** direct ascent of Mont Blanc de Courmayeur from the Brenva glacier, and other climbs / T. Graham Brown. London, 1929. Ill. Pp.34-49 of the *Alpine Journal*, vol.41 no.238.
GB.1881(64). f058.

First impressions: a series of letters from France, Switzerland, and Savoy, written in 1833-4, and addressed to the Rev. H. Raikes / John Davies. London, 1835.
Lloyd.566. f059.

First impressions on a tour upon the Continent in the summer of 1818, through parts of France, Italy, Switzerland, the borders of Germany, and a part of French Flanders / Marianne Baillie. London, 1819. Ill.
Lloyd.821. f060.

First over Everest: the Houston-Mount Everest Expedition, 1933 / P.F.M. Fellowes [et al.]; an account of the filming of the flight, by Geoffrey Barkas. 5th impr. London, 1933. Ill., maps, ports.
GB.1091. f061.

First steps in general knowledge. Pt 2: The surface of the earth / Sarah Tomlinson. London, [ca 1858].
GB.21. f062.

The **first** ten years: Swiss Foundation for Alpine Research. [Zug], 1951. Ill., ports.
Lloyd.1621(3). f063.

First to the top of the world: Admiral Peary at the North Pole / Tom Lisker. New York, 1978. Ill.
GB/A.2128. f064.

Fishes and tunicates. Pt.B: Ascidiacea / A.G. Huntsman. Ottawa, 1922. [Report of the Canadian Arctic Expedition, 1913-18; 6.]
GB/A.2139(9). f065.

Five miles high: the story of an attack on the second highest mountain in the world / by the members of the first American Karakoram expedition, Robert H. Bates, Richard L. Burdsall [et al.]; [edited by Robert H. Bates]. New York, 1939. Ill., maps, ports.
GB.921. f066.

Five months in the Himalaya: a record of mountain travel in Garhwal and Kashmir / A.L. Mumm. London, 1909.
GB.1191. f067.

Fjell i Norge / Ragnar Frislid. Oslo, 1969. Ill.
GB/B.238. f068.

La **flora**. Milano, 1958. Ill., maps. [Conosci l'Italia; 2.]
GB/B.560. f069.

La **flora** del Cadore: catalogo sistematico delle piante vascolari / Renato Pampanini; pubblicato a cura della Magnifica Comunità di Cadore [da] G. Negri e P. Zangheri. Forlì, 1958. Map, port.
GB/B.271. f070.

Flora der Südalpen: vom Gardasee zum Comersee / Hans Pitschmann, Herbert Reisigl. 2., erg. Aufl. Stuttgart, 1965. Ill.
GB/A.139. f071.

The **flora** of Prince Charles Foreland, Spitzbergen / R.N. Rudmose-Brown. [Edinburgh, 1908.] Pp.312-20 of *Trans. Bot. Soc. Edin.*, vol.23, 1908.
GB.1335(50). f072.

The **flora** of Switzerland for the use of tourists and field-botanists / August Gremli; translated from the 5th ed. by Leonard W. Paitson. London, 1889. Translated from *Excursionsflora für die Schweiz*.
Lloyd.231. f073.

The **flora** of the Alps: being a description of all the species of flowering plants indigenous to Switzerland, and of the Alpine species of the adjacent mountain districts of France, Italy and Austria, including the Pyrenees / Alfred W. Bennett. London, 1896. 2v; ill.
Lloyd.665-6. f074.

Floran och vegetationen i Kiruna / Herman G. Simmons. Stockholm, 1910.
GB/A.1843. f075.

Flore alpine / Henry Correvon. 8e éd. Neuchâtel, 1967. Ill. [Les beautés de la nature.]
GB/A.1566. f076.

Flore coloriée portative de touriste dans les Alpes / L. Schröter, avec texte par C. Schröter. 10e et 11e éd. Zürich, [1904]. Ill.
GB/A.1739. f077.

Flore fossile des environs de Lausanne / Charles Th. Gaudin, Ph. de la Harpe. Lausanne, 1856. Extrait du *Bulletin de la Société vaudoise des sciences naturelles*, séance du 4 juillet 1855.
Lloyd.687. f078.

The **flower-fields** of Alpine Switzerland: an appreciation and a plea / George Flemwell. London, 1911.
Lloyd.984.   f079.

Flowers from the upper Alps, with glimpses of their homes / Elijah Walton; with descriptive text by T.G. Bonney. 5th ed. London, 1882. Ill.
Lloyd.1524.   f080.

Flowers of modern voyages and travels. Vol.3. [London, 1828.] Ill.
GB.82 (impf.).   f081.

Fole e folletti delle Dolomiti / Severino Casara. Bologna, [1966]. Ill. [Voci dai monti; 7.]
GB/A.849.   f082.

Il **folklore**: tradizioni, vita e arti popolari / a cura di Paolo Toschi. Milano, 1967. Ill. [Conosci l'Italia; 11.]
GB/B.569.   f083.

Folklore e leggenda della Val di Fassa / Gianfranco Valentini. 2a ed. Bologna, 1971. [Le Alpi; 14.]
GB/A.1311.   f084.

Follow the North Star / Tay Thomas. Garden City, N.Y., 1960. Ill., maps, ports.
GB/A.1776.   f085.

Fonderie et exploitation des mines de fer de la vallée de Sixt. Description topographique et minéralogique de la vallée de Sixt / [Jean F. Albanis Beaumont]. [N.p., n.d.]
Lloyd.1620(20).   f086.

Fontana di giovinezza / Eugenio Guido Lammer; traduzione di Raffaello Prati. 2a ed. Milano, 1944. 2v; ill. [Montagna; 6-7.]
GB/A.554-5.   f087.

Footloose in the Swiss Alps / William E. Reifsnyder; with sections by Rachel Burbank. 2nd rev. ed. San Francisco, 1979. Ill., maps. [A Sierra Club totebook.]
GB/A.1676(13).   f088.

The **foreign** freaks of five friends / C.A. Jones. London, 1882. Ill.
Lloyd.572.   f089.

The **foreign** tour of Messrs. Brown, Jones and Robinson / Richard Doyle. London, 1854.
Lloyd.1497.   f090.

A **foreign** view of England in the reigns of George I & George II: the letters of Monsieur César de Saussure to his family / translated and edited by Madame Van Muyden. London, 1902.
GB.516.   f091.

Forerunners to Everest: the story of the two Swiss expeditions of 1952 / René Dittert, Gabriel Chevalley, Raymond Lambert; English version by Malcolm Barnes. London, 1954. Ill., maps, ports. Translated from *Avant-premières à l'Everest*.
GB.714; Lloyd.952.   f092.

The **forest** cantons of Switzerland: Lucerne, Schwyz, Uri, Unterwalden / J. Sowerby. London, 1892. Map.
Lloyd.354.   f093.

La **formation** des limites entre le Dauphiné et la Savoie, 1140-1760: contribution à l'étude de la géographie historique du sudest de la France / Louis Jacob. Paris, 1906. Maps.
GB.1329(17).   f094.

Formes et couleurs: revue internationale des arts, du goût et des idées. No.2, 1947: Montagne. Lausanne, 1947. Ill.
GB/C.5(3).   f095.

Forschung am Nanga Parbat, Deutsche Himalaya-Expedition 1934 / Richard Finsterwalder, Walter Raechl, Peter Misch, Fritz Bechtold. Hannover, 1935. Ill., maps, ports. Published by the Geographische Gesellschaft, Hannover.
GB.1140.   f096.

A **fortnight** in the Pyrenees, Luchon to San-Sebastian / comte Henry Russell-Killough. Pau, 1868. Map.
Lloyd.1617(19).   f097.

A **fortnight's** journal / Henry Herbert; with a short account of the manner of his death on one of the Jura Mountains, August 2, 1837. London, 1838.
GB.330; Lloyd.507.   f098.

A **fortnight's** journal / Henry Herbert; with a short account of the manner of his death on one of the Jura Mountains, August 2, 1837. London, 1838. A different issue from f098.
Lloyd.506.   f099.

Forty-six days in Switzerland and the north of Italy / [George Clowes]. London, 1856. Maps.
GB.553; Lloyd.702.   f100.

Fossili / J.F. Kirkaldy; [traduzione di Carlo Palau]. [Turin], 1971. Translated from *Fossils in colour*.
GB/A.1050(5).   f101.

Fotografare la natura / David Linton; traduzione di Alfredo Suvero. Bologna, 1976. Ill. [Biblioteca di scienze naturali; 2.] Translated from *Photographing nature*.
GB/A.2020(13).   f102.

Le **fou** d'Edenberg: roman / Samivel. Paris, 1967.
GB/A.1115(4).   f103.

[**Four** coloured prints to illustrate Albert Smith's *Ascent of Mont Blanc* / engraved by George Baxter.] [N.p., n.d.]
Lloyd.1593(3).   f104.

Four months' camping in the Himalayas / W.G.N. van der Sleen; translated by M.W. Hoper. London, 1929. Ill. Translated from *Vier maanden kampeeren in den Himalaya*.
GB.1147.   f105.

Fra il ghiacciaio e la luna: romanzo / A. den Doolard; [tradotto da Ada Salvatore]. Milano, 1954. Translated from *De groote verwildering*.
GB/A.1548.   f106.

Fragmente von Wanderungen in der Schweiz / Carl Grass. Zürich, 1797. Ill.
GB/A.700.   f107.

Fragments inédits de Mme. Necker de Saussure / A.S. Genève, 1848. Pp.266-89 of *Bibliothèque universelle de Genève. Littérature et sciences morales et politiques*.
Lloyd.1610(8).   f108.

Fragments of Italy and the Rhineland / T.H. White. London, 1841.
Lloyd.266.   f109.

Fram öfver Polarhafvet: den norska polarfärden 1893-96 / af Fridtjof Nansen; med ett tillägg af Otto Sverdrup; bemyndigad öfversättning från norskan under tillsyn af A.G. Nathorst. Stockholm, 1897. 2v.
GB/A.2187.   f110.

Francis Fox Tuckett / W.A.B. Coolidge. Lyon, [1913?]. Port. Extrait de la *Revue alpine* de septembre 1913.
GB.1335(11); GB.1340(32).   f111.

Francis Fox Tuckett, 1834-1913 / W.A.B. Coolidge. Torino, 1913. Estratto dalla *Rivista del Club Alpino Italiano*, vol.32 no.10, 1913.
GB.1340(33).   f112.

The **Franklin** expedition, or Considerations on measures for the discovery and relief of our absent adventurers in the Arctic regions / William Scoresby. London, 1850. Maps.
GB.868; GB.1029.   f113.

Die **Franklin-Expeditionen** und ihr Ausgang: Entdeckung der nordwestlichen Durchfahrt durch MacClure sowie Auffindung der Ueberreste von Sir John Franklin's Expedition durch Kapitan Sir Leopold McClintock. 4. durchgesehene Aufl. von Fr. Kiesewetter. Leipzig, 1879. Ill., map. [Buch der Reisen und Entdeckungen; 2.]
GB/A.1593.   f114.

The **Franz** Josef glacier, New Zealand / George Edward Mannering. Christchurch, [n.d.]. Ill.
Lloyd.1621(1).   f115.

The **French** Alps / edited by Findlay Muirhead and Marcel Monmarché. London, 1923. Maps. [Blue guides.]
GB.61.   f116.

Fridtjof Nansen / Wolfgang Sonntag; norsk utgave ved Liv Hansen Høyer. Oslo, 1947.
GB/A.1842.   f117.

Fridtjof Nansen: polarforskaren och människovännen / Paul Wetterfors. 2a uppl. Uppsala, 1932. Ill., map, ports.
GB/B.524(5).   f118.

Fridtjof Nansens saga / Jon Sørensen. Oslo, 1931. Ill., ports., facsim.
GB/A.1861.   f119.

Friends in solitude / Percy Withers. London, 1930. [Travellers' library.]
GB.215.   f120.

Friendship's Offering of Sentiment and Mirth. 1844. London, 1844.
GB.708.   f121.

Friluftsliv: blad av dagboka / Fridtjof Nansen. Oslo, 1940.
GB/A.2085.   f122.

Friuli-Venezia Giulia / Giorgio Valussi. 2a ed. riv. e aggiornata. Torino, 1971. Ill., maps. [Le regioni

d'Italia; 5.]
GB/B.550. f123.

From Basle to Bex / Y.S.N. [i.e. Mary Dutton].
Southsea, [ca 1865]. [Tourists' tickets.]
GB/C.5(12). f124.

From London Bridge to Lombardy, by a
macadamised route / W.R. Richardson. London,
1869. Ill., map.
Lloyd.732. f125.

From Skiddaw top on Jubilee bonfire night.
[London, 1887.] Pp.154-64 of the *Cornhill
Magazine*, 1887.
GB.1881(32). f126.

From the Alps to the Andes: being the auto-
biography of a mountain guide / Matthias
Zurbriggen; from the Italian by M.A. Vialls.
London, 1899. Ill.
GB.825; Lloyd.986. f127.

From Zermatt to Zinal and back / [T.G. Bonney].
[Cambridge, 1861.] Extracted from the *Eagle*, vol.3
no.14.
Lloyd.1594(7). f128.

Una **frontiera** da immaginare / Andrea Gobetti.
Milano, 1976. Ill. [Exploits.]
GB/A.1967(2). f129.

Frost and fire / John Francis Campbell. Edinburgh, 1865. 2v.
Lloyd.977-8. f130.

The **frosty** Caucasus: an account of a walk
through part of the range and of an ascent of
Elbruz in the summer of 1874 / F. C. Grove.
London, 1875. Ill., map.
GB.385; Lloyd.456; Lloyd.456A. f131.

Frozen future: a prophetic report from Antarctica
/ edited by Richard S. Lewis, Philip M. Smith.
New York, 1973. Ill., maps.
GB/A.1746. f132.

The **frozen** ship, or Clint Webb among the sealers
/ W. Bert Foster. Chicago, 1913. Ill.
GB/A.1960. f133.

The **frozen** stream, or An account of the nature,
properties, dangers and uses of ice, in various
parts of the world. London, 1846. Ill.
Lloyd.34. f134.

Fuga sul Kenya / Felice Benuzzi. 2a ed. Bologna,
1966. Ill. [Voci dai monti; 6.]
GB/A.848. f135.

Fuglefjell / Carl Schøyen. Oslo, 1929.
GB/A.1873. f136.

Führer / G. Grosjean. Bern, 1968. Ill. Published by
the Schweizerisches Alpines Museum, Bern.
GB/A.516(10). f137.

Führer durch das Dachsteingebirge und die
angrenzenden Gebiete des Salzkammergutes und
Ennstales / Alfred Radio-Radiis. 4. Aufl. Wien,
1932. Ill.
GB/A.1357. f138.

Führer durch die Mont-Blanc-Gruppe / Wilhelm
Martin, Paul Reuschel, Richard Weitzenbock.
Wien, 1913. Ill., maps.
Lloyd.194-5. f139.

Führer durch die Ortler-Gruppe: Täler — Hütten
— Berge / Lois Koll, [Dieter Drescher]. 3. Aufl.
München, 1969. Ill., maps.
GB/A.1050(13). f140.

Führer durch die Pragser-Dolomiten / Anton
Schwingshackl. [N.p., 1971?] Ill., map.
GB/A.801(6). f141.

Führer durch die Sextener Dolomiten: Hütten-
wege, Obergänge und Gipfel / Alois Haydn.
München, [1969?]. Ill., map. [Kleine Dolomiten-
Wanderführer.]
GB/A.1468(14). f142.

Führer durch die Urner-Alpen / verfasst vom
Akademischen Alpen-Club Zürich; heraus-
gegeben vom Schweizer Alpen-Club. [Zurich],
1905. 2v; ill. [Clubführer des Schweizer Alpen-
Club.]
GB/A.1359-60; Lloyd.183 (wanting v.1). f143.

Führer durch Graubünden: Touristik, Kurorte,
Sportplätze, Eisenbahnen, Automobilrouten / F.
Hasselbrink; herausgegeben vom Verkehrsverein
für Graubünden. Chur, [1920?]. Ill., maps.
GB/A.942(11). f144.

Führer von Zermatt und Umgebungen:
Beschreibung — Geschichte — Sagen / Alfred
Ceresole. 2. Aufl. Zürich, [ca 1890]. Ill., maps.
GB/A.701. f145.

Führerlose Gipfelfahrten / Paul Hübel. München, 1927. Ill.
GB.1082.   f146.

Führerlose Gipfelfahrten in den Hochalpen, dem Kaukasus, dem Tian-schan und den Anden / Hans Pfann. 4. Aufl. Berlin, [1943]. Ill., port.
GB.573.   f147.

Die **Fünffingerspitze** als Typus eines Modeberges / Louis Norman-Neruda. Die Langkofelgruppe / Oscar Schuster. [N.p., 1895-96.] Ill. Pp.[120]-37, 1895, and pp.277-319, 1896, of *Zeitschrift des Deutschen und Osterreichischen Alpenvereins*.
GB.1386.   f148.

Fünfzig Jahre Alpenclub Gerliswil / Fridolin Züsli. Emmenbrücke, 1969. Ill.
GB/B.245(29).   f149.

Fünfzig Jahre Bergsteiger: Erlebnisse und Gedanken / Fritz Rigele. Berlin, 1935. Ill.
GB/A.411.   f150.

Fünfzig Jahre Sektion Bonn des Deutschen und Osterreichischen Alpenvereins: 1884-1934. Bonn, [1934]. Ill., map.
GB/B.119(2).   f151.

Fünfzig Jahre Sektion Zimmerberg S A C 1922-1972. Thalwil, [1972]. Ill.
GB/A.938(3).   f152.

Fünfzig Kinder- und Hausmärchen / gesammelt durch die Brüder Grimm. Kleine Ausg. Leipzig, [n.d.]. Ill.
Lloyd.39.   f153.

Fuori delle strade battute / E.R. Blanchet; traduzione di Matelda Cozzani. Milano, 1935. Ill. [Montagna; 13.]
GB/A.1440.   f154.

A **further** contribution to the bibliography of Mont Blanc, 1786-1853 / Henry F. Montagnier. [London], 1916. Ports. Reprinted from the *Alpine Journal*, May 1916.
GB.1741(2); Lloyd.1602(6); Lloyd.1602(6)A.   f155.

Further explorations in the Caucasus / A.F. Mummery, H.W. Holder, C.T. Dent, D.W. Freshfield. London, [1889]. Ill., map. From the *Proceedings of the Royal Geographical Society and Monthly Record of Geography*, June no., 1889.
Lloyd.1620(22).   f156.

Eine **Fussreise** vor 60 Jahren / nach einem Manuscript Dr. S. Brunner's mitgetheilt von A. Wäber. [Bern, 1892.] Pp.[139]-83 of the *Jahrbuch des Schweizer Alpenclub*, Jahrg.27.
GB.1881(6).   f157.

-G-

Gabrisse: journal d'un gardien de cabane / Aug. Vautier. Lausanne, 1933.
GB.252. g001.

Gaddings with a primitive people: being a series of sketches of Alpine life and customs / W.A. Baillie-Grohman. London, 1878.
Lloyd.450-1. g002.

Galena and associated ore minerals from the cryolite at Ivigtut, South Greenland / Sven Karup-Møller, Hans Pauly. Copenhagen, 1979. Ill., map. [Meddelelser om Grønland. Geoscience; 2.]
GB/A.1818. g003.

Gales, ice and men: a biography of the steam barkentine *Bear* / Frank Wead. New York, 1937. Ill., maps.
GB/A.1906. g004.

La **gallina** di cartone: racconti di montagna / Carlo Arzani. Lecco, 1971.
GB/B.312(10). g005.

Det **gamle** Grønlands nye perlustration, eller natural-historie / Hans Egede. Kjøbenhavn, 1741. Ill., map.
GB/A.1882. g006.

Gaping Ghyll in 1904 / M. Botterill. [Leeds, 1929.] Map. Pp.309-10 of the *Yorkshire Ramblers' Club Journal*, vol.5 no.18.
GB.1332(34). g007.

La **gara** verso il Polo Nord / Giotto Dainelli. Torino, 1960. Ill., maps, ports. [La conquista della terra; 7.]
GB/B.432. g008.

Garhwal Himalaya: expédition suisse 1939 / André Roch; publié sous les auspices de la Fondation suisse d'explorations alpines. Neuchâtel, 1947. Ill., maps. [Montagne.]
GB/A.168. g009.

Gasherbrun 4° : Baltoro, Karakorum: una spedizione alle montagne del Pakistan organizzata e finanziata nel 1958 dal Club Alpino Italiano, diretta da Riccardo Cassin / raccontata da Fosco Maraini, valendosi di diari, appunti, ricordi suoi e di Walter Bonatti [et al.]. Bari, 1960. Ill., maps, ports.
GB.1102. g010.

The **gazetteer** of Sikhim / edited in the Bengal Government Secretariat. Calcutta, 1894. Ill., maps.
GB.1248. g011.

Die **Gebirge**: Vortrag / Albert Heim. Basel, 1881. Ill. [Oeffentlige Vorträge; Bd.6 Hft.7.]
GB/A.1052(2). g012.

Der **Gebirgsbau** der Alpen / E. Desor. Wiesbaden, 1865. Ill.
GB/A.513. g013.

Der **Gebirgsbau** der Westalpen / Carl Diener. Wien, 1891. Maps.
GB/A.1122. g014.

Die **Gebirgsgruppe** des Monte Cristallo: ein Beitrag zur Kenntnis der südtirolischen Dolomit-Alpen / W. Eckerth. 2., erw. und umgearb. Aufl. Prag, 1891. Ill., maps.
GB/A.378. g015.

Die **Gefahren** der Alpen: praktische Winke für Bergsteiger / Emil Zsigmondy. Leipzig, 1885. Ill.
GB.939. g016.

Gefahrten der Renntiere / Farley Mowat; übertragen von Heinz Geck. Stuttgart, 1954. Ill. Translated from *People of the deer*.
GB/A.417. g017.

Geiger, pilote des glaciers / Hermann Geiger. [Paris], 1967. Ill. [Sempervivum; 44.]
GB/A.161. g018.

Der **Geltengrat**, das Heremence- und Bagnethal, das Einfischthal und der Weissthorpass / Melchior Ulrich. Zürich, 1853. Map. Pp.35-74 of the *Mittheilungen der Naturforschenden Gesellschaft in Zürich*, no.82-3.
GB.1881(76). g019.

Gemmi bis Petersgrat / bearbeitet von Fred Müller und W. Diehl. 5. Aufl. Bern, 1571. Ill. [Hochgebirgsführer durch die Berner Alpen; 2.] Published by the Schweizer Alpenclub, Sektion Bern.
GB/A.989(2). g019.1.

Gemsen-Eier: Alpin-humoristisches in Wort & Bild / E. Bayberger, Herausgeber. Kempten, 1895-98. 3v (in 1).
Lloyd.392. g020.

A **general** collection of the best and most interesting voyages and travels / John Pinkerton. London, 1809. Extracts from v4-5. Contains:

Saussure's *An account of the attempts that have been made to attain the summit of Mont Blanc*; L. Ramond's *Journey to the summit of Mont Perdu*; and Coxe's *Travels in Switzerland*.
Lloyd.1483.   g021.

General description of my late tour through France, Switzerland and Germany, accompanied by my aunt and elder sister / E.D. Wynne Jones. Rhyl, [1868?]. Ill., port.
GB/A.1913.   g022.

General guide to the United States and Canada / Daniel Appleton and Co. New York, 1888. Ill., maps.
Lloyd.279.   g023.

A **general**, historical, and topographical description of Mount Caucasus: with a catalogue of plants indigenous to the country / translated from the works of Dr. Reineggs and Marshal Bieberstein, by Charles Wilkinson. London, 1807. 2v (in 1); ill., map.
Lloyd.941.   g024.

A **general** outline of the Swiss landscapes / [Rowley Lascelles]; with miscellaneous notes and illustrations from M. de Saussure and others. 3rd ed., rev. and enl. London, 1812.
GB/A.546.   g025.

General-Tarif für die Führer und Träger der Schweizer Alpen / unter Mitwirkung der Sektionen aufgestellt durch das Central-Comité des Schweizer Alpen-Clubs. 2: Berner-Oberland. Neuchâtel, 1899.
Lloyd.1615(5).   g026.

Genève à travers les siècles / Guillaume Fatio. Genève, 1900. Ill.
Lloyd.1498.   g027.

Genève au 18me siècle: suivi d'une notice sur les hôtelleries et auberges de la ville de Genève / Charles Louis Perrin. Genève, 1909. Ill., ports.
Lloyd.1616(12).   g028.

Genève de 1788 à 1792: la fin d'un régime / Henri Fazy. Genève, 1917.
Lloyd.1607(6).   g029.

Genève et la Révolution: les Comités provisoires, 28 décembre 1792-13 avril 1794: le Gouvernement constitutionnel, l'annexion, la société économique 1794-1814 / Marc Ernest Peter. Genève, 1921. 2v; ill., map.
Lloyd.1291 (wanting v.2).   g030.

Genti e cose della montagna: novelle e capitoli / Giuseppe Giacosa. Sesto S. Giovanni, 1917.
GB/A.444.   g031.

Geografia dell'Alpi / G. Nangeroni, C. Saibene. Lecco, 1953. Ill. [Dispensa / Club Alpino Italiano, Commissione Nazionale Scuole di Alpinismo; 2.]
GB/A.2022(6).   g032.

The **Geographical** Journal, including the Proceedings of the Royal Geographical Society. Vol.85 no.4-vol.131 pt.3. London, 1935-65. An imperfect set.
GB.1463-1502.   g033.

Géographie des Alpes / Pierre George. Paris, 1942. Ill., maps. [Géographie de la France.]
GB/A.181(8).   g034.

Geography of the Himalaya / S.C. Bose. Rev. ed. New Delhi, 1972. Ill., maps. [India, the land and the people.]
GB/A.2021(5).   g035.

The **geography** of the Polar regions, consisting of A general characterization of Polar nature / Otto Nordenskjöld; and A regional geography of the Arctic and the Antarctic / Ludwig Mecking. New York, 1928. Ill. [Special publication / American Geographical Society; 8.]
GB/A.1869.   g036.

A **geological** excursion to central Spitzbergen / Gerard de Geer. Stockholm, 1910. Ill., maps. Translated from *Guide de l'excursion au Spitzberg*. Published by the International Geological Congress, 1910.
GB.1335(39).   g037.

Geological travels in some parts of France, Switzerland, and Germany / Jean André de Luc; translated from the French manuscript. London, 1813. 2v; maps.
GB/A.619-20.   g038.

Géologie de Zermatt et sa situation dans le système alpin. Géologie du massif du Simplon / [Karl Schmidt]. Genève, 1895. A review. Extrait des *Archives des sciences physiques et naturelles*, novembre 1895.
GB/A.514(15).   g039.

Geologische Beschreibung der in Blatt XX des Eidg. Atlasses enthaltenen Gebirge von Graubünden / G. Theobald. Bern, 1866.
GB/B.382. g040.

Geologische Beschreibung der in den Blættern X und XV des Eidg. Atlasses enth. Gebirge von Graubünden / G. Theobald. Bern, 1864.
GB/B.381. g041.

Geologische Briefe aus den Alpen / Bernhard von Cotta. Leipzig, 1850. Ill.
GB/A.439. g042.

Geologische Briefe aus und über die Schweiz: mit steter Rücksicht auf die allgemeinen Naturverhältnisse der Erde / J. Meyer. 2. Ausg. Leipzig, 1858. Originally published as *Physik der Schweiz*.
GB/A.1467. g043.

Geologische und topographische Wanderungen im Aare- und Rhonegebiet in den Jahren 1877, 1878 und 1879 / Edmund von Fellenberg. Bern, 1880. Ill. Separatabdruck aus dem *Jahrbuch des S.A.C.*, Bd.14-15.
Lloyd.1615(21). g044.

Geologisches über die Stadt Zürich und ihre Umgebung / Leo Wehrli. [N.p., 1909.] Ill. Separatdruck aus der *Festschrift für den Deutschen Verein für öffentliche Gesundheitspflege*.
GB/A.1052(1). g045.

Geology: meteorology: botany: bird life: equipment: maps, &c.: rock and snow craft: photography: Sir Hugh Munro's classified tables of the 3000ft mountains of Scotland / edited by James Reid Young. Edinburgh, 1921. Ill. [Scottish Mountaineering Club guide; 1A.]
GB.1332(40). g046.

Geomorphological observations at Kangerdlugssuaq, East Greenland / Charles Kent Brooks. Copenhagen, 1977. Ill., maps. [Meddelelser om Grønland. Geoscience; 1.]
GB/A.1818. g047.

German conversation-grammar: a practical method of learning the German language / Emil Otto; revised by Franz Lange. 26th ed. London, 1895. [Method Gaspey-Otto-Sauer for the study of modern languages.]
Lloyd.692. g048.

Germano-Helveto-Sparta, oder Kurtz-deutliche Grund-Zeichnung dess alt-teutschen Spartier-Lands, das ist Schweitzerland / Johann Casper Steiner. Zug, 1684.
Lloyd.5. g049.

Gesammelte Schriften alpinen und vermischten Inhalts / Karl Hofmann; herausgegeben von Joh. Stüdl. Gera, 1871.
GB/A.825. g050.

Gesammelte Schriften des Freiherrn Hermann von Barth; herausgegeben von Carl Bünsch und Max Rohrer. München, [1926]. Ill., maps.
GB/B.133. g051.

Geschichte der alpinen Literatur: ein Abriss / Aloys Dreyer. München, 1938. [Jahresgabe der Gesellschaft alpiner Bücherfreunde; 25.]
GB.897. g052.

Geschichte der Begrundung des Gotthardunternehmens / Martin Wanner. Bern, 1880. Map.
GB/A.1126. g053.

Geschichte der physischen Geographie der Schweiz bis 1815 / Bernhard Studer. Bern, 1863.
GB.596. g054.

Geschichte der russischen geographischen Entdeckungen: gesammelte Aufsätze / L.S. Berg; [übersetzt von Rolf Ulrich]. Leipzig, 1954. Ill. [Ergebnisse und Probleme der modernen Wissenschaften.] Translated from *Ocherki po istorii russkikh geograficheskikh otkritii*.
GB/A.1498. g055.

Geschichte der Schweiz / Carl Grosse, Marquis von Pharmusa. Halle, 1791. 2v; port.
GB.103-4. g056.

Geschichte des Baues der Gotthardbahn / Martin Wanner. Luzern, 1885.
GB/A.1125. g057.

Geschichte des Bergbau's der östlichen Schweiz / Placidus A. Plattner. Chur, 1878.
GB/A.638. g058.

Geschichte des Deutschen und Oesterreichischen Alpenvereins / Johannes E. Emmer. [Munich?], 1894. Ill., ports. Pp.177-256 of an unidentified issue of the *Zeitschrift des Deutschen und Oesterreichischen Alpenvereins*.
GB.1880(28) (impf.). g059.

Geschichte des Reisens in der Schweiz: eine culturgeschichtliche Studie / Gustav Peyer. Basel, 1885.
GB.113. g060.

I **ghiacciai** del gruppo Ortles-Cevedale (Alpi centrali) / Ardito Desio, con la collaborazione di Severino Belloni e di Augusto Giorcelli. Torino, 1968. 2v; ill., maps.
GB/B.322-3. g061.

I **ghiacciai** dell'Alto Adige / Fausto Stefenelli. Bolzano, 1958. Ill. Published by the Club Alpino Italiano.
GB/A.1295(18). g062.

I **ghiacciai** della Valle d'Aosta / M. Vanni, C. Origlia, F. De Gemini. Torino, 1953. Ill., maps. Estratto dal *Bollettino del Comitato Glaciologico Italiano*, 2a ser. n.4, 1953.
GB/A.1409. g063.

Ghiacciai e vette / Emile Javelle; traduzione di Ettore Cozzani. Milano, [1947]. Ill. [Montagna; 24.] Translated from *Souvenirs d'un alpiniste*.
GB/A.550. g064.

Ghiaccio neve roccia / Gaston Rébuffat; traduzione di Rosalba Donvito Gossi. Bologna, 1980. Ill. [Montagne; 9.] Translated from *Glace, neige et roc*.
GB/B.591. g065.

Ghiaccio neve roccia 1961 / redattore responsabile: Charles Spillmann. Milano, 1961. Ill., maps, ports.
GB/B.442. g066.

Le **gibier** des montagnes françaises / Marcel Couturier. [Paris], 1964. Ill. [Sempervivum; 40.]
GB/A.192. g067.

Gino Watkins / J.M. Scott. 4th ed. London, 1937. Ill., maps, ports. [Black jacket books.]
GB.230. g068.

I **giorni** grandi / Walter Bonatti. [Milan], 1971. Ill.
GB/B.398. g069.

Die **Gipfel** schweigen: eine Liebeserklärung an die Julischen Alpen: Roman / Heinz Zechmann. Graz, [1965]. Ill.
GB/A.172. g070.

Gipfel über den Wolken: Lhotse und Everest / Albert Eggler. Bern, [1956]. Ill., maps. Published by the Swiss Foundation for Alpine Research.
GB.1126. g071.

Gipfelsturm im Karakorum / Józef Nyka, Andrzej Paczkowski, Andrzej Zawada. 2. Aufl. Leipzig, 1979.
GB/A.1984. g072.

Gipfelstürmer / Bilder von Vilém Heckel; Text von Otto Jelinek; Deutsch von Friedrich Runge. Prag, [1956].
GB/B.242. g073.

Gipfelwärts: ein junger Bergführer erzählt / Paul Etter. 2. Aufl. Frauenfeld, 1969. Ill.
GB/A.452. g074.

Die **Gipfelwelt** der Haute-Route zwischen Mont-Blanc und Saas-Fee / André Roch; die Ubertragung besorgte Max Oechslin. Zürich, 1944. Ill. Translated from: *La haute route*.
GB/B.452. g075.

Gita a Squillace eseguita dalla Sezione Calabrese del Club Alpino Italiano nel giorno 9 marzo 1879 / A. Spinola. Catanzaro, 1879.
GB/A.1351(6). g076.

Una **gita** autunnale nel 1846 pei monti del Tirolo italiano e tedesco: note a Cinzio Di Evaldo. Milano, 1862.
GB/A.1349(9). g077.

Give me the hills / Miriam Underhill. Riverside, Conn., [1971]. Ill.
GB/A.2062. g078.

Gjennem isbaksen: atten år med Roald Amundsen / Helmer Hanssen. Oslo, 1942.
GB/A.2083. g079.

Glaciaire et périglaciaire de l'Ata Sund, nord-oriental Groenland / Marc Boyé. Paris, 1950. [Actualités scientifiques et industrielles. Expéditions polaires françaises. Missions Paul-Emile Victor; 1.]
GB/A.1737. g080.

Glacial epochs and warm polar climates. [London, 1878.] Pp.223-54 of the *Quarterly Review*, Sept. 1878.
GB.1332(33). g081.

Il **glacialismo** attuale nel bacino del Breil / Manfredo Vanni. [Rome, 1931.] Ill. Estratto dal *Bollettino del Comitato Glaciologico Italiano*, n.11, anno 1931.
GB/B.313(5). g082.

Glacier Bay: the land and the silence / Dave Bohn; edited by David Brower. San Francisco, [1967]. Ill., ports. [Sierra Club exhibit format series; 16.]
GB/B.506. g083.

The **glacier** land / from the French of Alexandre Dumas; by Mrs. W.R. Wilde. London, 1852. [Bookcase; 7.] Translated from *Impressions de voyage*.
GB.297; Lloyd.351.   g084.

Glacier pilot: the story of Bob Reeve and the flyers who pushed back Alaska's air frontiers / [Beth Day]. 5th printing. [New York], 1968. Ill., maps, ports.
GB/A.1664.   g085.

Glacier-dammed lake investigations in the Hullet Lake area, South Greenland / Alastair G. Dawson. Copenhagen, 1983. Ill., maps. [Meddelelser om Grønland. Geoscience; 11.]
GB/A.1818(11).   g086.

Les **glaciers** / Frédéric Zurcher, Elie Margollé. 2e éd. rev. et augm. Paris, 1870. Ill. [Bibliothèque des merveilles.]
GB.233.   g087.

Les **glaciers** / Frédéric Zurcher, Elie Margollé. 3e éd., rev. et augm. Paris, 1875. Ill.
Lloyd.481.   g088.

Glaciers des Alpes / Robert C. Bachmann. Lausanne, 1979.
GB/B.504.   g089.

Les **glaciers** et les montagnes / Stanislas Meunier. Paris, [1920?]. [Bibliothèque de philosophie scientifique.]
GB/A.915(8).   g090.

Glaciers in China / edited by Chi Jian-mei, Ren Bing-hui. Shanghai, 1980. Ill.
GB/B.546.   g091.

The **glaciers** of Gunversdahl, Justedal / T.G. Bonney. Cambridge, [1870]. Extracted from the *Eagle*, no.37, 1870.
Lloyd.801.   g092.

The **glaciers** of the Alps / John Tyndall. London, 1863. Pp.77-125 of the *Quarterly Review*, no.227, July 1863.
GB.1747; GB.1881(45).   g093.

The **glaciers** of the Alps: being a narrative of excursions and ascents, an account of the origin and phenomena of glaciers, and an exposition of the physical principles to which they are related / John Tyndall. London, 1860. Ill.
GB.500; Lloyd.690; Lloyd.690A.   g094.

The **glaciers** of the Alps: being a narrative of excursions and ascents / John Tyndall. New ed. London, 1896. Ill.
GB.465.   g095.

The **glaciers** of the Alps (Part I), and Mountaineering in 1861 / John Tyndall. London, 1911. Ill. [Everyman's library. Science.]
GB.154.   g096.

The **glaciers** of the Bernina: read before the Alpine Club / E.N. Buxton. [London, 1864.] Pp.339-52 of the *Alpine Journal*, vol.1, 1864.
GB.1737(3) (impf.).   g097.

Le **glaçon** du Polaris: aventures du capitaine Tyson racontées d'après les publications américaines / W. de Fonvielle. 2e éd. Paris, 1877. Ill., map, ports.
GB/A.2152.   g098.

A **glance** at some of the beauties and sublimities of Switzerland / John Murray. London, 1829.
GB.356; Lloyd.396.   g099.

The **Glasgow** University Album. 1836. Glasgow, 1836.
Lloyd.313.   g100.

Glen Brittle memorial hut appeal / British Mountaineering Council. [Stockport], 1959.
GB.1322(9).   g101.

Glencoe. [Edinburgh, 1960.] Ill., ports. P.39 of *Scottish Field*, July 1960.
GB.1334(36) (impf.).   g102.

Die **Gletscher** der Alpen: autorisirte deutsche Ausgabe / John Tyndall. Braunschweig, 1898. Ill. Translated from *The glaciers of the Alps*.
GB/A.70.   g103.

Die **Gletscher** der Jetztzeit: eine Zusammenstellung und Prüfung ihrer Erscheinungen und Gesetze / Albert Mousson. Zürich, 1854.
GB/A.424(4).   g104.

Die **Gletscher** der Schweiz nach Gebieten und Gruppen geordnet: ein Auszug aus dem auf Anordnung des Schweizer Alpenclub in Bearbeitung genommenen Gletscherbuche. Les glaciers de la Suisse / J.J. Siegfried. Zürich, 1874.
GB.1325(6).   g105.

Die **Gletscher** und die erratischen Blöcke / F.J. Hugi. Solothurn, 1843.
GB.1330(8).   g106.

Das **Gletscherbuch**: Rätzel und Romantik, Gestalt und Gesetz der Alpengletscher / Walther Flaig. Leipzig, 1938. Ill.
GB/A.1496.   g107.

Gletscherfahrten in den Berner Alpen / Abraham Roth. Berlin, 1861. Ill.
GB.60(1); GB.67.   g108.

Die **Gletschermühlen** auf Maloja / Christian Tarnuzzer. Chur, 1896. Separat-Abdruck aus dem 39. *Jahresbericht der Naturforschenden Gesellschaft Graubünden's*.
GB/A.514(17).   g109.

Glimpses of the Wonderful: Christmas annual. Ser.3. London, 1847. Ill.
GB.65.   g110.

The **glittering** mountains of Canada: a record of exploration and pioneer ascents in the Canadian Rockies, 1914-1924 / J. Monroe Thorington. Philadelphia, 1925. Ill., maps, ports., facsims.
GB.947.   g111.

The **glories** of the Minya Konka: magnificent snow peaks of the China-Tibetan border are photographed at close range by a National Geographic Society expedition / Joseph F. Rock. Washington, 1930. Ill. Pp.[385]-437 of the *National Geographic Magazine,* vol.58 no.4, October 1930.
GB.1333(14).   g112.

Glückliche Tage auf hohen Bergen: die viertausender der schweizer Alpen / Walter Schmid. 6. Aufl. Bern, [n.d.]. Ill.
GB/A.374.   g113.

Godfrey Allan Solly, 1858-1942 / J.M.D. [London, 1942.] Pp.64-6 of the *Climbers' Club Journal,* N.S. vol.7 no.1.
GB.1339(14[2]).   g114.

Goethe, Scheffel und C.F. Meyer im Banne der Alpen / Carl Camenisch. 2. ill. Aufl. Samaden, 1911.
GB/A.1051(8).   g115.

Goethes schweizer Reisen / Wilhelm Bode. Leipzig, 1922. Ill.
GB/A.1404.   g116.

Gogarth / Alec Sharp. [Dunblane], 1977. Ill., maps. [Climbers' Club guides to Wales; 7.]
GB/A.1589(33).   g117.

Gogarth: 1981 supplement / Geoff Milburn. 2nd ed. [N.p.], 1981. [Climbers' Club guides to Wales.]
GB/A.1589(34).   g118.

Going high, the story of man and altitude / Charles S. Houston. Burlington, Vt., 1980. Ill.
GB/B.528(10).   g119.

Gold hunting in Alaska / Joseph Grinnell; edited by Elizabeth Grinnell. Elgin, Ill., 1901. Ill., ports.
GB/A.1710.   g120.

Goldau et son district / Carl Zay; extrait traduit de l'allemand. 2e éd. Lucerne, 1817. Translated from *Goldau und seine Gegend*.
Lloyd.1615(14).   g121.

Das **goldene** Buch der Alpen / die Zusammenstellung des Bildteiles besorgte Ulrich Link. München, 1959. Ill.
GB/B.597.   g122.

Der **Gornergrat** und die Walliser Alpenpässe mit geschichtlichen Notizen / Fritz Bühler. Luzern, 1894.
GB/A.1142.   g123.

Gottes unerforschliche Rathschlüsse bei der Lebensrettung der einen und dem Untergange der andern bei dem grossen Bergsturze über Goldau und seine Umgebung im Kanton Schwyz / Martin Ulrich. Altorf, 1836. Map.
GB/A.762.   g124.

Das **Gottesackerplateau**: ein Karrenfeld im Allgäu: Studien zur Lösung des Karrenproblems / Max Eckert. Innsbruck, 1902. Ill., maps. [Wissenschaftliche Ergänzungshefte zur Zeitschrift des D. und O. Alpenvereins; Bd.1 Hft.3.]
GB/B.1.   g125.

Der **Gotthard** / Carl Spitteler. Frauenfeld, 1897.
GB/A.189.   g126.

Der **Gotthard** und das Tessin mit den oberitalischen Seen / Eduard Osenbrüggen. Basel, 1877.
GB/A.678.   g127.

Die **Gotthard**-Bahn, Beschreibendes und Geschichtliches / H.A. Berlepsch. Gotha, 1881. Map. [Petermann's Geographische Mitteilungen. Ergänzungsheft; 65.]
GB/B.390(6).   g128.

Gotthardbahn. Kilchberg, [ca 1920]. Ill. [Souvenir-albums édition illustrato; 32.]
GB/B.313(6).   g129.

Der **Gotthardvertrag** im Nationalrat / Referat von A. v. Planta im Namen der Mehrheit der national-rätlichen Kommission, betreffend Staatsvertrag vom 13. Oktober 1909. Bern, 1913.
GB/A.1199(6).   g130.

Le **grain** du glacier / F.A. Forel. Genève, 1882. Extrait des *Archives des sciences physiques et naturelles*, avril 15 1882.
GB/A.514(2).   g131.

Il **Gran** Cervino: antologia di Alfonso Bernardi. Bologna, 1963. Ill., ports., facsims. [Montagne; 2.]
GB.1052.   g132.

Gran Paradiso / E. Andreis, R. Chabod, M.C. Santi. Roma, 1939. Ill., maps. [Guida dei monti d'Italia.]
GB/A.1625; GB/A.1805.   g133.

Il **Gran** Paradiso / Franco Fini, Gigi Mattana; contributi di Silvio Bruno [et al.]. Bologna, 1977. Ill.
GB/B.592.   g134.

Gran Paradiso: itinerari alpinistici e sci-alpinistici / Franco Brevini. Aosta, 1981. Ill., maps.
GB/A.1911(12).   g135.

Gran Sasso d'Italia / C. Landi Vittorj, S. Pietro-stefani. Roma, 1943. Ill., maps. [Guida dei monti d'Italia.]
GB/A.775.   g136.

Gran Sasso d'Italia / C. Landi Vittorj, S. Pietro-stefani. 3a ed. ampliata e aggiornata. Milano, 1972. Ill., maps. [Guida dei monti d'Italia.]
GB/A.1063.   g137.

Grand Hôtel Couttet et du Parc, [Chamonix]. Paris, [n.d]. Prospectus.
GB.1326(4).   g138.

Le **grand** messager boiteux des quatre parties du monde, almanach géographique, historique, constructif et amusant, pour l'an de grâce 1823. Belfort, [1822].
Lloyd.1591(8).   g139.

Le **grand** pic de Belledone / L. Xavier Drevet. Grenoble, 1876. Ill., map. [Bibliothèque du touriste en Dauphiné.]
GB/A.835(9).   g140.

Le **Grand** Saint-Bernard: trajet direct de Londres à Brindisi avec jonction à la Mediterranée par le col de Tende / baron Marius de Vautheleret. Paris, 1884. Map.
GB/A.827.   g141.

Le **Grand** Saint Bernard, ou Essai historique sur ce que l'hospice du Grand Saint-Bernard offre de plus intéressant / par un ecclésiastique du diocèse de Lion. [N.p.], 1830.
GB/A.1462.   g142.

Le **grand** vertige: roman / Pierre Mélon. Neuchâtel, 1951. Ill.
GB/A.1318.   g143.

La **Grande** Civetta / a cura di Alfonso Bernardi. Bologna, 1971. Ill., maps. [Montagne; 8.]
GB/A.911.   g144.

La **grande** conquête / James Ramsey Ullman; traduction de J. et F. Germain. Grenoble, 1948. Ill., maps. Translated from *High conquest*.
GB/A.136.   g145.

La **grande** crévasse: roman / R. Frison-Roche. [Grenoble], 1968. Ill.
GB/A.1317.   g146.

La **grande** ronde autour du Mont-Blanc / Sami-vel. Grenoble, 1981. Ill., map.
GB/B.532.   g147.

Grande traversata delle Alpi: percorso e posti tappa dalla valle del Po alla Dora Baltea / a cura del Comitato Promotore GTA [Grande Traversata delle Alpi]. Torino, 1981. Ill., maps. Published by Centro Documentazione Alpina.
GB/A.2033(6).   g148.

Les **grandes** Alpes ensoleillées / P. et G. Veyret. [Paris], 1970. Ill. [Le monde en images.]
GB/A.826.   g149.

Les **grandes** ascensions des Pyrénées d'une mer à l'autre: guide spécial du piéton / comte Henri Russell-Killough. Paris, [1866]. Maps.
GB/A.1930.   g150.

Grandes Jorasses — Géant — Rochefort — Leschaux — Talèfre / Gino Buscaini, Lucien Devies. 4e éd. Paris, 1979. Ill. [Guide Vallot. La chaîne du Mont Blanc; 4.]
GB/A.2013/4.   g150.1.

Grandes Jorasses, Sperone Walker: 40 anni di storia alpinistica / Alessandro Gogna. Bologna,

1969. Ill. [Voci dai monti; 15.]
GB/A.950. g151.

Grandes Murailles: cronaca di una spedizione alpina / Guido Monzino. Milano, 1957. Ill., map, ports.
GB/B.497. g152.

Grandes routes et chemins écartés: rencontres sur les routes grisonnes à la pointe du Tessin / Pierre Grellet. Lausanne, 1946. Ill.
GB/A.1155. g153.

Grandi guide italiane dell'arco alpino / Enrico Camanni. Torino, 1985. [Quaderni di cultura alpina.]
GB/B.654. g154.

Grandi imprese sul Cervino / Giuseppe Mazzotti. Milano, 1934. Ill. [Montagna; 10.]
GB.1325(3). g155.

Grandi imprese sul Cervino / Giuseppe Mazzotti. 2a ed. Milano, 1944. Ill. [Montagna; 10.]
GB.1327(12). g156.

Les **grands** sommets des Alpes de la Tarentaise dans l'histoire / W.A.B. Coolidge. Lyon, 1911. Extrait de la *Revue alpine* d'avril 1911.
GB.1340(22). g157.

Graubünden in der deutschen Dichtung: Auswahl und Einleitung / Carl Camenisch. Leipzig, 1925.
GB/A.1175. g158.

Graubünden und Veltlin: Reisetaschenbuch für Freunde der Alpenwelt / Iwan Tschudi. 7. Aufl. St. Gallen, 1868. Maps. [Schweizerführer.]
GB/A.1386. g159.

Die **Grauen** Hörner: Inaugural-Dissertation / Konstantin Tolwinski. Zürich, 1910. Ill.
GB/A.1052(13). g160.

The **great** beast: the life of Aleister Crowley / John Symonds. 3rd impr. London, 1952. Ports.
GB.1047. g161.

Great days in the Rockies: the photographs of Byron Harmon, 1906-1934 / edited by Carol Harmon and the Peter Whyte Foundation; with a biography by Bart Robinson, and an appreciation by Jon Whyte. Toronto, 1978. Ill.
GB/A.1919. g162.

A **great** effort / J.M. Edwards. [London], 1941. Pp.9-13 of the *Climbers' Club Journal*, N.S. vol.6 no.3.
GB.1339(22[2]). g163.

Great Gable, Borrowdale, Buttermere / C.J. Astley-Cooper [et al.]. Manchester, 1937. [Climbing guides to the English Lake District; 3.] Published by the Fell and Rock Climbing Club of the English Lake District.
GB.48(3); GB.49. g164.

Great moments in mountaineering / Ronald Clark. London, 1956. Ill.
GB.295. g165.

A **great** mountain painter / Arnold Lunn. [Uxbridge, 1928.] Ill. Pp.409-[17] of the *British Ski Year Book*, vol.4 no.9.
GB.1881(74). g166.

Great North Atlantic Telegraph route. London, 1866. Map.
Lloyd.1583(5). g167.

Great Norwegian expeditions / Thor Heyerdahl, Søren Richter, Hj. Riiser-Larsen. Oslo, [1954]. Ill., maps, ports.
GB/A.1742. g168.

The **great** plateau: being an account of exploration in central Tibet, 1903, and of the Gartok expedition, 1904-1905 / C.G. Rawling. London, 1905. Ill., maps, ports.
GB.820; GB.1030 (impf). g169.

Great Slave Lake area, Northwest Territories / G.H. Blanchet. Ottawa, 1926. Ill., map. Published by the Department of the Interior, North West Territories and Yukon Branch.
GB/B.528(1). g170.

The **Great** Smokies and the Blue Ridge: the story of the Southern Appalachians / edited by Roderick Peattie; contributors: Edward S. Drake [et al.]. New York, 1943. Ill., map.
GB/A.1961. g171.

The **Great** St. Bernard / C.E. Johnstone. [N.p., n.d.] Ill. Pp.72-4 of an unidentified periodical.
GB.1336(30). g172.

The **Greely** Arctic Expedition as fully narrated by Lieut. Greely, U.S.A., and other survivors: full account of the terrible sufferings on the ice, and awful tales of cannibalism / George Lippard

Barclay. Philadelphia, 1887. Ill.
GB/B.440(13). g173.

Green mountains and Cullenbenbong / Bernard
O'Reilly. Brisbane, 1952. Ill.
GB/A.1560. g174.

Greenland then and now / Erik Erngaard;
translation: Mona Giersing. Copenhagen, 1972.
Ill., maps. Translated from *Grønland i tusinde år*.
GB/B.443. g175.

Grenoble et ses Alpes / Paul et Germaine Veyret.
Paris, 1962. Ill., map.
GB/A.481. g176.

Grenoble et ses montagnes / Jean Jacques Chevallier. Grenoble, [1938].
GB/C.22(23). g177.

Grenzen des Menschenmöglichen: Alleingänger
am Berg / Helmut Dumler. Salzburg, 1970. Ill.
GB/A.471. g178.

Le **Grépon** / Gilbert Robino. [N.p.], 1972.
GB/B.570(9). g179.

Le **Grigne** / Claudio Cima. Bologna, 1971. Ill.,
map. [Itinerari alpini; 5]
GB/A.867(9). g180.

Die **Grill's** aus der Ramsau: eine deutsche Führer-
familie: zum fünfzigjährigen Führerjubiläum
Johann Grills des jüngeren / W.F. Berchtesgaden,
[ca 1930]. Ports. Published by the Deutscher
Alpenverein, Sektion Berchtesgaden.
GB/B.312(6). g181.

Les **grimpeurs** des Alpes: un recueil d'excursions
alpestres publié par le Club alpin de Londres /
traduit par El. Dufour. Paris, 1862. [Bibliothèque
contemporaine.] Translated from *Peaks, passes and
glaciers*.
Lloyd.1612(12). g182.

Grindelwald. Dresden, 1892. Ill. Photographs.
GB/A.1972. g183.

Grindelwald — Meiringen — Grimsel — Münster
/ bearbeitet von Rudolf Wyss unter Mitwirkung
einiger Herren der Sektion Zofingen SAC. 2. Aufl.
Bern, 1964. Ill., maps. [Hochgebirgsführer durch
die Berner Alpen; 5.] Published by the Schweizer
Alpenclub, Sektion Bern.
GB/A.989(6). g183.1.

Grindelwald — Meiringen — Grimsel — Münster
/ bearbeitet von Rudolf Wyss unter Mitwirkung
einiger Herren der Sektion Zofingen SAC. 3. Aufl.
[Zurich], 1975. Ill. [Hochgebirgsführer durch die
Berner Alpen; 5.] Published by the Schweizer
Alpenclub, Sektion Bern.
GB/A.989(7). g183.2.

Grindelwald in winter, 1887 / Sir Charles Sherrington. [London, 1950.] A photostat of pp.10-4 of
the *Alpine Journal* for 1950.
GB.1315(15). g184.

Grindelwalder Bergführer: 75 Jahre Führerverein
Grindelwald: Festschrift zum Jubiläum 1973 /
Samuel Brawand. Grindelwald, [1973]. Ill.
GB/B.366(4). g185.

Les **Grisons** et la haute Engadine / William Rey.
Genève, 1850.
GB/A.804(3). g186.

Grisons incidents in olden times / Beatrix L.
Tollemache. London, 1891.
Lloyd.453. g187.

Grivola e Gran Paradiso / Giovanni Bobba.
Torino, 1892. Estratto dal *Bollettino del Club Alpino
Italiano*, vol.25 no.58, 1891.
GB/B.289(16). g188.

Die **Grödener** Alpen / Karl Schulz. Rosengarten
und Marmolata Gruppe / Ludwig Darmstädter.
[Berlin, 1894.] Ill. Pp.[350]-98 of *Erschliessung der
Ostalpen*, Bd.3.
GB.1379. g189.

Das **Grödner** Thal / Franz Moroder. St.Ulrich in
Gröden, 1891. Maps. Published by der Deutscher
Alpenverein, Sektion Gröden.
Lloyd.346. g190.

Groenland: univers de cristal / Louis Rey. Paris,
1974. Ill., maps.
GB/B.524(12). g191.

Grønlands historiske mindesmærker / [edited by
Finnur Magnusson, C.C. Rafn]. København, 1976.
3v; ill., maps. Facsimile reprint of the Copenhagen, 1838-45 ed.
GB/A.1491-3. g192.

Das **grosse** Alpenwanderbuch: Wandern, Bergsteigen und Skifahren in den schönsten Gebieten
von Osterreich und Deutschland / Hermann
Molterer. Wels, [1966]. Ill., maps.
GB/C.25. g193.

Das **grosse** Ostalpenbuch / herausgegeben von Karl Lukan mit Beiträgen von Willi End [et al.]. Wien, 1969. Ill. Originally published as *Die Julische Alpen im Bilde*.
GB/B.240. g194.

Die **grossen** kalten Berge von Szetschuan: Erlebnisse, Forschungen und Kartierungen im Minya-Konka-Gebirge / Eduard Imhof; herausgegeben von der Schweizerischen Stiftung für alpine Forschungen. Zürich, 1974. Ill., maps. [Montes mundi; 1.]
GB/B.481. g195.

Die **grossen** Ski Stationen der Alpen / Walter Pause; unter Mitarbeit von Kurt Gramer. München, [1967]. Ill.
GB/B.114. g196.

Der **Grossvenediger** in der Geschichte des Alpinismus / Otto Knorr. München, 1932. Ill.
GB/B.451. g197.

Groupes de Trélatête et de Miage (entre les cols de Miage, de la Seigne et du Bonhomme) / Pierre Henry, Marcel Ichac, avec la collaboration de Paul Gayet-Tancrède. Paris, 1933. Ill., maps. [Guide Vallot. Description de la haute montagne dans le massif du Mont-Blanc; 7.]
GB/A.1802. g198.

Groupes de Triolet et d'Argentière, entre les cols de Pierre-Joseph et du Chardonnet / Lucien Devies, Pierre Henry, Pierre Dalloz. Paris, 1936. Ill. [Guide Vallot. Description de la haute montagne dans le massif du Mont-Blanc; 6.]
GB/A.1803. g199.

Groupes du Chardonnet et du Tour, entre les cols du Chardonnet et de Balme / Pierre Dalloz, Marcel Ichac, Pierre Henry. Paris, 1937. Ill. [Guide Vallot. Description de la haute montagne dans le massif du Mont Blanc; 6 bis.]
GB/A.1801. g200.

Groupes du Mont-Blanc et de la Tour Ronde / Jacques Lagarde. Paris, 1930. Ill., maps. [Guide Vallot. Description de la haute montagne dans le massif du Mont Blanc; 4.]
GB.89; Lloyd.146. g201.

Die **Grundlagen** des Alpinismus: ein Leitfaden des Bergsteigens. Osnovy al'pinzma: posobie dlia nachinaiushchikh al'pinistov / W. Abalakow; übersetzt von Hellmut Schöner. Leipzig, 1952. Ill.
GB/A.414. g202.

I **gruppi** di combattimento: Cremona, Friuli, Folgore, Legnano, Mantova, Piceno (1944-1945). Roma, 1974.
GB/A.2041. g203.

Il **gruppo** Caserine-Cornaget (o gruppo delle Pregoiane) nelle Prealpi Clautane / Tullio Trevisan, Sergio Fradeloni. Bologna, 1973. Ill., maps. Estratto da *Le alpi venete*, n.2/1971-n.1/1972.
GB/B.377(11). g204.

Il **gruppo** Castello-Provenzale / Gian Piero Motti, Alessandro Gogna. Bologna, 1975. Ill., map. [Itinerari alpini; 26.]
GB/A.1468(19). g205.

Gruppo del Catinaccio: dirupi di Larséc / Dante Colli, Gino Battista. Bologna, 1982. Ill., maps. [Itinerari alpini; 55.]
GB/A.1589(31); GB/A.1589(35). g206.

Gruppo del Catinaccio: guida escursionistica / Luca Visentini. 2a ed. Bolzano, 1979. Ill.
GB/A.1997. g207.

Il **gruppo** del Gran Paradiso. Torino, 1894. Maps. Published by the 26th Congresso Alpino, 1894.
GB/A.1416. g208.

Il **gruppo** del Gran Paradiso: la topografia storica e cartografica e la storia descrittiva ed alpina sino al 1860 / W.A.B. Coolidge. Torino, 1909. Maps. Estratto dal *Bollettino del C.A.I.* pel 1908, vol.39 n.72.
GB.1340(19). g209.

Il **gruppo** del Gran Paradiso nella storia: appendice agli articoli sullo stesso gruppo pubblicati nel *Bollettino C.A.I.*, n.72 / W.A.B. Coolidge. [Turin, 1909.] Pp.217-9 of the *Bollettino del Club Alpino Italiano*, 1909.
GB.1880(48). g210.

Il **gruppo** del Marguareis, Alpi Liguri: guida alpinistica / Sandro Comino. Mondovì, 1963. Ill., maps.
GB/A.1361. g211.

Il **gruppo** del Velino / Enrico Abbate. [Turin, 1898.] Map. Pp.[27]-42 of the *Bollettino del Club Alpino Italiano*, vol.31 no.64.
GB.1881(15). g212.

Gruppo dell'Adamello / Mario Bernasconi. Bergamo, 1929. Ill. [Guide sciistiche / Sci Club

Milano; 1.] At head of title: Sci Club Milano, con il patrocinio della Sezione di Milano del Club Alpino Italiano.
GB/A.1964(1). g213.

Gruppo della Marmolada: escursionismo / Luca Visentini. Bolzano, 1980. Ill.
GB/A.1977. g214.

Il **gruppo** della Paganella: guida per rocciatori / Heinz Steinkötter. Trento, [1969?]. Ill., map.
GB/A.1050(6). g215.

Gruppo della Schiara / Piero Rossi, con la collaborazione di G. Angelini. Bologna, 1967. Ill., map. [Itinerari alpini; 1.]
GB/A.802(12). g216.

Gruppo Monte Rosa / Amilcare Bertolini, Giuseppe F. Gugliermina. Monza, 1925. Ill. Published by the Club Alpino Italiano, Sezione Universitaria.
GB/A.1295(14). g217.

Gruppo Vedrette Giganti: descrizione ed itinerari / Guido Brizio. Roma, 1929. Ill., map. Published by the Club Alpino Italiano, Sezione di Roma.
GB/A.828(7). g218.

Gruss aus den Bergen. München, 1898. A postcard.
GB/A.2076(11). g219.

La **guerra** d'Italia. Milano, 1916-24. 6v; ill., ports.
GB/B.588. g220.

La **guerra** delle nazioni, 1914-1918. Milano, 1933-34. 12v (in 6); ill., ports.
GB/B.594. g221.

La **guerra** in Africa orientale, giugno 1940-novembre 1941 / Ministero della Difesa, Stato Maggiore, Esercito, Ufficio Storico. 2a ed. Roma, 1971. Maps.
GB/A.2042. g222.

Guida ad una gita entro la Vallesesia per cui si osservano alcuni luoghi e tutte le parrocchie che in essa vi sono / Girolamo Lana. Bologna, 1972. Facsimile reprint of the Novara, 1840 ed.
GB/A.1120. g223.

Guida ai bagni ed alle acque minerali di Courmayeur: con alcuni cenni sulle terme di Pré-St.Didier / Giovanni Antonio Giusta. Aosta, 1875.
GB/A.66. g224.

Guida ai monti dell'Alto Adige / Achille Gadler. Trento, 1980. Ill. [Guide Panorama.] Col patrocinio del Club Alpino Italiano, Sezione Alto Adige.
GB/A.2019(5). g225.

Guida ai nodi / Mario Bigon, Guido Regazzoni. Milano, 1981. Ill.
GB/A.2047. g226.

Guida ai rifugi e bivacchi in Valle d'Aosta / Cosimo Zappelli. Aosta, 1979. Ill., maps.
GB/A.2020(15). g227.

Guida al lago di Como ed alle strade Stelvio e Spluga / Cesare Cantù. Como, 1847. Map.
GB/A.776. g228.

Guida al tempo in montagna / Adolf Schneider. Bologna, 1981. Ill., maps. Translated from *Wetter und Bergsteigen*.
GB/A.2032(5). g229.

Guida al Val d'Ambiéz, Dolomiti di Brenta / Giorgio Armani. Trento, 1978. Ill., map.
GB/A.1911(16). g230.

Guida alla fotografia in montagna / Robert Löbl; traduzione Anita Terragni de Eccher. Bologna, 1978. Ill. Translated from *Fotografieren im Gebirge*.
GB/A.2023(2). g231.

Guida alla rassegna del centenario, Museo di Palazzo Braschi, Roma / Club Alpino Italiano, Sezione di Roma. Roma, 1973. Ill.
GB/A.1350(7). g232.

Guida alla tecnica di roccia / Paolo Lazzarin. Milano, [1980]. Ill.
GB/A.2022(7). g233.

Guida alle Alpi Apuane / Cesare Zolfanelli, Vincenzo Santini. Firenze, 1874. Ill.
GB/A.516(5). g234.

Guida alle Alpi centrali italiane / compilata per cura di Brusoni prof. Edmondo. Vol.3: Valli Ossolane e Alpi Ossolane. Milano, 1908. Ill., maps. [Pubblicazione del Club Alpino Italiano, Sezione di Como.]
GB/A.854. g235.

Guida alle località teatro della guerra / Walther Schaumann. Cortina, 1972-78. 3v (in 4); ill., maps, facsims. Translated from *Schauplätze des Gebirgskrieges*.
GB/A.1996; GB/A.1050(10) (another copy of v.1). g236.

Guida alle palestre di roccia e ghiaccio dell'Appennino bolognese / Maurizio Marsigli; a cura della Lega Montagna ARCI-UISP e del Gruppo Alpinistico Corvacci. [Corvacci? 1975?] Ill., maps.
GB/A.2021(12).   g237.

Guida allo Stelvio, ossia Notizie sulla nuova strada da Bormio all'incontro colla postale di Mals con alcuni cenni sul rilevamento dei progetti di strade montane e sulla esecuzione pratica delle gallerie perforanti / Giovanni Donegani. [Bologna, 1980.] Ill., map. Facsimile reprint of the Milan, 1842 ed.
GB/B.570(2).   g238.

La **guida** alpina / Luigi Spiro; traduzione di Ademaro Barbiellini Amidei. Bergamo, 1926. Ill.
GB/A.1326.   g239.

Guida alpina del Bassanese e delle montagne limitrofe, canale di Brenta, Sette Comuni, Grappa Marostica, Possagno, Feltre / Plinio Fraccaro. Bassano, 1909. Ill.
GB/A.2.   g240.

Guida alpinistica escursionistica del Trentino occidentale / Achille Gadler. Trento, 1981. Ill. Col patrocinio della S.A.T. Società Alpinisti Tridentini.
GB/A.2019(4).   g241.

Guida alpinistica escursionistica del Trentino orientale / Achille Gadler. Trento, 1982. Ill. Col patrocinio della S.A.T. Società Alpinisti Tridentini.
GB/A.2076(3).   g242.

Guida da Milano a Ginevra pel Sempione / Ferdinando Artaria. Milano, 1822. Ill., map.
GB/B.282.   g243.

Guida degli itinerari dell'Adamello, versante bresciano, e dell'alta via camuna, gruppo Ortles-Cevedale / R. Floreancigh, F. Ragni. [Brescia], 1980. Ill. Published by the Club Alpino Italiano, Sezione di Brescia.
GB/A.2018(5).   g244.

Guida dei castelli dell'Alto Adige / Marcello Caminiti. [Rovereto, 1964.] Ill.
GB/A.1051(1).   g245.

Guida dei monti d'Italia: Alpi centrali. Vol.1: Alpi retiche occidentali / Luigi Brasca [et al.]. Brescia, 1911. Ill., maps. Published by the Club Alpino Italiano.
Lloyd.1617(23).   g245.1.

Guida dei monti d'Italia: Alpi centrali. Vol.2: Regione dell'Ortler / Aldo Bonacossa. Milano, 1915. Ill., maps. Published by the Club Alpino Italiano.
Lloyd.1617(24).   g245.2.

Guida dei rifugi alpini del C.A.I. in provincia di Bolzano / Ente Provinciale per il Turismo, Bolzano, Club Alpino Italiano, Comitato Coordinamento Trentino-Alto Adige. Bolzano, 1951. Ill., maps.
GB/A.1295(19).   g246.

Guida dei sentieri e rifugi, Trentino orientale / Adolfo Valcanover, Tarcisio Deflorian. [Trento], 1981. Ill., maps. Published by the Società degli Alpinisti Tridentini.
GB/A.2018(17).   g247.

Guida dei sentieri e segnavia alpini della provincia di Torino. 3a ed. [Turin], 1980. Ill., maps. Published by the Commissione Sentieri e Segnavia Alpini.
GB/A.2018(6).   g248.

Guida del lago di Garda. 2a ed. Milano, 1950. Ill.
GB/A.1030.   g249.

Guida del lago Scaffaiolo e dell'Alto Crinale dall'Oppio all'Abetone / Giovanni Bortolotti. Bologna, [1950]. Ill., maps. [Guide dell'Appennino settentrionale.]
GB/A.1207.   g250.

Guida del Monte Emilius / Osvaldo Cardellina. Aosta, 1978. Ill., maps.
GB/A.1965(2).   g251.

Guida del Trentino / Ottone Brentari. Bologna, 1971. 4v; maps. A facsimile reprint of the Bassano, 1890-1902 ed.
GB/A.856-9.   g252.

Guida dell'Abruzzo / Enrico Abbate. Roma, 1903. Maps.
GB/A.20.   g253.

Guida dell'Alto Appennino bolognese-modenese-pistoiese dalle Piastre all'Abetone / Giovanni Bortolotti. Bologna, 1963. Ill., maps. [Guide dell'Appennino settentrionale.]
GB/A.1347.   g254.

Guida dell'Alto Appennino modenese e lucchese dall'Abetone alle Radici (Lago Santo modenese ed Orrido di Botri) / Giovanni Bortolotti. 2a ed. riv.

Bologna, 1961. [Guide dell'Appennino setten-
trionale.] Published by the Club Alpino Italiano,
Sezioni di Lucca e Modena.
GB/A.1270(5). g255.

Guida dell'Alto Appennino parmense-lunigia-
nese dal passo del Lagastrello alla Cisa (Crinale
dei Laghi — Monchio delle Corti — Corniglio
Lago Santo — Lunigiana nord-orientale —
Comano) / Giovanni Bortolotti. Bologna, 1966.
Ill., maps. [Guide dell'Appennino settentrionale.]
Published by the Club Alpino Italiano.
GB/A.1349(18). g256.

Guida dell'Appennino reggiano. Reggio-Emilia,
1930. Ill., map. [Guide.]
GB/A.867(1). g257.

Guida dell'Appennino reggiano / G. Pighini, O.
Siliprandi, A. Steiner. 2a ed. Reggio Emilia, [1953].
Ill., maps.
GB/A.1351(3). g258.

Guida dell'Appennino reggiano, Emilia / Alessandro Brian. Genova, [ca 1930]. Ill., maps.
GB/A.835(15). g259.

Guida della regione autonoma della Valle
d'Aosta. Guide de la région autonome de la vallée
d'Aoste / Mario Aldrovandi. Torino, 1964. Ill.,
maps.
GB/A.1350(1). g260.

Guida della regione dolomitica / testo a cura del
dott. Piero Rossi. Sesto San Giovanni, [ca 1967].
Ill., maps.
GB/A.1199(1). g261.

Guida della regione dolomitica / testo a cura del
dott. Piero Rossi. Sesto S. Giovanni, [ca 1973]. Ill.,
map.
GB/A.1270(11). g262.

Guida della valle di Ampesso e dei suoi dintorni.
Bologna, 1982. Ill., maps, music. Facsimile reprint
of the Ampezzo, 1905 ed.
GB/A.2019(3). g263.

Guida delle Alpi Apuane / L. Bozano, E. Questa,
G. Rovereto. 2a ed. con la collaborazione di
Bartolomeo Figari. Genova, 1921. Maps.
GB/A.434(5). g264.

Guida delle Alpi biellesi: la descrizione
dell'ambiente, 58 percorsi nelle valli del Viona,
dell'Elvo, dell'Oropa, del Cervo, del Sessera e di
Postua, 10 percorsi dell'alta via biellese, 10 escursioni di sci alpinismo / Giancarlo Regis, Renza
Piana Regis. Biella, 1981. Ill., maps.
GB/A.2018(1). g265.

Guida delle Alpi misteriose e fantastiche / Serge
Bertino. Milano, [1972]. Ill.
GB/A.1277. g266.

Guida delle Alpi occidentali. Vol.1, vol.2 pt.1 /
Martelli e Vaccarone. Vol.2 pt.2 / Bobba e Vaccarone. Torino, 1889-96. 2v (in 3); maps. Published
by the Club Alpino Italiano, Sezione di Torino.
GB/A.17-9; Lloyd.275 (v.1 only). g267.

Guida delle Alpi ticinesi: gruppo della Mesolcina
e della Calanca. 2a ed., compilata da membri della
Sezione Leventina; edita dal Club Alpino Svizzero. Bellinzona, 1932. Ill., map.
GB/A.1025. g268.

Guida delle Pale di S. Martino: catena di S.
Martino e massiccio centrale / Samuele Scalet,
Giulio Faoro, Lionello Tirindelli. Cremona, 1970.
Ill., maps. [Guide; 1.]
GB/A.1066. g269.

Guida delle palestre di roccia del Pre-Appennino
fabrianese. Jesi, 1973. Ill., maps. Published by the
Club Alpino Italiano, Sezione di Jesi.
GB/A.1295(3). g270.

Guida delle Prealpi Giulie: distretti di Gemona,
Tarcento, S. Daniele, Cividale e S. Pietro, con
Cormôns, Gorizia e la valle dell'Isonzo / Olinto
Marinelli [et al.]. Udine, 1912.
GB/A.2004. g271.

Guida delle valli del Sangone e della Chisola / a
cura di Piero Pollino. [Turin], 1972. Ill., maps. [Il
Piemonte e le sue valli.]
GB/A.1281(11). g272.

Guida delle valli di Lanzo / a cura di Piero
Pollino. 2a ed. corr. Torino, 1970. Ill., maps. [Il Pie-
monte e le sue valli.]
GB/A.1281(6). g273.

Guida delle valli di Susa: edizione italiana / a
cura di Piero Pollino. Torino, 1968. Ill., maps. [Il
Piemonte e le sue valli.]
GB/A.1281(10). g274.

La **guida** dello sciatore / a cura di Carlo Boleso.
13a ed. 1970-71. Milano, 1970.
GB/B.290(9). g275.

Guida di Bolzano / edita dalla Azienda Autonoma di Soggiorno e Turismo della Città Bolzano. Bolzano, 1951. Ill., maps.
GB/A.1911(17). g276.

Guida di congressi alpini, V Internazionale e XVII Nazionale, Torino, agosto-settembre 1885. Turin, [1885].
GB/A.1354. g277.

Guida di Monte Baldo / Ottone Brentari. Bologna, [1971]. Ill., map. Facsimile reprint of the Bassano, 1893 ed.
GB/A.965. g278.

Guida escursionistica alle Alpi Carniche occidentali / Rino Gaberscik. Genova, 1978.
GB/A.2022(9). g279.

Guida escursionistica delle valli del Santerno, Sillaro e Senio / a cura della Sezione di Imola del Club Alpino Italiano; patrocinio degli Enti Provinciali del Turismo di Bologna e Ravenna. Imola, 1981. Ill., maps. [Imola nostra; 1.]
GB/A.2020(10). g280.

Guida illustrata della Valsassina / Fermo Magni. Lecco, 1904. Ill.
GB/A.6. g281.

Guida illustrata della Valsesia e del Monte Rosa / Federico Tonetti. Varallo, [1891]. Ill.
GB/A.21. g282.

Guida illustrata di Vallombrosa e suoi contorni / Ranieri Agostini. Firenze, 1893. Ill., map.
GB/A.835(12). g283.

Guida illustrata, turistica, descrittiva di Lecco e paesi finitimi / Ariberto Villani. [Lecco, ca 1930.] Ill.
GB/A.1024. g284.

La **guida** P.L.M. delle Alpi: centri di turismo e d'alpinismo. Paris, [ca 1947]. Ill., maps. Published by the Chemin de Fer de Paris à Lyon et à la Méditerranée.
GB/A.835(3). g285.

Guida ricordo di Numana / Cesare Romiti. Osimo, 1927. Ill.
GB/A.1349(3). g286.

Guida sci alpinistica della Valle d'Ayas / Dino Barattieri, Gian Origlia. Torino, 1965. Ill. Published by the Ski Club Torino.
GB/B.312(27). g287.

Guida sci-alpinistica del Canavese. Rivarolo Canavese, 1972. Ill., maps. Published by the Club Alpino Italiano.
GB/A.1050(3). g288.

Guida sciistica dell'Alto Adige. Bolzano, [1963?]. Ill. With *Fascicolo aggiuntivo: aggiornamenti 1958-1963*. Published by the Ente Provinciale per il Turismo, Bolzano.
GB/A.828(5-6). g289.

Guida sciistica delle Orobie / L.B. Sugliani. 2a ed. Bergamo, 1971. Ill., maps.
GB/A.2038. g290.

Guida sciistica di Madonna di Campiglio: Bondone, Paganella, Gruppo di Brenta, Presanella / Ettore Castiglioni. Torino, 1946. Ill., map. At head of title: Sci Club Milano.
GB/A.1964(2). g291.

Guida storico-alpina del Cadore / O. Brentari. Bologna, 1981. Facsimile reprint of the Bassano, 1886 ed.
GB/A.1965(7). g292.

Guida storico-alpina di Bassano — Sette Comuni, Canale di Brenta, Marostica, Possagno / Ottone Brentari. Bologna, 1968. Facsimile reprint of the Bassano, 1885 ed.
GB/A.510. g293.

Guida storico-alpina di Belluno — Feltre — Primiero — Agordo — Zoldo / Ottone Brentari. Bassano, 1887. Map.
GB/A.3. g294.

Guida storico-alpina di Vicenza, Recoaro e Schio / Ottone Brentari, Scipione Cainer. 2a ed., riv. e corr. Vicenza, 1888. Ill., maps.
GB/A.1564. g295.

Guida-itinerario alle Prealpi Bergamasche compresa la Valsassina ed i passi alla Valtellina ed alla Valcamonica. 3a ed. Milan, 1900. 2v; ill., maps. [Manuale Hoepli.] Published by the Club Alpino Italiano, Sezione di Bergamo.
GB/A.820-1. g296.

Le **guide** blanc: itinéraires pour skieurs / éditeur responsable: H.C. Golay. 1971. Genève, [1970]. [Guides Pierre du Tagui.]
GB/A.802(15). g298.

Guide bleu illustré des Alpes françaises: Dauphiné-Savoie / Stéphane Juge. Paris, 1894. Ill.,

map, port.
Lloyd.341.   g299.

Guide d'alpinisme en Chablais de l'excursion facile à la varappe pure / édité sous le patronage de la Section Léman du Club alpin français et de la Société des eaux d'Evian. Thonon-les-Bains, 1939. Ill., map.
GB/A.2017(1).   g300.

Guide d'escalades dans le Jura / élaboré pour le Club alpin suisse par Maurice Brandt. [N.p., 1966.] 2v; ill.
GB/A.1202-3.   g301.

Guide de la chaîne du Mont Blanc à l'usage des ascensionnistes / Louis Kurz. Neuchâtel, 1892.
GB/A.2153.   g302.

Guide de la chaîne du Mont Blanc à l'usage des ascensionnistes / Louis Kurz. 2e éd., rev. et augm. Neuchâtel, 1914. Ill.
GB.70; Lloyd.69.   g303.

Guide de la chaîne du Mont Blanc à l'usage des ascensionnistes / Louis Kurz. 3e éd., rev. et mise à jour par Marcel Kurz. Lausanne, 1927.
GB.71.   g304.

Guide de la chaîne du Mont Blanc à l'usage des ascensionnistes / Louis Kurz. 4e éd., rev. et mise à jour par Marcel Kurz. Lausanne, 1935.
GB.72.   g305.

Guide de la chaîne frontière entre la Suisse et la Hte Savoie / publié par la Section genevoise du Club alpin suisse avec l'appui du Comité central du Club alpin suisse et de la Société pour le développement de la connaissance des Alpes. Vol.1: Massif Oche-Bise — massif Arvouin-Bellevue — massif Ouzon-Grange — massif Géant-Hautforts. Genève, 1928. Ill.
GB/A.1569.   g306.

Guide de la vallée du Trient: excursions-escalades de la Dent-du-Midi au Mont-Blanc / Auguste Wagnon. 3e éd. Genève, 1903. Ill., map.
Lloyd.655.   g307.

Guide de Tarentaise et Maurienne / Jeanne et Bernard Leclerc. Lyon, 1949. 2v; ill.
GB/A.1639.   g308.

Guide des Alpes fribourgeoises / édité par le Club alpin suisse, Section Moleson, avec l'appui du Comité central. Lucerne, 1951. Ill., maps.
GB/A.2000.   g309.

Guide des Alpes valaisannes / Marcel Kurz. Vol.1: Du col Ferret au col de Collon. Lausanne, 1923. Ill., maps. Published by the Club alpin suisse.
GB/A.1640(1).   g310.

Guide des Alpes valaisannes / Marcel Kurz. Vol.1: Du col Ferret au col Collon. 2e éd., 2e tirage et un supplément. Zollikon, 1963. Ill.
GB/A.1206.   g311.

Guide des Alpes valaisannes / Marcel Kurz. Vol.3a: Du col de Théodule au Monte Moro. 2e éd. Lucerne, 1937. Ill. Published by the Club alpin suisse.
GB/A.1640(3a).   g311.1.

Guide des Alpes valaisannes / Marcel Kurz. Vol.3b: Du Strahlhorn au Simplon. 2e éd. Lucerne, 1937. Ill. Published by the Club alpin suisse.
GB/A.1640(3b).   g311.2.

Guide des Alpes valaisannes / Marcel Kurz. Vol.4: Du col de Simplon au col de la Furka. Lausanne, 1920. Ill. Published by the Club alpin suisse.
GB/A.1640(4).   g311.3.

Guide des escalades du massif des Cerces / Suzy Péguy, Michel Pichot et le Syndicat des guides de la Guisane. [N.p., 1972.] Ill.
GB/A.1288.   g312.

Guide des loisirs en montagnes de France / réalisé par Robert Chastagnol en collaboration avec Pierre Mazeaud, Pierre Curchod, Jacques Thiébault. Paris, 1969. Ill., maps.
GB/B.252(1).   g313.

Guide des montagnes corses / Michel Fabrikant; ouvrage publié sous le patronage du Club alpin français et de la Fédération française de la montagne. Paris, [1965-71]. 2v; ill., maps.
GB/A.1037-8.   g314.

Guide des montagnes corses: randonnées pédestres et escalades / Michel Fabrikant. Grenoble, 1982. Ill., maps. [Cartes et guides de Corse.]
GB/A.2165(6).   g315.

Guide des Préalpes franco-suisses: chaîne frontière entre le Valais et la Haute-Savoie / Pierre Bossus. Genève, 1964. Ill., maps. Published by the Schweizer Alpenclub, Section genevoise.
GB/A.1027.   g316.

Guide des Pyrénées basques: promenades, ascensions, escalades / Miguel Angulo. Pau, [1980]. Ill., maps.
GB/A.1965(6).   g317.

Guide des voyageurs en Europe / Mr. Reichard. Nouv. éd. rev. & augm. Weimar, 1802. 2v; maps.
Lloyd.730-1.   g318.

Guide du Haut-Dauphiné: supplément / W.A.B. Coolidge, H. Duhamel, F. Perrin. Grenoble, 1890.
Lloyd.1616(21).   g319.

Guide du massif des Ecrins (Meije, Ecrins, Ailefroide, Pelvoux, Bans, Olan, Muzelle) / Lucien Devies, Maurice Laloue. Grenoble, 1946. 2v; ill.
GB/A.1627-8.   g320.

Guide du massif des Ecrins: Meije, Ecrins, Ailefroide, Pelvoux, Bans, Olan, Muzelle / Lucien Devies, Maurice Laloue. 2e éd. Paris, 1951. 2v; ill. At head of title: Groupe de Haute Montagne.
GB/A.1809-10.   g321.

Guide du naturaliste dans les Alpes / J.P. Schaer [et al.]. Neuchâtel, 1972. Ill., maps. [Guides du naturaliste.]
GB/A.1039.   g322.

Guide du touriste: vingt-cinq Belges au Mont-Blanc: itinéraires détaillés de 12 et de 15 jours en Suisse / Joë Diericx de Ten-Hamme. Bruxelles, 1869. Ill., map.
GB.682; Lloyd.938.   g323.

Guide du voyageur en Suisse / Richard. Paris, 1824.
GB/A.801(13).   g324.

Guide du voyageur en Suisse / [Thomas Martyn]; traduit de l'anglois. Genève, 1788. Translated from *Sketch of a tour through Swisserland*.
GB/A.802(6).   g325.

Guide du voyageur en Suisse: itinéraire tracé par Ebel. [N.p., ca 1820.]
Lloyd.149-50.   g326.

Guide en Suisse, illustré. 4e éd., refondue, rev. et complétée jusqu'en 1880. Leipsic, [1880]. Ill., maps. [Guides Meyer.]
GB/A.27.   g327.

Guide for travellers in the plain and on the mountain / Charles Boner. London, [1866]. Ill.
Lloyd.161.   g328.

Guide Lampugnani: ferrovia del Sempione da Milano e Torino a Losanna-Ginevra: Öberland Bernese / Giovanni Lampugnani. Milano, [1905?]. Ill., maps.
GB/A.768.   g329.

Guide of Freiburg in Breisgau, Baden. Freiburg, [1901]. Ill., maps.
Lloyd.1613(15).   g330.

Guide pittoresque et historique du voyageur dans le département de l'Isère et les localités circonvoisines / P. Fissont, Auguste Vitu. Grenoble, 1856. Ill., map.
GB/A.35.   g331.

Guide pratique de l'ascensionniste sur les montagnes qui entourent le lac de Genève / Charles Schaub, Moise Briquet. 3e éd., rev. et augm. Genève, 1893.
GB/A.1205.   g332.

Guide pratique de la montagne / Bertrand Kempf. 2e éd. rev. et corr. Paris, 1968. Ill., maps.
GB/A.464.   g333.

Guide sur le chemin de fer du St. Gothard et sur ses lignes accessoires / Max Koch von Berneck. Zurich, [1883?]. Ill., maps. Translated from *Führer auf der Gotthardbahn*.
Lloyd.1613(4).   g334.

Guide through Switzerland and Savoy, or A new and complete geographical, historical and picturesque description of every remarkable place in these countries / George Downes. Paris, 1827.
GB.13.   g335.

Guide through Switzerland and Savoy, or A new and complete geographical, historical and picturesque description of every remarkable place in these countries / George Downes. Paris, 1828.
Lloyd.16.   g336.

Guide to Carisbrooke Castle / H. Martyn Dodd. London, [1882]. Ill., port.
GB/A.990(3).   g337.

Guide to climbs in the Upper Engadine / W.J. Gyger. 3rd ed. Samaden, [1925?].
GB/A.2076(1).   g338.

Guide to Cook's excursions and tours to Paris, Switzerland, and Italy / Thomas Cook. 7th ed. London, [1869]. Maps.
Lloyd.1584(1).   g339.

Guide to Craig-y-Barns, Dunkeld / R. Campbell, N. MacNiven. [Edinburgh, n.d.] Published by the Edinburgh University Mountaineering Club.
GB.1318(18). g340.

Guide to Isle of Skye. Edinburgh, [1951]. Ill., maps. Published by the Scottish Youth Hostels Association.
GB.1325(14). g341.

Guide to Lucerne, the Lake, and its environs / J.C. Heer. 7th ed. Lucerne, 1898. Ill., map.
GB/A.2021(8). g342.

Guide to Mount Kenya and Kilimanjaro / edited by Iain Allan. 4th ed., completely rev. Nairobi, 1981. Ill., maps.
GB/A.2021(11). g343.

Guide to Nepal / J.H. Elliott. 3rd ed. Calcutta, 1969. Ill., maps.
GB/A.529. g344.

Guide to Switzerland / W.A.B. Coolidge; with a cycling supplement by Charles L. Freeston. London, 1901. Ill., maps. [Black's guide books.]
GB/A.855. g345.

Guide to Switzerland / William Paterson. 4th ed. Edinburgh, 1888. Maps.
GB/A.802(4). g346.

Guide to the broads and rivers of Norfolk and Suffolk, Great Yarmouth, Lowestoft, Norwich. London, [1951]. Ill. [Ward, Lock & Co.'s illustrated guide books.]
GB.1325(7). g347.

Guide to the collections of gemstones in the Museum of Practical Geology / W.F.P. McLintock. 2nd ed. London, 1923. Ill.
Lloyd.1251. g348.

Guide to the Colorado mountains / edited by Robert M. Ormes. Denver, 1952. Ill., maps.
GB/A.1915. g349.

A **guide** to the Eastern Alps / John Ball. London, 1868. Ill., maps. [The Alpine Guide; 3.]
GB/A.952. g350.

A **guide** to the Eastern Alps / John Ball. New ed. London, 1869. Ill., maps. [The Alpine Guide; 3.]
Lloyd.278. g350.1.

A **guide** to the Eastern Alps / John Ball. New ed. London, 1870. Ill., maps. [The Alpine Guide; 3.]
Lloyd.317B. g350.2.

A **guide** to the lakes in Cumberland, Westmorland, and Lancashire / by the author of *The antiquities of Furness* [i.e. Thomas West]. London, 1778.
Lloyd.367. g351.

Guide to the new system of Alpine & Italian tourist tickets established by Mr. Cook, with descriptions of Alpine routes, and the principal railways of northern & central Italy: designed as an appendix to the *Guide to Cook's tours in France, Switzerland and Italy*. London, [1869]. Map.
Lloyd.1584(2). g352.

A **guide** to the Pyrenees: especially intended for the use of mountaineers: with addition of an appendix, March 1864 / Charles Packe. 2nd ed., rewritten and much enl. London, 1864. Maps.
Lloyd.213; Lloyd.284. g353.

Guide to the Tyrol: comprising pedestrian tours made in Tyrol, Styria, Carinthia, and Salzkammergut, during the summers of 1852 and 1853 / Richard Stephen Charnock. London, 1857. Map.
Lloyd.207. g354.

Guide to the walks and climbs around Arolla / Walter Larden. London, 1908. Ill.
GB.27. g355.

A **guide** to the Western Alps / John Ball. New ed. London, 1866. Ill., maps. [The Alpine Guide; 1.]
Lloyd.276. g356.

A **guide** to the Western Alps / John Ball. New ed. London, 1870. Ill., maps. [The Alpine Guide; 1.]
Lloyd.316. g356.1.

A **guide** to the Western Alps / John Ball. New ed. London, 1877. Ill., maps. [The Alpine Guide; 1.]
GB.243. g356.2.

Guide touristique de Courmayeur / Alessio Nebbia. Courmayeur, 1931. Ill., maps. Published by the Istituto Geografico De Agostini, Sezione Calcocromia.
GB.164. g357.

Guide-itinéraire au Mont-Blanc, à Chamonix et dans les vallées voisines / Venance Payot. Genève, 1857. Map.
Lloyd.143. g358.

Guide-itinéraire au Mont-Blanc, à Chamonix et dans les vallées voisines / Venance Payot. Genève, [1869]. Map.
GB.76. g359.

Guides des vallées vaudoises du Piémont. Torre Pellice, 1898. Ill., map. Published by the Société vaudoise d'utilité publique.
GB/A.10.   g360.

Guido Rey: il maestro / Sandro Prada. Rocca San Casciano, 1956. [Le Alpi; 23.]
GB/A.1333.   g362.

Guillaume Tell, ou La Suisse libre / M. de Florian; mit grammatischen Erläuterungen und einem Wortregister zum Behufe des Unterrichts. Leipzig, 1815.
GB/A.1468(6).   g363.

The **Gurkhas**: their manners, customs and country / W. Brook Northey, C.J. Morris. London, 1928. Ill., map.
GB.922; GB.969.   g364.

-H-

H.E. Kretschmer / F.A. Pullinger. [London, 1948.] Port. Pp.361-3 of the *Climbers' Club Guide*, N.S. vol.8 no.3.
GB.1339(10).   h001.

The **Haast** is in South Westland / John Pascoe. Wellington, 1968. Ill., maps, ports.
GB/A.1880.   h002.

Habitations lacustres des temps anciens et modernes / Frédéric Troyon. Lausanne, 1860. Ill. [Société d'histoire de la Suisse romande. Mémoires et documents; 17.]
Lloyd.858.   h003.

Die **Haftung** bei Skiunfällen in den Alpenländern / Peter Kleppe. München, 1967.
GB/A.143.   h004.

Hand Atlas für Reisende in das Berner Oberland. Atlas portatif à l'usage des voyageurs dans l'Oberland bernois. Bern, 1816. Ill., maps.
GB.1311(4); GB/A.159.   h005.

Handbook / Midland Association of Mountaineers. 1958-1959. [Birmingham], 1958.
GB.1325(22).   h006.

Handbook / Rucksack Club. 1948, 1952, 1955, 1960-62. Manchester, [1948-62].
GB.1325(15-20).   h007.

Handbook for Central Europe, or Guide for tourists through Belgium, Holland, the Rhine, Germany, Switzerland, and France / Francis Coghlan. London, 1844. Map.
Lloyd.371.   h008.

Handbook for travellers in Scotland / edited by Scott Moncrieff Penney. 7th ed. London, 1898. [Murray's handbook.]
Lloyd.315.   h009.

A **handbook** for travellers in Southern Germany: being a guide to Bavaria, Austria, Tyrol. London, 1837. Map. [Murray's handbook.]
Lloyd.307.   h010.

A **handbook** for travellers in Switzerland. London, 1838. [Murray's handbook.]
Lloyd.286; Lloyd.286A,B.   h011.

A **handbook** for travellers in Switzerland. A new ed., rev. and corr. London, 1842. [Murray's handbook.]
GB.205; Lloyd.287. h012.

A **handbook** for travellers in Switzerland. A new ed., rev. and corr. London, 1843. [Murray's handbook.]
GB.245; Lloyd.288. h013.

A **handbook** for travellers in Switzerland. 3rd ed. London, 1846. [Murray's handbook.]
Lloyd.289. h014.

A **handbook** for travellers in Switzerland. 3rd ed., corr. London, 1847. [Murray's handbook.]
Lloyd.290. h015.

A **handbook** for travellers in Switzerland. 5th ed., corr. & augm. London, 1852. [Murray's handbook.]
Lloyd.291. h016.

A **handbook** for travellers in Switzerland. 6th ed. London, 1854. [Murray's handbook.]
GB.196; Lloyd.292. h017.

A **handbook** for travellers in Switzerland. 7th ed. London, 1858. [Murray's handbook.]
GB.197; Lloyd.293; Lloyd.293A,B. h018.

A **handbook** for travellers in Switzerland. 8th ed. London, 1858. [Murray's handbook.]
GB.198. h019.

A **handbook** for travellers in Switzerland. 10th ed. London, 1863. [Murray's handbook.]
Lloyd.294. h020.

A **handbook** for travellers in Switzerland. 12th ed. London, 1867. [Murray's handbook.]
Lloyd.295. h021.

A **handbook** for travellers in Switzerland. 15th ed., rev. London, 1874. [Murray's handbook.]
Lloyd.296. h022.

A **handbook** of Mr. Albert Smith's ascent of Mont Blanc: first represented at the Egyptian Hall, Piccadilly, March 15, 1852. [London, 1852?] Ill.
GB.10; GB.1335(13); GB.1335(20); GB.1335(21); Lloyd.1593(4). h023.

A **handbook** of Mr. Albert Smith's ascent of Mont Blanc: first represented at the Egyptian Hall, Piccadilly, March 15, 1852. [London, 1852?] A different issue from h023.
Lloyd.1593(4A). h024.

A **handbook** of Mr. Albert Smith's ascent of Mont Blanc: first represented at the Egyptian Hall, Piccadilly, March 15, 1852. 4th ed. [London, 1853.] Ill.
GB.1335(14); GB.1335(15). h025.

A **handbook** of Mr. Albert Smith's ascent of Mont Blanc: first represented at the Egyptian Hall, Piccadilly, March 15, 1852. 5th ed. [London, 1853.] Ill.
GB.1335(16). h026.

A **handbook** of Mr. Albert Smith's ascent of Mont Blanc: first represented at the Egyptian Hall, Piccadilly, March 15, 1852. London, [1856]. Ill.
GB.1335(17); Lloyd.1593(5). h027.

A **handbook** of Mr. Albert Smith's ascent of Mont Blanc: first represented at the Egyptian Hall, Piccadilly, 1852. [London? 1856?]
GB.397. h028.

A **handbook** of Mr Albert Smith's ascent of Mont Blanc: first represented at the Egyptian Hall, Piccadilly, 1852. [London? 1858.] Ill.
GB.1335(18). h029.

Handbook of travel / edited by George Cheever Shattuck. 2nd ed. Cambridge, Mass., 1935. Published by the Harvard Travellers Club.
GB.221. h029.1.

Handbook to the health resorts of Switzerland / Hans Loetscher. Zurich, 1887. Ill., maps.
GB/A.1021. h030.

Handbuch der Gebirgskunde für angehende Geognosten / Joseph Brunner. Leipzig, 1803. Ill., map.
GB/A.2198. h031.

Handbuch der Gletscherkunde / Albert Heim. Stuttgart, 1885. Ill., map. [Bibliothek geographischer Handbücher.]
GB/A.787. h032.

Handbuch des alpinen Sport / Julius Meurer. Wien, 1882. Ill., map.
Lloyd.308. h033.

Handbuch des Alpinismus / Josef Ittlinger. Leipzig, [ca 1915]. Ill. [Bibliothek für Sport und Spiel; 18.]
GB/A.52. h034.

Handbuch für Reisende in der Schweiz / Robert Glutz-Blotzheim; herausgegeben von C. Schoch. 6. verb. Aufl. Zürich, 1830. Map.
Lloyd.355.   h035.

Die Hände am Fels: mein alpinistisches Tagebuch / Andrea Oggioni; übersetzt von Ernst Müller; bearbeitet und herausgegeben von Carlo Graffigna. Rüschlikon-Zürich, [1967]. Ill. Translated from *Le mani sulla roccia*.
GB/B.232.   h036.

Hannibal once more / Douglas W. Freshfield. London, 1914. Ill., maps.
Lloyd.979.   h037.

Hannibal's march through the Alps / Spenser Wilkinson. Oxford, 1911. Maps.
Lloyd.1190.   h038.

Hannibal's passage of the Alps / by a member of the University of Cambridge [Henry Lawes Long]. London, 1830. Map.
GB/A.900.   h039.

Harper's hand-book for travellers in Europe and in the East / W. Pembroke Fetridge. Year 18. New York, 1879. 3v; maps.
GB/A.816 (wanting v.1-2).   h040.

Harry Ayres: mountain guide / Michael Mahoney. Christchurch, 1982. Ill., maps, ports.
GB/A.2096.   h041.

Harvard Mountaineering / Harvard Mountaineering Club. Vol.1 no.2-16, June 1928-May 1963. Cambridge, Mass., [1928-63]. Wanting no.3,7.
GB.1645(12-24).   h042.

The Harvard Mountaineering Club Bulletin. Vol.5 no.1,3, vol.7 no.1,3. Cambridge, Mass., 1947-52.
GB.1322(12-4).   h043.

Haupt-Scenen aus der lyrischen Oper *Die Schweizer-Familie* / Joseph Weigl; welche so verbunden sind, dass selbe ein Ganges bilden, und den Sinn der completten Oper klar darstellen, vom Herrn Schütz. London, [n.d.].
Lloyd.1572(2).   h044.

Haute montagne / John Tyndall; traduction de Bernard Lemoine. Neuchâtel, 1946. Ill. [Montagne.]
GB/A.1319.   h045.

Haute montagne / Pierre Dalloz. Paris, 1931. Ill.
GB.1319(8).   h046.

La haute route / Maurice Chappaz. Lausanne, 1974.
GB/A.1466.   h047.

La Haute Savoie: récits de voyage et d'histoire / Francis Wey. Paris, 1866. Ill.
GB/C.48.   h048.

Haute Tinée, Barcelonnette / Vincent Paschetta. 3e éd. Grenoble, 1973. Ill. [Guide Paschetta des Alpes-Maritimes.]
GB/A.1270(8).   h049.

La haute-route: Chamonix — Zermatt — Saas Fee / André Roch. Lausanne, 1963. Ill. [Merveilles de la Suisse.]
GB/B.265.   h050.

Haute-Savoie hors piste: 83 courses à ski / recueillies par Jean-Maurice Seigne; suivies d'une description systématique des avalanches par Michael Schmilinsky. Genève, 1979. Ill., map. Published by the Club alpin académique de Genève.
GB/A.2017(6).   h051.

The heart of a continent: a narrative of travels in Manchuria, across the Gobi Desert, through the Himalayas, the Pamirs, and Chitral, 1884-94 / Sir Francis Younghusband. 3rd ed. London, 1896. Ill., maps, ports.
Lloyd.1203.   h052.

The heart of a continent / Sir Francis Younghusband. Rev. London, 1937.
GB.792.   h053.

The heart of the Antarctic: being the story of the British Antarctic Expedition 1907-1909 / Ernest Shackleton. New and rev. ed. London, 1910. Ill., map, ports.
Lloyd.564.   h054.

The heart of the White Mountains: their legend and scenery / Samuel Drake Adams. London, 1882. Ill., maps.
Lloyd.1476.   h055.

Heath's Book of Beauty / edited by the Countess of Blessington. 1846. London, [1846]. Ill.
GB.978.   h056.

Heaton Works Journal / C.A. Parsons & Co. Vol.8 no.49, Christmas 1959. Newcastle upon Tyne,

1959. Ill., ports. Contains: *The lands of perpetual cold*, by H. Lister.
GB/B.478(2). h057.

Die **Heilquellen** und Kurorte der Schweiz: in historischer, topographischer, chemischer und therapeutischer Beziehung / Conrad Meyer-Ahrens. Zürich, 1860. 2v (in 1).
GB/A.57. h058.

Die **Heilquellen** und Kurorte der Schweiz und einiger der Schweiz zunächst angrenzenden Gegenden der Nachbarstaaten / Dr. Meyer-Ahrens. 2. umgearb. und sehr verm. Ausg. Zürich, 1867. Ill.
GB/B.387. h059.

Die **Heilquellen** von Passugg: eine historisch-legendäre Erzählung / E. Redelsberger-Gerig. [N.p., ca 1910.] Ill. Separatabdruck aus *Graubünden*.
GB/A.1115(3). h060.

Hellzapoppin': arrampicare nel Lazio / F. Antonioli, S. Ardito, G. Pietrollini. Roma, 1981. Ill., maps.
GB/A.1964(7). h061.

Helvetia antiqua et nova, seu Opus describens I. Helvetiam, II. antiquiora Helvetiæ loca, III. populos Helvetijs finitimos / Johannes Baptistes Plantinus. [Bern], 1656.
GB.105. h062.

Helvetia antiqua et nova: generalem Helvetiae antiquae, et novae quoad conjuncta et partes descriptionem Helvetiorum originem, nomina, mores, religionem, politiam, virtutem bellicam, aliasque antiquitates continens / Johannes Baptistes Plantinus. [Zurich], 1737.
Lloyd.1615(12). h063.

Helvetiae stoicheiographia, orographia et oreographia, oder Beschreibung der Elementen, Grenzen und Bergen des Schweitzerlands / Johann Jacob Scheuchzer. Zürich, 1716-18. 3v.
Lloyd.759 (wanting v.3). h064.

Helvetiorum respublica: diversorum autorum quorum nonnulli nunc primum in lucem prodeunt. [Leiden], 1627.
GB.4. h065.

Helvetischer Almanach für das Jahr 1815. Zürich, [1814]. Ill.
GB/A.817. h066.

Helvetischer Calender für das Jahr 1781[-1814]. Zürich, [1781-1814]. Map. Wanting the issues for 1790,1795,1799-1813.
GB/A.106-21, GB.394. h067.

Here and there among the Alps / Hon. Frederica Plunket. London, 1875.
Lloyd.390; Lloyd.548. h068.

Here and there in Italy, and over the border / Linda Villari. London, 1893.
Lloyd.569. h069.

"Here comes the *Polly"* / Ethel Anderson Becker. Seattle, 1971.
GB/B.503. h070.

Here is the far North / Evelyn Stefansson. New York, 1957. Ill., maps, ports.
GB/A.1874. h071.

L'**hermite** en Suisse, ou Observations sur les moeurs et les usages suisses au commencement du XIXe siècle / [edited by Alexandre Martin]. Paris, 1829-30. 3v; ill. Attributed to Etienne de Jouy.
GB/A.1337-9. h072.

The **heroes** of the Arctic and their adventures / Frederick Whymper. 10th ed., rev. London, 1899. Ill., map. Published by the Society for Promoting Christian Knowledge.
GB/A.1583. h073.

Herrn Bourret [sic] Schilderung seiner Reise nach den savoyischen Eisgebirgen / A.C. Bordier; aus dem Französischen, mit Anmerkungen und Zusätzen [by H.A.O. Reichard]. Gotha, 1775. 2v (in 1). Translated from *Voyage pitoresque aux glacières de Savoye fait en 1772*, par Mr. B. [Marc Théodore Bourrit].
GB/A.931. h074.

Heures pyrénéennes / Maurice Jeannel. Pau, 1972. Ill.
GB/A.1035(2). h075.

Les **heures** valaisannes / Edmond Bille. Berne, 1931. Ill. Published by the Schweizer Bibliophilen-Gesellschaft.
GB/B.366(3). h076.

The **high** adventure of Mr. Randall / J. Monroe Thorington. [New York, 1945.] Ports. Reprinted from the *American Alpine Journal*, vol.5 no.3, 1945.
GB.1337(8). h077.

The **High** Alps / T.G. Bonney. London, 1878. 2v; ill. [Picturesque Europe; 55-6.]
GB.1334(40-1).   h078.

The **High** Alps: a natural history of ice and snow / A.E.H. Tutton. London, 1931. Ill., map. Originally published as *The natural history of ice and snow*.
GB.900.   h079.

The **High** Alps in winter, or Mountaineering in search of health / Mrs Fred Burnaby. London, 1883. Ill., maps, port.
GB.311; Lloyd.415; Lloyd.415A.   h080.

The **High** Alps of New Zealand, or A trip to the glaciers of the Antipodes with an ascent of Mount Cook / William Spotswood Green. London, 1883. Ill., maps.
Lloyd.559; Lloyd.559A.   h081.

The **High** Alps without guides: being a narrative of adventures in Switzerland / A.G. Girdlestone. London, 1870. Maps.
GB.629; Lloyd.812; Lloyd.812A,B,C.   h082.

High altitude / J.W. [i.e. James Waller]. Edinburgh, 1939. Pp.558-80 of *Blackwood's Magazine*, no.1482, April 1939.
GB.1339(23); GB.1339(24).   h083.

High conquest: the story of mountaineering / James Ramsey Ullman. London, 1942. Ill., maps.
GB.767.   h084.

High heaven / Jacques Boell; translated by Dilys Owen. London, 1947. Ill., maps.
GB.685.   h085.

High in the thin cold air: the story of the Himalayan expedition, led by Sir Edmund Hillary, sponsored by World Book Encyclopedia / Sir Edmund Hillary, Desmond Doig. Garden City, N.Y., 1962.
GB/A.2101.   h086.

The **high** level glacier route from Chamounix to Zermatt. [London, 1862.] Chapter 4 of *Peaks, passes and glaciers, being excursions by members of the Alpine Club*, ser.2 vol.1.
GB.568.   h087.

High life and towers of silence / Elizabeth Main. London, 1886. Ill.
GB.269; Lloyd.373; Lloyd.373A,B.   h088.

High mountain peaks in China newly opened to foreigners / supervised by Chinese Mountain-eering Association. [Beijing?], 1981. Ill., ports.
GB/A.2022(2).   h089.

High odyssey: the first solo winter assault of Mt. Whitney and the Muir Trail area, from the diary of Orland Bartholomew and photographs taken by him / Eugene A. Rose. Berkeley, [1974]. Ill.
GB/A.1910.   h090.

The **High** Tatras: photographs / K. Gelba, B. Straka; texts by J. Simko. Prague, 1953. Ill.
GB/B.572.   h091.

The **high-roads** of the Alps: a motoring guide to one hundred mountain passes / Charles L. Freeston. London, [1910]. Ill., maps.
Lloyd.893.   h092.

The **highest** Andes: a record of the first ascent of Aconcagua and Tupungato in Argentina / E.A. Fitzgerald; with chapters by Stuart Vines and contributions by Professor Bonney [et al.]. London, 1899. Ill., maps.
Lloyd.1490.   h093.

Highland days / Tom Weir. London, 1948. Ill., maps.
GB.635.   h094.

Hilfeleistung bei Unfällen im Gebirge / Hermann Angerer. Innsbruck, 1950. Ill. Published by the Osterreichischer Alpenverein.
GB/A.1381(7).   h095.

Hill-writings of J.H. Doughty / collected by H.M. Kelly. Manchester, 1937. Ports. Published by the Rucksack Club.
GB.686.   h096.

Hills and the sea / Hilaire Belloc. 7th ed. London, 1913.
GB.209.   h097.

Himalaja rad te imam / Zoran Jerin. Ljubljana, 1978. Ill., map.
GB/A.1988.   h098.

Der **Himalaja** ruft / Sir Francis Younghusband; Ubersetzung aus dem Englischen von Heinrich Erler. Berlin, [1936]. Ill., maps.
GB/A.418.   h099.

Himalaja-Nachrichten / P.A. [Munich, 1936.] Pp.691-4 of *Der Bergsteiger*, vol.6 no.12, Sept. 1936.
GB.1338(2).   h100.

Himálaya / Piero Ghiglione. [Pt.1]: Karakoram. Novara, [1946]. Ill. [Le grandi montagne.] Published by the Istituto Geografico De Agostini.
GB.1334(2).   h101.

Himalaya / traduction et adaptation: Arlette Ivakovick. Paris, 1980. Ill. Translated from the Italian.
GB/B.598.   h102.

Himalaya: sciences de la terre: actes du Colloque international no. 268 / organisé dans le cadre des colloques internationaux du Centre national de la recherche scientifique, Sèvres — Paris du 7 au 10 décembre 1976 par C. Jest. Paris, 1977. Ill., maps. [Colloques internationaux du Centre national de la recherche scientifique; 268.]
GB/B.570(4).   h103.

The **Himalaya**: three points of view: reviews / R.A.H. [i.e. R.A. Hodgkin]. [London, 1939.] Pp.62-4 of the *Climbers' Club Journal*, N.S. vol.6 no.1.
GB.1338(11).   h104.

Himalaya 1933-1935 / Marcel Kurz. [Paris], 1936. Ill., maps. Pp.243-55 of *Alpinisme*, année 11 n.42.
GB.1337(20).   h105.

Himalaya 1935/1936 / Marcel Kurz; übersetzt von Paul Montandon. Bern, 1937. Ill. Sonderabdruck aus *Die Alpen*, 1937, Hft 11 und 12.
GB.1318(4).   h106.

Himalaya 1937, avec report 1935 / Marcel Kurz. Melun, 1939. Ill., map.
GB.1337(19).   h107.

Himalaya 1937, mit Nachtrag 1936 / Marcel Kurz. Bern, 1939. Ill. Sonderdruck aus *Die Alpen*, 1939, Hft 1 und 2.
GB.1318(29).   h108.

[The **Himalaya** from the air / photographs by Keeichi Yamada; explanations and maps by Yoshimi Yakushi.] Tokyo, 1975. Ill., map. Titlepage and text in Japanese.
GB/B.436.   h109.

Himalaya mountains. [London, 1931-32.] Pp.237-8 of Dent's *Everyman's encyclopaedia*, new and rev. ed., vol.7.
GB.1322(1-2).   h110.

L'**Himalaya**, troisième pôle: les '8.000' de la terre / G.O. Dyhrenfurth; avec la collaboration d'Erwin Schneider. Paris, 1953. Ill. [Bibliothèque géographique.]
GB.1330(4).   h111.

Himalayan assault: the French Himalayan expedition, 1936 / [edited by Henry de Ségogne]; translated by Nea E. Morin. London, 1938. Ill., maps, ports. Translated from *L'expédition française à l'Himalaya*.
GB.913.   h112.

The **Himalayan** districts of Kooloo, Lahoul, and Spiti / A.F.P. Harcourt. London, 1871. Ill., map.
GB.276.   h113.

Himalayan endeavour / edited by B.G. Verghese. Bombay, 1962. Ill.
GB/A.2052(8).   h114.

The **Himalayan** gazetteer / Edwin T. Atkinson. Repr. Delhi, 1973. 3v (in 6); map. Originally published as *The Himalayan districts of the North Western Provinces of India*.
GB/A.1253-8.   h115.

Himalayan holiday: a trans-Himalayan diary, 1939 / Peter Young. London, [1946]. Ill., maps.
GB.599.   h116.

The **Himalayan** Journal: records of the Himalayan Club / edited by Kenneth Mason. Vol.1 no.1, vol.2. Calcutta, 1929-[30].
GB.1306(1-2).   h117.

Himalayan journals, or Notes of a naturalist in Bengal, the Sikkim and Nepal Himalayas, the Khasia Mountains / Joseph Dalton Hooker. London, 1854. 2v; ill., maps, port.
GB.742-3; GB.945-6; Lloyd.963-4; Lloyd.1034-5.
                                               h118.

Himalayan pilgrimage: a study of Tibetan religion by a traveller through western Nepal / David Snellgrove. 2nd ed. Boulder, Colo., 1981. Ill.
GB/A.2060.   h119.

Himalayan quest: the German expedition to Siniolchum and Kanga Parbat / edited by Paul Bauer; translated by E.G. Hall. London, 1938. Ill., maps, ports. Translated from *Auf Kundfahrt im Himalaja*.
Lloyd.1311.   h120.

Himalayan wanderer / Hon. C.G. Bruce. London, 1934. Ill., ports.
GB.903; Lloyd.997.   h121.

Himalayan wanderer / Hon. C.G. Bruce. London, [1934]. A prospectus.
GB.1305(16). h122.

Himalayas / Yoshikazu Shirakawa; essay, *The great Himalayas*, by Kyuya Fukada, New York, 1971. Ill., maps.
GB/C.59. h123.

The **Himalayas**: an illustrated summary of the world's highest mountain ranges / David Mordecai. Calcutta, 1966. Ill.
GB/C.5(4). h124.

The **Himalayas**: profiles of modernisation and adaptation / edited by S.K. Chaube. New Delhi, 1985.
GB/A.2196. h125.

Hindu-Koh: wanderings and wild sport on and beyond the Himalayas / Donald Macintyre. Edinburgh, 1889. Ill.
GB.1002. h126.

Hindu-Koh: wanderings and wild sport on and beyond the Himalayas / Donald Macintyre. New ed. Edinburgh, 1891. Ill.
Lloyd.648. h127.

Hindukus: v krajine posledneho ticma / Alojz Halas, Frantisek Kele. Bratislava, 1978. Ill.
GB/B.595(3). h128.

Hindukusch: Osterreichische Forschungs-expedition in den Wakhan 1970 / herausgegeben von Karl Gratzl. 2. Aufl. Graz, 1974. Ill., map.
GB/B.401. h129.

Hints and notes practical and scientific for travellers in the Alps, being a revision of the general introduction to the *Alpine Guide* / John Ball. New ed., prepared on behalf of the Alpine Club by W.A.B. Coolidge. London, 1899.
Lloyd.380; Lloyd.380A. h129.1.

Hints for pedestrians / Medicus [i.e. G.C. Watson]. London, [1843]. Ill.
Lloyd.1616(8). h130.

Histoire, antiquités, usages, dialectes des Hautes Alpes, précédés d'un essai sur la topographie de ce département, et suivis d'une notice sur M. Villars / par un ancien préfet [baron Jean C.F. de Ladoucette]. Paris, 1820. Ill., maps, port.
GB/A.823. h131.

Histoire d'une promenade en Suisse et en France / Frédéric Dollé. Paris, 1837.
GB/A.1260. h132.

Histoire de Genève, depuis son origine jusqu'à nos jours / Albin Thourel. Genève, 1832-33. 3v; ports.
Lloyd.829-31. h133.

Histoire de la vallée d'Aoste / André Zanotto. Aoste, 1968. Ill.
GB/A.1280. h134.

Histoire des Alpes: perspectives nouvelles. Geschichte der Alpen in neuer Sicht / publiée sous la direction de Jean-François Bergier pour la Journée nationale des historiens suisses — Schweizer Historikertag, 19 mai 1979. Basel, 1979. Ill., map. Sonderausgabe von *Schweizerische Zeitschrift fur Geschichte*, vol.29, 1979.
GB/A.1675(3). h135.

Histoire des Helvétiens, aujourd'hui connus sous le nom de Suisses, ou Traité sur leur origine, leurs guerres, leurs alliances, & leur gouvernement / M. le baron d'Alt de Tieffenthal. Fribourg en Suisse, 1749-53. 10v.
GB/A.1390-9. h136.

Histoire du Cervin par l'image: avec reproductions de vieilles estampes et de tableaux modernes. 1: La montagne / Charles Gos. Lausanne, 1923. Ill.
GB.1330(10). h137.

Histoire du Mont Iseran: discours / Henri Ferrand. Grenoble, 1893. Extrait du *Bulletin de la Société de statistique des sciences naturelles et des arts industriels du département de l'Isère*.
Lloyd.1290. h138.

Histoire du Mont-Blanc: conférences faites à Paris / Charles Durier. Paris, 1873.
GB.1323(1); Lloyd.249. h139.

Histoire du passage des Alpes par Annibal, dans laquelle on détermine la route de ce général / Jean André de Luc. Genève, 1818. Map.
GB.541; Lloyd.1585(1). h140.

Histoire du passage des Alpes par Annibal / Jean André de Luc. 2e éd. corr. et augm. Genève, 1825.
Lloyd.784. h141.

Histoire et description de la Bibliothèque publique de Genève / Eusèbe Henri Gaullieur.

Neuchâtel, 1853. Extrait de la *Revue suisse*, année 1852.
Lloyd.1603(5). h142.

Histoire et description de la Suisse et du Tyrol / M. Ph. de Golbéry. Paris, 1838. Ill., map, ports. [L'univers. Histoire et description de tous les peuples. Europe; 3.]
Lloyd.728. h143.

Histoire et géographie de la vallée d'Aoste / Italo Cossard. 7e éd. Aoste, 1968. Ill.
GB/B.377(5). h144.

Histoire illustrée des grands voyages au XIXe siècle: voyages de Ross, Parry, Back, Franklin, Hayes aux régions arctiques, de Du Chaillu, Speke, Lejean & Cameron à travers l'Afrique / éd. rev. par J. Tribouillard. Rouen, 1883. Ill., maps, ports.
GB/A.1785. h145.

Histoire naturelle des glacières de Suisse / Gottlieb Sigmund Gruner; traduction libre par M. de Kéralio. Paris, 1770. Ill., maps. Translated from *Die Eisgebirge des Schweizerlandes*.
GB.1226; Lloyd.1301; Lloyd.1397. h146.

Histoire populaire du canton de Genève / H. Denkinger-Rod. Genève, 1905. Ill., maps, ports., facsims.
Lloyd.1461. h147.

Histoire populaire, religieuse et civile de la vallée d'Aoste, la première et la plus antique terre du royaume d'Italie / l'abbé Henry. 3e éd. Aoste, 1967. Ill.
GB/A.1279. h148.

Histoire, topographie, antiquités, usages, dialectes des Hautes-Alpes / baron J.C.F. de Ladoucette. Marseille, 1973. Ill., maps. Facsimile reprint of the Paris, 1848 ed.
GB/A.1342. h149.

Histoires d'en-haut / Fernand Gigon. Neuchâtel, 1933.
GB/A.455(10). h150.

Historia naturalis Helvetiæ curiosa, in VII. sectiones compendiosè digesta / Johannes Jacobus Wagnerus. [Zurich], 1680.
GB.395; Lloyd.12. h151.

Historiarum libri qui supersunt / Polybius; Isaacus Casaubonus emendavit, latine vertit, & commentariis illustravit. [Paris], 1609. Text in Greek and Latin.
GB.1294. h152.

Historic errors and doubts: a paper read before the Liverpool Literary and Philosophical Society, January 11th, 1869 / Frederick J. Jeffery. Liverpool, [1869].
Lloyd.1574(5). h153.

Historic tinned foods. 2nd ed. Greenford, [1939]. Ill., map, ports., facsims. [Publication / International Tin Research and Development Council; 85.]
GB.804. h154.

An **historical** document: the Führerbuch of Ferdinand Imseng / J.P. Farrar. [London], 1916. Ill., ports., facsims. Reprinted from the *Alpine Journal*, May 1916.
GB.1335(8); Lloyd.1605(16); Lloyd.1605(16)A. h155.

Historical documents IV: The Führerbücher of Peter Knubel / J.P. Farrar. [London], 1918. Ill., ports. Reprinted from the *Alpine Journal*, February 1918.
Lloyd.1605(17). h156.

An **historical** narrative of a most extraordinary event which happened at the village of Bergemoletto in Italy: where three women were saved out of the ruins of a stable, in which they had been buried thirty-seven days by a heavy fall of snow / Ignazio Somis. London, 1765. Ill. Translated from *Ragionamento sopra il fatto avenuto in Bergemoletto*.
Lloyd.222. h157.

An **historical** sketch of the Italian Vaudois / Hill D. Wickham. London, 1847. Map.
Lloyd.269. h158.

Historique de la percée du Mont-Blanc / [rédigé par Paul Guichonnet]. Aoste, 1962-67. 2v; ill.
GB/A.1352-3. h159.

Historique de la vallée d'Aoste / Jean Baptiste de Tillier. Aoste, 1968. Ill.
GB/A.1282. h160.

Historique du pays d'Aoste, suivi de la topographie de ce pays et d'une notice sur les anciens monuments qu'il renferme / J.M.F. Orsières. Aoste, 1920. Port.
GB/B.377(14). h161.

Historisch-romantische Schilderungen aus der westlichen Schweiz / Franz Kuenlin. Zürich,

1840. 4v.
GB/A.915(4). h162.

Historische, geographische und physikalische Beschreibung des Schweizerlandes / [edited by T.S. Wyttenbach]; aus dem Französischen übersetzt [by L. Fr. König]. Bern, 1782-83. 3v.
GB/A.754-6. h163.

Die **historische** Topographie der Schweiz in der künstlerischen Darstellung / Paul Hilber. Frauenfeld, 1927. Ill.
GB/A.2028. h164.

Historischer Calender, oder der Hinkende Bott enthaltend eine getreue Erzählung verschiedener im vergangenen Jahr sich zugetragenen politischen und andern Neuigkeiten auf das Gnadenreihe Christ-Jahr 1823 / Antoni Sorgmann. Vivis, [1822].
Lloyd.1591(10). h165.

Historischer Kalender, oder der Hinkende Bott, auf das Jahr Christi 1823. Bern, [1822].
Lloyd.1591(9). h166.

The **history** of a mountain / Elisée Reclus; translated by Bertha Ness and John Lillie. London, 1881. Ill. Translated from *Histoire d'une montagne*.
Lloyd.485. h167.

History of a six weeks' tour / Percy Bysshe Shelley [or rather, by Mary Shelley and Percy B. Shelley]. London, 1817.
Lloyd.83. h168.

History of a six weeks' tour through a part of France, Switzerland, Germany and Holland / [Mary Shelley, Percy Bysshe Shelley]. London, 1817.
GB.66; Lloyd.115. h169.

History of Alaska / Henry W. Clark. New York, 1930. Ill., maps.
GB/A.1733. h170.

The **history** of Italy and Switzerland / Julia Corner; adapted for youth, schools, and families. London, [1841]. Ill., map.
Lloyd.191. h171.

The **history** of Lapland: containing a geographical description, and a natural history of that country / John Scheffer; translated from the last edition in Latin. Also *A journey into Lapland, Finland, &c.*, written by Dr. Olof Rudbeck in the year 1701.

London, 1704. Ill., map. Translated from: *Lapponia*.
GB/A.2126. h172.

A **history** of mountaineering in the Alps / Claire Eliane Engel. London, 1950. Ill.
GB.1113. h173.

A **history** of mountains, geographical and mineralogical / Joseph Wilson. London, 1807-10. 3v; ill.
GB.1276-8; Lloyd.1499-501. h174.

The **history** of Rasselas, Prince of Abissinia / Samuel Johnson. New ed. Edinburgh, 1789.
GB.165. h175.

The **history** of Switzerland, from the conquests of Caesar to the abdication of Buonaparte. London, 1825.
GB/A.1384. h176.

The **history** of the altimetry of Mont Blanc / Sir Gavin de Beer. [London, 1956.] From *Annals of Science*, vol.12 no.1, March 1956.
GB.1318(20). h177.

The **history** of the city and state of Geneva, from its first foundation to this present time / Jacob Spon; faithfully collected from several manuscripts of Jacobus Gothofredus, Monsieur Chorier, and others. London, 1687. Ill. Translated from *Histoire de la ville et de l'estat de Genève*.
Lloyd.1495; Lloyd.1504; Lloyd.1518. h178.

The **history** of the Col de Tenda / W.A.B. Coolidge. [London], 1916. Reprinted from the *English Historical Review*, vol.36.
GB.1340(39). h179.

The **history** of the Evangelical churches of the valleys of Piemont / Sir Samuel Morland. London, 1658. Port.
Lloyd.1411 (impf.). h180.

The **history** of the Helvetic Confederacy / Joseph Planta. 2nd ed. London, 1807. 3v; map.
Lloyd.1017-9. h181.

History of the Swiss Confederation, with appendices on Tell and Winkelried: a sketch / W.A.B. Coolidge. [N.p.], 1887. Reprinted from the *Encyclopaedia Britannica*.
Lloyd.1616(17). h182.

De **hittills** funna flytbojarne från Andrée-expeditionen / A.G. Nathorst. [Stockholm], 1900.

Ill., map. Ur *Ymer*, årg.1900 h.3.
GB.1329(35). h183.

Ho Pasang!: österreichische Bergsteiger in Westnepal / Rudolf Jonas; unter Mitarbeit der Expeditionsteilnehmer Hannes Beyer [et al.]. Wien, 1954. Ill., maps.
GB/A.2054. h184.

Hoch über Tälern und Menschen: im Banne der Bernina / Walther Flaig. Stuttgart, [1925]. Ill., map.
GB/B.294. h185.

Hochalpenstudien: gesammelte Schriften / F.F. Tuckett; Übersetzung von Aug. Cordes. Leipzig, 1873-74. 2v; ill., map, port.
GB.217-8; Lloyd.270 (wanting v.1). h186.

Das **Hochgebirge** der Schweiz / Ed. Osenbrüggen. 3. erw. Aufl. Basel, [1875]. Ill.
GB/B.428. h187.

Das **Hochgebirge** des Dauphiné / W.A.B. Coolidge, H. Duhamel, F. Perrin. 4. durchgesehene und 1. authorisierte deutsche Ausg., herausgegeben vom Österreichischen Alpenklub. Wien, 1913. [Alpenklub-Ausgabe; 1.] Translated from *The Central Alps of the Dauphiny*.
Lloyd.190. h188.

Das **Hochgebirge** von Grindelwald: Naturbilder aus der schweizerischen Alpenwelt / Christoph Aeby, Edm. v. Fellenberg und Gerwer. Coblenz, 1865. Ill., map.
GB.1211; Lloyd.1038. h189.

Hochgebirgsführer durch die nordrhätischen Alpen / Walther Flaig. Bd.1: Rhätikon. Dornbirn, 1924.
Lloyd.79. h191.

Hochgebirgswanderungen in den Alpen und im Kaukasus / Andreas Fischer; herausgegeben, mit Lebensbild und Bericht der letzten Fahrt versehen von Ernst Jenny. [2nd ed.] Frauenfeld, 1913. 2v; ill., maps.
GB.480 (wanting v.2). h192.

Hochgebirgswanderungen in den Alpen und im Kaukasus / Andreas Fischer; herausgegeben von Ernst Jenny. Frauenfeld, 1913. 2v; ill., maps, port. A different ed. from h192.
GB.481 (wanting v.2). h193.

Hochschwab / Peter und Stefanie Rieder. München, 1968. Ill. [Alpenvereinsführer. Reihe: Nordliche Kalkalpen; Bd. Hochschwab.]
GB/A.2017(8). h194.

Hochschwabführer / im Einvernehmen mit dem Verein Turner Bergsteiger Graz herausgegeben von Eduard Mayer und Ludwig Obersteiner. Wien, 1922. Ill. Based on *Führer durch die Hochschwabführer*, by August von Böhm.
Lloyd.147. h195.

Die **Hochstrassen** der Alpen / Kurt Mair. Berlin, 1930. 2v; ill.
GB/A.157-8. h196.

Der **Hochtourist** in den Ostalpen / L. Purtscheller, H. Hess. Leipzig, 1894. 2v; maps. [Meyers Reisebücher.] Published by the Bibliographisches Institut, Leipzig.
GB/A.772-3. h197.

Der **Hochtourist** in den Ostalpen / Ludwig Purtscheller, Heinrich Hess. 3. Aufl. Leipzig, 1903. 3v; maps. [Meyers Reisebücher.]
Lloyd.71 (wanting Bd.1-2). h198.

Der **Hochtourist** in den Ostalpen / L. Purtscheller, H. Hess. 4. Aufl. Leipzig, 1910-11. 3v; maps. [Meyers Reisebücher.]
Lloyd.72-4. h199.

Der **Hochtourist** in den Ostalpen / begründet von Ludwig Purtscheller und Heinrich Hess. 5. Aufl., neu herausgegeben im Auftrag des Deutschen und Osterreichischen Alpenvereins unter der Schriftleitung von Hanns Barth. Leipzig, 1925-28. 8v. [Meyers Reisebücher.]
Lloyd.75 (v.4 only); GB/A.200 (v.7 only). h200.

Die **Hochwasser** im September und October 1868 im bündnerischen Rheingebiet / J.W. Coaz. Leipzig, 1869. Ill.
GB/A.803(7). h201.

Die **Höfats** im Algau / J. Joseph Enzensperger. [Munich, 1896.] Ill. Pp.[212]-33 of the *Zeitschrift des Deutschen und Oesterreichischen Alpenvereins*, 1896.
GB.1367(2). h202.

Hofer, the Tyrolese / by the author of *Claudine* [i.e. M.E.B.]. London, 1824. Ill.
Lloyd.204. h203.

Das **Hohelied** der Berge / Herman Hiltbrunner. Zürich, [1944].
GB/A.1588. h204.

Die **Hohen** Tauern: Einleitung / Eduard Richter. Die Schober Gruppe / G. Geyer. Goldberg und Ankogel Gruppe / August von Böhm. Die Niederen Tauern / Hans Wödl. [Berlin, 1894.] Ill., map. Pp.[130]-294 of *Erschliessung der Ostalpen*, Bd.3.
GB.1377. h205.

Höhengänge: drei Erzählungen aus den Alpen / Walther Nithack-Stahn. Halle a.d.S., 1915.
GB/A.5. h206.

Höhenklima und Bergwanderungen in ihrer Wirkung auf den Menschen: Ergebnisse experimenteller Forschungen im Hochgebirge und Laboratorium / N. Zuntz, A. Loewy, Frans Müller, W. Caspari. Berlin, 1906. Ill.
GB/B.18. h207.

Höhenrundweg 'Hochpustertal': Sommer-Winter / Italo De Candido. Bologna, 1979. Ill., maps. [Itinerari alpini; 46.]
GB/A.1589(26). h208.

A **holiday** in Switzerland / Dora M. Jones. [London, 1898.] Pp.344-50 of the *Young Woman*, June 1898.
GB.1336(8). h209.

Holiday memories / Joseph H. Fox. Wellington, Somerset, 1908.
Lloyd.1396; Lloyd.1396A. h210.

Holiday rambles / Thomas Read Wilkinson. Manchester, 1881. Ill.
Lloyd.895. h211.

A **holiday** tour: being a few weeks passed among the Swiss and Italian lakes / Bunny. London, 1868.
Lloyd.825. h212.

The **holidays**: being the summer and tourist 'extra' of the *Westminster Budget*. [London, n.d.]
GB.1334(32). h213.

Holidays in Tyrol: Kufstein, Klobenstein, and Paneveggio / Walter White. London, 1876. Map.
Lloyd.701. h214.

Holidays on high lands, or Rambles and incidents in search of Alpine plants / Hugh Macmillan. 2nd ed., rev. and enl. London, 1873.
Lloyd.320. h215.

The **holocene** vegetational development of the Godthåbsfjord area, west Greenland / Bent Fredskild. Copenhagen, 1983. Ill., maps. [Meddelelser om Grønland. Geoscience; 10.]
GB/A.1818(10). h216.

The **holocene** vegetational development of Tugtuligssuag and Qeqertat, northwest Greenland / Bent Fredskild. Copenhagen, 1985. [Meddelelser om Grønland. Geoscience; 14.]
GB/A.1818(14). h217.

Holy Himalaya: the religion, traditions, and scenery of a Himalayan province, Kumaon and Garhwal / E. Sherman Oakley. Edinburgh, 1905. Ill.
GB.526. h218.

The **holy** mountain: being the story of a pilgrimage to Lake Manas and of initiation on Mount Kailas in Tibet / Bhagwan Shri Hamsa; translated from the Marathi by Shri Purohit Swami. London, 1934. Ill., port.
GB.535. h219.

Home climbs: a paper read before the A.C. [i.e. Alpine Club] December 1918 / W.P. Haskett Smith. London, [1918]. Reprinted from the *Climbers' Club Journal*, vol.2 no.4.
Lloyd.1620(17). h220.

Home rule in Greenland / Isi Foighel. Copenhagen, 1980. Port. [Meddelelser om Grønland. Man & society; 1.]
GB/A.1820/1. h221.

Hommage à Mr de Saussure sur son ascension et ses expériences physiques au sommet du Mont-Blanc / M. Marignié. Genève, 1787.
GB.461(2). h222.

L'**homme** et la montagne / Jules Blache. 11e éd. [Paris], 1942. Ill.
GB/A.2032(2). h223.

L'**homme** et la montagne / Marcel Rouff. Paris, 1925.
GB/A.1157. h224.

L'**homme** et le Mont Blanc / Etienne Guidetti. [Paris], 1957. Ill., maps. [Bibliothèque des Guides bleus.]
GB/A.902. h225.

Hommes, cimes et dieux: les grandes mythologies de l'altitude et la légende dorée des montagnes à travers le monde / Samivel. [Paris], 1973. Ill.
GB/A.1136. h226.

Hon. Treasurer's statement, year ended 31st December, 1961 / Alpine Club. [London, 1962.]
GB.1319(16). h227.

The **Hong** Kong Mountaineering Club expedition to the Snow Mountains of New Guinea / Jack Baines. [N.p., 1972.] Ill.
GB/A.2048(5). h228.

The **Hong** Kong mountaineering expedition to Lamjung Himal, Spring 1974. Hong Kong, [1975?]. Ill., map.
GB/A.1974(5). h229.

Horaire du chemin de fer à Crémaillère Chamonix-Montenvers. Bellegarde, 1932.
GB.1326(6). h230.

Hors des chemins battus: ascensions nouvelles dans les Alpes / E.R. Blanchet. Paris, 1932. Ill.
GB.1327(11). h231.

Hospice of St. Bernard: a prize poem / Joseph Arnould. Oxford, 1834.
Lloyd.328. h232.

L'**hôtel** des Neuchâtelois: un épisode de la conquête des Alpes / Charles Gos. Lausanne, 1928. Ill., ports.
GB.1323(2). h233.

The **hour** of the angel / Joanna Cannan. London, 1949. [Pan books; 102.] Originally published as *Ithuriel's hour*.
GB.1328(4). h234.

Hours of exercise in the Alps / John Tyndall. London, 1871.
GB.443; Lloyd.613; Lloyd.613A,B. h235.

Hours of exercise in the Alps / John Tyndall. 2nd ed. London, 1871.
GB.444; Lloyd.614. h236.

Hours of exercise in the Alps / John Tyndall. New York, 1872. Ill.
GB.448. h237.

Hours of exercise in the Alps / John Tyndall; [edited by Mrs. Tyndall]. New ed. London, 1899.
GB.449. h238.

Hovedregister 1944-1968 til den Norske Turistforenings årbøker og medlemsblad / utarbeidet av Andreas Backer og Bjorn Ruud. Oslo, 1968.
GB/A.1674. h239.

How Franz redeemed his promise / [P.W. Thomas]. [London, 1886.] Pp.414-24 of the *Cornhill Magazine*, Oct. 1886.
GB.1881(78). h240.

How Jacques Balmat ascended Mont Blanc / Frank Barrett. [London, 1879.] Ill. Pp.726-30 of *Cassell's Family Magazine*, 1879.
GB.1646(26). h241.

How to become an alpinist / Frederick Burlingham. London, [1914]. Ill., port.
GB.357. h242.

How to climb Triglov. Ljubljana, 1979. Ill.
GB/A.2018(8). h243.

How to use the aneroid barometer / Edward Whymper. London, 1891.
GB.1045; Lloyd.1191; Lloyd.1191A. h244.

How to visit Switzerland: a guide-book to the chief scenes of interest in Switzerland / edited by Henry S. Lunn and W. Holdsworth Lunn. 4th ed., rev. and enl. London, 1898. Ill., maps. Incorporates the *J.E.M. guide to Switzerland*.
GB/A.802(11). h245.

How we did Mont Blanc / George F. Brown. [London, 1865.] Reprinted from the *Cornhill Magazine*.
GB.885. h246.

How we did them in seventeen days: to wit: Belgium, the Rhine, Switzerland, & France / described and illustrated by one of ourselves [i.e. Richard Marrack]; aided, assisted, encouraged and abetted by the other [i.e. Edmund G. Harvey]. Truro, [1876]. Ill., music.
Lloyd.412. h247.

How we spent the summer, or A 'voyage en zigzag' in Switzerland and Tyrol, with some members of the Alpine Club / from the sketch book of one of the party [i.e. Elizabeth Tuckett]. 2nd ed. London, 1864. Map.
GB.1290; Lloyd.1531. h248.

How we spent the summer, or A 'voyage en zigzag' in Switzerland and Tyrol, with some members of the Alpine Club / from the sketch book of one of the party [i.e. Elizabeth Tuckett]. London, 1873. Ill., map.
GB/B.531. h249.

The **Hudson** Bay route to Europe / Robert Bell. Winnipeg, 1909.
GB/B.440(17). h250.

Hudson's Bay, or A missionary tour in the territory of the Hon. Hudson's Bay Company / John Ryerson. Toronto, 1855. Ill., port.
GB/A.1935. h251.

Hulme Hall, session 1914-1915. [Manchester, 1914.] List of staff and students.
GB.1319(2). h252.

The **human** side of immigration / John Graham Brooks. [New York, 1907.] Pp.633-8 of the *Century Magazine*, vol.73, March 1907.
GB.1332(20). h253.

Hundert Jahre Bergführerverein Pontresina / verfasst im Auftrage des Bergführervereins Pontresina, von Charles Golay. Samedan, 1971. Ill.
GB/B.289(27). h254.

Hundert Jahre Faulhorn 1830-1930: Festschrift / Johannes Jegerlehner, Martin Nil, Samuel Brawand. Interlaken, 1930. Ill.
GB/A.803(5). h255.

Hundert Jahre Sektion Salzburg Osterreichischen Alpenverein, 1869-1969 / Redaktion: Erwin Niedermann. [Salzburg, 1969.]
GB/C.22(1). h256.

A **hundred** and three hikes in southwestern British Columbia / David Macaree. 2nd printing. Seattle, 1974. Ill., maps. Published by the British Columbia Mountaineering Club.
GB/B.525(7). h257.

Hut hopping in the Austrian Alps / William E. Reifsnyder. San Francisco, [1973]. Ill. [A Sierra Club totebook.]
GB/A.1676(14). h258.

Hval- og robbefangsten udi Strat-Davis, ved Spitsbergen, og under eilandet Jan Mayn, samt dens vigtige fordele / Carl Pontoppidan. Kiøbenhavn, 1785. Ill.
GB/A.1940. h259.

Hvalbåtliv / Fridtjov Barth Larsen. Oslo, 1935. Ill.
GB/B.524(10). h260.

-I-

I become a 'tiger': the life story of Sherpa Tenzing. London, 1955. Ill. Extracted from his *Man of Everest*. Pp.25-33 of *Illustrated*, April 23 1955.
GB.1334(28). i001.

I photograph mountains / Frank S. Smythe. London, 1939. Ill. Pp.557-9 of the *Listener*, vol.21 no.531, 16 March 1939.
GB.1334(5). i002.

I vinteroplag på Labrador / Thorolf Coldevin. Oslo, 1935.
GB/A.2078. i003.

Ice and its natural history / John Young Buchanan. London, [1908].
Lloyd.1609(3). i004.

The **ice** axe murders / Glyn Carr. London, [1958].
GB.298. i005.

The **ice** experience / Jeff Lowe. Chicago, 1979. Ill.
GB/A.1974(8). i006.

Ice on my palette / Maurice Conly; text by Neville Peat. Christchurch, 1977.
GB/B.607. i007.

Ice-caves of France and Switzerland: a narrative of subterranean exploration / G.F. Browne. London, 1865. Ill.
Lloyd.774. i008.

The **icebergs** or glaciers of the frozen ocean. [Edinburgh], 1785. Pp.161-2 of the *Scots Magazine*, April 1785.
GB.1313(10). i009.

Icebound: the *Jeannette* Expedition's quest for the North Pole / Leonard F. Guttridge. Annapolis, Md., 1986. Ill.
GB/A.2208. i010.

Iceland, or The journal of a residence in that island, during 1814 and 1815 / Ebenezer Henderson. Edinburgh, 1818. 2v; ill., map.
Lloyd.853-4. i011.

Ich und die Berge: ein Wanderleben / Theodor Wundt. Berlin, [1917]. Ill.
GB/A.425. i012.

Idyllen, Volkssagen, Legenden und Erzählungen aus der Schweiz / Johann Rudolf Wyss. Bern,

1815-22. 2v; ill.
GB/A.734-5. i013.

Idyllic Switzerland / George Carless Swayne. [Edinburgh], 1891. Pp.639-44 of *Blackwood's Magazine*, May 1891.
GB.1332(36). i014.

Igloo tales / Edward L. Keithahn. Lawrence, Kan., 1945. Ill.
GB/A.1784. i015.

Iglulik and Caribou Eskimo texts / Knud Rasmussen; [translated by W. Worster and W.E. Calvert]. New York, 1976. Ill. [Thule expedition, 5th, 1921-1924. Report; vol.7 no.3.]
GB/A.1834. i016.

L'île de Saint Pierre / Jules Baillods. Neuchâtel, 1931. Ill.
GB/B.338(20). i017.

Illustrated guide to the valleys of the Biellese region to the south of Monte Rosa / Pia Padovani, Emilio Gallo. Turin, 1900.
Lloyd.1614(8). i018.

Illustrated moss flora of Arctic North America and Greenland. 1: Polytrichaceae / editor Gert S. Morgensen. Copenhagen, 1985. [Meddelelser om Grønland. Bioscience; 17.]
GB/A.1819(17). i019.

Illustrations of the atmospherical origin of epidemic disorders of health and of its relation to the predisponent constitutional causes / T. Forster. Chelmsford, 1829.
GB.697(1). i020.

Illustrations of the passes of the Alps, by which Italy communicates with France, Switzerland, and Germany / William Brockedon. London, 1828-29. 2v.
Lloyd.1481-2; Lloyd.1542-3; Lloyd.1542A-3A. i021.

Illustrations of the passes of the Alps, by which Italy communicates with France, Switzerland and Germany / William Brockedon. London, [1877]. Ill.
GB.1263-4. i022.

Illustrations of the Vaudois, in a series of views / engraved by Edward Finden, from drawings by Hugh Dyke Acland; accompanied with descriptions. London, 1831. Map.
Lloyd.1298. i023.

Illustrierter Führer durch das Säntis-Gebiet / Gottlieb Lüthi, Carl Egloff; mit einem naturgeschichtlichen Anhang von Dr. Emil Bächler. 5. rev. und neu illustr. Aufl. St. Gallen, 1925. Ill., map.
Lloyd.370. i024.

Illustrierter Führer über die Lötschberg-Bahn nach dem Berner Oberland ins Wallis und nach Italien / herausgegeben von der Direktion der Berner Alpenbahn-Gesellschaft. Bern, 1925. Ill., maps.
GB/A.1351(12). i025.

Illustrierter Reisebegleiter für die Alpenstrasse des Klausen und ihre Zufahrtslinien / J. Knobel. Glarus, 1900.
GB/A.758(3). i026.

Illustriertes Bündner Oberland / Christian Tarnuzzer; mit einem geschichtlichen Beitrag von J.C. Muoth. Zürich, 1903. Map. Published by the Bündner-Oberländer-Verkehrsverein.
GB/A.1199(13). i027.

Illustrirte Zeitung für kleine Leute. Bd.2. Halle, [n.d.].
GB.1011. i028.

Im Banne der Dachstein-Südwand / Kurt Maix. 8. Aufl. Salzburg, 1969. Ill.
GB/A.438. i029.

Im Banne der Jungfrau / Konrad Falke. Zürich, 1909. Ill.
GB/A.95. i030.

Im Banne der Pole: ein Heldenbuch von Polarforschern und ihren Fahrten / Franz Graf Zedtwitz. Berlin, 1938. Ill., maps.
GB/A.2048(2). i031.

Im Banne der Spinne: im Winter durch die Eigerwand: 6. März bis 12. März 1961, der erste Dokumentar-Bericht / Toni Hiebeler. München, 1961. Ill., ports.
GB.316. i032.

Im Banne des Eismeers: grönländische Jagd- und Reiseerlebnisse / Alfred Leverkus. [Cologne, 1909?] Ill., maps.
GB/A.1612. i033.

Im Banne des Nanga Parbat: Bildband der deutsch-österreichischen Willy-Merkl-Gedächtnisexpedition 1953 zum Nanga Parbat / heraus-

gegeben von Karl M. Herrligkoffer. München, 1953.
GB/B.245(27).   i034.

Im extremen Fels: 100 Kletterführen in den Alpen / Walter Pause, Jurgen Winkler. München, 1970. Ill.
GB/B.258.   i035.

Im Fels und Eis der Mont Blanc-Gruppe / Guido Mayer. Bern, 1920. Ill. Pp.[3]-29 of the *Jahrbuch des Schweizer Alpenclub*, 1919.
GB.1229(1).   i036.

Im Hochgebirge: Wanderungen / Emil Zsigmondy; herausgegeben von K. Schulz. Leipzig, 1889. Ill.
GB.1231; Lloyd.1393.   i037.

Im Kalkfels der Alpen: 100 klassische Gipfeltouren in den Kalkalpen / Walter Pause. 4. Aufl. München, [1966]. Ill.
GB/B.236.   i038.

Im Kampf um den Berg: spannende Bergerlebnisse. Zürich, 1934. Ill.
GB/A.2031(5).   i039.

Im Kampf um den Himalaja: der erste deutsche Angriff auf den Kangchendzönga 1929 / Paul Bauer. 2. Aufl. München, 1931. Ill., maps.
GB.1059.   i040.

Im Kampf um Tschomo-lungma den Gipfel der Erde: der Himalaja und sein höchster Gipfel, Mount Everest oder Tschomo-lungma / Walther Flaig, unter Mitarbeit von Franz Zorell. Stuttgart, [1923]. Ill., maps.
GB/A.964.   i041.

Im Kaukasus: Bergbesteigungen und Reiseerlebnisse im Sommer 1914 / Carl Egger. Basel, 1915. Ill.
GB/A.1595.   i042.

Im Lande der Dolomiten / [edited by] Walther Amonn. Bolzano, 1928. Ill.
GB/C.7.   i043.

Im schweren Fels: 100 Genusskletereien in den Alpen / Walter Pause. 5., neubearb. Aufl. München, [1967]. Ill., maps.
GB/A.171.   i044.

Im Treibeisgürtel: ein Jahr als Arzt unter Eskimos / Arne Høygaard; übertragen von Elisabeth Ermel. Braunschweig, [1940]. Ill. Translated from *Innenfor drivisen*.
GB/B.248.   i045.

Im Zauber des Hochgebirges: alpine Stimmungsbilder, bergländischer Familienschatz / Otto Hartmann. 7. bis 11. verb. und verm. Aufl. Regensburg, [ca 1924]. 2v; ill., maps.
GB/B.116-7.   i046.

Images de la montagne: de l'artiste cartographe à l'ordinateur: catalogue et essais: exposition organisée par la Bibliothèque nationale avec le concours de l'Institut géographique national. Paris, 1984.
GB/B.520(11).   i047.

Images de la Suisse; oeuvres et études / Paul Valéry [et al.]. Marseille, [1943]. [Cahiers du sud.]
GB/A.1483.   i048.

Immagini della Valle d'Aosta nei secoli: mostra organizzata dall'Azienda Autonoma di Soggiorno e Turismo di Aosta: catalogo / a cura di Ada Peyrot con la collaborazione del Comitato Organizzatore, Aosta, Palazzo Vescovile, 29 luglio / 29 settembre 1971. Torino, 1971. Ill.
GB/B.338(10).   i049.

...immer noch 1000 Meilen zum Pazifik: die Abenteuer des Alexander Mackenzie / Hans-Otto Meissner. Stuttgart, [1966]. Ill., maps.
GB/A.477.   i050.

The **Imperial** Trans-Antarctic Expedition. London, [1914]. Ill., map.
GB/B.632.   i051.

Impressione di un anziano su due vie al M. Bianco / Piero Ghiglione. Torino, 1949. Ill. Pp.81-5 of *Scandere*, 1949.
GB.1331(50).   i052.

Impressions de voyage / Alexandre Dumas. Nouv. éd., rev. et corr. Paris, 1841. 2v (in 1).
GB.214.   i053.

Impressions de voyage: le Corricolo / Alexandre Dumas. Paris, 1851. 2v (in 1).
Lloyd.247.   i054.

Impressions de voyage: le Spéronare / Alexandre Dumas. Paris, 1855. 2v (in 1).
Lloyd.246.   i055.

Impressions de voyage: Suisse / Alexandre Dumas. Paris, 1859. 3v (in 1). [Oeuvres complètes d'Alexandre Dumas.]
Lloyd.245.   i056.

Impressions de voyage: Suisse / Alexandre Dumas. Nouv. éd. Paris, 1868-74. 2v. [Oeuvres complètes d'Alexandre Dumas.]
GB/A.800(3-4).   i057.

Impressions de voyage: Suisse / Alexandre Dumas. Nouv. éd. Paris, 1891-96. 3v. [Oeuvres complètes d'Alexandre Dumas.]
GB.225-7.   i058.

An **impromptu** ascent of Mont Blanc / W.H. Le Mesurier. London, 1882. Ill., map.
GB.884; Lloyd.921.   i059.

In alta montagna / Ildefonso Clerici. Milano, 1929. Ill.
GB/A.942(2).   i060.

In and beyond the Himalayas: a record of sport and travel in the abode of snow / S.J. Stone. London, 1896.
GB.1032.   i061.

In den Hochalpen: Erlebnisse aus den Jahren 1859-1885 / Paul Güssfeldt. 3. Aufl. Berlin, 1892. Ill.
GB.588.   i062.

In den Hochgebirgen Asiens und Siebenbürgens: Jagderlebnisse und Forschungsreisen / Alexander Florstedt. 4. Aufl. Neudamm, 1928. Ill., maps.
GB/A.1613.   i063.

In der polnischen Tatra / Józef Nyka. Warszawa, 1971. Ill.
GB/A.1284.   i064.

In Eis und Urgestein: 100 klassische Gipfeltouren in den Zentralalpen / Walter Pause. 5. Aufl. München, [1964]. Ill.
GB/B.234.   i065.

In icebound seas, or The voyage of the *Constance* rescue ship: a story of Arctic adventure / M. Gillies. London, [1860?].
GB/A.2109.   i066.

In isles of the far North: the early entrance of the Gospel on Greenland's snow-clad shores, Iceland's frozen fields, Lapland's icebound vales, Labrador's lone land, and Faroe's sea-girt isles. Kilmarnock, [ca 1914]. Ill.
GB/A.1764.   i067.

In Kenya, da -5 a +5000 metri di quota / Benedetto Lanza. Firenze, 1970. Ill., map. At head of title: Spedizione Mares-G.R.S.T.S. in Kenya e Tanzania, 1968. Reprinted from *l'Universo*, vol.50 no.1-3, 1970.
GB/B.338(13).   i068.

In Lessinia / Gianni Faè. [Lessinia], 1969. Ill., maps.
GB/A.1295(13).   i069.

In memoriam: reprinted from the *Alpine Journal*. May 1929-Nov. 1948. London, 1929-48. Wanting May 1930-May 1935, May 1936, May 1938-Nov.1938, Nov.1939-May 1948.
GB.1316(1-12).   i070.

In memoriam: Colin Fletcher Kirkus / A.B. Hargreaves. London, 1943. Port. Pp.168-73 of the *Climbers' Club Journal*, N.S. vol.7 no.2.
GB.1339(4).   i071.

In memoriam: Henry Fairbanks Montagnier, 1877-1933. [London, 1933.] Port. Pp.349-54 of the *Alpine Journal*, no.45.
GB.1133(3) (impf.).   i072.

In memoriam: J.E.Q. Barford / B.M. Crowther. [London, 1948.] Port. Pp.355-60 of the *Climbers' Club Journal*, N.S. vol.8 no.3.
GB.1337(4).   i073.

In memoriam: Josef Bollinger, 1873-1943. [London, 1944.] Ports. Reprinted from the *Alpine Journal*, vol.54 no.268, May 1944.
GB.1313(40).   i074.

In memoriam: Joseph Lochmatter / J.P. Farrar. [London], 1916. Port. Reprinted from the *Alpine Journal*, November 1915.
Lloyd.1602(1).   i075.

In memoriam: R.L. Beaumont / R.A.H. [i.e. Robert A. Hodgkin]. [London, 1939.] Port. Pp.55-6 of the *Climbers' Club Journal*, N.S. vol.6 no.1.
GB.1338(28).   i076.

In memoriam: Richard Wilfred Broadrick. Brighton, [1903?]. Port.
Lloyd.1613(21).   i077.

In memoriam: W. Cecil Slingsby, 1849-1929. [Leeds, 1930.] Ports. Pp.67-9 of the *Yorkshire*

Ramblers' Club Journal, vol.6 no.19.
GB.1881(22); GB.1881(23).   i078.

In montibus sanctis: studies of mountain form and of its visible causes: collected and completed out of *Modern painters* / John Ruskin. Orpington, 1884-85. 2v.
Lloyd.1621(12-3).   i079.

In praise of Switzerland: being the Alps in prose and verse / Harold Spender. London, 1912. [Constable's anthologies.]
GB.980.   i080.

In praise of walking / [Thoreau, Burroughs, Hazlitt, Whitman]. London, 1905.
Lloyd.1612(10).   i081.

In Rupert's Land / memoirs of Walter Traill; edited by Mae Atwood. Toronto, 1970.
GB/A.2120.   i082.

In Schnee und Eis: Soldaten erleben das Hochgebirge / Herbert Maeder. Frauenfeld, 1973. Ill.
GB/A.1250.   i083.

In search of the magnetic North: a soldier-surveyor's letters from the North-West 1843-1844 / John Henry Lefroy; edited by George F.G. Stanley. Toronto, 1955. Map. [Pioneer books.]
GB/A.1618.   i084.

In Tälern und Höhen des Himalaja: Jagden und Reisen in Kaschmir und Ladak / Hans Meyer-Illmersdorf; nach den Tagebüchern herausgegeben von A. Berger. Berlin, 1926. Ill., map.
GB/A.1060.   i085.

In the Alaska-Yukon gamelands / J.A. McGuire. Cincinnati, 1921. Ill., ports.
GB/A.1775.   i086.

In the Alsatian mountains: a narrative of a tour in the Vosges / Katherine Lee. London, 1883. Map.
Lloyd.609.   i087.

In the forbidden land: an account of a journey in Tibet, capture by the Tibetan authorities, imprisonment, torture, and ultimate release / A. Henry Savage-Landor. London, 1898. 2v.
GB.1003-4.   i088.

In the heart of the Canadian Rockies / James Outram. New York, 1923. Ill., port., maps.
GB.701; Lloyd.922.   i089.

In the high Himalayas: sport and travel in the Rhotang and Baralacha, with some notes on the natural history of that area / Hugh Whistler. London, 1924. Ill.
GB.972.   i090.

In the Himalayas and on the Indian plains / Constance F. Gordon-Cumming. New ed. London, 1886.
GB.545.   i091.

In the ice world of Himálaya / Fanny Bullock Workman, William Hunter Workman. London, 1900. Ill., maps, ports.
Lloyd.1115.   i092.

In Valpellina / Canzio E., Mondini F., Vigna N. Torino, 1899. Ill. Pp.[1]-96 of the *Bollettino del Club Alpino Italiano*, vol.32.
GB.1333(3) (impf.).   i093.

In Valpellina / Canzio E., Mondini F., Vigna N. Torino, 1899. Ill. Estratto dal *Bollettino del C.A.I.*, vol.32 no.65.
GB.1333(4).   i094.

In Valsesia: album d'un alpinista. Borgosesia, 1973. Ill., maps. Facsimile reprint of the Biella, 1878 ed. Published by the Club Alpino Italiano, Sezione di Varallo.
GB/B.390(2).   i095.

In Valsesia: la Val Grande ed il Monte Rosa / Giuseppe Lampugnani. Torino, 1907. Ill. Estratto dal volume *La Valsesia*, pubblicato a cura del Club Alpino Italiano, Sezione di Varallo.
GB.1188(5).   i096.

Inauguration of the Cabane Britannia. [N.p.], 1913. Published by the Association of British Members of the Swiss Alpine Club.
Lloyd.907; Lloyd.926; Lloyd.926A,B,C.   i097.

Incidents of travel in Central America / John L. Stephens. 12th ed. New York, 1844. 2v.
GB.942-3.   i098.

Incidents of travel in Egypt, Arabia Petræa and the Holy Land / J.L. Stephens. People's ed. Edinburgh, 1839.
GB.1179(4); GB.1180(3).   i099.

Incidents of travel in Greece, Turkey, Russia and Poland / J.L. Stephens. People's ed. Edinburgh, 1839.
GB.1177(1).   i100.

Le **incisioni** rupestri di Monte Bego / Ausilio Priuli. [Turin], 1984. [Quaderni di cultura alpina.]
GB/B.640.   i101.

The **incomparable** valley: a geologic interpretation of the Yosemite / François E. Matthès; edited by Fritiof Fryxell. Berkeley, 1950. Ill.
GB.1159.   i102.

Incontro con il Trentino / Gino Scrinzi. Calliano, [1971?]. Ill., maps.
GB/A.1041.   i103.

Incontro con Merano / H. Frass; testo a cura di Willy Dondio. Bolzano, 1973. Ill.
GB/C.5(11).   i104.

Index to the *Himalayan Journal*, volumes 1-35. [Bombay? 1979?] Published by the Himalayan Club.
GB/A.2019(7).   i105.

[**India**: a topographical photograph album.] [N.p., ca 1870.] Many photographs by Samuel Bourne.
GB/B.633.   i106.

India and Tibet: a history of the relations which have subsisted between the two countries from the time of Warren Hastings to 1910 / Sir Francis Younghusband. London, 1910. Ill., maps.
GB.1005.   i107.

The **Indian** Alps and how we crossed them: being a narrative of two years' residence in the Eastern Himalayas and two months' tour into the interior / by a lady pioneer [i.e. Nina Elizabeth Mazuchelli]. London, 1876. Ill.
Lloyd.1358.   i108.

The **Indian** Peaks Wilderness Area: a hiking and field guide / John A. Murray. Boulder, Colo., 1985.
GB/A.1974(3).   i109.

Indicatore turistico, alpinistico, sciistico del Piemonte / Adolfo Hess; edito per cura dell'Ente Provinciale per il Turismo. Torino, 1938. Map.
GB/A.2017(13).   i110.

Indice generale delle dieci annate 1884-1893 del *Bollettino del C.A.I.* / compilato da Luigi Vaccarone. 1894-1903 / compilato da Federico Federici. [Turin, 1893-1909.] Pp.[343]-81 of vol.27 no.60 and pp.[i]-xlviii of vol.40 no.73 of the *Bollettino del Club Alpino Italiano*.
GB.1329(8-9); GB.1881(10-1).   i111.

Indische Gletscherfahrten: Reisen und Erlebnisse im Himalaja / Kurt Boeck. Stuttgart, 1900. Ill., maps.
GB/A.203.   i112.

Indische Gletscherfahrten: Reisen und Erlebnisse im Ost- und West-Himalaja / Kurt Boeck. Leipzig, 1923. Ill., map.
GB/A.798.   i113.

Indische schetsen / P. Heering. 2. dr. Leiden, 1897.
GB/A.1381(2).   i114.

The **influence** of mountains upon the development of human intelligence: the seventeenth W.P. Ker Memorial Lecture delivered in the University of Glasgow / Geoffrey Winthrop Young. Glasgow, 1957.
GB.1313(22).   i115.

Information and directions for travellers on the Continent / Mariana Starke. 5th ed., rev. London, 1824. Originally published as *Travels on the Continent*.
GB/A.967.   i116.

Gli **infortunii** della montagna: manuale pratico ad uso degli alpinisti, delle guide e dei portatori / Oscar Bernhard; traduzione con note ed aggiunto, Riccardo Curti. Milano, 1900. Ill. [Manuali Hoepli.] Translated from *Samariterdienst*.
GB/A.1031.   i117.

The **innocent** on Everest / Ralph Izzard. London, 1954. Ill.
GB.555.   i118.

Inquiry into the decrease of the food-fishes; B: The propagation of food-fishes in the waters of the United States, 1875-1876 / Commission of Fish and Fisheries, U.S.A. Washington, 1878. Ill. [Report of the Commission of Fish & Fisheries, U.S.A.]
GB/A.1970.   i119.

Inscriptions from Swiss chalets: a collection of inscriptions found outside and inside Swiss chalets, storehouses and sheds / Walter Larden. Oxford, 1913. Ill.
Lloyd.954.   i120.

Das **Inselschiff**: eine Zeitschrift für die Freunde des Insel-Verlages. Jahrg.1-17, 1920-1936. Leipzig, 1920-36. Wanting Jahrg.9-12.
GB/A.396-408.   i121.

Inside the real Lakeland / A. Harry Griffin. Preston, 1961. Ill., map.
GB.1064.   i122.

Instructions pour un voyageur qui se propose de parcourir la Suisse / [J.G. Ebel]; traduit par le traducteur du *Socrate rustique* [i.e. Jean R. Frey des Landres]. Basle, 1795. 2v (in 1); ill. Translated from *Anleitung auf die nützlichste und genussvollste Art die Schweitz zu bereisen*.
Lloyd.111.   i123.

Instructions to those climbing Mount Kilimanjaro / Mountain Club of East Africa. Moshi, 1937.
GB/B.602(9).   i124.

Integrated mountain development / editors Tej Vir Singh, Jagdish Kaur; consulting editors: Jack D. Ives, Bruno Messerli. New Delhi, 1985.
GB/A.2204.   i125.

Intellectual culture of the Copper Eskimos / Knud Rasmussen; [translated by W.E. Calvert]. New York, 1976. Ill. [Thule expedition, 5th, 1921-1924. Report; 9.]
GB/A.1836.   i126.

Intellectual culture of the Iglulik Eskimos / Knud Rasmussen. New York, 1976. Ill. [Thule expedition, 5th, 1921-1924. Report; vol.7 no.1.]
GB/A.1832.   i127.

An **interesting** narrative of the travels of James Bruce, Esq. into Abyssinia to discover the source of the Nile: abridged from the original work. To which are added notes and extracts, from the travels of Dr. Shaw, M. Savary, and the memoirs of Baron de Tott. 2nd American ed. Boston, 1798.
GB/A.2088.   i128.

Interlaken / Gerber. Zürich, [1895?]. Ill. [Swiss scenes.]
GB/A.1817(5).   i129.

International mountain rescue handbook / Hamish MacInnes. New York, 1972. Ill., maps.
GB/B.528(9).   i130.

Introduction to the *Alpine Guide* / John Ball. New ed. London, [1873?].
Lloyd.1617(2).   i130.1.

Introductionis in universam geographiam, tam veterem quam novam, libri VI / Philippus Cluverius. Ed. ult. prioribus emend. [Paris], 1635.
GB.3.   i131.

Introduzione alla montagna / Giuseppe Mazzotti. Treviso, 1946. Ill. [Biblioteca alpina; 1.]
GB.1327(9).   i132.

Investigation of the fur-seal and other fisheries of Alaska: report from the Committee on Merchant Marine and Fisheries of the House of Representatives. Washington, 1889. Ill., maps. [Report / United States. Congress. House; 3883.]
GB/A.1735.   i133.

Invito al Cansiglio: la montagna di Vittorio Veneto / Giuseppe Mazzotti. Treviso, 1965. Ill.
GB/A.1035(8).   i134.

Invito al Frignano: l'Appennino modenese: folklore, arte, e natura dell' antica e gloriosa montagna modenese / Franco Mantovi; documentazione a cura di Graziano Manni. Modena, 1973.
GB/B.376.   i135.

Invito al Monviso: idee per una monografia sulla valle del Po / Giacinto Bollea. Saluzzo, 1971. Ill.
GB/B.377(7).   i136.

Invito alla montagna / Rosella Vacchino. Torino, 1973. Ill. [Manuali e guide pratiche Gribaudi; 85.]
GB/A.1468(2).   i137.

Invito alla Valle Vigezzo / studi di autori vari; coordinati a cura di Paolo Norsa. Domodossola, 1970. Ill., maps.
GB/A.1049.   i138.

Invito in Val Gardena / Arturo Tanesini. [Novara, 1936.] Ill., map. Published by the Istituto Geografico De Agostini.
GB/A.1002.   i139.

Ireland / edited by M.J.B. Baddeley and C.S. Ward. 2nd ed. London, 1890. Maps. [Thorough guide series].
Lloyd.110.   i140.

Irish Mountaineering: journal of the Irish Mountaineering Club. 1958-59, 1979-82. [Dublin, 1959-83?]
GB/B.528(18), GB/A.2052(4).   i141.

Ishavsodyssé: minnen och upplevelser från Golfströmsexpeditionen 1936 / Carl Eric Odelberg, Claes Chr. Olrog. Stockholm, 1936. Ill., map.
GB/B.524(6).   i142.

Island, Hvitramannaland, Grönland und Vinland, oder Der Norrmänner Leben auf Island und Grönland und deren Fahrten nach Amerika schon

über 500 Jahre vor Columbus: vorzüglich nach altscandinavischen Quellenschriften / Karl Wilhelmi. Amsterdam, 1967. Map. Facsimile reprint of the Heidelberg, 1842 ed.
GB/A.1609.   i143.

Island of Skye / edited by E.W. Steeple, Guy Barlow and Harry Macrobert. Edinburgh, 1923. Ill. [Scottish Mountaineering Club guide; 3A.]
GB.1309(1).   i144.

Island of Skye / edited by E.W. Steeple [et al.]; with a revised appendix on new climbs by William M. Mackenzie, J.K.W. Dunn. 2nd ed., rev. Edinburgh, 1948. [Scottish Mountaineering Club guide.]
GB.779.   i145.

The **Israel** of the Alps: a history of the persecutions of the Waldenses / Alexis Muston; translated by William Hazlitt. London, 1852. Ill. Translated from *L'Israël des Alpes*.
GB.324; Lloyd.530.   i146.

Isviddernas hjältar: polarforskningens historia genom tiderna berättad för ungdom i alla åldrar / Axel Ahlman. Lund, 1928.
GB/A.2079.   i147.

L'**Italia** e le regioni polari / Silvio Zavatti. Ancona, 1981. Ill., facsim. [Documenti; 7.]
GB/A.1990.   i148.

L'**Italia** fisica. Milano, 1957. Ill., maps. [Conosci l'Italia; 1.]
GB/B.559.   i149.

Italia in Patagonia: spedizione italiana alle Ande patagoniche, 1957-1958 / Guido Monzino. Milano, 1958. Ill.
GB/B.498.   i150.

L'**Italia** storica. Milano, 1961. Ill., maps. [Conosci l'Italia; 5.]
GB/B.563.   i151.

Italian Alps: sketches in the mountains of Ticino, Lombardy, the Trentino, and Venetia / Douglas W. Freshfield. London, 1875. Ill., maps.
GB.408; GB.409; Lloyd.699; Lloyd.699A.   i152.

Italian Alps: sketches in the mountains of Ticino, Lombardy, the Trentino, and Venetia / Douglas W. Freshfield. Le Alpi italiane; traduzione di Giovanni Strobele. Trento, 1971. Ill. Facsimile reprint

of the London, 1875 ed. English and Italian text.
GB/B.525(5).   i153.

The **Italian** valleys of the Pennine Alps: a tour through all the romantic and less-frequented 'vals' of northern Piedmont, from the Tarentaise to the Gries / S.W. King. London, 1858. Ill., maps.
GB.598; Lloyd.783; Lloyd.783A.   i154.

Italiani sulle montagne del mondo / Mario Fantin. Bologna, 1967. Ill.
GB/B.341.   i155.

Italien: eine Wanderung von den Alpen bis zum Aetna / Karl Stieler, Eduard Paulus, Woldemar Kaden. 2. Aufl. Stuttgart, 1880. Ill., map.
GB/C.109.   i156.

Italy: mountain holidays / [Mariano Ticconi]. Rome, [1979?]. Ill., maps.
GB/B.501(11).   i157.

Italy from the Alps to Naples / Karl Baedeker. Leipsic, 1904.
Lloyd.107.   i158.

Iter helveticum: being a journal of the doings of a cabinet of five fellow travellers in Switzerland, during September 1886 / by their Lord Chancellor [i.e. William Anderton Brigg]. Keighley, 1887.
GB.284; Lloyd.344; Lloyd.344A.   i159.

Itinéraire d'un voyage fait en Suisse en 1803 / P.J. Gerard. Bruxelles, 1804. Map.
Lloyd.86.   i160.

Itinéraire de Chamouni, de Sixt, des deux Saint Bernard et des vallées autour du Mont-Blanc / J.P. Pictet-Mallet. Genève, 1840. Map.
Lloyd.334.   i161.

Itinéraire de Genève, des glaciers de Chamouni, du Valais et du canton de Vaud / Marc Théodore Bourrit. Genève, 1808.
GB/A.1385.   i162.

Itinéraire de Genève, Lausanne et Chamouni / Marc Théodore Bourrit. Genève, 1791.
GB.84 (impf.); Lloyd.63.   i163.

Itinéraire de Genève, Lausanne et Chamouni / Marc Théodore Bourrit. 3e éd. [Geneva, 1808.]
GB.157 (impf.).   i164.

Itinéraire de la Suisse, du Mont-Blanc, de la vallée de Chamonix, et des vallées italiennes / Paul Joanne. Paris, 1884. 2v; ill., maps. [Guides Joanne.]
GB/A.2158.   i165.

Itinéraire de la vallée de Chamonix, d'une partie du Bas-Vallais et des montagnes avoisinantes / Jacob P. Berthoud Van Berchem. Lausanne, 1790. Maps.
Lloyd.199; Lloyd.199A,B.   i166.

Itinéraire de la vallée de Chamouni, d'une partie du Bas-Valais et des montagnes avoisinantes / [Jacob P. Berthoud van Berchem]. Genève, 1805. Maps.
GB.239.   i167.

Itinéraire des ascensions du Dauphiné / d'après le *Guide du Haut-Dauphiné* de Coolidge, Duhamel et Perrin complété et mis à jour par Jeanne et Tom de Lépiney. [Paris], 1924. 5v. Published by the Club alpin français, Groupe de haute montagne.
Lloyd.1606(19-23).   i168.

Itinéraire descriptif et historique de la Suisse, du Mont Blanc, de la vallée de Chamonix, du Grand Saint-Bernard et du Mont-Rose / Adolphe Joanne. Paris, 1853. Maps. [Guides Richard.]
GB/A.1264.   i169.

Itinéraire descriptif, historique et archéologique de la Maurienne et de la Tarentaise: discours prononcé à l'Académie delphinale, séance du 31 décembre 1878 / Henri Ferrand. Grenoble, 1879. Ill., map.
Lloyd.1624(9).   i170.

Itinéraire du Mont-Righi et du lac des 4 Cantons, précédé de la description de la ville de Lucerne et de ses environs / Joseph Maria Businger; traduit par H. de C*** [i.e Henry de Crousaz]. Lucerne, 1815. Ill., maps. Translated from *Die Stadt Luzern und ihre Umgebungen.*
Lloyd.500.   i171.

Itinéraire du pays de Vaud, du gouvernement d'Aigle, et du comté de Neuchâtel et Vallengin. Berne, 1794. Map.
GB/A.828(2).   i172.

Itinéraire du St Gothard, d'une partie du Vallais et des contrées de la Suisse, que l'on traverse pour se rendre au Gothard / Christian von Mechel. Basle, 1795. Ill.
Lloyd.597.   i173.

Itinéraire du voyage à Chamouny, autour du Mont-Blanc, au Grand et au Petit St.-Bernard, et autour du lac de Genève. Genève, [1845]. Map.
GB.9.   i174.

Itinéraire général de la France: Franche-Comté et Jura / Paul Joanne. Ed. de 1888 avec des renseignements pratiques mis au courant. Paris, [1891]. Maps. [Guides Joanne.]
GB/A.766.   i175.

Itinéraire général de la France: Vosges et Ardennes / Adolphe Joanne. Paris, 1868. Maps. [Guides Joanne.]
GB/A.901.   i176.

Itinéraire topographique et historique des Hautes-Pyrénées, principalement des établissemens thermaux / par A. A*** [i.e. A. Abadie]. Paris, 1819. Ill.
Lloyd.633.   i177.

Itinéraires autour de Locarno / Alexandre Cingria. Lausanne, 1945.
GB/B.338(21).   i178.

Itinerari alpinistici / direzione: Achille Boroli, Adolfo Boroli; direzione editoriale: Mario Nilo; testi e illustrazioni forniti dalla *Rivista della Montagna.* Novara, 1977. Ill., maps.
GB/B.589.   i179.

Itinerari del Carso triestino / Carlo Chersi. 6a ed. Trieste, 1970. Ill., maps. Published by the Ente Provinciale per il Turismo, Trieste, and the Società Alpina delle Giulie.
GB/A.1050(11).   i180.

Itinerari dell'Appennino (dal Cimone al Catria) / presentazione di Athos Vianelli. Bologna, 1980. Ill., maps. Facsimile reprint of the Bologna, 1888 ed. Published under the auspices of the Club Alpino Italiano, Sezione di Bologna.
GB/A.1964(4).   i181.

Itinerari di gite effettuabili da Milano in 1, 2 e 3 giorni. Milano, [1921]. Published by the Club Alpino Italiano, Sezione di Milano.
GB/A.800(2).   i182.

Itinerari escursionistici nei Monti Lucretili / Gilberto De Angelis, Marinella De Santi. Roma, 1980. Ill., map. Estratto da *Monti Lucretili*, a cura di G. De Angelis e P. Lanzara.
GB/A.2022(10).   i183.

Itinerari escursionistici nelle Alpi Orobie / Angelo Gamba. Bologna, 1975. Ill., maps. [Itinerari alpini; 23.]
GB/A.1351(17).   i184.

Itinerari sci alpinistici dell'Appennino bolognese e modenese: dal Corno alle Scale al Cimone / Alberto Malusardi. [Bologna? 1979?] Ill., map.
GB/A.2020(7).   i185.

Itinerari sci-alpinistici dalla Croce Arcana al passo di Pradarena. Lucca, [1980?]. Ill., maps.
GB/A.2019(9).   i186.

Itinerari sci-alpinistici dell'Adamello / a cura di Innocente Spinoni, Franco Solina, Franco Maestrini. Breno, 1979. Ill.
GB/A.2019(12).   i187.

Itinerari sciistici di valle Po e valle Varaita / M. Bressy. [N.p.], 1928. Ill., map.
GB/A.1349(8).   i188.

Itinerari sui monti pavesi. Pavia, [1963]. Ill., maps. Published by the Club Alpino Italiano, Sezione di Pavia.
GB/A.1295(7).   i189.

Itinerario del XLII Congresso degli Alpinisti Italiani 5-12 settembre 1913: cinquantesimo anniversario del Club Alpino Italiano / Giovanni Bobba, Agostino Ferrari. [Turin, 1913.] Ill., maps.
GB.1325(21).   i190.

Itinerario islandese / M. Vanni. Torino, 1967. Ill. Published by the Associazione Italiana Insegnanti di Geografia, Sezione Lombarda.
GB/B.312(28).   i191.

Itinerario-profilo del passo del Pordoi / Ottone Brentari. Milan, 1906. Ill. Published by the Touring Club Italiano.
GB/A.860(8).   i192.

Itinerarium für das Excursionsgebiet des S.A.C. von 1871: der St. Gotthard. St. Gallen, [1871].
GB/A.1200(1).   i193.

Itinerarium für das Excursionsgebiet des S.A.C. für 1882 und 1883: die westlichen Berner Kalk-Alpen und der westliche Theil des Finsteraarhorn-Central Massivs / bearbeitet und durch geologische und mineralogische Notizen vervollständigt von Edmund v. Fellenberg. Bern, 1882. Published by the Schweizer Alpenclub.
GB/A.181(9).   i194.

Itinerarium für das Excursionsgebiet des S.A.C. 1885 und 1886: kritisches Verzeichniss der Gesammtliteratur über die Berner Alpen: speciell über den centralen Theil des Finsteraarhorn-Massivs. Bern, 1889. 2v (in 1). Beilage zu *Jahrbuch*

S.A.C. 24. 2. Nachtrag zum *Kritischen Verzeichniss*.
GB/A.878.   i195.

Itinerarium für das Excursionsgebiet des S.A.C. 1888: Graue Hörner — Calanda — Rungelspitz / F. Becker. Glarus, 1888. Published by the Schweizer Alpenclub.
GB/A.181(10).   i196.

Itinerarium für die Albulagruppe 1893-95 / Ed. Imhof. Bern, [1896?]. Published by the Schweizer Alpenclub.
GB/A.181(12).   i197.

Itinerarium historico-politicum, quod ex inclyta Ad Moen. Francofordia, per celebriores Helvetiae et regni Arelatensis urbes in universam extenditur Italiam / Johannes Jacobus Grasserus. [Basel], 1624.
GB/A.915(5).   i198.

An **itinerary**, containing his ten yeeres travell through the twelve dominions of Germany, Bohmerland, Switzerland, Netherlands, Denmarke, Poland, Italy, Turky, France, England, Scotland & Ireland / Fynes Moryson. Glasgow, 1907-08. 4v; ill., maps, ports. Facsimile reprint of the London, 1617 ed.
Lloyd.1152-5.   i199.

An **itinerary** of Germany, or Traveller's guide through that country: to which is added an itinerary of Hungary and Turkey / M. Reichard. New ed. enl., by M. Pezzl. Paris, 1826. Map. Translated from *Guide de l'Allemagne*.
Lloyd.15.   i200.

-J-

The **J.E.M.** guide to Switzerland: the Alps and how to see them / edited by J.E. Muddock. 2nd ed. London, 1882. Ill., maps.
GB/A.567; Lloyd.189. j002.

J.J. Graham Brown, M.D. Edinburgh, 1905. Port. From *Scottish Life Notes*, no.6, April 1905.
GB.1315(10). j003.

J.J. Graham Brown, M.D. Edin., F.R.C.P. Edin., F.R.S. / R.M'K.J. Edinburgh, 1912. Port. Pp.48-9 of the *Gambolier*, vol.5 no.4.
GB.1336(34). j004.

Jacques Balmat, or The first ascent of Mont Blanc: a true story / T. Louis Oxley. London, 1881.
GB.280. j005.

Jacques Balmat du Mont-Blanc / Rochat-Cenise. Paris, 1929. [Bibliothèque du hérisson.]
GB.1323(9). j006.

Jacques de Lépiney / Jean Escarra. [London, 1943.] Pp.181-9 of the *Climbers' Club Journal*, N.S. vol.7 no.2.
GB.1339(13). j007.

Jæger og fangstmand / Finn Kristoffersen. København, 1969. Ill., maps.
GB/B.524(2). j008.

The **Jägerhorn**, the Jägerjoch, and the Lyskamm from Gressonay / [C.E. Mathews]. [N.p., 1868.]
Lloyd.1581(6). j009.

Jahrbuch / Schweizer Alpenclub. Jahrg.1-58, 1864-1923. Bern, 1864-1924.
GB/A.262-341, GB/B.3-10 (wanting Jahrg.45,49); Lloyd.1366-71 (Jahrg.45,49,55-58); Lloyd.1365 (another copy of Jahrg.41). j010.

Jahrbuch / Schweizer Alpenclub. Beilagen. Bd.38-45. Bern, 1903-10.
Lloyd.1372-9; Lloyd.1374A (another copy of Bd.41). j011.

Jahrbuch / Schweizer Alpenclub. Repertorium und Ortsregister für die Jahrbücher I bis XX / zusammengestellt von Otto v. Bülow. Bern, 1886. Map.
GB/A.342. j012.

Jahrbuch vom Thuner- und Brienzersee / herausgegeben vom Uferschutzverband, Thuner- und Brienzersee. 1972- . Interlaken, [1972-].
GB/A.1275. j013.

Jahres-Bericht / Alpenvereinssektion Bayerland. Nr.25, 1933/34. München, 1935.
GB.1305(18). j014.

Jahres-Bericht / Schweizer Alpenclub, Sektion Bern. 1906-1911, 1922. Bern, 1907-23.
Lloyd.1618(27-33). j015.

Jahresbericht / Akademischer Alpenclub Bern. Nr.32, 1936-37. [Bern, 1937.]
GB.1647(6). j016.

Jahresbericht / Akademischer Alpen-Club Zürich. Nr.37,42, 1932,1937. Zürich, 1932-37.
GB.1647(7-8). j017.

Jahresbericht / Akademischer Alpen-Verein Berlin. Nr.25-32, 1927/28-1934/35. [Berlin], 1928-35. Wanting no.26-7.
GB.1647(1-3). j018.

James W. Puttrell, 1869-1939 / G.D.A. [London, 1941.] Pp.41-3 of the *Climbers' Club Journal*, N.S. vol.6 no.3.
GB.1339(15[1]). j019.

Japanese literature / Clay MacCauley; paper, read in part at a meeting of the Yokohama Literary Society, October 21st, 1898. Yokohama, 1898.
Lloyd.1624(11). j020.

Japanische Bergfahrten: Wanderungen fern von Touristenpfaden / Wilhelm Steinitzer. München, 1918.
GB/A.501. j021.

Jean Antoine Carrel: il 'padre' di tutte le guide / Attilio Viriglio. Bologna, 1948. Ill. [Le Alpi; 3.]
GB/A.987(1). j022.

Jean Conrad Escher de la Linth: portrait d'un républicain. Genève, 1852. A review of *H.C. Escher von der Linth*, by J.J. Hottinger. Tiré de la *Bibliothèque universelle de Genève*, mai 1852.
GB.1335(25); Lloyd.923. j023.

Jenseits begangener Pfade: neue Bergfahrten in den Alpen / E.R. Blanchet; Übertragung von Heinrich Erler. Berlin, [ca 1942]. Ill. Translated from *Hors des chemins battus*.
GB/A.419. j024.

Jo Vagand, le cristallier: aventure d'un chercheur de cristaux dans les Alpes / Benoît Bickel. Neuchâtel, 1965.
GB/A.1375.   j025.

Johann Madutz, 1800-1861: ein Pionier der schweizer Alpen: eine biographische Skizze / W.A.B. Coolidge. Bern, 1917.
GB.1335(9).   j026.

John Addington Symonds: a biography, compiled from his papers and correspondence / Horatio F. Brown. 2nd ed. London, 1903. 2v; ill., ports.
GB.540.   j027.

John Buchan's Annual / edited by John Buchan. [No.2]: Great hours in sport. London, 1921.
GB.791.   j028.

John Bunyan, his life, times and work / John Brown; with illustrations by E. Whymper. 2nd ed. London, 1886.
GB.1076.   j029.

John Tyndall as a mountaineer / Claud Schuster. [London], 1945. Reprinted from *Life and work of John Tyndall*, by A.S. Eve and C.H. Creasey.
GB.1333(26).   j030.

Joies de la montagne / réalisé sous la direction de L. Devies et L. Terray. Paris, 1964. Ill. [Joies et réalités.]
GB/B.262.   j031.

Jordklodens udforskning: geografisk forskning og geografiske opdagelser i det nittende aarhundrede / Otto Nordenskjöld. Kjøbenhavn, 1920.
GB/A.1844.   j032.

Josias Simler et les origines de l'alpinisme jusqu'en 1600 / W.A.B. Coolidge. Grenoble, 1904. Ill., map, ports., facsims. The *De Alpibus commentarius*, by Josias Simler, with a French translation, notes, introduction and appendices by W.A.B. Coolidge.
GB.1205; Lloyd.1314; Lloyd.1314A.   j033.

Un **jour** au creux du vent: voyage des écoles supérieures des jeunes filles de Neuchâtel le 10 juillet, 1866 / Auguste Bachelin, Guillaume dr., E. Desor [et al.]. Neuchâtel, 1866. Ill. [Courses scolaires; année 3.]
GB/C.46.   j034.

Journal / Birmingham University Mountaineering Club. No.4, 1962. [Birmingham, 1962.]
GB.1333(10).   j035.

Journal / Edinburgh University Mountaineering Club. 1953-1961/62. [Edinburgh, 1953-62.]
GB.1645(64-70); GB.1645(71) (another copy of 1954/55); GB.1645(72) (another copy of 1960/61).
                                              j036.

Journal / Gritstone Club. Vol.1 no.3-vol.4 no.1. [N.p.], 1922-30.
GB.1646(18-25).   j037.

Journal / Manchester University Mountaineering Club. 1928/29-1930, 1964/65. [Manchester, 1929-65].
GB.1322(4-5), GB/B.528(19).   j038.

Journal / University College of North Wales Mountaineering Club. 1968. [Bangor], 1968.
GB/A.1974(2).   j039.

A **journal** abroad in 1868 / Fanny M. Trench. London, [1868].
Lloyd.640.   j040.

Journal d'un voyage à Chamouni & à la cime du Mont-Blanc, en juillet et aoust 1787 / Horace Bénédict de Saussure; [edited by E. Gaillard and H.F. Montagnier]. Lyon, 1926. Ill., port., facsim.
GB.1081; GB.1331(45); GB.1331(46); Lloyd.1595(1); Lloyd.1595(1)A.   j041.

Journal d'un voyage de Genève à Londres, en passant par la Suisse, entremêlé d'avantures tragiques / Mr. G.D.C. [i.e. Gaudard de Chavannes]. [N.p.], 1783.
GB/A.765.   j042.

Journal d'un voyage en Savoie et dans le Midi de la France en 1804 et 1805 / Henri de la Bédoyère. 2e éd., rev., corr., augm. Paris, 1849. Ill.
GB/A.805(3).   j043.

Journal d'une course faite aux glaciers du Mont Rose et du Mont Cervin, en société de MM. Studer, Agassiz [et al.], renfermant une notice sur les glaciers, par M. Agassiz / E. Desor. [Geneva], 1840. Ill. Tiré de la *Bibliothèque universelle de Genève*, mai 1840.
GB/A.793(2).   j044.

Journal descriptif, en croquis de vues pittoresques, faits dans un voyage en Savoye du 10 au 21 août 1837 / Louis Pierre Baltard. [N.d., 1837.]
Lloyd.1528.   j045.

Journal du dernier voyage du cen. Dolomieu dans les Alpes / Tønnes Christian Bruun-Neergaard. Paris, 1802.
Lloyd.700.   j046.

Journal du voyage en Italie, par la Suisse & l'Allemagne en 1580 & 1581 / Michel de Montaigne; avec des notes par M. de Querlon. Rome, 1775. 3v.
Lloyd.49-51.   j047.

Journal historique du voyage de M. de Lesseps depuis l'instant où il a quitté les frégates françoises au port Saint-Pierre & Saint-Paul du Kamtschatka, jusqu'à son arrivée en France, le 17 octobre 1788. Paris, 1790. 2v; ill., map.
GB/A.1693.   j048.

A **journal** kept during a summer tour for the children of a village school / by the author of *Amy Herbert* [i.e. Elizabeth M. Sewell]. London, 1852. 3v; maps.
Lloyd.261-3.   j049.

Journal of a second voyage for the discovery of a north-west passage from the Atlantic to the Pacific: performed in the years 1821-22-23, in His Majesty's Ships *Fury* and *Hecla* / William Edward Parry. London, 1824. Ill., maps.
GB.1250.   j050.

Journal of a tour in France, Switzerland, and Lombardy, crossing the Simplon, and returning by Mont Cenis to Paris, during the autumn of 1818. London, 1821. 2v; ill.
Lloyd.528-9.   j051.

Journal of a tour in Germany, through the Tyrol, Salzkammergut, the Danube, Hungary, &c. during August, September, and October, 1839 / [Frederick J. Monson]. [London, 1839.]
Lloyd.285.   j052.

Journal of a tour in Iceland, in the summer of 1809 / William Hooker. 2nd ed., with additions. London, 1813. 2v; ill., maps.
Lloyd.809-10.   j053.

Journal of a tour in Italy, and also in part of France and Switzerland from October, 1828, to September, 1829 / James P. Cobbett. London, 1830.
Lloyd.602.   j054.

Journal of a tour in pursuit of pleasure through part of France and Switzerland, in the year 1833 / R. Lambton Surtees. [Durham, 1833.]
GB/A.805(2).   j055.

Journal of a tour in the Highlands and Western Islands of Scotland in 1800 / John Leyden; edited by James Sinton. Edinburgh, 1903.
GB.335.   j056.

Journal of a tour made by a party of friends in the autumn of 1825, through Belgium, up the Rhine, to Frankfort and Heidelberg, and across the eastern side of France to Paris / T.B. [i.e. Thomas Brightwell]. Norwich, 1828.
Lloyd.1011.   j057.

Journal of a tour through part of the snowy range of the Himala mountains, and to the sources of the rivers Jumna and Ganges / James Baillie Fraser. London, 1820. Map.
Lloyd.1493.   j058.

Journal of a tour through parts of France, Italy, and Switzerland in the years 1823-4 / John Willes Johnson. [London, 1824?]
GB.199(2).   j059.

Journal of a tour to Italy: containing an account of the eruptions of Mount Vesuvius / M. de la Condamine. Dublin, 1763. Translated from *Journal d'un voyage en Italie*.
GB/A.933.   j060.

Journal of a tour to Italy / M. de la Condamine. London, 1763. Translated from *Journal d'un voyage en Italie*.
Lloyd.251.   j061.

The **journal** of a tour to the Hebrides, with Samuel Johnson / James Boswell. 2nd ed., rev. and corr. London, 1785.
GB.664.   j062.

The **journal** of a tour to the Hebrides / James Boswell. 3rd ed., rev. and corr. London, 1786.
GB.666.   j063.

The **journal** of a tour to the Hebrides / James Boswell. 6th ed., rev. and corr. London, 1813. Port.
GB.665.   j064.

Journal of a voyage to Peru, a passage across the cordillera of the Andes, in the winter of 1827, performed on foot in the snow: and a journey across the pampas / Charles Brand. London, 1828. Ill.
Lloyd.879; Lloyd.1611(10).   j065.

The **journal** of Baron von Gersdorf: extract. [London, 1957.] Pp.[367]-82 of *The first ascent of*

Mont Blanc, by T. Graham Brown.
GB.1093.   j066.

Journal of Herbert Edward Pretyman written during his expedition to the Kittar Mountains, between Kenneh, on the Nile, and the Red Sea, 1891. London, 1892. Ill., map, port.
Lloyd.813.   j067.

The **journal** of Horace Bénédict de Saussure. [N.p., n.d.] Ill. Pp.[383]-91 of an unidentified work.
GB.1745.   j068.

Journal of six weeks' adventures in Switzerland, Piedmont, and on the Italian lakes / W.L. [i.e. William Longman] and H.T. [i.e. Henry Trower]; June, July, August, 1856. London, 1856. Map.
GB.434; Lloyd.652; Lloyd.652A,B,C.   j069.

The **Journal** of the Fell and Rock Climbing Club of the English Lake District. Vol.6 no.2-vol.19 no.3; no.17-56 of series. [Manchester], 1923-62.
GB.1342-55.   j070.

The **Journal** of the Midland Association of Mountaineers. Vol.2 no.1- , 1947- . [N.p.], 1947- . Continues: *Bulletin*.
GB/A.1637.   j071.

The **Journal** of the Mountain Club of South Africa. No.43, 1950- . Cape Town, 1950- . Wanting no.58, 1955. Continues: *The annual of the Mountain Club of South Africa*.
GB/A.2160.   j072.

Journal of the Yukon 1847-48 / Alexander Hunter Murray; edited with notes by L.J. Burpee. Ottawa, 1910. [Publications of the Canadian Archives; 4.]
GB/A.1675(10).   j073.

Journal officiel du tir. No.1-19. Genève, 1851. Wanting no.4.
GB.1023.   j074.

Journals of excursions in the Alps: the Pennine, Graian, Cottian, Rhetian, Lepontian and Bernese / William Brockedon. London, 1833. Map.
GB.413; Lloyd.522.   j075.

Journals of excursions in the Alps: the Pennine, Graian, Cottian, Rhetian, Lepontian, and Bernese / William Brockedon. 3rd ed. London, 1845. Map.
GB/A.393.   j076.

Journals of travels in parts of the late Austrian Low Countries, France, the pays de Vaud, and Tuscany, in 1787 and 1789 / Lockhart Muirhead. London, 1803.
GB/A.627.   j077.

A **journey** across the Alps, in a letter to a friend / Abraham Hayward. London, [ca 1835]. Originally published as *Some account of a journey across the Alps*.
GB.78.   j078.

A **journey** beyond the Rocky Mountains in 1835, 1836 and 1837 / Samuel Parker. Corr. and extended. Edinburgh, 1841.
GB.1178(1).   j079.

A **journey** from Merut in India, to London, through Arabia, Persia, Armenia, Georgia, Russia, Austria, Switzerland, and France, during the years 1819 and 1820 / Thomas Lumsden. London, 1822. Map.
GB.689.   j080.

A **journey** in Carniola, Italy, and France, in the years 1817, 1818 / W.A. Cadell. Edinburgh, 1820. 2v; ill., maps.
Lloyd.1164-5.   j081.

A **journey** into various parts of Europe: and a residence in them, during the years 1818, 1819, 1820, and 1821: with notes, historical and classical / Thomas Pennington. London, 1825. 2v.
Lloyd.1159-60.   j082.

A **journey** to Katmandu, the capital of Nepaul, with the camp of Jung Bahadoor: including a sketch of the Nepaulese ambassador at home / Laurence Oliphant. London, 1852. Map.
GB.141; GB.192.   j083.

A **journey** to Switzerland, and pedestrian tours in that country: including a sketch of its history, and of the manners and customs of its inhabitants / Lewis Agassiz. London, 1833.
GB.931 (impf.); Lloyd.937.   j084.

A **journey** to the sacred mountain of Siao-Outai-Shan, in China / A. Henry Savage Landor. [London, 1894.] Pp.[393]-409 of the *Fortnightly Review*, N.S. vol.56.
GB.1336(12).   j085.

A **journey** to the source of the river Oxus / John Wood. New ed., edited by his son [Alexander Wood]; with an essay on the geography of the

valley of the Oxus, by Henry Yule. London, 1872. Maps.
GB.929. j086.

A **journey** to the Western Islands of Scotland / [Samuel Johnson]. London, 1775.
GB.594. j087.

A **journey** to the Western Islands of Scotland / Samuel Johnson; with remarks by Donald M'Nicol. Glasgow, 1817. Port.
GB.597. j088.

Jubiläumsschrift 1874-1974 / Schweizer Alpenclub, Sektion Blümlisalp. [Thun], 1974. Ill.
GB/A.1323(8). j089.

Jugend in Fels und Eis: ein Ehrenmal gewidmet dem Helden vom Matterhorn Toni Schmid von seinen Kameraden / bearbeitet von Hans Baumeister. München, 1934. Ill.
GB.1139. j090.

Jugend-Album: Blätter zur angenehmen und lehrreichen Unterhaltung im häuslichen Kreise. Neue Folge. Bd.1,5. Stuttgart, [n.d.]. Ill.
GB.955-6. j091.

Julische Alpen: die schönsten Berg- und Kletterfahrten / Hellmut Schöner. 3. Aufl. München, 1966. Ill., map.
GB/A.1062. j092.

Die **Julische** Alpen im Bilde / Julius Kugy. Graz, 1934.
GB/A.446. j093.

Jungborn: Bergfahrten und Höhengedanken eines einsamen Pfadsuchers / Guido Eugen Lammer. 2. stark verm. und veränderte Aufl. München, 1923. Ill., port.
GB.1121. j094.

Junger Mensch im Gebirg: Leben — Schriften — Nachlass / Leo Maduschka. München, 1936. Ill., ports., facsims.
GB.811; GB.812. j095.

The **Jungfrau** disaster. London, 1887. Pp.687-8 of *Chambers's Journal*, 22 Oct. 1887.
GB.1333(43). j096.

Die **Jungfrau**, mein Berg / selbsterlebtes skizziert von A.W. Diggelmann. [Zurich, 1958.]
GB/C.14. j097.

Jungfrau railway, Switzerland. [N.p., 1952?] Ill.
GB/B.528(6). j098.

Le **Jura** et le pays franc-comtois / G. Fraipont. Paris, [1897]. Ill. [Les montagnes de France.]
GB/B.530. j099.

The **juvenile** travellers: containing the remarks of a family during a tour through the principal states of Europe / Priscilla Wakefield. 5th ed. London, 1806.
Lloyd.248. j100.

-K-

K2 / Fulvio Campiotti. Milano, 1954. Ill., ports.
GB/A.2009.   k001.

K2: la montagna degli Italiani / Massimo Orlando, Franco Laffi. Venezia, 1985.
GB/A.2190.   k002.

K2: la victoire suspendue / Bernard Mellet. Grenoble, 1980. Ill., map. [Aventures extraordinaires.]
GB/B.600.   k003.

K2: the savage mountain / Charles S. Houston, Robert H. Bates and members of the Third American Karakoram Expedition. London, 1955. Ill., maps.
GB.796.   k004.

Kalaallit inngerutaannik nipilersortarnerannillu immikkoortiterineq. Klassifikation af traditionel grønlandsk musik. Classification of traditional Greenland music / Michael Hauser, H.C. Petersen. Copenhagen, 1985. Ill. [Meddelelser om Grønland. Man & society; 7.]
GB/A.1820/7.   k005.

Die **Kaltwasser-Gamsmutter** aus dem Kaltwassertal, Ost- und Nordwand / Julius Kugy. [Vienna], 1914. Ill. Pp.[1]-7 of the *Osterreichische Alpenzeitung*, Jahrg.36, Nr.897.
GB.1317(10).   k006.

Kamerad am Seil / Max Liotier. Zürich, 1969. Ill. Translated from *Celui qui va devant*.
GB/B.249.   k007.

Kamet conquered / Frank S. Smythe. London, 1932. Ill., map. [Black jacket books.]
GB.1088.   k008.

Kampen om Tirich Mir / Vlastimil Smida. Stockholm, 1969. Ill., maps.
GB/A.2066.   k009.

Kampf in den Bergen: das unvergängliche Denkmal der Alpenfront / Luis Trenker. Berlin, 1931. Ill. Originally published as *Berge in Flammen*.
GB/A.1488.   k010.

Kampf um den Himalaja: das Ringen der Deutschen um den Kantsch, den zweithöchsten Berg der Erde / Paul Bauer. München, 1934. Ill., maps.
GB.1074.   k011.

Kampf um den Himalaja: das Ringen der Deutschen um den Kantsch, den zweithöchsten Berg der Erde / Paul Bauer. München, 1952. Ill., maps.
GB.1068.   k012.

Der **Kampf** um den Nord- und Südpol: Berichte über Expeditionen nach Norden und Süden / Axel Ahlman. Berlin, [1928?]. Ill., ports. [Gefion Verlags populärwissenschaftliche Serie.]
GB/A.2045.   k013.

Der **Kampf** um die Eiger Nordwand: illustrierter Bericht über die Bergtragödien im Sommer 1935 und 1936 / Otto Zwahlen. 3. Aufl. Basel, 1936.
GB.1325(28).   k014.

Kampf um die Sextner Rotwand / Oswald Ebner; im Anhang: das Kriegstagebuch des Bergführers Sepp Innerkofler. Bregenz, 1937. Ill., maps, ports., facsims.
GB.1058.   k015.

Der **Kampf** um die Weltberge / herausgegeben von Th. Herzog, unter Mitarbeit führender Bergsteiger. München, [1934]. Ill.
GB.677.   k016.

Der **Kampf** ums Matterhorn: Tatsachenroman / Carl Hänsel. Stuttgart, [1929].
GB.1320(6).   k017.

Kamtchatka: skildringar från en treårig forskningsfärd / Sten Bergman. Stockholm, [ca 1923]. Ill., maps, ports.
GB/A.1781.   k018.

Kananaskis country: a guide to hiking and skiing trails / Tony & Gillean Daffern. Calgary, 1979. Ill., maps.
GB/B.525(10).   k019.

The **Kananaskis** Valley hikers' and x-c skiers' guide / C. Ruth Oltmann. Seebe, Alba, 1978. Ill., maps.
GB/B.525(12).   k020.

Kangbacen / Joze Andlovic [et al.]. Ljubljana, 1976. Ill.
GB/A.1991.   k021.

Kangchenjunga: the untrodden peak / Charles Evans. London, 1956. Ill., maps, ports.
GB.893; GB.990.   k022.

The **Kangchenjunga** adventure / Frank S. Smythe. London, 1930. Ill.
GB.1090. k023.

The **Kangchenjunga** adventure / Frank S. Smythe. [London], 1930. Prospectus.
GB.1329(26). k024.

Der **Kanton** Graubünden, historisch, statistisch, geographisch dargestellt für einheimische und fremde Reisende / J.K. von Tscharner. Chur, 1842. Ill.
GB/A.724. k025.

Der **Kanton** Graubünden, historisch, geographisch, statistisch geschildert: ein Hand- und Hausbuch für Kantonsbürger und Reisende / G.W. Röder, P.C.v. Tscharner. St.Gallen, 1838. [Gemälde der Schweiz; Hft.15 Abt.1.]
GB/A.1383. k026.

Der **Kanton** Solothurn, historisch, geographisch, statistisch geschildert: ein Hand- und Hausbuch / V. Peter Strohmeier. St. Gallen, 1836. [Gemälde der Schweiz; 10.]
GB/A.725. k027.

Der **Kanton** Uri, historisch, geographisch, statistisch geschildert: ein Hand- und Hausbuch für Kantonsbürger und Reisende / herausgegeben von Karl Franz Lusser. St.Gallen, 1834. [Gemälde der Schweiz; 4.]
GB/A.815. k028.

Kanton Wallis: Führer-Buch nach dem Polizei-Reglement vom 1. Februar 1882: ausgegeben an Herrn Peter Anton Perren, no.140. [N.p., 1882.]
Lloyd.141. k029.

Kanton Wallis: Führer-Buch nach dem Polizei-Reglement vom 1. Februar 1882: ausgegeben an Herrn Peter Anton Perren, no.140. [N.p., 1894?] Port.
Lloyd.142. k030.

Karakoram Himalaya: sommets de 7000 / André Roch. Neuchâtel, 1945. Ill., maps. [Montagne.] Published by the Swiss Foundation for Alpine Research.
GB.1305(4). k031.

The **Karakorams** and Kashmir: an account of a journey / Oscar Eckenstein. London, 1896.
GB.392; Lloyd.590. k032.

Die **Karawanken**: Steiner Alpen, Sulzbacher Alpen, Sannthaler Alpen / August von Böhm. [N.p., ca 1900.] Pp.[602]-33 of an unidentified publication.
GB.1384. k033.

Die **Karnischen** Alpen / Karl Diener. Die Friulaner Alpen. Die Liener Dolomiten / Philipp Wilhelm Rosenthal. Die Julischen Alpen / Julius Kugy. [Berlin, 1894.] Ill. Pp.[540]-600 of *Erschliessung der Ostalpen*, Bd.3.
GB.1383. k034.

Die **Karwendel** Gruppe. Das Kaiser Gebirge / Heinrich Schwaiger. [Berlin, 1893.] Ill. Pp.[188]-225, [239]-62 of *Erschliessung der Ostalpen*, Bd.1.
GB.1370. k035.

Katalog der Zentralbibliothek des Schweizer Alpenclub. Zürich, 1925. With 1.-4. Supplement, 1926/30-1952/63.
GB/A.995(5-9); GB.1332(3) (another copy of 1. Supplement). k036.

Kataloge der Alpenvereins Bücherei, München: Autorenkatalog. Boston, 1970. 3v.
GB/C.34-6. k037.

Kataloge der Alpenvereins Bücherei, München: Sachkatalog. Boston, 1970. 3v.
GB/C.37-9. k038.

Kaukasische Reisen und Studien: neue Beiträge zur Kenntnis des kaukasischen Landes / Carl von Hahn. Leipzig, 1896.
GB/A.77. k039.

Kebnekaise / text och foto: Tore Abrahamsson. Stockholm, 1968.
GB/A.386. k040.

The **Keepsake**. 1832,1840,1845-46,1848,1853. London, [1832-53].
GB.1083 (1832); Lloyd.1228 (1840); GB.1084-5 (1845-46); GB/B.140 (1848); Lloyd.1229 (1853).
k041.

Kenneth, or The rear guard of the Grand Army / by the author of *Scenes and characters* [i.e. Charlotte M. Yonge]. Copyright ed. Leipzig, 1860. [Series for the young; 1.]
GB/A.912. k042.

Der **Kilchherr** von Saas / Adolf Fux. 3. Aufl. Bern, [1959].
GB/A.368. k043.

Kilimanjaro, montagna dello splendore: dai ricordi di un medico alpinista / Giovanni Balletto. Bologna, 1974. Ill., port.
GB/A.2011.   k044.

Killing no murder / [Edward Sexby, Silius Titus]. [N.p., n.d.]
Lloyd.480 (impf.).   k045.

Kim / Rudyard Kipling. London, 1930.
GB.190; GB.531.   k046.

Kimberlite and lamproite dykes from Holsteinborg, West Greenland / Barbara H. Scott. Copenhagen, 1981. Ill., maps. [Meddelelser om Grønland. Geoscience; 4.]
GB/A.1818.   k047.

Kinabalu / R.C. Evans. London, 1947. Map. Pp.165-70 of the *Climbers' Club Journal*, N.S., vol.8 no.2.
GB.1337(3).   k048.

Kinematograph lecture on the Mount Everest Expedition 1922 / J.B.L. Noel. [London, 1922.] Joint meeting of the Royal Geographical Society and the Alpine Club, 21 November 1922.
GB.1313(27).   k049.

The **king** of mysteries, or The world's wonderland: a thrilling narrative of the many efforts and attempts to pierce through and unravel the dark shroud of unfathomable mystery enveloping the icy regions of the Arctic Circle / A.G. Feather. Philadelphia, 1891. Ill., maps.
GB/A.1714.   k050.

Kingdom of adventure: Everest: a chronicle of man's assault on the earth's highest mountain / narrated by the participants; with an accompanying text by James Ramsey Ullman. New York, [1947]. Ill., maps, ports.
Lloyd.913; Lloyd.913A,B.   k051.

Kleine Reisen im Schweizerland: Beyträge zur Topographie und Geschichte desselben / Hans Rudolf Maurer. Zürich, 1794.
GB/A.785.   k052.

Kleiner Führer durch die Zillertaler Alpen und die Tuxer Voralpen: Talorte, Hütten, Ubergänge, Gipfel / Erich Raitmayr. München, [1953]. Ill., map.
GB/A.1676(16).   k053.

Kleinere Schriften / Alexander von Humboldt. Stuttgart, 1853.
GB.674 (impf.).   k054.

Kletterführer: Zittauer und andere Gebirge: Zittauer Gebirge, Erzebirge, Vogtland, Ostthüringen, Thüringer Wald, Hanz, Halle (Saale), Leipziger Kletterschule / Autorenkollektiv unter Leitung von Hans Pankotsch. 3. Aufl. Berlin, 1980.
GB/A.2005.   k055.

Kletterführer durch das steirische Alpenvorland: Weinzodl, Kanzel, Pfaffenkogel, Rablgrat, Ratengrat / Franz Berghold. Graz, [1967]. Ill.
GB/A.153.   k056.

Das **Klettern** im Fels / Franz Nieberl. München, 1909. Ill.
GB/A.53.   k057.

Klettern ist mein Beruf / Cesare Maestri. Frauenfeld, 1963. Ill. Translated from *Arrampicare è il mio mestiere*.
GB/A.2068.   k058.

Klubführer: geologische Wanderungen durch die Schweiz / Julius Weber; herausgegeben von Schweizer Alpen Club. Zürich, [1913]. 2v.
GB/A.727-8.   k059.

Klubhütten-Album: Beilage zum *Jahrbuch S.A.C.*, Bd. 46. [Berne], 1911. Ill., maps.
Lloyd.395.   k060.

The **knapsack** guide for travellers in Switzerland. New ed., rev. London, 1864. Maps.
Lloyd.201.   k061.

The **knapsack** guide for travellers in Switzerland. New ed., rev. London, 1867. Ill., maps.
GB/A.782; Lloyd.202.   k062.

Komm mit mir ins Wallis / Walter Schmid. 10. Aufl. Bern, 1968. Ill.
GB/A.388.   k063.

Kongl. Maj:ts nådiga privilegium för et compagnie eller slutit bolag til idkande af hwalfiskfänge wid Gronland och Straet Davis, med mera. Gifwit then 1 Junii 1774. Stockholm, 1774.
GB/A.2033(8).   k064.

Kongur 81: the British Mount Kongur Expedition to China / organised by the Mount Everest Foundation; sponsored by Jardine, Matheson & Co. Ltd. [N.p.], 1981.
GB/A.1323(10).   k065.

Kontinentale Niveauveränderungen im Norden Europas / Gerard de Geer. Stockholm, 1912. Map. Extrait du *Compte rendu du XI:e Congrès géologique international*.
GB.1335(40). k066.

Kronika von der loblichen Eidgnoschaft, ir Härkomen und sust seltzam Stritten und Geschichten / colligiert und in Geschrift vervasst von Peterman Etterlin. Zum zweyten Mal herausgegeben und erläutert von Johann Jakob Sprengen. Basel, 1752.
Lloyd.1512. k067.

Kuling fra nord: en værvarslers erindringer / Sverre Petterssen. Oslo, 1974.
GB/A.1859. k068.

Kulu and Lahoul / Hon. C.G. Bruce. London, 1914. Ill., map.
GB.876; Lloyd.1003. k069.

The **Kumaon** Himalayas / M.S. Randhawa. New Delhi, 1970. Ill.
GB/A.869. k070.

Kung Karls Land / A.G. Nathorst. [Stockholm], 1899. Ill., maps. From *Ymer*, 1899 h.1.
GB.1335(54). k071.

Die **Kur-** und Seebad-Anstalt Waldhaus-Flims und ihre Umgebungen im Graubündner Vorderrheinthal / Ed. Killias. Zürich, [1895?]. [Swiss scenes.]
GB/A.1817(10). k072.

Kurz gefasste Schweizer-Geographie, samt den Merkwürdigkeiten in den Alpen und hohen Bergen / Gabriel Walser. Zürich, 1770.
GB/A.478. k073.

-L-

L.S.E.M.C. [London School of Economics Mountaineering Club] Journal. No.2. [London, 1956.]
GB.1310(1). l001.

Labske piskovce / Zdenko Feyfar, uvod a texty k vyobrazenim napsal Jan Smid. Praha, 1981. Ill.
GB/A.2121. l002.

Lac des IV. Cantons. Luzern, [n.d.]. A folding panorama.
GB/A.198. l003.

Le **lac** des Quatre-Cantons et ses rives classiques: souvenir de la navigation à vapeur sur le lac des IV Cantons. Lucerne, 1853. Ill., map.
GB/A.780. l004.

Ladakh / Géraldine Doux-Lacombe. Paris, 1981. Ill., maps. [Collection des guides Delta-Flammarion.]
GB/A.2020(3). l005.

Ladakh / Raphaël Gaillarde; texte de Christian Delacampagne. Paris, 1980. Ill.
GB/A.2016. l006.

Ladakh, Pianeta, Tibet: guida / curata per Loisirs Animazione Culturale da Ermanno Sagliani e Elio Bertolina; col patrocinio dell'Ufficio Nazionale del Turismo Indiano e di Air India. Milan, 1980. Ill., map.
GB/A.2023(3). l007.

Ladies' Alpine Club, 1907-1957. [Reading, 1957.] Ill., map, ports.
GB/B.528(17). l008.

Ladies in debate: being a history of the Ladies' Edinburgh Debating Society, 1865-1935 / edited by Lettice Milne Rae. Edinburgh, 1936. Ill., ports.
GB.991. l009.

Lady Franklin visits Sitka, Alaska, 1870: the journal of Sophia Cracroft, Sir John Franklin's niece / edited by R.N. DeArmond. Anchorage, 1981. Ill.
GB/A.2100. l010.

Lady mountaineers / Francis Gribble. London, 1897. Ports. Pp.683-7 of the *Lady's Realm*, vol.2 no.12.
GB.1332(18). l011.

A **lady's** tour round Monte Rosa, with visits to the Italian valleys: in a series of excursions in 1850-56-58 / [Mrs Henry Warwick Cole]. London, 1859. Ill., map.
GB.483; Lloyd.667; Lloyd.667A,B.   1012.

Il **Lago** Maggiore e dintorni / Luigi Boniforti; corografia e guida, storica, artistica, industriale. Torino, 1972. Ill. Facsimile reprint of the Torino, 1857? ed.
GB/A.1293.   1013.

Il **lago** Scaffaiolo e il suo nuovo rifugio. Bologna, 1926. Ill. Published by the Club Alpino Italiano, Sezione di Bologna. Cinquantenario della Sezione di Bologna, 1875-1925.
GB/B.312(21).   1014.

The **lake** dwellings of Switzerland and other parts of Europe / Ferdinand Keller; translated and arranged by John Edward Lee. London, 1866. Ill., maps.
Lloyd.1272.   1015.

The **lake** dwellings of Switzerland and other parts of Europe / Ferdinand Keller; translated and arranged by John Edward Lee. 2nd ed., greatly enl. London, 1878. 2v; ill., maps.
Lloyd.1273-4.   1016.

Lake Geneva and its literary landmarks / Francis Henry Gribble. London, 1901. Ill., ports.
Lloyd.1116; Lloyd.1116A.   1017.

The **Lake** of Geneva: a poem, moral and descriptive, in seven books: with notes historical and biographical / Sir Samuel Egerton Brydges. Geneva, 1832. 2v; ill.
GB/A.702-3.   1018.

Land des Lichtes / Albert Herrlich. München, 1937. A prospectus.
GB.1329(6).   1019.

The **land** of desolation: being a personal narrative of adventure in Greenland / Isaac I. Hayes. London, 1871. Ill., map, ports.
Lloyd.999.   1020.

The **land** of the cliff-dwellers / Frederick H. Chapin. Boston, 1892. Ill., map.
GB/A.2157.   1021.

The **land** of the Gurkhas, or The Himalayan kingdom of Nepal / W. Brook Northey; with a chapter by C.G. Bruce. Cambridge, [1937]. Ill.,

map, ports.
GB.932.   1022.

The **land** of the lama / David Macdonald. London, 1929.
GB.710.   1023.

Landbuch des Kantons Appenzell-Ausserroden: nach dem auf dem Rathhause in Trogen befindlichen Original abgedrückt. Trogen, 1828.
GB/A.1090.   1024.

Landing the treasures, or Results of the polar expedition. !!! / George Cruikshank. London, [1819]. A hand-coloured engraving.
GB/B.439(4).   1025.

Das **Landleben** / C.C.L. Hirschfeld. 3. verb. Aufl. Frankfurt, 1787.
GB/A.580(2).   1026.

The **Landquart-Davos** Railway / J. Hauri. Zürich, [1895?]. Ill. [Swiss scenes.]
GB/A.1817(8).   1027.

The **lands** of silence: a history of Arctic and Antarctic exploration / Sir Clements Markham. Cambridge, 1921.
GB.1125.   1028.

Lands of the thunderbolt: Sikhim, Chumbi and Bhutan / Earl of Ronaldshay. London, 1923.
GB.950.   1029.

The **Landscape** Annual. 1830. London, 1830. Contains *The tourist in Switzerland and Italy*, by Thomas Roscoe.
GB.482; Lloyd.619.   1030.

Languard-Rundschau: ein hypsometrisches Verzeichniss von Gipfeln und Gräten der Alpenkette zwischen Montblanc und Grossglockner, welche vom Piz-Languard im Ober-Engadin ausgesehen werden / Johann Baptist Ladner. Chur, 1858.
GB.147(4).   1031.

Lapland and its reindeer, with some account of the manners, customs, and peculiarities of its inhabitants. London, 1835.
GB/A.2197.   1032.

Lapland journey / Halliday Sutherland. New York, 1938. Ill.
GB/A.1772.   1033.

Lappland: dess natur och folk: efter fyra somrars vandringar i bilder och text / Carl Anton Pettersson. Stockholm, 1866.
GB/C.113. 1034.

Lapplands resa år 1732 / Carl Linnaeus. Stockholm, 1975.
GB/A.1852. 1035.

Il **Lario**, disegni a sanguigna / Franco Belluschi; testo di Giuseppe Ghielmetti. Como, 1968. Ill. [Acque e terre; 1.]
GB/C.5(5). 1036.

Last ascent of Mont Blanc [by Martin Barry]. London, 1835. Pp.34-6 of no.702 and pp.53-5 of no.703 of the *Mirror*.
GB.1313(15). 1037.

The **last** climb of the season / H.H. Jennings. London, 1902. Ill. Pp.304-8 of *Travel*, vol.7 no.79, Nov. 1902.
GB.1333(40). 1038.

Last of lands: Antarctica / J.F. Lovering, J.R.V. Prescott. Carlton [Australia], 1979. Ill.
GB/A.2048(9). 1039.

The **last** step: the American ascent of K2 / Rick Ridgeway. Seattle, 1980.
GB/A.1980. 1040.

The **last** voyage of Capt. Sir John Ross to the Arctic regions: for the discovery of a north west passage: performed in the years 1829-30-31-32 and 33 / Robert Huish. London, 1836. Ill., map, port.
GB.954. 1041.

Last voyage of the *Unicorn* / Delbert A. Young. Toronto, 1969. Ill.
GB/A.2173. 1042.

Late Weichselian and Flandrian biostratigraphy and chronology from Hochstetter Forland, northeast Greenland / Svante Björck, Thomas Persson. Copenhagen, 1981. Ill., maps. [Meddelelser om Grønland. Geoscience; 5.]
GB/A.1818. 1043.

Latemàr, Oclini, Altopiano / Aldo Gross, Dante Colli. Bologna, 1979. Ill. [Itinerari alpini; 45.]
GB/A.1589(21). 1044.

Die **Lauinen** der Schweizeralpen / J. Coaz. Bern, 1881. Ill., map.
GB/A.957. 1045.

Laure, ou Lettres de quelques personnes de Suisse / [François M.S. Constant]. Londres, 1787. 5v.
GB/A.586-90. 1046.

Laurins Rosengarten: Sagen aus den Dolomiten / Franz S. Weber. Bozen, [1914].
GB/A.516(13). 1047.

Lays and legends of the Rhine / J.R. Planché. London, 1832. Ill.
GB/A.939. 1048.

Lays from an Australian lyre / Austral [i.e. Annie Wilson]. London, [1882?].
GB.279. 1049.

[**Leaflets** concerning the animated pictures of the ascent of Mont Blanc by the Alpine Bioscope Expedition shown at the Palace Theatre, London.] [London, 1902.]
GB.1329(44-5). 1050.

Leaves from a Greenland diary / Ruth Bryan Owen. New York, 1935. Ill., ports.
GB/A.1854. 1051.

Leaves from *Rowan*'s logs: cruises on west coast of Scotland / R.B. Carslaw. 2nd impr. London, [1945]. Ill., map, ports.
GB.328. 1052.

Leaves from the Alpine notebooks of A.T. Malkin. In memoriam, Arthur Thomas Malkin / H. Pasteur. London, [1890]. Reprinted from the *Alpine Journal*, Feb., May and Aug., 1890.
Lloyd.786. 1053.

Leaves from the diary of the late Mr. A.T. Malkin. London, [1890].
Lloyd.862; Lloyd.862A. 1054.

Leben und Schriften / Stephan Steinberger (Pater Corbinian); herausgegeben und biographisch eingeleitet von Joseph Braunstein. München, 1929.
GB/A.2035. 1055.

Die **Lechthaler** Alpen. 1: Rothwand Gruppe / Anton Spiehler. 2: Parseyer Kette / C. Deutsch. [Berlin, 1893.] Pp.[96]-118 of *Erschliessung der Ostalpen*, Bd.1.
GB.1368(1). 1056.

Lecture entitled Jottings on my journeys in Switzerland / J. Manton Smith. [London, 1896.] Ill., music.
GB/A.677; GB/A.863. 1057.

A **lecture** on Switzerland / W. Longman. London, 1857.
GB.388; Lloyd.641; Lloyd.653; Lloyd.653A,B,C.
1058.

Lectures on landscape delivered at Oxford in Lent term, 1871 / John Ruskin. Sunnyside, 1897.
GB.1296.
1059.

Leeds University Climbing Club Journal. No.2, 1945-46. [Leeds, 1946.]
GB.1313(17).
1060.

Leeds University Union Climbing Club Journal. 1973-1974. [Leeds], 1973-74.
GB/A.1791(10); GB/A.1974(6) (another copy of the 1974 issue).
1061.

Legatio rhaetica / Carlo Pasquale. [Paris], 1620.
GB/A.596.
1062.

A **legend** of Broadstairs / [G.B.W.]. Broadstairs, [n.d.].
Lloyd.1574(6).
1063.

The **legend** of St. Bernard: a poem. Norwich, [1840?].
Lloyd.1606(14).
1064.

La **légende** du Mont Iseran: étude d'histoire topographique / W.A.B. Coolidge. Paris, 1901. Ill. Extrait de l'*Annuaire du Club alpin français*, vol.27, 1900.
GB.1340(7).
1065.

Légendes des Alpes vaudoises / Alfred Cérésole. Lausanne, 1885. Ill.
GB/B.332.
1066.

Les **légendes** du glacier: recueillies dans le Lötschental / Johan Siegen; traduction française de J. Bohy. Lausanne, [n.d.]. Ill. Translated from *Gletschermärchen*.
GB.1325(4).
1067.

Légendes et récits recueillis sur les bords du Lys / J.J. Christillin. Aosta, 1970. Ill.
GB/C.22(22).
1068.

Légendes valaisannes / recueillies et adaptées par Solandieu. Lausanne, [1919]. Ill.
Lloyd.1205.
1069.

Légendes valaisannes: d'après les *Walliser Sagen* de la Société d'histoire du Haut-Valais. Paris, 1931. Ill.
GB/A.1369.
1070.

Legends and tales of the Harz Mountains / Toofie Lauder. London, 1881.
Lloyd.386.
1071.

Legends of the Pike's Peak region: the sacred myths of the Manitou / Ernest Whitney assisted by William S. Alexander. Denver, 1892. Ill.
GB/A.2165(5).
1072.

La **leggenda** del Bernina / Lorenzo Pescio. Torino, [1963]. [Lucciole; 3.]
GB/A.455(8).
1073.

La **leggenda** della 'Crête à Collon' / W.A.B. Coolidge; versione italiana di W. Laeng. Torino, 1915. Estratto dalla *Rivista del Club Alpino Italiano*, vol.34 n.1, anno 1915.
GB.1340(43).
1074.

Leggende alpine / Constantino Burla. Torino, 1967. Ill.
GB/A.455(9).
1075.

Leggende del Trentino / Giovanna Borzaga. Trento, 1971. Ill. [Leggende d'Italia.]
GB/A.1042.
1076.

Leggende del Trentino / Luigi Menapace. 2a ed. Trento, 1972. Ill.
GB/B.377(10).
1077.

Leggende delle Alpi / Maria Savi-Lopez. Torino, 1889. Ill.
GB/A.427.
1078.

Leggende delle Alpi Lepontine e dei Grigioni / Aurelio Garobbio. [Bologna], 1969. Ill. [Le Alpi.]
GB/A.938(2).
1079.

Leggende delle Dolomiti / Giovanna Zangrandi. Milano, 1951. [Leggende d'Italia; 5.]
GB/A.1171.
1080.

Lehmann und Schultze in der Schweiz: ein komischer Bädeker für Schweizerreisende / herausgegeben von der Redaction des Komikers. Berlin, 1863. Ill.
GB/A.545.
1081.

Le **Léman**, ou Voyage pittoresque, historique et littéraire à Genève et dans le canton de Vaud, Suisse / Bailly de Lalonde. Paris, 1842. 2v.
GB/A.806(1-2).
1082.

Lepcha land, or Six weeks in the Sikhim Himalayas / Florence Donaldson. London, 1900. Ill., map.
GB.788.
1083.

The **Lepontine** Alps / W. Martin Conway, W.A.B. Coolidge. London, 1892. [Conway and Coolidge's climbers' guides; 3.]
GB.1324(3); Lloyd.19; Lloyd.19A. 1084.

A **letter** addressed to the members of the Alpine Club / Edward Whymper. London, 1900.
Lloyd.1592(1); Lloyd.1592(1)A,B; Lloyd.1602(30); Lloyd.1602(31). 1085.

Letter from the Secretary of the Treasury, transmitting, in response to the House resolution of the 22nd instant, a copy of the report of Henry W. Elliott on the condition of the fur-seal fisheries of Alaska, together with all maps and illustrations accompanying said report. Washington, 1896. Ill., maps.
GB/A.1730. 1086.

Letter of application for the Chair of Practice of Medicine in the University of Edinburgh / J.J. Graham Brown. Edinburgh, 1914.
GB.1317(2). 1087.

Letter to the Right Hon. the Lord President of the Court of Session / Henry Cockburn. [Edinburgh], 1838.
Lloyd.1610(5). 1088.

La **letteratura** dell'alpinismo / Enrico Camanni. Bologna, 1985. [Idee di alpinismo; 6.]
GB/A.2194. 1089.

Letters and journals of the late Alexander Menzies / arranged and supplemented by his father [William John Menzies]. Edinburgh, 1888. Port.
Lloyd.915. 1090.

Letters and other documents relating to the death of the Rev. W.G. Watson. [London, 1860?]
Lloyd.184. 1091.

Letters, descriptive of a tour through some parts of France, Italy, Switzerland, and Germany, in 1816, with incidental reflections on some topics connected with religion / John Sheppard. Edinburgh, 1817.
Lloyd.867. 1092.

Letters during a tour through some parts of France, Savoy, Switzerland, Germany, and the Netherlands, in the summer of 1817 / Thomas Raffles. Liverpool, 1818. Port.
Lloyd.540; Lloyd.540A. 1093.

Letters during a tour through some parts of France, Savoy, Switzerland, Germany and the Netherlands, in the summer of 1817 / Thomas Raffles. 5th ed. London, 1832. Port.
GB.7. 1094.

Letters during the course of a tour through Germany, Switzerland and Italy, in 1791 and 1792: with reflections on the manners, literature, and religion of those countries / Robert Gray. London, 1794.
Lloyd.948. 1095.

Letters from an absent brother, containing some account of a tour through parts of the Netherlands, Switzerland, northern Italy, and France, in the summer of 1823. 2nd ed. London, 1824. 2v. Some of the letters signed: D.W., i.e. Daniel Wilson.
GB.474-5; Lloyd.479 (bound in 1). 1096.

Letters from high latitudes / Lord Dufferin. 3rd ed. London, 1857.
Lloyd.814. 1097.

Letters from high latitudes: being some account of a voyage, in 1856, in the schooner yacht *Foam* to Iceland, Jan Mayen, and Spitzbergen / Lord Dufferin. New York, 1878. Ill., port.
GB/A.1622. 1098.

Letters from Italy / Joel Tyler Headley. London, 1845.
Lloyd.579. 1099.

Letters from Italy / Mariana Starke. 2nd ed., rev., corr., and enl. London, 1815. 2v.
Lloyd.1173-4. 1100.

Letters from Italy, describing the customs and manners of that country, in the years 1765, and 1766: to which is annexed, an admonition to gentlemen who pass the Alps, in their tour through Italy / Samuel Sharp. 3rd ed. London, [1767].
Lloyd.673; Lloyd.736. 1101.

[**Letters** from Michael Joseph Chasseur to Canon Georges Carrel, reproduced from typewriting, in connexion with the ascent of the Matterhorn in 1865, some of which were subsequently published in the *Alpine Journal*, vol.51. no.259, Nov.1939.] [N.p.], 1939.
Lloyd.1398. 1102.

Letters from Switzerland, 1833 / [Philip H. Stanhope, Earl Stanhope]. Carlsruhe, 1834.
GB.315. 1103.

Letters from Switzerland and France: written during a residence of between two and three years in different parts of those countries. London, 1821. Ill.
GB.873; Lloyd.1602(10). 1104.

Letters from Switzerland and Italy, during a late tour / by the author of *Letters from the East* [i.e. John Carne]. London, 1834.
GB.630. 1105.

Letters from the Pyrenees, during three months' pedestrian wanderings amidst the French and Spanish mountains, in the summer of 1842 / T. Clifton Paris. London, 1843. Ill.
Lloyd.607. 1106.

The **letters** of Gertrude Bell / selected and edited by Lady Bell. London, 1927. 2v; ill., ports.
GB.1103-4. 1107.

Letters of Lady M—y W—y M——e [i.e. Lady Mary Wortley Montagu]: written during her travels in Europe, Asia and Africa, to persons of distinction. London, 1763-67. 4v.
Lloyd.89-92. 1108.

Letters written during a journey to Switzerland in the autumn of 1841 / Mrs Ashton Yates. London, 1843. 2v.
GB.429-30; Lloyd.683-4. 1109.

Letters written during the late voyage of discovery in the western Arctic Sea / by an officer of the expedition. London, 1821. Attributed to William Nelson Griffiths.
GB/A.1672. 1110.

Lettre de M. Bourrit à Miss Craven sur deux voyages faits au sommet du Mont-Blanc: l'un, par le professeur de Saussure, l'autre, par M. le chevalier Beaufoix. [Geneva, 1787.]
GB.461(3). 1111.

Lettre de M. Bourrit à Miss Craven sur deux voyages faits au sommet du Mont-Blanc: l'un par M. le professeur de Saussure, l'autre, par M. le chevalier Beaufoix; et relation de celui que M. Bourrit a fait en Piémont, par la fameuse mer de Glace du Montanvert. San Remo, 1911.
GB.1314(6). 1112.

Lettre de Monsieur le général de St. Saphorin écrite à Monsieur le comte de Marsay à Genève, le 21. octobre en 1734. [N.p., 1735.]
GB.1158(2). 1113.

Lettre de Mr. le comte de Marsay écrite aux magnifiques Seigneurs, Sindics et Conseil de la république de Genève, le 5me. décembre 1736. [N.p., 1736.]
GB.1158(3). 1114.

Lettres à M.W. Melmoth, sur l'état politique, civil, et naturel de la Suisse / William Coxe; traduites de l'anglois [by Louis F.E. Ramond de Carbonnières], et augmentées des *Observations faites dans le même pays*, par le traducteur. Paris, 1782. 2v. Translated from *Sketches of the natural, civil, and political state of Swisserland*.
GB.655-6. 1115.

Lettres d'une famille suisse / [Herminie Chavannes]. Lausanne, 1841. 2v (in 1); ill.
GB/A.670. 1116.

Lettres de deux amans, habitans d'une petite ville au pied des Alpes / Jean Jacques Rousseau. Amsterdam, 1761. 6v.
GB.398-403. 1117.

Lettres de H.B. de Saussure à sa femme / commentées par E. Gaillard et H.F. Montagnier. Chambéry, 1937.
GB/B.338(19). 1118.

Lettres écrites de Suisse, d'Italie, de Sicilie et de Malthe / par M.*** [i.e. J.M. Roland de la Platière] à Mlle. *** à Paris, en 1776, 1777 & 1778. Amsterdam, 1780. 6v.
GB/A.715-20. 1119.

Lettres physiques et morales, sur les montagnes et sur l'histoire de la terre et de l'homme / Jean André de Luc. La Haye, 1778.
GB.574. 1120.

Lettres physiques et morales, sur les montagnes et sur l'histoire de la terre et de l'homme / Jean André de Luc. [N.p.], 1778.
GB.241; Lloyd.615. 1121.

Lettres sur la route de Genève à Milan par le Simplon, écrites en 1809 / George Mallet. 2e éd., corr. et augm. Paris, 1816.
GB/A.561. 1122.

Lettres sur la Suisse / H. Sazerac, G. Engelmann. Pt.1: Oberland bernois. Paris, 1823. Ill.
Lloyd.1544; Lloyd.1566(2). 1123.

Lettres sur la Suisse / P.L.C.L.D.C. [i.e. comte Léopoldo Curti]. Altona, 1797. 2v.
GB/A.685-6. 1124.

Lettres sur la Suisse, addressées à Madame de M*** par un voyageur françois, en 1781. Genève, 1783. 2v; map.
GB/A.789-90.   1125.

Lettres sur la Suisse écrites en 1819, 1820 et 1821 / M. Raoul-Rochette. 2e éd. Paris, 1823. 2v; ill.
GB.450-1; Lloyd.733-4.   1126.

Lettres sur la Suisse écrites en 1819, 1820 et 1821 / Désiré Raoul-Rochette. 4e éd., rev. et corr. Paris, 1828. 3v.
Lloyd.776-8.   1127.

Lettres sur la Suisse et le pays des Grisons / Louis Alceste de Chapuys Montlaville. Paris, 1826.
GB/A.917(1).   1128.

Der **letzte** Achttausender: Dhaulagiri-Expedition 1958 / Kaspar Winterhalter. Bern, [1959]. Ill., maps.
GB/A.370.   1129.

Letzte Fahrt / Kapitän Scott. Leipzig, 1913.
GB/A.2188.   1130.

Das **Letzte** im Fels / Domenico Rudatis; die Ubersetzung aus dem Italienischen besorgten Emmeli Capuis und Max Rohrer. München, 1936. Ill.
GB/A.431.   1131.

Leuchtende Berge: ein Farbbuch der Alpen / Jos. Jul. Schätz. München, [1954]. Ill.
GB/B.326.   1132.

Leuchtende Gipfel: Roman / Rudolf Haas. Leipzig, 1925.
GB/A.36.   1133.

Leysin, the Vaudese Alps, Switzerland: 1450 meters: a sanatorium and a high altitude health resort for summer and winter cures. Paris, 1893. Ill.
Lloyd.1618(23).   1134.

Lhasa: an account of the country and people of central Tibet and of the progress of the mission sent there by the English government in the year 1903-4 / written, with the help of all the principal persons of the mission, by Perceval Landon. Colonial ed. London, 1905. 2v; ill., maps, ports.
GB.1105-6.   1135.

Lhasa: an account of the country and people of central Tibet and of the progress of the mission sent there by the English government in the year 1903-4 / written, with the help of all the principal persons of the mission, by Perceval Landon. New and rev. ed. (Colonial ed.). London, 1906. Ill., maps, ports.
GB.1035.   1136.

Lhasa and its mysteries: with a record of the expedition of 1903-1904 / L. Austine Waddell. London, 1905.
GB.1026.   1137.

The **library** catalogue of the Scott Polar Research Institute, Cambridge, England. Boston, 1976. 19v.
GB/C.62-80.   1138.

The **library** catalogue of the Scott Polar Research Institute, Cambridge, England. 1st supplement. Boston, 1981. 5v.
GB/C.100-4.   1139.

Il **libro** dell'Alpe / Giuseppe Zoppi. 8a ed. Firenze, 1953.
GB/A.1750.   1140.

Lichens from central east Greenland / Eric Steen Hansen. Copenhagen, 1982. Ill., map. [Meddelelser om Grønland. Bioscience; 9.]
GB/A.1819.   1141.

Life and letters of James David Forbes / John Campbell Shairp, Peter Guthrie Tait, A. Adams-Reilly. London, 1873. Ill., map, ports.
GB.859; Lloyd.996.   1142.

The **life** and travels of Mungo Park: comprising an original memoir of his early life, a reprint of the *Travels in the interior of Africa*, written by himself, and an original narrative of his second journey: also, an original account of the progress of African discovery from the death of Park till the year 1838. Edinburgh, 1838. Map.
GB.1176(2).   1143.

The **life** and travels of Thomas Simpson, the Arctic discoverer / Alexander Simpson. Toronto, 1963. Maps. [Canadian heritage series. Library ed.; 3.]
GB/A.2155.   1144.

The **life** and work of John Ruskin / W.G. Collingwood. London, 1893. 2v; ill., ports.
GB.1257-8.   1145.

Life and work of John Tyndall / A.S. Eve, C.H. Creasy; with a chapter on Tyndall as a mountaineer by Lord Schuster. London, 1945. Ill., ports.
GB.862.   1146.

Life at the bottom: the people of Antarctica / John Langone. Boston, 1977. Map.
GB/A.1893.   1147.

Life eternal / Geo. B. [N.p., n.d.]
GB.1337(18).   1148.

Life in the Antarctic: sixty photographs by members of the Scottish National Antarctic Expedition. London, 1907. [Gowan's nature books; 10.]
GB/A.1468(10).   1149.

The **life** of Benvenuto Cellini / written by himself and translated by Thomas Nugent. London, 1771. 2v; port. Translated from *La vita di Benvenuto Cellini.*
GB.631-2.   1150.

The **life** of Horace Benedict de Saussure / Douglas W. Freshfield with the collaboration of Henry F. Montagnier. London, 1920. Ill., maps, ports.
GB.1109; Lloyd.1224; Lloyd.1224A.   1151.

Life with the Esquimaux: the narrative of Captain Charles Francis Hall from the 29th May, 1860, to the 13th September, 1862: with the discovery of actual relics of the expedition of Martin Frobisher and deductions in favour of yet discovering some of the survivors of Sir John Franklin's expedition. Popular ed. London, 1865. Ill., maps.
GB.331 (impf.).   1152.

La **ligia** grischa: treis maletgs dramatics / Maurus Carnot. [N.p.], 1924.
GB/A.1161.   1153.

La **limite** supérieure des polis glaciaires dans les Alpes, réponse à M.A. Schlagintweit / E. Desor. Neuchâtel, 1855. Extrait du IIIme vol. du *Bulletin de la Société des sciences naturelles de Neuchâtel.*
GB/A.793(1).   1154.

Linda of Chamouni, or Not 'Formosa': an operatic incongruity / Alfred Thompson. [London, 1869.]
Lloyd.347.   1155.

Lines written to beguile hours of indisposition, on the Isle of St. Pierre, Lake of Bienne, Switzerland / Edwin John James. London, [1832].
Lloyd.1602(11).   1156.

Le **Linththal** et le Tödi / Aline Martel. Paris, 1891. Ill. Extrait de l'*Annuaire du Club alpin français*, vol.17, 1890.
Lloyd.1620(6).   1157.

The **Lion**: university magazine. No.3, May 1859. Cambridge, 1859.
Lloyd.1605(9).   1158.

The **lipid** metabolism in Greenlanders / H.O. Bang, Jørn Dyerberg. Copenhagen, 1981. [Meddelelser om Grønland. Man & society; 2.]
GB/A.1820/2.   1159.

List of books in the Library / Fell and Rock Climbing Club of the English Lake District. [Ambleside], 1962.
GB.1305(15).   1160.

List of books in the Library: list of slides / Fell and Rock Climbing Club of the English Lake District. [Ambleside], 1947.
GB.1305(14).   1161.

List of members / Alpine Club. 1859,1959, 1961,1962. London, [1859]-1962.
GB.19, GB.1321(29-31).   1162.

List of members / Alpine Club. Additions and corrections to the 1942 (1953, 1956) list. London, [1943-58].
GB.1321(36-39).   1163.

List of members / Geologists' Association. 1868. London, 1868.
Lloyd.1605(18).   1164.

List of members / Royal Forth Yacht Club. 1951. Edinburgh, 1951.
GB.1326(32).   1165.

List of members with rules / Geographical Club. Sept.1939, Sept.1946, July 1948, Aug.1957, Nov. 1959. [London, 1939-59.]
GB.1341(10), GB.1307(3-5), GB.1326(17).   1166.

List of members, rules, meets, etc. / Fell and Rock Climbing Club of the English Lake District. 1923, 1925-26, 1939-40, 1948, 1954, 1961-62, 1964. [Kendal], 1923-64.
GB.1305(5-13).   1167.

List of office-bearers and members of the Scottish Mountaineering Club. 1950/51, 1953, 1955, 1960. Edinburgh, [1951-60].
GB.1325(30-3).   1168.

A **list** of the honorary members and fellows of the [Royal Geographical] Society, corrected to 30th September 1938. London, [1938]. With 1st supplement.
GB.1329(12-13).   1169.

A **list** of the writings, not being reviews of books, dating from 1868 to 1912 and relating to the Alps or Switzerland, of W.A.B. Coolidge. Grindelwald, 1912.
GB.1333(24). 1170.

List of tourist class passengers, R.M.S. *Aquitania*, 2nd June, 1934. [London? 1934.]
GB.1326(8). 1171.

List of tourist class passengers, R.M.S. *Mauretania*, September 26, 1934. [London? 1934.]
GB.1326(9). 1172.

A **list** of travels, tours, etc., relating to Scotland / Arthur Mitchell. [Edinburgh, 1902.] From the *Proceedings of the Society of Antiquaries in Scotland*, vol.35.
GB.918. 1173.

Liste et adresses des membres / Club alpin français, Groupe de haute montagne. 1933, 1935-7. Paris, [1933-37].
Lloyd.1621(14-7). 1174.

Listino n.03: attrezzatura per alpinismo, sci e sci-alpinismo disponibile al 1-3-1955 / Bottega dell'Alpinista e dello Sciatore. [Courmayeur, 1955.]
GB.1329(28). 1175.

The **Literary** and Statistical Magazine for Scotland. Vol.1. Edinburgh, 1817.
Lloyd.850. 1176.

Literary life and select works of Benjamin Stillingfleet / [edited by William Coxe]. London, 1811. 2v (in 3); ill., ports.
GB.626-8; Lloyd.901-3. 1177.

The **Literary** Souvenir / edited by Alaric A. Watts. 1833. London, 1833.
GB.471. 1178.

La **littérature** alpestre en France et en Angleterre aux XVIIIe et XIXe siècles / Claire Eliane Engel. Chambéry, 1930. Ill.
GB.1330(5); Lloyd.1620(8). 1179.

The **little** mountaineers of Auvergne, or The adventures of James and Georgette / altered from the French. London, 1801.
Lloyd.221. 1180.

Livat folk / John Giæver. 3. oppl. Oslo, 1974.
GB/A.2080. 1181.

Living below zero: a guide to all personnel in mountainous and other low-temperature regions. [London], 1946. [Air Ministry pamphlet; 194.]
GB.1313(30). 1182.

Living with Lepchas: a book about the Sikkim Himalayas / John Morris. London, 1938. Ill., map.
GB.759. 1183.

Livingstone of the Arctic / Dudley Copland. Ottawa, 1967.
GB/A.2183. 1184.

Livingstone's last journey / Reginald Coupland. London, 1945. Maps, ports.
GB.748. 1185.

Livres curieux & rares, manuscrits, enluminures, reliures anciennes: gravures anciennes principalement des écoles française & anglaise: Helvetica: sujets de genres vues & costumes, livres & recueils illustrés: oeuvres des artistes suisses / C.A. Mincieux. Genève, [n.d.]. 3v (in 1).
Lloyd.1605(11); Lloyd.1605(11)A (v.3). 1186.

Locarno and its valleys / J. Hardmeyer. Zurich, [1886]. Ill., maps. [Illustrated Europe.]
GB/A.760(3). 1187.

Log of the auxiliary schooner yacht *Northern Light* commanded by John Borden, Borden-Field Museum Alaska-Arctic Expedition, 1927. Chicago, 1929. Ill.
GB/B.429. 1188.

The **log** of the schooner *Bowdoin* / A.R. Horr; introductions and interpolations by Donald B. MacMillan. Cleveland, Ohio, 1947. Ill., maps, ports.
GB/A.1905. 1189.

Lombardia / Roberto Pracchi. Torino, 1960. Ill., map. [Le regioni d'Italia; 2.]
GB/B.548. 1190.

The **London** lectures / Mountaineering Association. 7th annual series. October 1954 to March 1955. London, [1954]. A prospectus.
GB.1330(1). 1191.

Longs Peak: its story and a climbing guide / Paul W. Nesbit. 8th ed., rev. Boulder, Colo., 1972. Ill.
GB/A.1791(5). 1192.

Looking far north: the Harriman expedition to Alaska 1899 / William H. Goetzmann, Kay Sloan.

Princeton, 1982. Ill., maps, ports.
GB/B.635(7). 1193.

Looking south: New Zealand Antarctic Society's first fifty years, 1933-1983 / Neville Peat. Wellington, 1983. Ill., maps, ports.
GB/A.2139(7). 1194.

The **Lord's** Prayer of an Unternaldener [sic] / invented by John Martin Usteri; engraved by Marquard Wocher. [N.p.], 1805. Ill.
Lloyd.1399. 1195.

A **lost** village in the Bernese Oberland / W.A.B. Coolidge. [N.p., n.d.] Corrected proof sheets.
GB.1340(55). 1196.

Louis Lachenal: ein Leben für die Bergen / Gérard Herzog. Bern, [1963]. Ill. Translated from *Carnets du vertige*.
GB/A.371. 1197.

La **luce** delle vette: romanzo alpino / Francesco Cavazzani. Milano, 1954.
GB/A.515(3). 1198.

Lucerne & lac des IV Cantons. Lucerne, [ca 1905]. Ill., map. [Edition 'Illustrato'.]
GB/A.2048(7). 1199.

The **Lucerne-Rigi** Rail at Vitznau, Lake of the Four Cantons / H.A. Berlepsch. Zurich, [1895?]. [Swiss scenes.]
GB/A.1817(2). 1200.

La **lumière** de la montagne: roman / Robert Claude. Louvain, [1934]. Ill. [Collection Jéciste; 13.]
GB/A.1199(11). 1201.

Lundy rock climb / Robert Moulton. 3rd ed. [N.p.], 1980. Ill., maps. Published by the Royal Navy and Royal Marines Mountaineering Club.
GB/A.1676(20). 1202.

La **lunga** strada agli '8000' / Cesare Ottin Pecchio. [N.p., 1971.] Ill., maps.
GB/B.319. 1203.

The **lure** of Alaska / Harry A. Franck accompanied by Harry A. Franck, jr. 3rd printing. New York, 1939. Ill., map, ports.
GB/A.1698. 1204.

The **lure** of Alaska / Harry A. Franck accompanied by Harry A. Franck, jr. Garden City, N.Y.,
1943. Ill., map, ports.
GB/A.1660. 1205.

The **lure** of the map / W. Powell James. London, [1920].
GB.158. 1206.

Lure of the North / Richard Finnie. Philadelphia, 1940. Ill., map, ports., facsim.
GB/B.517. 1207.

La **lutte** pour le Cervin: roman de faits / Carl Haensel; traduction de Marcel Travey. Genève, [1920?]. Port.
GB/A.915(7). 1208.

Lys og skygger i Sjøgata / John Giæver. Oslo, 1969.
GB/A.2081. 1209.

-M-

M. Bianco, 4810m.: 1a ascensione per la cresta SO. delle Bosses / Hans Pfann. [Turin, 1911.] P.334 of the *Rivista del Club Alpino Italiano*, vol.30.
GB.1880(45).   m001.

M. Dumollet sur le Mont-Blanc / Samivel. Lyon, 1946.
GB/A.124.   m002.

El **macizo** central de los picos de Europa / J.M. Boada. Madrid, 1935. Ill.
GB/B.493.   m003.

The **Mackenzie** Eskimos: after Knud Rasmussen's posthumous notes / edited by H. Ostermann. New York, 1976. Ill. [Thule expedition, 5th, 1921-1924. Report; vol.10 no.2.]
GB/A.1838.   m004.

Mademoiselle d'Angeville: notice biographique / Mary Paillon. Paris, 1894. Pp.[401]-34 of the *Annuaire du Club alpin français*, 1893.
GB.1738(2); Lloyd.988; Lloyd.1620(13).   m005.

Mænd i is og øde: danske ekspeditioner til Grønland i vort århundrede / Chr. Winther. Copenhagen, 1963.
GB/B.602(7).   m006.

Magasin d'éducation et de récréation. 1864. Paris, 1864.
GB/A.2048(11).   m007.

Magazine / Glasgow University Mountaineering Club. 1952-53. [Glasgow, 1952-53.]
GB.1332(16-7).   m008.

Magic Ladakh: an intimate picture of a land of topsy-turvy customs & great natural beauty / 'Ganpat' (i.e. M.L.A. Gompertz). London, 1928. Ill., map.
GB.719.   m009.

Magica Valle d'Aosta / Carlo Moriondo, Renato Willien. Torino, 1970. Ill.
GB/B.317.   m010.

Magico Appennino: immagini, racconti e itinerari da Gran Sasso, Sibillini, Maiella, Parco Nazionale d'Abruzzo e dalle altre montagne dell'Italia centrale / Stefano Ardito. Bolzano, 1984. Ill., map.
GB/A.2162.   m011.

Il **magico**, il divino, il favoloso nella religiosità alpina / Piercarlo Jorio. Ivrea, 1984. Ill., maps. [Quaderni di cultura alpina; 8.]
GB/B.639.   m012.

Magie de la montagne: un choix des plus belles photographies des Alpes européennes / Max Albert Wyss; adaptation française de David Rosset. Paris, 1967. Ill.
GB/B.241.   m013.

Mahlerische Reise auf der neuen Kunst-Strasse aus dem Etschthal im Tÿrol über das Stilfser-Joch durch das Veltlin längs dem Comersee nach Maÿland / herausgegeben von J. J. Meÿer. Zürich, 1831. Ill., map.
GB/B.230 (impf.).   m014.

Les **maîtres** de la gravure suisse / Daniel Baud-Bovy. Genève, 1935. Ill.
Lloyd.1622(1).   m015.

Majesté des Alpes / [photographs by] Yoshikazu Shirakawa; texte de Max A. Wyss; [version française de Georges A. Rosset]. Lausanne, 1973. Ill. [Bibliothèque des arts.]
GB/B.369.   m016.

Major E.A.M. Wedderburn / A.M. Greenwood. [London, 1946.] Pp.72-4 of the *Climbers' Club Journal*, N.S. vol.8 no.1.
GB.1337(2).   m017.

Makalu / Jean Franco. [London], 1957. A prospectus.
GB.1329(50).   m018.

Makalu: Expedition in die Stille / Hermann Warth, Dietlinde Warth. St. Ottilien, 1979.
GB/A.1684.   m019.

Makalu pilier ouest / Robert Paragot, Yannick Seigneur. [Paris], 1972. Ill., maps. [Sempervivum; 57.]
GB/A.988(4).   m020.

The **making** of a mountaineer / George Ingle Finch. 2nd impr. London, [1924].
GB.1115.   m021.

Malerische Reise durch einen grossen Theil der Schweiz vor und nach der Revolution / Reichard. Jena, 1805. Ill.
GB/A.641.   m022.

Malerische Reise durch einen grossen Theil der Schweiz vor und nach der Revolution / Reichard.

Neue Ausg. Gotha, 1827. Ill.
GB/A.636. m023.

Das **malerische** Schweizerland: Ansichten mit einem Worte zur Charakteristik der Schweiz / August Lewald. 2. Aufl. Karlsruhe, 1844.
GB/A.480. m024.

Malerisches Relief des klassischen Bodens der Schweiz / nach der Natur gezeichnet und radiert von Friedrich Wilhelm Delkeskamp; kommentiert von Eduard Imhof. Zürich, 1978.
GB/C.91. m025.

Mali planinarski terminoloski rjecnik / Stanislav Gilic. 2. izd. Rijeka, 1978.
GB/A.1964(10). m026.

Mallory et son Dieu / Joseph Peyré. Genève, 1947.
GB/A.495(1). m027.

Das **Maltathal** in Kärnthen: Ersteigung des Hochalpenspitzes / Anton von Ruthner. Wien, 1861. Separatabdruck aus den *Mittheilungen der k.k. Geographischen Gesellschaft*, Jahrg.5.
GB.1130(6). m028.

Man against the desolate Antarctic / Lord Mountevans. New York, 1951.
GB/A.2174. m029.

Man at great altitudes / Yandell Henderson. [London], 1926. A review of *The respiratory function of the blood*, by Joseph Barcroft. Pp.747-8 of *Nature*, vol.117 no.2952.
GB.1319(22). m030.

The **man** of Alaska: Peter Trimble Rowe / Thomas Jenkins. New York, 1943. Ill., maps, ports.
GB/A.1617. m031.

Man on the Matterhorn / edited by M. Dodderidge; from Edward Whymper's *Scrambles amongst the Alps*. London, 1940. Ill., map. [Journeys and adventures.]
GB.153. m032.

Manfred, a dramatic poem / Lord Byron. London, 1817.
GB.572. m033.

Männer des sechsten Grades / Aurelio Garobbio; übersetzt von Corrado Dapponte. Rüschlikon-Zürich, 1966. Ill. Translated from *Uomini del sesto grado*.
GB/B.233. m034.

Mantle of the skies: the Southern Alps of New Zealand / Philip Temple. [Christchurch], 1971.
GB/B.335. m035.

A **manual** of the thermometer / John Henry Belville. London, 1850.
Lloyd.1616(18). m036.

Manuale arrampicatore / Carlo Franchetti; testo riordinato da Alberto Fumagalli. Monza, 1924. Ill. [Manuali del Club Alpino Italiano, Sezione Universitaria.]
GB/A.1349(7). m037.

Manuale del trapper / Andrea Mercanti. Milano, 1976. Ill.
GB/A.1989. m038.

Manuale dell'alpinista / Felice Boffa. [Florence, 1965.] Ill., maps.
GB/A.1349(17). m039.

Manuale della montagna / a cura del C.A.I. Roma, 1939. Ill., maps. At head of title: Centro Alpinistico Italiano, Sede Centrale.
GB/A.2022(1). m040.

Manuale di speleologia / a cura della Società Speleologica Italiana. Milano, 1978. Ill. [La vostra via; 144.]
GB/A.2008. m041.

Manuale popolare dell'alpinista / Carlo Baudino. Roma, 1931. Ill. [Biblioteca dello sport; 3.]
GB/A.802(10). m042.

Manualetto di istruzioni scientifiche per alpinisti. Milano, 1934. Ill. Published by the Club Alpino Italiano.
GB/A.1468(16). m043.

Manuel d'alpinisme / publié avec la collaboration du Groupe de haute montagne [of the Club alpin français]. Chambéry, 1934. 2v.
GB/A.1098-9. m044.

Manuel d'alpinisme / Schweizer Alpenclub. Zurich, 1943.
GB/A.524. m045.

Manuel de l'étranger qui voyage en Suisse. Ed. corr. et augm. Zuric, 1799.
GB/A.652. m046.

Manuel du voyageur en Italie. Nouv. éd. corr. et augm. en 1838. Milan, [1838].
Lloyd.33. m047.

Manuel du voyageur en Suisse / J.G. Ebel; traduit de l'allemand [by J. Gaudin]. 2e éd., enrichie de toutes les additions et corrections de la troisième édition originale. Zurich, 1810-11. 4v; ill., maps. Translated from *Anleitung auf die nützlichste und genussvollste Art die Schweitz zu bereisen*.
GB.488-91; Lloyd.359-62; Lloyd.722-5.   m048.

Manuel du voyageur en Suisse / J.G. Ebel; traduit de l'allemand [by Jean Gaudin]. 3e éd. française. Paris, 1816. Maps. Translated from *Anleitung auf die nützlichste und genussvollste Art die Schweitz zu bereisen*.
GB/A.218.   m049.

Manuel du voyageur en Suisse / J.G. Ebel; traduit de l'allemand [by Jean Gaudin]. 3e éd. Zurich, 1818. Translated from *Anleitung auf die nützlichste und genussvollste Art die Schweitz zu bereisen*.
Lloyd.363-5.   m050.

Manuel du voyageur en Suisse / J.G. Ebel; traduit de l'allemand [by Jean Gaudin]. 4e éd. Paris, 1818. Translated from *Anleitung auf die nützlichste und genussvollste Art die Schweitz zu bereisen*.
Lloyd.236.   m051.

Manuel du voyageur suisse / J.G. Ebel. Nouv. éd. augm. Paris, 1830-31. Ill., map. Translated from *Anleitung auf die nützlichste und genussvollste Art die Schweitz zu bereisen*.
Lloyd.237.   m052.

Manuel du voyageur en Suisse / J.G. Ebel. Paris, 1836. Translated from *Anleitung auf die nützlichste und genussvollste Art die Schweitz zu bereisen*.
GB.22.   m053.

Manuel du voyageur en Suisse (le nouvel Ebel). Paris, 1840. Map. Translated from *Anleitung auf die nützlichste und genussvollste Art die Schweitz zu bereisen*.
Lloyd.238.   m054.

Manuel du voyageur en Suisse / J.G. Ebel. Nouv. éd. rev., mise en ordre et augm. par Richard. Paris, 1843. Translated from *Anleitung auf die nützlichste and genussvollste Art die Schweitz zu bereisen*.
Lloyd.217.   m055.

Manuel du voyageur en Suisse / Robert Glutz-Blotzheim. 3e éd. française augm. Zurich, 1828. Translated from *Handbuch für Reisende in der Schweiz*.
Lloyd.420.   m056.

Manuel pour les savans et les curieux qui voyagent en Suisse / Besson; avec des notes par M. W***. [i.e. Jacob S. Wyttenbach]. Berne, 1786. 2v (in 1). Originally published as *Discours sur l'histoire naturelle de la Suisse*.
Lloyd.421.   m057.

Manuscripts in the Scott Polar Research Institute, Cambridge, England: a catalogue / edited by Clive Holland. New York, 1982. [Garland reference library of social science; 123.]
GB/A.2077.   m058.

Marble Island and the north-west coast of Hudson's Bay / Robert Bell. Toronto, 1887. Reprinted from the *Proceedings of the Canadian Institute, Toronto*.
GB/A.1966(2).   m059.

The **marches** of Hindustan: the record of a journey in Thibet, trans-Himalayan India, Chinese Turkestan, Russian Turkestan, and Persia / David Fraser. Edinburgh, 1907. Ill., maps.
GB.640; GB.926.   m060.

Mariner of the North: the life of Captain Bob Bartlett / George Palmer Putnam. New York, 1947.
GB/A.1662.   m061.

Marion and Prince Edward Islands: report on the South African biological & geological expedition, 1965-1966 / edited by E.M. van Zinderen Bakker, J.M. Winterbottom, R.A. Dyer. Cape Town, 1971. Ill., maps.
GB/B.310.   m062.

Marmolada / Bepi Pellegrinon. Belluno, 1979. [Andar per monti; 1.]
GB/A.2017(10).   m063.

Marmolada / P. Rossi, Bepi Pellegrinon, Arturo Andreoletti. Bologna, 1965. Ill.
GB/C.22(17).   m064.

Martigny and the valleys of the Dranse, the Great St. Bernard / F.O. Wolf. Zürich, [1880?]. Ill., maps. [Valais and Chamounix; 7.]
GB/A.760(1).   m065.

Les **martyrs** du pôle / H. de Graffigny. Paris, [ca 1934]. Ill.
GB/A.1685.   m066.

Masherbrum: beyond Camp IV / R.A. Hodgkin. London, 1939. Ill. Pp.5-9 of the *Climbers' Club*

Journal, N.S. vol.6 no.1, 1939.
GB.1339(28). m067.

Masherbrum, 1938 / T. Graham Brown. London, [1940]. Ill., maps. Reprinted from the *Geographical Journal*, vol.95 no.2, February 1940.
GB.1332(6); Lloyd.1620(7). m068.

The **Massacre** of Glenco, being a true narrative of the barbarous murther of the Glenco-men faithfully extracted from the records of Parliament. 2nd ed. London, 1704. Ascribed to George Ridpath or Charles Leslie.
GB.464. m069.

Der **Massentourismus**: soziologische und wirtschaftliche Aspekte unter besonderer Berücksichtigung schweizerischer Verhältnisse / Christian Fink. Bern, 1970. Ill. [St. Galler Beiträge zum Fremdenverkehr und zur Verkehrswirtschaft. Reihe Fremdenverkehr; 2.]
GB/A.860(3). m070.

I **massi** erratici nella regione dei Tre Laghi. Pavia, 1914. Ill. Published by the Club Alpino Italiano, Sezione di Milano.
GB/B.289(3). m071.

Il **massiccio** del Monte Bianco: le 100 più belle ascensioni / Gaston Rébuffat; [traduzione di Rosalba Donvito Gossi]. Bologna, 1974. Ill. Translated from *Le massif du Mont Blanc: les 100 plus belles courses*.
GB/B.410. m072.

Il **massiccio** dell'Alto Delfinato: le 100 più belle ascensioni ed escursioni / Gaston Rébuffat; traduzione di Rosalba Donvito Gossi. Bologna, 1978. Ill., maps. Translated from *Le massif des Ecrins*.
GB/B.576. m073.

Le **massif** d'Ambin / W.A.B. Coolidge. Lyon, 1897. Map. Extrait de la *Revue alpine*, mars 1897.
GB.1340(1). m074.

Le **massif** d'Avérole / W.A.B. Coolidge. Lyon, 1902. Ill.
GB.1340(10). m075.

Le **massif** de Bellecôte / W.A.B. Coolidge. Paris, 1905. Ill., map. Extrait de *La Montagne*, vol.1, 1905.
GB.1340(12). m076.

Massif de l'Argentéra / Michel Dufranc. Grenoble, 1970. Ill. [Guide Paschetta des Alpes-Maritimes. Alpinisme.]
GB/A.1295(1). m077.

Le **massif** de la Vanoise / Charles Maly. Paris, 1976. Ill. [Les cent plus belles courses et randonnées.]
GB/B.582. m078.

Le **massif** de Méan-Martin, Haute-Maurienne / W.A.B. Coolidge. Lyon, 1901. 2v. Pp.[1]-17, 41-8 of the *Revue alpine*, année 7 no.1-2.
GB.1340(5-6). m079.

Le **massif** des Ecrins / Lucien Devies, François Labande, Maurice Laloue. Tom.1: Meije — Ecrins. 3e éd. Paris, 1969. Map.
GB/A.968. m080.

Le **massif** des Ecrins / Lucien Devies, François Labande, Maurice Laloue. Tom.2: Ailefroide, Pelvoux, Bans, Olan, Muzelle. 3e éd. Paris, 1971. Ill.
GB/A.969. m081.

Le **massif** du Mont Blanc: étude sur sa constitution géodésique et géologique, sur ses transformations et sur l'état ancien et moderne de ses glaciers / E. Viollet-le-Duc. Paris, 1876. Ill.
GB.1160. m082.

Le **massif** du Mont-Blanc: paysages caractéristiques et documentaires / Charles Vallot. Tom.1: Parcours des vallées et des hauts alpages. Versailles, [1921?]. Ill.
Lloyd.1269. m083.

Le **massif** du Mont Blanc: paysages caractéristiques et documentaires / Joseph Vallot. Tom.2: La haute chaîne. [Paris, 1922.] A prospectus.
GB.1318(16). m084.

Le **massif** du Mont-Blanc: vallées et sommets / Henry de Ségogne. Marseille, 1947. Ill.
GB/B.109. m085.

Le **massif** du Toubkal / Jean Dresch, Jacques de Lépiney, avec le concours de Théophile Jean Delaye. Rabat, 1938. Ill., maps. [Guide alpin de la montagne marocaine.]
Lloyd.1617(5). m086.

Massif du Vercors: Royans: itinéraires à pied et à ski / S. Sarthou, J. J. Bach. Grenoble, [1978]. Ill. [Cartes et guides du Dauphiné.]
GB/A.1911(3). m087.

Massif du Vercors: Royans: itinéraires à pied et à ski / S. Sarthou, J. J. Bach. Grenoble, 1980. Ill.
GB/A.2020(8). m088.

Massif et Parc national de la Vanoise: itinéraires à pied et à ski / O. Gumuchian, L. Martin. 3e éd. [Grenoble], 1973. Ill. [Cartes et guides de Savoie.] GB/A.802(7). m089.

Massif et Parc national de la Vanoise: itinéraires à pied et à ski / O. Gumuchian, L. Martin. 7e éd. Grenoble, 1979. Ill., maps. [Cartes et guides de Savoie.] GB/A.1911(4). m090.

Massifs de Chartreuse, Belledonne, Maurienne: itinéraires à pied et à ski / J. J. Bach, L. Martin. Grenoble, 1973. Ill., maps. [Cartes et guides du Dauphiné et de Savoie.] GB/A.1295(2). m091.

Massifs de Chartreuse, Belledonne, Maurienne: itinéraires à pied et à ski / J. J. Bach, L. Martin. 5e éd. Grenoble, 1980. Ill. [Cartes et guides du Dauphiné et de Savoie.] GB/A.1911(8). m092.

Les **massifs** de la Grande-Chartreuse et du Vercors: étude d'économie montagnarde / Jules Blache. Grenoble, 1932. Ill. Pp.1-387 of the *Bulletin de la Société scientifique du Dauphiné*, tom.52. GB/A.98. m093.

Massifs des Ecrins et Haut Dauphiné: itinéraires à pied et à ski / O. Gumuchian, L. Martin. 4e éd. rev. et augm. Grenoble, 1979. Ill., maps. [Cartes et guides du Dauphiné.] GB/A.1911(7). m094.

Massifs du Chablais, Faucigny & Genevois: itinéraires à pied et à ski / J. J. Bach. [Grenoble], 1972. Map. [Cartes et guides de Savoie.] GB/A.1270(3). m095.

Massifs du Chablais, Faucigny et Genevois: itinéraires à pied et à ski / J. J. Bach. 3e éd. Grenoble, 1977. Ill. [Cartes et guides de Savoie.] GB/A.1911(9). m096.

Massifs du Haut Dauphiné: itinéraires à pied et à ski / O. Gumuchian, L. Martin. [Grenoble, 1971.] [Cartes et guides du Dauphiné.] GB/A.942(6). m097.

Massifs du Queyras & Haute Ubaye: itinéraires à pied et à ski / J. Cadier, R.H. Gros. 2e éd. [Grenoble, 1972.] Map. [Cartes et guides du Dauphiné.] GB/A.1270(12). m098.

Massifs du Queyras et Haute Ubaye: itinéraires à pied et à ski / J. Cadier, R.H. Gros. 6e éd. Grenoble, 1979. Ill., map. [Cartes et guides du Dauphiné.] GB/A.1911(5). m099.

Les **massifs** entre l'Arc et l'Isère / Emile Gaillard. Chambéry, 1969-70. 2v; ill., maps. GB/A.1265-6. m100.

Massifs Mont-Blanc, Aravis, Beaufortain, Haute Route: randonnées à ski / Ph. et M. Baltardive. Grenoble, 1979. Ill., maps. GB/A.1911(2); GB/A.2019(8). m101.

Massifs Mont-Blanc, Beaufortain, Aravis, Val d'Arly: itinéraires pédestres / J. J. Bach. 2e éd. [Grenoble], 1973. [Cartes et guides de Savoie.] GB/A.802(8). m102.

Massifs Mont-Blanc, Beaufortain, Aravis, Val d'Arly: itinéraires pédestres / J. J. Bach. 5e éd. Grenoble, 1979. Ill. [Cartes et guides de Savoie.] GB/A.1911(6). m103.

Master mariner and Arctic explorer: a narrative of sixty years at sea from the logs and yarns of Captain J.E. Bernier. Ottawa, 1939. GB/A.2202. m104.

Masterpieces of Alpine landscape / Vittorio Sella; exhibition of photographs at the Alpine Club. London, [n.d.]. Lloyd.1609(8). m105.

Material culture of the Copper Eskimo / D. Jenness. Ottawa, 1946. [Report of the Canadian Arctic Expedition, 1913-18; 16.] GB/A.2139(10); GB/B.440(16). m106.

Das **Mätteliseppi**: eine Erzählung / Heinrich Federer. Berlin, 1916. Port. [Grote'sche Sammlung von Werken zeitgenössischer Schriftsteller; 125.] GB/A.39. m107.

The **Matterhorn** / Guido Rey; translated from the Italian by J.E.C. Eaton. London, 1907. Ill. Lloyd.1469; Lloyd.1469A. m108.

The **Matterhorn** / Guido Rey. 2nd ed. London, 1908. Lloyd.1394. m109.

The **Matterhorn** / Guido Rey; translated from the Italian by J.E.C. Eaton. 3rd impr. London, 1913. GB.1219. m110.

The **Matterhorn** / Guido Rey; revised and two additional chapters by R.L.G. Irving. Oxford, 1946. Ill., ports.
GB.618. m111.

Das **Matterhorn** / Guido Rey; geologische Erläuterungen von Vittorio Novarese; deutsche Übersetzung von Otto Hauser. Stuttgart, 1905. Ill.
GB/B.316. m112.

Matterhorn: roman / Joseph Peyré. Paris, 1947. Ill. [La vie exaltante; 42.]
GB/A.43. m113.

Das **Matterhorn** und seine Geschichte / Theodor Wundt. Berlin, [1897]. Ill. Published by the Deutscher Alpenverein, Sektion Berlin.
GB/B.120. m114.

Matthew Henson, black explorer / Edward F. Dolan jr. New York, 1979. Ill.
GB/A.2129. m115.

Maurice Crettez: guide légendaire / Ernest Christen. Genève, 1952. Ill., port. Published by the Swiss Foundation for Alpine Research.
GB.1329(10). m116.

The **mauvais** pas: a scene in the Alps, illustrating a passage in the novel of Anne of Geirstein [sic] / Edward Stanley. Macclesfield, [1829?]. Reprinted from *Blackwood's Magazine*, Sept. 1829.
Lloyd.885. m117.

Mavor abbreviated by the application of a new principle to his system of universal stenography, an entirely new & complete book of short hand, adapted to every purpose of neat and expeditious writing / I.H. Clive. 2nd ed. London, 1814.
GB/A.1969(2). m118.

Mazama: a record of mountaineering in the Pacific North-West. Annual number. Vol.2 no.4, Dec.1905. Portland, 1905.
GB.1329(4). m119.

Med kanon og kamera efter storhvalen / Aasmund Slaattelid. Oslo, 1938. Ill.
GB/A.1857. m120.

Un **médecin** de montagne: roman / Georges Sonnier. Paris, 1963.
GB/A.1158. m121.

Médecine et montagne / Jean Rivolier. Paris, 1956. Ill. [Sempervivum; 30.]
GB/A.390. m122.

Medicine for mountaineering / edited by James A. Wilkerson. Repr. Seattle, 1972. Ill.
GB/A.1008. m123.

Medicine for mountaineering / edited by James A. Wilkerson. 2nd ed. Seattle, 1975. Ill.
GB/A.2076(2). m124.

La **Meije** / Henri Isselin. Paris, [1967]. Ill. [Sempervivum; 31.]
GB/A.469. m125.

Meije: récit / Georges Sonnier. Paris, 1952. [Bibliophiles de la montagne; 2.]
GB/A.1144. m126.

La **Meije** — 3983m. / Gilbert Robino. 2e éd. [N.p.], 1973. Ill.
GB/B.570(6). m127.

Mein Alpenfahrt / Wilhelm Junk. Berlin, 1878. Ill.
GB/C.30. m128.

Mein Osterreich, mein Heimatland: illustrierte Volks und Vaterlandskunde des Osterreichischen Kaiserstaates / unter Mitwirkung hervorragender Schriftsteller herausgegeben und ridigiert von Siegmund Schneider; nach dessen Tode fortgeführt von Benno Imendörffer. Wien, 1915.
GB/B.610. m129.

Mein Sommer 1826: Reise in das Oberland: Lager bei Thun: Deftleen des Leberberges: als Seitenstück zu der Fusspromenade durch das Schweizerland in militairischer Beziehung vom Jahr 1822: ein freundliches Wort an die Waffenbrüder und an alle Eidgenossen / Wieland. Basel, 1827.
GB/A.801(3). m130.

Meine Berge: das Bergbuch / Luis Trenker unter Mitarbeit von Walter Schmidkunz. Berlin, [1931]. Ill.
GB/B.237. m131.

Meine Reise durch das Wallis und Pays de Vaud, im Jahre 1803 / C.H. Hölder. Stuttgart, 1805.
GB.155. m132.

Meine Reise durch die Schweiz: eine Sammlung von 792 Ansichten der schönsten Punkte der Schweiz nach Photographien: mit begleitendem Text und Supplement: der Bodensee. Neuenburg, 1898. Ill.
GB/B.402. m133.

Meine Reise über den Gotthard nach den borromäischen Inseln und Mailand: und von da zurück über das Val Formazza, die Grimfel und das Oberland im Sommer 1801 / [Hölder]. Stuttgart, 1803-04. 2v.
GB/A.559-60. m134.

Meine Wege in den Alpen / Geoffrey Winthrop Young; übertragen von Helen Hinrich, Alexander Perrig. Bern, [n.d.]. Translated chapters from his *On high hills*, and *Mountains with a difference*.
GB/A.373. m135.

Der **Meister** und die Jugend: Vergangenes und Gegenwärtiges / Gustav Renker. [Vienna], 1926. Pp.[81]-4 of the *Osterreichische Alpenzeitung*, Jahrg.47 Nr.1049.
GB.1317(8). m136.

Melbourne illustrated and Victoria described: the visitors handbook of facts and figures: a new series of original photographic views of Melbourne with a full description of each illustration and a concise statistical account of the Colony of Victoria as it was and as it is / compiled and published by H. Perkins and Co. Melbourne, [n.d.]. Ill.
GB/A.381. m137.

Mellom rein og varg / Thorfinn Solberg. 5. tusen. Oslo, 1942. Map.
GB/A.1860. m138.

Mementoes, historical and classical, of a tour through part of France, Switzerland, and Italy, in the years 1821 and 1822. London, 1824. 2v.
GB/A.530-1. m139.

A **memoir** of Felix Neff, pastor of the High Alps; and of his labours among the French Protestants of Dauphiné / William Stephen Gilly. 3rd ed. London, 1833. Map.
Lloyd.206; Lloyd.206A. m140.

Mémoire historique sur la vie et les écrits de Horace Bénédict de Saussure, pour servir d'introduction à la lecture de ses ouvrages / Jean Senebier. Genève, [1801].
GB.386; GB.1312(30); Lloyd.1603(7). m141.

Mémoire sur les groupes du Cantal, du Mont-Dore, et sur les soulèvemens auxquels ces montagnes doivent leur relief actuel / M. Dufrenoy et Elie de Beaumont. Paris, 1833. Maps. Extrait des *Annales des mines*, sér.3 tom.3.
GB.1315(6). m142.

Mémoires de la Société royale académique de Savoie. Tom.10. Chambéry, 1841.
GB/A.424(2). m143.

Mémoires et lettres sur la guerre de la Valteline / Henri, duc de Rohan; publiés & accompagnés de notes par M. le baron de Zur-Lauben. Genève, 1758. 3v.
GB/A.664-6. m144.

Mémoires et voyages, ou Lettres écrites à diverses époques, pendant des courses en Suisse, en Calabre, en Angleterre, et en Ecosse / M. de Custine. Paris, 1830. 2v.
GB/A.633-4. m145.

Memoirs / Benvenuto Cellini; translated by Thomas Roscoe. London, 1903. [Unit library; 24.] Translated from *Vita di Benvenuto Cellini*.
GB.114. m146.

Memoirs of a mountaineer: Helvellyn to Himalaya, and Lhasa: the holy city / F. Spencer Chapman. London, 1945. Ill., ports.
GB.323. m147.

Memoirs of a mountaineer: Helvellyn to Himalaya, and Lhasa: the holy city / F. Spencer Chapman. London, 1951. Ill., ports.
GB.536. m148.

Memoirs of Hans Hendrik, the Arctic traveller, serving under Kane, Hayes, Hall and Nares, 1853-76 / written by himself; translated from the Eskimo language by Henry Rink; edited by George Stephens. London, 1878.
GB/A.2175. m149.

Memoirs of the life of Andrew Hofer: containing an account of the transactions in the Tyrol during the year 1809 / taken from the German [of Joseph Hormayr] by Charles Henry Hall. London, 1820. Map., port.
Lloyd.1206. m150.

Memoria sobre los trabajos de perforación del túnel de los Alpes / José Echegaray, Manuel Pardo, Luis Vasconi. Madrid, 1863. Ill.
GB/B.416. m151.

Memoriale del geografo, ossia Dizionario universale compendiato di geografia antica e moderna, astronomico, fisico e politico / Giuseppe Carraro. Firenze, 1884.
GB/A.637. m152.

Memorials of a tour on the Continent: to which are added miscellaneous poems / Robert Snow. London, 1845.
GB.391; Lloyd.657.   m153.

Memorials of Henry Douglas Freshfield. [N.p.], 1892. Ports., facsim.
Lloyd.894.   m154.

Memorie / Società Geografica Italiana. Vol.5-9. Roma, 1895-99.
GB/A.604-8.   m155.

Memorie della corte di Mattarella o sia del Borgo di Duomo d'Ossola e sua giurisdizione / Giovanni Capis. 2a ristampa. Domodossola, 1968.
GB/A.1056.   m156.

Memorie storiche della città di Fossano / Giuseppe Muratori. Torino, [1972]. Facsimile reprint of the Turin, 1787 ed.
GB/B.385.   m157.

Memorie storiche di Borgomanero e del suo mandamento / Vincenzo De-Vit. [2nd ed., rev. and repr.] Torino, 1974. Facsimile reprint of the Prato, 1880 ed.
GB/A.1575.   m158.

Memories: from Philadelphia to Charlestown, Maryland via Nome, Alaska / Louis H. Eisenlohr, Riley Wilson. Philadelphia, 1918. Ill., ports., facsims.
GB/A.1773.   m159.

Memories of a long life / T.G. Bonney. Cambridge, 1921.
Lloyd.919.   m160.

A **memory** of the Mischabel: the Täsch-Horn by the south face / Geoffrey Winthrop Young. London, 1920. Pp.737-57 of the *Cornhill Magazine*, N.S., vol.48.
GB.1881(51).   m161.

Memsahb in Himalaja / Hettie Dyhrenfurth. Leipzig, 1931. Ill., ports.
GB.537.   m162.

Men against the clouds: the conquest of Minya Konka / Richard L. Burdsall, Arthur B. Emmons, with contributions by Terris Moore and Jack Theodore Young. London, 1935. Ill., maps.
GB.765.   m163.

Men against the clouds: the conquest of Minya Konka / Richard L. Burdsall, Arthur B. Emmons,

with contributions by Terris Moore and Jack Theodore Young. Rev. ed. Seattle, 1980. Ill., maps.
GB/A.1791(6).   m164.

The **men** at Cary Castle: a series of portrait sketches of the Lieutenant-Governors of British Columbia from 1871 to 1971 / S.W. Jackman. Victoria, B.C., 1972. Ill.
GB/A.2146.   m165.

Men, books and mountains: essays / Leslie Stephen; collected, and with an introduction, by S.O.A. Ullman. London, 1956.
GB.821.   m166.

Men, women and mountains: days in the Alps and Pyrenees / Claud Schuster. London, 1931.
GB.1137.   m167.

Der **Mensch** am Berg: von der Freude, dem Kampf und der Kameradschaft der Bergsteiger: ein Bildbericht / Hans Franz mit Wörtern von Kurt Maix. München, [1935].
GB.1034.   m168.

Der **Mensch** auf den Hochalpen: Forschungen / Angelo Mosso. Leipzig, 1899. Ill. Translated from *Fisiologia dell'uomo sulle Alpi*.
GB/A.103.   m169.

Der **Mensch** und die Berge: eine Weltgeschichte des Alpinismus / Karl Ziak. 2. neu bearb. Aufl. Salzburg, [1956]. Ill.
GB/A.208.   m170.

Menschen am Matterhorn / Walter Schmid. 3. Aufl. Bern, 1966. Ill., maps.
GB/A.377.   m171.

Menschen der Berge / Hans Leifhelm. Graz, [1936]. Ill. [Die deutschen Bergbücher; 5.]
GB/A.448.   m172.

Menschen im Hochgebirge: Festgabe für Hans Pfann zum 60. Geburtstage, 4. August 1933 / bearbeitet von Hans Baumeister; herausgegeben von der Sektion Bayerland des Deutschen und Osterreichischen Alpenvereins. München, 1933. Ill., ports.
GB.1142.   m173.

[**Menu** cards for the annual dinners of the Scottish Mountaineering Club, the Alpine Club, and other organizations, 1896-1962.] [N.p., 1896-1962.]
GB.1330(11).   m174.

La **mer** libre du pôle: voyage de découvertes dans les arctiques exécuté en 1860-1861 / J. J. Hayes; traduit par Ferdinand de Lanoye. Paris, 1868. Ill., maps. Translated from *Open polar sea*.
GB/A.1632. m175.

Merano e il Meranese con la Passiria e la Val d'Ultimo / Felice Nunziata. Trento, 1939. Maps. [Collana di piccole guide locali dell'Alto Adige; 4.]
GB/A.9. m176.

The **'Meraviglie'** / Matthew Moggridge; read before the International Prehistoric Congress, August 1868. London, 1868. Ill.
Lloyd.846. m177.

Meravigliose storie vere di solidarietà alpina: antologia internazionale / Sandro Prada presenta. Milano, 1967. Ill.
GB/A.1371. m178.

A **merchant's** holiday, or A rapid journey over the Alps and Apennines to the battle-fields of Italy, and the cities of Rome and Naples / [James Monteith?]. London, 1861.
GB.550; Lloyd.789. m179.

The **Merchants'** Magazine and Commercial Review. Vol.3, July 1840. New York, 1840. Contains: *Discovery of the Northwest Passage: Dease and Simpson's Arctic land expedition*.
GB/A.1791(3). m180.

Mercurius helveticus: fürstellend die denk- und schauwürdigsten vornemsten Sachen und Seltsamkeiten der Eidgnossschaft / J. Jacob Wagner. Zürich, 1701. Ill.
GB/A.669. m181.

Meroplankton in Jørgen Brønland Fjord, north Greenland / Ole G. Norden Andersen. Copenhagen, 1984. Ill. [Meddelelser om Grønland. Bioscience; 12.] Contribution from the Danish Peary Land Expeditions, leader: Eigil Knuth.
GB/A.1819(12). m182.

Les **merveilles** de la Suisse: tourisme: I. Le Valais / Ed. Vittoz. Lausanne, [ca 1925]. 24v; ill.
Lloyd.1262. m183.

Merveilles, Tende, Gordolasque / Vincent Paschetta. 7e éd. Grenoble, 1973-74. Ill. [Guide Paschetta des Alpes-Maritimes. 2: Randonnées et alpinisme; vol.a.]
GB/A.1350(10). m184.

Merveilles, Tende, Gordolasque / Vincent Paschetta. 11e éd. Grenoble, 1978. Ill. [Guide Paschetta des Alpes-Maritimes. 2: Randonnées et alpinisme.]
GB/A.1911(10). m185.

Mes aventures alpines / Geoffrey Winthrop Young; traduit de l'anglais par Bernard Lemoine. Neuchâtel, [1926]. [Montagne.]
GB/A.167. m186.

Mes deux courses dans le champ d'excursions / W.A.B. Coolidge. [Bern, 1901.] Extrait de l'*Annuaire du Club alpin suisse*, année 36.
GB.1340(50). m187.

Mes escalades dans les Alpes et le Caucase / A.F. Mummery; traduit par Maurice Paillon. Paris, [1903]. Ill., maps, port. Translated from *My climbs in the Alps and Caucasus*.
Lloyd.1620(15). m188.

Mes étapes d'alpinisme / Charles Lefebure. 2e éd. Paris, 1904. Ill., ports. Published by the Club alpin français.
GB.1181; GB.1208. m189.

Mesozoic rocks and crystalline schists in the Lepontine Alps / T.G. Bonney. [N.p., 1894.] From the *Quarterly Journal of the Geographical Society* for August 1894, vol.1.
GB/A.514(10). m190.

Mesures hypsométriques dans les Alpes exécutées à l'aide du baromètre / E. Plantamour. Genève, 1860. Extrait des *Mémoires de la Société de physique et d'histoire naturelle de Genève*, tom.15 pt.2.
GB.1336(35). m191.

Meteora Felsen / Dietrich Hasse, Heinz Lothar Stutte. München, 1977. Ill., maps. [Wander- und Kletterführer; 1.]
GB/A.2018(12). m192.

Meteoritic iron, telluric iron and wrought iron in Greenland / Vagn Fabritius Buchwald, Gert Mosdal. Copenhagen, 1981. [Meddelelser om Grønland. Man & society; 9.]
GB/A.1820/9. m193.

Eine **Methode** zur flächendeckenden Kartierung von Schneehöhen unter Berück sichtigung von reliefbedingten Einflüssen / Urs Witmer. Bern, 1984. [Geographica bernensia; G21.]
GB/B.651. m194.

Mezzo secolo d'alpinismo / Tita Piaz. 3a ed. Bologna, 1952. Ill., port. [Le Alpi; 1.]
GB.1323(3).   m195.

La **mia** vita nel lavoro, per la musica, sui monti / Giulio Kugy; traduzione di Ervino Pocar. Bologna, 1969. Translated from *Arbeit, Musik, Berge: ein Leben*.
GB/A.945.   m196.

Michel Gabriel Paccard und der Montblanc / Karl Egger. Basel, 1943. Ill., ports., facsims.
Lloyd.828; GB.1315(16-7) (positive and negative photolithographic copies of pp.84-9); GB.1315(18) (positive photolithographic copy of pp.84-9).
                                               m197.

Midst Himalayan mists / R.J. Minney. Calcutta, 1920.
GB.741.   m198.

A **midsummer** ramble in the Dolomites / Amelia B. Edwards. 2nd ed. London, [1889]. Ill., map.
GB/A.1545.   m199.

Mid-winter on an Alpine peak / Mrs. Aubrey Le Blond. [London, 1904.] Ill. Pp.[19]-25 of the *Badminton Magazine*, Jan. 1904.
GB.1332(31).   m200.

Le **mie** montagne / Walter Bonatti. Bologna, [1962]. Ill.
GB.998.   m201.

Le **mie** scalate nelle Alpi e nel Caucaso / A.F. Mummery; traduzione di Adolfo Balliano. Torino, 1965. Ill. [La piccozza e la penna; ser.3 no.2.] Translated from *My climbs in the Alps and Caucasus*.
GB/B.338(1).   m202.

I **miei** viaggi nella Terra del Fuoco / Alberto M. De Agostini. Torino, [1923]. Ill., maps.
GB/B.284.   m203.

The **military** operations at Cabul, which ended in the retreat and destruction of the British Army, January 1842: with a journal of imprisonment in Afghanistan / Vincent Eyre. 3rd ed. London, 1843. Map.
GB.522.   m204.

Min Grönlandstripp / Robert af Klinteberg. Stockholm, 1969. Ill., map.
GB/B.524(4).   m205.

Mineralogische Bemerkungen von den Karpathen / Johann Ehrenreich von Fichtel. Wien, 1791. 2v (in 1); map.
GB/A.2123.   m206.

Mineralogy of the Werner Bjerge alkaline complex, east Greenland / C. Kent Brooks [et al.]. Copenhagen, 1982. Ill., maps. [Meddelelser om Grønland. Geoscience; 7.]
GB/A.1818.   m207.

Le **miniere**: un tempo in efficienza nella Vallata Zoldana / Antonio Balestra. [N.p, n.d.] Facsimile reprint of the Vicenza, 1934 ed.
GB/A.455(7[2]).   m208.

Minimus in altis: autour du Mont-Blanc: étapes de la caravane minimoise août 1882 / Pierre Bauron. Lyon, 1883. Ill.
GB.781.   m209.

The **mint**: a day-book of the R.A.F. Depot between August and December 1922, with later notes / 352087 A/C Ross [T.E. Lawrence]. London, 1955.
GB.1170.   m210.

Minutes of a committee meeting of the Royal Air Force Mountaineering Association, 24th November 1950. [London, 1950.] With Minutes of the Annual General Meeting, 24th November, 1961.
GB.1331(37).   m211.

Minutes of the seventieth Annual General Meeting of the Scottish Mountaineering Club, December 6th, 1958. [Edinburgh], 1958.
GB.1331(32).   m212.

Mirabilia, or The wonders of nature and art: comprising upwards of three hundred of the most remarkable curiosities and phenomena in the known world: with an appendix: selected from the researches of eminent travellers, historians, and naturalists / Joseph Taylor. London, 1829. Ill.
GB.275.   m213.

The **Mirror** of Literature, Amusement, and Instruction. Vol.38. London, 1841.
GB.620.   m214.

[**Miscellaneous** notices of lectures and dinners held in honour of the Mount Everest Expedition, 1921.] [London, 1921-22.]
GB.1319(18-21).   m215.

Miscellaneous observations and opinions on the Continent / by the author of *The Life of*

Michelangelo [i.e. Richard Duppa]. London, 1825. Ill.
GB.848.   m216.

Miscellaneous verses and sonnets / R.E. Egerton Warburton. London, 1859.
Lloyd.253.   m217.

The **miscellany**: a book for the field or the fireside: amusing tales and sketches / Albert Smith. London, 1850.
Lloyd.1616(13).   m218.

A **missing** page in Alpine history / Richard J.F. Edgcumbe. London, 1893. Pp.249-57 of the *National Review*, October 1893.
GB.1880(25).   m219.

Missionary travels and researches in South Africa: including a sketch of sixteen years' residence in the interior of Africa / David Livingstone. London, 1857. Ill., maps, port.
GB.988.   m220.

Mit Byrd zum Südpol / Paul Siple; Übersetzung von Felix Beran. Zürich, 1933. Ill. [Was Jungens erzählen; 15.] Translated from *A boy scout with Byrd*.
GB/A.1626.   m221.

Mit glücklichen Augen: aus den Aufzeichnungen eines romantischen Bergsteigers / Walter Pause. 2. Aufl. [Munich], 1949. Ill.
GB/A.429.   m222.

Mitglieder-Verzeichnis / Schweizer Alpenclub, Sektion Bern. Februar 1905. Bern, 1905.
Lloyd.1617(11).   m223.

Mitteilungen / Deutscher und Osterreichischer Alpenverein. N.F. Bd.1-27, 1885-1911. München, 1885-1911. Ill.
GB/B.543.   m224.

Mitteilungen des Deutschen Alpenvereins. Jahrg. 1938 Folge 1-12, N.F. Jahrg.1 Hft.8. München, 1938-49. Wanting Jahrg.1938 Folge 2,3,8.
GB.1644(30-9).   m225.

Mitteilungen-Jugend am Berg / Deutscher Alpenverein. Jahrg.20-25, 1968-73. München, 1968-73. Ill., maps.
GB/B.288(1-12), GB/A.2071.   m226.

Mittheilungen des Oesterreichischen Alpen-Vereines / redigirt von Edmund v. Mojsisovics,

Paul Grohmann. Vienna, 1863-64. 2v; ill.
Lloyd.368-9.   m227.

La **mode** de formation et le régime des lacs suisses en général et de quelques petits lacs en particulier / Léon W. Collet. Genève, 1916. Extrait du *Globe*, tom.55.
Lloyd.1624(5).   m228.

Modèle qui offre la restauration du Colisée de Rome tel qu'il étoit originairement; de la soixantième partie de la réalité mesure linéaire / commencé par Charles Lucangeli et terminé par Paul Dalbono. Rome, 1815.
Lloyd.1578(3).   m229.

Modern antiquities: comprising sketches of early Buffalo and the Great Lakes: also sketches of Alaska / Barton Atkins. Buffalo, 1898. Ill.
GB/A.1723.   m230.

Modern mountaineering / [C.T. Dent]. [Edinburgh, 1897.] Pp.33-59 of the *Edinburgh Review*, July 1897.
GB.1881(21).   m231.

Modern mountaineering / George D. Abraham. London, 1933. Ill.
GB.332.   m232.

Modern painters / John Ruskin. Vol.4: Of mountain beauty. London, 1856.
GB.1232.   m233.

Modern painters / John Ruskin. Vol.4: Of mountain beauty. 2nd ed. London, 1868.
GB.1233.   m234.

Moderne arktisk forskning / Gunnar Seidenfaden. København, 1938. Ill., maps, ports.
GB/A.1877.   m235.

Les **moeurs** genevoises de 1700 à 1760, d'après tous les documents officiels / Charles du Bois-Melly. 2e. éd. augm. Genève, 1882.
Lloyd.413.   m236.

Moir's guide book to the tramping tracks and routes of the Great Southern Lakes and fiords of Otago and Southland. 5th ed. / edited by Lawrence D. Kennedy, Gerald Hall-Jones. Wellington, 1979-84. 2v; ill., maps, ports. Published by the New Zealand Alpine Club.
GB/B.635(1-2).   m237.

Un **mois** dans les Alpes de Genève à Nice / Albert Dauzat. Paris, [1922]. Ill., maps.
GB/A.1173.   m238.

Un **mois** de voyage en Suisse pour 200 francs, donnant tous les renseignements nécessaires au voyageur en Suisse / Adolphe Desbarrolles. Paris, 1840. Map.
GB/A.800(12).   m239.

Mon carnet de courses / André Roch. Lausanne, 1948. [Collection alpine; 8.]
GB.1307(8).   m240.

The **Monastery** of the Great St. Bernard / Etoile [i.e. Edward Mitchell]. [N.p., 1891.] Pp.[472]-7 of *Good Words*, July 1891.
GB/A.797(6).   m241.

Le **monde** des Alpes, ou Description pittoresque des montagnes de la Suisse, particulièrement des animaux qui les peuplent / F. de Tschudi. 2e éd. rev. et corr. par O. Bourrit. Bâle, 1870. Ill.
GB/A.1898.   m242.

Mondo alpino / Giotto Dainelli. Milano, 1930. Ill. *L'illustrazione italiana*, primavera 1930.
GB/C.58.   m243.

Monografia del terreno, Alta Durance, Drac, Drôme. Roma, 1881-83. 2v. At head of title: Corpo di Stato Maggiore.
GB/A.1966(5).   m244.

Monograph of the shallow-water starfishes of the North Pacific coast from the Arctic Ocean to California / Addison Emery Verrill. Washington, 1914. 2v; ill. [Harriman Alaska series; 14.] [Smithsonian Institution publication; 2140.]
GB/B.490-1.   m245.

Monsieur Dumollet sur le Mont-Blanc: les aventures surprenantes de Monsieur Dumollet (de Saint-Malo) durant son voyage de 1837 aux glacières de Savoie et d'Helvétie / extraites du cahier de ses mémoires, recueillies, annotées et corrigées par Samivel. Chamonix, 1972. Ill.
GB/B.389.   m246.

Le **Mont** Aiguille (2086m.) / Bernard Caillat. [N.p.], 1972. Ill.
GB/B.570(11).   m247.

Le '**Mont** Alban' / W.A.B. Coolidge. Lyon, 1911. Extrait de la *Revue alpine*, février 1911.
GB.1340(4).   m248.

Mont Blanc / Albert Smith. Edinburgh, 1852. Pp.35-55 of *Blackwood's Edinburgh Magazine*, vol.71 no.335.
Lloyd.1593(1).   m249.

Mont Blanc / Albert Smith. London, 1852.
GB.126; GB.278; GB.127 (impf.); Lloyd.258.
                                                                     m250.

Mont Blanc / Albert Smith; with a memoir of the author by Edmund Yates. London, [1860]. Ill. Originally published as *The story of Mont Blanc*.
GB.106; GB.133; Lloyd.154; Lloyd.166.   m251.

Der **Mont** Blanc / Hans Pfann. Wien, 1912. Ill., map. Pp.124-45 of the *Zeitschrift des Deutschen und Osterreichischen Alpenvereins*, Bd.43.
GB.1742.   m252.

Mont Blanc / J.D. [i.e. J. Dornford]. London, 1821. Pp.[451]-62, 505-[17] of the *New Monthly Magazine*, vol.1.
GB.1736(1).   m253.

Mont Blanc / Roger Tissot. London, [1924]. [The picture guides.]
GB.523.   m254.

Mont Blanc: a comedy, in three acts / Henry and Athol Mayhew; part of the plot derived from *Le voyage de M. Perrichon*, by MM. E. Labiche, E. Martin. London, 1874.
Lloyd.1604(3).   m255.

Mont Blanc: a part of Underwood and Underwood's stereoscopic tour through Switzerland / personally conducted by M.S. Emery. New York, [1902]. Ill., maps.
GB/A.1883(8).   m256.

Mont Blanc: a treatise on its geodesical and geological constitution: its transformations: and the ancient and recent state of its glaciers / Eugène Viollet-le-Duc; translated by B. Bucknall. London, 1877. Ill. Translated from *Le massif du Mont Blanc*.
GB.852: Lloyd.990.   m257.

Mont Blanc: an irregular lyric poem / Thomas Sedgwick Whalley. Bath, 1788.
Lloyd.1303.   m258.

Le **Mont** Blanc: ascensions d'hiver et d'été: études dans la haute montagne / Paul Güssfeldt; traduction de D. Delétra. Genève, 1899. Ill., map.
GB/A.1079.   m259.

Mont Blanc: attempts and ascents, 1762-1854. The ascent of Mont Blanc: a list of selected accounts in English, 1779-1853 / [T. Graham Brown]. [London, 1957.] Pp.433-60 of *The first ascent of Mont Blanc*, by T. Graham Brown and Sir Gavin de Beer.
GB.1075. m260.

[**Mont** Blanc: Brenva face, 1927-1928.] Paris, 1930. *Alpinisme*, no.18, 1930. Title supplied by T. Graham Brown.
GB.1254. m261.

Mont Blanc: Italian ode / translated into English verse by an Italian alpinist [i.e. Sebastiano Fenzi]. Firenze, 1879.
GB.1335(68); Lloyd.1616(3). m262.

Mont Blanc and its Aiguilles / William Cecil Slingsby. Burnley, [1893]. Extracts from a paper read before the Burnley Literary & Scientific Society, Nov. 1893.
GB.887; Lloyd.882. m263.

Mont Blanc and its glaciers. Edinburgh, [1854]. [Chambers's Repository of instructive and amusing tracts; 81.]
GB.349; GB.1335(65). m264.

Mont Blanc, and other poems / Mary Ann Browne. London, 1827.
GB.1067; Lloyd.1204; Lloyd.1204A. m265.

Mont Blanc and the Aiguilles / C. Douglas Milner. London, 1955. Ill., maps.
GB.1062. m266.

Mont Blanc and the valley of Chamonix: together with a short account of the vallies of Sixt, Samoens and St. Gervais, revised since the late fire of Chamonix / by a resident in the Alps. Geneva, 1855. Ill., map.
Lloyd.1613(22). m267.

Mont Blanc aux sept vallées / Roger Frison-Roche, Pierre Tairraz. [Paris], 1968. Ill., map. [Les beaux pays.]
GB/A.1294. m268.

Mont Blanc by the Brenva / R.W. Lloyd. [London], 1913. Ill. Reprinted from the *Alpine Journal*, May 1912.
Lloyd.1602(24). m269.

Le **Mont** Blanc, ou Description de la vue et des phénomènes que l'on peut apercevoir du sommet de Mont Blanc / A. Bravais. Paris, [1854]. Ill.
GB.147(1); GB.267. m270.

Mont Blanc sideshow: the life and times of Albert Smith / J. Monroe Thorington. Philadelphia, 1934. Ill., ports., facsims.
GB.975. m271.

Mont Blanc — Trélatête / Lucien Devies, Pierre Henry, Jacques Lagarde. Grenoble, [1946]. Ill. [Guide Vallot. La chaîne du Mont Blanc; 1.]
GB.92; GB/A.1813. m272.

Mont Blanc — Trélatête / Lucien Devies, Pierre Henry, Jacques Lagarde. 2e éd. Grenoble, 1951. Ill. [Guide Vallot. La chaîne du Mont Blanc; 1.]
GB.95. m273.

Mont Blanc — Trélatête / Lucien Devies, Pierre Henry. 3e éd. Paris, 1973. Ill. [Guide Vallot. La chaîne du Mont Blanc; 1.]
GB/A.1100. m274.

Mont Blanc — Trélatête / Lucien Devies, Pierre Henry. 4e éd. Paris, 1978. Ill. [Guide Vallot. La chaîne du Mont Blanc; 1.]
GB/A.2013/1. m275.

The **Mont** Blanc Twelfth Night characters: taken from Mr. Albert Smith's entertainment, *The ascent of Mont Blanc* / Albert Smith, Cuthbert Bede. [N.p., 1855?] Ill.
Lloyd.1624(3). m276.

Der **Mont** Blanc und seine Ersteigung von Courmayeur / W. Dechy. [Bern, 1878.] Pp.[181]-218 of the *Jahrbuch des Schweizer Alpenclub*, 1878.
GB.1880(26). m277.

Mont Blanc vom Brenvagletscher / Ludwig Hall. Frühjahrsskituren im Berner Oberland / Josef Dahinden. [N.p., n.d.] Ill. Pp.273-86 of an unidentified publication.
GB.1318(14). m278.

Le **Mont** Blanc vu par les écrivains et les alpinistes / choix de textes par Claire Eliane Engel. [Paris], 1965. Ill., ports. [Editions d'histoire et d'art.]
GB/B.528(8). m279.

For titles starting **Mont-Blanc**, see nos.m290-m303.2.

Mont Blank [sic] revisited / Wilfrid Noyce. [London], 1956. Pp.10-5 of *Mountaineering*, vol.2 no.9.
GB.1881(65). m280.

Mont Brouillard 4053 m., Punta Baretti 4026 m., Grandes Jorasses 4205 m., Punta Margherita 4066 m. / Karl Blodig. [Munich, 1928.] Pp.308-34 of his *Viertausenders*, 3rd ed.
GB.1881(42). m281.

Le Mont Cenis: ode à S.M. le roi de Piémont / Henri Derville. Souvenir du Mont Blanc / Jacques Balmat. Chambéry, 1858.
Lloyd.883. m282.

Le Mont Cenis et le Saint-Gothard / Louis Hymans. Verviers, [1884?]. [Bibliothèque Gilon.]
GB/A.801(9). m283.

Der Mont Cenis (Fréjus) / V. Barbier; übersetzt von J.H. Zürich, [1887?]. Ill., maps. [Europäische Wanderbilder; 117-20.]
GB/A.1351(9). m284.

Le Mont Cervin / Guido Rey; ouvrage traduit par L. Espinasse-Mongenet. 2e éd. rev. Paris, 1906. Ill. Translated from: *Il Monte Cervino*.
GB.264; GB/A.122. m285.

Le Mont Pelvoux: monographie historique; le Meije et ses noms divers / W.A.B. Coolidge. Grenoble, 1902. Extrait de l'*Annuaire de la Société des touristes du Dauphiné*, 1901.
GB.1340(9). m286.

Il Mont Pourri, m.3788, Alta Savoia: prima ascensione italiana / Giovanni Bobba. Torino, 1901. Estratto dalla *Rivista Mensile del C.A.I.*, vol.20 n.6, 1901.
GB/B.289(2). m287.

Le Mont Redessau dans l'histoire / W.A.B. Coolidge. Aoste, 1919. Extrait du *Bulletin de la Société de la flore valdôtaine*, n.13.
GB.1340(54). m288.

Mont Vélan e Grand Combin / Agostino Ferrari. [Turin, 1909.] Ill. Pp.[123]-78 of the *Bollettino del Club Alpino Italiano*, vol.40 n.73.
GB.1880(47). m289.

Le Mont-Blanc / Charles Durier. Paris, 1877. Ill., maps, ports., facsims.
GB.1184; Lloyd.1275. m290.

Le Mont-Blanc / Charles Durier. 3e éd. Paris, [1881]. Ill., maps, ports., facsims.
GB.1323(10). m291.

Le Mont-Blanc / Charles Durier. 4e éd. rev. et augm. Paris, 1897. Map.
Lloyd.265; Lloyd.265A. m292.

Le Mont-Blanc / Charles Durier. 8e éd., annotée et illustrée par Joseph Vallot et Charles Vallot. Paris, 1923. Ill.
GB.1316(13). m293.

Le Mont-Blanc: conférences faites devant la Société [scientifique et littéraire des instituteurs de France] / Maurice de Thierry. Paris, 1896.
Lloyd.1216. m294.

Der Mont-Blanc: Darstellung der Besteigung desselben am 31. Juli, 1. und 2. August 1859: ein Blick in die Eislandschaften der europäischen Hochalpen / Wilhelm Pitschner. 2. Aufl. Genf, 1864. Ill.
GB.1096 (impf.); Lloyd.1242 (impf.). m295.

Le Mont-Blanc: deuxième ascension scientifique de M. W. Pitschner du 30 août au 16 septembre 1861: relation sommaire / vicomte Camille de Catelin; publiée par les soins de la Compagnie des guides de Chamonix. Annecy, 1861.
Lloyd.1602(5). m296.

Mont-Blanc: jardin féerique / Gaston Rébuffat. [Paris], 1962. Ill., ports., facsims.
GB.1153. m297.

Mont-Blanc: première ascension par l'arête de l'Innominata / Giuseppe F. Gugliermina. Bern, 1923. Ill. Pp.[147]-53 of *Alpina*, Jahrg.31 Nr.6.
GB.1881(37). m298.

Le Mont-Blanc: route classique et voies nouvelles / Claire Eliane Engel. Neuchâtel, [1939]. Ill.
GB.1320(8). m299.

Le Mont-Blanc: route classique et voies nouvelles / Claire Eliane Engel. Ed. rev. et augm. Neuchâtel, 1946. Ill. [Montagne.]
GB.1309(5); GB.1310(3). m300.

Le Mont-Blanc (4,807m.) / Gilbert Robino. 2e éd. [N.p.], 1973. Ill.
GB/B.570(14). m301.

Le Mont-Blanc aérien / Georges René Albert Benoist, F. Seive. Grenoble, [1935?]. Ill.
GB/B.368. m302.

Le Mont-Blanc de près et de loin / Daniel Baud-Bovy. Grenoble, [1903.] Ill.
GB.1331(48). m303.

Le **Mont-Blanc** et le col du Géant / Horace Bénédict de Saussure; annoté par E. Gaillard et Henry F. Montagnier. Lyon, 1927. Ill.
GB.1331(47); Lloyd.1595(2).   m303.1.

Le **Mont-Blanc** jadis, aujourd'hui / éd. réalisée par Chantal et Jean-Jacques Mallaret, Hyacinthe Vulliez. Paris, 1977. Ill.
GB/A.1597(1).   m303.2.

The **Montafun**. [London, 1886.] Pp.282-93 of the *Cornhill Magazine*, vol.7, Sept.1886.
GB.1881(55).   m304.

La **montagna** / Carla Garello Guarisco. Torino, 1967. [ZUM; 2.]
GB/A.1964(11).   m305.

La **montagna** / Maurice Zermatten. Scuole svizzere di alpinismo / Michel Vaucher; traduzione italiana di Carlo Calgari. Zurigo, 1968. Ill. Published by the Ufficio Nazionale Svizzero del Turismo.
GB/B.377(34).   m306.

Montagna: atti di 6 tavole rotonde e 215 film / G. Tonella, G. Grassi. Trento, 1971. Ill.
GB/A.1321.   m307.

Montagna: fonte di gioia e di vita, scuola d'altruismo e di bontà: impressioni e ricordi di un alpinista / Bartolomeo Figari. Bologna, 1956.
GB/B.289(26).   m308.

Montagna: G.I.S.M. annuario. 1963,1965,1969-70/71. Lecco, 1964-71. Published by the Gruppo Italiano Scrittori di Montagna.
GB/B.312(13-6).   m309.

La **montagna**: nelle sue modificazioni, nella sua vita e nella sua importanza di fronte all'economia della terra e della società / Virgilio Monti. Milano, [1913?]. Ill. [Biblioteca popolare di coltura; 9.]
GB/A.1468(13).   m310.

Montagna: una parola magica / Tito Livraghi. Bologna, 1971. Ill.
GB/A.942(7).   m311.

La **montagna** a mani nude / René Desmaison; traduzione di Giancarlo Barberis. [Milan], 1972. Translated from *La montagne à mains nues*.
GB/A.995(3).   m312.

La **montagna** bolognese del medio evo / Arturo Palmieri. Bologna, [1972]. Facsimile reprint of the Bologna, 1929 ed.
GB/A.1300.   m313.

La **montagna** del Bolognese: tra le valli del Samoggia e dell'Idice / Natale Calanchi [et al.]; coordinamento editoriale di Renzo Renzi. Bologna, [1980?]. Ill.
GB/A.2023(10).   m314.

La **montagna** è là: breve storia dell'alpinismo / G.C. Zuccarelli. Torino, [1960].
GB/A.500.   m315.

La **montagna** e le sue risorse terapeutiche / Plinio Schivardi. Milano, [ca 1870].
GB/A.516(1).   m316.

La **montagna** è una parte di me / Pierre Mazeaud; traduzione di Spiro Dalla Porta Xidias. Bologna, [1967]. Ill., ports. [Voci dai monti; 12.]
GB/A.853.   m317.

La **montagna** nei manifesti e nei francobolli di ieri e di oggi: mostra internazionale, Treviso, Salone di Trecento, 29 aprile-7 maggio 1967 / [organizzazione generale della mostra, Giuseppe Mazzotti]. Treviso, 1967. Ill.
GB/A.1350(11).   m318.

La **montagna** nella pittura / Ulrich Christoffel; traduzione del dott. Giuseppe Curonici. Berna, 1963. Ill. Translated from *Der Berg in der Malerei*. Published by the Schweizer Alpenclub.
GB/A.997.   m319.

La **montagna** non ha voluto / A. de Saint Loup; traduzione di E. Cozzani. Milano, 1950. [Montagna; 27.] Translated from *La montagne n'a pas voulu*.
GB/A.551.   m320.

La **montagna** parlò al cuore / Luigi Bianchi. Lecco, 1971. Ill.
GB/A.836(10).   m321.

Montagna poca / Franco Brevini. Milano, 1972. Ill. [Quaderni alpini; 1.]
GB/B.366(5).   m322.

La **montagna** veronese nella poesia / Gianni Faè. Verona, 1973.
GB/A.1115(7).   m323.

Montagna viva / Lina Castelli. Torino, 1941.
GB/A.1034(14).   m324.

Montagnards / Pierre Mélon. Lyon, 1949. Ill. [Vertige.]
GB/A.1156. m325.

Les **montagnards** de la nuit: roman / Roger Frison-Roche. Paris, 1968.
GB/A.987(5). m326.

Montagne / Andrée Martignon. 12e éd. Paris, 1930. [Livres de nature; 14.]
GB/A.1468(7). m327.

La **montagne** / J. Michelet. 3e éd. Paris, 1868.
GB/A.1362. m328.

La **montagne** / J. Michelet. Paris, 1885. Ill. [Petite bibliothèque Charpentier.]
GB.6. m329.

La **montagne** / ouvrage publié sous la direction de Maurice Herzog; avec la collaboration de Pierre Courthion [et al.]. Paris, 1956. Ill.
GB/B.19. m330.

La **montagne** / Roger Canac. Paris, 1968. [Peuple et culture.]
GB/A.434(6). m331.

Montagne / Roger Frison-Roche, Pierre Tairraz. Paris, 1975. Ill.
GB/B.418. m332.

La **montagne**: revue mensuelle du Club alpin francais. No.151-366. Paris, 1933-54. Continued by *La montagne et alpinisme* (m346).
GB.1609-24 (1933-54) (impf.); Lloyd.1415-28 (no.151-339) (impf.). m333.

La **montagne**: roman / Jean Claude Fontanet. Paris, 1970.
GB/A.1308. m334.

La **montagne** à mains nues / René Desmaison. Paris, 1971. Ill.
GB/A.1292. m335.

La **montagne** à travers les âges: rôle joué par elle: façon dont elle a été vue / John Grand-Carteret. Grenoble, 1903-04. 2v; ill., maps, ports., facsims.
Lloyd.1491-2. m336.

La **montagne** à travers les livres: Bibliothèque de Grenoble, février-avril 1976. [Grenoble, 1976.]
GB/B.528(15). m337.

La **montagne** aux écritures / Frison-Roche. [Paris], 1970. Ill. [Bivouacs sous la lune.]
GB/A.988(1). m338.

Montagne bianche e uomini rossi: diario della spedizione al Caucaso organizzata dalla Sezione di Trieste del Club Alpino Italiano nel 1929 / Andrea Pollitzer de Pollenghi. Milano, 1932. Ill., maps.
GB/A.1132. m339.

La **montagne** des autres: alpinisme en pays kurde / Bernard Amy. [Paris], 1972. Ill., maps.
GB/A.987(3). m340.

Montagne di Groenlandia: monografia storico-esplorativa e geografico-alpinistica / Mario Fantin. Bologna, 1969. Ill., maps. [Collana CISDAE.] Published by the Centro Italiano Studio Documentazione Alpinismo Extra-europeo.
GB/B.318; GB/B.613. m341.

Le **montagne** di Lecco / Riccardo Cassin, Annibale Rota. Lecco, 1981. Ill.
GB/B.558. m342.

La '**montagne**' du Cenis: profil de l'ancien chemin muletier par le col du Grand Mont Cenis: documents et cartes inédits, notes, photographies / M.A. de Lavis-Trafford. Saint-Jean-de-Maurienne, [1956]. Ill. Extrait des *Mémoires et documents de la Société savoisienne d'histoire et d'archéologie*, tom.77, 1952-54, p.107-22, 1956.
GB/A.836(4). m343.

Montagne e valli incantate / Aurelio Garobbio. [Rocca San Casciano, 1963.] Ill. [Le Alpi.]
GB/A.842. m344.

Montagne — e volontà: diario alpinistico / Angelo Ursella; a cura di Beppe e Italo Zandonella; [revisione generale del testo, Marcello Rossi]. 2a ed. Crocetta del Montello, 1973. Ill.
GB/A.1291. m345.

La **montagne** et alpinisme: revue du Club alpin français et du Groupe de haute montagne. No. 17,44, avril 1958, oct.1963. Paris, 1958-63. Continues *La montagne* (m333).
GB.1625-6. m346.

La **montagne** et l'homme / Georges Sonnier. Paris, 1970. Ill.
GB/A.877. m347.

Montagne meravigliose / Severino Casara. Bologna, [1965]. Ill. [Voci dai monti; 4.]
GB/A.846. m348.

Montagne pour un homme nu / Pierre Mazeaud. [Grenoble], 1971. Ill. [Sempervivum; 52.]
GB/A.995(1).   m349.

Les **montagnes** / Albert Dupaigne. 5e éd. Tours, 1883. Ill., maps.
GB/A.102.   m350.

Montagnes: la vie aux hautes altitudes / Henri Gaussen, Paul Barruel. Paris, 1955. Ill. [La nature vivante; 5.]
GB/B.153.   m351.

Montagnes arides du Wakhan / Henri Agresti [et al.]. [N.p., 1970.] Ill., maps.
GB/B.288(19).   m352.

Les **montagnes** de la terre / Roger Frison-Roche. Paris, [1964]. 2v; ill.
GB/B.280-1.   m353.

Les **montagnes** du monde / publié par la Fondation suisse pour l'exploration alpine. Vol. 1-2. Zürich, 1946-47.
GB.1330(6-7).   m354.

Montagnes héroiques: histoire de l'alpinisme / Aimé Michel. [N.p.], 1953.
GB/A.2200.   m355.

Montagnes, ma vie / Giusto Gervasutti. Nouv. éd. Genève, 1978. Ill., maps. [Les Alpes et les hommes; 3,] Translated from *Scalate nelle Alpi*.
GB/A.1607.   m356.

Montagnes Pyrénées / Jean Louis Pérès, Jean Ubiergo. [Paris], 1973. Ill., maps.
GB/A.1128.   m357.

'**Montagnes** valdôtaines, vous êtes mes amours': storia di una vacazione / Giuseppe Mazzotti. Treviso, 1951. [Biblioteca alpina; 5.]
GB/A.1295(11).   m358.

Les **montagnes** vues par les géographes et les naturalistes de langue française au XVIIIe siècle / Numa Broc. Paris, 1969. [Comité des travaux historiques et scientifiques. Mémoires de la Section de géographie; 4.]
GB/B.312(5).   m359.

Montanaia / Spiro Dalla Porta Xidias. Bologna, 1957. Ill. [Il semprevivo; 4.]
GB/A.995(4).   m360.

Las **montañas** / Lorus J. Milne, Margery Milne, los redactores de *Life* en español. Mexico City,

1963. Translated from *The mountains*.
GB/B.599.   m361.

Der **Montblanc**: Studien im Hochgebirge, vornehmlich in der Montblanc-Gruppe / Paul Güssfeldt. Berlin, 1894. Ill., map.
GB.1095; Lloyd.1210.   m362.

Der **Montblanc**: zur Erinnerung an seine erste Ersteigung vor 150 Jahren / Wilhelm Lohmüller. [Munich, 1936.] Ill. Pp.4-10 of *Der Bergsteiger*, vol.7 no.1, Oct.1936.
GB.1338(21).   m363.

Montblanc-Gruppe: die beliebtesten und schwierigsten Anstiege auf die wichtigsten Gipfel der Montblanc-Gruppe / Franz Königer. 5., verb. Aufl. München, 1967. Published by the Deutscher Alpenverein, Sektion Bayerland.
GB/A.942(17).   m364.

Monte Api '78: spedizione alpinistico-scientifica nell'Himalaya del Nepal della Scuola Nazionale di Alpinismo 'Agostino Pallavicini' del Club Alpino Italiano, Sezione di Milano / Alberto Bianchi [et al.]; col patrocinio del Comune di Milano e del Club Alpino Italiano, Sezione di Milano. Milano, 1981. Ill., maps.
GB/A.2022(4).   m365.

Il **Monte** Baldo / Eugenio Turri. Verona, 1971. Ill.
GB/A.1302.   m366.

Il **Monte** Baldo / Vincenzo Chiappini. Verona, 1956. Ill., maps. [Le guide; 40.]
GB/A.1295(17).   m367.

Monte Bego: storia di una montagna / Enzo Bernardini. Bordighera, 1971. Ill.
GB/B.290(6).   m368.

Il **Monte** Bianco / Piero Ghiglione. Novara, 1947. Ill. [Le grandi montagne.] Published by the Istituto Geografico De Agostini.
GB.1334(27).   m369.

Monte Bianco / Renato Chabod [et al.]. Milano, 1968-74. 2v; ill., maps. [Guida dei monti d'Italia.]
GB/A.1946.   m370.

Il **Monte** Bianco: ai piedi del gigante / Giotto Dainelli. Torino, 1926. Ill., map.
GB.1322(15).   m371.

Monte Bianco: ascensione del Colle del Gigante per il M. Blanc du Tacul — vetta — ed il M. Maudit — épaule / Adolfo Hess. Torino, 1898.

Pp.[1]-15 of the *Rivista Mensile del Club Alpino Italiano*, vol.17 no.1.
GB.1881(16). m372.

Il **Monte** Bianco: antologia / Alfonso Bernardi. Bologna, 1965-66. 2v; ill. [Montagne; 4-5.]
GB/A.134-5. m373.

Il **Monte** Bianco esplorato 1760-1948: notizie storico-alpinistiche e relazioni originali dei primi salitori / Giuseppe F. Gugliermina. Bologna, [1973]. Ill.
GB/B.380. m374.

Il **Monte** Cervino / Guido Rey; nota geologica di Vittorio Novarese. Milano, 1904. Ill.
GB.1334(1). m375.

Monte Civetta: guida turistico-alpinistica / Vincenzo Dal Bianco. Padova, 1956. Ill., maps.
GB/A.1029. m376.

Monte Ortigara: guida a un campo di battaglia / Gianni Pieropan. Cortina d'Ampezzo, 1979. Ill., map.
GB/A.2018(9). m377.

Monte Pasubio: guida sentieri, segnavia, rifugi. 2a ed. Vicenza, 1964. Ill. Published by the Federazione Italiana Escursionismo.
GB/A.1034(10). m378.

Monte Piana: storia, escursioni e paesaggio: museo all'aperto degli anni 1915-1917 / Walther Schaumann; traduzione a cura di Carlo Milesi. Cortina, 1978. Ill., maps.
GB/A.2019(6). m379.

Il **Monte** Rosa / Franco Fini. Bologna, 1983. Ill.
GB/B.577. m380.

Monte Rosa / S. Saglio, F. Boffa. Milan, 1960. Ill. Published by the Club Alpino Italiano and the Touring Club Italiano.
GB/A.774. m381.

Monte Rosa 1865-1965. Sion, 1965. Ill. Published by the Schweizer Alpenclub, Sektion Monte Rosa.
GB/A.1330. m382.

Il **Monte** Rosa al XVIII secolo / W.A.B. Coolidge. Torino, 1907. Ill. Estratto dalla *Rivista Mensile del C.A.I.*, vol.26 n.4, 1907.
GB.1340(17). m383.

Monte Rosa & Gressoney / Vittorio Sella, Domenico Vallino. Biella, [1890]. Ill.
GB/A.914. m384.

Monte Rosa e Gressoney / V. Sella, D. Vallino. Ivrea, 1983.
GB/B.624. m385.

Eine **Monte** Rosa-Uberschreitung / George Ingle Finch. Bern, 1920. Ill. Pp.[30]-40 of the *Jahrbuch des Schweizer Alpenclub*, 1919.
GB.1229(2). m386.

Der **Monte-Rosa**: eine topographische und natur-historische Skizze, nebst einem Anhange der von Herrn Zumstein gemachten Reisen zur Ersteigung seiner Gipfel / Ludwig, Freiherrn v. Welden. Wien, 1824. Ill., map.
GB.782; Lloyd.1589(1). m387.

Das **Monte-Rosa** und Matterhorn — Mont-Cervin — Gebirg / Christian Moritz Engelhardt. Paris, 1852. Ill., maps.
GB.1244; Lloyd.1146; Lloyd.1146A; Lloyd.1565(2). m388.

Monte-Rosa-Ostwand / Hermann Franke. [Munich, 1936.] Ill. Pp.683-5 of *Der Bergsteiger*, vol.6 no.12, Sept.1936.
GB.1338(31). m389.

A **month** in France and Switzerland, during the autumn of 1824 / John Smith. London, 1825.
Lloyd.868. m390.

A **month** in Switzerland / F. Barham Zincke. London, 1873.
GB.310; Lloyd.387; Lloyd.387A. m391.

A **month** in Switzerland, in 1874 / T. Sopwith. Hexham, 1875.
GB.1327(13). m392.

A **month** in the Himalayas, from 12th May to 11th June 1933. Meerut, [1933?].
GB/A.2180. m393.

I **monti** del Chesio / Giovanni Desimoni. Torino, [1938]. Ill., map. [Itinera montium; 2.]
GB/A.1034(3). m394.

I **monti** della Valle Aurina: escursioni e salite / Lucio Alberto Fincato, Mario Galli. Brunico, 1979. Ill., maps.
GB/A.2019(15). m395.

Monti e poggi toscani: nell'occasione del 39°
Congresso degli Alpinisti Italiani. Firenze, 1908.
Ill.
GB/B.298.   m396.

Monti, laghi, marine. Roma, 1908. Ill. Published
by the Associazione Nazionale Italiana per il
Movimento dei Forestieri.
GB/A.799(16).   m397.

I monti Sarentini / Bruno Nice. Roma, 1950. Ill.
[Studi sul 'Maso Chiuso' alto-atesino; 1.]
[Memorie di geografia antropica; vol.5 fasc.1.]
Published by the Consiglio Nazionale delle
Ricerche.
GB/B.403(8).   m398.

Montreux / Alfred Cérésole. Zurich, [ca 1886]. Ill.,
maps. Published by the Société d'utilité publique
de Montreux.
GB/A.1349(5).   m399.

Montreux / E. Rambert [et al.]. Neuchâtel, 1877.
Ill.
GB/A.1363.   m400.

Monviso / Severino Bessone, Felice Burdino.
Bologna, 1971. Ill., maps. [Itinerari alpini; 7.]
GB/A.867(11).   m401.

Monviso re di pietra / Ezio Nicoli. Bologna, 1972.
Ill., maps.
GB/B.353.   m402.

The moonland: Ladakh: a travellers' guide. New
Delhi, 1981. Ill., map.
GB/A.2023(7).   m403.

Moonlight on Brenva / Mike Banks. London,
1955. Ill. Pp.217-38 of his Commando climber.
GB.1881(39).   m404.

Die Moränen-Landschaft / E. Desor. Schaffhausen, 1874. Map.
GB/A.1468(5).   m405.

Morecambe Bay: proposed harbour of refuge and
port: remarks on the importance of establishing a
harbour of refuge in Lancaster Sound and a port
of commerce at Heysham / George Elliot, James
A. Paynter. London, [ca 1850].
Lloyd.1583(18).   m406.

Mot ukjent land: Norvegia-ekspedisjonen 1929-
1930 / Hj. Riiser-Larsen. Oslo, 1930.
GB/A.2084.   m407.

The Mount Aspiring region / Graham Bishop.
[Wellington], 1981. Ill., maps. Published by the
New Zealand Alpine Club.
GB/B.635(4).   m408.

Mount Cook alpine regions / L.R. Hewitt, M.M.
Davidson. 2nd (rev.) ed. [Christchurch, 1972.] Ill.
GB/A.2076(12).   m409.

The Mount Cook guidebook: a climber's guide to
the Mt Cook region / Hugh Logan. [Wellington],
1982. Ill., map. Published by the New Zealand
Alpine Club.
GB/B.635(3).   m410.

Mount Everest: der Angriff, 1922 / C.G. Bruce
und anderen Teilnehmern; Deutsch von W.
Rickmer Rickmers. Basel, 1924. Ill., maps.
Translated from The assault on Mount Everest.
GB/A.1899.   m411.

Mount Everest: the reconnaissance, 1921 / C.K.
Howard-Bury and other members of the Mount
Everest Expedition. London, 1922. Ill., maps.
GB.1289.   m412.

Mount Everest, 1938 / H.W. Tilman. Cambridge,
1948. Ill., maps.
GB.835; Lloyd.946; Lloyd.946A.   m413.

Mount Everest Reconnaissance Expedition 1951:
Special supplement, The Times. London, 1951.
GB.1298(1); GB.1912(8).   m414.

Mount Foraker / T. Graham Brown; read in an
abridged form before the Alpine Club, February 5,
1935. [London, 1935.] Ill. Reprinted from the
Alpine Journal, May and November 1935.
GB.706; GB.721; GB.1313(20); Lloyd.1612(4).

                                                       m415.

Mount Gerizim: the one true sanctuary / Jacob,
son of Aaron, High Priest of the Samaritans;
translated from the Arabic by Abdullah Ben Kori;
edited by William E. Barton. Oak Park, Ill., 1907.
Reprinted from the Bibliotheca sacra for July 1907.
GB.1305(3).   m416.

Mount McKinley conquered by new route:
landing by plane on a glacier, climbers pioneer a
western approach to North America's loftiest
peak / Bradford Washburn. Washington, 1953. Ill.,
ports. Pp.219-48 of the National Geographic
Magazine, vol.104 no.2, August 1953.
GB.1333(30).   m417.

Mount McKinley National Park, Alaska: season June 10 to September 15, [1935]. Washington, 1935. Ill., maps. Published by the National Park Service.
GB.1338(16). m418.

Mount Olympus / Francis P. Farquhar, Aristides E. Phoutrides. San Francisco, 1929.
GB/B.611. m419.

Mount Pilatus: Switzerland's far-famed mountain peak. Alpnachstad, [ca 1955]. Ill.
GB/A.836(5). m420.

Mount Qomolangma: the highest in the world / Zhang Rongzu. Beijing, 1981.
GB/A.2052(5). m421.

The **Mount** Rainier National Park / Bob and Ira Spring; text by Harvey Manning. Seattle, [1975?]. Ill., maps.
GB/B.602(3). m422.

Mount Robson and beautiful Jasper Park, Canada. Winnipeg, [1910?]. Published by Grand Trunk Pacific Railway, General Passenger Department.
Lloyd.1617(6). m423.

Mount St. Elias and its glaciers / Mark Brickell Kerr. [New York, 1891.] Ill., map. Pp.[361]-72 of *Scribner's Magazine*, vol.9, March 1891.
GB.1336(21). m424.

Mountain adventures in the various countries of the world: selected from the narratives of celebrated travellers / founded on a compilation by Zurcher and Margollé. London, 1869. Ill. Translated from *Les ascensions célèbres*.
GB.318; Lloyd.423; Lloyd.423A,B,C. m425.

Mountain ascents in Westmoreland and Cumberland / John Barrow. Chipping Norton, 1885.
Lloyd.949. m426.

Mountain ascents in Westmoreland and Cumberland / John Barrow. London, 1886.
GB.309; Lloyd.518. m427.

A **mountain** called Nun Kun / Bernard Pierre; translated by Nea Morin and Janet Adam Smith. London, 1955. Ill., maps. Translated from *Une montagne nommée Nun-Kun*.
GB.600. m428.

Mountain climbing / Edward L. Wilson, Edwin Lord Weeks [et al.]. London, 1897. Ill. [Out of doors library.]
GB.513. m429.

The **Mountain** Club Annual. No.7-9, 1901/2-1904/5. Cape Town, 1902-05. Continued by *The Annual of the Mountain Club of South Africa*.
GB/A.2160. m430.

Mountain craft / edited by Geoffrey Winthrop Young. London, 1920. Ill.
Lloyd.1037. m431.

Mountain craft / edited by Geoffrey Winthrop Young. 4th ed. London, 1920. Ill.
GB.948. m432.

Mountain Craft: the journal of the Mountaineering Association. No.27,51-81, Apr./Jun.1955, Apr./Jun.1961-Autumn 1968. London, 1955-68.
GB/B.605; GB.1322(19) (another copy of no.57).
m433.

Mountain holidays / Janet Adam Smith. London, 1946. Ill., maps, ports.
GB.694. m435.

Mountain holidays in Norway. [London], 1953. Ill. Published by the Norway Travel Association.
GB/A.1597(7). m436.

Mountain jubilee / Arnold Lunn. London, 1943. Ill.
GB.699. m437.

Mountain jubilee: Switzerland and the English, by Arnold Lunn / H.E. Kretschmer. [London, 1944.] A review. Pp.323-5 of the *Climbers' Club Journal*, N.S. vol.7 no.3.
GB.1337(10). m438.

Mountain life. No.1, April 1972. Reading, 1972. Ill. Published by the British Mountaineering Council.
GB/B.602(1). m439.

Mountain lure / George Basterfield. Kendal, 1947. Ill., port.
GB.619; GB.636. m440.

Mountain memories: a pilgrimage of romance / W. Martin Conway. London, 1920. Ill.
GB.1116; Lloyd.1250. m441.

Mountain motives and values / R.A. Hodgkin. [London, 1943.] Pp.110-6 of the *Climbers' Club Journal*, N.S. vol.7 no.2, 1943.
GB.1339(12). m442.

Mountain panoramas from the Pamirs and Kwen Lun / M. Aurel Stein. London, 1908. Ill., map.
GB/B.513.   m443.

Mountain passages / Jeremy Bernstein. Lincoln, Neb., 1978.
GB/A.1916.   m444.

Mountain paths / H.E.G. Tyndale. London, 1948. [New Alpine library.]
Lloyd.881.   m445.

Mountain prospect / R. Scott Russell. London, 1946. Ill., maps, ports.
GB.608; Lloyd.788.   m446.

A **mountain** 'sanctuary' in Piedmont / Emily Constance Cook. [N.p., 1895.] Pp. 246-55 of *Charities Review*, March 1895.
GB/A.797(3).   m447.

The **mountain** scene / Frank S. Smythe. London, 1937. Ill.
GB.1253.   m448.

Mountain search and rescue techniques /. W.G. May. Boulder, Colo., 1973. Ill., map.
GB/B.525(4).   m449.

Mountain solitude / Charles Gos. [London], 1939. Ill. Reprinted from the *Alpine Journal*, May 1939.
GB.1339(33).   m450.

The **mountain** top: an illustrated anthology from the prose and pictures of Frank S. Smythe. London, 1947.
GB.68.   m451.

The **mountain** way: an anthology in prose and verse / collected by R.L.G. Irving. London, 1938. Ill.
GB.427.   m452.

Mountain weather for climbers / David J. Unwin. Leicester, 1978. Ill., map.
GB/A.1676(12).   m453.

The **mountain** world / edited by Marcel Kurz, Malcolm Barnes. 1953, 1954, 1955, 1958/59. London, 1953-58. Ill., maps, ports. Published by the Swiss Foundation for Alpine Research.
GB.1122-4 (1953,1955,1958/59); Lloyd.1245-6 (1953,1954).   m454.

Mountain-falls / W. Martin Conway. [London, 1894.] Pp.[821]-8 of the *Contemporary Review*, vol.66.
GB.1336(11).   m454.1.

Mountaineering / C.T. Dent; with contributions by W.M. Conway, D.W. Freshfield [et al.]. London, 1892. Ill. [Badminton library.]
GB.1166; Lloyd.570; Lloyd.570A; Lloyd.1281; Lloyd.1281A.   m455.

Mountaineering / C.T. Dent; with contributions by W.M. Conway, D.W. Freshfield [et al.]. 3rd ed. London, 1900. Ill. [Badminton library.]
GB.360.   m456.

Mountaineering / Claude Wilson. London, 1893.
GB.333; Lloyd.203A.   m457.

Mountaineering / Claude Wilson. London, 1893. [All England series.]
Lloyd.203.   m458.

Mountaineering / Claude Wilson. London, 1893. [All England series.] A different issue from m458.
Lloyd.541; Lloyd.541A.   m459.

Mountaineering / Sydney Spencer (editor), E.R. Blanchet, Olaf Bloch [et al.]. London, [1934]. Ill., maps. [Lonsdale library; 18.]
GB.912; Lloyd.904.   m460.

Mountaineering / T.A.H. Peacocke. London, 1941. Ill. [Sportsman's library; 29.]
GB.307.   m461.

Mountaineering / W. Martin Conway. [London, 1898.] Ill. Pp.23-49 of the *Encyclopaedia of sport*.
GB.1336(27).   m462.

Mountaineering: a bibliography of books in English to 1974 / compiled by Chess Krawczyk. Metuchen, 1977.
GB/A.1502.   m463.

Mountaineering: the bulletin of the British Mountaineering Council. Vol.1 no.3-4, Jan.-April 1948. [London], 1948.
GB.1313(38-9).   m464.

Mountaineering: the freedom of the hills / editor, Ed Peters; revision committee, Roger Anderson [et al.]. 4th ed. Seattle, 1983. Ill.
GB/A.2131.   m465.

Mountaineering adventure: the dangers of avalanche, glacier, crevasse, and precipice / Francis Gribble. [N.p., n.d.] Ill. Pp.[417]-28 of an unidentified periodical.
GB.1336(31).   m466.

Mountaineering and exploration in the Japanese Alps / Walter Weston. London, 1896. Ill., maps. Lloyd.1222. m467.

Mountaineering art / Harold Raeburn. London, [1920]. GB.373. m468.

Mountaineering ballads / A.C. Downer. London, [1905]. GB.1335(28). m469.

Mountaineering below the snow-line, or The solitary pedestrian in Snowdonia and elsewhere / M. Paterson. London, 1886. Ill. Lloyd.335. m470.

Mountaineering clubs 1857-1907 / A.J. Mackintosh. London, 1907. Reprinted from the *Alpine Journal*, August 1907. GB.1306(11); GB.1306(12); GB.1306(13). m471.

A **mountaineering** expedition to the Himalaya of Garhwal / T.G. Longstaff. London, 1908. Ill. Pp.[361]-95 of the *Geographical Journal*, vol.31 no.4. GB.1337(15). m472.

Mountaineering handbook: a complete and practical guide for beginner or expert. London, 1950. Ill. Translated from *Bergsteigen*. Published by the Association of British Members of the Swiss Alpine Club. GB.296. m473.

Mountaineering holiday / Frank S. Smythe. London, 1940. Ill. GB.891; Lloyd.1016. m474.

Mountaineering in 1861: a vacation tour / John Tyndall. London, 1862. Ill. GB.617; Lloyd.805; Lloyd.808; Lloyd.808A,B. m475.

Mountaineering in China / compiled by the People's Physical Cultural Publishing House. Peking, 1965. Ill. GB/B.390(12). m476.

Mountaineering in Colorado: the peaks about Estes Park / Frederick H. Chapin. Boston, 1889. Ill. Published by the Appalachian Mountain Club. Lloyd.596. m477.

Mountaineering in Colorado: the peaks about Estes Park / Frederick H. Chapin. 2nd ed. London, 1890. Ill. Lloyd.694. m478.

Mountaineering in Scotland / W.H. Murray. London, 1947. Ill., maps. GB.692. m479.

Mountaineering in Scotland, by W.H. Murray / G.A. Dummett. [London, 1948.] A review. Pp.396-400 of the *Climbers' Club Journal*, N.S. vol.8 no.3. GB.1337(9). m480.

Mountaineering in the Sierra Nevada / Clarence King. London, 1872. GB.255; Lloyd.785. m481.

Mountaineering in the Sierra Nevada / Clarence King. New ed. London, 1874. Maps. Lloyd.577. m482.

Mountaineering in the Sierra Nevada / Clarence King. [New ed., rev.] New York, 1923. GB.615. m483.

Mountaineering library of Dr. G. I. Meyer. [N.p., n.d.] GB.1334(35). m484.

Mountaineering memories / H. Preston-Thomas. Edinburgh, 1895. Pp.92-103 of *Blackwood's Magazine*, no.957. GB.1329(16); GB.1881(77). m485.

Mountaineering memories of the past / G.P. Baker. [N.p.], 1951. Ill., ports. GB.732; Lloyd.911. m486.

Mountaineering records / E. Hornby. Liverpool, 1907. GB.675; Lloyd.886; Lloyd.886A. m487.

Mountaineering tragedies / Edward Whymper. London, 1909. Ill. Pp.[49]-56 of the *Strand Magazine*, vol.37 no.217, Jan.1909. GB.1333(5). m488.

Mountaineering without guides: the conclusion of a lecture to the Yorkshire Ramblers' Club / Charles Pilkington. Leeds, 1897. GB.1335(36); GB.1335(37); Lloyd.992. m489.

The mountaineer's gadgeteer / R. Burns, Ltd. [Manchester, n.d.] GB.1327(2). m490.

The mountaineer's week-end book / Showell Styles. London, [1951]. Ill., music. GB.303. m491.

The **mountains**. 7. [New York, 1873.] Ill. Pp.669-80 of *Harper's New Monthly Magazine*, April 1873.
GB.1332(35). m492.

The **mountains** and lakes of Switzerland: with descriptive sketches of other parts of the Continent / Anna Eliza Bray. London, 1841. 3v.
Lloyd.533-5. m493.

The **mountains** and lakes of Switzerland, the Tyrol and Italy / George E. Hering. London, 1847. Ill.
GB/C.27. m494.

Mountains and men / Leonard H. Robbins. New York, 1931. Ill., maps, ports.
GB.520. m495.

Mountains and mountain-climbing: records of adventure / by the author of *The Mediterranean illustrated* [i.e. W.H. Davenport Adams]. London, 1883. Ill.
GB.462; GB.463. m496.

Mountains and mountaineering: a list of the writings, 1917-1947, of J. Monroe Thorington. [N.p.], 1947.
GB.1337(12). m497.

The **mountains** of Cogne / George Yeld, W.A.B. Coolidge. London, 1893. Map. [Conway and Coolidge's climbers' guides; 7.]
GB.1324(2); Lloyd.23; Lloyd.23A. m498.

The **mountains** of northeastern Tasmania: a study of alpine geomorphology / Nel Caine. Rotterdam, 1983.
GB/A.2177. m499.

The **mountains** of Oregon / W.G. Steel. Portland, 1890. Ill.
GB/A.2159. m500.

Mountains of the Middle Kingdom: exploring the peaks of China and Tibet / Galen Rowell. San Francisco, 1983. Ill.
GB/B.628. m501.

The **mountains** of the whirlpool / J. Monroe Thorington. London, 1925. Ill., map, ports. Reprinted from the *Alpine Journal*, November 1924.
GB.1880(42). m502.

The **mountains** of youth / Arnold Lunn. London, 1925.
GB.866. m503.

Mountains, rain and snow / R.C. Nichols. [N.p., 1873.] From the *Alpine Journal*, vol.6, 1873.
Lloyd.933; Lloyd.933A. m504.

Mountains with a difference / Geoffrey Winthrop Young. London, 1951. Ill. [New Alpine library.]
GB.688. m505.

Mountaintop kingdom: Sikkim / photographs by Alice S. Kandell; text by Charlotte Y. Salisbury. Delhi, 1972. Ill.
GB/B.396. m506.

Moved on! from Kashgar to Kashmir / P.S. Nazaroff; rendered into English from the Russian by Malcolm Burr. London, 1935. Ill., map.
GB.722. m507.

Mozley and Tyndall on miracles: an essay / William Fowler. London, 1868.
Lloyd.1606(12). m508.

Mr. Albert Smith's ascent of Mont Blanc in miniature. London, 1854. A peepshow, with accompanying *Handbook of the miniature Mont Blanc*, edited by Madame de Chatelain. 2nd ed., 1855.
GB/C.120. m509.

Mr. Albert Smith's ascent of Mont Blanc, proceeding to Chamouni via the Rhine and Baden, and returning by Paris: Egyptian Hall, Piccadilly. [London, 1853.] A programme.
GB.1335(22). m510.

Mr. Albert Smith's Mont Blanc, Naples, Pompeii, and Vesuvius: Egyptian Hall, Piccadilly. [London, 1858.] A programme.
GB.1335(23). m511.

Mr. Smythe: The valley of flowers. Peaks and valleys, by F.S. Smythe / R.A.H. [i.e. R.A. Hodgkin]. [London, 1939.] A review. Pp.69-70 of the *Climbers' Club Journal*, N.S. vol.6 no.1.
GB.1339(29). m512.

Mt. McKinley: the pioneer climbs / Terris Moore. [College, Alaska, 1967.] Ill., maps, ports.
GB/A.1912. m513.

The **Mt.** Pilatus railway / J. Hardmeyer. Zurich, [1895?]. Ill. [Swiss scenes.]
GB/A.1817(6). m514.

Mt. Whitney / Thomas Winnett. 2nd ed. Berkeley, 1978. Ill.
GB/A.1589(10). m515.

Mummery / Attilio Viriglio. Bologna, [1953]. Ill. [Le Alpi; 13.]
GB/A.800(13). m516.

Munchausen at the Pole, or The surprising and wonderful adventures of a voyage of discovery consisting of some of the most marvellous exploits ever performed by man / Capt. Munchausen. London, 1824. Ill.
GB/A.2049. m517.

Munchausen on the Jungfrau. New ed., with notes [by Hereford B. George and Charles E. Mathews]. London, [n.d.].
Lloyd.1581(9). m518.

Murailles et abîmes / Jurg Weiss; traduit de l'allemand par Elizabeth A. Cuenod. Neuchâtel, 1946. Ill. [Montagne.]
GB/A.166. m519.

Das **Murmeltier** mit dem Halsband: Tagebuch eines Philosophen / Eugène Rambert; aus dem Französischen übertragen von Alfred Graber. München, 1929. Ill.
GB/A.4. m520.

Le **musée** suisse: album de la littérature et des arts. 2e livr., février 1853. Genève, 1853. Contains *Une ascension à la cime du Mont Blanc*, by comte Henri de Tilly.
GB.1334(33); Lloyd.1503. m521.

My Alpine jubilee, 1851-1907 / Frederic Harrison. London, 1908. Port.
GB.256; Lloyd.509. m522.

My Alpine scrapbook / W.A.B. Coolidge. No.12: The first recorded Grindelwald guide: Peter Baumann, 1800-1853. [N.p., n.d.]
GB.1340(59). m523.

My climbing adventures in four continents / Samuel Turner. 2nd impr. London, 1913.
GB.428. m524.

My climbs in the Alps and Caucasus / A.F. Mummery. London, 1895. Ill.
GB.1238; Lloyd.1391; Lloyd.1391A,B; Lloyd.1455; Lloyd.1455A,B. m525.

My climbs in the Alps and Caucasus / A.F. Mummery. 3rd ed. London, 1895.
GB.1237. m526.

My climbs in the Alps and Caucasus / A.F. Mummery. London, [1913]. [Nelson's shilling library.]
GB.73. m527.

My diary: being notes of a Continental tour / K.H. [i.e. Kirkwood Hevat?]. [N.p., 1878?]
GB.182; Lloyd.255. m528.

My first glacier pass / A.C. [Cambridge, 1868.] Pp.390-8 of *Macmillan's Magazine*, vol.8 no.47.
GB.1880(5). m529.

My four-thousands / Eustace Thomas. Manchester, 1929. Ill. Pp.[330]-6 of the *Rucksack Club Journal*, vol.6 no.3.
GB.1880(3). m530.

My hardest rock climb / Frank S. Smythe. [London, 1940.] Chapter 7 of his *Adventures of a mountaineer*.
GB.1339(27). m531.

My home in the Alps / Mrs Main. London, 1892.
Lloyd.475; Lloyd.475A. m532.

My journey to Lhasa / Alexandra David-Neel. London, 1927. Ill., ports. Translated from *Voyage d'une Parisienne à Lhassa*.
GB.849. m533.

My life among the Eskimos: Baffinland journeys in the years 1909 to 1911 / Bernhard Hantzsch; translated from the German original and edited by Leslie H. Neatby. Saskatoon, 1977. Ill., map, port. [Mawdsley memoir series / Institute for Northern Studies; 3.]
GB/B.486. m534.

My notebook: Switzerland / John MacGregor. Frankfort o.M., 1837.
GB.29; Lloyd.37. m535.

My old playground revisited: a tour in Italy in the spring of 1881 / Benjamin E. Kennedy. London, 1882. Ill.
Lloyd.501. m536.

My summer in the Alps, 1913 / William Williams. New York, 1914. Ill.
GB/A.1670. m537.

My travels abroad / Mrs Conrad Pestalozzi. Zürich, 1856.
GB/A.803(4). m538.

My way was North: an Alaskan autobiography / Frank Dufresne. New York, 1966. Ill.
GB/A.1657. m539.

The **mystery** rivers of Tibet: a description of Tibet, its peoples, fauna, & flora / F. Kingdon Ward. London, 1923. Ill., maps.
GB.761. m540.

-N-

Naar onbekend midden-Azië: tusschen Karakorum en Hindu-Kush / P.C. Visser. Rotterdam, 1926. Ill., maps.
GB/A.871. n001.

Nachbarn des Nordwinds / Kurt Lütgen. [Brunswick], 1968.
GB/A.1848. n002.

Nachrichten von den Eisbergen im Tyrol / Joseph Walcher. Frankfurt, 1773. Ill.
Lloyd.1617(22). n003.

Några upplysningar till den nya kartan öfver Beeren eiland / A.G. Nathorst. Stockholm, 1899. Ill., maps. Reprinted from *Ymer*, årg.1899, h.2.
GB.1880(13). n004.

Nahanni / Roger Frison-Roche. Grenoble, 1969. Ill., maps. [Romans et récits de Roger Frison-Roche.]
GB/A.988(5). n005.

Nalunaerutit. Grønlandsk lovsamling. Ser.A, nr.1-2, 1959. [Copenhagen, 1959.]
GB/A.1864. n006.

The **names** of Zermatt / W.A.B. Coolidge. [London, 1912.] Reprinted from the *English Historical Review*, July 1912.
GB.1340(40). n007.

Nanda Devi / Charles S. Houston. [New York, 1937.] Ill. Reprinted from the *American Alpine Journal*, vol.3 no.1, 1937.
GB.1339(31). n008.

Nanda Devi / Eric Shipton. London, 1936. Ill.
GB.981. n009.

Nanda Devi / N.E. Odell. [N.p., 1936.] Ill., map. Reprinted from the *Canadian Alpine Journal*, 1936.
Lloyd.1624(4). n010.

Nanda Devi / N.E. Odell. London, 1937. Ill. Pp.118-23 of the *Climbers' Club Journal*, N.S. vol.5 no.2.
GB.1339(26). n011.

Nanda Devi: 3e expédition française à l'Himalaya / J.J. Languepin, L. Payan. Paris, 1952. Ill., maps, ports.
GB/B.602(6). n012.

Nanda Devi: 'the blessed goddess Nanda' / N.E. Odell. London, 1937. Ill., maps, ports. Pp.257-74 of the *Geographical Magazine*, vol.5 no.4.
GB.1339(3). n013.

Nanda Devi and the Ganges watershed / Eric Shipton. [London], 1935. Ill., maps. Reprinted from the *Geographical Journal*, vol.85 no.4.
GB.1339(2). n014.

The **Nanda** Devi group and the sources of the Nandakgini / T.G. Longstaff. Notes on a visit to western Tibet in 1926 / Hugh Ruttledge. Notes on the channel connecting the Lakes Manasarowar and Rakas / R.C. Wilson. London, 1928. Ill., maps. Reprinted from the *Geographical Journal*, vol.71 no.5, May 1928.
GB.1337(17). n015.

Nandu Jayal and Indian mountaineering: a tribute to Major Narendra Dhar Jayal. Poona, [1975?].
GB/A.2213. n016.

Nanga Parbat: Berg der Kameraden: Bericht der deutschen Himalaja-Expedition 1938 / aus Tagebüchern von Bruno Balke, Fritz Bechtold [et al.]; herausgegeben von der Deutschen Himalaja-Stiftung München. Berlin, [1943]. Ill.
GB/A.460. n017.

Nanga Parbat adventure: a Himalayan expedition / Fritz Bechtold; translated from the German by H.E.G. Tyndale. London, 1935. Ill.
GB.1171. n018.

Nansen / Anna Gertrude Hall. New York, 1940. Ill., ports.
GB/A.1715. n019.

Nansens røst: artikler og taler / Fridtjof Nansen. Oslo, 1945. 3v.
GB/A.1634-6. n020.

Nares Strait and the drift of Greenland: a conflict in plate tectonics / ed. P.R. Dawes, J.W. Kerr. Copenhagen, 1982. Ill., maps. [Meddelelser om Grønland. Geoscience; 8.]
GB/A.1818(8). n020.1.

Narrative of a journey from Caunpoor to the Boorendo Pass in the Himalaya mountains, via Gwalior, Agra, Delhi, and Sirhind / Sir William Lloyd; and Captain Alexander Gerard's account of an attempt to penetrate by Bekhur to Garoo, and the Lake Manasarowara; edited by George Lloyd. London, 1840. 2v; maps.
GB.667-8. n021.

Narrative of a journey from Caunpoor to the Boorendo Pass in the Himalaya mountains / William Lloyd; and Captain Alexander Gerard's account of an attempt to penetrate by Bekhur to Garoo and the Lake Manasarowara. London, 1846. 2v (in 1); maps.
GB.968. n022.

Narrative of a journey from Santiago de Chile to Buenos Ayres in July and August, 1821 / [Edward Hibbert]. London, 1824.
Lloyd.592. n023.

Narrative of a journey from the village of Chamouni, in Switzerland, to the summit of Mount Blanc, undertaken on Aug.8, 1787 / Mark Beaufoy. London, 1817. From *Annals of Philosophy*, vol.9, 1817.
GB.662(1); Lloyd.877. n024.

Narrative of a journey from the village of Chamouni, in Switzerland, to the summit of Mont Blanc, undertaken on the 8th of August, 1787: read to the Royal Society / Mark Beaufoy; with a note by Douglas W. Freshfield. [London], 1916. Ill., port. Reprinted from the *Alpine Journal*, November 1915.
GB.660. n025.

Narrative of a journey to the shores of the polar sea, in the years 1819-20-21-22 / Sir John Franklin. 3rd ed. London, 1824. 2v.
GB.1050-1. n026.

Narrative of a journey to the summit of Mont Blanc, made in July, 1819 / William Howard. Baltimore, 1821.
GB.238; Lloyd.1609(10). n027.

Narrative of an ascent of Mont Blanc in August, 1830 / Edward Bootle Wilbraham. London, 1832.
GB.1881(62); Lloyd.491. n028.

Narrative of an ascent of Mont Blanc in August, 1830 / Edward Bootle Wilbraham. [N.p., 1832?]
GB.320; Lloyd.510. n029.

A **narrative** of an ascent to the summit of Mont Blanc / H.H. Jackson. [London, 1827.] Pp.458-69 of the *New Monthly Magazine*, vol.19.
GB.623(6). n030.

Narrative of an ascent to the summit of Mont Blanc, August 18th, 1822: with an appendix, upon the sensations experienced at great elevations / Frederick Clissold. London, 1823.
GB.616; GB.1335(32); Lloyd.1581(8); Lloyd. 1581(8)A. n031.

A **narrative** of an ascent to the summit of Mont Blanc made during the summer of 1827 by William Hawes and Charles Fellows / [Sir Benjamin Hawes]. London, 1828. Facsim.
GB.1108; Lloyd.1231A; Lloyd.1295. n032.

A **narrative** of an ascent to the summit of Mont Blanc made during the summer of 1827 by William Hawes and Charles Fellows / [Sir Benjamin Hawes]. London, 1828. A different issue from n032.
Lloyd.1230A; Lloyd.1231. n032.1.

A **narrative** of an ascent to the summit of Mont Blanc made during the summer of 1827 by William Hawes and Charles Fellows / [Sir Benjamin Hawes]. London, 1828. A different issue from n032 and n032.1.
Lloyd.1230. n032.2.

Narrative of an ascent to the summit of Mont Blanc, on the 8th and 9th August, 1827 / John Auldjo. London, 1828. Ill., maps.
GB.1280; Lloyd.1494; Lloyd.1494A. n033.

Narrative of an ascent to the summit of Mont Blanc, on the 8th and 9th August, 1827 / John Auldjo. 2nd ed. London, 1830.
GB.874; Lloyd.983; Lloyd.1177. n034.

Narrative of an ascent to the summit of Mont Blanc, on eighth and ninth of August, 1827 / John Auldjo. 3rd ed. London, 1856. Ill.
GB.235(2); GB.1328(1); Lloyd.299; Lloyd.1573(1). n035.

Narrative of an ascent to the summit of Mont Blanc, on the eighth and ninth of August, 1827 / John Auldjo. 4th ed. London, 1867. Ill.
GB.203. n036.

Narrative of an attempt to reach the North Pole, in boats fitted for the purpose, and attached to His Majesty's Ship *Hecla*, in the year 1827, under the command of Captain William Edward Parry. London, 1828. Ill., maps.
GB.1251. n037.

Narrative of an excursion on the chain of Mount Blanc / C.E. Mathews. Birmingham, [1862]. Reprinted from the *Birmingham Daily Gazette* of July 10th 1862.
Lloyd.1581(5). n038.

Narrative of an excursion to the mountains of Piemont, and researches among the Vaudois, or Waldenses / William Stephen Gilly. London, 1824. Ill., maps, facsims.
Lloyd.1414. n039.

Narrative of an excursion to the mountains of Piemont, and researches among the Vaudois, or Waldenses / William Stephen Gilly. 2nd ed. London, 1825. Ill., maps, facsims.
GB/A.197. n040.

Narrative of an excursion to the mountains of Piemont, and researches among the Vaudois, or Waldenses / William Stephen Gilly. 3rd ed. London, 1826. Ill., maps, facsims.
Lloyd.851. n041.

Narrative of an excursion to the mountains of Piemont / William Stephen Gilly. 4th ed. London, 1827.
GB.715. n042.

Narrative of an excursion to the summit of Mont Blanc, August 26th, 1825 / Edmund J. Clark, Markham Sherwill. [London, 1825-26.] 2v. From the *New Monthly Magazine*, vol.16, 1825-26.
GB.623(1-2). n043.

Narrative of an expedition to the Zambesi and its tributaries and of the discovery of the lakes Shirwa and Nyassa, 1858-1864 / David and Charles Livingstone. New York, 1865.
GB.1007. n044.

A **narrative** of Arctic discovery, from the earliest period to the present time / John J. Shillinglaw. 2nd ed. London, 1851.
GB.473. n045.

Narrative of the Arctic land expedition to the mouth of the Great Fish River, and along the shores of the Arctic Ocean, in the years 1833, 1834, and 1835 / Sir George Back. London, 1836. Map.
GB.1049. n046.

Narrative of the ascent to the summit of Mont Blanc, of the 25 July, 1827 / Sir Charles Fellows. London, 1827. Ill., facsim.
GB.1286; Lloyd.1489; Lloyd.1489A; Lloyd.1505; Lloyd.1506. n047.

Narrative of the shipwreck of the *Jean*, of Peterhead, at Greenland, 18th April, 1826 / James Cumming. Aberdeen, 1826.
GB/A.1969(1).   n048.

A **narrative** of the voyages round the world, performed by Captain James Cook: with an account of his life / Andrew Kippis. London, 1839. Originally published as *The life of Captain James Cook*.
GB.15.   n049.

Narratives of an ascent of Mont Blanc in 1819 / Jeremiah van Rensselaer, William Howard; with a note by Henry F. Montagnier. [London], 1920. Ill., facsim. Reprinted from the *Alpine Journal*, March 1920.
GB.1335(12); Lloyd.1602(4).   n050.

Narratives of ascents of Mont Blanc and Monte Rosa in 1855 / Edward Hyde Greg; with a note by Godfrey A. Solly. [London], 1920. Reprinted from the *Alpine Journal*, November 1920.
GB.1740; Lloyd.1602(7).   n051.

Natur-Geschichte des Schweizerlandes, samt seinen Reisen über die Schweizerische Gebürge / Johann Jacob Scheuchzer; aufs neue herausgegeben, und mit einigen Anmerkungen versehen von Joh. Georg Sulzer. Zürich, 1746. 2v. Originally published as: *Beschreibung der Natur-Geschichten des Schweizerlandes*.
Lloyd.856-7.   n052.

Natural history: the magazine of the American Museum of Natural History. Vol.41 no.4, Apr.1938. New York, 1938. Includes *The highest mountain ever climbed*, by Arthur B. Emmons, and *A ticket to the Arctic*, by Richard Finnie.
GB/B.520(1).   n053.

Naturbilder aus den rhätischen Alpen: ein Führer durch Graubünden / G. Theobald. 2. verm. und verb. Aufl. Chur, 1862. Ill., maps.
GB/A.547.   n054.

Naturbilder aus den rhätischen Alpen: ein Führer durch Graubünden / G. Theobald. 3. verm. und verb. Aufl. bearbeitet von Chr. Tarnuzzer. Chur, 1893. Ill., maps.
Lloyd.737.   n055.

La **nature** alpine: exposé de géographie physique / René Godefroy. Grenoble, 1940.
GB/A.99.   n056.

Der **Naturfreund** und der Bergsteiger in Vulkangebieten / Karl Sapper. Ulm-Donau, 1941. Ill.
GB/A.449.   n057.

Die **Naturgeschichte** Helvetiens in der alten Welt / Gottlieb Sigmund Gruner. Bern, 1773.
GB/A.1078.   n058.

Naturhistorische Alpenreise / Fr. Jos. Hugi. Solothurn, 1830. Ill., maps.
GB.407; Lloyd.671; Lloyd.1611(5).   n059.

Die **Naturkräfte** in den Alpen, oder Physikalische Geographie des Alpengebirges / Friedrich Pfaff. München, 1877. Ill. [Die Naturkräfte. Eine naturwissenschaftliche Volksbibliothek; 24.]
GB/A.523.   n060.

Naturschilderungen, Sittenzüge und wissenschaftliche Bemerkungen aus den höchsten Schweizer-Alpen, besonders in Süd-Wallis und Graubünden / Christian Moritz Engelhardt. Paris, 1840. Ill.
GB.634; Lloyd.1145; Lloyd.1565(1).   n061.

A **near** thing in the Dolomites / Frank S. Smythe. London, 1930. Pp.408-16 of *Blackwood's Magazine*, no.1373, March 1930.
GB.1881(57).   n062.

Nebo nad strechou sveta / Marcel Belica. Bratislava, 1979.
GB/B.520(7).   n063.

De **nederlandsche** Pool-expeditie 1882-83 / Maurits Snellen; uitgeven door B.J.G. Volck. Utrecht, 1886.
GB/B.609.   n064.

Neige et roc / Gaston Rébuffat. Paris, 1959. Ill. [Tout par l'image; 20.]
GB/A.1558.   n065.

Neiges éternelles / C. Egmond d'Arcis. Neuchâtel, 1945.
GB.1321(48); GB/A.1351(7).   n066.

Nel centenario delle guide di Alagna, 1872-1972 / Erminio Ragozza. Biella, [1972]. Ill.
GB/B.377(17).   n067.

Nel Pantheon valsesiano: un avventuriero geniale: G.B. Fassola; un mazziniano eroico: Giacomo Antonini; un musicista insigne: Carlo Fasso / Luigi Fasso. Varallo, 1961. [Quaderni della Società Valsesiana di Cultura; 5.]
GB/B.312(25).   n068.

Nell'Uganda e nella catena del Ruwenzori: relazione preliminare sulle osservazioni geologiche fatte durante la spedizione di S.A.R. il duca degli Abruzzi nell'anno 1906 / Alessandro Roccati. Roma, 1907. Estratto dal *Bollettino della Società Geologica Italiana*, vol.26 fasc.2, 1907.
GB/B.289(1). n069.

Nella catena del Monte Bianco: ricordi di ascensioni / Agostino Ferrari. Torino, 1900. Ill. Estratto dal *Bollettino del C.A.I.* pel 1900, vol.33 n.66.
Lloyd.1620(29). n070.

Nelle Dolomiti con prefazione e versi / Gino Cucchetti. Bolzano, 1929.
GB/B.496. n071.

Nelle valli di Genova: romanzo / Giovanna Borzaga. Trento, 1970. Ill.
GB/A.502. n072.

Nepal / Perceval Landon. London, 1928. 2v; ill., maps, ports., music.
GB.1192-3; GB.1194-5. n073.

Nepal / Robert Rieffel. Paris, 1980. Ill., maps. [Les grands voyages.]
GB/A.2020(2). n074.

Il **Nepal** e la HN '79: spedizione italiana all' Annapurna Fang — m.7650, Himalaya del Nepal / Arturo Bergamaschi. [Ancona?], 1980. Ill., maps.
GB/A.1986. n075.

Nepal Himalaya / H.W. Tilman. Cambridge, 1952. Ill., maps.
GB.915; Lloyd.950. n076.

Netsilik Eskimos: social life and spiritual culture / Knud Rasmussen; [translated by W.E. Calvert]. New York, 1976. Ill. [Thule expedition, 5th, 1921-1924. Report; vol.8 no.1-2.]
GB/A.1835. n077.

Neuchâtel et ses environs / Auguste Bachelin. Zürich, [1883?]. Ill., map. [Europe illustrée; 28, 28a.]
Lloyd.1615(22). n078.

Neue Alpina: eine Schrift der schweizerischen Naturgeschichte, Alpen- und Landwirthschaft gewiedmet / herausgegeben von Johan Rudolf Steinmuller. Vol.1-2. Winterthur, 1821-27. Ill. Continues: *Alpina: eine Schrift der genauern Kenntniss der Alpen gewiedmet.*
GB/A.1400-1. n079.

Neue Beyträge zur nähren Kenntniss des Schweizerlandes / H. von Orell. Hft.1. Zürich, 1791.
GB/A.698(2). n080.

Neue Briefe über die Schweitz / C.C.L. Hirschfeld. Hft.1. Kiel, 1785. Ill.
GB/A.732. n081.

Neue deutsche Alpen-Zeitung / redigirt von Richard Issler. Bd.1 Nr.1-Bd.11 Nr.10, Juli 1875-Oktober 1880. Wien, 1875-80.
GB/B.141-9. n082.

Neue Kronik der kais. kön. v. oestr. Stadt Konstanz am Bodensee. 2. Aufl. Konstanz, 1798.
GB.138. n083.

Der neue Sammler, ein gemeinnütziges Archiv für Bünden / herausgegeben von der Okonomischen Gesellschaft daselbst. Jahrg.1-7. Chur, 1805-12.
GB/A.538-44; GB/A.942(10) (another copy of Jahrg.3 Bd.1). n084.

Neue schweizerische Spaziergänge / Leonard Meister. St. Gallen, 1790.
GB.45(2). n085.

Neue und vollständige Topographie der Eydgnossschaft / David Herrliberger. Frankfurt a.M., 1928. 2v. Facsimile reprint of the Zurich, 1754-73 ed.
GB/A.623-4. n086.

Neue Untersuchungen über die physicalische Geographie und die Geologie der Alpen / Adolph Schlagintweit, Hermann Schlagintweit. Leipzig, 1854. 2v. With atlas.
GB/C.82-3. n087.

Neuer Führer um den Bodensee und zu den Burgen des Höhgaus / Ottmar Fr.H. Schönhuth. Lindau, 1851. Map.
GB/A.979. n088.

Neues Land: vier Jahre in arktischen Gebieten / O. Sverdrup. Leipzig, 1903. 2v; ill., maps.
GB/A.2125. n089.

Die **neuesten** Briefe aus der Schweiz, in das väterliche Haus nach Ludwigsburg: nebst einem Gemälde des Bergsturzes am Rigi und Lauwerzer-See. München, 1807. 2v (in 1); ill.
GB/A.942(12). n090.

Nevado Caraz / [Mario Cristofolini, Ulisse Marzatico]. Trento, 1972. Ill.
GB/B.338(11).   n091.

The **new** ascent of Mont Blanc. London, [1854?]. Ill.
GB.5; Lloyd.4.   n092.

A **new** ascent of Piz Bernina and climbs in 1930 / T. Graham Brown. [London], 1931. Ill. Reprinted from the *Alpine Journal*, May 1931.
GB.1305(24); Lloyd.1612(3).   n093.

New climbs. 1966-70. [N.p.], 1966-70. *Climbers' Club Bulletin*, ser.3, no.3-7. 1966-69 edited by Nigel Rogers; 1970 edited by Ian Roper.
GB/A.1676(4-8).   n094.

New climbs. 1973. [N.p.], 1973. Published by the British Mountaineering Council; edited by Tony Moulam.
GB/A.1676(9).   n095.

New climbs. 1974. [N.p.], 1974. Edited by Caroline Deketelaere.
GB/A.1676(10).   n096.

New climbs in Norway: an account of some ascents in the Sondmore district / E.C. Oppenheim. London, 1898. Ill.
Lloyd.672; Lloyd.672A.   n097.

The **new** Eldorado: a summer journey to Alaska / Maturin M. Ballou. Boston, 1889.
GB/A.1728.   n098.

The **New** Excitement, or A book to induce young people to read. 1838. Edinburgh, 1838.
GB.18.   n099.

New expeditions: Mont Blanc group / T. Graham Brown. London, 1928. Ill. Pp.372-5 of the *Alpine Journal*, vol.40 no.237.
GB.1881(20).   n100.

New expeditions and topographical notes for the summer of 1867: notes communicated by F.F. Tuckett. London, [1868]. Advance proof of the article contained in the *Alpine Journal*, vol.4, May 1868.
GB.1880(8); Lloyd.1581(3); Lloyd.1583(4).   n101.

New fragments / John Tyndall. London, 1892.
GB.456.   n102.

The **new** graving dock, Millbrook, Southampton, for the Southern Railway Company, to be opened by H.M. King George V. July 1933: a series of drawings / Sydney R. Jones. London, 1933.
Lloyd.1462.   n103.

A **new** journey through Greece, Ægypt, Palestine, Italy, Swisserland, Alsatia, and the Netherlands / written by a French officer [i.e. Charles de Sainte-Maure]; now first done into English. London, 1725.
GB/A.759.   n104.

The **New** Monthly Magazine and Literary Journal. Vol.1, 16-17, 19, 1821, 1826, 1827. London, 1821-27.
Lloyd.1218-21.   n104.1.

The **new** Northland / L.P. Gratacap. New York, 1915. Ill.
GB/A.1726.   n105.

New plants from the Andes / Edmund G. Baker. [London, 1890.] Ill. Reprinted from the *Journal of Botany* for June 1890.
GB.612(4).   n106.

A **new** route up Mont Blanc without guides / Frank S. Smythe. London, 1928. Pp.[719]-42 of *Blackwood's Magazine*, vol.224 no.1858.
GB.1881(35); GB.1881(36).   n107.

A **new** voyage to Italy / François Maximilien Misson. 5th ed., with additions. London, 1739. 2v (in 4); ill. Translated from *Nouveau voyage d'Italie*.
GB.501-4.   n108.

New Voyages and Travels; consisting of originals, translations, and abridgments. Vol.1-9. London, [1819-23].
Lloyd.792-800.   n108.1.

The **New** Zealand Alpine Journal. Vol.1-8, 15-17, 19, 23- , 1892-1939/40, 1953-58, 1961, 1969- . Christchurch, 1892- .
GB/A.2164 (v.6-8, 17, 19, 23-); Lloyd.970-6 (v.1-5, 15-17); Lloyd.970A (another copy of v.1); Lloyd.971A (another copy of v.3 no.15); Lloyd.972A (another copy of v.4 no.17).   n109.

New Zealand Alpine Journal. Jubilee illustrated supplement. Christchurch, 1941.
Lloyd.1602(3).   n109.1.

New Zealand and the Antarctic / L.B. Quartermain. Wellington, 1971. Ill., maps, port.
GB/A.1601.   n110.

Newsletter / Austrian Alpine Club. No.33- ,
New Year 1972- . London, [1972-].
GB/B.426.   n111.

Newsletter / Chicago Mountaineering Club.
Vol.10 no.3-vol.13 no.5, June 1956-June 1959.
[Chicago], 1956-59. Wanting vol.10 no.5-6, vol.11
no.3, vol.13 no.2.
GB.1646(1-17).   n112.

Newsletter / Royal Air Force Mountaineering
Association. No.2/64, 1st July 1964. [London],
1964.
GB.1334(4).   n113.

Newsletter / Scottish Mountaineering Club. 4th
October 1961. Glasgow, 1961.
GB.1334(29).   n114.

[**Newspaper** cuttings and supplements relating to
the Mount Everest reconnaissance expeditions of
1951 and 1952, the Swiss expedition of 1952 and
the ascent of 1953.] [N.p., 1951-53.] 6v.
Lloyd.1548-53.   n115.

[**Newspaper** cuttings from *The Times* of April 30,
May 1,2 and 16, 1958, containing obituaries, etc. of
R.W. Lloyd.] [London], 1958.
GB.1341(19).   n116.

[**Newspaper** cuttings relating to the Mont Blanc
exhibition in the Egyptian Hall, Piccadilly, put on
by Albert Smith.] [N.p., 1853-54.]
Lloyd.1593(2).   n117.

[**Newspaper** cuttings with a few manuscript items
relating to mountaineering, collected by P.W.
Thomas.] [N.p., 1878-94.] 3v.
Lloyd.1509-11.   n118.

Nice et région: renseignements artistiques,
historiques et touristiques / Vincent Paschetta. 7e
éd. entièrement refondue. Nice, 1962. Ill., maps.
GB/A.2021(2).   n119.

Nice et sa région: guide du Syndicat d'initiative,
Office de tourisme de Nice. 9e éd. Grenoble,
[1973?]. Ill. [Guide Paschetta des Alpes-Maritimes;
3.]
GB/A.2021(3).   n120.

Niederschläge und Schneelagerung in der Arktis
/ Max Friedrich. Leipzig, 1891.
GB/B.440(11).   n121.

A **night** at the Grande Chartreuse / Joyce E.
Muddock. [London, 1891.] Pp. [268]-76 of the
Strand Magazine, March 1891.
GB/A.797(7).   n122.

A **night** on the Carnedds: a tale of the hills / E. Ll.
J. Chester, [1935].
GB/A.2076(9).   n123.

Nilakantha: the first ascent / Narinder Kumar.
New Delhi, 1979. Ill.
GB/A.2057.   n124.

No picnic on Mount Kenya / Felice Benuzzi. 4th
ed. London, 1952. Ill., map, port.
Lloyd.900.   n125.

I **nodi** che servono per la nautica, il campeggio,
l'alpinismo, la pesca / Mario Bigon, Guido
Regazzoni. Milano, 1979. Ill. [Oscar Mondadori;
4.]
GB/A.2020(4).   n126.

Noi della montagna: romanzo d'una vita / Luis
Trenker. Milano, 1949. [Montagna; 26.]
GB/A.549.   n127.

Nomenclature historique du Weisshorn / W.A.B.
Coolidge. [N.p., 1917.]
GB.1340(48).   n128.

Les **noms** de lieux de la région du Mont-Blanc /
Roland Boyer. [N.p.], 1979.
GB/A.1740.   n129.

Les **noms** de lieux des montagnes françaises /
Léon Maury. Paris, 1929.
GB/A.100.   n130.

Le **nord** de la Sibérie: voyage parmi les peuplades
de la Russie asiatique et dans la mer glaciale /
l'amiral de Wrangell; traduit du russe par le
prince Emmanuel Galitzin. Limoges, [ca 1830]. Ill.
GB/B.489.   n131.

Il **Nordend**, 4612m.: seconda ascensione da
Macugnaga e discesa a Zermatt / Carlo Restelli.
Torino, 1894. Ill. Pp. [37]-58 of the *Bollettino del
Club Alpino Italiano*, vol.27 no.60.
GB.1881(13).   n132.

Nordöstliche Dolomiten / Gunther Langes. 3.
Aufl. München, 1970. Ill., maps. [Dolomiten-
Kletterführer; 2a.]
GB/A.1050(14).   n133.

Nordover med hurtigruten: historie og hver-
dagsbilder gjennom femti år / Reidar Stavseth.

Oslo, 1943. Ill., map.
GB/A.1867.   n134.

Der **Nordpol** als Völkerheimat: nach den
Ergebnissen der prähistorischen, etymologischen
und naturwissenschaftlichen sowie insbesondere
der Veda- und Avesta-Forschungen Tilaks
dargestellt / Georg Biedenkapp. Jena, 1906.
GB/B.440(12).   n135.

Nordpolfahrten Fridtjof Nansen's, seiner
Vorgänger und Nachfolger / nach dem
norwegischen Originalwerk *Fridtjof Nansen* von
W.C. Drogger und N. Rolfsen übersetzt und auf
Grund neuer Quellenstudien ergänzt von Eugen
von Enzberg. Berlin, [1902]. Ill.
GB/A.2024.   n136.

Nordvestpassagen: beretning om Gøja-
ekspeditionen, 1903-1907 / Roald Amundsen;
med et tillæg av Godfred Hansen. Kristiania, 1907.
Ill., maps, ports.
GB/A.1734.   n137.

Norge. [N.p., ca 1900.] Ill. A book of photographs.
GB/C.114.   n138.

Norika: neues ausführliches Handbuch für
Alpenwanderer und Reisende durch das
Hochland in Oesterreich ob der Enns: Salzburg,
die Gastein, die Kammerguter, Lilienfeld,
Mariazell, St. Florian und die obere Steyermark /
Helmina von Chezy. München, 1833. Ill., map.
GB/A.1795.   n139.

Norsk fjellsport, 1948 / utgitt av Norsk Tindeklub
i anledning av klubbens 40-års jubileum;
[redaksjonskomité: C.W. Rubenson, Hans H.
Røer]. Oslo, 1948.
GB/A.2058.   n140.

Norsk fjellsport, 1958 / utgitt av Norsk Tindeklub
i anledning av klubbens 50-års jubileum;
[redaksjonskomité: Bror W. Bommen et al.]. Oslo,
1958.
GB/A.2059.   n141.

Den **Norske** Turistforenings aarbok. 1918-68.
Kristiania, 1918[-68].
GB/B.131.   n142.

The **North** American Alps, Canadian Rockies,
Mount Robson route: new trails for the tourist, the
alpinist and sportsman. Winnipeg, 1915. Ill., map.
Lloyd.1618(2).   n143.

North American Indians: being letters and notes
on their manners, customs, and conditions,
written during eight years' travel amongst the
wildest tribes of Indians in North America, 1832-
1839 / George Catlin. Edinburgh, 1926. 2v; ill.
GB.1197-8.   n144.

The **North** Cascades National Park / Bob and Ira
Spring; text by Harvey Manning. Seattle, [1975?].
Ill., maps.
GB/B.602(4).   n145.

The **north** coast of Spitzbergen, western part /
Gerard de Geer. Stockholm, 1913. Map. Reprinted
from *Ymer*, 1913, h.3.
GB.1335(4).   n146.

North Face in winter / Toni Hiebeler; translated
by Hugh Merrick. London, [1962]. Ill. Translated
from *Im Banne der Spinne*.
GB.845.   n147.

The **North** Oxfordshire Archaeological Society /
Philip Hookins. Banbury, [1868].
Lloyd.1583(16).   n148.

The **North** Pole: its discovery in 1909 under the
auspices of the Peary Arctic Club / Robert E.
Peary. Toronto, 1910.
GB/A.2098.   n149.

North Pole boarding house / as told by Elsie
McCall Gillis to Eugenie Myles. Toronto, 1951. Ill.,
ports.
GB/A.1722.   n150.

North Switzerland including the Righi, Zurich
and Lucerne / John Ball. London, 1873. Maps.
[Ball's Alpine guides.]
GB/A.709.   n150.1.

North to the Orient / Anne Morrow Lindbergh.
7th printing. New York, 1935. Ill., maps.
GB/A.1865.   n151.

The **north-east** face of Finsteraarhorn / G. Hasler.
London, 1922. Ill. Reprinted from the *Alpine
Journal*, May 1922.
GB.1312(25).   n152.

The **North-West** Passage, 1940-1942 and 1944: the
famous voyages of the Royal Canadian Mounted
Police Schooner *St Roch* / Henry Larsen.
[Vancouver, 1954.] Ill., map.
GB/B.635(11).   n153.

Northern adventure / Jean McGill. Cobalt, Ont., 1976. Ill., maps, ports.
GB/A.1597(14).   n154.

The **northern** barrier of India: a popular account of the Jummoo and Kashmir territories / Frederic Drew. London, 1877.
GB.560.   n155.

The **northern** Cambrian Mountains, or A tour through North Wales / Thomas Compton. [2nd ed. enl.] London, 1820. Ill.
GB/B.365.   n156.

The **Northern** Exploration Company, Ltd. [London, 1913.] Maps. A prospectus.
GB.1336(36).   n157.

Northern regions, or Uncle Richard's relation of Captain Parry's voyages for the discovery of a north-west passage, and Franklin's and Cochrane's overland journeys to other parts of the world. New York, 1827. Ill.
GB.232.   n158.

A **northern** summer, or Travels round the Baltic, through Denmark, Sweden, Russia, Prussia, and part of Germany, in the year 1804 / John Carr. Abridged. Glasgow, 1806. Ill.
GB.346.   n159.

Northern vagabond: the life and career of J.B. Tyrrell / Alex Inglis. Toronto, 1978.
GB/A.1747.   n160.

The **Northland**: studies of the Yukon and the Northwest Territories / John Wolforth. [Toronto, 1968.] Ill., maps. [Curriculum resources books series; 11.]
GB/A.1675(11).   n161.

The **Northwest** Territories: administration — resources — development. Ottawa, 1943. Published by the Bureau of Northwest Territories and Yukon Affairs.
GB/B.478(5).   n162.

Norway and its glaciers, visited in 1851: followed by journals of excursions in the High Alps of Dauphiné, Berne, and Savoy / James D. Forbes. Edinburgh, 1853. Ill., maps.
GB.1213; Lloyd.1310.   n163.

Norway and Sweden / Karl Baedeker. 6th ed. Leipsic, 1895. Translated from *Schweden und Norwegen*.
Lloyd.98.   n164.

Norway eclipse expedition, July 25th to August 24th, 1896. [London?, 1897.] Ill.
GB/A.1741.   n165.

Norway in 1848 and 1849: containing rambles among the fjelds and fjords of the central and western districts / Thomas Forester; with extracts from the journals of M.S. Buddulph. London, 1850. Ill., maps.
GB.979.   n166.

Norway log. [N.p.], 1928.
GB/A.1675(6).   n167.

Norway, the northern playground / William Cecil Slingsby. Edinburgh, [1904]. A prospectus.
GB.1306(15).   n168.

Norwegen, Grönland, Dänemark, Schleswig: Probleme nordischer Politik / Gustav Smedal. Oslo, 1942. Maps. Translated from *Nordisk samarbeide og Danmarks sydgrense*.
GB/A.1870.   n169.

Norwegen und seine Gletscher: nebst Reisen in den Hochalpen von Bern, Savoyen und der Dauphiné / James D. Forbes; aus dem Englischen von Ernst A. Zuchold. 2. Ausg. Leipzig, 1858. Ill., map. Translated from *Norway and its glaciers*.
GB.334.   n170.

Nos montagnes. Unsere Berge. Le nostre vette. Nossas muntagnas: revue du Club suisse de femmes alpinistes. Jahrg.28, Nr.279. Zürich, 1949.
GB.1329(19).   n171.

Nos Pyrénées: récits de montagne / Charles Boutonnet et les membres des groupes 'Ski et montagne' de l'A.S.P.T.T. de Toulouse. Toulouse, 1966. Ill.
GB/A.148.   n172.

Nostalgie di Penna Nera / Ugo Di Vallepiana. 2a ed. Roma, 1933.
GB/A.804(4).   n173.

A **note** on the law of gravitation / Frank S. Smythe. [London], 1928. Port. Pp.14-27 of the *Faraday House Journal*, Michaelmas Term, 1928.
GB.1880(2).   n174.

Note sur l'édicule placé au sommet du Mont Blanc / Jules Janssen. Paris, [1892]. Extrait des *Comptes rendus des séances de l'Académie des Sciences*, t.114, séance du 1er février 1892.
GB/B.260(5).   n175.

Note sur l'observatoire du Mont Blanc / Jules Janssen. Paris, [1891-92]. 2v. Extrait des *Comptes rendus des séances de l'Académie des Sciences*, t.113, 115; séance du 2 novembre 1891, 28 novembre 1892.
GB/B.260(4,6). n176.

Note sur la relation de Paccard — perdue / Henry F. Montagnier; traduit par Henri Ferrand. Lyon, 1921. Translated from *Dr Paccard's lost narrative*. Extrait de la *Revue alpine* du 4e trimestre 1920.
GB.1133(2); GB.1329(38). n177.

Note sur un projet d'observatoire au Mont Blanc / Jules Janssen. Paris, [1819]. Extrait des *Comptes rendus des séances de l'Académie des Sciences*, t.113, séance du 27 juillet 1891.
GB/B.260(3). n178.

Notes abroad and rhapsodies at home / by a veteran traveller [i.e. W. Rae Wilson]. London, 1837. 2v; ill.
Lloyd.726-7. n179.

Notes and reflections during a ramble in Germany / by the author of *Recollections in the Peninsula* [i.e. Joseph Moyle Sherer]. London, 1826.
GB/A.791. n180.

Notes for travellers in Tyrol and Vorarlberg / George Bradshaw. New ed. London, [n.d.]. Ill., maps.
Lloyd.125. n181.

Notes from a knapsack / George Wherry. Cambridge, 1909. Ill.
Lloyd.474. n182.

[**Notes** from the *Yorkshire Ramblers' Club Journal*, vol.5 no.15, 1922, on Clogwyn du'r Arddu.] [Leeds, 1922.]
GB.1880(37). n183.

Notes of a campaign in the Alps, 1927 / Frank S. Smythe. Leeds, 1929. Ill. Pp.282-6 of the *Yorkshire Ramblers' Club Journal*, vol.5 no.18.
GB.1881(47[2]). n184.

Notes of a continental tour made in the summer of 1873 / [Joseph Jordan]. Walsall, [1873]. Reprinted from the *Walsall Advertiser*.
Lloyd.644. n185.

Notes of a course of six lectures [at the Royal Institution] on ice, water, vapour, and air / John Tyndall; Christmas, 1871-2. London, [1872]. Ill.
Lloyd.811. n186.

Notes of a journey from Berne to England through France: made in 1796 / A.D. [i.e. Andrew Douglas]. Notes of a journey made by M.D. [i.e. M. Douglas]. London, 1797. 2v (in 1).
Lloyd.689. n187.

Notes of a ramble through France, Italy, Switzerland, Germany, Holland, and Belgium: and of a visit to the scenes of *The lady of the lake* / by a lover of the picturesque [i.e. Edward Wilkey]. London, 1836.
GB/A.616. n188.

Notes of a season at St.Moritz in the Upper Engadine, and of a visit to the baths of Tarasp / I. Burney Yeo. London, 1870. Ill., map.
Lloyd.505; Lloyd.505A. n189.

Notes of a short journey in France and southern Switzerland / by the Family Eight. [N.p., 1868.]
GB.219. n190.

Notes of a tour in Switzerland, in the summer of 1847 / Baptist W. Noel. London, 1848. Ill.
GB.570; Lloyd.735. n191.

Notes of a tour in the valleys of Piedmont, in the summer of 1854 / Baptist W. Noel. London, 1855. Map.
GB.251; Lloyd.326. n192.

Notes of a tour on the Continent, in August and September 1869 / Mrs Robert Milne. Aberdeen, 1870. Ports.
Lloyd.775. n193.

Notes of a trip to Kedarnath, and other parts of the snowy range of the Himalayas, in the autumn of 1853. Edinburgh, [1854].
GB.1315(8). n194.

Notes of travels in Europe, in the years 1856-1864 inclusive / Alexander Rivington. London, 1865. Ill., port.
GB.59; Lloyd.85; Lloyd.85A. n195.

Notes of wanderings in the Himmala / Pilgrim. Agra, 1844. Map. Attributed to T.J. Saunders and —— Baron.
GB.762. n196.

Notes on a journey through France, from Dieppe through Paris and Lyons, to the Pyrenees, and back through Toulouse, in July, August and

September, 1814 / Morris Birkbeck. 2nd ed., with an appendix. London, 1815.
Lloyd.1150.   n197.

Notes on a journey through France / Morris Birkbeck. 4th ed. London, 1815.
Lloyd.1123.   n198.

Notes on a journey through the Western Himalaya / T.G. Longstaff. London, [1907]. From the *Geographical Journal*, February 1907.
GB.1337(16).   n199.

Notes on certain glaciers in north-west Kashmir / Sir H.H. Hayden. [Calcutta], 1907. Ill., maps. From the *Records, Geological Survey of India*, vol.35 pt.3, 1907.
GB.1317(11).   n200.

Notes on fossils from Prince Charles Foreland, brought home by Dr William S. Bruce in 1906 and 1907 / G.W. Lee. Edinburgh, 1908. Ill. Reprint from the *Proceedings of the Royal Physical Society of Edinburgh*, session 1907-1908, vol.17 no.4.
GB.1335(51).   n201.

Notes on the district of Menteith for tourists and others / R.B. Cunninghame Graham. London, 1895.
GB.1325(8).   n202.

Notes on the early history of the Dent du Requin / J.P. Farrar. London, 1927. Ill. Reprinted from the *Alpine Journal*, May 1927.
GB.1335(64).   n203.

Notes on the lesser climbing of England / E.C. Pyatt. [London, 1946.] Ill. Pp.40-8 of the *Climbers' Club Journal*, N.S. vol.8 no.1, 1945/6.
GB.1337(5).   n204.

Notes on the microscopic structure of some rocks from the Andes of Ecuador, collected by E. Whymper / T.G. Bonney. [London, 1884.] 5v. From the *Proceedings of the Royal Society*, no.229-34, 1884.
GB.612(3).   n205.

Notes on the seal and whale fishery of 1900 / Thomas Southwell. [London, 1901.] Reprinted from the *Zoologist*, no.717, March 1901.
GB.1335(45).   n206.

Notes sur l'alpinisme: massif du Mont-Blanc / Emile Fontaine. Tours, 1930. Ill., ports., facsims.
GB.1306(6); Lloyd.1608(4).   n207.

Notes sur la Suisse et une partie de l'Italie / comte Théobald Walsh. Paris, 1823.
GB/A.801(7).   n208.

Notes sur le versant de la Brenva du Mont Blanc / Jacques Lagarde. Lyon, 1922. Ill. Pp.[157]-70 of the *Revue alpine*, vol.23 no.4.
GB.1329(20[2]).   n209.

Notes sur les inconvénients et les difficultés du tunnel étudié sous le Mont-Blanc et de ses lignes d'accès projetées: avantages incontestables d'un chemin de fer international par le Simplon / D. Colladon. Genève, 1880. Ill.
Lloyd.916.   n210.

Notes, taken during a month's trip, in August, 1844: embracing the voyage from Clyde to Liverpool. Glasgow, 1842.
Lloyd.1616(16).   n211.

Notes taken during different journeys, made in the years 1792-3-4-5-6 into Switzerland, Italy and Germany / A.D. [i.e. Andrew Douglas]. Notes taken by Mrs D. [i.e. M. Douglas]. 2 pt. London, 1798.
Lloyd.1196.   n212.

Notfälle in den Bergen: Verhütung und Erstversorgung / Siegfried Weller, Gottfried Neureuther. Stuttgart, 1967. Ill.
GB/A.455(2).   n213.

Notice biographique sur Jacques Balmat dit Mont-Blanc / Michel Carrier. Genève, 1854. Port.
GB.586; Lloyd.645; Lloyd.991; Lloyd.991A; Lloyd.1583(1).   n214.

Notice biographique sur Mr. Marc Théodore Bourrit / Charles Bourrit. Genève, 1836. Port.
Lloyd.1529.   n215.

Notice de la vie et des écrits de George Louis Le Sage / George Louis Le Sage; rédigée d'après ses notes par Pierre Prévost; suivie d'extraits de sa correspondance avec divers savans et personnes illustres. Genève, 1805.
Lloyd.1604(5).   n216.

Notice et tables destinées à accompagner le baromètre répétiteur / baron Jules Pierre Al. d'Avout. Paris, 1857. Ill.
Lloyd.1613(14).   n217.

Notice historique sur la Grande Chartreuse, avec cinq nouvelles vues dessinées d'après nature et lithographiées par Champin: introduction à

l'ouvrage de M. Champin, intitulé *Excursion à la Grande Chartreuse* / C*** [i.e. Felix Crozet]. Paris, 1839.
Lloyd.1606(8).   n218.

Notice historique sur les cinquante premières années de la Section genevoise du Club alpin suisse. Genève, 1915. Ill.
GB/A.1150.   n219.

[**Notice** of a meet] / Scottish Mountaineering Club. 17/3/1922. Edinburgh, 1922.
GB.1334(34).   n220.

Notice of a paper laid before the Geological Society on the structure of the Alps and adjoining parts of the Continent, and their relation to the secondary and transition rocks of England / William Buckland. London, [1821]. Article 9, pp.450-68, *Annals of Philosophy*, June 1821.
Lloyd.980.   n221.

[**Notice** of meetings] / Alpine Club. 1931. [London, 1931.]
GB.1327(6).   n222.

[**Notice** of reception, meeting and dinner, etc. 1948] / Scottish Mountaineering Club. Edinburgh, 1948. With *Account of receipts and expenditure, 1948*.
GB.1318(1).   n223.

[**Notice** of the Annual General Meeting and balloting list] / Royal Geographical Society. 14th June 1948. [London, 1948.]
GB.1333(1).   n224.

Notice sur les altitudes du Mont-Blanc et du Mont-Rose, déterminées par des mesures barométriques et géodésiques / François Joseph Delcros. [Paris, 1851.] Extrait de l'*Annuaire météorologique de la France*, année 1851.
GB.1130(2).   n225.

Notice sur les glaciers, les moraines et les blocs erratiques des Alpes / Ch. Godeffroy. Paris, 1840.
GB/A.424(1).   n226.

Notice sur les glaciers, les moraines, et les blocs erratiques des Alpes, par Ch. Godeffroy. Etude sur les glaciers, par L. Agassiz. Théorie des glaciers de la Savoie, par M. le chanoine Rendu / [A. Favre]. [Geneva, 1841.] A review.
GB/A.424(3).   n227.

Notices géologiques et paléontologiques sur les Alpes vaudoises et les régions environnantes /

Eugène Renevier. Lausanne, 1865. Maps. Tiré du *Bulletin de la Société vaudoise des sciences naturelles*, tom.8.
Lloyd.1606(4).   n228.

[**Notices** of meets] / Scottish Mountaineering Club. 1951-61. Edinburgh, 1951-61.
GB.1331(28); GB.1331(36).   n229.

[**Notices** of various meets, dinners, etc.] / Rucksack Club. [Manchester], 1950-62.
GB.1331(40).   n230.

[**Notices** re applications for membership] / Scottish Mountaineering Club. Glasgow, 1951-57.
GB.1331(31).   n231.

Notiziario / Club Alpino Italiano, Sezione Ligure. 15 ottobre 1946-luglio-dicembre '67. Genova, [1946-67.] Ill.
GB/A.903-9.   n232.

Notiziario mensile / Club Alpino Italiano, Sezione di Torino. Anno 1 no.2-anno 2 no.1, febb.1939-genn.1940. Torino, 1939-40. Wanting anno 1, no.3, 5, 9-12.
Lloyd.1620(32-36).   n232.1.

Notizie naturali e civili su la Lombardia. Vol.1. Milano, 1844. Map.
GB/A.868.   n233.

Nouveau guide en Suisse / H.A. Berlepsch; traduit sur l'édition de 1863. Hildburghausen, [n.d.]. Ill., map. [Guides-Meyer; 2.] Translated from *Neuestes Reisebuch für die Schweiz*.
Lloyd.314.   n234.

Un **nouveau** passage de Saint-Christophe à la Grave / W.A.B. Coolidge. Grenoble, [1884]. From *Les Alpes françaises*, no.11, 25 octobre, 1884.
Lloyd.1283.   n235.

Nouveau voyage en Suisse / Helene Maria Williams; traduit par J.B. Say. Paris, 1798. Translated from *A tour in Switzerland*.
GB/A.1283.   n236.

Nouveau voyage vers le septentrion: où l'on représente le naturel, les coutumes, & la religion des Norwegiens, des Lapons, des Kiloppes, des Russiens, des Borandiens, des Syberiens, des Zembliens, des Samoïedes, &c. / [Pierre Martin de la Martinière]. Amsterdam, 1708. Ill.
GB/A.1788.   n237.

Nouveaux mémoires du baron de Pöllnitz, contenant l'histoire de sa vie, et la relation de ses premiers voyages. Nouv. éd. Francfort, 1738. 2v (in 1); ill.
GB/A.737.   n238.

Nouveaux voyages en zigzag à la Grande Chartreuse / Rodolphe Töpffer. Paris, 1854. Ill.
GB/B.367.   n239.

Nouveaux voyages en zigzag, à la Grande-Chartreuse, autour du Mont Blanc / Rodolphe Töpffer. 5e éd. Paris, 1886. Ill.
Lloyd.1475.   n240.

Nouvel abrégé de tous les voyages autour du monde depuis Magellan jusqu'à d'Urville et Laplace 1519-1832 / E. Henri Garnier. Bruxelles, 1837. 2v (in 1); ill.
GB/A.487.   n241.

Le **nouvel** anabaptiste, ou L'agriculteur-pratique: almanach nouveau pour l'an 1823 / par un ami des champs. Montbélard, [1822].
Lloyd.1591(4).   n242.

Nouvel itinéraire des vallées autour du Mont-Blanc / J.P. Pictet-Mallet. Genève, 1808. Map.
GB.156; Lloyd.163.   n243.

Nouvel itinéraire des vallées autour du Mont-Blanc / J.P. Pictet-Mallet. Genève, 1818. Map.
GB.117; Lloyd.333; Lloyd.333A.   n244.

Nouvel itinéraire des vallées autour du Mont-Blanc / J.P. Pictet-Mallet. 2e éd., rev., augm. Genève, 1829. Map.
Lloyd.162.   n245.

Nouvel itinéraire portatif de Suisse, d'après Ebel et les sources les plus récentes. Paris, 1827. Maps. [Collection européenne de nouveaux itinéraires portatifs.]
GB.12.   n246.

Nouvelle ascension du Grand-Paradis et promenades alpines / P.J. Frassy. Torino, 1870. Extrait du *Bollettino del Club Alpino Italiano*, no.15, 2e semestre 1869.
Lloyd.1217.   n247.

Nouvelle description de l'Oberland bernois à l'usage des voyageurs / [Rod. Walthard]. Berne, 1838. Maps.
GB.1092.   n248.

Nouvelle description des glacières, vallées de glace et glaciers qui forment la grande chaîne des Alpes de Savoye, de Suisse et d'Italie / Marc Théodore Bourrit. Nouv. éd., rev. et augm. Genève, 1787. 3v; ill., maps.
GB.421-3; GB.576 (bound in 1); Lloyd.625-7; Lloyd.630-2.   n249.

Nouvelle description des vallées de glace et des hautes montagnes qui forment la chaîne des Alpes pennines & rhétiennes / Marc Théodore Bourrit. Genève, 1785. 3v; ill., maps.
Lloyd.549-50 (bound in 2); GB.517 (v.3 only).   n250.

Nouvelle description générale et particulière des glacières, vallées de glace et glaciers qui forment la grande chaîne des Alpes de Suisse, d'Italie & de Savoye / Marc Théodore Bourrit. Nouv. éd., corr. & augm. d'un troisième volume. Genève, 1785. 3v; ill., map.
Lloyd.554-6.   n251.

Nouvelle flore coloriée de poche des Alpes et des Pyrénées / Ch. Flahault. Paris, 1906-12. 3v; ill. [Bibliothèque de poche du naturaliste; 2, 16, 21.]
GB/A.2076(8).   n252.

Nouvelles escalades dans les Alpes, 1910-1914: premières du Taeschhorn, face sud — Grépon, mer de Glace — Grandes Jorasses, col des Hirondelles, etc. / Geoffrey Winthrop Young; traduction de Bernard Lemoine. Neuchâtel, [ca 1935]. Ill. [Montagne.]
GB/A.1374.   n253.

Nouvelles études et expériences sur les glaciers actuels: leur structure, leur progression et leur action physique sur le sol / Louis Agassiz. Paris, 1847.
Lloyd.1299.   n254.

Nouvelles études et expériences sur les glaciers actuels: leur structure, leur progression et leur action physique sur le sol: atlas / Louis Agassiz. Paris, 1847.
Lloyd.1547.   n255.

Nouvelles excursions et séjours dans les glaciers et les hautes régions des Alpes, &c.: coupe idéale du système alpin / E. Desor. Neuchâtel, 1845.
GB.254; Lloyd.353.   n256.

Nouvelles genevoises / Rodolphe Töpffer. 3e éd. Paris, 1851. Ill.
Lloyd.1267.   n257.

Nouvelles genevoises / Rodolphe Töpffer. 5e éd. Paris, [1877?]. Ill.
Lloyd.1401.   n258.

Nova Helvetiae tabula geographica / Johann Jacob Scheuchzer; [edited by] Arthur Dürst. Zurich, 1971.
GB/A.1036.   n259.

Novant'anni della Sezione di Roma del Club Alpino Italiano, pubblicato per il centenario del C.A.I., 1863-1963. [Rome, 1963.] Ill.
GB/B.289(6).   n260.

La **Novara** sacra / Carlo Bescapè; tradotta in italiano con annotazioni e vita dell'autore da Giuseppe Ravizza. Bologna, 1973. Ill. Facsimile reprint of the Novara, 1878 ed.
GB/B.405.   n261.

Novelle e paesi valdostani / Giuseppe Giacosa; a cura di Vanni Bramanti. Firenze, 1971.
GB/A.1259.   n262.

Nozioni di alpinismo / [Ugo Manera et al.]. Torino, 1969. Ill. Published by the Club Alpino Italiano, Sezione di Torino, Sottosezione G.E.A.T.
GB/A.1051(5).   n263.

Nozioni mediche elementari per l'alpinista / Emilio Giani. Milano, 1933. Published by the Club Alpino Italiano, Comitato Scientifico, Commissione Medico-Fisiologica.
GB/A.1034(1).   n264.

Nozioni topografiche del Monte Rosa ed ascensioni su di esso / Giovanni Gnifetti. Torino, 1845.
GB.993; Lloyd.1586; Lloyd.1589(2).   n265.

Nozioni topografiche del Monte Rosa ed ascensioni su di esso / Giovanni Gnifetti. 2a ed., con note ed aggiunte. Novara, 1858.
Lloyd.1577(2).   n266.

La **nuit** des drus / Charles Gos. Lausanne, 1929.
GB.1323(4); Lloyd.1615(13).   n267.

The **numerical** system of classification [of mountain climbs] / H.E. Kretschmer. [London, 1943.] Pp.154-62 of the *Climbers' Club Journal*, N.S. vol.7 no.2.
GB.1339(9).   n268.

Numismatic history of England, from 1066 to the present time: in two papers, read before the Historic Society of Lancashire and Cheshire /

Frederick J. Jeffery. Liverpool, 1867. Ill.
Lloyd.1574(4).   n269.

Nuova guida della Valle d'Aosta / [Renato Willien]. Torino, [1973]. Ill., maps.
GB/A.799(5).   n270.

Nuove ascensioni nel gruppo del Monte Bianco: Aiguille de la Brenva m.3207.: Mont de Jetoula m.3345 e 3365 c.a / Adolfo Hess. Torino, 1898. Ill. Pp.466-76 of the *Rivista Mensile del Club Alpino Italiano*, vol.17 no.11.
GB.1881(17).   n271.

Nuove tavole barometriche per il calcolo facile e spedito delle altezze con un cenno sull'uso dell'aneroide / E.F. Bossoli; aggiuntovi l'elenco delle altezze dei principali monti e passi delle Alpi, compilato dal nobile Francesco Lurani. Milano, 1881. Published by the Club Alpino Italiano, Sezione di Milano.
GB/A.1165.   n272.

Nuovissima guida dei viaggiatori in Italia / Epimaco e Pasquale Artaria. 3a ed. accr. e corr. Milano, 1834. Ill., maps.
GB/A.788.   n273.

-O-

O, Alpenluft! Sang und Klang aus den Bergen / Georg Lang. Frankfurt a.M., 1891.
GB/A.584. o001.

Ober-Engadin: Album mit 40 Ansichten. Kilchberg, [ca 1930]. Ill.
GB/B.366(11). o002.

Das **Oberengadin**: sein Climat und seine Quellen als Heilwerthe / A. Biermann. Leipzig, 1875.
GB/A.1468(9). o003.

Das **Oberengadin**: tourist's guide to the Upper Engadine / M. Caviezel; translated by A.M.H. London, 1877. Map.
GB/A.671; Lloyd.219; Lloyd.219A. o004.

Oberengadin mit seinen Gletschern / R. Guler. Zürich, [ca 1880]. Ill.
GB/A.1147. o005.

The **Oberland** and its glaciers: explored and illustrated with ice-axe and camera / Hereford Brooke George. London, 1866. Ill., map.
GB.1240; Lloyd.1390; Lloyd.1390A; Lloyd.1477.
o006.

L'**Oberland** bernois sous les rapports historique, scientifique et topographique: journal d'un voyageur / publié par P. Ober. Berne, 1854. 2v.
GB.375-6. o007.

Observations des hauteurs faites avec le baromètre, au mois d'aoust 1751: sur une partie des Alpes en présence, et sous les auspices de milord comte de Rochford [i.e. Benjamin Thompson, Count Rumford] / John T. Needham. [Turin, 1751.]
GB/B.288(17). o008.

Observations made in Savoy, in order to ascertain the height of mountains by means of the barometer: being an examination of Mr. de Luc's rules, delivered in his *Recherches sur les modifications de l'atmosphère* / Sir George Shuckburgh; read at the Royal Society, May 8 and 15, 1777. London, 1777. Pp.513-97 of *Philosophical Transactions*, vol.67.
GB.1247; Lloyd.1621(7). o009.

Observations météorologiques faites au col du Géant du 5 au 18 juillet 1788 / Horace Bénédict de Saussure. Genève, 1891. Ill. *Mémoires de la Société de physique et d'histoire naturelle de Genève*, volume supplémentaire, 1890, no.9.
GB/B.390(3). o010.

Observations on Mount Vesuvius, Mount Etna, and other volcanos: in a series of letters, addressed to the Royal Society: to which are added, explanatory notes by the author, hitherto unpublished / Sir William Hamilton; [edited by Thomas Cadell]. London, 1772. Ill., map.
GB.299. o011.

Observations on Mount Vesuvius, Mount Etna, and other volcanos: in a series of letters, addressed to the Royal Society: to which are added, explanatory notes by the author, hitherto unpublished / Sir William Hamilton; edited by Thomas Cadell. London, 1774. Ill., map.
Lloyd.419. o012.

Observations on several parts of Great Britain, particularly the High-lands of Scotland, relative chiefly to picturesque beauty, made in the year 1776 / William Gilpin. 3rd ed. London, 1808. 2v; ill., maps.
GB.815-6. o013.

Observations on the intellectual culture of the Caribou Eskimos / Knud Rasmussen. New York, 1976. Ill. [Thule expedition, 5th, 1921-1924. Report; vol.7 no.2.]
GB/A.1833. o014.

Observations on waders (Charadriidae) at Scoresby Sund, east Greenland / J. de Korte, C.A.W. Bosman, H. Meltofte. Copenhagen, 1981. Ill., maps. [Meddelelser om Grønland. Bioscience; 7.]
GB/A.1819. o015.

Un **observatoire** au Mont-Blanc / Jules Janssen. Paris, 1892.
GB/B.260(7). o016.

L'**observatoire** du Pic-du-Midi: monographie à l'usage des touristes / Camille Dauzère. Toulouse, 1921. Published by the Université de Toulouse.
GB/A.455(6). o017.

Occasional papers on the theory of glaciers, now first collected and chronologically arranged: with a prefatory note on the recent progress and present aspect of the theory / James D. Forbes. Edinburgh, 1859. Ill.
GB.966; Lloyd.1193. o018.

L'**océan** Arctique: voyages d'exploration au pôle Nord / J. Hayes; abrégés par H. Vattemare. Paris, 1880. [Bibliothèque des écoles et des familles.]
GB/A.2091.   o019.

Ocherki po istochnikovedeniiu Sibiri / A.I. Andreev. 2-oe izd. ispr. i dop. Moskva, 1960-65. 2v; port. At head of title: Akademiia nauk SSSR, Institut istorii, Leningradskoe otdelenie.
GB/A.1770.   o020.

Die **Oetzthaler** Gruppe / Heinrich Hess. [Berlin, 1893?] Ill. Pp.[245]-376 of *Erschliessung der Ostalpen*, Bd.2.
GB.1378.   o021.

Oeuvres / chevalier de Boufflers. La Haye, 1781.
GB/A.1167.   o022.

Oeuvres alpines / Théodore Camus. Chambery, 1930. Ill.
GB/A.1153.   o023.

Of gods and glaciers: on and around Mt. Rataban / Man Mohan Sharma. New Delhi, 1979.
GB/A.1682.   o024.

Of men and mountains / William O. Douglas. London, 1951. Map.
GB.822.   o025.

Of the inhabitants of Chamouni, their manners, customs, &c.: abridged from vol.3 of *Voyages dans les Alpes* / Horace Bénédict de Saussure. Edinburgh, 1787. Pp.235-9 of the *Scots Magazine*, vol.49.
GB.1743.   o026.

Off the mill: some occasional papers / G.F. Browne. London, 1895.
GB.410; Lloyd.539.   o027.

Official handbook / Royal Forth Yacht Club. 1949, 1952, 1954-56, 1958, 1962, 1964. London, [1949-64].
GB.1326(24-31).   o028.

Die **ohnlängst** in Nürnberg befindlichen und nach der Natur abgezeichneten Bildnüsse, der aus der Strasse David in Gröndländischen, Familie. Nurnberg, [ca 1760].
GB/C.111.   o029.

L'**Oisans** au Moyen-Age: étude de géographie historique en haute montagne d'après des documents inédits suivie de la transcription des textes / André Allix. Paris, 1929. Map.
GB/A.74.   o030.

L'**Oisans** il y a vingt ans: souvenirs / W.A.B. Coolidge. Grenoble, 1893.
Lloyd.1226.   o031.

The **old** glaciers of Switzerland and North Wales / A.C. Ramsay. London, 1859. Ill., map.
Lloyd.1602(17).   o032.

The **old** glaciers of Switzerland and North Wales / A.C. Ramsay. London, 1860. Ill., map.
Lloyd.264; Lloyd.280.   o033.

Old Merry's travels on the Continent. London, [1869]. Ill.
Lloyd.113.   o034.

The **old** whaling days: a history of southern New Zealand from 1830-1840 / Robert McNab. Auckland, 1975. [New Zealand classics.]
GB/A.1758.   o035.

Oltre il sentiero: le Aquile di S. Martino (le guide del primiero) / Elio Conighi, Antonino Vischi, Gino Callin. Trento, 1972. Ill.
GB/B.384.   o036.

Oltre il sentiero: le guide della valle di Fassa / Gino Callin, Elio Conighi, Antonino Vischi. Trento, 1972. Ill.
GB/B.349.   o037.

Omaggio al XXXII. Congresso degli Alpinisti convocato nei giorni 1 a 7 settembre 1901 in Brescia. Brescia, 1901.
GB/B.390(13).   o038.

L'**ombre** de Chamossaire / F.A. Forel. Genève, 1885. Pp.291-4 of l'*Echo des Alpes*, no.4, 1885.
GB.1306(21).   o039.

Omegna e il corso dello Strona / Franco Barbero. Como, 1970. Ill., map. [Minima turistica Piemonte: il Novarese, lago d'Orta; 2.]
GB/A.835(11).   o040.

On Alexander's track to the Indus: personal narrative of explorations on the north-west frontier of India / Aurel Stein. London, 1929. Ill., maps.
GB.1117.   o041.

On Alpine heights and British crags / George D. Abraham. Boston, 1916.
GB/A.2108.   o042.

On climbing / Charles Evans. Woodstock, [1956]. GB/A.2211.   o043.

On foot through Tyrol in the summer of 1855 / Walter White. London, 1856.
Lloyd.696.   o044.

On Helvellyn with the shepherds. [London, 1890.] Pp.379-94 of the *Cornhill Magazine*, Oct.1890.
GB.1880(33).   o045.

On high hills: memories of the Alps / Geoffrey Winthrop Young. London, 1927. Ill.
GB.1015; GB.1016.   o046.

On high hills: memories of the Alps / Geoffrey Winthrop Young. 2nd ed. London, 1927.
GB.941.   o047.

On high hills: memories of the Alps / Geoffrey Winthrop Young. 5th ed. London, 1947.
GB.785 (impf); GB.786 (impf).   o048.

On high hills, [by] G. Winthrop Young / M.S. Gotch. Liverpool, 1928. A review. Pp.226-8 of the *Climbers' Club Journal*, N.S. vol.3 no.2.
GB.1881(46).   o049.

On mountain-climbing for professional men / Cecil Kent Austin. Boston, 1907. Ill. Reprinted from the *Boston Medical and Surgical Journal*, vol.156 no.25, June 20, 1907.
Lloyd.1612(9).   o050.

On rock and ice: mountaineering in photographs / André Roch. London, 1947.
Lloyd.1289.   o051.

On ropes and knots / edited by J.P. Farrar. [N.p.], 1913. Ill.
GB.1306(5); Lloyd.1602(20).   o052.

On some cases of the conversion of compact 'greenstones' into schists / T.G. Bonney. [N.p, 1894.] From the *Quarterly Journal of the Geographical Society* for May 1894, vol.1.
GB/A.514(9).   o053.

On some relics of the guides lost on Mont Blanc / J.J. Cowell; read before the Alpine Club. [London, 1864.] Pp.332-9 of the *Alpine Journal*, vol.1, 1864.
GB.1737(2).   o054.

On the admiration of mountains, in Gesner's pamphlet *On milk and substances prepared from milk*; a description of the Riven Mountain, commonly called Mount Pilatus; translated by H.B.D. Soulé; together with *On Conrad Gesner* and *The mountaineering of Theuerdank*, by J. Monroe Thorington; [edited by W. Dock]. San Francisco, 1937. Ill.
GB.1272.   o055.

On the conformation of the Alps / John Tyndall. [London, 1864.] From the *Philosophical Magazine* for October 1864.
GB/A.514(1).   o056.

On the crystalline schists and their relation to the mesozoic rocks in the Lepontine Alps / T.G. Bonney. [N.p., 1890.] Ill. From the *Quarterly Journal of the Geological Society* for May 1890, vol.46.
GB/A.514(5).   o057.

On the direction of the wind at the Royal Observatory, Greenwich, in the twenty years ending December 1860 / James Glaisher. [London, 1861.] From the *Proceedings of the British Meteorological Society*, Nov.20. 1861.
GB.1307(9).   o058.

On the effects of elevation and floods on health: and the general health of Oxford, compared with that of other districts / G.A. Rowell. London, 1866.
Lloyd.1583(9).   o059.

On the extraordinary cold weather at the end of 1860 and beginning of 1861 / James Glaisher. [London, 1861.] From the *Report of the Meteorological Society* for 1861.
GB.1307(12).   o060.

On the fells of the Lake District / Claude E. Benson. [London, 1901.] Ill. Pp.[484]-500 of the *Badminton Magazine* for May 1901.
GB.1312(23).   o061.

On the frontier and beyond: a record of thirty years' service / Sir Frederick O'Connor. London, 1931.
GB.917.   o062.

On the geological relations of the secondary and primary rocks of the chain of Mont Blanc / James D. Forbes. [Edinburgh], 1856. Pp.[189]-203 of the *Edinburgh New Philosophical Journal*, April 1856.
GB.1880(59).   o063.

On the Jöstedal-Bræ glaciers in Norway / C.M. Doughty. London, 1866. Map.
Lloyd.1605(13).   o064.

On the nature and causes of the physiological phenomena, comprised in the term 'mountain sickness': more especially as experienced among the higher Alps / Stanhope Templeman Speer. [London], 1853. Pp.49-53 and 80-7 of the *Provincial Medical and Surgical Journal*, Jan.21 & 28, 1853.
GB.1331(44). o065.

On the pressure of the wind in strong winds and in gales, at the Royal Observatory, Greenwich, from the year 1841 to 1860 / James Glaisher. [London, 1862.] From the *Proceedings of the British Meteorological Society*, Jan.15, 1862.
GB.1307(11). o066.

On the weather from October 1859 to December 1860 / James Glaisher. London, 1862. From the *Report of the Meteorological Society* for 1861.
GB.1307(13). o067.

On the 'White Pass' pay roll / the President of the White Pass & Yukon route. Chicago, 1908. Ill.
GB/A.1701. o068.

On thermometric observations in the Alps / John Ball. [London? n.d.] From the *Proceedings of the British Meteorological Society*.
GB.1307(10). o069.

Once in the Eastern Alps / J. Monroe Thorington. [Boston, 1948.] Ill. Extracted from *Appalachia*, June 1948.
GB.1337(13). o070.

Onze jours aux Pyrénées centrales / racontés et illustrés par les congressistes de la Réunion générale du Club alpin français 1934. Toulouse, 1934. Ill. Published by the Section des Pyrénées centrales du C.A.F.
GB/A.1381(6). o071.

Ood-le-uk the wanderer / Alice Alison Lide, Margaret Alison Johansen. New York, 1930. Ill., map.
GB/A.1902. o072.

Op en om den Mont Blanc / P.C. Visser. Rotterdam, 1918. Ill.
GB.1333(12). o073.

The **open** polar sea: a paper read before the Albany Institute / George Rogers Howell. Albany, N.Y., 1884.
GB/B.440(22). o074.

The **opening** of the Canadian North, 1870-1914 / Morris Zaslow. Toronto, [1971]. Ill. [The Canadian centenary series.]
GB/A.1759. o075.

L'**opera** del Club Alpino Italiano nel primo suo cinquantennio, 1863-1913 / pubblicato per cura del Consiglio Direttivo. Torino, 1913. Ill., ports.
Lloyd.1621(4). o076.

Opportunities / Sir John Hunt. [London], 1941. Map. Pp.5-8 of the *Climbers' Club Journal*, N.S. vol.6 no.3.
GB.1339(22[1]). o077.

Ora d'andare: poesie di montagna / Mario Perucca. [Romano Canavese], 1972. Ill.
GB/B.377(4). o078.

Ordeal by ice: the search for the Northwest Passage / Farley Mowat. Rev. ed. Toronto, 1977. Ill., maps, ports. [The top of the world; 1.]
GB/A.1605. o079.

Das **Originalpanorama** eines Theils der Unterwaldner und Berner Alpen: von Aarburg aus aufgenommen von J.B. Micheli du Crest / J.H. Graf. [Bern, 1892.] Pp.[245]-52 of the *Jahrbuch des Schweizer Alpenclub*, Jahrg.27.
GB.1881(60). o080.

L'**origine** des lacs suisses / Bernhard Studer. [N.p.], 1864. Tiré de la *Bibliothèque universelle et revue suisse, Archives des sciences phys. et nat.*, t.19.
Lloyd.1606(5). o081.

L'**origine** des Préalpes romandes et les zones de sédimentation des Alpes de Suisse et de Savoie / Emile Haug. Lausanne, 1894. Extrait des *Archives des sciences physiques et naturelles*, août 1894.
GB/A.514(8). o082.

Les **origines** du Grand Combin et du Mont Collon et la légende de la 'Crête à Collon' / W.A.B. Coolidge. Aoste, 1913. Extrait du *Bulletin de la Société de la flore valdôtaine*, no.9.
GB.1340(35). o083.

Le **origini** storiche di Arolla / W.A.B. Coolidge; versione italiana di W. Laeng. Torino, 1914. Estratto dalla *Rivista del Club Alpino Italiano*, vol.33 n.10, anno 1914.
GB.1340(45). o084.

Ornament narodov Sibiri kak istoricheskii istochnik po materialam XIX-nachala XXv.: narody Severa i Dal nego Vostoko / S.V. Ivanov. Leningrad, 1963. [Trudy Instituta etnografii; nov.

ser. 81.] At head of title: Akademiia nauk SSSR.
GB/A.1786.   o085.

Ornithological observations in northeast Greenland between 74° 30' and 76° 00' N. lat., 1976 / Hans Meltofte, Magnus Elander, Christian Hjort. Copenhagen, 1981. Ill., maps. [Meddelelser om Grønland. Bioscience; 3.]
GB/A.1819.   o086.

Oro fra le rocce: romanzo / Irmgard Wurmbrand; traduzione di Violante Zovetti. Milano, 1946. [Montagna; 23.]
GB/A.552.   o087.

Ortlergruppe: ein Führer für Täler, Hütten und Berge / Peter Holl. 5., völlig neu bearb. Aufl. München, 1981. Ill., maps. [Alpenvereinsführer. Reihe: Zentralalpen.]
GB/A.1965(8).   o088.

Ortles-Cevedale / Luciano Viazzi. Bologna, 1981. Ill., maps.
GB/B.539.   o089.

Ortsregister zu Amthors *Alpenfreund*: erste Serie, Band 1-11. Gera, 1879.
GB/A.1457.   o090.

Oscillations des quatre grands glaciers de la vallée de Chamonix et énumération des ascensionnistes au Mont Blanc / Venance Payot. Genève, 1879. Map.
Lloyd.1616(22).   o091.

Osservazioni geologiche sulle Alpi Marittime e sugli Apennini Liguri / Angelo Sismonda. [N.p.], 1841. Maps. Offprint from *Memorie della Reale Accademia delle Scienze di Torino*, ser. 2 tom. 4.
GB/B.501(15).   o092.

L'Ossola e le sue valli; guida turistica, storica, artistica / Giovanni De-Maurizi. 2a ed. riv. e ampliata a cura di Franco Ferraris. Domodossola, [1954]. Ill., map.
GB/A.1059.   o093.

L'Ossola inferiore: notizie storiche e documenti / raccolti da Bianchetti Enrico. Domodossola, 1969. 2v; map. Facsimile reprint of the Rome, 1878 ed.
GB/A.1005-6.   o094.

Ostafrikanische Gletscherfahrten: Forschungsreisen im Kilimandscharo-Gebiet / Hans Meyer. Leipzig, 1890. Ill., maps.
GB/B.435.   o095.

Osterreichische Alpen Zeitung: Organ des Alpen-Club Oesterreich Jahrg.1 Nr.1-Jahrg.74 Folge 1335, 1879-1964. Wien, [1879-1964]. Also called: *Organ des Oesterreichischen Alpenclub*. Wanting 1906.
GB/B.154-226 (Jahrg.1-74, 1879-1956); GB.1580-1608 (Folge 1069-1335, 1928-64) (impf.); Lloyd. 1402-9 (another copy of Folge 969-1118, 1129-1271/72); Lloyd.1953A (another copy of Folge 1255).   o096.

Die **österreichischen** Alpen: eine zusammenfassende Darstellung / O. Abel, F. Bruckner [et al.]; herausgegeben von Hans Leitmeier. Leipzig, 1928. Ill., maps.
GB/B.125.   o097.

Der **Ostgrat** der Aiguille du Plan / J.H. Bell. Bern, 1930. Ill. Separatdruck aus D*ie Alpen*, Jahrg. 6 Hft 11, 1930.
GB.1322(6).   o098.

Osttirol: Grossvenediger, Grossglockner: ein Wanderführer / Louis Oberwalder. Innsbruck, 1956. Maps.
GB/A.1807.   o099.

Ottanta itinerari di escursionismo-alpinismo, sci alpinismo in Valle d'Aosta / Osvaldo Cardellina. Aosta, 1977. Ill., maps.
GB/A.1964(5).   o100.

Otztaler Alpen: ein Führer für Täler, Hütten und Berge / Heinrich E. Klier, Henriette Prochaska. München, 1953. Ill., maps. [Alpenvereinsführer. Reihe: Zentralalpen.]
GB/A.1808.   o101.

Où le Père a passé / Pierre Puiseux. Paris, 1928. 2v.
GB/A.1091-2.   o102.

Où règne la lumière / Georges Sonnier. Paris, 1946. Ill.
GB/A.1154.   o103.

Oued Djaret: una delle più antiche stazioni di arte rupestre del Sahara / Giuseppe Rivalta. Bologna, [1981?]. Ill., maps.
GB/A.2022(5).   o104.

Oulx e Cesana / Ettore Doglio. Torino, 1933. Ill., map. [Guida delle valli di Susa; 2.]
GB/A.1034(4).   o105.

Our Arctic province: Alaska and the Seal Islands / Henry W. Elliott. New York, 1886. Ill., maps.
GB/A.1669.   o106.

Our Everest adventure: the pictorial history from Kathmandu to the summit / Sir John Hunt. Leicester, 1954.
Lloyd.1288. o107.

Our life in the Swiss highlands / John Addington Symonds and his daughter Margaret. 2nd ed. London, 1907.
GB.1027. o108.

Our lost explorers: the narrative of the *Jeannette* Arctic expedition as related by the survivors, and in the records and last journals of Lieutenant De Long: also an account of the *Jeannette* search expeditions, their discoveries, the burning of the *Rodgers* &c. &c. / revised by Raymond Lee Newcomb. Hartford, Conn., 1883. Ill., maps.
GB/A.2147. o109.

Our western archipelago / Henry M. Field. New York, 1895. Ill., maps.
GB/A.1704. o110.

Ouresiphoites helveticus, sive Itinera alpina tria: in quibus incolæ, animalia, plantæ et quicquid per Alpes helveticas & rhaeticas rarum sit, & notatu dignum, exponitur, & iconibus illustratur / Johannes Jacobus Scheuzerus. Londini, 1708. 3v (in 1); ill., port.
GB.1301. o111.

Ouresiphoites helveticus, sive Itinera per Helvetiae alpinas regiones facta. annis 1702-1711 / Johannes Jacobus Scheuzerus. [Leiden], 1723. 4v; ill., maps, port.
GB.1216-7 (bound in 2); Lloyd.1005 (bound in 1); Lloyd.1304-5 (bound in 2); Lloyd.1304A-5A (bound in 2). o112.

Out for a holiday with Cook's excursion, through Switzerland and Italy / Arthur Sketchley. London, [1870].
Lloyd.1614(6). o113.

The **Outer** Hebrides / Mathew Botterill. [Leeds, 1930.] Ill. Pp.13-8 of the *Yorkshire Ramblers' Club Journal*, vol.6 no.19, 1930.
GB.1881(33); GB.1881(34). o114.

An **outline** of the Canadian eastern Arctic: its geography, peoples and problems / J. Lewis Robinson. Ottawa, 1944. Published by the Bureau of Northwest Territories and Yukon Affairs, Lands, Parks and Forests Branch.
GB/B.478(4). o115.

Outline sketches in the High Alps of Dauphiné / T.G. Bonney. London, 1865. Ill., map.
GB.1200; Lloyd.1296; Lloyd.1296A. o116.

The **outpost** of the lost: an Arctic adventure / David L. Brainard; edited by Bessie Rowland James. Indianapolis, 1929. Maps.
GB/A.1793. o117.

Over some Alpine passes: memories of 1908 / W.C. Berwick Sayers. [Croydon], 1913.
GB/A.181(2). o118.

Over the Alps, by the St. Gothard Pass / Charles Hardwick. [N.p., n.d.]
GB.1335(56); Lloyd.1612(8). o119.

Over the Alps on a bicycle / Elizabeth Robins Pennell. London, 1898. Ill.
Lloyd.791. o120.

Over the Alps to Rome and a group of Italian cities / Robert Best. London, 1867.
Lloyd.197. o121.

Over the Gemmi / Thomas Stanley. London, 1889. Pp.[287]-98 of *East and West*, no.4, Sept. 1889.
GB.1881(52). o122.

Over the Pyrenees: a bicyclist's adventures / Alfred M. Bolton. London, 1883.
Lloyd.1613(6). o123.

Over the roof of Europe: climbing Mont Blanc / notes and photographs by Frank S. Smythe. London, 1940. Pp.342-[7] of the *Geographical Magazine*, vol.10 no.5, March 1940.
GB.1339(30). o124.

Over the sea and far away, being a narrative of wanderings round the world / Thomas Woodbine Hinchliff. London, 1876. Ill.
GB.1066; Lloyd.1180; Lloyd.1180A. o125.

Over Tyrolese hills / Frank S. Smythe. London, 1936. Ill.
GB.958. o126.

Overland, inland, and upland: a lady's notes of personal observations and adventure / A.U. London, 1873. Ill.
Lloyd.526. o127.

Ovras da Giachen Caspar Muoth. Pt 1. Glion, 1931.
GB/A.1162. o128.

Oxford and Cambridge mountaineering, 1921, 1928-1929. Cambridge, [1921-29]. Ill. Published by the University of Oxford Mountaineering Club. 1921 edited by Raymond Greene, Eliot Wallis; 1928-29 edited by J.L. Longland.
Lloyd.1603(4) (1921); GB/A.1035(4) (1928-29).
o129.

Oxford mountaineering essays / edited by Arnold Lunn. London, 1912.
GB.344. o130.

-P-

På verdens top / Hans Ruesch. Kjøbenhavn, 1950. GB/B.525(3). p001.

Paccard wider Balmat, oder Die Entwicklung einer Legende: ein Beitrag zur Besteigungs geschichte des Mont Blanc / Heinrich Dübi. Bern, 1913. Facsim.
GB.1329(29); GB.1329(30-31) (positive and negative photostats of Textbeilage II). p002.

Paccard's diary / Michel Gabriel Paccard. [N.p., n.d.]. Typewritten, with a carbon copy.
Lloyd.1459-60. p003.

Il **paesaggio** / Aldo Sestini. Milano, 1963. Ill., maps. [Conosci l'Italia; 7.]
GB/B.565. p004.

Il **paese** delle montagne: spedizione organizzata dalla sezione CAI-UGET nell'Himalaya del Nepal per il centenario del Club Alpino Italiano. Torino, 1966. Ill.
GB/A.972. p005.

Pagine biellesi / Pietro Paolo Trompeo. [Biella], 1967.
GB/B.403(3). p006.

Die **Pala** Gruppe / Gustav Euringer. [Berlin, 1894.] Ill. Pp.[399]-440 of *Erschliessung der Ostalpen*, Bd.3.
GB.1382. p007.

Pale di San Martino. Vol.1: Mulàz Stia, Facobòn, Bureloni, Vezzana, Cimón della Pala / Bepi Pellegrinon. Bologna, 1971. Ill., map. [Itinerari alpini; 6.]
GB/A.867(10). p008.

Pale di San Martino. Vol.2: Val Canali, Coro, Croda Granda, Agnèr, Pape, Pale di San Lucano / Gabriele Franceschini, Bepi Pellegrinon. Bologna, 1974. Ill., map. [Itinerari alpini; 16.]
GB/A.1351(4). p009.

Palestre di arrampicamento genovesi / Euro Montagna. Genova, 1963. Ill., maps.
GB/A.1028. p010.

Palette / Mary Paillon. Paris, 1905. Extrait de *La Montagne, revue mensuelle du Club alpin français*, vol.1 numéro du 20 mai 1905.
Lloyd.1620(10). p011.

The **Pamirs**: being a narrative of a year's expedition on horseback and on foot through Kashmir, Western Tibet, Chinese Tartary, and Russian Central Asia / Earl of Dunmore. 2nd ed. London, 1893. 2v; ill., map, port.
GB.363-4. p012.

[**Pamphlets**, magazine articles, etc., relating to Mont Blanc.] [N.p., n.d.]. 6v.
Lloyd.1596-1601. p013.

Panorama de la pierre du Couvercle, 2705m. / Club alpin français, Section de Chamonix. [Chamonix, n.d.]
GB.1326(5). p014.

Panorama de Mürren. Zürich, [ca 1900]. Photograph.
GB/A.1841. p015.

Panorama des Alpes bernoises, pris sur le Niesen près de Thoune. Berne, [1900?].
GB/A.2051. p016.

Panorama des Alpes, pris sur le Mayinghorn ou Torrenthorn en Valais / dessiné d'après nature par R. Ritz; lithographié par J. Jacottet. Vévey, [ca 1864].
GB.1134. p017.

Panorama des Maderaner-Thales im Kanton Uri nach einer hinterlassenen Zeichnung des verstorbenen Georg Hoffmann: dazu ein Führer in die Gebirge des Maderaner-Thales / verfasst von einigen Mitgliedern der Basler Section des Schweizerischen Alpenclubs. Basel, 1865.
GB/A.824. p018.

Panorama du massif de l'Oisans / cliché de M. Emile Piaget pris de la roche du Grand Galibier. Lyons, [n.d.]. Published by the Société des guides Pol.
GB.1326(10). p019.

Panorama du Mont Righi / R. Dikenmann. Zurich, [n.d.].
GB.1326(20). p020.

Panorama du Pilate. Genève, [ca 1880]. 1v. of photographs.
GB/A.2122. p021.

Panorama of Switzerland as viewed from the summit of Mont Righi / drawn from nature by Henry Keller. Also a circular view of the country, by General Pfyffer; with descriptive notices of the most remarkable objects. London, [n.d.].
GB.1242. p022.

Das **Panorama** von Bern: Schilderung der in Berns Umgebungen sichtbaren Gebirge / G. Studer. Bern, 1850. Ill.
GB.210. p023.

Les **panoramas** du Mont Blanc / Robert Perret. Chambéry, 1929. Ill., map.
GB/B.427. p024.

Par le détroit de Bering / Gontran de Poncins. Paris, 1953. Ill., map, ports. [L'homme sur la terre.]
GB/A.1589(12). p025.

Paradise North: an Alaskan year / Henry D. Barrow. New York, 1956. Ill., map.
GB/A.1756. p026.

Parbati-Himalaya: la spedizione romana al Lal Qilà / Paolo Consiglio. Bologna, 1966. Ill., maps.
GB/A.1549. p027.

Le **Parc** national de la Vanoise. Chambéry, 1967. Ill., maps. Published by the Conseil d'administration du Parc national de la Vanoise.
GB/B.253. p028.

Il **Parco** Nazionale del Gran Paradiso / Giulio Berutto. Torino, 1979-81. 2v; ill., maps. [Guide I.G.C.; 3.] Published by the Istituto Geografico Centrale.
GB/A.1964(12). p029.

Parco Nazionale delle Dolomiti Bellunesi: itinerari nelle Alpi Feltrine, Monti del Sole, Schiara, Tamer-S. Sebastiano, Prampèr-Spiz de Mezzodi, Bosconero / Giuliano Dal Mas, Bruno Tolot. Cortina d'Ampezzo, [1978?]. Ill., maps. [Guida dell'escursionista; 3.]
GB/A.2017(3). p030.

Un **parco** per Tovel / [P. Consiglio, D. De Riso]. Roma, 1971. Ill., maps. [Documenti di Italia nostra; 6.]
GB/B.337(5). p031.

Le **parcours** du Haut Rhône, ou La julienne et l'ail sauvage / Charles Albert Cingria, Paul Monnier. Fribourg, 1944. Ill.
GB/A.1223. p032.

Pareti d'inverno / Giovanni Rusconi; a cura di Aurelio Garobbio. Milano, [1973]. Ill.
GB/A.1249. p033.

Parlano i monti / Antonio Berti. 2a ed. Bologna, 1972.
GB/A.876.   p034.

La **parlata** di Moena nei suoi rapporti con Fiemme e con Fassa: saggio fonetico e fonematico / Luigi Heilmann. Bologna, 1955. Map. [Università degli Studi di Bologna. Facoltà di Lettere e Filosofia. Studi e ricerche; n.s., 1.]
GB/A.1445.   p035.

La **paroi** occidentale de l'Argentera: premières ascensions / Victor de Cessole. Nice, 1903. Extrait du 23me *Bulletin de la Section des Alpes-Maritimes du Club alpin français.*
Lloyd.1594(8).   p036.

Parois d'escalade au Québec / Eugénie Lévesque, Jean Sylvain. Québec, 1978. Ill. [Collection des guides pratiques.]
GB/A.1883(1).   p037.

Parole agli alpinisti / Angelo Manaresi. Roma, 1932. Ill.
GB/B.289(13).   p038.

Paropàmiso: spedizione romana all'Hindu-Kush ed ascensione del Picco Saraghar, 7350m. / Fosco Maraini. Bari, 1963. Ill., maps. [All'insegna dell'orizzonte; 20.]
GB/A.1073.   p039.

Parthenäis, oder Die Alpenreise: ein idyllisches Epos in zwölf Gesängen / Jens Baggesen. Amsterdam, [1807].
GB/A.875.   p040.

Parthenäis, oder Die Alpenreise: ein idyllisches Epos in zwölf Gesängen / Jens Baggesen. Leipzig, 1819. 2v (in 1); ill.
GB/A.1616.   p041.

Particulars of sale of the fine Highland sporting estate of Glenaven in the counties of Banff and Aberdeen. Seller's solicitors: John C. Brodie. Edinburgh, [1931]. Ill., map.
Lloyd.1621(2).   p042.

La **partie** suisse de la chaîne du Mont-Blanc: intinéraire du champ d'excursions du Club alpin suisse pour 1900 et 1901 / Louis Kurz, Eugène Colomb. Neuchâtel, 1900. Ill.
GB.1325(5); Lloyd.1617(18).   p043.

The **Pass** of St. Gothard and the Italian lakes / John Ball. London, 1873. Maps. [Ball's Alpine guides.]
GB/A.710.   p043.1.

The **passage** of the mountain of Saint Gothard: a poem (Passage du Mont Saint-Gothard) / Georgiana, Duchess of Devonshire; traduit par M. l'abbé de Lille. [Paris, 1802.] Ill.
Lloyd.1523; Lloyd.1523A.   p044.

The **passage** of the Saint Gothard / Georgiana, Duchess of Devonshire; with an Italian translation by G. Polidori. London, 1803.
Lloyd.200.   p045.

The **passages** of the Alps in 1518 / Jacques Signot. [N.p, 1915.] His *La totale et vraie description de tous les passaiges des Gaules ès Ytalies*, with notes by W.A.B. Coolidge. Reprinted from the *English Historical Review,* October 1915.
GB.1340(58); Lloyd.1620(2).   p046.

Passagier auf der Reise in Deutschland, der Schweiz, nach Venedig, Amsterdam, Brüssel, Kopenhagen, Paris, St. Petersburg und Stockholm: ein Reise-Handbuch für jedermann / Reichard. 11. Aufl., von neuem durchgesehen, berichtigt und ergänzt von F. Herbig. Berlin, 1841. Map.
GB/A.1022.   p047.

Passato, presente e futuro nella legislazione sul Club Alpino Italiano. Bologna, 1957. Published for the Club Alpino Italiano, Sede Centrale.
GB/A.1468(15).   p048.

Pässe und Strassen in den schweizer Alpen: topographisch-historische Studien / Raphael Reinhard. Amsterdam, 1971. Facsimile reprint of the Lucerne, 1903 ed.
GB/A.874.   p049.

Passion des hautes cimes / René Dittert. Lausanne, 1945. Ill., map. [Collection alpine; 4.]
GB.1310(4); GB.1310(5).   p050.

Il **passo** di Pagarí nella storia / W.A.B. Coolidge. Torino, 1913. Estratto dalla *Rivista del Club Alpino Italiano*, vol.32 n.5, anno 1913.
GB.1340(31).   p051.

The **past** and the future land: an account of the Berger Inquiry into the Mackenzie Valley pipeline / Martin O'Malley. Toronto, 1976. Ill.
GB/A.1620.   p052.

Pastelli di monte / Attilio Viriglio. Torino, [ca 1950].
GB/B.289(14). p053.

Patchwork / Basil Hall. London, 1841. 3v.
GB.508-10; Lloyd.679-81; Lloyd.679A-81A.
p054.

Pater Placidus A. Spescha: sein Leben und seine Schriften: mit Unterstützung von Behörden und Vereinen / herausgegeben von Fried. Pieth und Karl Hager; mit einem Anhang von Maurus Carnot. Bern, 1913. Ill., ports.
GB/A.614. p055.

Paterfamilias's diary of everybody's tour: Belgium and the Rhine, Munich, Switzerland, Milan, Geneva and Paris / [Martin Tupper]. London, 1856.
Lloyd.223. p056.

Paul-Emile Victor présente Groenland 1948-1949. Paris, 1951. Ill.
GB/B.439(1). p057.

Paura in montagna / C.F. Ramuz; traduzione di Giuseppe Zoppi. 3a ed. Milano, 1945. [Montagna; 2.]
GB/A.495(2). p058.

Le **paysage** morainique: son origine glaciaire et ses rapports avec les formations pliocènes d'Italie / E. Desor. Paris, 1875. Maps.
Lloyd.1620(1). p059.

Paysages romanesques / Henry Bordeaux. Paris, [1906].
GB/A.1351(1). p060.

Paysages suisses: les lacs / Gonzague de Reynold. Genève, 1818. Ill.
GB/C.57. p061.

The **peak** of Tenerife. [London, 1888.] Pp.157-77 of *Cornhill Magazine*, N.S. vol.11, 1888.
GB.1306(17). p062.

A **peak** to climb: the story of South African mountaineering / José Burman. Cape Town, 1966. Ill. Published by the Mountain Club of South Africa.
GB/A.128. p063.

Peaks and glaciers of Nun Kun: a record of pioneer-exploration and mountaineering in the Punjab Himalaya / Fanny Bullock Workman, William Hunter Workman. London, 1909. Ill., map.
GB.1111. p064.

Peaks and passes: summaries of six mountaineering tours accomplished between 1869 and 1876 / Anna Pigeon, Ellen Abbot. London, 1885.
Lloyd.239; Lloyd.239A. p065.

Peaks and pleasant pastures / Claud Schuster. Oxford, 1911.
GB.965. p066.

Peaks and precipices: scrambles in the Dolomites and Savoy / Guido Rey; translated from the Italian by J.E.C. Eaton. London, 1914. Ill., ports.
GB.1220; Lloyd.1355. p067.

The **peaks** and valleys of the Alps: from water-colour drawings / Elijah Walton; descriptive text by T.G. Bonney. London, 1868.
Lloyd.1562. p068.

Peaks, passes, and glaciers / edited by John Ball. London, 1859. Ill., maps. Published by the Alpine Club.
GB.652; GB/A.482; Lloyd.815; Lloyd.815A. p069.

Peaks, passes, and glaciers / edited by John Ball. 2nd ed. London, 1859. Ill., maps. Published by the Alpine Club.
Lloyd.816. p069.1.

Peaks, passes, and glaciers: a series of excursions by members of the Alpine Club / edited by John Ball. 3rd ed. London, 1859. Published by the Alpine Club.
GB.505; GB/A.123. p070.

Peaks, passes, and glaciers / edited by John Ball. 4th ed. London, 1859. Ill., maps. Published by the Alpine Club.
Lloyd.817. p070.1.

Peaks, passes, and glaciers / edited by John Ball. 5th ed. London, 1860. Published by the Alpine Club.
GB.246; GB.247; Lloyd.332. p071.

Peaks, passes and glaciers. Ser.2 / edited by Edward Shirley Kennedy. London, 1862. 2v; ill., maps. Published by the Alpine Club.
GB.653-4; Lloyd.818-9; Lloyd.818A-9A; Lloyd. 818B-9B. p072.

Peaks, passes and glaciers. Ser.3 / edited by A.E. Field, Sydney Spencer. London, 1932. Ill. Published by the Alpine Club.
GB.842; GB.864; Lloyd.820.   p073.

Peaks, passes & glaciers / selected and annotated by E.H. Blakeney. London, [1926]. [Everyman's library; 778.]
GB.174.   p074.

Peasant art in Switzerland / Daniel Baud-Bovy; translated by Arthur Palliser. London, 1924. Ill., facsims. Translated from *L'art rustique en Suisse*.
Lloyd.1623(2).   p075.

The **peasants** of Chamouni: containing an attempt to reach the summit of Mont Blanc, and a delineation of the scenery among the Alps. London, 1823.
GB.393; Lloyd.54.   p076.

The **peasants** of Chamouni: containing an attempt to reach the summit of Mont Blanc, and a delineation of the scenery among the Alps. 2nd ed. London, 1826.
GB.34; Lloyd.55; Lloyd.55A.   p077.

Pechuck: Lorne Knight's adventures in the Arctic / Richard G. Montgomery. Caldwell, Idaho, 1948. Ill., map.
GB/A.1619.   p078.

The **pedestrian**: a summer's ramble in the Tyrol, and some of the adjacent provinces / Charles Joseph La Trobe. London, 1832. Map.
Lloyd.1122.   p079.

Pedestrianism, or An account of the performances of celebrated pedestrians during the last and present century, with a full narrative of Captain Barclay's public and private matches, etc. Aberdeen, 1813.
GB.621 (impf.)   p080.

Pedestrianism in Switzerland / [James D. Forbes]. [London, 1857.] Pp.[285]-323 of the *Quarterly Review*, vol.101 no.202, April 1857.
GB.1042.   p081.

A **peep** at the Continent, or A six weeks' tour through parts of Belgium, Rhenish Prussia, Savoy, Switzerland and France, including six days in Paris, in the summer of 1834 / Edward S. Dublin, 1835.
GB/A.953.   p082.

A **peep** at the mountains: the journal of a lady. Leicester, [1871].
GB/A.802(5).   p083.

A **peep** at the Pyrenees / by a pedestrian: being a tourist's note-book. London, 1867. Map.
Lloyd.208.   p083.1.

Peking to Lhasa: the narrative of journeys in the Chinese Empire made by George Pereira / compiled by Sir Francis Younghusband from notes and diaries. London, 1925. Ill., maps, port.
GB.813.   p084.

Les **pèlerinages** de Suisse: Einsiedeln, Sachslen, Maria-Stein / Louis Veuillot. Bruxelles, 1839.
GB/A.558.   p085.

Pen & pencil sketches of the Lakes. Windermere, [1885?]. Ill.
GB/A.990(2).   p086.

Pencillings by the way: being a tour on the Rhine and in Switzerland / John Longmore. Worcester, 1872. Ill.
GB.281; GB.282.   p087.

Pennine Alps, including Mont Blanc and Monte Rosa / John Ball. New ed. London, 1875. Maps. [Ball's Alpine guides.]
GB.236; GB/A.707.   p088.

People of the deer / Farley Mowat. Rev ed. Toronto, 1977. Ill., map, ports. Reprint of v.1 of his *Death of a people — the Ihalmiut*.
GB/A.1762.   p089.

People of the Noatak / Claire Fejes. New York, 1966. Ill., maps.
GB/A.1695.   p090.

Per l'alpinismo: vade-mecum SUCAI. Monza, 1913. Published by the Club Alpino Italiano, Stazione Universitaria.
GB/A.1034(2).   p090.1.

Per l'alpinismo: vade-mecum S.U.C.A.I. 3a ed. Monza, 1919. Ill. [Manualetti / Club Alpino Italiano, Stazione Universitaria.]
GB/A.1468(11).   p091.

Per le montagne dell'Alto Adige: piccola guida delle passeggiate e delle escursioni / Hanspaul Menara, Hannsjörg Hager; a cura dell'Ufficio Provinciale per il Turismo di Bolzano. Bolzano, 1981. Ill.
GB/A.2018(10).   p092.

Peralba, Chiadenis, Avanza / Spiro Dalla Porta Xidias, Sergio De Infanti. Bologna, 1974. Ill. [Itinerari alpini; 16.]
GB/A.1349(1). p093.

I **percorsi** degli Alpini in guerra sul Paterno / Camillo e Tito Berti; con note di guerra di Antonio Berti; a cura della Fondazione Antonio Berti e della Sezione di Padova del C.A.I. Cortina, 1977.
GB/A.1964(8). p094.

Père Murray and the hounds: the story of Saskatchewan's Notre Dame College / Jack Gorman. Sydney, B.C., 1977. Ill., ports.
GB/A.1909. p095.

Peregrinando in Val di Susa / M. Zanone. Torino, [1962]. Ill. [Italia.]
GB/A.498. p096.

Peregrinazioni nel bacino della Thuile / Giovanni Bobba. Torino, 1897. Ill. Published by the Club Alpino Italiano, Sezione di Torino.
GB/B.289(20). p097.

I **pericoli** dell'alpinismo, e norme per evitarli / Cesare Fiorio, Carlo Ratti. Torino, 1889. Ill. Published by the Club Alpino Italiano.
Lloyd.1265. p098.

I **pericoli** in montagna / Paulcke-Dumler. Milano, 1972. Ill. Translated from *Gefahren der Alpen*.
GB/A.1051(2). p099.

The **perilous** adventures of Quintin Harewood and his brother Brian, in Asia, Africa and America / by the author of *Paul Preston's voyages and travels in Europe*. London, 1839. Ill.
Lloyd.14. p100.

A **personal** narrative of a journey to the source of the River Oxus, by the route of the Indus, Kabul, and Badakhshan, performed in the years 1836, 1837, and 1838 / John Wood. London, 1841. Map.
GB.1006. p101.

Personal narrative of an excursion to the hospice of the Great St. Bernard: read before the Liverpool Literary and Philosophical Society / R. Hibbert Taylor. Liverpool, 1846.
GB.1335(58). p102.

A **personal** narrative of the discovery of the North-West Passage / Sir Alex. Armstrong. London, 1857. Map.
GB.910. p103.

Il **peso** dello zaino / Giulio Bedeschi. Milano, 1966.
GB/A.489. p104.

Peter Freuchen's adventures in the Arctic / edited by Dagmar Freuchen. New York, 1960. Ill., maps, ports.
GB/A.1718. p105.

Peterli and the mountain / Georgia Engelhard. Philadelphia, [1954]. Ill.
Lloyd.1202. p106.

Petersgrat — Finsteraarjoch — Unteres Studerjoch / O.A. Hug [et al.]. 2. neubearb. Aufl. des *Hochgebirgsführer durch die Berner Alpen* von W.A.B. Coolidge und H. Dübi. Bern, 1931. Ill., maps. [Hochgebirgsführer durch die Berner Alpen; 4.] Published by the Schweizer Alpenclub, Sektion Bern.
GB.163. p107.

Petersgrat — Finsteraarjoch — Unteres Studerjoch — Galmilücke / O.A. Hug [et al.]. Neu nearbeitet von Daniel Bodmer. 5., ergänzte Aufl. des *Hochgebirgsführer durch die Berner Alpen* von W.A.B. Coolidge und H. Dübi. Bern, 1970. Ill., maps. [Hochgebirgsführer durch die Berner Alpen; 4.] Published by the Schweizer Alpenclub, Sektion Bern.
GB/A.989(5). p107.1.

Petit carême de Massillon / Jean Baptiste Massillon. Paris, 1823. Port. [Collection des classiques françois.]
Lloyd.2. p108.

Petit guide panoramique des roches / J. Arrecgros. 2e éd. Neuchâtel, 1968. Ill.
GB/A.1050(7). p109.

Petits et grands sommets de Savoie: 63 itinéraires alpins en été / Charles Cabaud. Chambéry, 1971.
GB/A.910. p110.

Petits hommes, grandes montagnes / H. De Amicis; traduit de l'italien par E. Gaillard. Chambéry, 1927. Ill.
GB/A.1211. p111.

Les **petits** montagnards de 39-45 / Raoul Sylvestre. Annecy, 1965.
GB/A.1589(11). p112.

Les **petits** voyageurs en Suisse, ou Description pittoresque de cette contrée / D. Prieur de

Sombreuil. Paris, 1840. Ill.
GB/A.1480.   p113.

Petrology of the coastal dykes at Tugtilik, southern east Greenland / John C. Rucklidge, Charles Kent Brooks, Troels F.D. Nielson. Copenhagen, 1980. Ill., map. [Meddelelser om Grønland. Geoscience; 3.]
GB/A.1818.   p114.

Die **Petronella-Kapelle** in Grindelwald / W.A.B. Coolidge. Grindelwald, 1911. Ill., map.
GB.1335(7).   p115.

Pfade zur Höhe: Zehnjahrbuch der Alpinistengilde / geleitet von Fritz Kolb. Wien, [1930]. Ill. Published by the Alpinistengilde.
GB/A.92.   p116.

The **phanerozoic** development of the Kangerdlugssuaq area, east Greenland / Charles Kent Brooks, Troels F.D. Nielsen. Copenhagen, 1982. Ill., maps. [Meddelelser om Grønland. Geoscience; 9.]
GB/A.1818(9).   p117.

[A **photograph** of the original charcoal drawing by Kathleen Shackleton of T. Graham Brown.] [N.p.], 1937.
GB.1912(4); GB.1912(5).   p118.

[**Photograph** taken from the top of Mount Everest] / British Everest Expedition, 1975. [London? 1975?]
GB/B.520(5).   p119.

A **photographic** record of the Mount Jolmo Lungma Scientific Expedition. Peking, 1974. Ill., map.
GB/B.453.   p120.

A **photographic** record of the Mount Shishma Pangma Scientific Expedition. Peking, 1966. Ill., map.
GB/B.527.   p121.

Photographische Aufnahmen im Dachsteingebirge und seinen nächsten Umgebungen: ausgeführt in den Jahren 1877, 1884 u. 1885 / Friedr. Simony. [N.p., 1885?]
GB/C.60.   p122.

[**Photographs** of the titlepage of Franz Joseph Lochmatter's Führer-Buch and of the pages containing testimonials.] [N.p., n.d.] Port.
Lloyd.1613(17).   p123.

[**Photographs** of the titlepage of Joseph Bollinger's Führer-Buch and of the pages containing testimonials.] [N.p., n.d.] Port.
Lloyd.1613(18).   p123.1.

[**Photographs**, slides and postcards, mainly relating to mountaineering, collected by T. Graham Brown.] [N.p., n.d.] 6v.
GB.1912(12-37); GB.1929-34.   p124.

Photography and mountain climbing / Matthew Surface. [N.p., 1896.] Ill. Pp.106-[11] of the *American Year Book of Photography*, 1896.
GB.1881(29).   p125.

A **physician**'s holdiay [sic], or A month in Switzerland in the summer of 1848 / John Forbes. London, 1849. Ill., map.
GB.506; Lloyd.621.   p126.

A **physician**'s holiday, or A month in Switzerland in the summer of 1848 / John Forbes. 2nd ed. rev. and corr. London, 1850. Ill., map.
GB.507.   p127.

A **physician**'s holiday, or A month in Switzerland in the summer of 1848 / John Forbes. 3rd ed. London, 1852. Ill., map.
GB.249.   p128.

Physikalisch-metallurgische Abhandlungen über die Gebirge und Bergwerke in Ungarn: nebst einer Beschreibung des steirischen Eisenschmetzens und Stahlmachens von einem Ungenannten / Johann Jacob Ferber. Berlin, 1780. Ill.
GB.579(1).   p129.

The **physiography** of Arctic Canada, with special reference to the area south of Parry Channel / J. Brian Bird. Baltimore, [1967]. Ill., maps.
GB/A.1885.   p130.

Physiological effects of high altitudes / Clinton Dent. London, 1893. Pp.46-8 of the *Geographical Journal*, vol.1 no.1.
GB.1338(14).   p131.

A **phytogeographical** study of south Greenland: vascular plants / Jon Feilberg. Copenhagen, 1984. Ill., maps. [Meddelelser om Grønland. Bioscience; 15.]
GB/A.1819(15).   p132.

Picchi, colli e ghiacciai / [edited by] Irene Affentranger, Adolfo Balliano. Torino, 1961. Ill.
GB/A.503.   p133.

Picchi e burroni: escursioni nelle Alpi / Giuseppe Corona. Torino, 1876.
Lloyd.441. p134.

Piccole corna rosse: storia vera di due caprioli Pippo e Bambi / Paolo Cavagna. [N.p.], 1971. Ill.
GB/A.1281(3). p135.

Piccole Dolomiti e monte Pasubio / Gianni Pieropan. Milano, 1978. Ill., maps. [Guida dei monti d'Italia.]
GB/A.1950. p136.

The pictorial illustrations of de Saussure's Mont-Blanc ascent / Carl Egger. [N.p.], 1946. A review of the book by Henry L'Evêque and Christian von Mechel. From Die Alpen no.9-10, 1946.
Lloyd.1382. p137.

A picture history of mountaineering / Ronald W. Clark. London, 1956. Ports. [Hulton's picture histories.]
GB.1260. p138.

The picture of Everest: reproductions of photographs of the Everest scene / chosen and explained by Alfred Gregory. [London], 1954.
Lloyd.1452. p139.

Picture of Italy: being a guide to the antiquities and curiosities of that classical and interesting country: containing sketches of manners, society and customs / Henry Coxe. London, 1815. Ill., maps.
Lloyd.185. p140.

A picture of the Empire of Buonaparte, and his federate nations, or The Belgian traveller: being a tour through Holland, France and Switzerland, during the years 1804-5, in a series of letters from a nobleman to a minister of state / edited by the author of the Revolutionary Plutarch [i.e. ———— Stewarton]. Middletown, Conn., 1807.
GB/A.628. p141.

Pictures from Italy / Charles Dickens. Paris, 1846.
GB/A.722. p142.

Pictures in Tyrol and elsewhere: from a family sketch-book / by the author of A voyage en zigzag &c. [i.e. Elizabeth Tuckett]. London, 1867. Ill., ports.
Lloyd.738. p143.

Pictures of Cuba / William H. Hurlbert. London, 1855.
GB.235(1). p144.

Pictures of life at home and abroad / Albert Smith. London, 1853. [Bentley's railway library.]
Lloyd.1614(7). p145.

A picturesque and descriptive tour in the mountains of the High Pyrenees: comprising views of the most interesting scenes, from original drawings taken on the spot: with some account of the bathing establishments in that department of France / Joseph Hardy. London, 1825. Map.
GB.1094; Lloyd.1208; Lloyd.517. p146.

Picturesque and historical recollections during a tour through Belgium, Germany, France and Switzerland in the summer vacation of 1835 / Matthew O'Conor. London, 1837. Ill.
Lloyd.324. p147.

A picturesque description of Switzerland / Marquis de Langle. London, [1791]. Translated from Tableau pittoresque de la Suisse.
GB.213; Lloyd.604. p148.

A picturesque tour by the new road from Chiavenna, over the Splügen, and along the Rhine, to Coira, in the Grisons: views / C.G. Esq. [i.e. George Clowes]. London, 1826. Ill.
Lloyd.1520. p149.

Picturesque tour from Geneva to Milan, by way of the Simplon: illustrated with views of the most striking scenes and of the principal works belonging to the new road constructed over that mountain / Frederic Shoberl. London, 1820. Ill., map.
Lloyd.1456. p150.

A picturesque tour through France, Switzerland, on the banks of the Rhine, and through part of the Netherlands: in the year 1816. London, 1817. Maps.
GB.657; Lloyd.760. p151.

Pièces relatives aux troubles actuels de Genève. [N.p., 1782.]
Lloyd.339. p152.

Piemonte e Valle d'Aosta. Vol.1. Milano, 1962. Ill., maps.
GB/B.338(6). p153.

La Pietra di Bismantova: Appennino reggiano / Gino Montipò. Bologna, 1976. Ill., map. [Itinerari alpini; 29.] At head of title: G.A.B. Gruppo Amici di Bismantova.
GB/A.1468(22). p154.

Pietro Strigini / Giuseppe Lampugnani. [Varallo, 1941.] Port. Omaggio della Sezione di Varallo del Centro Alpinistico Italiano.
GB/B.440(7). p155.

Pilati Montis historia in pago lucernensi Helvetiæ siti / Mauritius Antonius Cappellerius. [Basel], 1767. Ill., maps, music.
GB.661; Lloyd.1036. p156.

Pilatus: eine Erzählung aus den Bergen / Heinrich Federer. Berlin, 1916. [Grote'sche Sammlung von Werken zeitgenössischer Schriftsteller; 108.]
GB/A.40. p157.

Der **Pilatus** und seine Geschichte / P.X. Weber. Luzern, 1913. Ill., map.
GB/A.506. p158.

Der **Pilatus** und seine Umgebungen: Souvenir für Touristen. Luzern, 1867. Ill., music.
GB/A.583. p159.

A **pilgrimage** into Dauphiné: comprising a visit to the monastery of the Grande Chartreuse: with anecdotes, incidents, and sketches from twenty departments of France / George M. Musgrave. London, 1857. 2v; ill., port.
Lloyd.482-3. p160.

Pillar of the sky / Hugh Merrick. [London], 1941.
GB.347. p161.

Pillar Rock and neighbourhood / H.M. Kelly. New and rev. ed. Manchester, 1935. [Climbing guides to the English Lake District; 1.] Published by the Fell and Rock Climbing Society of the English Lake District.
GB.48(1); GB.51. p162.

Pillar Rock and neighbouring climbs: a climbers' guide / H.M. Kelly. Barrow-in-Furness, [1923]. [Climbers' guides to the English Lake District; 2.] Published by the Fell and Rock Climbing Club of the English Lake District.
GB.1328(7). p163.

Pink, mauve, but no purple: reviews / R.A.H. [i.e. R.A. Hodgkin]. [London, 1938.]
GB.1338(10). p164.

Piolet et ski. Pickel und Ski. 1936. [Zurich, 1935.] 2v.
GB.1319(12-3). p165.

A **pioneer** in the High Alps: Alpine diaries and letters / F.F. Tuckett, 1856-1874; [edited by E. Howard, W.A.B. Coolidge]. London, 1920. Ill., ports.
GB.877; Lloyd.994. p166.

Pioneer work in the Alps of New Zealand: a record of the first exploration of the chief glaciers and ranges of the Southern Alps / Arthur P. Harper. London, 1896. Ill., maps.
GB.898; Lloyd.1043. p167.

The **pioneers** of the Alps / [edited] by C.D. Cunningham, W. de Abney. London, 1877. Ports.
GB.1297; Lloyd.1525; Lloyd.1525A; Lloyd.1539; Lloyd.1539A. p168.

The **pioneers** of the Alps / [edited by] C.D. Cunningham, W. de Abney. 2nd ed. London, 1888. Ports.
GB.1268; Lloyd.1479. p169.

Pioniere der Alpen: 30 Lebensbilder der grossen schweizer Bergführer, von Melchior Anderegg bis Franz Lochmatter, 1827 bis 1933 / Carl Egger. Zürich, [1946]. Ports.
Lloyd.715. p170.

Pionieri sull'Alpe: scalate di grandi alpinisti narrate alla gioventù / Walter Maestri. Roma, 1949. Ill.
GB/A.870. p171.

Les **pionniers** du Club alpin: étude historique / C. Morf. Lausanne, 1875.
GB/A.801(12). p172.

Il **pioppo** bianco ed altre leggende alpine / Ezio Flori. Firenze, 1940. Ill.
GB/A.455(1). p173.

Piramidi di terra nel Trentino-Alto Adige / Giuliano Perna. Calliano, 1970. Ill.
GB/B.338(12). p174.

Le **più** belle leggende dell'Alto Adige: storia, folclore, tradizioni, credenze, riti e costumanze popolari / Lucillo Merci. 3a ed. Calliano, 1973. Ill.
GB/A.1303. p175.

The **Piz** Bernina in January / Frank S. Smythe. Uxbridge, [1928]. Reprinted from *The Times* of January 24th, 1928. Pp.286-8 of the *British Ski Year Book*, vol.4 no.9.
GB.1881(58). p176.

Piz Languard und die Bernina-Gruppe bei Pontresina, Oberengadin: Skizzen aus Natur und Bevölkerung: zugleich als Wegweiser für Wanderungen / entworfen durch Ernst Lechner. Leipzig, 1858. Ill., map.
GB.419; Lloyd.1610(10).					p177.

Piz Languard und die Bernina-Gruppe / Ernst Lechner. 2. Aufl., erw. Bearb. Leipzig, 1865. Ill., map.
GB/A.934(1).					p178.

Pizzo Bernina: prima ascensione per il canalone meridionale della Forcola Scerscen-Bernina / Alfredo Corti. Torino, 1918. Ill. Estratto dalla *Rivista del Club Alpino Italiano*, vol.37 n.7, 8 e 9, anno 1918.
GB.1333(44).					p179.

Le **Placche** / Gruppo Condor di Lecco. Lecco, [1982?]. Ill., maps.
GB/A.2033(1).					p180.

The **plagiary** 'warned': a vindication of the drama, the stage, and public morals, from the plagiarisms and complications of John Angell James in a letter to the author / [Joseph Parkes]. Birmingham, 1824.
Lloyd.682.					p181.

Planktonic choanoflagellates from the Disko Bugt, west Greenland, with a survey of the marine nanoplankton of the area / Helge Abildhauge Thomsen. Copenhagen, 1982. Ill., maps. [Meddelelser om Grønland. Bioscience; 8.]
GB/A.1819.					p182.

Play and work in the Alps / Elizabeth Robins Pennell, Joseph Pennell. New York, 1891. Pp.194-211 of the *Century Illustrated Monthly Magazine*, vol.42 no.2.
GB.1336(20); GB/A.797(2); Lloyd.1659(9).	p183.

The **playground** of Europe: a collection, with additions and alterations, of articles [reprinted from] *Fraser's Magazine*, the publications of the Alpine Club, and the *Cornhill Magazine* / Sir Leslie Stephen. London, 1871. Ill.
GB.412; Lloyd.342; Lloyd.502; Lloyd.502A.	p184.

The **playground** of Europe: the delights of Alpine rambling / Sir Leslie Stephen. New ed. London, 1894. Ill. [Silver library.]
GB.374.					p185.

The **playground** of Europe: the delights of Alpine rambling / Sir Leslie Stephen. New ed., new impression. London, 1899. Ill. [Silver library.]
GB.327; GB.358 (impf.).				p186.

The **playground** of Europe, by Sir Leslie Stephen. [London, 1871.] A review. Pp.276-80 of *Chambers's Journal*, 1871.
GB.1881(72).					p187.

Plezalni vzponi vzhodne Julijske Alpe / uredili: Tomaz Banovec [et al.]. Ljubljana, 1970. Ill.
GB/A.835(5).					p188.

Pobezhdennye vershiny: sbornik sovetskogo al'pinizma. 1973/74-1975/78. Moscow, 1976-81. Ill.
GB/A.1900.					p189.

The **poems** of Mr. Gray / with notes by Gilbert Wakefield. London, 1786.
GB.1044.					p190.

Poems upon several occasions / Thomas Parnell; published by Mr. Pope; to which is prefixed, the life of Dr. Parnell. London, 1774.
Lloyd.126.					p191.

Poésies helvétiennes / Mr. B***** [i.e. Philippe S. Bridel]. Lausanne, 1782. Also attributed to Jean Bridel and A.C. Bondier.
Lloyd.871.					p192.

The **poetical** works of Sir Walter Scott. Leipzig, 1861. 2v. [Collection of British authors; 545.]
GB/A.485 (wanting v.2).				p193.

Poetische Reise 1837. [London? 1837.]
GB/A.672; Lloyd.1286.				p194.

La **Pointe** Lagarde, ou Les plaisirs d'un alpiniste au cours d'une première ascension / Pierre Dalloz. Strasbourg, 1926. Ill.
GB/A.1051(7).					p195.

The **Pointe** Percée / B.H. Kemball-Cook. London, 1941. Pp.18-21 of the *Climbers' Club Journal*, N.S. vol.6 no.3.
GB.1339(21).					p196.

Pokorennye giganty / P.S. Rototaev. Izd. 2. perer. i dop. Moskva, 1975.
GB/A.1565.					p197.

The **polar** and tropical worlds: a description of man and nature in the polar and equatorial regions of the globe / G. Hartwig; edited, with additional chapters, by A.H. Guernsey. New ed. Guelph, 1874. Ill., maps, ports., facsim.
GB/A.1623.					p198.

Polar Geography. Vol.1-3, 1977-79. Washington, 1977-79. Continued by *Polar Geography and Geology*.
GB/B.636.   p199.

Polar Geography and Geology. Vol.4- , 1980- . Washington, 1980- . Continues *Polar Geography*.
GB/B.636.   p200.

The polar passion: the quest for the North Pole / [edited by] Farley Mowat. Rev. ed. Toronto, 1977.
GB/A.1603.   p201.

Polar secrets: a treasury of the Arctic and Antarctic / edited by Seon Manley, Gogo Lewis. New York, 1968. Ill., maps, ports.
GB/A.1932.   p202.

Polar shiphandling / Edwin A. McDonald. Washington, 1965. Ill. Published by the Arctic Institute of North America.
GB/B.390(10).   p203.

The Polar Times. No.40-74, June 1955-June 1972. [N.p.], 1955-72. Ill., ports. Wanting no.43, 44, 46, 63.
GB/B.478(7).   p204.

Polar whaling: a sea-letter narrative of a cruise in the Okhotsk Sea in 1849 / William Henry Holmes. Mystic, Conn., 1948. Ill. [Publication / Marine Historical Association; vol.2 no.5.]
GB/A.1791(2).   p205.

Polarfahrten: die wichtigsten Entdeckungsreisen in den Eismeeren mit Berichten der Forscher und ihrer Gefahrten / Paul Gerhard Zeidler. Berlin, 1927. Ill., maps.
GB/A.2089.   p206.

Polarfeber / Einar Sverre Pedersen; [översättning från det norska manuskriptet av Elsie och Håkan Tollet]. Stockholm, 1969. Ill., ports.
GB/A.1856.   p207.

Polarforskningens eventyr / L.P. Kirwan; [oversat af Hagmund Hansen og Iver Gudme]. København, 1963. Ill., maps. [Fremads rejsebøger.] Translated from *The white road*.
GB/A.1858.   p208.

Polarkreis Süd-Polarkreis Nord: als Walfisch- und Seelenfänger rund um die beiden Amerika / Carl Kircheiss. Leipzig, 1933. Ill., maps.
GB/A.1666.   p209.

Die Polarwelt nach den vorzüglichsten neuern Reisewerken / E. Scheuermann. Tl.1: Der Reisebilder. Schaffhausen, 1852.
GB/A.60.   p210.

Die Polarwelt und ihre Nachbarländer / Otto Nordenskjold. Leipzig, 1909. Ill.
GB/A.1876.   p211.

Le pôle et l'équateur: études sur les dernières explorations du globe / Lucien Dubois. Paris, 1863. Map.
GB/A.2151.   p212.

Le pôle meurtrier: journal du capitaine Scott / ouvrage adapté de l'anglais par Ch. Rabot. Paris, 1914. Ill., map.
GB/B.477.   p213.

Poles and tails, or English vagabondism in Switzerland in the summer of 1854 / by two of the vagabonds. London, 1855. Ill.
Lloyd.416.   p214.

Pont suspendu de Fribourg, Suisse: notice / Chaley. Paris, 1839.
Lloyd.758.   p215.

Pontresina / G.F. Browne. [N.p., 1895.] Pp.388-98 of the *National Review*, May 1895.
GB/A.797(12).   p216.

Pontresina und Engelberg: Aufzeichnungen aus den Jahren 1826-1863 / Gottlieb Studer; Festgabe der Section Bern des S.A.C. an die Theilnehmer des Clubfestes in Bern 21.-23. September 1907. Bern, 1907. Ill.
GB/A.814.   p217.

Populations and breeding schedules of waders, Charadrii, in high arctic Greenland / Hans Meltofte. Copenhagen, 1985. [Meddelelser om Grønland. Bioscience; 16.]
GB/A.1819(16).   p218.

Porlezza: il suo lago e la sua valle / Alverio Gualandris. 2a ed. Como, 1970. Ill., map. [Mimima lariana; 11.]
GB/A.867(6).   p219.

Port-Tarascon: dernières aventures de l'illustre Tartarin / Alphonse Daudet. Paris, 1890. [Collection Guillaume.]
Lloyd.1201.   p220.

La **porta** delle Dolomiti: Zambana: Fai: Paganella / Antonio Pranzelores. Trento, 1929. Ill., map.
GB/A.1034(19). p221.

Portantina che porti quel morto: ed altri racconti alpini / Eugenio Sebastiani; sotto gli auspici della Sezione di Fiume del Club Alpino Italiano. Firenze, 1930. Ill.
GB/A.1212. p222.

The **Portillon** d'Oc, and Pic des Posets / Charles Packe. [N.p., n.d.]
GB.1314(8) (impf.). p223.

Portrait of an ice cap with human figures / J.M. Scott. London, 1953. Ill.
GB.515. p224.

Portrait of the Dalai Lama / Sir Charles Bell. London, 1946. Ill., maps, ports.
GB.713. p225.

Das **Poschiavino-Thal**: Bilder aus der Natur und dem Volksleben: ein Beitrag zur Kenntniss der italienischen Schweiz / Georg Leonhardi. Leipzig, 1859. Ill., map.
GB/A.799(12). p226.

Posets — Maladeta (du Cinca à la Noguera Ribagorzana) : Peña Montanesa, Cotiela, Turbón, Posets, Eristé, Aneto, Malibierne, Forcanada / André Armengaud, Augustín Jolis; traduit de l'espagnol par Bernard Clos. Pau, 1967. Ill., maps. At head of title: Centre excursionniste de Catalogne, Club alpin catalan.
GB/A.1204; GB/A.2001. p227.

The **possibility** of approaching the North Pole asserted / Hon. Daines Barrington; with an appendix, containing papers on the same subject, and on a North West Passage, by Colonel Beaufoy. New ed. London, 1818. Map.
GB.984. p228.

Postes alpestres suisses: vallée d'Hérens: route postale du Grand St. Bernard. Berne, 1932. 2v. Published by the Direction générale des postes suisses.
GB.1326(33-4). p229.

Les **postes** suisses: leur développement jusqu'en 1912. Zofingue, [1914]. Ill. Published by the Direction générale des postes suisses.
GB/B.289(11). p230.

Postscript to adventure / Claud Schuster. London, 1950. Ill. [New Alpine library.]
GB.789; GB.790 (impf.). p231.

Postumia ed il fantastico mondo sotterraneo delle sue celebri grotte / G.A. Perco, Sergio Gradenigo. Postumia, 1927. Ill.
GB/A.799(3). p232.

Pour apprendre soi-même à skier / [Georges Joubert]. [Paris], 1970. Ill.
GB/A.803(3). p233.

Poznanie Tatr: szkice z rozwoju wiedzy o Tatrach do polowy XIX wieku / Józef Szaflarsky. Warszawa, 1972. Ill., maps.
GB/A.1567. p234.

A **practical** Swiss guide: the whole of Switzerland / by an Englishman in Switzerland [i.e. Alexander T. Gregory]. London, 1856. Ill., map.
GB/A.960; Lloyd.1614(11). p235.

A **practical** Swiss guide / [Alexander T. Gregory]. 9th ed. London, 1864.
Lloyd.1614(12). p236.

Practical Swiss guide: red book for Switzerland, the adjoining districts of Savoy, Piedmont, North Italy, the routes from London by France, Belgium, Holland, and the Rhine / by an Englishman abroad [i.e. Alexander T. Gregory]. London, 1869. Ill., maps.
Lloyd.1614(13). p237.

Practical Swiss guide: English red book for Switzerland, Savoy, Piedmont, North Italy: the route from London by France, Belgium, Holland, and the Rhine / [Alexander T. Gregory]. London, 1874. Ill., maps.
GB/A.769. p238.

A **practical** word about Switzerland: principally addressed to visitors to the Paris Exhibition. [London, 1867.] Pp.13-20 of *London Society*, July 1867.
GB.1332(37). p239.

Praeterita: outlines of scenes and thoughts perhaps worthy of memory in my past life / John Ruskin. Orpington, 1885-88. 3v; ill.
GB.1282-3 (wanting v.1). p240.

A **prairie** tragedy: the fate of Thomas Simpson, the Arctic explorer / Alex. McArthur. Winnipeg, 1887. Read before the Historical and Scientific

Society of Manitoba (Transaction no.26).
GB/B.528(4).   p241.

Prampèr-Mezzodì / Giovanni Angelini. [N.p.],
1968. Ill., maps. [Le Alpi venete.]
GB/B.338(15).   p242.

Les **Préalpes** du Sud: Vercors — Verdon —
Devoluy / Patrick Cordier. Paris, 1981. Ill., maps.
[Les cent plus belles courses et randonnées.]
GB/B.584.   p243.

Préalpes et Alpes vaudoises / Théo Chevalley.
Lausanne, 1971. Ill. [Guide de tourisme pédestre.]
GB/A.867(5).   p244.

Préalpes franco-suisses: chaîne frontière entre le
Valais et la Haute-Savoie / guide élaboré pour le
CAS par Pierre Bossus. Zurich, 1979. Ill., maps.
[Guides du Club alpin suisse.]
GB/A.2044.   p245.

The **Pre-basaltic** sediments and the lower basalts
at Kangerdlussuaq, east Greenland / Troels F.D.
Nielsen [et al.]. Copenhagen, 1981. Ill., map.
[Meddelelser om Grønland. Geoscience; 6.]
GB/A.1818.   p246.

Preliminary report on scientific work carried out
on the London School of Economics
Mountaineering Club Himalayan Expedition,
1956. [London], 1956.
GB.1322(7).   p247.

Preliminary report on the aerial mineral
exploration of northern Canada / G.H. Blanchet.
Ottawa, 1930. Ill., maps. Published by the
Department of the Interior, North West Territories
and Yukon Branch.
GB/B.528(2).   p248.

Premier de cordée: roman / Roger Frison-Roche.
Montréal, [1946].
GB/A.23.   p249.

Premier de cordée / R. Frison-Roche. [Paris],
1963. Ill.
GB/A.1281(8).   p250.

Premier voyage à la cime, Mont-Blanc, le 8 août
1786: reproduction phototypographique d'un des
rares exemplaires connus du Prospectus de
souscription à l'ouvrage du Dr. Paccard: propriété
du Dr. H. Maillart, Genève. [N.p., n.d.]
GB.750; Lloyd.1606(15).   p251.

Première ascension à la tête du Rutor: 3486m. /
Gottlieb Studer; adapté du texte allemand par
W.A.B. Coolidge. [N.p., 1920.] Extracted from
Augusta Praetoria, 1920.
GB.1340(56).   p252.

La **première** ascension du Cervin: interview de M.
Ed. Whymper: récit complet de la gatastrophe
[sic] de 1865: détails inédits / Jules Monod.
Zermatt, 1895. Port. From the *Journal et liste des
étrangers de Zermatt*, année 1895, 25 août.
GB.1318(19).   p253.

La **première** ascension du Mont Blanc, du glacier
de la Brenva, route de la Sentinelle (1er et 2
septembre, 1927) / T. Graham Brown. Berne, 1928.
Extrait de la revue *Les Alpes*, année 4 fascicule 10,
1928.
Lloyd.1620(26).   p254.

La **première** caravane d'Arcueil: récit du voyage
de la caravane scolaire de l'Ecole Albert-le-Grand
pendant les vacances de l'année 1878 / Eug. Ebel,
G. Muleur. Paris, 1879. Ill., music.
GB/A.1072.   p255.

Les **premières** ascensions du Pavé — 3831 — et du
Fifre — 3630. II: Le Fifre / W.A.B. Coolidge.
Grenoble, 1901. Pp.[97]-106 of the *Revue des Alpes
dauphinoises*, année 4 no 5.
GB.1340(49).   p256.

Les **premiers** guides de Courmayeur, soit
Contribution à l'histoire des guides de
Courmayeur avant la fondation du Bureau le 6
juillet 1868: suivi de l'Alpinisme et le clergé
valdôtain en 1907 / abbé Henry. Aoste, 1908. Port.
GB.1188(4).   p257.

Premiers voyages à Chamouni / lettres de
Windham et de Martel 1741-1742 publiées et
annotées par M. Henri Ferrand. Lyon, 1912. Map,
facsim. Extrait de la *Revue alpine* de février et mars
1912. A photocopy.
GB/B.290(13).   p258.

Premiers voyages au Mont-Blanc / H.B. de
Saussure, M.-T. Bourrit; textes choisis et présentés
par Daniel May. [Geneva, 1973.] Ill.
GB/A.1285.   p259.

Premiers voyages en zigzag / Rodolphe Töpffer.
4e éd. Paris, 1855. Ill. Originally published as
Voyages en zigzag.
GB.1249.   p260.

Premiers voyages en zigzag, ou Excursions d'un pensionnat en vacances dans les cantons suisses et sur le revers italien des Alpes / par R. Töpffer. 5e éd. Paris, 1859. Ill. Originally published as *Voyages en zigzag*.
GB/B.487. p261.

Près des névés et des glaciers: impressions alpestres / Charles Gos. 2e éd. Paris, [1912]. Ill.
GB/A.836(6). p262.

Presanella / Dante Ongari. Milano, 1978. Ill., maps. [Guida dei monti d'Italia.]
GB/A.1952. p263.

The **present** state of the world: Switzerland / Tobias Smollett. [London, 1768.] Extracted from his *The present state of all nations*.
Lloyd.855. p264.

Presolana 1870-1970 / Angelo Gamba. Bergamo, 1971. Ill. Published by the Club Alpino Italiano, Sezione di Bergamo.
GB/B.313(1). p265.

[**Press** cuttings dealing mainly with mountaineering.] [N.p., n.d.] 38v.
GB.1935-72. p266.

La **presse** grenobloise (1788-1888): exposition / Pierre Vaillant. Grenoble, 1964. Ill., ports. At head of title: Bibliothèque municipale de Grenoble.
GB/B.528(14). p267.

Le **prestige** du passé / texte et mise en pages de Robert Berton. Genova, 1967. Ill.
GB/C.22(11). p268.

Preuss, l'alpinista leggendario / Severino Casara. Milano, 1970. [La vostra via sportiva; 21.]
GB/A.519. p269.

Priatelstvo v srdci Pamira / Ivan Fiala. Bratislava, 1982. Ill.
GB/B.520(8). p270.

Prière sur le Mont Blanc: chroniques de la montagne / Max Melou. [Paris], 1967. [Sempervivum; 42.]
GB/A.155. p271.

Les **prières** ecclésiastiques, et la manière de célébrer le service divin: avec les liturgies du batême, de la sainte cène, et du mariage: pour l'usage des églises du païs de Vaud. Berne, 1734.
GB.159(2). p272.

Le **prieuré** de Chamonix: histoire de la vallée et du prieuré de Chamonix du Xe au XVIIIe siècle / André Perrin; d'après les documents recueillis par A. Bonnefoy. Paris, 1887. Map, facsims. [Mémoires de l'Académie des sciences, belles-lettres et arts de Savoie; sér.3 tom.12.]
GB.1128; Lloyd.1302. p273.

La **prima** ascensione del Cervino per la cresta di Furggen / Mario Piacenza. [Turin, 1911.] Ill. Pp.320-6 of the *Rivista del Club Alpino Italiano*, vol.30.
GB.1880(50). p274.

La **prima** ascensione del Monte Bianco / T. Graham Brown, Sir Gavin de Beer; unica traduzione autorizzata di Mario Magistretti. Milano, 1960. Ill., maps, ports., facsims. Translated from *The first ascent of Mont Blanc*.
GB.1087. p275.

La **prima** frana-valanga del Monte Bianco sul ghiacciaio della Brenva, 14 novembre 1920 / Ubaldo Valbusa. Roma, 1931. From the *Bollettino della R. Società Geografica Italiana*, ser.6 vol.8 n.2, febbraio 1931.
Lloyd.1618(57). p276.

Le **prime** ascensioni al Monte Bianco: le avventurose scalate di un naturalista del '700 al gigante delle Alpi / H.B. de Saussure; traduzione a cura di Paolo Brogi. Milano, 1981. Ill., ports. [La biblioteca del viaggiatore.] Translated from *Voyages dans les Alpes*.
GB/A.1941. p277.

Prime giunte al saggio di bibliografia cadorina: dall'anno 1532 all'anno 1960 / Giovanni Fabbiani. Feltre, 1962.
GB/B.300. p278.

Prince Charles Foreland / William S. Bruce. Edinburgh, [1907]. Ill., map. Reprinted from the *Scottish Geographical Magazine* for March 1907.
GB.1335(49). p279.

Principal Forbes and his biographers / John Tyndall. London, 1873.
Lloyd.440; Lloyd.440A. p280.

I **principali** toponimi in Valtellina e Val Chiavenna / Renzo Sertoli Salis. Milano, 1955. [Raccolta di studi storici sulla Valtellina; 9.]
GB/B.119(9). p281.

I **principi** di Savoia attraverso le Alpi nel medioevo, 1270-1520: dai conti dei tesorieri e dei castellani dell'Archivio di Stato in Torino / Luigi Vaccarone. Torino, 1902. Pp.[1]-91 of the *Bollettino del Club Alpino Italiano*, vol.35 no.68.
GB.1880(52[1]) (impf.). p282.

The **prisoner** of Chillon, and other poems / Lord Byron. London, 1816.
GB.992. p283.

Prò Cascata del Toce / Giorgio Spezia. [N.p., ca 1910.]
GB/A.1035(7). p284.

Proceedings / Geologists' Association. Vol.6 no.1-5,7. London, 1879-80.
Lloyd.1608(10-15). p284.1.

Proceedings of a court of inquiry convened at the Navy Department, Washington, D.C., October 5, 1882, in pursuance of a joint resolution of Congress approved August 8, 1882, to investigate the circumstances of the loss in the Arctic seas of the exploring steamer *Jeannette*. Washington, 1883.
GB/A.1705. p285.

Proceedings of Symposium on Qinghai-Xizang (Tibet) Plateau, May 25-June 1, 1980: abstracts. [Taipei, 1980.] Published by the Organizing Committee, Symposium on Qinghai-Xizang (Tibet) Plateau, Academia Sinica.
GB/B.520(6). p286.

Proceedings of the Norwegian-Netherlands Symposium on Svalbard, [Arctic Centre, University of Groningen, Netherlands, November 1978]. [Groningen], 1980.
GB/B.524(1). p287.

Prof. F.W. Oliver, F.R.S. / Agnes Arber. St. Albans, [1951]. Reprinted from *Nature*, vol.168, November 10, 1951.
GB.1313(32). p288.

Professor Crum Brown. [N.p., n.d.] A photograph, extracted from an unidentified book.
GB.1317(7). p289.

Professor Forbes' account of his recent observations on glaciers. [N.p., 1842-45.] With other extracts by and about Forbes.
GB.614. p290.

Professor Helmholtz on ice and glaciers: a summary of the scientific portion of *On ice and glaciers* / John Tyndall. [London, 1865.] From the *Philosophical Magazine* for December 1865.
Lloyd.1581(2). p291.

Professor Tyndall's observations on the Mer de Glace. [London, 1859.] Pp.[261]-78 of the *Philosophical Transactions of the Royal Society* for 1859.
GB.1341(16) (impf.). p292.

Programme / Mountaineering and Mountain Rescue Course, Lochaber Mountaineering Club, 20th-22nd, 27th-29th November, 1959. [Fort William? 1959.]
GB.1331(41). p293.

Programme des courses / Schweizer Alpenclub, Section genevoise. 1931, 1954-55. [Geneva, 1931-55.]
GB.1326(13-5). p294.

Programme of meetings / Royal Geographical Society. [London, 1946-57.]
GB.1326(42-51). p295.

Programme of Mr. Albert Smith's ascent of Mont Blanc, August 12th & 13th 1851. Paris, [1851]. A fan.
GB.1330(12). p296.

A **progress** in mountaineering: Scottish hills to Alpine peaks / J.H.B. Bell. Edinburgh, 1950. Ill., maps.
GB.823. p297.

A **progress** in mountaineering: Scottish hills to Alpine peaks / J.H.B. Bell. [Edinburgh, 1950.] A prospectus.
GB.1315(12). p298.

La **progressione** in sicurezza della cordata / Umberto De Col, Armando Dallago. 2a ed. Cortina, 1981. Ill.
GB/A.1983. p299.

Promenade au Mont-Blanc et autour du lac de Genève / [François Vernes?]. Londres, [ca 1795].
Lloyd.920. p300.

Promenade aux Alpes / C.A. Snoeck. [N.p., ca 1825.] Ill., maps.
GB/B.342. p301.

Promenade aux glaciers. [N.p., n.d.]
Lloyd.1606(9). p302.

Promenade dans la Suisse occidentale et le Valais / A.L.A. Fee. Paris, 1835.
GB/A.459. p303.

Promenade durch die Schweiz. Hamburg, 1793.
GB/A.803(6). p304.

Promenades au pays des Grisons, ou Choix des vues les plus remarquables de ce canton / dessinées d'après nature et lithographiées par Ed. Pingret; accompagnées d'un texte historique et descriptif par Mr. le vicomte de Senonnes. Paris, [1827]. Ill.
GB/C.33. p305.

Promenades en Suisse / A. Fee. Paris, 1836.
GB/A.1143. p306.

Promenades et excursions aux environs de Genève / F.T. [i.e. F. Thioly]. Genève, 1861.
Lloyd.1615(23). p307.

Promenades historiques dans le canton de Genève / Gaudy Le Fort. 2. éd. corr. et augm. Genève, 1849. 2v (in 1).
GB/A.712. p308.

Promenades neuchâteloises / Jules Baillods. Neuchâtel, 1925. Ill.
GB/A.1133. p309.

Promenades philosophiques et religieuses au Jura et à l'hospice du Grand St. Bernard, faisant suite aux *Promenades aux environs du Mont-Blanc* / C.E.F. Moulinie. Genève, 1820.
Lloyd.1568(2). p310.

Promenades philosophiques et religieuses aux environs du Mont-Blanc, précédées d'un itinéraire et d'une table des principales hauteurs des montagnes de cette contrée / C.E.F. Moulinie. Genève, [1817].
Lloyd.1568(1). p311.

Promenades philosophiques et religieuses aux environs du Mont-Blanc, précédées d'un itinéraire et d'une table des principales hauteurs des montagnes de cette contrée / C.E.F. Moulinie. Nouv. éd. Genève, 1820.
Lloyd.210. p312.

Propos d'un alpiniste / Charles Gos. Lausanne, 1922.
GB.1327(19); Lloyd.1614(14). p313.

Proposed Club hut: the site, Brackenclose Wood, Lingmell Ghyll, Wasdale / Fell and Rock Climbing Club of the English Lake District. [Barrow-in-Furness? 1935.] Ill.
GB.1313(7). p314.

Proposed new rules / Alpine Club. 1903, 1945, 1946. London, [1903-46].
Lloyd.1606(13) (1903); GB.1321(34) (1945); GB.1321(35) (1946). p315.

Proposed rules / Alpine Club. [London, 1857.]
GB.1318(7). p317.

Proposta per un parco del Pasubio e delle Piccole Dolomiti / [a cura del Comitato Promotore, sotto gli auspici dell'Ente Provinciale per il Turismo di Vicenza]. Vicenza, 1972. Ill., maps.
GB/B.313(11). p318.

Prosäische Schriften / Friederike Brun. Zurich, 1799-1801. 4v (in 3); ill.
GB/A.928-30. p319.

Prospectus and programme / Royal Scottish Geographical Society. 1936-37, 1937-38. [Edinburgh, 1936-37.]
GB.1341(7-8). p320.

La **protection** des plantes alpines / Victor de Cessole. Nice, 1904. Published by the Club alpin français, Section des Alpes Maritimes.
GB/A.803(2). p321.

Provisional report / Special Committee on Equipment for Mountaineers, Alpine Club. London, 1891.
GB.1312(22); Lloyd.1609(7). p322.

Pubblicazione commemorativa della Società degli Alpinisti Tridentini — Sezione del C.A.I. — nel suo cinquantenario 1872-1922. Trento, [1922]. Ill.
GB/B.291. p323.

The **Public** Schools Alpine Sports Club year book. 1924-28. London, 1924-28. Continued from *Public Schools Winters Sports Club year book.*
Lloyd.406-9; Lloyd.407A (another copy of the 1925 issue). p324.

The **Public** Schools Winter Sports Club year book. 1907,1909. London, 1907-09. Continued as *Public Schools Alpine Sports Club year book.*
Lloyd.404-5. p325.

The **Pullen** Expedition in search of Sir John Franklin: the original diaries, log, and letters of Commander W.J.S. Pullen / selected and

introduced by H.F. Pullen. Toronto, 1979. Maps.
GB/A.1667.   p326.

Pumo Ri: der schönste Berg der Erde: die Erst-
besteigung des 7145 Meter hohen Himalaya
Gipfels durch die Deutsch Schweizerische Nepal
Himalaya Expedition, 1962 / Gerhard Lenser.
Zürich, 1963. Ill.
GB/A.2053.   p327.

La **Punta** Bianca — m.3890 circa: pagine di vita
alpina / Guido Rey. [Turin, 1899.] Ill. Pp.[173]-212
of the *Bollettino del Club Alpino Italiano*, no.65.
GB.1333(28[1]).   p328.

The **Purcell** Range of British Columbia / J.
Monroe Thorington. New York, 1946. Ill., maps.
Published by the American Alpine Club.
GB.1053.   p329.

Puteshestvie Flota Kapitana Sarycheva po
Sieverovostochnoi chasti Sibiri, Ledovitomu
moriu i Vostochnomu okeanu v prodolzhenie
os'mi liet' pri Geograficheskoi i Astronomicheskoi
morskoi Ekspeditii, byvshei pod nachal'stvom
Flota Kapitana Billingsa s 1785 po 1793 god /
[Gavriil Sarychev]. Sanktpeterburg, 1802. 2v; ill.,
maps.
GB/A.1926.   p330.

Pyrénées / F. Schrader; [edited by Edouard
Privat, under the direction of Maurice Heid];
ouvrage publié sous les auspices de l'Académie
de Béarn. Toulouse, 1936. 2v; ill.
GB/A.163-4.   p331.

Pyrénées / P. Joanne. Paris, 1898. Maps. [Guides-
Joanne.] [Guides-diamant.]
GB/A.1591.   p332.

Les **Pyrénées** / Patrice de Bellefon. Paris, 1976. Ill.
[Les cent plus belles courses et randonnées.]
GB/B.585.   p333.

The **Pyrenees**: a description of summer life at
French watering places / Henry Blackburn. Paris,
1867. Ill., map, music.
Lloyd.1278; Lloyd.1300.   p334.

The **Pyrenees**: a description of summer life at
French watering places / Henry Blackburn. New
ed. corr. to 1880. London, 1881. Ill., map.
Lloyd.586.   p335.

Les **Pyrénées**: développement de la connaissance
géographique de la chaîne: thèse / Pierre Camena

d'Almeida. Amsterdam, 1969. Facsimile reprint of
the Paris, 1893 ed.
GB/A.941.   p336.

Pyrenees, Andorra, Cerdagne: a guide to the
mountains for walkers and climbers / Arthur
Battagel. Reading, 1980. Ill., maps.
GB/A.1904.   p337.

Pyrénées centrales / auteur-éditeur: R. Ollivier;
[édité sous le patronage de la Fédération française
de la montagne et avec l'aide technique du
Groupe pyrénéiste de haute montagne]. Pau,
1965-69. 3v; ill., maps.
GB/A.578.   p338.

Les **Pyrénées** du pic d'Anie au Canigou en 30
excursions, ou 140 jours de pyrénéisme / Pierre
Soubiron; avec la collaboration de Raymond
d'Espouy pour la partie cartographique.
Toulouse, 1920. Maps. [Guide Soubiron.]
GB/A.1459(5).   p339.

Pyrenees high level route: Atlantic to
Mediterranean: mountain walking and trekking
guide for a complete traverse of the range in 45
day stages with 50 easier or harder alternatives
and variations / Georges Véron. Goring, 1981.
Maps. [Mountain guides to the Pyrenees.]
GB/B.528(11).   p340.

Pyrénées itinéraires-skieurs / Henri Favre, André
Fillol, Robert Ollivier. Pau, 1971-74. 4v; ill., maps.
Published by the Fédération française de la mon-
tagne.
GB/A.2018(4).   p341.

Les **Pyrénées**, les ascensions, et la philosophie de
l'exercise / Henri Russell-Killough. Pau, 1865.
GB.1329(46).   p342.

Les **Pyrénées** monumentales et pittoresques /
dessinées d'après nature et lithographiées par
Gorse. Pt.1: Luchon et ses environs. Luchon,
[1860?].
GB/C.28.   p343.

Pyrénées occidentales. 1: Aspe & Ossau /
rédaction générale: R. Ollivier. Pau, 1968. Ill.,
maps.
GB/A.1064.   p344.

The **Pyrenees**, with excursions into Spain /
Georgiana Lady Chatterton. London, 1843. 2v.
Lloyd.1032-3.   p345.

-Q-

Quando avevo le ali / Giuseppe Zoppi. 3a ed. riv. Milano, 1943. [Montagna; 12.]
GB/A.556. q001.

Quando la corda si ruppe: la storia di una grande tragedia / Ronald W. Clark; traduzione di Marisa Sughi. Milano, 1965. Ill. [La vostra via sportiva; 6.] Translated from *The day the rope broke*.
GB/A.1343. q002.

Quando le campane non suonano più / Viktor Rákosi; traduzione di Ignazio Balla, Ettore Cozzani. 2a ed. Milano, 1944. [Montagna; 16.]
GB/A.557. q003.

Quarant'anni di Giovane Montagna a Verona, 1929/1969. Verona, [1970]. Ill.
GB/B.337(6). 004.

Quaternary shells collected by the fifth Thule Expedition 1921-24 / Dan Laursen; translated by A. Mikkelsen. New York, 1976. Ill. [Thule expedition, 5th, 1921-1924. Report; vol.1 no.7.]
GB/A.1822. q005.

Quatre jours d'observations au sommet du Mont-Blanc / Jules Janssen; lu dans la séance publique annuelle des cinq Académies du 25 octobre 1893. Paris, [1893].
GB/B.260(9). q006.

Les **quatre** sources de la Reuss au Saint-Gothard / Rey. Paris, 1835. Map.
GB/A.803(8[2]). q007.

I **quattordici** '8000': antologia / Mario Fantin. Bologna, 1964. Ill. [Montagne; 3.]
GB/A.127. q008.

Le **quattro** vite di Reinhold Messner / Emanuele Cassarà. [Milan], 1981. Ill. [Exploits.]
GB/A.1967(4). q009.

I **quattromila** delle Alpi: 60 cime, la loro storia, i punti d'appoggio, le vie di salita / Karl Blodig, Helmut Dumler; traduzione: Gianguido Piani. 3a ed. riv. Bologna, 1979. Ill., maps. Translated from *Die Viertausender der Alpen*.
GB/B.557. q010.

A **queen** as mountaineer / Elsie Thornton Cook. [N.p., 1894.] Pp.[447]-53 of *English Illustrated*, February 1894.
GB/A.797(4). q011.

Quelques hommes et l'Himalaya / Guy Marester. Paris, [1950]. Ill., maps.
GB/A.1051(9). q012.

The **quest** for Cathay / Sir Percy Sykes. London, 1936. Ill., maps.
GB.1089. q013.

Questions archéologiques et historiques sur les Alpes de Savoie entre le lac Léman et le Mont Genèvre / C.A. Ducis. Annecy, 1871.
GB/A.1269. q014.

Le **Queyras**: splendeurs et calvaire d'une haute vallée alpine / A. Guillaume. Gap, 1968. Ill., maps.
GB/B.290(4). q015.

Quiet resting places in the Swiss Highlands: Evolena, Ferpècle, Arolla / Wynne E. Baxter. London, 1898. Ill.
GB/A.802(14). q016.

Quiet resting places in the Swiss Highlands: Evolena, Ferpècle, Arolla / Wynne E. Baxter. London, 1903. Ill.
Lloyd.1613(5). q017.

Quinze jours en Suisse: promenade d'un jeune peintre français dans les cantons du Midi. Paris, [1819?]. Ill.
GB/A.771. q018.

La **quistione** del passaggio delle Alpi elvetiche con una ferrovia / rapporto della Commissione nominata dal Consiglio Provinciale di Milano. Milano, 1862. Ill.
GB/B.352. q019.

-R-

Rabagaster under polarstjernen / John Giæver. Oslo, 1959.
GB/A.2082. r001.

Racconti a picco / Samivel; [traduzione] di Adolfo Balliano. Rocca San Casciano, 1956. Ill. [Le Alpi; 25.] Translated from *Contes à pic*.
GB/A.1573. r002.

Racconti per un bivacco / Carlo Arzani. Milano, 1968. Ill.
GB/B.338(7). r003.

Raetia, das ist ausführliche und wahrhaffte Beschreibung der dreyen loblichen Grawen Bündten und anderer retischen Völcker / Johann Guler von Weineck. Zurych, 1616. Ill., maps.
GB/B.394. r004.

La **ragazza** che voleva ripopolare la montagna / Sandro Prada. Cosenza, [ca 1960].
GB/A.1331; GB/C.22(15). r005.

Raid in sci: 73 itinerari di traversata dalle Alpi Marittime al Ticino / Gruppo Sci Alpinistico CAI-UGET di Torino. Torino, 1976. Ill., maps. [Biblioteca della montagna; 4.]
GB/A.2019(14). r006.

The **raiders**: being some passages in the life of John Faa, lord and earl of Little Egypt / S.R. Crockett. 7th ed. London, 1895. [The wayfarer's library.]
GB.534. r007.

Railway routes in Alaska: message from the President of the United States transmitting Report of Alaska Railroad Commission. Washington, 1913. 2v; maps. [U.S. 62d Congress, 3d session. House. Document; 1346.]
GB/A.1711-2. r008.

A **ramble** through Swisserland, in the summer and autumn of 1802 / [W.J. McNevin]. Glasgow, 1803.
Lloyd.662 (impf.). r009.

Rambles in France and Switzerland / Thomas Roscoe, Cyril Thornton. London, [ca 1840]. Ill.
GB/A.924. r010.

Rambles in Switzerland: with reminiscences of the Great St. Bernard, Mont Blanc and the Bernese Alps / William Dowsing. Kingston-upon-Hull, 1869. Ill.
GB.776; Lloyd.790; Lloyd.940; Lloyd.940A. r011.

Rambles in the Pyrenees: and a visit to San Sebastian / Frederic W. Vaux. London, 1838.
Lloyd.686. r012.

Rambles in the Rocky Mountains: with a visit to the gold fields of Colorado / Maurice O'Connor Morris. London, 1864.
Lloyd.688. r013.

Rambles in the romantic regions of the Hartz Mountains, Saxon Switzerland, &c. / Hans Christian Andersen; from the Danish by Charles Beckwith. London, 1848. Ill. Translated from *Skyggebilleder af en reise til Harzen*.
Lloyd.571; Lloyd.617. r014.

Rambles in the Vaudese Alps / F.S. Salisbury. London, 1916.
GB.319. r015.

Randonnées au Caroux / ouvrage réalisé par une équipe de la Section du Caroux du C.A.F; rédaction: Gérard Rey. Béziers, 1975. Maps. [Guides du Caroux; 1.]
GB/A.1964(13). r016.

Randonnées et ascensions: Chambéry, Bauges, Chartreuse. Chambéry, 1972. Maps. Published by the Club alpin français, Section de Savoie.
GB/A.1459(6). r017.

Randonnées et ascensions: Haute-Maurienne, Alpes Grées méridionales. [Paris], 1973. Maps. Published by the Club alpin français, Section de Savoie.
GB/A.1459(7). r018.

The **range** of the Tödi / W.A.B. Coolidge. London, 1894. [Conway and Coolidge's climbers' guides; 8.]
GB.1324(1); Lloyd.24. r019.

Le **rapt**: roman / Roger Frison-Roche. Paris, 1971. [Lumière de l'arctique; 1.]
GB/A.988(3). r020.

Rassegna di montagna: annuario / Club Alpino Italiano, Sezione di Lecco, Sottosezione di Belledo. 1965-1966. Turin, 1965-66.
GB/B.252(3). r021.

A **reading** party in Switzerland: with an account of the ascent of Mont Blanc, on the 12th and 13th

of August, 1851 / Francis Philips. Manchester, 1851.
GB.186; GB.187; Lloyd.259; Lloyd.259A,B.   r022.

Real stories: taken from the narratives of various travellers. London, 1827.
Lloyd.53.   r023.

La **Reale** Società Geografica Italiana e la sua opera dalla fondazione ad oggi, 1867-1936 / Enrico De Agostini. Roma, 1937. Ill.
GB/C.22(13).   r024.

Recent mountaineering. [London, 1901.] Pp.126-48 of the *Quarterly Review*, vol.194 no.387.
GB.1881(25).   r025.

Recherches géographiques et archæologiques sur le département des Basses-Alpes / D.M.J. Henry. Forcalquier, 1818. Ill., map.
GB/A.938(5).   r026.

Recherches géologiques dans les parties de la Savoie, du Piémont et de la Suisse voisines du Mont-Blanc / Alphonse Favre. Paris, 1867. 4v; maps.
GB/C.51-4.   r027.

Recherches sur la condensation de la vapeur aqueuse de l'air au contact de la glace et sur l'évaporation / Ch. Dufour, F.A. Forel. [Geneva? 1871.] Tiré des *Archives des sciences de la Bibliothèque universelle*, mars 1871.
GB/A.793(3).   r028.

Recherches sur les climats de l'époque actuelle et des époques anciennes particulièrement au point de vue des phénomènes glaciaires de la période diluvienne / baron Wolfgang Sartorius von Waltershausen. [N.p., 1866.] Tiré des *Archives des sciences de la Bibliothèque universelle*, septembre 1866.
Lloyd.1606(6).   r029.

Recherches sur les glaciers et sur les formations erratiques des Alpes de la Suisse / Henri Hogard. Epinal, 1858.
GB/B.239.   r030.

Récits et impressions d'alpinisme / Guido Rey; traduit de l'italien par Emile Gaillard. Mâcon, 1913.
GB.1330(9).   r031.

The **recollections** of a bishop / G.F. Browne. 2nd ed. London, 1915. Ports.
GB.853; Lloyd.958.   r032.

Recollections of a first visit to the Alps, in August and September, 1814 / Thomas Noon Talfourd. London, [1842?].
GB.69; Lloyd.88; Lloyd,93; Lloyd.94; Lloyd.94A,B; Lloyd.138.   r033.

Recollections of a great mountaineer and his mountains / George D. Abraham. Kendal, 1919. Ill., port. Offprint from the *Fell and Rock Climbing Club Journal*.
GB.1306(7).   r034.

Recollections of a journey through Tartary, Thibet, and China, during the years 1844, 1845, and 1846 / Evariste Régis Huc; a condensed translation by Mrs Percy Sinnett. London, 1852. Translated from *Souvenirs d'un voyage dans la Tartarie et le Thibet*.
GB.172.   r035.

Recollections of a tour: a summer ramble in Belgium, Germany and Switzerland / J.W. Massie. London, 1846.
Lloyd.639.   r036.

Recollections of an old mountaineer / Walter Larden. London, 1910. Ill.
GB.1012; Lloyd.1162.   r037.

Recollections of foreign travel, on life, literature, and self-knowledge / Sir Egerton Brydges. London, 1825. 2v.
Lloyd.349-50.   r038.

Recollections of 'old' Swinton, Lancashire / Peter Holland; edited by Alfred Hardy. Swinton, 1914. Ill.
Lloyd.444.   r039.

Record of expeditions: Alpine Journal / Alpine Club. 1909-1925. [London, 1910-26.] There are no records for 1914-1919.
GB.1765.   r040.

Record of expeditions in 1911 / J.P. Farrar. Colchester, 1912. For binding with the *Alpine Journal*.
GB.1315(11).   r041.

Records of a run through Continental countries: embracing Belgium, Holland, Germany, Switzerland, Savoy, and France / James Grant. London, 1853. 2v (in 1).
Lloyd.588.   r042.

The **Recreation**: a gift-book for young readers. 1842, 1843, 1847. Edinburgh, 1842-47.
GB.129-30 (1842, 1847); Lloyd.193 (1843).   r043.

The **red** sentinel of Mont Blanc / Frank S. Smythe. London, 1928. Pp.[1]-22 of *Blackwood's Magazine*, vol.224 no.1353.
GB.1881(43); GB.1881(44).   r044.

Redogörelse för den svenska expeditionen till Spetsbergen, 1890 / G. Nordenskiöld. Stockholm, 1892. Ill., map. [Bihang till K. Svenska Vet.-Akad. handlingar, bd.17 afd.2 nr 3.]
GB.1335(41).   r045.

Redogörelse för den tillsammans med G. de Geer år 1882 företagna geologiska expeditionen til Spetsbergen / A.G. Nathorst. Stockholm, 1884. Map. [Bihang till Kongl. Svenska Vetenskaps-Akademiens handlingar, bd.9 nr 2.]
GB.1335(42).   r046.

Reflections on Mr Varillas's *History of the revolutions that have hapned* [sic] *in Europe in matters of religion*. And more particularly on his ninth book that relates to England / Gilbert Burnet. London, 1689.
GB.46A(2).   r047.

Refuges accessibles en hiver et itinéraires d'accès / Club alpin français. [N.p, 1928.]
GB/A.1965(3).   r048.

Les **refuges** alpins dans le massif du Pelvoux en 1885 / H. Ferrand. Genève, 1885. Extrait de l'*Echo des Alpes*, no.4, 1885.
GB.1306(8).   r049.

Refuges des montagnes françaises et zones limitrophes / Jacques Meynieu; avec la collaboration de Claude Bourleaux, Michel Molin, Simone Marzio. [Paris], 1967. Ill., maps.
GB/A.199.   r050.

Regards vers l'Annapurna / Maurice Herzog, Marcel Ichac. Paris, 1951. Ill., map. [Les beaux pays.]
GB/A.2139(3).   r051.

La **regina** senza terre: leggenda canavesana / Remo Appia. Torino, 1970.
GB/A.804(5).   r052.

La **région** du Mont Lusitania au Spitzberg / Auguste Dubois. Neuchâtel, 1911. Ill. Extrait du tome 21 du *Bulletin de la Société neuchâteloise de géographie*, 1911-1912.
GB.1880(55).   r053.

Regione del Bernina / Alfredo Corti con la collaborazione di Aldo Bonacossa. Brescia, 1911. Ill., maps. [Guida dei monti d'Italia. Alpi centrali; vol.1 pt.4.] Published by the Club Alpino Italiano, Sezione di Milano.
GB/A.784.   r054.

La **regione** del lago Tana / Giotto Dainelli. Milano, 1939. Ill., map.
GB/A.1134.   r055.

Regione Másino — Bregáglia — Disgrázia / Aldo Bonacossa. Roma, 1936. Ill., maps. [Guida dei monti d'Italia.]
GB/A.1552.   r056.

Regione Másino — Bregáglia — Disgrázia / Aldo Bonacossa, Giovanni Rossi. Vol.1: Badile, Cengalo, Ligoncio, Manduino, Sciora. Milano, 1977. Ill. [Guida dei monti d'Italia.]
GB/A.1949.   r057.

Register zu David Herrliberger's *Topographie der Eydgnossschaft* / Fritz Spänhauer, U. Waldburger. Basel, 1929.
GB/A.792.   r058.

Règlement de la Compagnie des guides de Chamonix, loi du 11 mai 1852. Bonneville, 1858.
GB.418.   r059.

Règlement et tarif des postes dans les Etats romains: augmenté du service des postes de la Toscane, du Piémont, de la Lombardie, du royaume de Naples: et des routes de la Sicile et à travers les Alpes. Rome, 1841.
Lloyd.65.   r060.

Règlement UIAA pour la côtation des difficultés. Genève, 1973. Ill.
GB/B.377(9).   r061.

Regolamento / Club Alpino Italiano, Sezione di Torino. 1905, 1909, 1912-13. Torino, 1905-13.
Lloyd.1617(14-17).   r062.

Regolamento generale del Club Alpino Italiano approvato dall'assemblea dei delegati, 6 gennaio, 1883. Torino, 1883.
GB/B.403(20).   r063.

Regrets pour le triste despart de Seigneur Marquard Zehender, conseiller en la très-illustre république de Berne et resiouyssance pour

l'heureuse arriuée de Seigneur Burkheld Fischer son successeur au bailliage de Lausanne: le tout representé en façon de comédie au chasteau de Lausanne le 1. d'octobre 1630 / P.B.L. [i.e. Pierre Bosson]. [N.p.], 1632.
Lloyd.908. r064.

The **regular** Swiss round, in three trips / Harry Jones. London, 1865. Ill., map.
GB.96; Lloyd.144. r065.

The **regular** Swiss round, in three trips / Harry Jones. 2nd ed. London, 1868. Ill.
Lloyd.136. r066.

Reindeer trek / Allen Roy Evans. Toronto, 1935. Ill., map.
GB/A.1699. r067.

Reindeer-land: Arctic sketches / A. van Doren Honeyman. Plainfield, N.J., 1905. Ill. [Library of the great world.]
GB/A.1771. r068.

Reise auf den Glockner / J.A. Schultes. Wien, 1804. 4v; ill.
GB/A.654-7. r069.

Die **Reise** auf den Grossglockner / Franz Michael Vierthaler. München, 1938. Entnommen aus *Meine Wanderungen durch Salzburg, Berchtesgaden und Osterreich*, Tl.2.
GB.1315(2). r070.

Reise auf den Jungfrau-Gletscher und Ersteigung seines Gipfels von Joh. Rudolf Meyer und Hieronymus Meyer im Augustmonat 1811 unternommen: aus den Miszellen für die neueste Weltkunde besonders abgedruckt. [N.p., 1811.]
GB.420(3); GB.447; Lloyd.1579(1). r071.

Die **Reise** auf den St. Gotthardt / herausgegeben von W. von Normann. Heidelberg, 1826.
GB/A.515(5). r072.

Reise auf die Eisgebirge des Kantons Bern und Ersteigung ihrer höchsten Gipfel im Sommer 1812 / Rudolf Meyer; [edited by J.H.D. Zschokke]. Aarau, 1813. Map.
GB.420(2); Lloyd.1579(2); Lloyd.1611(7). r073.

Reise durch die Andes von Süd-Amerika, von Cordova nach Cobija im Jahre 1858 / J.J. von Tschudi. Gotha, 1860. Ill., map. [Ergänzungsheft zu Petermann's Geographischen Mittheilungen; 2.]
GB/B.15. r074.

Reise durch die Schweiz / John Carne; aus dem Englischen übersetzt von Wilhelm Adolf Lindau. Dresden, 1828.
GB/A.736. r075.

Reise durch die Schweiz und Italien mit der französischen Reserve-Armee / von einem Officier des General-Stabs [i.e. Victor-Donatien de Musset-Pathay]. Göttingen, 1801.
GB/A.1459(1). r076.

Reise durch einen Theil von Teutschland, Helvetien und Ober-Italien, im Sommer 1803: in Briefen an einen Freund / [H.C. Menu von Minutole?]. Berlin, 1804. 2v (in 1); ill.
GB/A.730. r077.

Reise durch einige Cantone der Eidgenossenschaft / Johann Michael Afsprung. Leipzig, 1784.
GB/A.597. r078.

Reise durch etliche Cantone der Schweitz: im Jahr 1789 / von einem Schweitzer [i.e. Johann Georg Müller]. Zürich, 1790.
GB/A.704. r079.

Reise eines Norddeutschen durch die Hochpyrenäen in den Jahren 1841 und 1842 / W.v. R. [i.e. Wilhelm von Rhetz]. Leipzig, 1843. 2v.
GB/A.1489-90. r080.

Reise in das Berner Oberland / J. Rud. Wyss. Bern, 1816-17. 2v; ill.
GB.650-1. r081.

Reise in die Alpen / F.N. König; begleitet mit naturhistorischen Beyträgen von Kuhn, Meisner, Seringe, Studer und Tscharner. Bern, 1814. Ill.
GB.420(1); Lloyd.1615(19). r082.

Reise in die weniger bekannten Thäler auf der Nordseite der Penninischen Alpen / Julius Froebel. Berlin, 1840. Ill., map.
GB.974; Lloyd.1580(1). r083.

Reise mehrer Schlesier in die Alpen der Schweitz und Tyrol's in Briefen des Grafen von P. Breslau, 1830.
GB/A.1465. r084.

Reise von Linththal über die Limmern-Alp nach Brigels / Karl von Schütz. Zurich, 1812.
GB.420(4). r085.

Reise von Wien durch die Schweiz nach Paris, durch Belgien und Deutschland zurück, 455

Meilen in 50 Tagen / Friedrich Drazic. Wien, 1847. GB/A.62.   r086.

Reise-Studien aus Italien, England und Schottland / Titus Ullrich. Berlin, 1893. GB/A.1643.   r087.

Reisen auf den Montblanc im August 1820 / Joseph von Hamel; aus dem Augusthefte der in Genf erscheinenden *Bibliothèque universelle* übersetzt. Basel, 1820. Translated from *Relation de deux tentatives récentes pour monter sur le Mont-Blanc*. Lloyd.1617(13).   r088.

Reisen in den Gebirgstock zwischen Glarus und Graubünden in den Jahren 1819, 1820 und 1822: nebst einem botanischen Anhang und lithographirten Zeichnungen / Johann Hegetschweiler. Zürich, 1825. Ill., map. Lloyd.562.   r089.

Reisen in den Savoyer Alpen und in anderen Theilen der Penninen-Kette nebst Beobachtungen über die Gletscher / James D. Forbes; bearbeitet von Gustav Leonhard. Stuttgart, 1845. Ill., maps. Translated from *Travels through the Alps of Savoy*. GB/A.415.   r090.

Reisen nach den Eisgeburgen von Faucigny in Savoyen / Jean André de Luc; aus dem Französischen übersetzt. Leipzig, 1777. Translated from *Relation de différents voyages*, extracted from *Recherches sur les modifications de l'atmosphère*. Lloyd.1613(2).   r091.

Reiseskizzen aus den Alpen und Karpathen / Carl von Sonklar. Wien, 1857. GB/A.211.   r092.

De **reizen** en lotgevallen van John Ross, op zijne ontdekkingstogten naar de noordpools gewesten. Amsterdam, 1837. Ill., map. GB/A.1896.   r094.

Relation abrégée d'un voyage à la cime du Mont-Blanc en août 1787 / Horace Bénédict de Saussure. Genève, [1787?]. GB.461(1); Lloyd.870; Lloyd.870A.   r095.

Relation abrégée d'un voyage à la cime du Mont-Blanc, &c. A short narrative of a journey to the summit of Mont-Blanc, by M. de Saussure. Edinburgh, 1788. A review. Pp.25-8 of the *Scots Magazine*, 1788, vol. 50. GB.1744.   r096.

Relation d'un accident fatal arrivé à un voyageur sur le glacier de Buet / M.A. Pictet. [N.p., 1808.] Extrait du no.112 de la *Bibliothèque britannique*. GB.584.   r097.

Relation d'un voyage du pôle arctique, au pôle antarctique, par le centre du monde. Amsterdam, 1721. Ill. GB/A.1878.   r098.

Relation de deux tentatives récentes pour monter sur le Mont-Blanc / Joseph von Hamel. Genève, [1820]. Extrait de la *Bibliothèque universelle*, août 1820. Lloyd.1606(18).   r099.

Relation de différents voyages dans les Alpes du Faucigny / Messieurs D. & D. [i.e. J.A. de Luc and Pierre Gédéon Dentand.] Maestricht, 1776. GB.151; GB.1321(52); Lloyd.209.   r100.

Relation de l'ascension sur la cime du Mont-Blanc (abrégée) / Horace Bénédict de Saussure. Genève, 1807. Originally published as *Relation abrégée d'un voyage à la cime du Mont-Blanc*. GB.175; Lloyd.283.   r101.

A **relation** of a journey to the glaciers, in the Dutchy of Savoy / Marc Théodore Bourrit; translated by C. and F. Davy. Norwich, 1775. Ill. Translated from *Description des glacières, glaciers et amas de glace du duché de Savoye*. GB.228; Lloyd.591; Lloyd.330.   r102.

A **relation** of a journey to the glaciers, in the Dutchy of Savoy / Marc Théodore Bourrit. 2nd ed. London, 1776. Translated from *Description des glacières, glaciers et amas de glace du duché de Savoye*. GB.1320(1); Lloyd.331.   r103.

A **relation** of a journey to the glaciers in the Dutchy of Savoy / Marc Théodore Bourrit; translated by Cha. and Fred. Davy. 3rd ed. Dublin, 1776. Translated from *Description des glacières, glaciers et amas de glace du duché de Savoye*. GB.152.   r104.

A **relation** of the death of the primitive persecutors / written originally in Latin by L.C.F. Lactantius; English'd by G. Burnet. Amsterdam, 1687. GB.46A(1).   r105.

A **relation** sent to the Royal Society of London, from some considerable merchants and persons worthy of credit who went to the top of the Pike of

Teneriff. London, 1787. Pp.66-8 of the *New London Magazine*, February 1787.
GB.1880(21).   r106.

Relations des troubles qui ont régné dans la ville de Genève pendant l'année mil sept cens trente-quatre. Rouen, 1736.
GB.1158(1).   r107.

Relations historiques et curieuses de voyages, en Allemagne, Angleterre, Hollande, Bohème, Suisse / Charles Patin. Lyon, 1674. Ill., map, port.
GB.40.   r108.

Relazione del Presidente Generale [Club Alpino Italiano] all'assemblea dei delegati. 1953-1965. [Turin? 1953-65.] Wanting the 1962 issue.
GB/B.403(25-36).   r109.

Remarks on antiquities, arts, and letters, during an excursion in Italy, in 1802 and 1803 / Joseph Forsyth. 3rd ed., from the 2nd London ed. London, 1824. 2v (in 1).
Lloyd.490.   r110.

Remarks on several parts of Europe: relating chiefly to the history, antiquities, and geography of those countries through which the author has travel'd / J. Breval. London, 1726. 2v (in 1); ill.
Lloyd.1537.   r111.

Remarks on several parts of Italy, &c. in the years 1701, 1702, 1703 / Joseph Addison. London, 1705.
GB.379; Lloyd.489.   r112.

Remarks on several parts of Italy, &c. in the years, 1701, 1702, 1703 / Joseph Addison. 5th ed. London, 1736. Ill.
Lloyd.157.   r113.

Remarks on several parts of Italy, &c. in the years, 1701, 1702, 1703 / Joseph Addison. London, 1753.
GB.81.   r114.

Reminiscences of a Continental trip / H.M. London, 1871.
Lloyd.1614(5).   r115.

Reminiscences of a student's life at Edinburgh in the seventies / Alisma [i.e. George Skelton Stephenson]. Edinburgh, 1918.
GB.274.   r116.

Reminiscences of Pen-y-Gwyrd / C.E. Mathews. [N.p.], 1902. Ill., ports. Reprinted from the *Climbers' Club Journal*.
Lloyd.884; Lloyd.884A.   r117.

Le **rendez-vous** d'Essendilene / Roger Frison-Roche. [Grenoble], 1966. Ill.
GB/A.1017.   r118.

Rendez-vous in Zermatt / Walter Schmid. 5. Aufl. Bern, 1965. Ill.
GB/A.365.   r119.

Rendu and his editors / John Tyndall. [London, 1874.] Pp.[135]-48 of the *Contemporary Review*, June 1874.
GB.1167.   r120.

Reply to Professor Tyndall's remarks, in his work *On the glaciers of the Alps*, relating to Rendu's *Théorie des glaciers* / James D. Forbes. Edinburgh, 1860.
Lloyd.1581(1); Lloyd.1602(12).   r121.

Report / Finance Sub-committee, Alpine Club. May 1947. London, [1947].
GB.1313(33).   r122.

Report / North Oxfordshire Archaeological Society. 1865, 1867. Banbury, [1865-67].
Lloyd.1583(14-5).   r123.

[**Report** and accounts, with list of members / Association of British members of the Swiss Alpine Club.] 1911, 1919, 1924-26, 1944-45, 1947, 1951. London, 1912-52.
Lloyd.1613 (7-11) (1911, 1919, 1924-26); GB.1325 (23-27) (1944-51).   r123.1.

Report of the Committee for 1944-1945 / Midland Association of Mountaineers. [Birmingham, 1945.]
GB.1313(6).   r124.

Report of the Council [of the Geological Society] for 1900. [London, 1900.] A proof.
Lloyd.1605(20).   r124.1.

Report of the Council [of the] Royal Geographical Society. 1947, 1949, 1950. London, 1948-51.
GB.1329(1); GB.1332(13-4).   r125.

Report of the cruise of the Revenue Marine Steamer *Corwin* in the Arctic Ocean in the year 1884 / M.A. Healy. Washington, 1889. Ill.
GB/B.547.   r126.

Report of the cruise of the Revenue Marine Steamer *Corwin* in the Arctic Ocean in the year 1885 / M.A. Healy. Washington, 1887. Ill., maps.
GB/B.492.   r127.

Report of the cruise of the U.S. Revenue Cutter *Bear* and the overland expedition for the relief of the whalers in the Arctic Ocean, from November 27, 1897, to September 13, 1898. Washington, 1899. GB/A.1652.   r128.

Report of the expedition to Hudson Bay and Cumberland Gulf in the steamship *Diana*, under the command of William Wakeham, Marine and Fisheries, Canada, in the year 1897. Ottawa, 1898. Ill., maps.
GB/A.2052(2).   r129.

Report of the Hudson's Bay expedition of 1886 under the command of Lieut. A.R. Gordon, R.N. Ottawa, 1887. Maps. Published by the Department of Marine and Fisheries, [Canada].
GB/B.440(18).   r130.

Report of the special committee on ropes, axes and alpenstocks: read before the [Alpine] Club on July 5, 1864. London, [1864].
GB.729(1).   r131.

Report of the special committee on ropes, axes and alpenstocks: read before the [Alpine] Club on July 5, 1864. [London], 1864. Pp.322-30 of the *Alpine Journal*, September 1864.
GB.729(2) (impf.); Lloyd.1583(3); Lloyd.1583(3)A.
                                                                 r132.

Report of Winfield S. Schley, Commander, U.S. Navy, commanding Greely Relief Expedition of 1884. Washington, 1887. Ill., maps, port.
GB/B.544.   r133.

Report on new whaling grounds in the southern seas / David Gray. Peterhead, 1891.
GB/A.2154.   r134.

Report on the expedition / Therkel Mathiassen. New York, 1976. Ill. [Thule expedition, 5th, 1921-1924. Report; vol.1 no.1.]
GB/A.1821.   r135.

Report on the London School of Economics Mountaineering Club Himalayan Expedition, 1956. [London, 1956.]
GB.1331(38).   r136.

A **report** on the resources of Iceland and Greenland / compiled by Benjamin Mills Peirce. Washington, 1868. Maps. At head of title: U.S. State Department.
GB/A.1323(9).   r137.

Report on the selection of a terminal port for the Hudson Bay Railway / F. Palmer. London, 1927. Ill., maps. Report of a survey conducted at the request of the Canadian Minister for Railways and Canals.
GB/B.501(12).   r138.

Report upon expedition to ascend Kamet — 25,447ft — and investigate the physiological effects of high altitude / A.M. Kellas. [N.p., 1920.]
GB/C.13.   r139.

[**Reports** and accounts, with lists of members] / Association of British Members of the Swiss Alpine Club. 1925, 1944, 1945, 1947, 1951. London, 1925[-52].
GB.1325(23-7).   r140.

Reports of agents, officers, and persons, acting under the authority of the Secretary of the Treasury, in relation to the condition of seal life on the rookeries of the Pribilof Islands, and to pelagic sealing in Bering Sea and the North Pacific Ocean, in the years 1893-1895. Washington, 1896. 2v; ill., maps. [U.S. 54th Congress, 1st session. Senate. Document; 137.]
GB/A.1696.   r141.

Die **Republik** Graubünden historisch-geographisch-statistisch dargestellt / H.L. Lehmann. Magdeburg, 1787-99. 2v (in 1).
GB/A.786.   r142.

La **république** des Suisses, contenans le gouvernement de Suisse, l'estat public des treize cantons, & de leurs confederez & autres gestes memorables, depuis l'Empereur Raoul de Habspourg, iusqu'à Charles V / descrite en latin par Iosias Simler de Zurich, & nouuellement mise en françois. Paris, 1578. Ill. Translated from *De republica Helvetiorum*.
GB.109; Lloyd.87.   r143.

La **république** des Suisses / Josias Simler; nouuellement mise en françois. Anvers, 1579. Ill. Translated from *De republica Helvetiorum*.
Lloyd.174.   r144.

Research in the Antarctic: a symposium presented at the Dallas meeting of the American Association for the Advancement of Science, December 1968 / Louis O. Quam, editor; Horace D. Porter, associate editor. Washington, 1971. Ill., maps.
GB/A.2116.   r145.

Research on glacier flow / G. Seligman. Stockholm, 1949. Reprinted from *Glaciers and climate, Geografiska annaler*, 1949, h.1-2.
GB.1337(14). r146.

Researches about atmospheric phenomena: annals of some remarkable aërial and Alpine voyages, including those of the author / Thomas Forster. London, 1832. Ill.
Lloyd.823. r147.

A **residence** in France: with an excursion up the Rhine, and a second visit to Switzerland / Fenimore Cooper. London, 1836. 2v. Originally published as *Sketches of Switzerland*, pt.2.
GB.454-5. r148.

La **restauration** des Alpes / P. Mougin. Paris, 1931. Ill., maps. At head of title: Ministère de l'agriculture. Direction générale des eaux et forêts. Eaux et génie rural.
GB/B.423. r149.

Die **Resterschliessung** der karnischen Voralpen / Wolfgang Herberg, Vincenzo Altamura. [N.p., ca 1953.] Ill., map.
GB/B.245(25). r150.

Retiche pievi / Aurelio Garobbio. Milano, 1936. Ill.
GB/A.1323(6). r151.

Retour à la montagne / Roger Frison-Roche. [2nd ed.]. Paris, 1968.
GB/A.1323(4). r152.

Retour à la montagne / Roger Frison-Roche. [Grenoble, 1957.] A prospectus.
GB.1332(21). r153.

Return from the Pole / Frederick A. Cook; the original manuscript edited, with an appraisal by Frederick J. Pohl. London, 1953. Ill., map, port., facsim.
GB.871. r154.

Return to the Alps / Max Knight; edited with selections from Alpine literature by David R. Brower. San Francisco, [1970?]. Ill. [The earth's wild places; 2.]
GB/B.507. r155.

Révélation de la montagne: les Alpes juliennes, les Dolomites, le massif de Clauta, les Alpes carniques / Julius Kugy; traduit par Paul du Bouchet. Neuchâtel, 1944. Ill. [Montagne.]
GB/A:169. r156.

[A **review** and analysis of Göran Wahlenberg's *Flora Carpatorum principalium*.] [London], 1817. Ill. Pp.140-8 of *Annals of Philosophy* vol.9, Feb.1817.
GB.1880(35). r157.

Revista peruana de andinismo y glaciología. 1969-1970, año 19 no.9: edición extraordinaria conmemorando el primer año del sismo del 31 mayo de 1970. Huaraz, [1971]. Ill. Published by the Instituto Nacional de Glaciología.
GB/A.1051(4). r158.

Revue alpine / Club alpin français, Section lyonnaise. Vol.1-32, 39, 1894-1931, 1933-38/40. Lyon, 1894-1940. Incomplete. Not published 1915-19.
GB/A.882-99 (v.1-20); GB.1634-42 (v.21-29); GB.1643(1) (no.317, 1938); Lloyd. 1430-43 (another copy of v.23/24, 27-32, 39); Lloyd.1430A (another copy of v.23 no.4) r159.

Revue alpine: bulletin du Club alpin belge. 2e sér. tom.8 no.25, déc.1931. Bruxelles, 1931.
GB.1332(41). r160.

Revue géologique suisse pour l'année 1894 / Ernest Favre, Hans Schardt. Genève, 1895. [Eclogae geologicae helveticae; 4,] Tiré des *Archives des sciences de la Bibliothèque universelle*, avril-juin 1895.
GB/A.514(14). r161.

Rhapsodie savoyarde / Jean Canault. Paris, 1950. Ill.
GB/C.5(2). r162.

Der **Rhätikon** / Wilhelm Strauss. [Berlin, 1893.] Ill. Pp.[21]-36 of *Erschliessung der Ostalpen*, Bd.1.
GB.1368(2). r163.

Die **Rhätische** Bahn, Rh.B: praktischer Reiseführer durch das Schweizer: Hochland Graubünden / Hermann Behrmann. 3. Aufl. Chur, 1910. Ill., maps.
GB/A.942(4). r164.

Das **Rheinwaldgebirge**: Itinerarium für den S.A.C., 1872. Basel, [1872].
GB/A.1200(2). r165.

Le **Rhin**: la contrée de sa naissance / texte original de Hermann Hiltbrunner adapté de l'allemand par J. Volmar. Neuchâtel, [ca 1929]. Ill., map. [Les Grisons; 1.]
GB/A.921. r166.

The **Rhine** from Rotterdam to Constance / Karl Baedeker. 16th ed. Leipsic, 1906. Translated from *Die Rheinlande*.
Lloyd.108.   r167.

Rhymes of a rolling stone / Robert Service. London, 1920.
Lloyd.128.   r168.

Ricerche petrografiche sulle valli del Gesso, valli di S. Giacomo / Alessandro Roccati. Torino, 1905. Published by the Accademia Reale delle Scienze.
GB/B.312(9).   r169.

Richard Wagner and the Alps / Josef Braunstein. [London, ca 1930.]
GB.1326(55).   r170.

Richtiges Bergsteigen in Fels und Eis: für Wanderer, Kletterer, Schifahrer: die Technik im Eis / Otto Eidenschink. 5. Aufl. München, 1967. Ill.
GB/A.434(7).   r171.

Richtiges Bergsteigen in Fels und Eis für Wanderer und Kletterer: die Technik im Fels / Otto Eidenschink. 6. Aufl. München, 1966. Ill.
GB/A.434(3).   r172.

Ricordi alpini / Carolina Palazzi-Lavaggi. Torino, 1890.
GB/A.1443.   r173.

Ricordi di un alpinista / Emilio Javelle: [traduzione di Mariuccia Zechinelli]. Treviso, 1947. Ill., port. [Biblioteca alpina; 4.] Translated from *Souvenirs d'un alpiniste*.
GB/A.1576.   r174.

Ricordi di una settimana di allenamento: les Aiguilles Rouges de Chamonix / J.A. Spranger. Firenze, 1912. Ill. Estratto dal *Bollettino della Sezione Fiorentina del C.A.I.*, anno 3 no.1, gennaio 1912.
GB.1329(48).   r175.

Ricordi di vita alpina / Ugo Di Vallepiana. Bologna, 1972. Ill. [Voci dai monti; 23.]
GB/A.1040.   r176.

Ricordo di Giulio Kugy: lo scopritore delle Alpi Giulie / Celso Macor. Gorizia, 1967. Ill.
GB/B.313(7).   r177.

Ricordo di Venezia. Venezia, [n.d.]. Photographs.
Lloyd.841.   r178.

La **ricostruzione** della montagna e il dominio sulle acque / Arturo Cigolla. Trento, 1928.
GB/A.1034(20).   r179.

The **Ried** Pass / T.G. Bonney. [Cambridge, 1874.] Extracted from the *Eagle*, no.50, 1874.
Lloyd.1594(6).   r180.

I **rifugi** alpini d'Italia / Agostino Ferrari. Monza, 1925. [Manuali del Club Alpino Italiano, Sezione Universitaria.] Published by the Club Alpino Italiano.
GB/A.1349(11).   r181.

I **rifugi** alpini dell'Alto Adige / Willy Dondio. Calliano, 1982. Map.
GB/A.2076(6).   r182.

I **rifugi** alpini dell'Alto Adige: rifugi, basi di partenza, itinerari di accesso, traversate, ascensioni / a cura di Willy Dondio. 2a ed. Bolzano, 1968. Ill. Published by the Ente Provinciale per il Turismo, Bolzano.
GB/A.1050(9).   r183.

I **rifugi** alpini delle nuove provincie / per cura di G.B. Calegari. Bolzano, 1924. Map. Published by the Club Alpino Italiano, Commissione Centrale Rifugi Alpini Nuove Provincie.
GB/B.403(18).   r184.

I **rifugi** del Club Alpino Italiano: le stazioni del Corpo Nazionale di Soccorso Alpino / Carlo Arzani. Milano, [1971]. Ill., maps. Published by the *Rassegna alpina*.
GB/A.1323(2).   r185.

I **rifugi** del Club Alpino Italiano: storia e descrizione illustrata con elenco dei rifugi costruiti in Italia da altre società alpine / Agostino Ferrari. Torino, 1905. Ill. From the *Bollettino del Club Alpino Italiano*, vol.37 no.70.
GB.1329(36) (impf.).   r186.

I **rifugi** della Sezione di Milano. Milano, 1929. Ill. Published by the Club Alpino Italiano, Sezione di Milano.
GB/B.289(17).   r187.

I **rifugi** delle Orobie / Angelo Gamba; a cura del Club Alpino Italiano, Sezione di Bergamo. Bergamo, 1966.
GB/A.799(9).   r188.

I **rifugi** e i bivacchi del Club Alpino Svizzero / Carlo Arzani. [N.p.], 1970. Ill.
GB/A.805(4).   r189.

Rifugi e sentieri alpini sulle Dolomiti della valle del Bóite. [Cortina d'Ampezzo?], 1981. Ill., maps. [Guida breve per l'escursionista.]
GB/A.1911(14). r190.

Rifugi, passeggiate, escursioni, vie ferrate del Cadore e suoi dintorni / Renato Zanolli. Treviso, 1979. Ill., maps. [Guida alpina delle Dolomiti; 2.]
GB/A.2017(11). r191.

Rifugi, passeggiate, escursioni, vie ferrate di Cortina d'Ampezzo e suoi dintorni / Franz Dallago, Renato Zanolli. Nuova ed. ampliata e aggiornata. Treviso, 1979. Ill., maps. [Guida alpina delle Dolomiti; 3.]
GB/A.2017(12). r192.

Un **rifugio** e otto montagne / Teresio Valsesia. [Macugnana], 1973. Published by the Club Alpino Italiano, Sezione di Macugnana.
GB/A.1295(8). r193.

Rigi: die Geschichte des meistbesuchten schweizer Berges / Willy Zeller. Bern, 1971. Ill. [Schweizer Heimatbücher; 154.]
GB/B.366(9). r194.

The **Rigi**, Lucerne, and the Vitznau railway / August Feierabend. Zurich, [1883.] Ill.
GB/A.990(1). r195.

Rilevamenti di ghiacciai e studi glaciologici compiuti in occasione dell'Anno Geofisico 1957-1958. Vol.1: Il ghiacciaio del Miage (massiccio del Monte Bianco). Torino, 1961. Ill., maps. Published by the Comitato Glaciologico Italiano.
GB/B.366(6). r196.

Rimembranze di un viaggio all'Alpe di S. Pellegrino e al Monte Orientale o Cimone negli Stati Estensi / Galdino Gardini. [Bologna], 1980. Facsimile reprint of the Bologna, 1852 ed.
GB/A.2165(9). r197.

Das **Ringen** um den Nanga Parbat 1856-1953: hundert Jahre bergsteigerischer Geschichte / Paul Bauer. München, [1955]. Ill., maps, ports.
GB.1114. r198.

Ringer Kunst: fünff und achtzig Stücke / durch Fabian von Auerswald zugericht. Wittemberg, 1539.
Lloyd.1478 (impf.). r199.

Ritmi dell'Alpe / Rino Bigarella. Vicenza, 1948.
GB/A.860(2). r200.

Ritorno ai monti: l'alpinismo come forma di vita — pensieri e immagini / Reinhold Messner; versione italiana di Willy Dondio. Bolzano, 1971. Translated from *Zurück in die Berge*.
GB/B.315. r201.

Ritorno alla montagna / Guido Devescovi. Milano, 1937. Ill.
GB/A.1350(6). r202.

Rivers of ice: a tale, illustrative of Alpine adventure and glacier action / R.M. Ballantyne. London, 1875. Ill.
Lloyd.235. r203.

Rivers of Iceland / R.N. Stewart. Reykjavik, 1950. Ill., map, ports.
GB/A.1850. r204.

Rivières: l'Areuse: le Doubs / Jules Baillods. [Neuchâtel, 1936.] Ill.
GB/A.1222. r205.

Rivista / Legione Trentina. Anno 6-7, 1930-31. Trento, 1930-31. Wanting anno 6 no.5,7,8 and anno 7 no.3,5,7-10.
GB/B.337(7-16). r206.

Rivista alpina italiana. Vol.1-3, 1882-1884. Bologna, 1970. Continued by: *Rivista mensile / Club Alpino Italiano*. Facsimile reprint of the Turin, 1882-84 ed.
GB/A.1246. r207.

Rivista alpina italiana / Club Alpino Italiano. Indice Generale, 1882-1954, a cura di Paolo Micheletti. Milano, [1957].
GB/A.1246. r208.

Rivista della montagna: pubblic. trimestrale del Centro Documentazione Alpina di Torino. Anno 1 n.2- , settembre 1970- . Torino, 1970- .
GB/A.1500. r209.

Rivista mensile / Club Alpino Italiano. Vol.4- , 1888- . Roma, 1888- . Vols.4-6 are facsimile reprints of the original, with the imprint Bologna, 1970. The GB run wanting v.8-18, 20, 23-5, 28, 38, 53-58, 65-7, and with 35, 44, 46-52, 59, 92-3 incomplete. Continues *Rivista alpina italiana*.
GB.1627-33; GB/A.1246; GB.1645(4-6) (further copies of odd issues); Lloyd. 1252-9 (v.35-57). r210.

[The **road** to Chogori: K2, 8611m.] [Tokyo, 1982.] In Japanese.
GB/B.520(10). r211.

The **road** to Lamaland: impressions of a journey to Western Tibet / M.L.A. Gompertz. London, [1926]. Ill., ports.
GB.923.   r212.

Roald Amundsen som han var / Odd Arnesen. Oslo, 1929. Ill., ports.
GB/A.1738.   r213.

Roberts' moving diorama of the polar expedition: being a series of views representing the progress of His Majesty's ships the *Hecla* and *Fury*. London, 1829. A playbill for the Theatre Royal, Covent Garden.
GB/C.92.   r213.1.

Le **Robinson** suisse / Johann David Wyss; nouvelle traduction de l'allemand, Elise Voiart. Paris, 1845. 2v (in 1).
GB/A.28.   r214.

Rocca Sbarua e M. Tre Denti / Gian Piero Motti. Torino, 1969. Ill., maps. Published by the Club Alpino Italiano, Sezione di Torino.
GB/A.1270(15).   r215.

Roccia e ghiaccio alpinismo / Carlo Negri. 4a ed. Milano, 1959. Ill.
GB/A.2023(4).   r216.

Rocher et glace: technique alpine / rédigé par Ruedi Schatz et Ernest Reiss pour le Comité central du Club alpin suisse; traduction de Pierre Vittoz. [Zurich], 1970. Ill.
GB/A.1146.   r217.

Rock climbing guide to Hong Kong / J.F. Bunnell. Hong Kong, 1959. Ill.
GB/A.1879.   r218.

Rock climbing in Great Britain / George and Ashley P. Abraham. [London, 1899.] Ill. Pp.[661]-71 of the *Wide World Magazine*, March 1899.
GB.1318(8).   r219.

Rock climbs: Glencoe and Ardgour / W.H. Murray. Edinburgh, 1949. Maps. [Scottish Mountaineering Club guide.]
GB.85.   r220.

Rock climbs in Jotunheimen, Norway. London, 1953. Ill. Published by the Norway Travel Association.
GB/A.1597(9).   r221.

Rock climbs in Lofoten, Norway. London, 1953. Ill. Published by the Norway Travel Association.
GB/A.1597(11).   r222.

Rock climbs in Nordmore, Norway. London, 1953. Ill. Published by the Norway Travel Association.
GB/A.1597(10).   r223.

Rock climbs on the Roches & Hen Cloud. Hanley, 1968. Ill. Published by the North Staffordshire Mountaineering Club.
GB/A.1597(6).   r224.

Rock for climbing / C. Douglas Milner. London, 1950. Ill.
GB.1169.   r225.

Rock-climber's guide to Donegal. [Dublin? 1962.] Published by the Irish Mountaineering Club.
GB/A.1965(12).   r226.

Rock-climbing guide to Dalkey / Irish Mountaineering Club. [Dalkey?], 1950. Map.
GB/B.440(21).   r227.

Rock-climbing in the English Lake District / Owen Glynne Jones. London, 1897. Ill., maps.
GB.1041; Lloyd.1186; Lloyd.1186A.   r228.

The **Rocky** Mountains of Canada, south / Glen W. Boles, with Robert Kruszyna and William L. Putnam. 7th ed. New York, 1979. Ill. Published by the American Alpine Club and the Alpine Club of Canada.
GB/A.1883(6).   r229.

Rodolphe Töpffer: biographie et extraits / Pierre Maxime Relave. Lyon, 1899. Ill.
GB/B.450.   r230.

Rodolphe Töpffer, où êtes-vous? / Gianni Valenza. [Turin, 1971.] Ill. Published by the Club Alpino Italiano. Pp.[35]-66 of *Scàndere*, 1971.
GB/B.338(4).   r231.

Le **roman** de montagne, ou L'alpinisme dans le roman / Bénédicte et Jean Michel Adam. Paris, 1977. Ill. [Textes pour aujourd'hui.]
GB/A.1597(3).   r232.

Le **roman** de montagne en France / Michel Ballerini. [Paris], 1973. Ill. [Sempervivum; 53.]
GB/A.1051(6).   r233.

The **romance** of adventure, or True tales of enterprise: for the instruction and amusement of the young. London, 1856. Ill.
GB.177.   r234.

The **romance** of mountaineering / R.L.G. Irving. London, 1935. Ill., maps.
GB.1071; Lloyd.1200. r235.

The **romance** of state-mapping / T. Pilkington White. [Edinburgh, 1888.] Pp.384-98 of *Blackwood's Magazine*, Sept. 1888.
GB.1881(26). r236.

Romance of the mountains / Ascott Robert Hope. London, [1888]. Ill.
Lloyd.410. r237.

Romance Switzerland / W.D. McCrackan. Boston, 1894.
Lloyd.32. r238.

Rondoy: an expedition to the Peruvian Andes / David Wall. [London, 1965.] Ill., maps, ports.
GB.905. r239.

The **roof** of the world, being the narrative of a journey over the high plateau of Tibet to the Russian frontier and the Oxus sources on Pamir / T.E. Gordon. Edinburgh, 1876. Ill., map.
GB/B.479. r240.

Rosengarten-, Geisler- und Langkofel-Gruppe / Gunther Langes. 6. Aufl. München, 1969. Ill., maps. [Dolomiten-Kletterführer; 1a.]
GB/A.1050(18). r241.

Rough notes of an excursion to the Soonderdoongee glacier in the Himalaya mountains, during the autumn of 1848 / H.B.T. [i.e. Henry B. Thornhill?]. London, 1858.
Lloyd.762. r242.

Round Kangchenjunga: a narrative of mountain travel and exploration / Douglas W. Freshfield. London, 1903.
GB.1206. r243.

Round mystery mountain: a ski adventure / Norman Watson, Edward J. King. London, 1935. Ill.
GB.901. r244.

La **route** des Alpes françaises / Henri Ferrand. La route des Alpes d'hiver, la route Napoléon / Paul Guiton. Grenoble, 1939. Ill. [Les beaux pays.]
GB/B.377(33). r245.

La **route** des Alpes françaises du Léman à la mer / Henri Ferrand. Grenoble, 1912. Ill., map.
GB/C.4. r246.

La **route** des Pyrénées françaises de la Méditerranée à l'océan / Henri Ferrand. Grenoble, 1914. Ill., map.
GB/B.337(18). r247.

La **route** du Simplon. Basle, 1823.
Lloyd.1611(1). r248.

La **route** du Simplon / Frédéric Barbey. Genève, 1906. Ill.
GB/B.356. r249.

Routes des Alpes françaises: itinéraires avec profils des pentes à l'échelle du 1/200,000 à l'usage des alpinistes, cyclistes et voituristes / H. Dolin. [N.p., ca 1897.]
GB/B.440(19). r250.

Routes in the Western-Himalayas, Kashmir, &c. / T.G. Montgomerie. 3rd ed., rev. and corr. Dehra Dun, 1909. Map.
GB/A.1928. r251.

The **Royal** Geographical Society: its foundation and history, work and publications, charter and bye-laws, and its house. Rev. London, 1937. Ill.
GB.1329(7). r252.

[**Royal** Geographical Society notices.] [London, n.d.]
GB.1326(11). r253.

Royal Institution of South Wales announce that Dr. Hooker, who accompanied the recent expedition in H.M.'s ships *Erebus* and *Terror* to explore the Antarctic seas has kindly consented to deliver an account of the principal incidents of the voyage. Swansea, 1846.
GB/C.118. r254.

The **royal** road to romance / Richard Halliburton. Indianapolis, 1925. Ill., maps, ports.
GB/A.2025. r255.

Ruapehu: a tribute to a mountain / J.C. Graham. Wellington, 1963. Ill., maps. [A Reed book.]
GB/A.1587. r256.

Rückblick auf die 40 jährige Tätigkeit [Deutscher und Osterreichischer Alpenverein, Sektion Bozen], 1869-1909 / H. Forcher-Mayr. Bozen, [1909]. Ill.
GB/B.403(1). r257.

The **Rucksack** Club Journal. Vol.1,8,11-14. Manchester, 1907-63.
GB.1356-61 (impf.). r258.

Der **Ruf** der Berge: die Erschliessung der Berner Hochalpen / Edmund von Fellenberg; Lebensbild versehen von Ernst Jenny. Erlenbach-Zürich, [1925]. Ill.
GB.442. r259.

Der **Ruf** des Nordens: Abenteuer und Heldentum der Nordpolfahrer / H.H. Houben. Berlin, 1927. Ill., map.
GB/A.1629. r260.

Rules / New Zealand Alpine Club. April 1933. [N.p., 1933.]
Lloyd.1617(3); Lloyd.1659(8). r261.

Rules and list of members / Alpine Club. 1866-1956, 1960. London, [1866-1960].
Lloyd.224-8 (1866-1956); GB.1321(1-3) (other copies of 1866, 1953, 1956); Lloyd.224A (another copy of 1906); LLoyd.226A-B (another copy of 1947-48); GB.1321(4-28) (other copies of 1926-42, 1944-50); GB.1321(33) (1960). r262.

Rules and list of members / Climbers' Club. 1937-40. [London], 1937-40.
Lloyd.1615(6-8). r262.1.

[**Rules** and list of members] / Gritstone Club. [N.p., ca 1946.]
GB.1327(3). r263.

Rules and regulations of the Gresham Club, with a list of members. 1915. [London, 1915.]
Lloyd.84. r264.

Rules for finding distances and heights at sea. [N.p., n.d.]
Lloyd.1583(8). r265.

Rules, list of members and officers / Climbers' Club. 1900, 1906, 1912, 1920, 1923, 1925, 1928, 1930, 1935. [London], 1900-35.
Lloyd.1618(35-43). r265.1.

Rules of the Cardiff and County Club, established 1866. Cardiff, 1954.
GB.1325(29). r266.

Rules of the Scottish Mountaineering Club: also hut regulations. 1935, 1950-51. Edinburgh, [1935-51].
GB.1325(11-3). r267.

A **run** through the Dolomites in 1876 / W.A.B. Coolidge. York, 1902. Reprinted from the *Yorkshire Ramblers' Club Journal*, no.4, 1902.
GB.1340(11). r268.

A **run** to Switzerland / Malcolm Douglas. [N.p.], 1874. Reprinted from the *Chelmsford Chronicle*.
Lloyd.1620(5). r269.

Rundsicht vom Gipfel des Säntis / Albert Heim. 8. Aufl. Revision und Reliefton von Ed. Imhof; herausgegeben vom Schweizer Alpenclub als Beilage zur Monatsschrift *Die Alpen*, Jahrgang 5 no.7, Juli 1929, zur Ehrung des Erstellers anlasslich seines 80. Geburtstages am 12. April 1929. Zürich, [1929].
GB.1329(11). r270.

Running water / A.E.W. Mason. London, [1914]. [The wayfarer's library.]
GB.191; GB.193. r271.

Running water / A.E.W. Mason. London, 1925. [The wayfarer's library.]
GB.321. r272.

Rural pickings, or Attractive points in country life and scenery / by the author of *Points and pickings of information about China* [i.e. George Mogridge]. London, 1846. Ill.
GB.207. r273.

Ruskin et les Anglais à Chamonix: causerie faite le 19 juillet 1938, à la 'Pierre à Ruskin' à l'occasion de l'arrivée en France de Leurs Majestés le roi et la reine d'Angleterre /Paul Payot. Bonneville, 1938. Port.
Lloyd.1620(14). r274.

Le **Russell** de la jeunesse: pages choisies du comte Henry Russell extraites de *Souvenirs d'un montagnard* / [edited by] Paul Mieille; avec introduction et notices biographiques d'Henry Beraldi et du Dr. Sabatier. Tarbes, 1930. Ill. [Pages choisies des grands écrivains français.]
GB/A.1381(5). r275.

Russell W. Porter, arctic explorer, artist, telescope maker / Berton C. Willard. Freeport, Me., 1976. Ill.
GB/A.1692. r276.

Rutas montañeras. Vol.1: Roncal, Zuriza. 2a ed. Pamplona, 1974. [Diario de Navarra; 4.]
GB/A.1468(8). r277.

Il **Ruwenzori**: viaggio di esplorazione e prime ascensioni delle più alte vette nella catena nevosa situata fra i grandi laghi equatoriali dell'Africa Centrale / Filippo De Filippi. Milano, 1908. Ill., maps.
GB/A.1551. r278.

-S-

S.A.C. Itinerarium für 1880-81: Orographie der Hohen Kalk-Alpen / Eugène Renevier; deutsche Uebersetzung von H. Schardt. Lausanne, 1880.
GB/A.181(11). s001.

S.U.M.C. Bulletin. No.1-2, Dec.1944-June 1945. [Sheffield], 1944-45.
GB.1331(39). s002.

Sa planina i gora: dojmovi i utisci / Vjekoslav Cvetisic. Kn.3. [Zagreb], 1930. Ill.
GB/A.799(6). s003.

Saas-Fee und Umgebung: ein Führer durch Geschichte, Volk und Landschaft des Saasthales / Heinrich Dübi. Bern, 1902. Ill., map.
GB.348. s004.

Sachregister zu Amthors *Alpenfreund*: erste Serie, Band 1-11. Gera, 1879.
GB/A.1458. s005.

Sacro Monte di Varallo / P. Galloni. Borgosesia, 1973. Ill.
GB/A.1380. s006.

Saggi sulla psicologia dell'alpinista: raccolta di autobiografie psicologiche di alpinisti viventi / [edited by] Adolfo Hess. Torino, 1914. Ill.
GB/A.1345. s007.

Saggio di bibliografia cadorina / Giovanni Fabbiani. Feltre, 1939.
GB/B.299. s008.

Saggio di corografia statistica e storica delle valli di Lanzo / Luigi Clavarino. Torino, 1972. Facsimile reprint of the Turin, 1867 ed.
GB/A.1310. s009.

Le **Sahara** / E.F. Gautier. 3e éd. Paris, 1950. Ill. [Bibliothèque scientifique.]
GB/A.1137. s010.

Saint Bernard et les origines de l'hospice du Mont-Joux (Grand-St-Bernard) / André Donnet. St Maurice, 1942.
GB/B.449. s011.

Saint Pauls: a monthly magazine / edited by Anthony Trollope. Vol.1, Oct.1867-Mar. 1868. London, 1868. Containing an article *Alpine climbing*.
Lloyd.1117. s012.

Saint-Martin-Vésubie, Valdeblore / Vincent Paschetta, Michel Dufranc. 6e éd. Grenoble, 1972. Ill. [Guide Paschetta des Alpes-Maritimes. 2: Randonnées et alpinisme; 2.]
GB/A.1349(13). s013.

Saint-Martin-Vésubie, Valdeblore / Vincent Paschetta. 10e éd. Grenoble, 1976. Ill., maps. [Guide Paschetta des Alpes-Maritimes. 2: Randonnées et ascensions. Circuits automobiles.]
GB/A.1911(11). s014.

Les **saisons** valaisannes / Maurice Zermatten. Neuchâtel, 1948. Ill.
GB/B.404. s015.

[**Sale** catalogue of ice-axes and crampons] / François Simond et fils. Chamonix, [n.d.].
GB.1326(3). s016.

Salire su ghiaccio / Yvon Chouinard; [traduzione di Paola Ornella Antonioli]. Bologna, 1979. Translated from *Climbing ice*.
GB/B.579. s017.

Salita al Monte Viso / Guglielmo Matkews [sic]; traduzione dall'inglese con note. Bologna, 1970. Map. Facsimile reprint of the Saluzzo, 1863 ed. Translated from pp.147-74 of ser.2 vol.2 of *Peaks, passes and glaciers*, published by the Alpine Club in 1862.
GB/A.516(4). s018.

Una **salita** al Monviso / lettera di Quintino Sella a B. Gastaldi. Torino, 1863. Estratto dall'*Opinione*, settembre 1863.
Lloyd.64; Lloyd.1616(11). s019.

Salita iemale al Gran Sasso d'Italia: lettera all'ing. Martiniori / Corradino Sella. Roma, 1880. Estratto dal giornale l'*Opinione*, n.14.
GB/A.1051(3). s020.

Salite in Moiazza / Giovanni Angelini. Vicenza, 1950. Ill., map. Published by the Club Alpino Italiano, Sezione Trivenete.
GB/B.312(26). s021.

Salute the skier: the hundred best ski runs in the Alps / Walter Pause; translated by Ruth Michaelis-Jena and Arthur Ratcliff. New York, 1963. Ill., maps. Translated from *Ski heil*.
GB/A.1914. s022.

Die **Salzburger** Alpen / Max Haushofer. Darmstadt, [ca 1860]. Ill.
GB/B.12. s023.

Die **Salzburger** Kalkalpen / Ludwig Purtscheller. Die Dachstein Gruppe / August von Böhm. [Berlin, 1893.] Pp.[263]-356 of *Erschliessung der Ostalpen*, Bd.1.
GB.1371. s024.

Samanala and its shadow. [London, 1886.] Pp.44-5 of the *Cornhill Magazine*, Jan. 1886.
GB.1880(32). s025.

I **samaritani** della roccia / Cesare Ottin Pecchio. Torino, 1970. Ill.
GB/C.5(7). s026.

Sámiid dilit: föredrag vid den Nordiska Samenkonferensen, Jokkmokk, 1953 / [redaktion Kalle Nickul, Asbjörn Nesheim, Israel Ruong]. Oslo, 1957. Ill., maps.
GB/B.524(3). s027.

Sammlung kurzer Reisebeschreibungen und anderer zur Erweiterung der Länder- und Menschenkenntniss dienender Nachrichten / Johann Bernoulli. Berlin, [1781]-85. 16v; ill., maps
GB/A.1230-43 (wanting v1-2). s028.

San Gottardo strada d'Europa / Jean Louis Bierman, Basilio M. Biucchi, Bruno Legobbe. Bellinzona, 1959. Ill. Published by the Nouvelle société helvétique.
GB/B.289(15). s029.

Il **Sasso** di Remenno: guida alpinistica ad una meravigliosa palestra di granito / Antonio Boscacci. [Sondrio?], 1977. Ill., maps. Published by the Club Alpino Italiano, Sezione Valtellinese.
GB/A.1966(7). s030.

Sassolungo e Sella: escursionismo e vie normali di salita alle principali cime / Luca Visentini. Bolzano, 1981. Ill., maps.
GB/A.1978. s031.

A **satchel** guide for the vacation tourist in Europe. Edition for 1883. Boston, 1883. Maps.
GB/A.383. s032.

Saussure aux Alpes. 1: Portrait de H.B. de Saussure / Charles Vallot. 2: Autour du Mont Blanc: extrait des *Voyages dans les Alpes* / H.B. de Saussure. Paris, 1938.
GB.1326(39). s033.

Savoie / Jacques Lovie. Paris, 1973. Ill.
GB/A.1278. s034.

Scafell group / A.T. Hargreaves. Manchester, 1936. [Climbing guides to the English Lake District; 2.] Published by the Fell and Rock Climbing Society of the English Lake District.
GB.48(2). s035.

Scalate nelle Alpi / Giusto Gervasutti. 2a ed. Torino, 1947. Ill.
GB.746. s036.

Scalate nelle Alpi: conquista del Cervino / Edward Whymper. Nuova ed. Torino, 1965. Ill. [La piccozza e la penna; ser.3 no.1.] Translated from *Scrambles amongst the Alps*.
GB/B.338(2). s037.

Scalate nelle Grigne / Claudio Cima. Bologna, 1975. Ill., maps. [Itinerari alpini; 24.]
GB/A.1351(14). s038.

Scalate su ghiaccio: classiche ed estreme sulle Alpi / Renzo Quagliotto. [N.p.], 1981. Ill., maps. [Guida alpinistica.]
GB/A.2021(6). s039.

Scalatori: le più audaci imprese alpinistiche da Whymper al 'sesto grado' / raccontate dai protagonisti; a cura di A. Borgognoni e G. Titta Rosa. Milano, 1939. Ill.
GB/B.245(28). s040.

Scándere / Club Alpino Italiano, Sezione di Torino. 1949-1971. Torino, [1949-71]. Wanting 1950, 1956, 1966-70.
GB/C.22(2-10); GB/B.403(9-12); GB/B.403(15). s041.

La **Scandinavie** et les Alpes / Ch. Victor de Bonstetten. Genève, 1826.
GB/A.465. s042.

Scarponate / Ubaldo Riva. Milano, 1933. [Montagna; 11.]
GB/A.495(3). s043.

La **scava**, or Some account of an excavation of a Roman town on the hill of Chatelet in Champagne. To which is added, A journey to the Simplon, by Lausanne, and to Mont Blanc / by the author of *Letters from Paris in 1791-2* [i.e. Stephen Weston]. London, 1818.
GB.985; Lloyd.1151. s044.

Scenarie der Alpen / Eberhard Fraas. Leipzig, 1892. Ill.
GB/A.1130. s045.

[**Scenery** in the Himalayas and the highlands of Perthshire.] [N.p., ca 1864.] A photograph album.
GB/C.115.   s046.

The **scenery** of Switzerland and the causes to which it is due / Sir John Lubbock. London, 1896. Ill., maps.
GB.340; Lloyd.573.   s047.

Scenery of the Grampian Mountains / George Fennell Robson. London, 1819. Ill., map.
Lloyd.1554.   s048.

Scenes & adventures at home and abroad, or Pleasing and instructive narratives, anecdotes, etc., etc., for young people. London, [n.d.]. Ill.
GB.131.   s049.

Scenes and impressions in Switzerland and the north of Italy: together with some remarks on the religious state of these countries, taken from the notes of a four months' tour during the summer of 1852 / D.T.K. Drummond. Edinburgh, 1853. Ill.
GB.339; Lloyd.352.   s051.

Scenes from the snow-fields: being illustrations of the upper ice-world of Mont Blanc, from sketches made on the spot in 1855, 1856, 1857, 1858: with historical and descriptive remarks, and a comparison of the Chamonix and St. Gervais routes / Edmund T. Coleman; the views lithographed and printed by Vincent Brooks. London, 1859.
GB.1301; GB.1302; GB.1303; Lloyd.1561.   s052.

Scenes of modern travel and adventure. London, 1845.
Lloyd.123.   s053.

Scenes of modern travel and adventure. London, 1851.
Lloyd.148.   s054.

Scenes of Scottish story / [selected by] William Ballingall. Edinburgh, 1874. Ill.
Lloyd.1357.   s055.

[**Scenes** of the Alps.] [England? 1855?] 4 coloured prints.
GB/B.445-8.   s056.

[**Scenes** of the Alps.] [N.p., 1910?] 12 postcards.
GB/A.2165(11).   s056.1.

Scènes vaudoises: journal de Jean-Louis / Alfred Cérésole. 2e éd. Lausanne, 1884. Ill.
GB/A.1208.   s057.

Schi-Fahrten im südlichen Schwarzwald / Henry Hoek, Heinrich Wallau. 2. verm. und verb. Aufl. München, 1911. Maps.
Lloyd.134.   s058.

Schiara: Dolomiti bellunesi / Piero Rossi. Milano, 1982. Ill., maps. [Guida dei monti d'Italia.]
GB/A.1948.   s059.

Schilderung der Gebirgsvölker der Schweitz / J.G. Ebel. Leipzig, 1798-1802. 2v; ill., map.
GB/A.532-3.   s060.

Schlechtwetter Fahrten / Othmar Gurtner. Bern, 1917. Ill.
GB.301.   s061.

Die **schöne** alte Schweiz: die Kunst der Kleinmeister / herausgegeben von R. Nicolas u. A. Klipstein. Lfg.1-4. Zürich, [n.d.]. Ill.
Lloyd.1621(19-22).   s062.

Schöne Bergwelt / Walter Pause. München, [1964]. Ill.
GB/B.231.   s063.

Schönheiten und Schrecknisse der schweizerischen Alpenwelt / J.B. Bandlin, Vogel von Clarus. 3. Aufl. Clarus, 1868.
GB/A.1461.   s064.

Die **Schule** der Berge / Geoffrey Winthrop Young; Deutsch von Rickmer Rickmers. Leipzig, 1925. Ill. Translated from *Mountain craft*.
GB.1152.   s065.

Die **Schutzhütten** des Deutschen und Osterreichischen Alpenvereins / herausgegeben vom Hauptausschuss des Deutschen und Osterreichischen Alpenvereins. Innsbruck, 1932. Ill., maps.
GB/B.134.   s066.

Die **Schutzhütten** des Deutschen und Osterreichischen Alpenvereins / herausgegeben vom Hauptausschuss des Deutschen und Osterreichischen Alpenvereins. München, [n.d.]. Ill., maps.
GB/B.126.   s067.

Die **Schweitz** in Bildern / nach der Natur gezeichnet von W.H. Bartlett und mit beschreibendem Text von Wilhelm Beattie, aus dem Englischen uebersetzt und mit Anmerkungen begleitet von Johann von Horn.

London, [1839]. 2v; ill., map. Translated from *Switzerland*.
GB/B.285-6. s068.

Die **Schweiz** / J.C. Heer. 2. Aufl. Bielefeld, 1902. Ill., map. [Land und Leute: Monographien zur Erdkunde; 5.]
GB/B.361. s069.

Die **Schweiz** / Johann Jacob Egli. Leipzig, 1886. Ill.
GB/A.47. s070.

Die **Schweiz** / Theodor Gsell-Fels. Hanover, 1978.
GB/B.511. s071.

Die **Schweiz**: das Paradies Europas / C.W. Schmidt. Berlin, [1930]. Ill., map.
GB/B.229. s072.

Die **Schweiz**: ein Handbuch zunächst für Reisende: mit einem Anhang, enthaltend die Beschreibung der interessantesten Punkte der Nachbarlande der Schweiz / L.v. Bollman. Stuttgart, 1837. Ill., map.
GB/A.1298. s073.

Die **Schweiz**: Handbüchlein für Reisende, nach eigener Anschauung und den besten Hülfsquellen bearbeitet. Koblenz, 1844. Ill., map.
GB/A.752. s074.

Die **Schweiz**: ihre Geschichte, Geographie und Statistik. Abt.1: Die Geschichte der Schweiz / E.H. Gaullieur; aus dem Französischen von H. Graefe und G. Fr. Reiss. Genf, 1856. Ill.
GB/B.413. s075.

Die **Schweiz**: ihre Geschichte, Geographie und Statistik. Abt.2: Die malerische Schweiz / von Ch. Schaub und E.H. Gaullieur, sowie von einigen andern Professoren und Mitgliedern der Schweizerischen Historischen Gesellschaft; aus dem Französischen von G. Fr. Reiss. Genf, 1857. Ill.
GB/B.414. s076.

Die **Schweiz**: Landschaft und Baukunst / Martin Hürlimann. Zürich, [1931]. Ill. [Orbis terrarum.]
GB/C.12. s077.

Schweiz: rese-anteckningar i bref: jemte redo-görelser för landets statsförfattning, forsvars-väsen, m.m., från våren 1866 / S.A. Hedlund. Stockholm, 1866. Ill.
GB/A.520. s078.

Die **Schweiz** aus der Vogelschau: Abbildungen / herausgegeben und eingeleitet von Otto Flückiger. Zürich, 1924. Maps.
Lloyd.1485. s079.

Die **Schweiz** in ihren klassischen Stellen und Hauptorten geschildert / H. Zschokke. 2. durchges. und erg. Aufl. St. Gallen, 1858. Ill.
GB/A.626. s080.

Die **Schweiz** wie Goethe sie sah: eine Bilder-sammlung für Freunde des Dichters und der alten Schweiz / mit Einführung von Wilhelm Bode. Leipzig, 1922. Ill.
GB/A.1405. s081.

Die **Schweizer** Ansichten, 1653-1656 / Jan Hackaert; zweiundvierzig Faksimilewiedergaben bearbeitet und kommentiert von Gustav Solar; herausgegeben von der Zentralbibliothek Zürich und dem Schweizerischen Institut für Kunst-wissenschaft. Zürich, 1981. Ill.
GB/C.105. s082.

Schweizer Bergführer erzählen. Zürich, [1936]. Ports.
GB.521. s083.

Schweizer Bilder / Jean Gaberell. Thalwil-Zürich, [1930]. 2v; ill. Wanting Bd.1.
GB.1269. s084.

Schweizer Bilder / Julius Lowenberg. Berlin, 1834. Ill., maps.
GB.994. s085.

Schweizer Führer: durch die Schweiz in 8 Tagen / Leo Woerl. Würzburg, [1888]. Maps.
GB/A.963. s086.

Schweizer Wanderbuch / Heinrich Tgetgel. Bd.9: Cur, Arosa, Lenzerheide: Routenbeschreibungen von Wanderwegen, Spazierwegen, Fern-wanderungen. Bern, [1953]. Ill., maps.
GB/A.1199(5). s087.

Schweizer-Reisen in 14 Abschnitten / Engelbert Hipp. Tuttlingen, 1911. Ill., maps.
GB/A.942(3). s088.

Die **schweizerische** Alpenwelt: für junge und alte Freunde der Alpen dargestellt / August Feierabend. Bielefeld, 1873. Ill.
GB/A.196. s089.

Schweizerische Landesausstellung: Bern 1914: das schweizerische Postwesen in seiner Entwicklung bis zum Jahr 1912 / herausgegeben von der Schweizerischen Oberpostdirektion. Zofingen, [1914]. Ill.
GB/B.312(17). s090.

Schweizerische Stiftung für Alpine Forschungen: 1939 bis 1970: Rückblick auf ihre 30jährige Tätigkeit. Zürich, 1972. Ill.
GB/B.395. s091.

Schweizerische Touristenblätter / Alfred Müller. Leipzig, 1857.
GB/A.1172. s092.

Die **schweizerischen** Alpenpässe und die Postkurse im Gebirge: offizielles illustriertes Posthandbuch / herausgegeben von der Schweiz. Postverwaltung. 2. verm. Aufl. Bern, 1893. Ill., maps.
GB/A.461. s093.

Schweizerisches Archiv für Volkskunde. Vol.1-31, 1897-1931. Zürich, 1897-1931. Title varies: v.1-4, 1897-1900; v.22-26, 1918-1926; v.28-31, 1928-31, as *Archives suisses des traditions populaires.*
GB/A.1418-39. s094.

Schweizerisches Künstler-Lexikon. Dictionnaire des artistes suisses / redigiert unter Mitwirkung von Fachgenossen von Carl Brun. Frauenfeld, 1905-17. 4v. Published by the Schweizerischer Kunstverein.
Lloyd.1360-3. s095.

Schweizerland vor hundert Jahren: Tafeln nach Originalstichen / Gabriel Lory père et fils; Einführung von C. von Mandach. Bern, [1935].
Lloyd.1622(5). s096.

Schweizerreise / Frank Heller. Kopenhagen, 1949. Ill.
GB/A.1224. s097.

Schweizersche Spaziergänge / Leonard Meister. St. Gallen, 1789.
GB.45(1). s098.

Sci / Ugo Ottolenghi di Vallepiana. 3a ed. [Monza?], 1926. Ill. [Manuali SUCAI.] Published by the Istituzione Nazionale Alpina Universitaria SUCAI.
GB/A.828(4). s099.

Sci alpinismo / a cura di Claude e Philippe Traynard. Milano, 1980. [Sportiva; 76.] Translated from *Ski de montagne.*
GB/A.2032(6). s100.

Sci alpinismo in Val D'Ossola: 65 itinerari sci alpinistici nelle valli: Anzasca, Antrona, Bognanco, Sempione, Divedro, Antigorio, Formazza, Vigesso / Loris Bonavia, Mauro Previdoli. Domodossola, [1979?]. Ill., maps.
GB/A.1967(6). s101.

Sci competizione : la tecnica delle tre discipline : slalom, gigante e discesa / Franco e Mario Cotelli. Milano, 1979. Ill. [La vostra via sportiva; 66.]
GB/A.1985. s102.

Sci di fondo / Fulvio Campiotti, Giulio De Florian; con la collaborazione della Scuola Alpina della Guardia di Finanza di Predazzo. 3a ed. Milano, 1980. Ill. [La vostra via sportiva; 44.]
GB/A.1982. s103.

Sci di fondo / Nemo Canetta, Giancarlo Corbellini. Bologna, 1977. Maps. [Itinerari alpini; 38.]
GB/A.1589(4). s104.

Sci di fondo / Nemo Canetta, Giancarlo Corbellini. Bologna, [1979?]. Ill., maps. [Itinerari alpini; 47.]
GB/A.1589(25). s105.

Sci-alpinismo in Adamello e Presanella / J. Casiraghi, M. Andreolli, R. Bazzi. Bologna, [1978]. Ill., maps. [Itinerari alpini; 39.]
GB/A.1589(1). s106.

Sci-alpinismo in Val d'Aosta / Pietro Giglio, Emile Noussan. Bologna, 1981.
GB/B.581. s107.

Sci-alpinismo nelle Alpi: le 'settimane' di Toni Gobbi nelle Alpi italiane, francesi, svizzere e austriache. Bologna, 1975. Ill., maps. [Itinerari alpini; 21.]
GB/A.1468(3). s108.

Sci-alpinismo nelle Dolomiti di Brenta / Marcello Andreolli, Jacques Casiraghi. Bologna, 1973. Ill. [Itinerari alpini; 15.]
GB/A.1199(19). s109.

Sci-alpinismo sull'Appennino tosco-emiliano: dal Corno alle Scale all'Alpe di Succiso / La Focolaccia (Gruppo alpinisti sciatori lucchesi). Bologna, 1979.
GB/A.1589(19). s110.

La **S'ciara** de Oro, monti di Val Belluna / Piero Rossi; con uno scritto di Dino Buzzati. Bologna, [1964]. Ill.
GB/B.379.   s111.

Sciare meglio / Georges Joubert, Jean Vuarnet; tradotto da M.G. Moneta Marchelli. Milano, 1969. Ill. [La vostra via sportiva; 20.] Translated from *Comment se perfectionner à ski*. Pubblicato con la collaborazione della rivista *Sci*.
GB/A.2010.   s112.

Science: men on ice in Antarctica / John Béchervaise. Melbourne, 1978. Ill., maps. [Australian life series; 2.]
GB/A.2048(3).   s113.

Scientific guide to Switzerland / J.R. Morell. London, 1867. Ill.
Lloyd.558.   s114.

The **scientific** observations of the Ross Sea Party of the Imperial Trans-Antarctic Expedition 1914-1917 / Fritz Loewe. Columbus, Ohio, 1963. [Reports / Ohio State University. Institute of Polar Studies; 5.]
GB/B.478(1).   s115.

Scientific reports / Australasian Antarctic Expedition, 1911-14; expedition leader: Sir Douglas Mawson. Series A: [Geography, physiography, glaciology, oceanography and geology]. Sydney, 1918-43. 26v; ill., maps.
GB/B.454-8.   s116.

Scientific reports / Australasian Antarctic Expedition, 1911-14; expedition leader: Sir Douglas Mawson. Series B: [Terrestrial magnetism and meteorology]. Sydney, 1925-47. 10v; ill., maps.
GB/B.459-65.   s117.

Scientific reports / Australasian Antarctic Expedition, 1911-14; expedition leader: Sir Douglas Mawson. Series C: [Zoology and botany]. Sydney, 1916-37. 54v; ill., maps.
GB/B.466-75.   s118.

Scizze einer mahlerischen Reise durch die Schweiz / aus dem Englischen eines Ungenannten; herausgegeben, mit einigen Anmerkungen u. einem doppelten Anhange, von Joh. Rud. Wyss. Bern, 1816.
GB/A.684; Lloyd.599.   s119.

Gli **scoiattoli** di Cortina / Piero Rossi. Bologna, 1965. Ill.
GB/B.392.   s120.

La **scoperta** delle Dolomiti, 1862 / Paul Grohmann; traduzione di Giuseppina e Toni Sanmarchi. Bologna, 1982. Ill., port. Translated from *Wanderungen in den Dolomiten*.
GB/A.1955.   s121.

Scoperta e conquista delle Alpi / Aurelio Garobbio. [Milan], 1955. Ill. [Il sestante.]
GB/A.1546.   s122.

The **Scottish** Himalayan Expedition / W.H. Murray. London, 1951. Ill., maps.
GB.705.   s123.

The **Scottish** Himalayan Expedition / W.H. Murray. [London, 1951.] A prospectus.
GB.1305(2).   s124.

The **Scottish** Mountaineering Club Journal. Vol.24-26 nos.140-147, vol.27 no.152, vol.28 no.155. Edinburgh, 1949-64.
GB.1362-6.   s125.

Scottish Spitsbergen Syndicate. [N.p., 1909?] A circular.
GB.1335(43).   s126.

Scrambles amongst the Alps / Edward Whymper; and, Down the Rhine / Lady Blanche Murphy. Cleveland, Ohio, [ca 1890]. Ill.
GB/A.1757.   s127.

Scrambles amongst the Alps in the years 1860-69 / Edward Whymper. London, 1871. Ill., maps, ports., facsim.
GB.879; GB.1025; Lloyd.1178.   s128.

Scrambles amongst the Alps in the years 1860-69 / Edward Whymper. 2nd ed. London, 1871. Ill., maps, ports., facsim.
GB.797.   s129.

Scrambles amongst the Alps in the years 1860-69 / Edward Whymper. 4th ed. London, 1893. Ill., maps, ports.
GB.1110; Lloyd.1215.   s130.

Scrambles amongst the Alps in the years 1860-69 / Edward Whymper. 5th ed. London, 1900. Ill., maps, ports.
GB.798; GB.799.   s131.

Scrambles amongst the Alps in the years 1860-69 / Edward Whymper. London, [1909]. Ill.
GB.77. s132.

Scrambles amongst the Alps: with additional illustrations and material from the author's unpublished diaries / Edward Whymper. 6th ed.; rev. and ed. by H.E.G. Tyndale. London, 1936. Ill., maps, ports.
GB.747. s133.

Scrambles amongst the Alps in the years 1860-69 / Edward Whymper. 4th ed. Zürich, 1965. Facsimile reprint of the London, 1893 ed.
GB/A.516(12). s134.

Scrambles in the Eastern Graians, 1878-1897 / George Yeld. London, 1900. Ill., map.
GB.604; GB.605; Lloyd.716; Lloyd.716A. s135.

[A **scrap** book.] [N.p., n.d.]
Lloyd.1464. s136.

Scritti alpinistici / Achille Ratti, ora Pio XI; raccolti e pubblicati in occasione del cinquantenario della Sezione di Milano del Club Alpino Italiano; [edited by Giovanni Bobba and Francesco Mauro]. Milano, [1923]. Port.
GB.1319(7). s137.

The **sea** to the Schwarzwald and back / M.T. Tudsbery. [N.p.], 1935. Ill. Reprinted from an unidentified periodical.
GB.1317(1). s138.

Seadragon: northwest under the ice / George P. Steele. New York, 1962. Ill., maps, ports.
GB/A.1656. s139.

Seal and salmon fisheries and general resources of Alaska. Washington, 1898. 4v; ill. Wanting vol.2.
GB/A.1731. s140.

Seal islands of Alaska. Washington, 1911. [U.S. 62d Congress, 1st Session. House. Documents; vol.5.]
GB/A.1590. s141.

The **search** for Sir John Franklin: a lecture delivered at the Russell Institution, January 15, 1851 / Charles Richard Weld. London, 1851.
GB/A.2176. s142.

A **search** for the apex of America: high mountain climbing in Peru and Bolivia including the conquest of Huahscarán / Annie Smith Peck. New York, 1911. Ill., map.
GB/A.1077. s143.

The **search** for the North Pole / Nellis M. Crouse. New York, 1947.
GB/A.1713. s144.

Seasons of the Eskimo: a vanishing way of life / Fred Bruemmer. Toronto, [1971]. Ill.
GB/B.529. s145.

Sechs Jungens tippeln zum Himalaja / Hans Queling. Frankfurt am Main, 1933. Ill.
GB/A.1924. s146.

Seconda controffensiva italo-tedesca in Africa settentrionale da El Agheila a El Alamein (gennaio-settembre 1942). 2a ed. Roma, 1971.
GB/A.2040. s147.

Seconde course à la vallée de Bagnes, et détails sur les ravages occasionnés par l'écoulement du lac de Mauvoisin, 21 juin 1818 / [Philippe S. Bridel?]. Vevey, [1818?]. Ill.
Lloyd.1576(2). s148.

Seconde notice sur la question Simplon ou Mont-Blanc: réponse à une lettre publiée par M. le sénateur Chardon / D. Colladon. Genève, 1880.
GB/A.836(8). s149.

Secondo Corso Nazionale Istruttori, Col d'Olen, giugno 1958 / C.A.I., Corpo Soccorso Alpino. [N.p., 1958.] Ill. Estratto dalla *Rivista mensile del Club Alpino Italiano*, n.5/6-7/8, 1958.
GB/B.440(1). s150.

Secourisme en montagne / sous la haute autorité du professeur Merle-d'Aubigné. 2e éd. Paris, 1972. Ill. Published by the Fédération française de la montagne.
GB/A.1115(2). s151.

Le **secours** en montagne de France. Grenoble, 1967. Published by the Fédération française de la montagne.
GB/A.1199(4). s152.

La **Section** de Chamonix du C.A.F. fondée le 14 août 1902. [Chamonix, 1926.]
GB.1326(7). s153.

Sécurité en paroi / Gianni Mazzenga; traduit par Gilbert Marcilhacy. Roma, 1967. Ill. Translated from *Sicurezza in roccia*.
GB/A.147. s154.

Die **Seen** der deutschen Alpen: eine geographische Monographie / Alois Geistbeck. Leipzig, 1885.
GB/C.2. s155.

Segantini, ou Le roman de la montagne / Raffaele Calzini; traduit par V. Modigliani. Genève, [1947]. Translated from *Segantini, romanzo della montagna*.
GB/A.860(1). s156.

Les **seigneurs** de la neige / Max Liotier. [Paris], 1970. Ill. [Sempervivum; 49.]
GB/A.804(6). s157.

Die **Seilknoten**: ihre Anwendung in Handwerk, in der Landwirtschaft, beim Wasser- und Bergsport / Otto Eggstein. 6. erw. Aufl. Luzern, 1966. Ill.
GB/A.455(3). s158.

Die **Seitenthäler** des Wallis und der Monterosa / Melchior Ulrich. Zürich, 1850.
Lloyd.1580(2). s159.

Sektion Bern S.A.C.: 75 Jahrfeier: die letzen 25 Jahre, 1913-1937. Bern, [1938]. Ill.
Lloyd.1618(44). s160.

Selbander zum Kilimandscharo / Walter Schmid. 3. Aufl. Bern, [1959]. Ill., maps.
GB/A.369. s161.

The **Select** Magazine, for the instruction and amusement of young persons. Vol.1-5, Jan./June 1822-Jan./June 1824. Wellington, Salop, 1822-24.
Lloyd.242-4 (impf.). s162.

Selected climbs in the Canmore area / Gregory Spohr. Banff, Alta, 1976. Ill., map. Published by the Alpine Club of Canada.
GB/A.1883(5). s163.

Selections from a forthcoming anthology [i.e. *Switzerland in English prose and poetry*] / Arnold Lunn. London, 1944. Pp.242-8 of the *Climbers' Club Journal*, N.S. vol.7 no.3.
GB.1337(23). s164.

Selections of the most remarkable phenomena of nature / edited by Henry G. Bell. Edinburgh, 1827. [Constable's miscellany; 12.]
GB.30. s165.

The **Selkirk** Mountains: a guide for mountain climbers and pilgrims / information by A.O. Wheeler. Winnipeg, 1912. Ill., maps, port.
GB/A.1589(38). s166.

The **Selkirks**: Nelson's mountains / J.F. Garden. Revelstoke, 1984.
GB/B.649. s167.

Sella- , Marmolata- und Pala-Gruppe / Gunther Langes. 6. Aufl. München, 1969. Ill., maps. [Dolomiten-Kletterführer; 1b.]
GB/A.1050(17). s168.

Le **selve** della montagna pistoiese: canti V / Giuseppe Tigri. 2a ed. Firenze, 1868.
GB/A.521. s169.

Une **semaine** au Mont Blanc, août 1893 / Paul Helbronner. Paris, 1894. Ill.
GB.1157; Lloyd.1620(18). s170.

Les **sensations** extraordinaires: à travers les périls de l'Alpe / Robert Sans-Terre. Genève, [ca 1940].
GB/A.1035(3). s171.

I **sentieri** dell'Enrosadira / Sandro Prada. Lecco, [1971]. Ill.
GB/A.1245. s172.

Sentieri e segnavia dell'Alto Adige. Trento, 1950. Ill., maps. Published by the Club Alpino Italiano, Comitato Coordinamento Trentino-Aldo Adige.
GB/A.516(8); GB/A.2018(14). s173.

Sepp Höltzl aus den Alpen / Alfred Rottauscher. Leipzig, 1924. [Die lustigen Bücher; 3.]
GB/A.26. s174.

Sergeant Bell, and his raree-show / Peter Parley. New ed. London, 1842.
GB.20. s175.

A **series** of letters written by the Rev. James Jackson to Mr. George Seatree and others, describing his wonderful octogenarian mountaineering and climbing exploits in Cumberland, 1874-1878. Penrith, 1906. Ill. Reprinted from the *Penrith Observer*, Nov. and Dec.1906.
GB.1312(21). s176.

Sesto grado: l'affermazione / Vittorio Varale; gli sviluppi / Reinhold Messner; i valori / di Domenico A. Rudatis. Milano, 1971. Ill. [La vostra via sportiva; 28.]
GB/A.977. s177.

Sette anni contro il Tirich / [Guido Machetto, Maria Ludovica Varvelli, Ricardo Varvelli]. [Milan], 1976. Ill. [Exploits.]
GB/A.1580(14). s178.

Settimane nazionali sci-alpinistiche d'alta montagna / organizzazione e direzione tecnica Toni Gobbi, collaboratore Giulio Salomone. [Turin, 1956.] Published by the Commissione Centrale per lo Sci-Alpinismo, Club Alpino Italiano.
GB.1313(13). s179.

Settimane sci-alpinistiche 1955, organizzate e dirette da Toni Gobbi: la haute route: i quattromila della Britannia: i 4000 del Rosa. [Courmayeur, 1955.] Published by the Club Alpino Italiano.
GB.1334(18). s180.

Settimo grado: clean climbing — arrampicata libera / Reinhold Messner. Nuova ed. Novara, 1983.
GB/A.2113. s181.

Settimo grado: racconti — idee — sentimenti / Arturo Tanesini. Milano, 1946. [Montagna; 22.]
GB/A.548. s182.

The **seven** lamps of architecture / John Ruskin. London, 1849. Ill.
GB.1228. s183.

Seven letters on the recent politics of Switzerland: originally published in the *Spectator* / George Grote. London, 1847.
GB.554. s184.

Seven pillars of wisdom: a triumph / T.E. Lawrence. 2nd ed. London, 1935. Ill., maps, ports.
GB.1196. s185.

Seven weeks in Belgium, Switzerland, Lombardy, Piedmont, Savoy, &c. / John Roby. London, 1838. 2v; ill., map.
Lloyd.658-9; Lloyd.658A-9A. s186.

Seven years in Tibet. [London, 1954.] A notice of a lecture at the Royal Geographical Society by Heinrich Harrer.
GB.1326(54). s187.

The **seventh** continent: Antarctica in a resource age / Deborah Shapley. Washington, 1985.
GB/B.645. s188.

La **Sezione** Agordina 1868-1968 / a cura della Sezione Agordina del C.A.I. nel suo primo centenario / Giovanni Angelini [et al.]. Bologna, 1968. Ill.
GB/B.313(10). s189.

La **Sezione** Napoletana del Club Alpino Italiano (1871-1971) / Pasquale Palazzo. [Naples], 1970. Ill.
GB/C.22(20). s190.

The **shameless** diary of an explorer / Robert Dunn. New York, 1907. Ill., map.
GB.302. s191.

Sharpe's London Journal. Vol.9-10. London, 1849-[50].
GB.1389-90. s192.

Sharpe's London Magazine: a journal for entertainment and instruction. Vol.3,7, 1846/47-1848. London, 1847-48.
GB.1387-8. s193.

The **shepherdess** of the Alps, a moral tale / Jean François Marmontel. London, 1776. Translated from *La bergère des Alpes*.
Lloyd.76. s194.

The **shepherdess** of the Alps, a moral tale / Jean François Marmontel. York, [1810?]. Translated from *La bergère des Alpes*.
Lloyd.151. s195.

Sherpa, Himalaya, Nepal / Mario Fantin; translated by R.S. Shluwalia. New Delhi, 1974. Ill. Translated from *Sherpa, Himalaya, Nepal* (Italian).
GB/B.499. s196.

Sherrington — the man / T. Graham Brown. St. Albans, [1947]. Reprinted from the *British Medical Journal*, November 22, 1947.
GB.1313(35). s197.

Shisha Pangma: eine deutsche Tibetexpedition bezwingt den letzten Achttausender / Manfred Abelein. Bergisch Gladbach, 1980. Ill., ports.
GB/B.534. s198.

Shores and Alps of Alaska / H.W. Seton Karr. London, 1887. Ill., maps.
GB.709. s199.

A **short** account of Mont Blanc and the Valley of Chamouni; serving to illustrate the models of those places, carved in wood, by J. Troye, and now exhibiting at the Museum, Piccadilly. London, 1817. Ill.
Lloyd.1578(4). s200.

Short stalks, or Hunting camps north, south, east, and west / Edward North Buxton. Ser.2. 2nd ed. London, 1893. Ill., maps.
GB.1098; GB.1099. s201.

Short stalks, or Hunting camps north, south, east, and west / Edward North Buxton. Ser.2. London, 1898. Ill., maps.
GB.1040.   s202.

Shpitsbergen v russkoi istorii i literature / A.F. Shidlovsky. St. Petersburg, 1912.
GB.1317(9).   s203.

Siberia and Central Asia / John W. Bookwalter. 2nd ed. New York, [1899]. Ill., map.
GB/A.1884.   s204.

Sibir' i ee sosedi v drevnosti / [otv. redaktor: V.E. Larichev]. Novosibirsk, 1970. Ill. [Drevniaia Sibir'; 3.] At head of title; Akademiia nauk SSSR, Sibirskoe otdelenie, Institut istorii, filologii i filosofii.
GB/A.1787.   s205.

Sicheres Klettern in Fels und Eis / Günter Sturm, Fritz Zintl. München, 1969. Ill.
GB/A.436.   s206.

Sicurezza in roccia / Gianni Mazzenga [con la collaborazione di Mario Bisaccia]. 2a ed. ampliata. Padova, 1973. Ill. Published by the Club Alpino Italiano, Sezione di Padova.
GB/B.377(12).   s207.

Un **siècle** d'ascensions au Mont-Blanc / Joseph Vallot. Paris, 1889. Ill., map, port. Extrait de l'*Annuaire du Club alpin français*, vol.15, 1888.
Lloyd.939.   s208.

Der **Sieg** des Lebens / Carl Eduard Wilhelm Bölsche. 9. Aufl. Stuttgart, [1905].
GB.1313(19).   s209.

Sierra Club Bulletin. Vol.4 no.4-vol.9 no.4, vol.29 no.5-vol.46 no.8, June 1903-Jan.1915, Oct.1944-Oct.1961. San Francisco, 1903-61. Incomplete.
GB.1530-5; GB/B.409(1-52).   s210.

La **Sierra** de Gredos: guía de los Galayos, el Circo de Gredos y otras zonas de interés / Miguel Angel Adrados, Emilio García Viel, Jerónimo Lopez. Madrid, 1981. Ill., maps.
GB/A.2021(14).   s211.

The **Sierra** Nevada: the range of light / edited by Roderick Peattie; contributors: David R. Brower [et al.]. New York, 1947. Ill., map. [American mountain series.]
GB/A.1923.   s212.

Sight-seeing in Germany and the Tyrol in the autumn of 1855 / Sir John Forbes. London, 1856.
Lloyd.664.   s213.

Sikhim & Bhutan: twenty-one years on the northeast frontier, 1887-1908 / John Claude White. London, 1909. Ill., map, port.
GB.1214.   s214.

Sikkim / [photographs by] Pietro Francesco Mele; text by Desmond Doig and Jean Perrin. Calcutta, 1971. Ill.
GB/B.397.   s215.

Die **silbernen** Götter des Cerro Gallan / Mathias Rebitsch. München, [1957]. A prospectus.
GB.1313(28).   s216.

Il **silenzio** ha le mani aperte: romanzo / Ettore Zapparoli. Torino, 1949.
GB/A.528.   s217.

Die **Silvretta** Gruppe / O. von Pfister. Die Ferwall Gruppe / W. Strauss. [Berlin, 1893?] Ill., map. Pp.[3]-65 of *Erschliessung der Ostalpen*, Bd.2.
GB.1373.   s218.

Le **Simplon**: promenade pittoresque de Genève à Milan / [Charles Malo]. Milan, [1825]. Ill.
Lloyd.1613(3).   s219.

Le **Simplon** et l'Italie septentrionale / J.L. Belin. 2e éd. Paris, 1843. Ill.
GB/A.183.   s220.

Sinfonie alpine: musicalità dell'alpinismo: saggio critico / Iginio Gobessi. Genova, [1950].
GB/A.1034(16).   s221.

Sir John Franklin's last Arctic expedition: the Franklin Expedition: a chapter in the history of the Royal Navy / Richard J. Cyriax. London, 1939. Maps.
GB.902.   s222.

Sir John Hawkwood: story of a condottiere / John Temple-Leader, Giuseppe Marcotti; translated by Leader Scott. Florence, 1889. Translated from *Giovanni Acuto*.
Lloyd.1465.   s223.

Sir Paul E. Strzelecki: the man who climbed and named Mt. Kosciusko / Marian Kaluski. [Sydney?], 1981. Port.
GB/B.635(8).   s224.

Six great mountaineers: Edward Whymper, A.F. Mummery, J. Norman Collie, George Leigh-Mallory, Geoffrey Winthrop Young, Sir John Hunt / Ronald W. Clark. London, 1956. Ports. ['Six great' series.]
GB.304.   s225.

Six mois dans l'Himalaya: le Karakorum et l'Hindu-Kush: voyages et explorations aux plus hautes montagnes du monde / J. Jacot Guillarmod. Neuchâtel, [1903].
GB/A.2181.   s226.

The six sisters of the valleys: an historical romance / William Bramley-Moore. 4th ed., rev. London, 1865. Ill.
Lloyd.565.   s227.

Six weeks in north and south Tyrol / William Longman. London, 1872. Map. Pp.720-31 of *Fraser's Magazine*, N.S. vol.6 no.36.
GB.1880(7).   s228.

Six weeks in Switzerland, with some mountain ascents / George Edward Mannering. Christchurch, [n.d.].
Lloyd.1620(31).   s229.

Sixty below / Tony Onraet. Toronto, 1944. Ill., map.
GB/A.1889.   s230.

Skeletal remains of the Central Eskimo / K. Fischer-Møller; [translated by W.E. Calvert]. New York, 1976. [Thule expedition, 5th, 1921-1924. Report; vol.3 no.1.]
GB/A.1826.   s231.

Sketch of a descriptive journey through Switzerland / [Rowley Lascelles]. To which is added The passage of S. Gotthard, a poem by the Duchess of Devonshire. New ed. Berne, 1816.
GB.673; GB/A.680; Lloyd.663; Lloyd.1610(11).
                                                           s232.

Sketch of a tour in Switzerland. London, 1797.
GB/A.635.   s233.

A sketch of a tour in Switzerland in a series of letters to a friend / John Hayden. London, 1859.
Lloyd.36.   s234.

A sketch of a tour on the Continent, in the years 1786 and 1787 / James Edward Smith. London, 1793. 3v.
Lloyd.765-7.   s235.

Sketch of a tour through Swisserland / T.M. [i.e. Thomas Martyn]. London, 1787. Map.
GB.139(1).   s236.

Sketch of a tour through Swisserland / T.M. [i.e. Thomas Martyn]; to which is added A short account of an expedition to the summit of Mont Blanc, by M. de Saussure, of Geneva; [translated by T. Martyn]. New ed. London, 1788. Map.
GB.234(1); Lloyd.1569(1); Lloyd.1569(1)A.
                                                           s237.

A sketch of the geography and geology of the Himalaya Mountains and Tibet / S.G. Burrard, H.H. Hayden. Calcutta, 1907-08. 4v; ill., maps.
GB.1337(21-2) (wanting pt.2,4).   s238.

Sketches descriptive of Italy in the years 1816 and 1817. With a brief account of travels in various parts of France and Switzerland / [Jane Waldie]. London, 1820. 4v.
Lloyd.271-4.   s239.

Sketches in Norway taken during a yachting cruise in the summer of 1852 / George M.W. Atkinson. Cork, 1852. Map.
GB/C.49.   s240.

Sketches of Highland character. Edinburgh, [1873]. Ill.
Lloyd.1449.   s241.

Sketches of manners, scenery &c. in the French provinces, Switzerland, and Italy: with an essay on French literature / John Scott. London, 1821.
Lloyd.1031.   s242.

Sketches of nature in the Alps / Friedrich von Tschudi. London, 1856. [Traveller's library; 1.] Translated from *Das Thierleben der Alpenwelt*.
Lloyd.325; Lloyd.325A,B; Lloyd.1573(2).
                                                           s243.

Sketches of Switzerland / by an American [i.e. James Fenimore Cooper]. Philadelphia, 1836.
Lloyd.402-3.   s244.

Sketches of the natural, civil, and political state of Swisserland: in a series of letters to William Melmoth / William Coxe. London, 1779.
GB.863; Lloyd.956.   s245.

Sketches of the natural, civil, and political state of Swisserland: in a series of letters to William Melmoth / William Coxe. 2nd ed. London, 1780.
GB.647.   s246.

Sketches of Vesuvius, with short accounts of its principal eruptions, from the commencement of the Christian era to the present time / John Auldjo. London, 1833. Ill., map.
GB.777; Lloyd.1184.   s247.

Sketching rambles, or Nature in the Alps and Apennines / Agnes and Maria E. Catlow. London, [1861]. 2v; ill.
GB.492-3; Lloyd.622-3.   s248.

Lo **ski** / H. Mückenbrünn, F. Hallberg; traduzione di Adolfo Balliano. Torino, 1931. Ill. Translated from *Le ski par la technique moderne.*
GB/A.828(1).   s249.

Ski: technique, compétition, montagne / James Couttet, en collaboration avec Philippe Gaussot. Chamonix-Mont Blanc, [1947]. Ill.
GB/B.312(18-20).   s250.

The **Ski** Club of Great Britain handbook. 1926-27. London, [1926].
GB.1310(2).   s251.

Ski de fond — randonnée et compétition / Hans Brunner, Alois Kalin. 3e éd. Lausanne, 1972. Ill.
GB/A.1058.   s252.

Ski trails in the Canadian Rockies: a guide to Banff, Jasper, Koolenay and Yoho Parks / Rick Kunelius, Dave Biederman. Rev. ed. Banff, Alta, 1981. Ill., maps.
GB/B.528(5).   s253.

Ski- und Bergkalendar. 1974 / [Bildauswahl und Texte von Walter Pause]. Stuttgart, [1973]. Ill.
GB/B.390(5).   s254.

Ski-Führer für die Silvretta- und Bernina-Gruppe. Chur, 1913. Ill. Published by the Akademischer Alpen-Club Zürich.
GB/A.508.   s255.

Ski-ing: the review of the British Ski Association. Vol.1 no.1, Dec.1912. London, 1912.
Lloyd.1605(8).   s256.

Ski-running / D.M.M. Crichton Somerville, W.R. Rickmers, E.C. Richardson. London, 1904. Ill., map.
Lloyd.944.   s257.

Ski-Touren im Ober-Engadin / Anton Willy. Chur, [1916].
GB/A.509.   s258.

Skizze einer Wanderung durch einen Theil der Schweiz und des südlichen Deutschlands / G. von Schultes. Bamberg, 1820. Ill.
GB/A.801(8).   s259.

The **sky** was his limit: the life and climbs of Sonan Gyatso / B.N. Mullik. Dehra Dun, 1970. Ill.
GB/A.1004.   s260.

Slæderejserne: Knud Rasmussens ekspeditions-beretninger 1902-1924 / under redaktion af Palle Koch. [Copenhagen], 1979. 4v.
GB/A.1679.   s261.

Sledging into history / David L. Harrowfield. Auckland, 1981.
GB/B.608.   s262.

Slight reminiscences of the Rhine, Switzerland, and a corner of Italy / [Mary Boddington]. London, 1834. 2v; ill.
Lloyd.637-8.   s263.

Snioland, or Iceland, its jokulls and fjalls / William Lord Watts. London, 1875. Ill., maps.
Lloyd.576.   s264.

Snow bridge / Mokuo Nagayama. Tokyo, 1976.
GB/B.528(12).   s265.

Snow dogs / Neville Peat. Christchurch, 1978. Ill.
GB/A.2099.   s266.

Snow on the Equator / H.W. Tilman. London, 1937. Ill, maps.
GB.909; Lloyd.998.   s267.

Snowdon biography / Geoffrey Winthrop Young, Geoffrey Sutton, Wilfrid Noyce; edited by Wilfrid Noyce. London, 1957. Ill., map.
GB.724.   s268.

Snowdon out of season, or The misadventures of a solitary mountain climber / Jacques Stafford. London, [1887]. Ill.
Lloyd.1617(10); Lloyd.1617(10A).   s269.

The **snows** of yesteryear: J. Norman Collie, mountaineer / William C. Taylor. Toronto, 1973. Ill.
GB/A.2136.   s270.

Soccorsi d'urgenza in attesa del medico / A. Peterlana e C. Sebesta. 2a ed. [N.p.], 1954. Ill.
GB/A.1355.   s271.

Il **soccorso** alpino in Italia / Scipio Stenico. [Trento], 1956. Ill. Published by the Corpo Soccorso Alpino.
GB/B.377(36).   s272.

Social life in Munich / Edward Wilberforce. 2nd ed. London, 1864.
GB/A.1382.   s273.

Social progress. [N.p., 1861].
Lloyd.1583(13).   s274.

Soirées fantastiques, Melville Island. Melville Island, 1853. A poster.
GB/C.110(1).   s275.

Les **soirées** helvétiennes, alsaciennes, et fran-comtoises / [Alexandre F. J. Masson]. Amsterdam, 1771.
GB/A.781.   s276.

Le **soldat** de la neige / Paul Achard. Paris, 1945. 2v; ill. [La vie exaltante; 24,30.]
GB/A.44-5.   s277.

Sole e neve nelle 4 valli ladine di Gardena, Fassa, Badia e Livinallongo / Carlo Artoni. 2a ed. Calliano, 1973. Ill., maps. [Montagne celebri.]
GB/B.363.   s278.

Solo il vento bussa alla porta / Aldo Gorfer. 2a ed. Trento, 1971. Ill.
GB/B.327.   s279.

Some account of a journey across the Alps / Abraham Hayward. London, [1834].
GB.216; Lloyd.114; Lloyd.114A,B.   s280.

Some account of a journey across the Alps: in a letter to a friend / Abraham Hayward. London, [1834]. A different ed. from s280.
Lloyd.124; Lloyd.257.   s281.

Some account of the dogs and of the Pass of the Great Saint Bernard: intended to accompany an engraving after a picture by Edwin Landseer / John Landseer. London, [1831].
Lloyd.156.   s282.

Some account of the valley of Chamouni, and of the ascent of Mont Blanc: storms and avalanches of the Alps. [London], 1837. 4v. Extracted from the *Saturday Magazine* supplements, no.320, 337, 347, 351.
GB.1259; GB.1336(29) (wanting v.4).   s283.

Some choice week-end and holiday retreats. Glasgow, [1900?] Ill., map. Published by the Public House Trust.
GB/A.2165(4).   s284.

Some early visits to Zermatt and Saas / W.A.B. Coolidge. London, 1907. Reprinted from the *Alpine Journal*, Nov.1906 and Feb.1907.
GB.1340(16); Lloyd.1602(9).   s285.

Some episodes of mountaineering / by a casual amateur [i.e. Edwin Lord Weeks]. [London?], 1894. Ill.
GB/A.797(1).   s286.

Some episodes of mountaineering / by a casual amateur [i.e. Edwin Lord Weeks]. [New York], 1894. Ill. Pp.[531]-53 of *Scribner's Magazine*, vol.15 no.5.
GB.1336(14).   s287.

Some high notes. [London, 1893.] Pp.608-20 of the *Cornhill Magazine*, 1893.
GB.1881(54).   s288.

Some letters: containing an account of what seemed most remarkable in Switzerland, Italy &c. / Gilbert Burnet. Rotterdam, 1686.
GB.306; Lloyd.356.   s289.

Some letters: containing an account of what seemed most remarkable in Switzerland / Gilbert Burnet. Rotterdam, 1687.
Lloyd.56.   s290.

Some letters, containing an account of what seemed most remarkable in travelling through Switzerland, Italy, some parts of Germany / Gilbert Burnet. London, 1689.
GB.46(1).   s291.

Some letters: containing an account of what seem'd most remarkable in travelling through Switzerland / Gilbert Burnet. London, 1724.
Lloyd.593.   s292.

Some mountain expeditions of the Parkers from 1860 to 1865 / J. P. Farrar. [London], 1916. Ports. Reprinted from the *Alpine Journal*, Feb., May 1916.
Lloyd.1606(10).   s293.

Some Oberland climbs in 1907 / H.V. Reade; read at the Alpine Club on April 7, 1908. London, 1908. Port.
Lloyd.1604(2).   s294.

Some remarks on the Alpine passes of Strabo / William John Law. London, 1846. Map.
Lloyd.1602(18). s295.

Sommer i Antarktis: blant pingviner, sel og hvalfangstminner / Lauritz Somme. Oslo, 1983. Ill., maps.
GB/B.629. s296.

Sommerski / Fritz Schmitt. München, 1934. Ill.
GB.1326(23). s297.

Sommets / [edited by] Félix Germain. [Mulhouse], 1959.
GB/A.2036. s298.

Son of the North / Charles Camsell. Toronto, 1954. Ill., maps, ports.
GB/A.1748. s299.

Die **Sondirung** des Montblancgipfels im Sommer 1891 / Xavier Imfeld. [Bern, 1892.] Pp.374-80 of the *Jahrbuch des Schweizer Alpenclub*, Jahrg.27.
GB.1881(59). s300.

Songs of a cragsman / George Basterfield. London, 1930. Published by the Fell and Rock Climbing Club of the English Lake District, London section.
GB.1318(2); GB.1318(3). s301.

Songs of a cragsman / George Basterfield. Barrow-in-Furness, 1935. Music.
GB.1338(30). s302.

The **songs** of Skye: an anthology / edited by B.H. Humble. 2nd ed. Stirling, 1944. Ill.
GB.116. s303.

The **songs** of the mountaineers / John Hirst. [Manchester, 1922.] A prospectus and order form.
GB.1313(2). s304.

Das **Sonnenland** und andre Erzählungen aus dem Nachlass / Hans Hoffmann. 2. Aufl. München, 1911.
GB/A.55. s305.

Sonnige Halden am Lötschberg / F. G. Stebler. [Bern], 1913. Ill., ports. [Monographien aus den Schweizeralpen. Beilage zum Jahrbuch des S.A.C.; 49.]
GB/B.119(4); Lloyd.1620(21). s306.

Sorapíss (Dolomiti orientali) / Camillo Berti. Bologna, [1968]. Ill., map. Estratto da *Le Alpi Venete*, n.2, 1968.
GB/B.338(9). s307.

Le **Soreiller** / Gilbert Robino. [N.p.], 1973. Ill.
GB/B.570(5). s308.

Sotto le grandi pareti: l'alpinismo come sport di competizione / Vittorio Varale. Bologna, 1969. Ill. [Voci dai monti; 16.]
GB/A.949. s309.

Il **sottobosco**: atlante di florula nemorale indicativa / Attilio Arrighetti. Calliano, 1970. Ill.
GB/A.1074. s310.

La **source** et le glacier du Rhône, en juillet 1834 / Rey. Paris, 1835.
GB/A.803(8[1]). s311.

Sous l'oeil des choucas, ou Les plaisirs de l'alpinisme / quatre-vingt dessins alpins de Samivel. Paris, 1972.
GB/B.337(1). s312.

South: man and nature in Antarctica: a New Zealand view / Graham Billing. Rev. ed. Wellington, 1969. Ill., maps.
GB/B.514. s313.

South American sketches, or A visit to Rio Janeiro, the Organ Mountains, La Plata, and the Paranà / Thomas Woodbine Hinchliff. London, 1863. Ill., map.
Lloyd.608; Lloyd.677. s314.

South Col: one man's adventure on the ascent of Everest, 1953 / Wilfrid Noyce. London, 1954. Ill., maps, ports.
GB.764. s315.

South to Samarkand / Ethel Mannin. 3rd impr. London, 1936. Ill.
GB.819. s316.

South-eastern France from the Loire to the Riviera and the Italian frontier, including Corsica / Karl Baedeker. 3rd ed. Leipsic, 1898.
Lloyd.109. s317.

South-western Alps including Dauphiné and Piedmont from Nice to the Little St. Bernard / John Ball. London, 1873. Maps. [Ball's Alpine guides.]
GB/A.705. s317.1.

The **Southern** Alps / John Pascoe. Pt.1: From the Kaikouras to the Rangitata. 2nd, rev. ed. Christchurch, 1956. Ill., maps. [New Zealand holiday guides; 3.]
GB/A.942(8). s318.

The **southern** Cordillera Real: a guide for mountaineers, skiers and walkers / R. Pecher, W. Schmiemann; translated from the German by Ewald Osers. Chur, 1977. Ill.
GB/A.2020(12). s319.

The **southern** Highlands / edited by J.D.B. Wilson; including an appendix on rock climbs in the Arrochar district by B.H. Humble and J.B. Nimlin. Edinburgh, 1949. Ill., map. [Scottish Mountaineering Club guide.]
GB.778. s320.

Souvenir de Chamonix. [N.p., n.d.] Ill.
Lloyd.137. s321.

Souvenir de Gavarnie / [Lucien Briet]. [Gèdre, ca 1900.] Ill. [Collection des albums Briet.]
GB/A.1936. s322.

Souvenir de la Suisse. [N.p., n.d.] Ill. Views.
GB/A.384. s323.

Souvenir de la Suisse. Zurich, [n.d.]. Ill.
Lloyd.11. s324.

Souvenir du lac des Quatre Cantons. Lucerne, [ca 1850]. Ill. Views.
GB/A.745. s325.

Souvenir du Mont-Blanc et de Chamouni. Genève, [n.d.]. Ill.
Lloyd.1616(20). s326.

Souvenir du Righi. Genève, [ca 1890]. Ill. Folding views.
GB/A.1163. s327.

Souvenirs d'un alpiniste / Emile Javelle; avec une notice biographique et littéraire par Eugène Rambert. 4e éd. Lausanne, 1906.
GB.271. s328.

Souvenirs d'un montagnard, 1858-1888 / comte Henry Russell-Killough. Pau, 1888.
Lloyd.714. s329.

Souvenirs d'un montagnard, 1858-1888 / comte Henry Russell-Killough. 2e éd., rev. et corr. Pau, 1908.
GB/A.104. s330.

Souvenirs d'un voyage dans les Pyrénées. Paris, 1835.
GB/A.2075. s331.

Souvenirs de voyage en 1832 et 1833. Paris, 1834. 2v.
GB/B.290(1-2). s332.

Souvenirs de voyages, les bords du Rhin, la Hollande, Anvers, l'Angleterre, l'Ecosse et Cherbourg / baron de Mengin-Fondragon. Paris, 1838.
GB/A.917(2). s333.

Souvenirs des Pyrénées: vues prises aux environs des eaux thermales de Bagnères-de-Bigorre, Bagnères-de-Luchon, Cauteretz, Saint-Sauveur, Barèges, les-Eaux-Bonnes, les-Eaux-Chaudes & Pau / dessinées d'après nature et lithog. par Victor Petit. Pau, [ca 1840]. Ill.
GB/C.97. s334.

Souvenirs des travaux du Simplon / Robert Ceard. Genève, 1837. Ill.
GB/C.47. s335.

Souvenirs du Mont-Blanc. Genève, [ca 1850]. Ill. Views.
GB/A.105. s336.

Souvenirs du Mont-Blanc et de la vallée de Chamonix. [N.p., n.d.] Ill.
Lloyd.1606(1). s337.

Souvenirs du Mont-Blanc et de la vallée de Chamonix. [N.p., n.d.] Ill. A different edition from s337.
Lloyd.1606(2). s338.

Souvenirs et récits de voyages: les Alpes françaises et la haute Italie / F.B. de Mercey. Paris, 1857.
GB/A.61. s339.

Souvenirs pour servir à la statistique du département de l'Isère / le baron d'Haussez. Bordeaux, 1828.
GB/A.2104(2). s340.

Souveränitätsfragen der Polargebiete: norwegische Interessen in den Eismeeren / Gustav Smedal. [Oslo], 1943.
GB/A.2052(6). s341.

Spanning the Atlantic / F. Lawrence Babcock. New York, 1931.
GB/A.1677. s342.

Spasatel'nye raboty v gorakh / Ferdinand Aloizovich Kropf. Moskva, 1966. Ill.
GB/A.129. s343.

Spaziergänge in den Alpen / Eugen Simmel. Leipzig, 1880. Ill.
GB/A.1325.   s344.

Spaziergänge in den Alpen: Wanderstudien und Plaudereien / J.V. Widmann. 2. veränderte und verm. Aufl. Frauenfeld, 1892.
GB/A.486.   s345.

Spectres lumineux: spectres prismatiques et en longueurs d'ondes destinés aux recherches de chimie minérale / Lecoq de Boisbaudran. Paris, 1874. 2v.
GB/A.2103.   s346.

La **spedizione** italiana all'Everest, 1973 / Guido Monzino; con il resoconto scientifico di Paolo Cerretelli. [Verona], 1976. Ill., maps.
GB/C.87.   s347.

Spedizioni d'alpinismo in Africa: atti delle spedizioni G.M. 1959/60, 1960/61, 1961/62, 1963/64, 1964/65 / Guido Monzino; fotografie, tratti geografici ed appunti storico-alpinistici di Mario Fantin; note dai diari dei componenti le spedizioni. Verona, 1966.
GB/B.263.   s348.

Spedizioni d'alpinismo in Groenlandia: atti delle spedizioni G.M. 1960-1961-1962-1963-1964 / Guido Monzino; fotografie, tratti geografici ed appunti storico-alpinistici di Mario Fantin; note dai diari dei componenti le spedizioni. Verona, 1966. Maps.
GB/B.264.   s349.

Speeches at Colchester, delivered at the dinner given to D.W. Harvey, Esq. Chelmsford, 1830.
GB.697(3).   s350.

La **speleologia** in terra bresciana / Dante Vailati. Brescia, 1979. Ill. [Schede Grafo.]
GB/A.2033(2).   s351.

The **spirit** of the hills / Frank S. Smythe. London, 1935. Ill.
GB.1008.   s352.

The **spirit** of the Matterhorn / Lord Queensberry. London, [1881?].
GB.1309(4); Lloyd.909; Lloyd.1611(8).   s353.

The **spirit** of travel / Charles Packe. London, 1857.
Lloyd.322; Lloyd.322A,B.   s354.

Le **Spitzberg**: aurore boréale sur l'île polaire / Julius Büdel, Walter Imber. Berne, 1968. Ill.
GB/B.301.   s355.

Le **Spitzberg** dans l'histoire diplomatique / Arnold Ræstad; traduit du norvégien par Charles Rabot. Paris, 1912. Maps. Extrait de *La Géographie*, t.25 no.5,6 et t.26 no.2.
GB.1336(2).   s356.

The **splendid** hills: the authorised life and the photographs of Vittorio Sella, 1859-1943 / Ronald Clark. London, [1948]. A prospectus.
GB.1332(22).   s357.

Sport and folklore in the Himalaya / H.L. Haughton. London, 1913.
GB.911.   s358.

Sport and travel in the Highlands of Tibet / Sir Henry Hayden, Cesar Cosson. London, [1927].
GB.609.   s359.

Sport in the Alps in the past and present: with some sporting reminiscences of the late Duke of Saxe-Coburg-Gotha / W.A. Baillie-Grohman. London, 1896. Ill.
Lloyd.1156.   s360.

Sport in the Crimea and Caucasus / Sir Clive Phillipps-Wolley. London, 1881.
Lloyd.1004.   s361.

Gli **sport** invernali visti dal medico / S. Vacchelli, C.F. Zanelli. Milano, 1950. Ill. [I libri della salute; 59.]
GB/A.1442.   s362.

Les **sports** de montagne et le droit / W. Rabinovitch. Paris, 1959.
GB/A.96.   s363.

Sports invernali: pattinaggio, slitta, bobsleigh, skeleton, skis / Nino Salvaneschi. Milano, 1911. Ill. [Manuali Hoepli.]
GB/A.1164.   s364.

St. Andrews and neighbourhood: a history and guide book / Walter Coutts. 2nd ed. St. Andrews, [n.d.]. Ill., map.
Lloyd.1616(14).   s365.

Das **St.** Antöniertal / G. Fient. St. Antönien, 1903. Ill.
GB/A.1199(9).   s366.

St Loup, Vallorbe, Covatanne: 3 écoles d'escalades vaudoises / Claude et Yves Rémy. Renens, 1975. Ill.
GB/A.1381(9).   s367.

The St. Moritz Post / edited by F. de Beauchamp Strickland. No.1-15, vol.4 no.1,10, Dec.7th 1886-March 15th 1887, Oct.27, Dec.29 1888. St. Moritz, 1886-88.
GB/B.484 (1886-87); Lloyd.1533 (1888).   s368.

St-Gervais-les-Bains et le Mont-Blanc: aperçus topographiques, pittoresques et scientifiques. Paris, 1839. Map.
GB.1335(19).   s369.

Staats und Erd Beschreibung der ganzen helvetischen Eidgenossschaft, derselben gemeinen Herrschaften und zugewandten Orten / Johann Conrad Fäsi. Zürich, 1765-68. 4v.
GB/A.629-32.   s370.

Staats und Erd Beschreibung der ganzen helvetischen Eidgenossschaft, derselben gemeinen Herrschaften und zugewandten Orten / Johann Conrad Fäsi. 2. verb. Aufl. Zürich, 1768. 4v.
GB/A.864 (v.1 only).   s371.

Staats- und Erdbeschreibung der schweizerischen Eidgenossschaft / Johann Conrad Füssli. Schafhausen, 1770-72. 4v.
GB/A.673-6.   s372.

Der Stadt Bern vornehmste Merkwürdigkeiten, samt einer kurzen Chronik der Geschichte dieser Stadt, von ihrem Ursprung bis auf des Jahr 1808 / S.v. W. Bern, 1808.
Lloyd.1575(2).   s373.

Die Stadt Luzern und ihre Umgebungen: in topographischer, geschichtlicher und statistischer Hinsicht / Joseph Maria Businger. Luzern, 1811. Ill., map.
Lloyd.603.   s374.

Statistique de la Suisse, ou Etat de ce pays et des vingt-deux cantons dont il se compose / Jean Picot. Genève, 1819.
GB/A.699.   s375.

Statistique de la Suisse, ou Etat de ce pays et des vingt-deux cantons dont il se compose / Jean Picot. Genève, 1819. A different issue from s375.
GB/A.944.   s376.

Statistique générale de la France: département du Mont-Blanc. Paris, 1807. Map. Published by the Ministère du Travail et de la Prévoyance Sociale.
GB/B.292.   s377.

Statistisches Jahrbuch der Schweiz / herausgegeben vom Statistischen Bureau des eidg. Departements des Innern. Jahrg.1, 1891. Bern, 1891. Maps. [Schweizerische Statistik; 80.]
GB/A.966.   s378.

Statuten / Schweizer Alpenclub; beraten und angenommen in den Delegiertenversammlungen vom 21. September und 13. December 1907 in Bern. Solothurn, 1907.
Lloyd.1612(15).   s379.

Statuten und Reglemente / Schweizer Alpenclub, Sektion Bern. Bern, 1908.
Lloyd.1617(12).   s380.

Statuti della Sezione 'Ampezzo' del Club Alpino Tedesco ed Austriaco colla sede in Cortina. Statuten der Section 'Ampezzo' des Deutschen und Oesterreichischen Alpenvereins mit dem Sitze in Cortina. Trento, 1882.
GB.1327(8).   s381.

Statuts / Club alpin français, Groupe de haute montagne. Paris, [n.d.].
Lloyd.1605(4).   s382.

Statuts / Schweizer Alpenclub; adoptés par l'Assemblée générale à Saint-Gall, le 2 septembre, 1866, et révisés par l'Assemblée des délégués les 28 août 1869, 20 août 1887, 26 septembre 1892 et 7 septembre 1895, suivis de divers règlements. Winterthur, 1903.
Lloyd.1602(16).   s383.

Stazzema: la perla dell'Alta Versilia e centro di escursioni alpine con preliminare illustrazione sull'Apuania e la regione versiliese e guida per gite / Guido Gherardi. Camaiore, 1935. Ill., port.
GB/A.799(15).   s384.

Stefansson and the Canadian Arctic / Richard J. Diubaldo. Montreal, 1978.
GB/A.2179.   s385.

La stella alpina nella leggenda e nel folklore / Giovanni Solinas. Verona, 1953. [Quaderni di Vita veronese; serie varia, 15.]
GB/B.403(4).   s386.

Stepping stones to the South Pole / J.R. Nichol. Sydney, 1948.
GB/A.2117. s387.

[Stereoscopic views of Arctic exploration.] Arlington, N.J., 1902.
GB/A.1589(9[1-20]). s388.

Die **Stimme** der Berge / Lubos Brchel. Salzburg, 1969. Ill.
GB/B.151. s389.

The **stones** of Venice / John Ruskin. New ed. London, 1873. 3v; ill.
GB.1221-3. s390.

Det **store** polardrama / Einar Lundborg, Knut Stubbendorff. København, 1928. Ill., ports.
GB/A.1791(9). s391.

Den **store** sledereise / Knud Rasmussen; oversatt av Halvdan Hydle. Oslo, 1938. Ill, map, ports. Translated from *Den store slæderejse.*
GB/A.1871. s392.

La **storia** dei tre Weissthor / W.A.B. Coolidge; versione italiana di G. Laeng. Torino, 1917. Ill. Estratto dalla *Rivista del Club Alpino Italiano,* vol.36 n.3-6, anno 1917.
GB.1340(57). s393.

Storia del territorio vicentino / Gaetano Maccá. Bologna, 1972. 14v (in 7). Facsimile reprint of the Caldogno, 1812-15 ed.
GB/A.1010-6. s394.

Storia del Trentino e dell'Alto Adige / Antonio Zieger. Trento, 1926. Ill.
GB/B.403(2). s395.

Storia della spedizione scientifica italiana nel Himàlaia, Caracorùm e Turchestàn cinese, 1913-14 / Filippo De Filippi; con capitoli aggiuntivi di Giotto Dainelli e J.A. Spranger. Bologna, 1924. Ill., maps.
GB.1235. s396.

Storia della Vallesesia e dell'Alto Novarese / Federico Tonetti; con note e documenti. Borgosesia, 1972. Map. Facsimile reprint of the Varallo, 1875-80 ed.
GB/A.1276. s397.

Storia della Valsesia: età contemporanea 1861-1943 / Enzo Barbano. Novara, 1967. Ill. Published by the Società Valsesiana di Cultura.
GB/A.996. s398.

Storia della Valtellina e della Val Chiavenna / Enrico Besta. Vol.1: Dalle origini alla occupazione grigiona. 2a ed. Milano, 1955. [Raccolta di studi storici sulla Valtellina; 7.]
GB/A.1378. s399.

Storia delle montagne / Ferdinand C. Lane; traduzione di Alberto Bargelesi. Milano, 1952. Ill. Translated from *The story of the mountains.*
GB/A.992. s400.

Storia delle montagne / Ferdinand C. Lane; traduzione di Alberto Bargelesi; revisione, per la parte alpinistica, di Carlo Ramella. Milano, 1953. Ill. Translated from *The story of the mountains.*
GB/A.873. s401.

Storia di Bassano e del suo territorio / Ottone Brentari. Bologna, 1967. Facsimile reprint of the Bassano, 1884 ed.
GB/B.400. s402.

Storia di Cortina d'Ampezzo: il leone sorride ancora / Mario Ferrucio Belli. Bologna, 1973. Ill.
GB/A.1286. s403.

Storia di Fiemme, e della magnifica comunità dalle origini all'istituzione dei comuni / Candido Degiampietro. Calliano, [1972]. Ill.
GB/A.955. s404.

Storia naturale in campagna / Paolo Lioy. Milano, 1901.
GB/A.828(3). s405.

Storie e leggende dell'Appennino e del Po / Aldo Cerlini. Reggio, 1939. Ill.
GB/A.517. s406.

Stories from Switzerland and the Tyrol. London, 1853. Ill.
Lloyd.173. s407.

Storm on the heights / Frank S. Smythe. London, 1937. Ill. Pp.402-12 of the *Strand Magazine,* Feb.1937.
GB.1336(32); GB.1336(33). s408.

A **storm** on the Pétéret Ridge / Frank S. Smythe. [Edinburgh, 1929.] Chapter 13 of his *Climbs and ski runs.*
GB.1335(62). s409.

The **story** of Alpine climbing / Francis Gribble. London, 1904. [The library of useful stories.]
GB.47. s410.

The **story** of an Alpine adventure / A.E. Metcalfe. [London, 1899.] Ill., ports. Pp.[453]-8 of the *Wide World*, Jan.1899.
GB.1336(3). s411.

The **story** of Borrowdale / Shelagh Sutton. Rev. Keswick, 1974. Ill., maps.
GB/A.2031(4). s412.

The **story** of Everest / W.H. Murray. London, 1953. Ill., maps.
GB.728. s413.

The **story** of Everest / W.H. Murray. 2nd ed. London, 1953. Ill., maps.
Lloyd.832. s414.

The **story** of Mont Blanc / Albert Smith. London, 1853. Ill.
GB.377; GB.378; Lloyd.589; Lloyd.589A. s415.

The **story** of Mont Blanc / Albert Smith. New York, 1853. Ill.
GB.353. s416.

The **story** of Mont Blanc / Albert Smith. 2nd ed., enl. London, 1854.
GB.202; Lloyd.230. s417.

The **story** of Mont Blanc / Albert Smith. Goring, 1974. Facsimile reprint of the London, 1853 ed.
GB/A.1596. s418.

The **story** of Mont Blanc / J.E. Muddock. [London, 1892.] Ill., port. Pp.[88]-108 of the *Strand Magazine*, July 1892.
GB.1881(63). s419.

The **story** of Mont Blanc: an address / delivered by C.E. Mathews at the Sutton Coldfield Institute, 20th January, 1896. Birmingham, [1896]. Ill.
GB.886; Lloyd.859. s420.

The **story** of Mont Blanc and A diary to China and back / Albert Smith. [London], 1859-60. 2v (in 1); ill., ports.
GB.170. s421.

Una **strada** che parte da Rimbianco / Aldo Depoli. Bologna, [1967]. Ill. [Voci dai monti; 8.]
GB/A.850. s422.

La **strada** è questa / Adolfo Balliano, Irene Affentranger. Bologna, 1957. Ill. [Il semprevivo; 2.]
GB/A.495(4). s423.

Strade delle Dolomiti: itinerari automobilistici della regione Trentino-Alto Adige / Remo Pedrotti. Rovereto, [1973]. Ill., maps.
GB/B.377(16). s424.

Strade e sentieri del Baldo e Lessini / Giordano Sabaini. Verona, 1959. Ill., maps. [Le guide; 59.]
GB/A.1349(19). s425.

Straight up: the life and death of John Harlin. New York, 1968. Ill., ports.
GB/A.2212. s426.

Strange sights in the Himalayas / Ellis Griffiths. [London, 1899.] Ill. Pp.[313]-23 of *Wide World*, vol.3 no.40.
GB.1336(4). s427.

Stratigraphy of Greenland / Lauge Koch. Copenhagen, 1929. Ill., maps.
GB/B.524(7). s428.

Stray leaves from an Arctic journal: to which is added the career, last voyage, and fate of Captain Sir John Franklin: being vol.1 of Osborn's *Narratives of voyage and adventure*. New ed. Edinburgh, 1865.
GB.258. s429.

Streiftog i Nord / Ebbe Munck. Copenhagen, 1959. Ill., ports.
GB/B.524(8). s430.

Streifzüge durch die norischen Alpen / F. Freiherrn v. Augustin. Wien, 1840. Ill.
GB/A.1597(13). s431.

De **strijd** tusschen Boer en Brit: de herinnering / C.R. de Wet. Amsterdam, 1902.
GB/A.1680. s432.

The **structure** of the Alps / Léon W. Collet. London, 1927. Ill., maps.
Lloyd.987. s433.

The **struggles** and adventures of Christopher Tadpole at home and abroad / Albert Smith. London, [1848]. Ill.
GB.827. s434.

Stubaier Alpen : ein Führer für Täler, Hütten und Berge / Wolfgang Rabensteiner, Heinrich E. Klier. München, 1953. Ill., maps. [Alpenvereinsführer. Reihe: Zentralalpen.]
GB/A.1806. s435.

Die **Stubaier** Gruppe / Ludwig Purtscheller. Die Sarnthaler Gruppe / Julius Pock. [Berlin, 1893?] Ill. Pp.[377]-495 of *Erschliessung der Ostalpen*, Bd.2.
GB.1375. s436.

Studies in both arts: being ten subjects drawn and described / John Ruskin. Orpington, 1895. Ill.
GB.1291.   s437.

Sturm auf den Südpol: Abenteuer und Heldentum der Südpolfahrer / H.H. Houben. Berlin, 1934.
GB/A.1678.   s438.

Sturm auf die Throne der Götter / Rudolf Skuhra. Berlin, [1938]. Ill.
GB/A.90.   s439.

A **sub-aqueous** moraine / H.W. Feilden. Leeds, [1894]. Reprinted from the *Glacialists' Magazine*, vol.2, August 1894.
GB.1880(11).   s440.

The **subalpine** kingdom, or Experiences and studies in Savoy, Piedmont, and Genoa / Bayle Saint John. London, 1856. 2v.
Lloyd.642-3.   s441.

Substance of the speech of General Sir John Doyle at the India House, upon the Hyderabad papers, on Friday, March 4, 1825. London, 1825.
Lloyd.898.   s442.

The '**substantial**' and 'wave' theories of sound: two letters / A. Wilford Hall, Sedley Taylor. London, 1891.
Lloyd.1605(14).   s443.

A **substitute** for the Alps / Sir Leslie Stephen. [N.p., 1894.] Pp.460-7 of the *National Review*, June 1894.
GB/A.797(9).   s444.

Subterranean climbers: twelve years in the world's deepest chasm / Pierre Chevalier; translated by E.M. Hatt. London, 1951. Ill., maps, ports. Translated from *Escalades souterraines*.
GB.861.   s445.

La **sud** del McKinley: Alaska '61, spedizione 'Città di Lecco' / Riccardo Cassin. Milano, 1965. Ill., map, ports.
GB/B.430.   s446.

Die **südlichen** Ortler-Alpen nach den Forschungen und Aufnahmen / Julius Payer. Gotha, 1869. Ill., maps. [Petermann's Geographische Mitteilungen. Ergänzungsheft; 27.]
GB/B.523(2).   s447.

Die **südlichen** Rheingletscherzungen von St. Gallen bis Aadorf: Inaugural-Dissertation / C.

Falkner; begutachet von Albert Heim. St. Gallen, 1910. Map.
GB/A.1052(15).   s448.

Südtiroler Wanderbuch: sechzig Wege am Etsch, Eisack und Rienz / Josef Rampold. 3. neubearb. Aufl. Innsbruck, 1970. Ill., maps.
GB/A.837.   s449.

Suggestions for the exploration of Iceland: an address delivered to the members of the Alpine Club, on April 4, 1861 / William Longman. London, 1861. Map.
GB.1335(44); Lloyd.1025; Lloyd.1581(10).   s450.

Sui campi di battaglia: la nostra guerra. 2a ed. Milano, [ca 1940]. Maps, ports. Published by the Touring Club Italiano. Introduzione alla serie delle guide dei campi di battaglia in 6 volumi.
GB/A.2033(5).   s451.

Sui campi di battaglia: guida storico-turistica. Vol.1: Il Cadore, la Carnia, l'alto Isonzo. 5a ed. Milano, 1942. Ill., maps, ports., facsims. Published by the Consociazione Turistica Italiana.
GB/A.2031(1).   s452.

Sui campi di battaglia: guida storico-turistica. Vol.2: Il Monte Grappa. 4a ed. Milano, [1940?] Ill., maps, ports., facsims. Published by the Touring Club Italiano.
GB/A.2048(1).   s453.

Sui campi di battaglia: guida storico-turistica. Vol.3: Il Trentino, il Pasubio, gli altipiani. 4a ed. Milano, 1937. Ill., maps, ports. Published by the Touring Club Italiano.
GB/A.2031(2).   s454.

Sui campi di battaglia: guida storico-turistica. Vol.4: Il medio e il basso Isonzo. 5a ed. Milano, 1939. Ill., maps, ports., facsims. Published by the Consociazione Turistica Italiana.
GB/A.2033(4).   s455.

Sui campi di battaglia: guida storico-turistica: il Piave e il Montello. Milano, 1929. Ill., maps, ports., facsims. Published by the Touring Club Italiano.
GB/A.2032(1).   s456.

Sui ghiacciai dell'Africa (Kilimangiaro, Kenya, Ruwenzori) / Mario Fantin. Bologna, 1968. Ill., maps.
GB/B.354.   s457.

Sui monti della Grecia immortale / Spiro Dalla Porta Xidias, Bianca Di Beaco. Bologna, 1965. Ill. GB/B.290(7). s458.

La **Suisse** / Adolphe Joanne. 2e éd. Paris, 1868. [Collection des Guides Joanne. Guides diamant.] Lloyd.41. s459.

La **Suisse** / Paul Guiton. Grenoble, 1930. Ill. [Les beaux pays.] GB/B.338(22). s460.

La **Suisse**: études et voyages à travers les 22 cantons / Jules Gourdault. Paris, 1879-80. 2v; ill. GB/C.88. s461.

Suisse: impressions de route / Léon Bovier. Bruxelles, 1906. GB/A.801(4). s462.

Suisse: les routes les plus fréquentées / P. Joanne. Paris, 1909. Maps. [Guides-Joanne.] GB/A.1463. s463.

La **Suisse**, ou Esquisse d'un tableau historique, pittoresque et moral des cantons helvétiques / G.B. Depping. 2. éd. rev. et augm. Paris, 1824. 4v. GB/A.746-9. s464.

La **Suisse** à pied: souvenirs de vacances offerts aux jeunes touristes / Charles Dehansy. Paris, [ca 1880]. Ill., map. GB/A.1121. s465.

La **Suisse** allemande et l'ascension du Mœnch / la comtesse Dora d'Istria. Paris, 1856. 4v; ill. GB.259-62. s466.

La **Suisse**, Chamonix et les vallées italiennes / Paul Joanne. Paris, 1887. Ill., maps. [Guides-Joanne.] GB/A.764. s467.

La **Suisse** circulaire: voyage dans la Suisse française, la Savoie, l'Oberland et la Suisse centrale / [H.A. de Conty]. 5e éd. [Paris, 1881.] Ill., maps. [Guides Conty.] GB/A.1268. s468.

La **Suisse** en miniature. [N.p., n.d.] Ill. Lloyd.3. s469.

La **Suisse** et le Tyrol: scènes de la vie des montagnes. Paris, [1850?]. Ill. GB/A.1903. s470.

La **Suisse** et les parties limitrophes de l'Italie, de la Savoie et du Tyrol / Karl Baedeker. 14e éd. rev. et corr. Leipzig, 1883. Maps. GB/A.778. s471.

La **Suisse** et les parties limitrophes de l'Italie, de la Savoie et du Tyrol / Karl Baedeker. 24e éd. Leipzig, 1905. GB/A.779. s472.

La **Suisse** et ses amis, by Claire Eliane Engel / Gavin de Beer. [Uxbridge, 1945.] A review. Pp.449-53 of the *British Ski Year Book*, vol.11 no.26. GB.1337(7). s473.

La **Suisse** historique politique et pittoresque / E.H. Gaullier, Ch. Schaub. Genève, 1855-56. 2v; ill. GB/B.287(1-2). s474.

La **Suisse** pittoresque et ses environs: tableau général, descriptif, historique et statistique des 22 cantons, de la Savoie, d'une partie du Piémont et du pays de Bade / Alexandre Martin. Paris, 1835. Ill., map, ports., music. Lloyd.1457; Lloyd.1457A. s475.

Sul granito della val Masino: ascensioni ed escursioni scelte / G. Miotti, G. Mottarella. Sondrio, 1982. Ill., maps. GB/A.2021(13). s476.

Sul rimboschimento alpino / Filippo Vallino. Torino, 1881. Estratto dal *Bollettino del Club Alpino Italiano*, no.47, anno 1881. GB/B.290(11). s477.

Sull'Appennino modenese: versi / Alfredo Testoni. Bologna, 1894. GB/A.1023. s478.

Sulle Alpi / Alessandro Dumas; [traduzione di Nerina Crétier]. Treviso, 1946. Ill. Translated from *Impressions de voyage*. GB/A.1376. s479.

Summary of accounts: abridged statement of receipts and payments of the Committee, January 1921-30th June, 1947 / Mount Everest Committee, Royal Geographical Society. [London], 1947. GB.1326(1). s480.

Summer and winter in the Pyrenees / by the author of *The women of England* [i.e. Sarah Ellis]. London, [1841]. Lloyd.708. s481.

Summer holidays in the Alps, 1898-1914 / W.E. Durham. London, 1916. Ill., ports. GB.1230. s482.

A **summer** in Alaska: a polar account of the travels of an Alaska exploring expedition along the great Yukon River, from its source to its mouth, in the British North-West Territory, and in the territory of Alaska / Frederick Schwatka. St. Louis, 1893. Ill., map, port.
GB/A.1659.   s483.

A **summer** in Skye / Alexander Smith. Edinburgh, 1880.
Lloyd.521.   s484.

A **summer** in the Pyrenees / James Erskine Murray. London, 1837. 2v.; ill.
Lloyd.1194-5.   s485.

Summer months among the Alps: with the ascent of Monte Rosa / Thomas W. Hinchliff. London, 1857. Ill., maps.
GB.533; Lloyd.685; Lloyd.685A.   s486.

A **summer** tour in the Grisons and Italian valleys of the Bernina / Mrs Henry Freshfield. London, 1862. Ill., maps.
Lloyd.538; Lloyd.538A,B.   s487.

Summer tours in Central Europe 1853-54, 1855- 56 / John Barrow. London, 1855-57. 3v (in 1); maps.
Lloyd.240.   s488.

Summit Magazine. Vol.2 no.9-vol.3 no.11, Sept.1956-Nov.1957. Huntington Park, 1956-57. Wanting vol.2 no.10-11.
GB.1644(18-29).   s489.

Summits of adventure: the story of famous mountain climbs and mountain climbers / John Scott Douglas. London, 1955. Ill.
GB.512.   s490.

Sunkrotema Leukon Oreon: Gigilos kai Volakias. Massif des Lefka Ori de Crète / Catherine Gueca. Athènes, 1972.
GB/B.377(1).   s491.

Sunny memories of foreign lands / Harriet Beecher Stowe. London, 1854. 2v; ill.
Lloyd.567-8.   s492.

Sunny memories of foreign lands / Harriet Beecher Stowe. Author's ed. London, 1854. Ill.
Lloyd.186.   s493.

Sunny scenes, or Recollections of Continental rambles among men and mountains / [R.R.]. London, [1863]. Ill.
Lloyd.44.   s494.

Sunset at midnight: autobiography / Arthur Grey Fullerton. Portland, 1969. Ill., ports., facsims.
GB/A.1778.   s495.

Sunset on Mont Blanc / Sir Leslie Stephen. [London, 1873.] Pp.457-66 of the *Cornhill Magazine*, vol.28, 1873.
Lloyd.1610(6).   s496.

Le **superstizioni** delle Alpi Venete con una lettera aperta al prof. Paolo Mantegazza / Giambattista Bastanzi. Bologna, 1973. [Classici di folk-lore; 4.] Facsimile reprint of the Treviso, 1888 ed.
GB/A.1323(3).   s497.

Supplement to *Vacation rambles*, consisting of recollections of a tour through France, to Italy, and homeward by Switzerland, in the vacation of 1846 / Thomas Noon Talfourd. London, 1854.
GB.195; Lloyd.304.   s498.

Sur l'Alpe fleurie: promenades poétiques et philosophiques dans les Alpes / George Flemwell; adapté par L. Marret et L. Capitaine. Paris, [1914]. Ill. Translated from *The flower-fields of Alpine Switzerland*.
GB/A.998.   s499.

Sur l'origine des Préalpes romandes, zone du Chablais et du Stockhorn / Hans Schardt. [Geneva], 1893. Extrait des *Archives des sciences physiques et naturelles*, déc.1893.
GB/A.514(6).   s500.

Sur la catastrophe de Saint-Gervals, 12 juillet 1892 / J. Vallot, A. Delebecque, L. Duparc. [Geneva, 1892.] Ill. From *Archives des sciences physiques et naturelles*, 3e période, t.28, septembre 1892.
GB.1312(26); Lloyd.1028.   s501.

Sur la montagne: Alpes et Jura / Fritz Berthoud. Nouv. éd. Paris, 1872.
GB/A.915(6).   s502.

Sur la théorie de l'affouillement glaciaire / Gastaldi, Mortillet. Sulla escavazione dei bacini lacustri compresi negli anfiteatri morenici: lettera del socio Gastaldi al socio Mortillet. Sur l'affouillement des anciens glaciers / réponse de Gabriel de Mortillet à M. Bartolomeo Gastaldi. Milan, 1863. Map. Dal vol.5 degli *Atti della Società Italiana di Scienze Naturali*.
Lloyd.803.   s503.

Sur le spectre tellurique dans les hautes stations, et en particulier sur le spectre de l'oxygène / Jules

Janssen. Paris, [1888]. Extrait des *Comptes rendus des séances de l'Académie des sciences*, t.107, séance du 29 octobre 1888.
GB/B.260(1). s504.

Sur les crêtes du Mont Blanc / Jacques et Tom de Lépiney. Chambéry, 1929. Ill., ports.
GB.1320(2). s505.

Sur les observations spéctroscopiques faites à l'observatoire du Mont Blanc, les 14 et 15 septembre 1893 / lettre de M.J. Janssen à M. le Président. Paris, [1893]. Extrait des *Comptes rendus des séances de l'Académie des sciences*, t.117, séance du 25 septembre 1893.
GB/B.260(8). s506.

Sur les pas du promeneur solitaire: randonnées pédestres sur le versant n.o. du Pilat. 2e éd. St. Etienne, 1972. Ill., maps. Published by the Club du jeune ami des animaux de la vallée du Gier.
GB/A.1270(9). s507.

Sur les variations périodiques des glaciers / F.A. Forel. Rome, 1883.
GB/A.793(5). s508.

A **survey** of early American ascents in the Alps in the nineteenth century / J. Monroe Thorington. [New York, 1943.] Ill., ports., facsims. Published by the American Alpine Club.
GB.1022. s509.

A **survey** of human exposure to mercury, cadmium and lead in Greenland / Jens C. Hansen. Copenhagen, 1981. Ill., maps. [Meddelelser om Grønland. Man & society; 3.]
GB/A.1820/3. s510.

Survey of northeast Greenland / I. P. Koch. Kobenhavn, 1916. [Danmark-ekspeditionen til Grønlands nordøstkyst 1906-1908; bd.6 nr.2.]
GB/A.1846. s511.

Der **Sustenpass** und seine Thäler / A. Baehler; mit einem Anhang: das Unglück am Sustenpass im Jahre 1899, von Dr J. Jegerlehner. Bern, 1899. Ill.
GB/A.758(1). s512.

Sustenstrasse: Meiringen – Wassen – Göschenen, Gadmental – Meintal – Reusstal / herausgegeben von der Generaldirektion der Post- Telegraphen- und Telephonverwaltung. 3. Aufl. Bern, 1948. Ill., maps.
GB/A.1351(13). s513.

La **Svizzera** / Voldemaro Kaden. Milano, 1921. Ill. GB/C.24. s514.

La **Svizzera** considerata nelle sue vaghezze pittoresche nella storia, nelle leggi e ne' costumi: lettere / Tullio Dandolo. Milano, 1833. [Viaggio per la Svizzera occidentale; 10.]
GB/A.1348. s515.

La **Svizzera** pittoresca e suoi dintorni: quadro generale descrittivo, istorico e statistico dei 22 cantoni, della Savoja, d'una parte del Piedmonte e del paese di Baden / Alexandre Martin. 2a ed. Mendrisio, 1838. Ill. Translated from *La Suisse pittoresque et ses environs*.
GB/B.278. s516.

La **Svizzera** pittoresca, o Corse per le Alpi e pel Jura a comentario del medio evo elvetico / Tullio Dandolo. Milano, 1846.
GB/A.840. s517.

Svizzera. Tirolo / de Golbery. [N.p., ca 1840.] [L'universo o storia e descrizione di tutti i popoli.] Translated from *Histoire et description de la Suisse et du Tyrol*.
GB/A.1007. s518.

Swiss allmends, being a second month in Switzerland / F. Barham Zincke. London, 1874.
Lloyd.388; Lloyd.388A. s518.1.

The **Swiss** emigrants: a tale / [Hugh Murray]. London, 1804.
GB/A.813. s519.

The **Swiss** emigrants: a tale / [Hugh Murray]. 2nd ed. London, 1806.
Lloyd.281. s520.

The **Swiss** expedition to Greenland, 1938 / André Roch. [London], 1939. Ill., map. Reprinted from the *Alpine Journal*, May 1939.
GB.1339(32). s521.

Swiss letters and Alpine poems / Frances Ridley Havergal; edited by J. Miriam Crane. London, [1881]. Music.
Lloyd.445; Lloyd.445A. s522.

Swiss letters and Alpine poems / Frances Ridley Havergal; edited by J. Miriam Crane. London, 1882. Music.
GB.562. s523.

Swiss men and Swiss mountains / Robert Ferguson. London, 1853. [Travellers library; 45.]
GB.200(2); Lloyd.303; Lloyd.303A,B; Lloyd.1571(2). s524.

Swiss mountain climbs / George D. Abraham. Cheaper ed. London, [1922]. Ill.
GB.220. s525.

Swiss notes / by five ladies. Leeds, 1875. Ill.
Lloyd.1287. s526.

Swiss pictures / [Samuel Manning]. London, [1866]. Ill.
GB.1261; GB/B.152; Lloyd.1458; Lloyd.1458A. s527.

Swiss pictures / Samuel Manning. New, enl. ed. London, [1879].
GB.1256. s528.

Swiss scenery from drawings by Major Cockburn. London, 1820. Ill.
Lloyd.1413; Lloyd.1484. s529.

Swiss travel: being chapters from Dumas' *Impressions de voyage* / edited by C.H. Parry. London, 1890.
Lloyd.256. s530.

Swiss travel and Swiss guide-books / W.A.B. Coolidge. London, 1889.
GB.370; Lloyd.542; Lloyd.542A. s531.

Switzerland. London, 1852. Map. [Bogue's guides for travellers; 2.]
Lloyd.47. s532.

Switzerland / [edited by] Doré Ogrizek and J.G. Rufenacht; text by Piero Bianco [et al.]; adapted and translated by Mary Bancroft. Zurich, [1947]. Ill.
GB/A.1358. s533.

Switzerland / Lina Hug, Richard Stead. London, 1890. Ill., maps, ports. [Story of the nations; 26.]
Lloyd.656. s534.

Switzerland / William Beattie; illustrated in a series of views taken by W.H. Bartlett. London, 1836. 2v.
Lloyd.1453-4. s535.

Switzerland / William Beattie; illustrated in a series of views taken by W.H. Bartlett. London, 1836. 2v (in 1). A different issue from s535.
Lloyd.1412 (impf.). s536.

Switzerland / William Beattie; illustrated in a series of views taken by W.H. Bartlett. London, 1839. 2v (in 1); map.
GB/B.328. s537.

Switzerland: historical and descriptive. London, [1853].
Lloyd.45. s538.

Switzerland: how to see it for ten guineas / Henry Gaze. London, [1861]. Ill.
GB.147(3); Lloyd.1613(16). s539.

Switzerland: interspersed with historical anecdotes, local customs, and a description of the present state of the country: with picturesque representations of the dress and manners of the Swiss: to which is added a short guide to travellers / Ann Yosy. London, 1815. 2v; music.
Lloyd.1276-7. s540.

Switzerland: its mountains and valleys / Woldemar Raden [sic, i.e. Kaden]. London, 1878. Ill.
Lloyd.1527. s541.

Switzerland: Neuchâtel: its lake, its mountains, and its vineyards / by a member of the Alpine Club. London, 1876.
Lloyd.1609(1). s542.

Switzerland: Neuchâtel: its lake, its mountains, and its vineyards / by a member of the Alpine Club. London, 1877.
Lloyd.887. s543.

Switzerland: official handbook of the Automobile Club of Switzerland / Karl Baedeker; edited by Oskar Steinheil; [translated by] Otto Baedeker and H.A. Piehler. Stuttgart, 1957. Ill., maps. [Baedeker's autoguides.]
GB/A.625. s544.

Switzerland: the country and its people / Clarence Rook. London, 1907. Ill.
Lloyd.1223. s545.

Switzerland: the traveller's illustrated guide prepared with the collaboration of experts and traffic organisations / Walter Stalder. 3rd English ed. Bern, 1949. Ill., maps.
GB/A.1160. s546.

Switzerland: water-colours by various artists. London, 1920. [Black's 'Water-colour' series.]
GB/A.861. s547.

Switzerland: with Chamonix and the Italian lakes / edited by Findlay Muirhead. London, 1923. 3v; maps. [Blue guides.]
Lloyd.95-7. s548.

Switzerland, or A journal of a tour and residence in that country, in 1817, 1818, and 1819: followed by an historical sketch on the manners and customs of ancient and modern Helvetia / Louis Simond. London, 1822. 2v. Translated from *Voyage en Suisse fait dans les années 1817, 1818 & 1819*.
Lloyd.981-2. s549.

Switzerland, or A journal of a tour and residence in that country, in 1817, 1818, and 1819: followed by an historical sketch on the manners and customs of ancient and modern Helvetia / Louis Simond. 2nd ed. London, 1823. 2v. Translated from *Voyage en Suisse*.
GB/A.394-5. s550.

Switzerland, and other poems / J.F. Hone. Gloucester, 1878.
Lloyd.374. s551.

Switzerland and Savoy. 2nd annual issue. London, 1853. Ill., map. [Bogue's guides for travellers; 2.]
Lloyd.48. s552.

Switzerland and the adjacent portions of Italy, Savoy and the Tyrol, etc. / Karl Baedeker. Coblenz, 1863. Translated from *Die Schweiz*.
Lloyd.99. s553.

Switzerland and the adjacent portions of Italy, Savoy and the Tyrol, etc. / Karl Baedeker. 2nd ed. Coblenz, 1864. Translated from *Die Schweiz*.
Lloyd.100. s554.

Switzerland and the adjacent portions of Italy, Savoy and the Tyrol, etc. / Karl Baedeker. 3rd ed. Coblenz, 1867. Translated from *Die Schweiz*.
Lloyd.101. s555.

Switzerland and the adjacent portions of Italy, Savoy and the Tyrol, etc. / Karl Baedeker. 5th ed. Coblenz, 1872. Translated from *Die Schweiz*.
Lloyd.102; Lloyd.102A. s556.

Switzerland and the adjacent portions of Italy, Savoy and the Tyrol, etc. / Karl Baedeker. 6th ed. Coblenz, 1873. Translated from *Die Schweiz*.
Lloyd.103. s557.

Switzerland and the adjacent portions of Italy, Savoy and the Tyrol, etc. / Karl Baedeker. 8th ed.

Coblenz, 1879. Translated from *Die Schweiz*.
Lloyd.104. s558.

Switzerland and the adjacent portions of Italy, Savoy and the Tyrol / Karl Baedeker. 14th ed. Leipsic, 1891. Translated from *Die Schweiz*.
GB/A.462. s559.

Switzerland and the adjacent portions of Italy, Savoy and the Tyrol / Karl Baedeker. 24th ed. Leipzig, 1911. Translated from *Die Schweiz*.
GB.79. s560.

Switzerland and the adjacent portions of Italy, Savoy and the Tyrol / Karl Baedeker. 25th ed. Leipzig, 1913. Translated from *Die Schweiz*.
GB/A.463. s561.

Switzerland and the Swiss / Mrs. Ashton Yates. London, [1842]. 2v (in 1).
GB.326. s562.

Switzerland as a holiday resort / H. Schütz Wilson. [N.p., 1886.] Pp.[225]-34 of *Fortnightly*, August 1886.
GB.1336(24). s563.

Switzerland, as I saw it / Henry Collings. London, [1876].
Lloyd.384; Lloyd.384A. s564.

Switzerland by pen & pencil. [London, 1878.] Articles and illustrations extracted from *London Society*, 1878.
Lloyd.1171. s564.1.

Switzerland in 1847: and its condition, political, social, moral, and physical, before the war / Theodore Mügge; translation abridged from the original, edited by Mrs. Percy Sinnet. London, 1848. 2v. Translated from *Die Schweiz und ihre Zustande*.
Lloyd.513-4; Lloyd.720-1. s565.

Switzerland in 1854-5: a book of travel, men, & things / W.G. Heathman. London, 1855.
GB.648; GB.957; Lloyd.773. s566.

Switzerland in miniature: description of the grand model of Switzerland, by Professor Gaudin, now exhibiting at the Egyptian Hall, Piccadilly. London, 1825. Ill.
GB.575; Lloyd.1587(2). s567.

Switzerland in the eighteenth century / Arnold Lunn. [London], 1943. Pp.86-90 of the *Climbers'*

Club Journal, vol.7 no.2.
GB.1339(8).   s568.

Switzerland in your pocket / A. Siegrist. [Zurich, 1954.] Ill., map.
GB/A.1199(3).   s569.

Switzerland, land of peace and liberty / edited by the Swiss Office for the Development of Trade; translation: R. Grandvoinet. 4th ed. Lausanne, 1949. Ill., ports., facsims.
Lloyd.1620(27).   s570.

Switzerland, the pioneer of the Reformation, or La Suisse allemande / comtesse Dora d'Istria; translated by H.G. London, 1858. 2v; port., facsim. Translated from *La Suisse allemande*.
Lloyd.875-6.   s571.

Switzerland, the South of France, and the Pyrenees / H.D. Inglis. London, 1837. Map.
GB.414; Lloyd.1244.   s572.

Switzerland, the south of France, and the Pyrenees in 1830 / Derwent Conway. Edinburgh, 1831. 2v; ill., map. [Constable's miscellany; 26-7.]
Lloyd.66-7.   s573.

Switzerland through the stereoscope: a journey over and round the Alps / Mabel Sarah Emery. New York, [1901]. Maps.
GB/A.1174.   s574.

The **Switzers** / William Hepworth Dixon. Copyrigth [sic] ed. Berlin, 1872.
Lloyd.233.   s575.

The **Switzers** / William Hepworth Dixon. 2nd ed. London, 1872.
GB.857.   s576.

Syenitic and associated intrusions of the Kap Edvard Holm region of Kangerdlugssuaq, East Greenland / W. A. Deer, D.R.C. Kempe and G.C. Jones. Copenhagen, 1984. Ill., maps. [Meddelelser om Grønland. Geoscience; 12.]
GB/A.1818(12).   s577.

Sylvain Saudan, skieur de l'impossible / Paul Dreyfus. [Paris], 1970. Ill. [Sempervivum; 50.]
GB/A.805(5).   s578.

Symposium on remote sensing in the polar regions: highlights of a symposium held at Easton, Maryland on March 6, 7, and 8, 1968 under the auspices of the Arctic Institute of North America. Washington, 1968.
GB/B.390(11).   s579.

Le **système** glaciaire des Alpes: guide / publié par A. Penck, E. Brückner, Léon du Pasquier. Neuchâtel, 1894. Extrait du *Bulletin de la Société des sciences naturelles de Neuchâtel*, séance du 7 avril 1894.
GB/A.514(11).   s580.

-T-

Table Mountain: our national heritage after three hundred years / C.A. Lückhoff; [in collaboration with Colin Gohl and M. Versveld]. Cape Town, 1951. Ill.
GB/B.421. t001.

Le **tableau** de la Suisse et autres alliez de la France és hautes Allemagnes: auquel sont descrites les singularités des Alpes, & rapportées les diuerses alliances des Suisses, particulierement celles qu'ils ont auec la France / Marc Lescarbot. Paris, 1618. Map.
GB/A.795. t002.

Tableau des Pyrénées françaises / M. Arbanère. Paris, 1828. 2v.
GB/A.602-3. t003.

Tableau historique et politique des deux dernières révolutions de Genève / [Sir Francis d'Ivernois]. Londres, 1789. 2v.
Lloyd.531-2. t004.

Tableau historique et politique des révolutions de Genève dans le dix-huitième siècle / par Mr. ...... [i.e. Sir Francis d'Ivernois]. Genève, 1782.
Lloyd.624; Lloyd.624A. t005.

Tableau historique, statistique et moral de la Haute-Italie et des Alpes qui l'entourent: précédé d'un coup d'oeil sur le caractère des empereurs, des rois et autres princes qui ont régné en Lombardie, depuis Bellovèse et César jusqu'à Napoléon premier / Ch. Denina. Paris, 1805.
GB.446. t006.

Tableau littéraire du massif du Mont-Blanc: le massif du Mont-Blanc dans la littérature française / Charles Vallot. Le massif du Mont-Blanc dans la littérature anglaise / Claire Eliane Engel. Chambéry, 1930. Ill.
GB.1314(5). t007.

Tableau pittoresque de la Suisse / marquis de Langle. Paris, 1790.
GB.283. t008.

Tableau pittoresque, scientifique et moral, de Nismes et de ses environs, à vingt lieues à la ronde / E.B.D. Frossard. Nismes, 1834-38. 3v (in 1); ill., map.
Lloyd.706. t009.

Tableaux topographiques, pittoresques, physiques, historiques, moraux, politiques, littéraires de la Suisse / Laborde. Paris, 1780-86. 2v (in 4).
Lloyd.1555-8; Lloyd.1555A-8A. t010.

Tageblätter unsrer Reise in und um den Harz / C.G. Horstig. Leipzig, 1805. Ill.
GB/A.1642. t011.

Tagebuch einer Reise durch die östliche, südliche und italienische Schweiz: ausgearbeitet in den Jahren 1798 und 1799 / Friederike Brun. Kopenhagen, 1800. Ill.
GB/A.663. t012.

Tagebuch einer Reise durch die Schweiz / von der Verfasserin von Rosaliens Briefen [i.e. Sophie de La Roche]. Altenburg, 1787.
GB/A.783. t013.

Tales about Europe / Peter Parley; edited by T. Wilson. 3rd ed. London, [n.d.]. Ill., maps.
Lloyd.58. t014.

Tales about Great Britain / Peter Parley. London, [n.d.].
GB.8. t015.

Tales and souvenirs of a residence in Europe / by a lady of Virginia [i.e. Judith Page Rives]. Philadelphia, 1842.
Lloyd.582. t016.

Tales from Switzerland / [Ann Yosy]. London, 1822-23. 3v.
GB/A.738-40. t017.

Tales of adventure and stories of travel of fifty years ago / [edited by J.C.]. London, 1893. Ill.
GB.532. t018.

Tales of adventure by sea and land / [W.D.]. London, 1847.
GB.212. t019.

Tales of Ardennes / Derwent Conway. London, 1825.
Lloyd.606. t020.

Tales of discovery / edited by William Anderson. Edinburgh, [1853]. Ill. Originally published as *Treasury of discovery, enterprise, and adventure*.
GB.134. t021.

Tales of the Great St. Bernard / [George Croly]. New York, 1829.
GB.424-5.   t022.

I **tamburi** e la valanga: racconti di montagna / Carlo Arzani. Bologna, 1972. Ill. [Voci dai monti; 25.]
GB/A.1263.   t023.

Támer — S. Sebastiano / Giovanni Angelini. Bologna, 1966. Ill., map. [Le Alpi venete.] Published by the Club Alpino Italiano, Sezione di Belluno e Val Zoldana.
GB/B.312(23).   t024.

La **tanaglia** bianca: novelle alpine / Attilio Viriglio. Torino, 1930.
GB/A.800(9).   t025.

Target: Arctic: men in the skies at the top of the world / George Simmons. Philadelphia, 1965. Ill., maps, ports.
GB/A.1797.   t026.

Tarif für die Beförderung der Reisenden und ihres Gepäckes im Berner Oberland, Juni 1890. Bern, 1890.
Lloyd.1613(12).   t027.

Tariffe gite ed ascensioni nella catena del Monte Bianco, stagione estiva 1949. Aosta, [1949]. Published by the Società delle Guide.
GB.1334(24).   t028.

Tartarin on the Alps / Alphonse Daudet; translated by Henry Frith. London, 1887. Ill. Translated from: *Tartarin sur les Alpes*.
GB.426; Lloyd.442; Lloyd.442A.   t029.

Tartarin sur les Alpes: nouveaux exploits du héros tarasconnais / Alphonse Daudet. Paris, 1885. Ill.
Lloyd.1207.   t030.

Tartarin sur les Alpes: nouveaux exploits du héros tarasconnais / Alphonse Daudet. Paris, 1886. Ill.
GB.272; Lloyd.488.   t031.

Tartarino sulle Alpi / Alphonse Daudet; [traduzione e riduzione di Elio D'Aurora]. Torino, 1959. Ill. Translated from *Tartarin sur les Alpes*.
GB/A.1344.   t032.

Taschen-Buch zu Schweizer-Reisen mit Hinweisung auf alle Sehens und Merkwürdigkeiten der Schweiz, eines Theiles von Savoyen und einiger anderer Orte angrenzender Länder und mit Angabe der Wirthshäuser / [Samuel Walcher].

2. ganz umgearb. und stark verm. Aufl. Glarus, 1833.
GB/A.668.   t033.

Taschen-Kalender für Schweizer Alpen-Clubisten. 1906, Jahrg.3. Zürich, [1906].
Lloyd.82.   t034.

Taschenbuch der Alpenvereins-Mitglieder. Wien, 1972- .
GB/A.1271.   t035.

Tat und Traum: ein Buch alpinen Erlebens / Oskar Erich Meyer. München, 1922.
GB/A.193.   t036.

Das **Tauernkraftwerk** Glockner-Kaprun der Tauernkraftwerke Aktiengesellschaft, Zell am See, Salzburg / J. Götz. 6. Aufl. [Zell am See], 1954. Ill.
GB/B.403(17).   t037.

Technique de l'alpinisme / Bernard Amy [et al.]; sous la direction de Bernard Amy. [Paris], 1977. Ill.
GB/A.1624.   t038.

La **technique** de l'alpinisme / Marcel Pourchier, Edouard Frendo. Grenoble, 1944. Ill.
GB/A.927.   t039.

Technique des chaînes de l'Oberland bernois [by H. Golliez]. Genève, 1896. A review. Extrait des *Archives des sciences physiques et naturelles*, août 1896.
GB/A.514(18).   t040.

The **technique** of Alpine mountaineering / publication of the UTO section of the S.A.C. [Schweizer Alpenclub]; English edition adapted by members of the Association of British Members of the S.A.C. Buckingham, [n.d.].
GB.63.   t041.

La **tecnica** dell'alpinismo / Andrea Mellano. Novara, 1978. Ill.
GB/B.480.   t042.

Tecniche di sopravvivenza / Brian Hildreth. Milano, 1979. Ill. [Guide pratiche; 16.] Translated from *How to survive*.
GB/A.2020(11).   t043.

Teen stormwind en steil wande: die beroemdste bergklimprestasies / Henri Snijders. [Cape Town], 1966. Ill.
GB/A.149.   t044.

Le **temple** de la nature / Henri Ferrand. Paris, 1924. Ill. Extrait du *Bulletin de la Section de géographie*, 1923.
GB.1329(14). t045.

Il **tempo** che torna / Guido Rey. Torino, 1929. Ill. [La piccozza e la penna.]
GB/A.1407. t046.

Tempo perso! / Scipione Giordano. Torino, 1880.
GB/A.1365. t047.

Ten days in August / J.M.L. Gavin. London, 1940. Pp.5-11 of the *Climbers' Club Journal*, N.S. vol.6 no.2.
GB.1338(9). t048.

Ten great mountains; Snowdon, Ben Nevis, Mount Cook, the Matterhorn, Ushba, Mont Blanc, Mount Logan, Nanga Parbat, Kangchenjunga, Mount Everest / R.L.G. Irving. London, 1942. Ill.
GB.738. t049.

Ten great mountains; Snowdon, Ben Nevis, Mount Cook, the Matterhorn, Ushba, Mont Blanc, Mount Logan, Nanga Parbat, Kangchenjunga, Mount Everest / R.L.G. Irving. London, 1947. Ill.
GB.739; GB.740. t050.

Ten scenes in the last ascent of Mont Blanc, including five views from the summit / sketched and lithographed by J.D.H.B. [i.e. J.D.H. Browne]. London, 1853.
GB.1300; Lloyd.1560. t051.

Ten thousand miles with a dog sled: a narrative of winter travel in interior Alaska / Hudson Stuck. 2nd ed. London, [1915]. Ill., map, ports.
GB.1013. t052.

Ten thousand miles with a dog sled: a narrative of winter travel in interior Alaska / Hudson Stuck. 2nd ed. New York, 1916. Ill., map, ports.
GB.567. t053.

Tent life with English gipsies in Norway / Hubert Smith. 2nd ed. London, 1874. Ill., map, music.
Lloyd.947. t054.

Une **tentative** d'ascension au Mont-Blanc en 1802 / Henry F. Montagnier. [Geneva, 1912.] From *L'Echo des Alpes*, no.1, 1912.
GB.1063; GB.1305(20); Lloyd.1183. t055.

Terra di Baffin: note e impressioni sulla prima spedizione italiana alla penisola di Cumberland / M.A. Sironi. Milano, 1973. Ill., maps. [Caleidoscopio.] Expedition organised by the Club Alpino Italiano.
GB/A.1550. t056.

Terribile Everest / Italo Neri, Ugo Martegani. Bologna, 1953. [Le Alpi; 16.]
GB/A.1572. t057.

Terza pagina sulla Valle d'Aosta / Rino Cossard. Roma, 1959. Ill.
GB/A.1323(7). t058.

Die **Tessiner-Alpen**: Itinerarium für den S.A.C. 1873. Basel, 1873. Published by the Schweizer Alpenclub.
GB/A.879(1). t059.

Textbook of geology: by Archibald Geikie / Charles Lapworth. London, [1883]. A review. Extracted from the *Geological Magazine*, Decade 11 vol.10, January and February, 1883.
Lloyd.1605(22). t060.

Texte zu der Sammlung von Schweizer-Kühreihen und Volksliedern / J.R. Wyss. 4., viel verm. Ausg. Bern, 1826.
Lloyd.1612(14). t061.

Das **Thal** Bergell, Bregaglia, in Graubünden: Natur, Sagen, Geschichte, Volk, Sprache etc.: nebst Wanderungen / Ernst Lechner. Leipzig, 1865. Ill., map.
GB/A.934(2). t062.

Thawing out the Eskimo / Adrian G. Morice; translated by Mary T. Laughlin. 2nd ed. Boston, 1943. Ill., maps, ports.
GB/A.1777. t063.

Théorie des glaciers de la Savoie / Louis Rendu. Chambéry, 1840. Extrait du tome 10 des *Mémoires de la Société royale académique de Savoie*.
Lloyd.598. t064.

Theory of the glaciers of Savoy / Louis Rendu; translated by Alfred Wills; to which are added the original memoir; and supplementary articles by P.G. Tait and John Ruskin; edited, with introductory remarks, by George Forbes. London, 1874. Map. Translated from *Théorie des glaciers de la Savoie*.
GB.906; Lloyd.995; Lloyd.995A. t065.

Le **Thevenon**, ou Les journées de la montagne / E. Bertrand. Neuchâtel, 1777.
GB/A.1296. t066.

They came to the hills / Claire Eliane Engel. London, 1952. Ill., ports.
GB.808.   t067.

Thirty years in the Arctic regions, or The adventures of Sir John Franklin. New York, 1860. Ill. The preface signed: D.W.B.
GB/A.1610.   t068.

This my voyage / Tom Longstaff. London, 1950. Ill., maps.
GB.949.   t069.

Thorild Wulffs grönländska dagböcker / utgivna av Axel Elvin. Stockholm, 1934.
GB/A.2052(7).   t070.

Thoughts in rhyme / the posthumous work of C.C. Colton; selected from the original manuscripts [by Markham Sherwill]. Paris, 1832.
Lloyd.1582(3).   t071.

A thousand mountains shining: stories from New Zealand's mountain world / edited by Ray Knox. Wellington, 1984.
GB/A.2169.   t072.

[**Three** Alpine views.] [N.p., n.d.] Extracted from unknown publications.
GB.1312(1-3).   t073.

Three days at Thoune / E. Bischoff. London, [1887].
Lloyd.422.   t074.

Three letters concerning the present state of Italy, written in the year 1687 / Gilbert Burnet. [N.p.], 1688.
GB.46(2).   t075.

A three months' tour in Switzerland and France: with a route to Chamouni, the Bernese Alps &c. / William Liddiard. London, 1832. Ill.
GB.927.   t076.

Three panoramic views of Ottacamund, the chief station on the Neilgherries / lithographed by W.L. Walton from drawings by Major McCurdy. London, [ca 1830]. Ill.
GB/C.96.   t077.

[**Three** pastels of Alpine scenes] / C. Marks. [N.p., n.d.]
GB.1912(1-3).   t078.

Three weeks from home, through France and Switzerland over the Alps to Milan, Florence, Rome, Naples, Pompeii, Genoa &c.: what I saw and what it cost me / John Bradbury. 2nd ed. Manchester, 1867.
Lloyd.1616(5).   t079.

Three weeks from home, through France and Switzerland over the Alps to Milan, Florence, Rome, Naples, Pompeii, &c.: what I saw and what it cost me / John Bradbury. London, [1886]. [Bradbury's shilling guides.]
Lloyd.1616(6).   t080.

Three weeks in Switzerland, with lines on the *Prisoner of Chillon* / Charles Cook. London, [n.d.].
Lloyd.327.   t081.

A three weeks tour in Savoy and Switzerland: written with the intention of showing a cheap and agreeable manner of travelling in those countries, with a list of the best hotels at the different towns. Geneva, 1844.
Lloyd.252.   t082.

Through Auvergne on foot / Edward Barker. London, 1884.
Lloyd.198.   t083.

Through Norway with a knapsack / W. Mattieu Williams. London, 1859. Ill., map.
Lloyd.503.   t084.

Through Norway with a knapsack / W. Mattieu Williams. London, 1859. Ill., map. A different edition from t084.
Lloyd.620.   t085.

Through the Canadian Pacific Rockies: a series of views illustrating the chief points of interest and the glorious mountain scenery seen in a journey through the Rocky and Selkirk Mountains. [Montreal? 1920?] Ill. Published for the Canadian Pacific Railway News Service.
GB/B.501(14).   t086.

Through the Dolomites from Venice to Toblach / Alexander Robertson. London, 1896. Ill., map.
Lloyd.312.   t087.

Through the heart of Asia over the Pamir to India / Gabriel Bonvalot; translated by C.B. Pitman. London, 1889. 2v. Translated from *Du Caucase aux Indes à travers le Pamir*.
GB.1150-1.   t088.

Through the Tyrol to Venice / Mrs. Newman Hall. London, 1860. Ill.
Lloyd.544. t089.

Thrutch: the Australasian climbing magazine. No.60, 62-3, 66-75, June 1973, Dec.1973-June 1974, June 1975-Winter 1978. [Beacon Hill, N.S.W.?], 1973-78.
GB/A.1791(11). t090.

Thulia: a tale of the Antarctic / J.C. Palmer. New York, 1843. Ill., music.
GB/A.1943. t091.

Thun und Thunersee. Zürich, [1895?] Ill. [Swiss scenes.]
GB/A.1817(4). t092.

Thusis. Samaden, [ca 1910]. Ill.
GB/A.1199(8). t093.

Thusis und die Hinterrhein-Thäler: Landschafts- und Geschichtsbilder / Ernst Lechner. Chur, 1875.
GB/A.799(8). t094.

Thusis und die Hinterrhein-Thäler: Landschafts- und Geschichtsbilder / Ernst Lechner. 2., erw. Aufl. Chur, 1897.
GB/A.758(2). t095.

Tianshan / edited and published by the Xinjiang People's Publishing House. Beijing, 1980. Ill., map.
GB/B.526. t096.

Tibet and Nepal / painted & described by A. Henry Savage Landor. London, 1905.
GB.951. t097.

Tibet, past & present / Sir Charles Bell. Oxford, 1924. Ill., maps, ports.
GB.888. t098.

Tibetan journey / Alexandra David-Neel. London, 1936. Ill., map.
GB.914. t099.

A **Tibetan** on Tibet: being the travels and observations of Mr. Paul Sherap (Dorje Zödba) of Tachienlu: with an introductory chapter on Buddhism and a concluding chapter on the devil dance / G.A. Combe. London, 1926.
GB.1019. t100.

Tibetan trek / Ronald Kaulback. London, 1934. Ill., port.
GB.860. t101.

Tike Saab / Guido Machetto. Cremona, 1972. Ill.
GB/A.1247; GB/A.1547. t102.

Til fjells: Stormarka, Hardangervidda, Sogn og Fjordane, Finnmarksvidda, Dovrefjell og Rondane, Jotunheimen / Andreas Backer. Oslo, 1944. Ill., maps.
GB/B.138. t103.

Tinder og banditter: opplevelser i Alperne og på Corsica / Alf B. Bryn. Oslo, 1943. Ill., map.
GB/A.209. t104.

Tirich Mir / Norwegian Himalaya Expedition; translated by Sölvi and Richard Bateson. London, 1952. Ill., maps, ports.
GB.832. t105.

Titian Ramsay Peale, 1799-1885, and his journals of the Wilkes expedition / Jessie Poesch. Philadelphia, 1961.
GB/B.615. t106.

To Mont Blanc, and back again / Walter White. London, 1854. Partly reprinted from Eliza Cook's Journal.
GB.108; GB.168; Lloyd.158; Lloyd.165. t107.

To stand at the Pole: the Dr. Cook-Admiral Peary North Pole controversy / William R. Hunt. New York, 1981. Ill., ports.
GB/A.2148. t108.

To the Alps of Chinese Tibet: an account of a journey of exploration up to and among the snow-clad mountains of the Tibetan frontier / J.W. Gregory, C.J. Gregory. London, 1923.
GB.684. t109.

To the Arctic by canoe, 1819-1821: the journal and paintings of Robert Hood, midshipman with Franklin / edited by C. Stuart Houston. Montreal, 1975. Ill.
GB/B.638. t110.

To the Arctic with the Mounties / Douglas S. Robertson. Toronto, 1934. Ill., map.
GB/A.1921. t111.

To the Committee of the Alpine Club. [London, 1937.] Report of a Committee appointed by the Committee of the Alpine Club to consider the relationship between the Alpine Club and the Mount Everest Committee.
GB.1334(8); GB.1334(9). t112.

To the Jungfrau peak by trolley: a wonderful Alpine railway / Ernst von Hesse-Wartegg. [New York, n.d.] Ill. Pp.245-53 of the *Century Magazine*, vol.72.
GB.1341(11). t113.

To the top of the continent: discovery, exploration and adventure in sub-arctic Alaska: the first ascent of Mt. McKinley, 1903-1906 / Frederick A. Cook. London, 1908. Ill., maps, ports.
GB.1072. t114.

To the untouched mountain: the New Zealand conquest of Molamenging, Tibet / Warwick Anderson. Wellington, 1983.
GB/A.2168. t115.

Tobogganing in the Engadine / Celia Lovejoy. [London, 1895.] Ill. Pp.[493]-500 of the *Strand Magazine*, vol.9 no.64.
GB.1336(10). t116.

De **tocht** van de *Krassin*, het authentieke verhaal van de avonturen der hulp-expeditie, welke werd uitgerust ter redding van de verongelukte Italia-bemanning / Valentin Suchanow; uit het russisch vertaald door S. van Praag. Amsterdam, 1929. Ill., map, ports.
GB/A.1765. t117.

Todeszone: erste Skibesteigung eines Acht-tausenders: Sieg, Tragödie, Nachspiel / Fritz Stammberger. St. Ottilien, 1972.
GB/A.1675(5). t118.

Der **Tödi-Rusein** und die Excursion nach Ober-sandalp: Beschreibung der am 30. Juli 1861 von Stacheler aus unternommenen Ersteigung / R. Theodor Simler. Bern, 1863. Ill., maps.
Lloyd.1606(7); Lloyd.1618(53). t119.

Top of Switzerland: 360° Panorama vom höchsten Punkt der Schweiz: panorama de 360° du point le plus élevé de Suisse / Emil Schulthess. Zurich, 1970. Ill.
GB/C.50. t120.

Top of the world. [London], 1931. Pp.[109]-10 of the *Faraday House Journal*, vol.14 no.4, 1931.
GB.1333(42). t121.

La **topografia** storica e cartografica del gruppo del Gran Paradiso sino al 1860 / W.A.B. Coolidge. Statistica delle prime ascensioni nel gruppo del Gran Paradiso / Agostino Agostino Ferrari. I minerali del gruppo del Gran Paradiso / Alberto

Pelloux. [Torino, 1908.] Map. Pp.[31]-188 of the *Bollettino del Club Alpino Italiano*, vol.39 no.72.
GB.1880(20). t122.

Topographia Helvetiæ, Rhætiæ et Valesiæ, das ist Beschreibung und eigentliche Abbildung der vornembsten Stätte und Platz in der hoch-löblichen Eydgenossschafft, Grawbündten, Walliss und etlicher zugswandten Orten / Matthæus Merian. Franckfurt, 1642. Ill., maps.
Lloyd.1508; Lloyd.1517. t123.

Topographische Mittheilungen aus dem Alpen-gebirge / G. Studer. 2. Ausg. Bern, 1844. 2v; ill.
GB.242 (wanting v2). t124.

Topography of the chain of Mont Blanc / [James D. Forbes]. [Edinburgh, 1865.] Maps. Pp.137-57 of the *North British Review*, March 1865.
GB.934; GB.935(2). t125.

Les **torrents** de la Savoie / P. Mougin. Grenoble, 1914. Ill., maps. Published by the *Société d'histoire naturelle de Savoie*.
GB/A.91. t126.

Toscana / Giuseppe Barbieri. Torino, 1964. Ill., maps. [Le regioni d'Italia; 8.]
GB/B.552. t127.

Le **tour** de Léman / Alfred de Bougy. Paris, 1846. Ill.
GB/B.320. t128.

Le **tour** du lac / Rodolphe Töpffer. Genève, 1841. Ill., map.
Lloyd.1567(1). t129.

Le **tour** du lac de Genève / George Mallet. Genève, 1824.
GB/A.515(1). t130.

Un **tour** en Suisse: histoire, science, monuments, paysages / Jacques Duverney. Tours, 1866. 2v (in 1); ill.
GB/A.494. t131.

Un **tour** en Suisse: histoire, science, monuments, paysages / Jacques Duverney. Tours, 1894. Ill.
GB/B.494. t132.

Tour in Austrian Lombardy, the northern Tyrol, and Bavaria, in 1840 / John Barrow. London, 1841.
Lloyd.600. t133.

A **tour** in France, Savoy, northern Italy, Switzerland, Germany and the Netherlands, in the

summer of 1825 / Seth William Stevenson. London, 1827. 2v.
GB.624-5; Lloyd.1197-8.   t134.

A **tour** in Holland, the countries on the Rhine, and Belgium: in the autumn of 1838 / William Chambers. Edinburgh, 1839.
GB.1178(3).   t135.

A **tour** in Holland, the countries on the Rhine, and Belgium: in the autumn of 1838 / William Chambers. 2nd ed. Edinburgh, 1842.
GB.1179(1).   t136.

A **tour** in Scotland, 1769 / Thomas Pennant. Chester, 1771. Ill.
GB.595.   t137.

A **tour** in Scotland, 1769 / Thomas Pennant. 3rd ed. Warrington, 1774.
GB.1144.   t138.

A **tour** in Scotland, and voyage to the Hebrides, 1772 / Thomas Pennant. Chester, 1774-76. 2v; ill., plans.
GB.1145-6.   t139.

A **tour** in Scotland, 1769: a tour in Scotland and voyage to the Hebrides, 1772 / Thomas Pennant. 4th ed. Dublin, 1775. 2v.
GB.577-8.   t140.

A **tour** in Switzerland, or A view of the present state of those cantons: with comparative sketches of the present state of Paris / Helen Maria Williams. London, 1798. 2v.
Lloyd.838-9.   t141.

A **tour** in Switzerland and various parts of the Continent / James Reid. [N.p.], 1878. Ill.
Lloyd.824; Lloyd.824A.   t142.

A **tour** in Switzerland, in 1841 / William Chambers. Edinburgh, 1842. [People's editions.]
GB.1179(2).   t143.

A **tour** in the Alps of Dauphiné, and a tour in the Carpathians / E. Hornby. Liverpool, 1906. 2v (in 1).
Lloyd.418.   t144.

The **tour** of Mont Blanc and of Monte Rosa: being a personal narrative, abridged from the author's *Travels in the Alps of Savoy*, &c. / James D. Forbes. Edinburgh, 1855. Ill., maps.
GB.140; GB.167; Lloyd.250.   t145.

Tour on the Continent, by rail and road, in the summer of 1852, through northern Germany, Austria, Tyrol, Austrian Lombardy, &c. / John Barrow. London, 1853. Map. [Traveller's library; 2.]
GB.200(1); Lloyd.1571(1).   t146.

Tour on the Continent in France, Switzerland, and Italy, in 1817 and 1818 / Roger Hog. London, 1824.
Lloyd.1149.   t147.

Tour over the Alps and in Italy / Albert Montémont. London, 1823. Translated from *Voyage aux Alpes et en Italie*.
GB.987; Lloyd.1181.   t148.

A **tour** through a part of the Netherlands, France, and Switzerland, in 1817 / Thomas Heger. London, 1820.
GB.875; Lloyd.807.   t149.

A **tour** through Italy: containing full directions for travelling in that interesting country / Thomas Martyn. London, [1791]. Map. Originally published as *The gentleman's guide in his tour through Italy*.
Lloyd.927.   t150.

A **tour** through parts of the Netherlands, Holland, Germany, Switzerland, Savoy, and France, in the year 1821-2 / Charles Tennant. London, 1824. 2v; port.
Lloyd.1023-4.   t151.

A **tour** through Sicily and Malta: in a series of letters to William Beckford / Patrick Brydone. Edinburgh, 1840.
GB.1177(2); GB.1179(3).   t152.

A **tour** through some parts of France, Switzerland, Savoy, Germany and Belgium, during the summer and autumn of 1814 / Richard Boyle Bernard. London, 1815.
Lloyd.712.   t153.

A **tour** to Great St. Bernard's and round Mont Blanc: with descriptions copied from a journal kept by the author, and drawings taken from nature. London, 1827. Ill., map.
GB.294; GB.396; Lloyd.306; Lloyd.306A.   t154.

Touren-Programm / Schweizer Alpenclub, Sektion Bern. 1950,1952. Bern, 1950-52.
Lloyd.1617(8-9).   t155.

Le **tourisme** aérien au Mont Blanc sur les avions de la Compagnie Air-Union-Aéronavale / Henri Bouché. Paris, 1928. Ill. Extrait de l'*Illustration* du 18 février 1928.
GB.1334(23). t156.

A **tourist** guide to Mount McKinley: the story 'Denali' — 'the great one': mile-by-mile through the Park over Mount McKinley Park Highway (formerly the Denali Highway): the record of McKinley climbs / Bradford Washburn. Rev. Anchorage, 1976. Ill.
GB/A.1675(2). t157.

The **tourist** in Ireland. [London], 1862. From nos.559, 561 and 563 of the *Leisure Hour*, 1862.
GB.1318(25-7) (impf.). t158.

The **tourist's** guide to Kashmir, Ladakh, Skardo, &c. / edited by Arthur Neve. 15th ed., rev. by E.F. Neve. Lahore, 1933. Maps.
GB.317. t159.

The **tourist's** handbook to Switzerland / Robert Allbut. London, 1884. Ill., maps.
GB/A.767. t160.

Tours in upper India, and in parts of the Himalaya Mountains: with account of the courts of the native princes / Major Archer. London, 1833. 2v.
GB.695-6. t161.

Tours to the British mountains, with the descriptive poems of Lowther, and Emont Vale / Thomas Wilkinson. London, 1824.
GB.384; Lloyd.375; Lloyd.547. t162.

Toute la montagne / Albert Dauzat. Paris, 1924.
GB/A.1199(7). t163.

Towards the North Pole / Fridtjof Nansen. [London, 1893.] Ill., ports. Pp.[614]-24 of the *Strand Magazine*, vol.6 no.36.
GB.1336(17). t164.

The **Town** and Country Miscellany. No.1-5, April-August, 1850. London, [1850].
Lloyd.543. t165.

Tra cielo e inferno: autobiografia d'un alpinista / Toni Hiebeler; traduzione di E. Erich Rieckhoff e Spiro Dalla Porta Xidias. Bologna, 1970. Ill. [Voci dai monti; 21.] Translated from *Zwischen Himmel und Hölle*.
GB/A.947. t166.

Tra i misteri del Cervino: la cresta sud del Picco Tyndall: ricordi di ascensioni / Giuseppe Lampugnani. [Turin, 1909.] Pp.[255]-84 of the *Bollettino del Club Alpino Italiano*, vol.40 n.73.
GB.1880(46). t167.

Tra i monti del Lazio e dell'Abruzzo / a cura della Sezione di Roma del Club Alpino Italiano a ricordo del cinquantenario della sua fondazione. Roma, 1924. Ill.
GB/B.288(15). t168.

Tra le rocce nascono i fiori / Spiro Dalla Porta Xidias. Bologna, 1967. [Voci dai monti; 10.]
GB/A.852. t169.

Tra zero e ottomila / Kurt Diemberger. Bologna, 1970. Ill. [Montagne; 7.]
GB/A.493. t170.

Traces in Scotland of ancient water-lines, marine, lacustrine and fluviatile, with some account of the drift materials on which these traces are imprinted / David Milne-Home. Edinburgh, 1882.
GB.1043. t171.

Trachten der Alpenländer. Wien, 1937. Ill.
GB/A.455(4). t172.

Tracings of the Alps / R.C. [i.e. Robert Chambers]. [London], 1848. Pp.[321]-6 of *Chambers' Edinburgh Journal*, no.255, New series.
GB.1881(18). t173.

Tracks for tourists / F.C. Burnand. London, 1864.
Lloyd.1615(16); Lloyd.1659(7). t174.

Il **traforo** del Sempione ed i passagi alpini / Antonio Ferrucci. Torino, 1906. Map.
GB/A.802(1). t175.

Trag le chamois / Micheline Morin. [N.p.], 1967. Ill.
GB/A.794. t176.

Tragédies alpestres / Charles Gos. Paris, [1939]. Ill.
GB.1320(7). t177.

Trails and tales of the North Land / John Crawford Cochrane. Toronto, 1934. Ill., map.
GB/A.2021(10). t178.

Trails of the Cordilleras Blanca and Huayhuash of Peru / Jim Bartle. [Healdsburg, Calif.], 1981. Ill., maps.
GB/A.2019(10). t179.

A **tramp** through Switzerland / Benjamin F. Leggett. New York, 1887.
Lloyd.454. t180.

Tramps in the Tyrol / H. Baden Pritchard. London, 1874. Ill.
GB.277; Lloyd.560. t181.

Trans-Himalaya: discoveries and adventures in Tibet / Sven Hedin. London, 1910-13. 3v; ill., maps.
GB.839-41. t182.

Transcaucasia and Ararat: being notes of a vacation tour in the autumn of 1876 / James Bryce. 2nd ed. London, 1877. Map.
Lloyd.414. t183.

Il **trapper** sulla neve / Andrea Mercanti. Milano, 1981. Ill.
GB/A.1993. t184.

Traumberge der Welt / Dölf Reist; Textbeiträge von Emil Egli [et al.]. 2. Aufl. Frauenfeld, 1974. Ill.
GB/B.371. t185.

Travel, adventure and sport. Edinburgh, [1889]. From *Blackwood's Magazine*.
GB.97-102; Lloyd.1615(11). t186.

Travel and adventure in the Territory of Alaska / Frederick Whymper. London, 1868. Ill., map.
Lloyd.1030. t187.

Travel and adventure in the Territory of Alaska / Frederick Whymper. 2nd ed. London, 1869. Ill., map.
GB.717. t188.

Travel and ascents in the Himalaya / W.W. Graham. London, 1884. Pp.430-47 of the *Proceedings of the Royal Geographical Society*, August 1884.
GB.1333(25). t189.

The **traveller**, or An entertaining journey round the habitable globe: being a novel and easy method of studying geography. 4th ed., with emendations and additions. London, [n.d.]. Ill., maps.
Lloyd.211. t190.

The **traveller's** fire-side: a series of papers on Switzerland, the Alps, &c. containing information and descriptions, original, and selected from French and Swiss authors / Samuel Miller Waring. London, 1819.
Lloyd.348. t191.

The **traveller's** guide in Switzerland: being a complete picture of that interesting country / Henry Coxe. London, 1816.
GB.28 (impf.); Lloyd.52 (impf.). t192.

The **traveller's** guide through Switzerland / J.G. Ebel. New ed., arranged and improved by Daniel Wall. London, 1819. Maps.
GB.404. t193.

Traveller's guide through Switzerland, chiefly compiled from the works of Ebel and Coxe / Galignani. Paris, 1818.
GB.23; Lloyd.42. t194.

The **traveller's** sketch book: containing upwards of forty illustrations reproduced from the *Graphic* of places and people in Europe. London, [n.d.].
Lloyd.647. t195.

Travellers in Switzerland / E.F. de Lantier; translated by Frederic Schoberl. London, 1804. 6v (in 3). Translated from *Les voyageurs en Suisse*.
GB/A.1168-70. t196.

Travellers in Switzerland: a chronological list of itineraries / Sir Gavin de Beer. London, 1949. Ill.
GB.800. t197.

Travelling sketches / Anthony Trollope. London, 1866. Reprinted from the *Pall Mall Gazette*.
GB.312; Lloyd.495. t198.

Travelling sketches in the north of Italy, the Tyrol, and on the Rhine / Leitch Ritchie. London, 1832. Ill. [Heath's Picturesque Annual for 1832.]
Lloyd.628; Lloyd.628A. t199.

Travelling sketches of the Rhine and in Belgium and Holland / Leitch Ritchie. London, 1833. Ill. [Heath's Picturesque Annual for 1833.]
Lloyd.629. t200.

Travels among the Alpine scenery / Dr. Cheever and J.T. Headley. London, 1855. Ill.
GB.188. t201.

Travels amongst the great Andes of the Equator / Edward Whymper. London, 1892. Ill., maps.
Lloyd.1169; Lloyd.1169A. t202.

Travels amongst the great Andes of the Equator / Edward Whymper. 2nd ed. London, 1892.
GB.1039. t204.

Travels amongst the great Andes of the Equator / Edward Whymper. Special ed. London, 1892. Ill.,

maps.
GB.1037; Lloyd.1166.   t205.

[**Travels** amongst the great Andes of the Equator /
Edward Whymper.] [London, 1892?] Maps.
GB.896 (proof copy); Lloyd.1168.   t205.1.

Travels amongst the great Andes of the Equator /
Edward Whymper. Supplementary appendix,
with contributions by H.W. Bates, T.G. Bonney [et
al.]. Special ed. London, 1891.
GB.1038; Lloyd.1167; Lloyd.1170.   t206.

Travels, comprising observations made during a
residence in the Tarentaise, and various parts of
the Grecian and Pennine Alps, and in Switzerland
and Auvergne, in 1820, 1821, and 1822 / R.
Bakewell. London, 1823. 2v; ill.
GB.690-1; Lloyd.864-5; Lloyd.864A-5A.   t207.

Travels from France to Italy, through the
Lepontine Alps / Albanis Beaumont. London,
1800. Ill.
Lloyd.1541; Lloyd.1541A.   t208.

Travels from Paris through Switzerland and Italy,
in the years 1801 and 1802 / [Joseph Sansom].
London, 1808.
Lloyd.1610(9); Lloyd.1659(3).   t209.

Travels in Alaska / John Muir. Boston, 1915. Ill.
GB.566.   t210.

Travels in Ceylon and continental India: including Nepal and other parts of the Himalayas, to the
borders of Thibet, with some notices of the overland route / Werner Hoffmeister. Edinburgh,
1848. Map. Translated from *Briefe aus Indien*.
GB.519; GB.610.   t211.

Travels in China 1966-71 / R. Alley. Peking, 1973.
GB/A.2007.   t212.

Travels in Hindustan and China / Howard
Malcolm. Edinburgh, 1840. Ill. First published in
Travels in South-eastern Asia.
GB.1180(2).   t213.

Travels in Hungary, with a short account of Vienna in the year 1793 / Robert Townson. London,
1797. Ill., map.
Lloyd.1410.   t214.

Travels in Iceland / Sir George Steuart Mackenzie. New ed., rev. by the author. Edinburgh, 1842.
GB.1178(2).   t215.

Travels in Italy, the Alps, and the Rhine / J.T.
Headley. Dublin, 1849.
GB/A.1673.   t216.

Travels in Ladâk, Tartary, and Kashmir / Henry
D. Torrens. London, 1862. Ill., maps.
GB.889.   t217.

Travels in northern Italy compiled from the most
recent authorities. Dublin, 1831. Ill.
GB/A.1479.   t218.

Travels in Russia, Tartary and Turkey / Edward
Daniel Clarke; with a memoir of the author, and
numerous additions and notes, prepared for the
present edition. Edinburgh, 1839. Originally
published as *Travels in various countries of Europe*.
GB.1176(1).   t219.

Travels in Switzerland / Alexandre Dumas;
translated by R.W. Plummer and A. Craig Bell;
edited by A. Craig Bell. London, 1958. Ill., port.
[Icon books.] Translated from *Impressions de voyage
en Suisse*.
GB.1320(5).   t220.

Travels in Switzerland, compiled from the most
recent authorities. Dublin, 1830. Ill.
GB/A.585.   t221.

Travels in Switzerland, compiled from the most
recent authorities. London, 1831. Ill.
Lloyd.40.   t222.

Travels in Switzerland, compiled from the most
recent authorities. London, [n.d.]. Ill.
Lloyd.46.   t223.

Travels in Switzerland, in a series of letters to
William Melmoth / William Coxe. London, 1789.
3v; ill., maps.
GB.644-6; Lloyd.755-7.   t224.

Travels in Switzerland / William Coxe. 2nd ed.
London, 1791. 3v; maps.
GB/A.598-600.   t225.

Travels in Switzerland, and in the country of the
Grisons: in a series of letters / William Coxe. 4th
ed. London, 1801. 3v.
GB.772-4; Lloyd.1187-9.   t226.

Travels in Switzerland, and in the country of the
Grisons / William Coxe; to which are added the
notes and observations of Mr. Ramond, translated
from the French. New ed. [Basel, 1802.] 3v; ill.,

map.
Lloyd.749-51 (impf.). t227.

Travels in Switzerland, Italy, and Dalmatia / by a lady. Hastings, 1862.
GB/A.801(2). t228.

Travels in the Burman Empire / Howard Malcolm. Edinburgh, 1840. Ill., map. First published in *Travels in south-eastern Asia*.
GB.1180(1). t229.

Travels in the central Caucasus and Bashan, including visits to Ararat and Tabreez and ascents of Kazbek and Elbruz / Douglas W. Freshfield. London, 1869. Ill., maps.
GB.580; Lloyd.889. t230.

Travels in the Himalayan provinces of Hindustan and the Panjab: in Ladakh and Kashmir: in Peshawar, Kabul, Kunduz, and Bokhara: from 1819 to 1825 / William Moorcroft, George Trebeck; prepared for the press, from original journals and correspondence, by Horace Hayman Wilson. London, 1841. 2v; map.
GB.1009-10. t231.

Travels in the Pyrenees / M. Ramond; translated by F. Gold. London, 1813. Translated from *Voyage dans les Pyrénées*.
Lloyd.869; Lloyd.1010. t232.

Travels in western North America, 1784-1812 / David Thompson; edited by Victor G. Hopwood. Toronto, 1971. Maps.
GB/A.1956. t233.

Travels into different parts of Europe, in 1791 and 1792: with familiar remarks on places — men — and manners / John Owen; [revised by W. Belsham]. London, 1796. 2v.
Lloyd.842-3. t234.

The **travels** of an English gentleman from London to Rome on foot. 5th ed. London, 1728.
GB/A.946. t235.

The **travels** of Richard and John Lander, into the interior of Africa, for the discovery of the course and termination of the Niger / Robert Huish. London, 1836.
GB/A.2102. t236.

Travels on the Continent: written for the use and particular information of travellers / Mariana Starke. London, 1820.
Lloyd.905. t237.

Travels thro' Germany, Bohemia, Swisserland, Holland, and other parts of Europe / Charles Patin. London, 1696. Ill., map, port. Translated from *Relations historiques et curieuses de voyage*.
Lloyd.70. t238.

Travels through France, Italy, Germany, and Switzerland / Gilbert Burnet. London, 1750.
GB.44; Lloyd.171. t239.

Travels through Germany, Bohemia, Hungary, Switzerland, Italy and Lorrain: giving a true and just description of the present state of those countries / Johann Georg Keysler; translated from the 2nd ed. of the German. 3rd ed. London, 1760. 4v; ill., map. Translated from *Reise durch Teütschland, Böhmen, Ungarn*.
Lloyd.739-42. t240.

Travels through Germany, Switzerland, Italy / Graf Friedrich Leopold zu Stolberg; translated by Thomas Holcroft. London, 1796-97. 2v; ill., map. Translated from *Reise in Deutschland, der Schweiz, Italien und Sicilien*.
Lloyd.1384-5. t241.

Travels through Switzerland, Italy, Sicily, the Greek Islands to Constantinople, through part of Greece, Ragusa, and the Dalmatian Isles; in a series of letters to Pennoyre Watkins / Thomas Watkins; in the years 1787, 1788, 1789. 2nd ed. London, 1794. 2v.
Lloyd.768-9. t242.

Travels through the Alps of Savoy and other parts of the Pennine chain, with observations on the phenomena of glaciers / James D. Forbes. Edinburgh, 1843. Ill., maps.
GB.1168. t243.

Travels through the Alps of Savoy, and other parts of the Pennine chain, with observations on the phenomena of glaciers / James D. Forbes. 2nd ed., rev. Edinburgh, 1845. Ill., maps.
GB.1212; Lloyd.1309; Lloyd.1349. t244.

Travels through the Alps / James D. Forbes. Edinburgh, 1855.
GB.60(3) (the introductory sketch only). t245.

Travels through the Alps / James D. Forbes. New ed., rev. and annotated by W.A.B. Coolidge. London, 1900. Ill., maps, port.
GB.1086; Lloyd.1199. t246.

Travels through the Rhætian Alps by Albanis Beaumont from Italy to Germany, through Tyrol. London, 1792. Ill.
GB.1299; Lloyd.1559. t247.

Traversata alpinistica delle piccole Dolomiti: rifugi, punti d'appoggio, vie d'accesso, itinerari / Cesco Zaltroni; traduzione in francese Marcello Cortiana. [Thiene], 1973. Ill., map. Published by the Club Alpino Italiano, Sezione di Thiene.
GB/A.1270(7). t248.

A **traverse** of the Barre des Ecrins, Dauphiné / Mrs Aubrey Le Blond. [London, 1902.] Ill. Pp.62-6 of *Travel*, June 1902.
GB.1336(1). t249.

A **traverse** of the Dent Blanche and first ascent of the Zinal face of the Oberschallijoch / R.W. Lloyd; read before the Alpine Club, May 3rd, 1921. London, 1921. Ill. Reprinted from the *Alpine Journal*, November 1921.
Lloyd.1602(21). t250.

A **traverse** of the Dent Blanche and the first direct ascent of the Aiguille de Bionnassay by the north face / R.W. Lloyd; read before the Rucksack Club, March 11, 1927 and The first direct ascent of the Aiguille de Bionnassay by the north face, read before the Alpine Club, December 13. 1926. London, 1927. Ill.
Lloyd.1602(2); Lloyd.1602(2)A,B,C. t251.

Une **traversée** au col de la Brenva / Jacques de Lépiney. Lyon, 1922. Ill. Pp.[141]-56 of the *Revue alpine*, vol.23 no.4.
GB.1329(20[1]). t252.

La **traversée** des Grands Charmoz de l'ouest à l'est / Emile Fontaine. Berne, 1925. Ill. Extrait de la revue du Club alpin suisse *Les Alpes*, octobre 1925.
Lloyd.1620(25). t253.

Le **tre** cime di Lavaredo: uomini — montagne — avventure / Helmut Dumler; traduzione di Silvana Aite e Spiro Dalla Porta Xidias. Bologna, 1972. Ill. [Voci dai monti.]
GB/A.1057. t254.

Tre mesi al di là delle Alpi / Geremia Bonomelli. Milano, 1901.
GB/A.1336. t255.

Tre mesi sotto le nevi del Giura: storia vera tradotta dall'inglese. Firenze, 1868.
GB/A.516(11). t256.

Le **tre** Venézie / L.V. Bertarelli. Milano, 1920. 2v; ill., maps. [Guida d'Italia del Touring Club Italiano; supplemento al n.7.]
GB/A.1811-2. t257.

Tre vette. Il ponte alato. Una via nova. La parete fiorita / Spiro Dalla Porta Xidias; con un saggio di Vittorio Frosini. [Trieste, 1944.]
GB/A.995(11). t258.

Treasurer's report / Geographical Club. Session 1946/47. [London], 1947.
GB.1318(30). t259.

A **treatise** on Hannibal's passage of the Alps, in which his route is traced over the Little Mont Cenis / Robert Ellis. Cambridge, 1853. Ill., maps.
Lloyd.1113. t260.

A **treatise** on the aneroid, a newly invented portable barometer: with a short historical notice on barometers in general / Edward J. Dent. London, 1859.
Lloyd.1583(7). t261.

The **Treaty** of Union of Scotland and England, 1707 / edited, with an introduction by George S. Pryde. London, 1950.
GB.161. t262.

Trekking 'alta via del Lario' / Sandro Gandola. [N.p.], 1983. Ill. Pubblicazione patrocinata dalla Sottosezione di Dongo del C.A.I.
GB/A.2076(5). t263.

Trekking en Himalaya / Tomoya Iozawa; traduit de l'anglais par Françoise et Frédérique Rebuffat. Paris, 1980. Ill., maps. Translated from *Himaraya torekkingu*.
GB/A.2015. t264.

Trent'anni di alpinismo: nella catena del Monte Bianco / Adolfo Hess. Novara, [1929]. Ill.
GB/C.18. t265.

Trent'anni nella Terra del Fuoco / Alberto M. De Agostini. Torino, [1955]. Ill., maps.
GB/B.261. t266.

Trentasette anni di vita sezionale in occasione del centenario del Club Alpino Italiano. Pisa, 1963. Ill. Published by the Club Alpino Italiano, Sezione di Pisa.
GB/B.403(6). t267.

Il **Trentino** nella preistoria del mondo alpino: dagli accampamenti sotto roccia alla città quadrata /

Bernardino Bagolini. Trento, 1980. Ill., maps.
GB/B.556. t268.

Le **très** cher frère Constantin Marie (Désiré Célestin Roulin) des Frères de l'Instruction Chrétienne de Ploërmel (1874-1926): un religieux éducateur, chez les Peaux-Rouges des montagnes Rocheuses, chez les Esquimaux de l'Alaska, au noviciat de Bitterne Park (Angleterre). Vannes, 1933. Ill., maps, ports.
GB/A.1789. t269.

Tribes of the Hindoo-Koosh / John Biddulph. Graz, 1971. Ill., map. [Quellen zur Entdeckungsgeschichte und Geographie Asiens; 2.] Facsimile reprint of the Calcutta, 1880 ed.
GB/B.476. t270.

Tricolore sulle più alte vette / Mario Fantin. Bologna, 1975. Ill. Published by the Club Alpino Italiano, Commissione Centrale delle Pubblicazioni.
GB/B.439(3). t271.

Triglav / a cura della Planinska Zveza Slovenije. [N.p., 1973.] Maps. [Escursioni e gite nelle Alpi Giulie orientali, Slovenia, Jugoslavia.]
GB/A.1281(9). t272.

A **trip** to Alaska: a narrative of what was seen and heard during a summer cruise in Alaskan waters / George Wardman. Boston, 1884.
GB/A.2170. t273.

Trip to Italy, during the long vacation. London, 1844.
GB.525; Lloyd.618. t274.

Trisul ski expedition / N. Kumar [et al.; edited by V.S. Nanda]. New Delhi, 1978.
GB/A.1981. t275.

Trois ascensions au Grand-Paradis / W.A.B. Coolidge. Grenoble, 1890. Map. Extrait de l'*Annuaire de la Société des touristes du Dauphiné*, année 1889.
Lloyd.1211. t276.

Trois cent quarante-deux heures dans les Grandes Jorasses / René Desmaison. [Paris], 1973. Ill. [L'aventure vécue.]
GB/A.1051(10). t277.

Trois curés en montagne / Jean Sarenne. Paris, 1950. Ill.
GB/A.1140. t278.

Trois jours de vacances: voyage des écoles industrielles dans le Jura neuchâtelois / Guillaume docteur, A. Bachelin, A. Biolley [et al.]. Neuchâtel, 1864. Ill. [Courses scolaires; année 1.]
GB/C.44. t279.

Trois jours en Savoie: congrès des Clubs Alpins à Annecy, août 1876 / François Descostes. Annecy, 1877.
GB/A.860(7). t280.

Troisième Congrès international d'alpinisme. [Chamonix, 1932.] 2v. Programmes of the Congress held in August 1932 at Chamonix; published by the Club alpin français.
GB.1334(21-2). t281.

A **true** and particular account, of the most surprising preservation, and happy deliverance, of three women who were buried thirty-seven day's [sic] at the village of Bergemoletto, in Italy / Ignazio Somis. London, 1768. Translated from *Ragionamento sopra il fatto avenuto in Bergemoletto*.
GB.110; Lloyd.214; Lloyd.214A,B. t282.

The **true** book about Everest / Eric Shipton. London, [1955]. Ill.
GB.305. t283.

True tales of mountain adventure for non-climbers young and old / Mrs Aubrey Le Blond. New York, 1903. Ill., ports.
Lloyd.966. t284.

True tales of mountain adventure for non-climbers young and old / Mrs Aubrey Le Blond. 3rd imp. London, 1906. Ill., ports.
GB.603. t285.

Trunk road for Hannibal: with an elephant over the Alps / John Hoyte. London, 1960. Ill., maps, ports.
GB.498. t286.

Tundra: selections from the great accounts of Arctic land voyages / [edited by] Farley Mowat. Toronto, 1977.
GB/A.1604. t287.

The **tundra** world / Theodora C. Stanwell-Fletcher. Boston, 1952. Ill. [An Atlantic Monthly pressbook.]
GB/A.1853. t288.

Der **Turist** in der Schweiz und dem angrenzenden Süd-Deutschland, Ober-Italien und Savoyen /

Iwan von Tschudi. 28. neu bearb. Aufl. St. Gallen, 1886. Maps.
Lloyd.120.   t289.

Turner in Switzerland / survey and notes with a checklist of the finished Swiss watercolours by Andrew Wilton; designed and edited by Walter Amstutz. Dübendorf, 1976. Ill.
GB/B.482.   t290.

Tutta montagna / Emanuele Cassarà con la collaborazione della Scuola Militare Alpina di Aosta. Milano, 1977. Ill. [La vostra via sportiva; 51.]
GB/A.1979.   t291.

Twenty years in Tibet: intimate and personal experiences / David Macdonald. London, 1932. Ill., maps, ports.
GB.760.   t292.

Two attempts to ascend Chimborazo / Alexander von Humboldt; translated from the German by Martin Barry. London, 1838. From nos. 878, 881, 883 and 884 of the *Mirror*.
GB.1313(14).   t293.

Two Caucasus climbs. 1: / R.A. Hodgkin. 2: Ushba / R.L. Beaumont. London, 1938. Ill., ports. Pp.169-75 of the *Climbers' Club Journal*, N.S. vol.5 no.3. R. A. Hodgkin's article is untitled.
GB.1338(27).   t294.

Two Dianas in Alaska / Agnes Herbert and a shikári. London, [1909].
GB.817.   t295.

Two expeditions to Mount St. Elias. 1: The expedition of the *New York Times*, 1886 / Frederick Schwatka. 2: The expedition of the National Geographic Society and the United States Geological Survey, 1890 / Israel C. Russell. [New York, 1891.] Ill., maps. Pp.[865]-84 of the *Century Magazine*, vol.41, April 1891.
GB.1329(42).   t296.

Two huts in the Antarctic / L.B. Quartermain. Wellington, 1963. Ill., maps.
GB/A.1966(3).   t297.

Two lady Alpine climbers: Mrs. Burnaby — Miss Walker / Edward Whymper. London, 1885. Ill., port. Pp.164-7 of the *Girl's Own Paper*, vol.7 no.311.
GB.1881(40).   t298.

Two men and a mountain / Sir Arnold Lunn. London, 1945. A review of *Brenva*, by T. Graham

Brown and *Climbs and ski runs*, by Frank S. Smythe. Pp.514-9 of the *New English Review*, vol.11 no.6.
GB.1331(49).   t299.

Two mountains and a river / H.W. Tilman. Cambridge, 1949. Ill., maps.
Lloyd.960.   t300.

Two new ascents of Mont Blanc / T. Graham Brown. Edinburgh, 1929. Pp.71-2 of the *Edinburgh Academy Chronicle*, vol.36 no.4, March 1929.
GB.1319(9).   t301.

[**Two** newsletters of the Schweizer Alpenclub, Sektion Bern, dated 5. Januar 1950 and 5. Januar 1952.] Bern, [1950-52].
Lloyd.1605(12).   t302.

[**Two** obituary notices of Edward Whymper, by J.E.C. Eaton and W.A.B. Coolidge.] [Turin, 1911.] Port. Pp.370-2 of the *Rivista del Club Alpino Italiano*, vol.30.
GB.1881(71).   t303.

Two seasons in Switzerland / Herbert Marsh. London, 1895. Ill.
GB.561; Lloyd.717; Lloyd.717A.   t304.

Two summers in the ice-wilds of eastern Karakoram / Fanny Bullock Workman, William Hunter Workman. London, 1917. Ill., maps.
GB.1070.   t305.

[**Two** views of Mount Etna, engraved by George Cooke.] London, 1809.
GB.1334(19-20).   t306.

Two years in the Antarctic / W. Kevin Walton. London, 1955. Ill., maps, ports.
GB.795.   t307.

Tyndall as a mountaineer / W. Martin Conway. [London, 1893.] Chapter 6 of *The life and work of John Tyndall*.
GB.1336(37).   t308.

The **Tyrol**: with a glance at Bavaria / Henry D. Inglis. London, 1833. 2v.
Lloyd.477-8.   t309.

Tyrol and the Tyrolese: the people and the land in their social, sporting and mountaineering aspects / W.A. Baillie-Grohman. London, 1876.
Lloyd.497; Lloyd.497A,B.   t310.

Tyrol and the Tyrolese / W.A. Baillie-Grohman. 2nd ed. London, 1877.
Lloyd.498; Lloyd.498A.   t311.

Le **Tyrol** et le pays des Dolomites / Jules Leclercq. Paris, 1880. Map.
Lloyd.1614(15).   t312.

The **Tyrol** jubilee in 1863. [London, 1864.] Pp.225-32 of the *Cornhill Magazine*, Aug. 1864.
GB.1332(38).   t313.

-U-

Uber alpine Randseen und Erosionsterrassen im besondern des Linthtales: Inaugural-Dissertation / Emil Gogarten; begutachtet von A. Heim. Gotha, 1910. Ill.
GB/A.1052(18).   u001.

Uber das Interessanteste der Schweiz / aus dem Französischen frey übersezt, berichtigt und vermehrt / [J.H.F. Ulrich]. Leipzig, 1777-80. 4v.
GB/A.1116-9.   u002.

Uber das Wesen der Gletscher, und Winterreise in das Eismeer / F.J. Hugi. Stuttgart, 1842.
GB/A.1444.   u003.

Uber dem Abgrund-Senkrecht bis überhängend: aus dem Leben eines passionierten Bergsteigers / Georges Livanos; übertragen von Kaspar von Almen. Rüschlikon bei Zürich, [n.d.]. Ill. Translated from *Au delà de la verticale*.
GB/A.422.   u004.

Uber den St. Gotthard: Reise-Skizzen / A.W. Grube. Berlin, [1871?]. Ill.
GB/A.1464.   u005.

Uber den Zmuttgrat auf das Matterhorn / Hans Lorenz. [N.p., n.d.] Ill.
GB/B.245(26).   u006.

Uber die Aiguille Blanche de Pétéret zum Montblanc / Willi Mayr. [N.p., 1928.] Pp.17-[31] of an unidentified periodical.
GB.1318(28).   u007.

Uber die orographische und geologische Structur der Gruppe des Monte-Rosa / Adolph von Schlagintweit. Leipzig, 1853. Ill.
GB.1317(3).   u008.

Uber die Schneegränze auf der mittäglichen Seite des Rosagebürges und barometrische Messungen / Friedrich Parrot. Nürnberg, 1817. Pp.368-424 of the *Journal für Chemie und Physik*, Bd.19.
Lloyd.1577(1).   u009.

Uber Eis und Schnee: die höchsten Gipfel der Schweiz und die Geschichte ihrer Besteigung / G. Studer. Bern, 1869-83. 4v.
GB.265-6 (bound in 2); GB.1327(14-6) (wanting v.1).   u010.

Uber Eis und Schnee: die höchsten Gipfel der Schweiz und die Geschichte ihrer Besteigung / G.

Studer. 2. Aufl. umgearbeitet und ergänzt von A. Wäber und H. Dübi. Bern, 1896-99. 3v; port. GB.300 (wanting v.2-3). u011

Uber Fels und Firn: Bergwanderungen / Ludwig Purtscheller; herausgegeben von H. Hess. München, 1901. Ill., port. GB.1245. u012

Uber Fels und Firn: die Bezwingung der mächtigsten Hochgipfel der Erde durch den Menschen: nach Berichten aus früherer und späterer Zeit für junge wie alte Freunde der Berge / Th. Schwarz. Leipzig, 1888. GB.834. u013

Uber Genf und den Genfer-See / Christian August Fischer. Berlin, 1796. GB/A.804(2). u014

Uber östliche Eiswege zum Mont Blanc-Gipfel / Walter Amstutz. [Berne, 1928.] Ill. Separatabdruck aus *Die Alpen*, Jahrg.4, Hft.8, 1928. Mit Ergänzungen. Lloyd.1308. u015

Ubergang aus dem Otzthale in das Pitzthal über den Hochvernagt- und Sechsegertenferner / Anton von Ruthner. Wien, 1859. Separat-Abdruck aus den *Mitteilungen der k.k. geographischen Gesellschaft*, Jahrg.3 Hft.2. GB.1130(5). u016

Die **Uberschreitung** des Berner Hochgebirges im Jahre 1712 / W.A.B. Coolidge. Bern, [1913]. Separatabdruck aus den *Blättern für bernische Geschichte, Kunst und Altertumskunde*. GB.1340(34). u017

Das **überseeische** Deutschland: die deutschen Kolonien in Wort und Bild. 2. Aufl. bearbeitet von Hauptmann a. d. Hutter [et al.]. Bd.1. Berlin, 1911. Ill., maps, ports. GB.1175. u018

The **ultimate** mountains: an account of four months' mountain exploring in the central Himalaya / Tom Weir. London, 1953. Ill., maps. GB.803. u019

Um den Kantsch: der zweite deutsche Angriff auf den Kangchendzönga, 1931 / Paul Bauer. München, 1933. Ill., map. GB.1073. u020

Um den Südpol / nach vorzüglichen Reisebeschreibungen ausgewählt und bearbeitet von Alexandrine Haenicke. Stuttgart, 1926. Ill., map. [Fahrten und Forschungen; 7.] GB/A.454. u021

Uncle Sam's attic: the intimate story of Alaska / Mary Lee Davis. Boston, 1930. Ill., maps, ports. GB/A.1732. u022

An **unconventional** guide for tourists: a fortnight in Switzerland: a free-and-easy account of a first visit to the Rigi, the Bernese Oberland, Chamouny, &c. / by the editor of the *Western Gazette* [i.e. Charles Clinker]. London, 1880. GB.735. u023

Under det nordligste Dannebrog: beretning om Dansk Nordøstgrønlands Ekspedition, 1938-39 / Eigil Knuth; udsendt af Alf Trolle, Ebbe Munck og Eigil Knuth. København, 1940. Ill., maps. GB/A.1866. u024

Under the management of Mr Charles Dickens: his production of *The frozen deep* / edited by Robert Louis Brannan. Ithaca, N.Y., 1966. Ill., facsim. GB/A.1655. u025

Under the mountains. [London, 1871.] Pp.63-85 of the *Cornhill Magazine*, July 1871. GB.1313(4). u026

Undersökningar beträffande den på Kung Karls Land funna stora flytbojen från Andrée-expeditionen. 1: Den Andréeska polarbojens drift till Kung Karls Land / A.G. Nathorst. 2: Fyndomständigheter, bojens identifiering, tekniska undersökningar etc. 3: Om växt- och djurlämningarna i Andrées polarboj / G. Lagerheim. Stockholm, 1900. Map. Ur *Ymer*, årg.1899, h.4. GB.1800(15). u027

Undiscovered Scotland: climbs on rock, snow, and ice / W.H. Murray. London, 1951. Ill., maps. GB.775. u028

Undiscovered Scotland / W.H. Murray. London, [1950]. A prospectus. GB.1315(9). u029

The **unexploited** West: a compilation of all the authentic information available at the present time as to the natural resources of the unexploited regions of northern Canada / Ernest J. Chambers. Ottawa, 1914. Ill., maps. Published by the Railway Lands Branch, Department of the Interior. GB/B.528(3). u030

An **unexplored** pass: a narrative of a thousand-mile journey to the Kara-koran Himalayas / B.K. Featherstone. London, [1926].
GB.1097.   u031.

Das **Unglück** an der Jungfrau vom 15. Juli 1887 / auf Veranlassung des Vorstandes der Section UTO S.A.C. dargestellt von F. Becker, A. Fleiner. 3. Aufl. Zürich, [1888?]. Ill., map, port.
Lloyd.1209.   u032.

United States polar exploration / edited by Herman R. Friis and Shelby G. Bale, Jr. Athens, Ohio, [1970]. Ill. [National Archives Conference; 1.] Published by the Conference on United States Polar Exploration, 1967, Washington D.C.
GB/A.1653.   u033.

The **universal** traveller, containing the popular features and contents of the best standard modern travels in the four quarters of the world / Samuel Prior. London, 1839. Ill.
GB.208.   u034.

The **universal** traveller, containing the popular features and contents of the best standard modern travels in the four quarters of the world / Samuel Prior. [London, n.d.] Ill.
GB.204 (impf.).   u035.

University of Edinburgh Gazette. Supplement April 1954. Report of the Expedition to Arctic Norway, 1953. Edinburgh, [1954].
GB.1334(3).   u036.

Unprotected females in Sicily, Calabria, and on the top of Mount Ætna / [Emily Lowe]. London, 1859. Ill.
Lloyd.525; Lloyd.525A.   u037.

The **unseen** universe, or Physical speculations on a future state / [Balfour Stewart, Peter G. Tait]. London, 1875.
GB.973.   u038.

Unsolved mysteries of the Arctic / Vilhjalmur Stefansson. New York, 1938. Maps.
GB/A.2149.   u039.

Unter den Dolomiten: Roman / Konrad Telmann. 12. Aufl. Dresden, 1907. 2v (in 1).
GB/A.1341.   u040.

Untersuchungen über den Mechanismus der Gebirgsbildung im Anschluss an die geologische Monographie der Tödi-Windgällen-Gruppe /

Albert Heim. Basel, 1878. 3v; maps.
GB/B.358-60.   u041.

Untersuchungen über die erste Bevölkerung des Alpengebirgs insbesondere der schweizerischen Urkantone, des Berner Oberlandes und des Oberwallis / J. Rudolf Burckhardt. [N.p., ca 1850.]
GB/B.312(11).   u042.

Untersuchungen über die Gletscher / Louis Agassiz. Solothurn, 1840-41. 2v; ill. Translated from *Etudes sur les glaciers*.
GB/C.55-6.   u043.

Unterwaldner Alpen und angrenzende Urner Alpen. Basel, 1875. Published by the Schweizer Alpenclub.
GB/A.879(3).   u044.

Unto the hills / Douglas W. Freshfield. London, 1914.
GB.201; Lloyd.241; Lloyd.241A,B,C.   u045.

Untrodden paths in Roumania / Mary Adelaide Walker. London, 1888. Ill.
Lloyd.1179.   u046.

Untrodden peaks and unfrequented valleys / Amelia Blandford Edwards. London, 1873.
Lloyd.1110; Lloyd.1125.   u047.

Untrodden peaks and unfrequented valleys / Amelia Blandford Edwards. 2nd ed. London, 1890.
GB.940.   u048.

The **unveiling** of Lhasa / Edmund Candler. London, 1905. Ill., map, ports. [Nelson's shilling library.]
GB.1036.   u049.

Uomini del Cervino / Francesco Cavazzani. Milano, 1955. Ill.
GB/A.1131.   u050.

Gli **uomini** del Rosa / Teresio Valsesia. Novara, 1972. Ill. Estratto da *Novara*, n.7-8, anno 1972.
GB/B.337(19).   u051.

Uomini e montagne / Sandro Prada. Bologna, 1951. Ill. [Le Alpi; 8.]
GB/A.1574.   u052.

Uomini e montagne: 50 capitoli ameni-amari, campestri e montanini / Mario Fierli. Torino, 1931.
GB/A.1579.   u053.

Uomini sul K2 / Achille Compagnoni. Milano, 1958. Ill. [Gli sport e gli sportivi.]
GB/A.1568.   u054.

Uomini sulla Annapurna / Maurice Herzog; traduzione di Enrico Peyronel. Milano, 1952. Ill., map. Translated from *Annapurna premier 8000*.
GB/A.860(9).   u055.

L'**uomo** e le Dolomiti: valle di Fassa: le più belle passeggiate, escursioni, traversate, facili ascensioni / P. Cavagna, T. Rizzi. Trento, [ca 1967]. Ill.
GB/A.1316.   u056.

L'**uomo** felice / Remo Appia. Rivarolo, 1964.
GB/A.455(11).   u057.

L'**uomo** sulle Alpi / Angelo Mosso. 3a ed. Milano, 1909. Originally published as *Fisiologia dell'uomo sulle Alpi*.
GB/B.257.   u058.

Un **uomo** va sui monti / Giorgio Brunner. Bologna, 1957. Ill. [Il semprevivo; 3.]
GB/A.495(5).   u059.

Up and down Mont Blanc. London, [1866]. Ill. Christmas extra double number of *Chambers's Journal*, 1866. Attributed to Sir Leslie Stephen.
GB.1239; GB.1336(26); Lloyd.1381.   u060.

Up Mont Blanc by the Brenva 'Poire' route: second ascent / R. Greloz. Birkenhead, 1938. Pp.31-3 of the *Mountaineering Journal*, vol.6 no.1.
GB.1317(4).   u061.

Up the Himalayas: mountaineering on the Indian Alps / W.W. Graham. [London, 1885.] From *Good Words*, Jan., Feb. and Mar. 1885.
GB.1318(6).   u062.

Upernivik ø: incontro con la Groenlandia / Piergiorgio Bosio, Giuseppe Patrucco; versione inglese a cura di Maria Paola Ferraguti Bazzini. [Ivrea], 1972. Ill. [Viaggi, paesi e tradizioni.]
GB/B.345.   u063.

Upon that mountain / Eric Shipton. London, 1944. Ill., maps.
GB.362.   u064.

Upon that mountain, by Eric Shipton / C.B.M. Warren. [London, 1944.] A review. Pp.318-22 of the *Climbers' Club Journal*, N.S. vol.7 no.3.
GB.1337(6).   u065.

The **Upper-Engadine** / J. Pernisch. Zürich, [1895?]. Ill. [Swiss scenes.]
GB/A.1817(9).   u066.

Upptäcktsresor i norra Polarhavet / Julius Payer; öfversättning och bearbetning af Th. M. Fries. Stockholm, 1877. Ill., maps, ports.
GB/A.1851.   u067.

Uso della carta topografica: orientamento — aerofotografie / Enrico Cecioni. 2a ed. Firenze, 1965. 2v; ill.
GB/A.1034(12-3).   u068.

USSR/USA Bering Sea Experiment / editor-in-chief: R. Ya. Kondrat'ev. Rotterdam, 1982. Ill., maps.
GB/A.2133.   u069.

-V-

Vacation rambles and thoughts: comprising the recollections of three continental tours: in the vacations of 1841, 1842, and 1843 / Thomas Noon Talfourd. London, 1845. 2v.
GB.527-8; Lloyd.634-5.   v001.

Vacation rambles and thoughts: comprising the recollection of three continental tours, in the vacations of 1841, 1842 and 1843 / Thomas Noon Talfourd. 2nd ed. London, 1845.
GB.487.   v002.

A **vacation** tour at the Antipodes, through Victoria, Tasmania, New South Wales, Queensland, and New Zealand, in 1861-1862 / B.A. Heywood. London, 1863. Ill., maps, port.
Lloyd.691.   v003.

A **vacation** tour in Switzerland / John Tyndall. London, [1862]. Ill.
GB.435; GB.499 (impf.); Lloyd.693.   v004.

Vacation tourists and notes of travels in 1860 / edited by Francis Galton. Cambridge, 1861. Ill., maps.
GB.960; Lloyd.1007.   v005.

Vacation tourists and notes of travel in 1861 / edited by Francis Galton. Cambridge, 1862. Maps.
GB.961; GB.962; Lloyd.878; Lloyd.1008.   v006.

Vacation tourists and notes of travel in 1862-3 / edited by Francis Galton. London, 1864.
GB.869.   v007.

Vade-mecum S.U.C.A.I. Monza, 1913. Ill. [Per l'alpinismo.] Pubblicazione del Club Alpino Italiano, Stazione Universitaria.
GB/A.1034(2).   v008.

Vademecum dell'alpinista / Felice Boffa. Milano, [1953?]. Ill.
GB/A.1381(8).   v009.

Værbitt sagaland / Håkan Morne; på norsk ved Øystein Orre Eskeland. Oslo, 1939. Ill., map.
GB/A.1868.   v010.

Vagabonding down the Andes: being the narrative of a journey, chiefly afoot, from Panama to Buenos Aires / Harry A. Franck. New York, 1917. Ill., map, ports.
GB/A.1686.   v011.

Le **vainqueur** du Mont Blanc: roman / A. den Doolaard; traduit par H. et P. Hofer-Bury. Paris, [1951]. Translated from *De groote verwildering*.
GB/A.938(1).   v012.

La **Val**. Trento, 1972. Ill. Published by the Centro Studi per la Val di Sole.
GB/B.377(18).   v013.

La **Val** Belluna: studio antropogeografico / Elio Migliorini. Roma, 1932. Ill. [Università di Roma. Istituto di Geografia. Pubblicazioni; ser.A num.2.]
GB/B.312(8).   v014.

Das **Val** d'Anniviers und das Bassin de Sierre: ein Beitrag zur physikalischen Geographie und Ethnographie der Walliser Alpen / Gustav Berndt. Gotha, 1882. Ill. [Petermann's Mittheilungen. Ergänzungsheft; 68.]
GB/C.5(8).   v015.

Val d'Anniviers, Val d'Hérens: descriptions de 42 itinéraires avec profils, croquis et photographies / Ignace Mariétan. 3e éd. Berne, 1967. Ill. [Guide suisse; 12.]
GB/A.516(14).   v016.

Le **val** d'Aoste. Novare, 1951. Ill., map. Published by the Bureau regional du tourisme de la vallée d'Aoste.
GB.1313(16).   v017.

Val d'Arno: ten lectures on the Tuscan art, directly antecedent to the Florentine Year of Victories / John Ruskin; given before the University of Oxford, 1873. Orpington, 1874. Ill.
GB.1135.   v018.

La **Val** di Genova e l'alta via di Lares-Carè Alto: l'ultimo paradiso delle Alpi / Luciano Viazzi. [Lecco], 1972. Ill., map.
GB/A.1054.   v019.

Val di Mello / Antonio Boscacci; con la collaborazione di J. Merizzi e di M. Ghezzi. Bologna, 1980. Ill., maps. [Itinerari alpini; 51.]
GB/A.1589(28).   v020.

Le **val** Ferret / Ernest Lovey-Troillet. Neuchâtel, [1946]. Ill.
GB/A.1270(6).   v021.

Val Gardena nelle Dolomiti / Edgard Moroder; [traduzione: Willy Dondio]. 2a ed. Calliano, [1972]. Ill., map. [Montagne celebri.]
GB/B.351.   v022.

Val Malenco / Ezio Pavesi. Bologna, 1969. [Le Alpi.]
GB/A.867(4). v023.

La **Val** Pusteria e le valli adiacenti: guida turistica / a cura di Giuseppe Puerari, Ernst Mariner. Bolzano, [n.d.]. Ill., map.
GB/A.7. v024.

Val Rosandra: rapporto sentimentale / Spiro Dalla Porta Xidias. Trieste, 1971.
GB/A.958. v025.

Val San Martino: storia, panorama economico sociale, guida turistica / Severino Bessone. Pinerolo, [1971]. Ill., maps.
GB/A.836(11). v026.

Val Vigezzo / Gianfranco Francese. Bologna, 1976. Ill., map. [Itinerari alpini; 28.]
GB/A.1468(21). v027.

Le **valanghe** dell'alta Valtournanche / Manfredo Vanni. Torino, [1962]. Ill., map. Estratto dal *Bollettino del Comitato Glaciologico Italiano*, 1961-62.
GB/B.338(8). v028.

Valberg (Beuil, Guillaumes, Péone): Haut-Var (Esteng, Pélens) / Vincent Paschetta. 3e éd. Grenoble, 1972. Ill. [Guide Paschetta des Alpes-Maritimes. 2: Randonnées et alpinisme; c.]
GB/A.1350(8). v029.

Valbrenta. 1: Canale del Brenta / Armando Scandellari. Bologna, 1981. Ill., map. [Itinerari alpini; 53.]
GB/A.1589(29). v030.

Valbrenta. 2: Valsugana / Armando Scandellari. Bologna, 1983. Ill., maps. [Itinerari alpini; 57.]
GB/A.2165(8). v030.1.

Valdagnesi sulle piccole Dolomiti / a cura di Nico Ceron. Vicenza, 1970. Ill., map. Published by the Club Alpino Italiano, Sezione di Valdagno.
GB/B.290(5). v031.

Valérie: comédie / MM. Scribe et Mélesville. Londres, 1828.
Lloyd.1572(3). v032.

La **Valganna** / Manfredo Vanni. Roma, 1917. Ill. Estratto dal *Bollettino della Reale Società Geografica Italiana*, fasc.1-3, 1917.
GB/A.1035(9). v033.

Valgrande / Luciano Rainoldi. Lecco, 1979. Ill., maps.
GB/A.2023(1). v034.

La **vallata** di Zoldo: escursione alpina / Riccardo Volpe. [N.p., n.d.] Facsimile reprint of the Belluno, 1884 ed.
GB/A.455(7[1]). v035.

La **Valle** Aurina / Eugenia Bevilacqua. Roma, 1955. Ill., maps. [Memorie di geografia antropica; vol.10 fasc.1.]
GB/B.312(4). v036.

La **valle** d'Aosta nei secoli: vedute e piante dal IV al XIX secolo: bibliografia, iconografia, repertorio degli artisti / Ada Peyrot. Torino, 1972.
GB/B.357. v037.

La **valle** dei Mocheni / Aldo Gorfer. 2a ed. Calliano, 1972. Ill.
GB/B.348. v038.

La **valle** del Cervino: guida alpinistica / Francesco Cavazzani. Milano, [1962]. Ill., maps.
GB/A.1065. v039.

Valle dello Spluga e valle di Lei: itinerari alpinistici / a cura di Giovanni De Simoni. Chiavenna, 1980. Ill., maps. Published by the Club Alpino Italiano, Sezione Valle Spluga.
GB/A.2018(2). v040.

La **valle** di Challant-Ayas: le sue antichità / Ugo Torra. 2a ed. Ivrea, 1963. Ill. [Archeografia e storia in valle d'Aosta.]
GB/A.1349(15). v041.

La **valle** di Champorcher: le sue antichità / Ugo Torra. Ivrea, 1961. Ill.
GB/A.1349(4). v042.

La **valle** di Gressoney: le sue antichità / Ugo Torra. 2a ed. Ivrea, 1966. Ill. [Archeografia e storia in valle d'Aosta.]
GB/A.1349(14). v043.

La **valle** di Ledro et le sue palafitte / Mario Ferrari, Gina Tomasi; a cura di Gino Scrinzi. Rovereto, 1969. Ill., maps.
GB/A.954. v044.

La **valle** di Rhêmes / Lorenzo Rossi di Montelera. Bologna, 1978. Ill., map. [Itinerari alpini; 40.]
GB/A.1589(6). v045.

La **valle** di St. Barthelemy / Giuseppe Garimoldi. Torino, 1962. Ill., map. Published by the Club

Alpino Italiano, Sezione di Torino.
GB/A.1034(6). v046.

Valle Formazza / Luciano Rainoldi. [Lecco?], 1974. Ill., maps.
GB/A.2031(3). v047.

La **valle** Gesso / Alessandro Gogna. Bologna, 1975. Ill., maps. [Itinerari alpini; 20.]
GB/A.1351(15). v048.

Valle Intelvi / Fernando Cavadini. 2a ed. Como, 1969. Ill., map.
GB/A.835(1). v049.

Valle Shaksgam e catene Aghil / Filippo De Filippi. Roma, 1929. Estratto dal *Bollettino della Reale Società Geografica Italiana*, ser.6 vol.6, luglio 1929.
GB.1880(40). v050.

Valle Susa e Sangone / Gian Carlo Grassi. Bologna, 1980. Ill., maps. [Itinerari alpini; 49.]
GB/A.1589(23). v051.

La **vallée** d'Aoste / Edouard Aubert. Paris, 1860. Ill.
GB.1293. v052.

La **vallée** de Monjoie et la découverte du Mont Blanc / Henri Baud. [N.p., n.d.] Facsim.
GB.1322(16). v053.

La **vallée** de Sixt et le Petit Saint Bernard / Jacques Louis Manget. Genève, 1851. Ill., map.
GB.147(2). v054.

La **vallée** de Valtornenche en 1867: notice / G. Carrel. Turin, 1868. Ill.
GB.1326(41). v055.

Une **vallée** insolite: Chamonix, le Mont Blanc, la Savoie: histoire des origines à 1860 / Roger Couvert du Crest. Annecy, 1971. 2v; ill.
GB/B.343-4. v056.

Les **vallées** rhétiques / texte original de Hermann Hiltbrunner adapté de l'allemand par Joh. Widmer. Paris, 1929. Ill., map. [Les Grisons; 2.]
GB/A.922. v057.

Vallesiæ descriptio, libri duo. De Alpibus commentarius. Accessit his appendix descriptionis Vallesiæ / Josias Simler. [Zurich], 1574.
Lloyd.133. v058.

Vallesiae et Alpium descriptio / Josias Simler. [Leiden], 1633.
GB.1; GB.2 (impf.); Lloyd.1. v059.

The **valley** of Aosta: a descriptive and historical sketch of an Alpine valley noteworthy in story and in monument / Felice Ferrero. New York, 1910. Ill., maps.
GB.565. v060.

The **valley** of Zermatt and the Matterhorn: a guide / Edward Whymper. London, 1897. Ill., maps.
GB.469; Lloyd.424; Lloyd.424A,B. v061.

The **valley** of Zermatt and the Matterhorn / Edward Whymper. 2nd ed. London, 1898.
Lloyd.425. v062.

The **valley** of Zermatt and the Matterhorn / Edward Whymper. 3rd ed. London, 1899.
Lloyd.426. v063.

The **valley** of Zermatt and the Matterhorn / Edward Whymper. 4th ed. London, 1900.
Lloyd.427; Lloyd.427A. v064.

The **valley** of Zermatt and the Matterhorn / Edward Whymper. 5th ed. London, 1901.
Lloyd.428. v065.

The **valley** of Zermatt and the Matterhorn / Edward Whymper. 6th ed. London, 1902.
Lloyd.429. v066.

The **valley** of Zermatt and the Matterhorn / Edward Whymper. 7th ed. London, 1903.
Lloyd.430. v067.

The **valley** of Zermatt and the Matterhorn / Edward Whymper. 8th ed. London, 1904.
Lloyd.431. v068.

The **valley** of Zermatt and the Matterhorn / Edward Whymper. 9th ed. London, 1905.
Lloyd.432. v069.

The **valley** of Zermatt and the Matterhorn / Edward Whymper. 10th ed. London, 1906.
Lloyd.433. v070.

The **valley** of Zermatt and the Matterhorn / Edward Whymper. 11th ed. London, 1907.
Lloyd.434. v071.

The **valley** of Zermatt and the Matterhorn / Edward Whymper. 12th ed. London, 1908.
Lloyd.435. v072.

The **valley** of Zermatt and the Matterhorn / Edward Whymper. 13th ed. London, 1909. Lloyd.436.   v073.

The **valley** of Zermatt and the Matterhorn / Edward Whymper. 14th ed. London, 1910. Lloyd.437.   v074.

The **valley** of Zermatt and the Matterhorn / Edward Whymper. 15th ed. London, 1911. Lloyd.438.   v075.

The **valleys** of Tirol: their traditions and customs and how to visit them / Rachel Harriette Busk. London, 1874. Maps.
Lloyd.584; Lloyd.584A.   v076.

The **valleys** of Turtman and Eifisch, val de Tourtemagne and val d'Anniviers / F.O. Wolf. Zurich, [1880?]. Ill., map. [Valais and Chamounix; 5.]
GB/A.760(2).   v077.

Le **valli** del Trentino: guida geografico, storico, artistico, ambientale / Aldo Gorfer. Calliano, 1975. 2v; ill., maps.
GB/A.2002-3.   v078.

Le **valli** dell'Adda e della Mera nel corso dei secoli / Enrico Besta. 2: Il dominio grigione a cura di Beatrice Besta e Renzo Sertoli Salis. Milano, 1964. [Storia della Valtellina e del contado di Chiavenna.]
GB/A.1379.   v079.

Le **valli** dell'Alto Lario: guida escursionistica / Sandro Gandola. Lecco, 1980. Ill., map.
GB/A.2018(16).   v080.

Le **valli** di Lanzo (Alpi Graie) / edizione fatta per cura del Club Alpino Italiano, Sezione di Torino. Torino, 1904. Ill.
GB/B.314.   v081.

Valli di Susa, Chisone e Germanasca: escursioni, ascensioni, traversate, trekking / Giulio Berutto. 2a ed. Torino, 1980. Ill. [Guide I.G.C.] Published by the Istituto Geografico Centrale.
GB/A.1911(13).   v082.

Valmadrera: montagne e itinerari alpinistici / Giorgio Tessari, Gian Maria Mandelli. Valmadrera, 1979. Ill., maps.
GB/A.2019(1).   v083.

Valmalenco: itinerari scelti / Alessandro Gogna, Lorenzo Marimonti. Bologna, 1977. 2v; ill., map.

[Itinerari alpini; 34-5.]
GB/A.1589(13-4).   v084.

Valsesia e lago d'Orta: descrizione geologica / Carlo Fabrizio Parona. Bologna, [1973]. Maps. Facsimile reprint of the Milan, 1886 ed.
GB/B.377(8).   v085.

Valsesia e Monte Rosa: guida alpinistica, artistica, storica / Luigi Ravelli. Bologna, [1970]. Ill., maps.
GB/A.867(12).   v086.

La **Valtornenche**: le sue antichità / Ugo Torra. Ivrea, 1973. Ill. [Archeografia e storia in valle d'Aosta.]
GB/A.1299.   v088.

Vanished civilizations: forgotten peoples of the ancient world / Henri Lhote, Roger Summers [et al.]; edited by Edward Bacon. London, [1963]. Ill., maps.
GB.1295.   v089.

A **vanished** dynasty: Ashanti / Sir Francis Fuller. London, 1921. Ill., map.
GB.880.   v090.

La **Vanoise**: parc national / Roger Frison-Roche, Pierre Tairraz. [Paris], 1972. Ill.
GB/A.1089.   v091.

Variantes: nouvelles et pastiches / Etienne Bruhl. Paris, 1951. [Sempervivum; 13.]
GB/A.1320.   v092.

Variation of the population structure of *Polygonum viviparum L.* in relation to certain environmental conditions / Peter Milan Petersen. Copenhagen, 1981. Ill. [Meddelelser om Grønland. Bioscience; 4.]
GB/A.1819(4).   v093.

Les **variations** périodiques des glaciers des Alpes / F.A. Forel. 2e rapport, [1881]. Berne, [1882]. Extrait de l'*Echo des Alpes*, année 18 no.2, 1882.
GB/A.793(4).   v094.

Les **variations** périodiques des glaciers des Alpes / F.A. Forel. 6e rapport, 1885. Berne, 1886. Extrait du *Jahrbuch des Schweizer Alpenclub*, vol.21.
GB/A.793(7).   v095.

Les **variations** périodiques des glaciers des Alpes / F.A. Forel. 7e rapport, [1886]. Berne, 1887. Extrait du *Jahrbuch des Schweizer Alpenclub*, vol.22.
GB/A.793(10).   v096.

Les **variations** périodiques des glaciers des Alpes / F.A. Forel. 8e rapport, 1887. Berne, 1888. Extrait du *Jahrbuch S.A.C.*, 23, 1887.
GB/A.793(11). v097.

Les **variations** périodiques des glaciers des Alpes / F.A. Forel. 9e rapport, 1888. Berne, 1889.
GB/A.793(12). v098.

Les **variations** périodiques des glaciers des Alpes / F.A. Forel. 10e rapport, 1889. Berne, 1890. Extrait du *Jahrbuch des S.A.C.*, année 25.
GB/A.793(14). v099.

Les **variations** périodiques des glaciers des Alpes / F.A. Forel. 11e rapport, 1890. Berne, [1891]. Separatabdruck aus dem *Jahrbuch des S.A.C.*, Jahrg.26.
GB/A.793(15). v100.

Les **variations** périodiques des glaciers des Alpes / F.A. Forel. 12e rapport, 1891. Berne, 1892. Separatabdruck aus dem *Jahrbuch des S.A.C.*, Jahrg.27.
GB/A.793(16). v101.

Les **variations** périodiques des glaciers des Alpes / F.A. Forel. 13e rapport, 1892. Berne, 1893. Extrait du *Jahrbuch des S.A.C.*, année 28.
GB/A.793(17). v102.

Les **variations** périodiques des glaciers: discours préliminaire / F.A. Forel. Geneve, 1895. Extrait des *Archives des sciences physiques et naturelles*, t.34.
GB/A.793(18). v103.

Les **variations** périodiques des glaciers: lettre à M. Fr. Schrader / F.A. Forel. Paris, 1887. Extrait de l'*Annuaire du Club alpin français*, vol.13.
GB/A.793(9). v104.

Various expeditions in 1914: Pennines / R.W. Lloyd. London, 1915. Reprinted from the *Alpine Journal*, November 1914.
Lloyd.1602(25). v105.

Vascos en el Everest / Felipe Uriarte. Bilbao, [1981]. Ill., maps, ports.
GB/B.587. v106.

Il **Vatnajökull**: il più grande ghiacciaio d'Europa: appunti di viaggio / Manfredo Vanni. Torino, [1964]. Ill. Estratto dal *Bollettino del Comitato Glaciologico Italiano*.
GB/B.338(16). v107.

Vatnajökull: kampen mellem ild og is / Niels Nielsen. København, 1937. Ill., maps.
GB/A.1791(8). v108.

Vegetation of the Angmagssalik district, southeast Greenland / F.J.A. Daniels. Copenhagen, 1982. Ill., maps. [Meddelelser om Grønland. Bioscience; 10.]
GB/A.1819. v109.

Das **Veltlin** nebst einer Beschreibung der Bäder von Bormio: ein Beitrag zur Kenntniss der Lombardei / Georg Leonhardi. Leipzig, 1860. Map.
GB/A.932. v110.

Die **Venetianer** Alpen: ein Beitrag zur Kenntnis der Hochgebirge / Wilhelm Fuchs. Solothurn, 1844.
GB/B.375. v111.

Veneto / Elio Migliorini. Torino, 1962. Ill., maps. [Le regioni d'Italia; 4.]
GB/B.549. v112.

The **Venlo** incident / S. Payne Best. London, [1950]. Ill., map, ports.
GB.794. v113.

Venticinque anni di vita della Società Alpinisti Vicentini. [Vicenza], 1971. Ill.
GB/B.338(18). v114.

Die **Vergletscherung** der deutschen Alpen, ihre Ursachen, periodische Wiederkehr und ihr Einfluss auf die Bodengestaltung / Albrecht Penck. Leipzig, 1882. Ill., maps.
GB/A.412. v115.

Verkehrsgeschichte der Alpen / P.H. Scheffel. Berlin, 1908-14. 2v.
GB/B.444; GB/B.270 (wanting v2). v116.

Il **vero** arrampicatore: lo stile di Emilio Comici e Arrampicare d'inverno in 274 immagini / Severino Casara. Milano, 1972. Ill.
GB/A.1251. v117.

Vers l'idéal par la montagne: souvenir de mes escalades de haute montagne en Europe et en Amérique / Myrtil Schwartz. Paris, 1924. Ill.
GB/B.110. v118.

Vers le pôle / Fridtjof Nansen; traduit et abrégé par Charles Rabot. Paris, [1897]. Ill., ports. Translated from *Fram over Polhavet*.
GB/A.1939. v119.

Il **versante** italiano del Monte Bianco / F. Mondini, G.F. e G.B. Gugliermina, E. Canzio. Torino, 1902. Ill., map. Published by the Club Alpino Italiano.
GB.1188(1).   v120.

Il **versante** italiano del Monte Bianco. 1: Storia alpinistica / F. Mondini. Torino, 1902. Ill. Pp.177-208 of the *Bollettino del Club Alpino Italiano*, vol.35 no.68.
GB.1880(52[2]) (impf.).   v121.

Verslag van den vijfden tocht van de *Willem Barents* naar de noordelijke ijszee in den zomer van 1882 / uitgebracht aan het bestuur der Vereeniging Willem Barents. Haarlem, 1883. Ill., map.
GB/A.2050.   v122.

Verso il Trentino / Ubaldo Valbusa. Torino, [ca 1920]. Ill.
GB/B.403(5).   v123.

Verso l'alto / Dougal Haston; traduzione e introduzione di Luciano Serra. [Milan], 1978. Ill. [Exploits.] Translated from *In high places*.
GB/A.1967(5).   v124.

Versuch einer Beschreibung des Bodensee's / Georg Leonhard Hartmann. 2. sehr verm. und verb. Aufl. St. Gallen, 1808.
GB/A.943.   v125.

Versuch einer critischen Verzeichnisz aller Schriften welche die Schweiz ansehen / Gottlieb Emanuel von Haller. Bern, 1759-70. 6v (in 5).
GB/A.1101-5.   v126.

Versuch einer historischen und physischen Beschreibung der helvetischen Eisbergen / Johann Georg Altmann. Zürich, 1751. Ill.
GB/A.151.   v127.

Versuch schweizerischer Gedichte / Albrecht von Haller. 3. verm. und veränd. Aufl. Danzig, 1743.
GB/A.651.   v128.

Versuch schweizerischer Gedichte / Albrecht von Haller. 11. verm. und verb. Aufl. Bern, 1777. Ill., port.
GB/A.2030.   v129.

Vertigine: romanzo / Stanislas de Saint Loup; traduzione di Ettore Cozzani. Milano, 1950. [Montagna; 28.] Translated from *Face nord*.
GB/A.553.   v130.

Vertikali / [sostavitel': V.A. Presnova]. Leningrad, 1979. Ill., ports.
GB/A.1676(1).   v131.

Vertrauliche Erzählung einer Schweizerreise im Jahr 1786 in Briefen / Ploucquet. Tübingen, 1787.
GB/A.581.   v132.

The **very** thought of Thee: the adventures of an Arctic missionary / Bernice Bangs Morgan. Grand Rapids, 1952. Ill., ports.
GB/A.1779.   v133.

Verzeichnis der Clubhütten des S.A.C.: Stand Ende Februar 1952 / zusammengestellt und herausgegeben vom Central-Comité Glarus. Kriens, 1952. Ill., map.
GB/A.2021(9).   v134.

Vesuvius in fury: causes and characteristics of the great eruption of April, 1906 / William P. Andrews. [New York, ca 1906]. Ill. From the *Century Magazine*.
GB.1341(12).   v135.

Vette: ricordi di esplorazioni e nuove ascensioni sulle Alpi, nei gruppi del Monte Rosa, del Cervino e del Monte Bianco dal 1896-1921 / G.F. e G.B. Gugliermina, Giuseppe Lampugnani. Ivrea, 1927. Ill. Published by the Club Alpino Italiano, Sezione di Varallo.
GB.1279.   v136.

Le **vette** solitarie: leggende delle Dolomiti di Brenta / Elena Tessadri. Torino, 1960. Ill.
GB/A.491.   v137.

La **Via** delle Bocchette / Giovanni Strobele. Rovereto-Bolzano, 1968. Ill., map.
GB/A.1050(1).   v138.

Viaggi nell'Appennino modenese e reggiano / Lazzaro Spallanzani; a cura di Pericle Di Pietro. Bologna, 1985.
GB/A.2195.   v139.

Viaggiatori inglesi in valle d'Aosta (1800-1860) / a cura di Piero Malvezzi. Milano, 1972. Ill. [Saggi di cultura contemporanea; 100.]
GB/A.970.   v140.

Viaggio ai monti di Parma (1804) / Antonio Boccia. [Parma], 1970. Ill. [Quaderni parmigiani; 2.]
GB/A.1048.   v141.

Viaggio del beato Odorico da Pardenone / a cura di Giorgio Pulle. Milano, 1931. Ill., maps. [Viaggi e scoperte di navigatori ed esploratori italiani; 17.]
GB/A.1974(7).   v142.

Viaggio di esplorazioni nei monti del Karakoram / conferenza letta da Luigi Amadeo di Savoia, duca degli Abruzzi, in Torino il 16 febbraio 1910. Torino, 1910. Ill., maps. Published by the Club Alpino Italiano.
GB/B.289(4).   v143.

Viaggio in Savoia, ossia Descrizione degli stati oltramontani di S.M. il re di Sardegna / Davide Bertolotti. Livorno, 1828. 2v.
GB/A.835(13-4); GB/A.516(2) (wanting v.2).
                                                     v144.

Vicenza illustrata: illustrierter Führer. Vicenza, [1902]. Ill.
GB/A.1034(5).   v145.

Victoire sur l'Everest / Sir John Hunt; traduit de l'anglais par Bernard Pierre. Paris, 1953. Ill., map, ports. [Bibliothèque de l'alpinisme.] Translated from *The ascent of Everest*.
Lloyd.1620(28).   v146.

Victoires au Cervin / Giuseppe Mazzotti; traduit par E. Gaillard. Nouv. éd. Neuchâtel, 1951. Ill. Translated from *Grandi imprese sul Cervino*.
GB/A.1406.   v147.

Victor-Emmanuel sur les Alpes: notices et souvenirs / Amato Gorret. 2e éd. rev. et augm. Turin, 1879. Ill., map.
GB.58.   v148.

The **Victorian** mountaineers / Ronald Clark. London, 1953. Ill., ports.
GB.766.   v149.

Viddenes folk: Samedikt / Carl Schøyen. Oslo, 1937.
GB/A.1849.   v150.

Vie attrezzate sulle Dolomiti / Hilde Frass; traduzione di Willy Dondio. Bologna, 1972. Ill., maps. [Itinerari alpini; 9.] Translated from *Die schönsten Klettersteige der Dolomiten*.
GB/A.942(16).   v151.

Le **vie** della sete: esplorazioni sahariane / Ardito Desio. Milano, 1950. Ill.
GB/B.252(2).   v152.

Le **vie** delle Alpi occidentali negli antichi tempi: ricerche e studi pubblicati su documenti inediti / Luigi Vaccarone. Bologna, 1970. Facsimile reprint of the Turin, 1884 ed.
GB/C.22(18).   v153.

Vie di ghiaccio in Dolomiti: guida alle più belle ascensioni su ghiaccio e misto nell'area dolomitica / Eugenio Cipriani. Bologna, [1986]. Ill., maps. [Itinerari alpini; 63.]
GB/A.1589(40).   v154.

Die **Viertausender** der Alpen / Carl Blodig. München, 1923. Ill.
GB.1118.   v155.

Die **Viertausender** der Alpen / Carl Blodig. 3. Aufl. München, [1928]. Ill.
GB.1119; GB.1120 (impf.).   v156.

Der **Vierwaldstättersee** / S. Blumer. [N.p., 1905?] Ill. Pp.228-39 of an unidentified work.
GB/A.1052(6).   v157.

Vierwaldstättersee. Lac des Quatre Cantons. Lucerne and the lake. Kilchberg, [ca 1930]. Ill.
GB/B.366(12).   v158.

Vierzig Jahre Sektion Halle des Deutschen und Osterreichischen Alpenvereins: Festschrift zum 14. Mai 1926. Halle a.d.S., [1926]. Ill., maps.
GB/B.127.   v159.

A **view** of society and manners in France, Switzerland and Germany / by a gentleman who resided several years in those countries [i.e. John Moore]. London, 1779. 2v.
GB.855-6; Lloyd.779-80.   v160.

A **view** of society and manners in France, Switzerland, and Germany / by a gentleman who resided several years in those countries [i.e. John Moore]. 2nd ed. corr. London, 1779. 2v.
Lloyd.781-2.   v161.

Views in India, chiefly among the Himalaya mountains / George Francis White; edited by Emma Roberts. London, 1838.
GB.1292.   v162.

Views in India, Himalaya mountains, taken during tours in the direction of Mussooree, Simla, the sources of the Jumna and Ganges, &c. &c., in 1829-31-32 / George Francis White. Delhi, 1985. 2v; ill. Facsimile reprint of the London, 1836-37 ed.
GB/B.647.   v163.

Views in Italy, during a journey in the years 1815 and 1816 / Herman Friedlander. London, 1821. Ill. GB/A.1370. v164.

Views in Switzerland drawn from nature / C. Bourgeois. London, 1822. Ill. GB/C.26. v165.

Views in the High Alps / Vittorio Sella. [N.p., n.d.] Ill. Lloyd.1563. v166.

Views in the Himalayas, drawn on the spot / Mrs W.L.L. Scott. London, 1852. Ill. GB/C.108. v167.

Views in the Tyrol / from drawings by Thomas Allom. London, [1836]. Ill. Lloyd.1400. v168.

[**Views** of Switzerland, Italy and France.] [N.p., n.d.] Ill. Lloyd.914. v169.

Views of the far famed Blue Mountains, N.S.W. [N.p., ca 1915.] Ill., ports. GB/B.501(13). v170.

Views to illustrate the route of Mont Cenis / drawn from nature, by Major Cockburn. London, 1822. Ill. Lloyd.1546. v171.

Views to illustrate the route of the Simplon / drawn from nature, by Major Cockburn. London, 1822. Ill. Lloyd.1545. v172.

Le **Vignemale** / Michel Marchal. 2e éd. [N.p.], 1973. Ill. GB/B.570(10). v173.

Vignettes: Alpine and eastern / Elijah Walton; the descriptive text by T.G. Bonney. Alpine series. London, 1873. Lloyd.1521. v174.

Vignettes: Alpine and eastern / Elijah Walton; the descriptive text by T.G. Bonney. Alpine series. 4th ed. London, 1882. Lloyd.1522. v175.

Vigolana e altopiano di Folgaria / Armando Scandellari. Bologna, 1986. [Itinerari alpini; 61.] GB/A.1589(37). v176.

Village life in Switzerland / Sophia Duberly Delmard. London, 1865. Lloyd.661. v177.

Les **vins**, la cuisine et les tavernes du Mont Blanc / Sergio Canavese; ont collaboré pour le texte et les graphiques: Paolo Grasso; pour la version française: Lucienne Faletto Landi. [Aosta, 1973.] Ill. GB/A.1281(7). v178.

Violanta Prevosti: geschichtlicher Roman / Silvia Andrea. Frauenfeld, 1905. GB/A.1149. v179.

The **violated** vision: the rape of Canada's North / James Woodford. Toronto, 1972. GB/A.1761. v180.

Visit of Canadian teachers to Italy, together with Gibraltar and Toulon, July 21st-August 9th, 1928: programme. London, [1928]. Published by the Overseas Education League. GB.1319(5). v181.

A **visit** to the Grande Chartreuse / Elisabeth Lecky. [N.p., 1891.] Pp.405-14 of *Nineteenth Century*, March 1891. GB/A.797(8). v182.

A **visit** to the summit of Mont Blanc, 25th, 26th, and 27th of August, 1825: in letters addressed to a friend / Markham Sherwill. [London, 1825-26.] From the *New Monthly Magazine*, vol.16, 1825-26. GB.623(3-5). v183.

Visitors' books / Elsie Thornton Cook. [N.p., ca 1890.] Pp.[334]-40 of *Good Words*. GB/A.797(5). v184.

Die **Visperthäler**, der Saasgrat und der Monte Rosa / Melchior Ulrich; vorgetragen den 22. Januar 1849. [Zurich, 1849.] Pp.291-321 of *Mittheilungen der Naturforschenden Gesellschaft in Zürich*, 1848. Lloyd.1602(8). v185.

Vittorio Sigismondi / D.A. Cojazzi. Torino, 1936. [Cristiani laici moderni; 5.] GB/A.515(4). v186.

Vitus Bering: the discoverer of Bering Strait / Peter Lauridsen; revised by the author and translated by Julius E. Olsen. Chicago, 1889. Maps. Translated from *Vitus J. Bering og de russiske opdagelsesrejser*. GB/A.1942. v187.

Vivere nelle Alpi / fotografie di Pepi Merisio; testi di Gino Carrara. Bologna, 1979. Ill.
GB/A.1901.   v188.

Vizille et le bassin inférieur de la Romanche: essai de monographie géographique / A. Allix. Grenoble, 1917.
GB/A.97.   v189.

Vocabolario bormino / Glicerio Longa; edizione a cura della Associazione Glicerio Longa. Tirano, 1975. Port. Facsimile reprint of the Perugia, 1913 ed.
GB/A.1966(4).   v190.

Vocation alpine: souvenirs d'un guide de montagne / Armand Charlet. Neuchâtel, 1949. Ill.
GB.1309(6).   v191.

La **voce** delle altezze / Armando Biancardi. [Rocca San Casciano, 1956.] Ill. [Le Alpi; 24.]
GB/A.841.   v192.

Voiage historique et politique de Suisse, d'Italie et d'Allemagne. Francfort, 1736-43. 3v; ill. With a dedication subscribed D********.
GB/A.742-4.   v193.

A **voice** from the Alps, or the Vaudois valleys: with scenes by the way of lands and lakes historically associated / Joseph Denham Smith. Dublin, 1854.
Lloyd.282.   v194.

The **voice** of the mountains / edited by Ernest A. Baker and Francis E. Ross. London, [1905]. [Wayfaring books.]
Lloyd.155.   v195.

Voir la montagne / Edmond Pidoux. [Lausanne], 1970. [Vie intérieure.]
GB/B.313(4).   v196.

Vollständiges Handbuch für Reisende durch die gesammte Schweiz / Adolph von Schaden. München, 1834. Ill., map.
GB/A.986.   v197.

[A **volume** of charts, maps, and plates illustrating Captain Cook's voyages.] London, [n.d.].
GB.1304 (impf.).   v198.

Vom Col de Collon bis zum Theodulpass / Heinrich Dübi. Zürich, 1921. Ill. [Clubführer durch die Walliseralpen; 2.] Published by the Schweizer Alpenclub.
GB.122.   v199.

Vom Engadin zum Comersee: Berge — Strassen — Pässe — Seen / Walther Flaig. 3. Aufl. Wien, [1955]. Ill. [Europas Ferienstrassen; 2.]
GB/A.180.   v200.

Vom Theodulpass bis zum Schwarzenberg-Weisstor. Vom Strahlhorn bis zum Simplon / H. Dübi. St. Gallen, 1916. 2v. [Clubführer durch die Walliseralpen; 3 a-b.] Published by the Schweizer Alpenclub.
GB.123-4; Lloyd.196,129.   v201.

Von Bergen, Sonnen- und Nebelländern: Erlebnisse in europäischen und aussereuropäischen Hochgebirgen / Carl Diener. München, 1929. Port. [Grosse Bergsteiger.]
GB/A.441.   v202.

Von Hütte zu Hütte: 100 alpine Höhenwege und Übergänge / Walter Pause. 12. durchgesehene Aufl. München, 1969. Ill.
GB/B.247.   v203.

Von Hütte zu Hütte: Führer zu den Schutzhütten der deutschen und österreichischen Alpen / herausgegeben von Josef Moriggl; unter Mitwirkung der Sektionen des Deutschen u. Osterreichischen Alpenvereins und der übringen hüttensbesitzenden Vereine. Leipzig, 1911-13. 4v; ill., maps.
GB/A.1411-4.   v204.

Von Jugendwandern und Bergsteigertum: eine Geschichte des bayerischen Jugendherbergeswerkes / Ernst Enzensperger. [Munich, 1951?] Ill., port.
GB/A.615.   v205.

Von Macugnaga über die Dufourspitze nach Zermatt / Ludwig Becker. [Bern, 1904.] Ill. Pp.[63]-81 of the *Jahrbuch des Schweizer Alpenclub*, Jahrg.39.
GB.1881(79).   v206.

Von Menschen, Bergen und andern Dingen / Josef Ittlinger. München, 1922.
GB/A.51.   v207.

Von Spitzbergen zur Sahara: Stationen eines Naturforschers in Spitzbergen, Lappland, Schottland und Algerien / Charles Martins; autorisirte und unter Mitwirkung des Verfassers übertragene Ausgabe für Deutschland; aus dem Französischen von A. Bartels. 2. Aufl. Jena, 1872. Ill. Translated from *Du Spitzberg au Sahara*.
GB/A.527.   v208.

Vor den Toren des Himmels: von den Alpen zur Annapurna / Lionel Terray; übertragen und mit einem Nachwort von Herbert Stifter. 2. Aufl. München, [1965]. Ill., maps. Translated from *Les conquérants de l'inutile*.
GB/A.450.   v209.

Vorstellung der vornemsten Gletscher und Eisbergen in der Schweiz, oder Der Alp-Topographie / David Herrliberger. Abschnitt 1. Chur, 1774. Ill.
GB.676.   v210.

Les **Vosges** / Gustave Fraipont. Paris, [1895]. Ill., map. [Les montagnes de France.]
GB/B.251.   v211.

Voyage à Geneve et dans la vallée de Chamouni, en Savoie / P.X. Leschevin. Paris, 1812. Port.
GB.1316(15); Lloyd.636; Lloyd.1603(8).   v212.

Voyage à la Val-Sainte de Notre-Dame de la Trappe, dans le canton de Fribourg, en Suisse, peu de temps avant que sa Majesté l'empereur et roi Napoléon ordonnât la dissolution de ce monastère / George Tarenne. Paris, 1812.
Lloyd.675.   v213.

Voyage à Lucerne et dans la Suisse orientale / Henry de Lalaubie. Paris, 1866.
GB/A.1018.   v214.

Un **voyage** au cercle polaire / Léonie Ferland. Montréal, [ca 1940].
GB/A.1675(7).   v215.

Un **voyage** au Giétroz, vallée de Bagnes, Valais, Suisse, en 1863 / Eugène Besse. Sion, 1864.
Lloyd.1574(2).   v216.

Voyage au Mont-Blanc / René de Chateaubriand. Nouv. éd. suivie d'une étude sur Chateaubriand et la montagne, par Gabriel Faure. Grenoble, 1920.
GB/A.1115(5).   v217.

Voyage autour du Mont Blanc dans les vallées d'Hérens, de Zermatt et au Grimsel: autographie / R.T. [i.e. Rodolphe Töpffer]. [N.p.], 1843.
GB.639.   v218.

Voyage aux mers polaires à la recherche de Sir John Franklin / J.R. Bellot. Nouv. éd. Paris, 1880.
GB/A.2092.   v219.

Voyage d'Italie / Maximilien Misson. Ed. augm. Amsterdam, 1743. 4v; ill.
GB/A.563-6.   v220.

Voyage d'un amateur des arts, en Flandre, dans les Pays-Bas, en Hollande, en France, en Savoye, en Italie, en Suisse, fait dans les années 1775-76-77-78 / par M. de La R*** [i.e. Roche]. Amsterdam, 1783. 4v.
GB/A.658-61.   v221.

Voyage d'un artiste en Suisse à 3 francs 50 par jour / Adolphe Desbarrolles. 3e éd. Paris, 1865. [Bibliothèque contemporaine.]
GB/A.799(11).   v222.

Voyage d'un convalescent dans le département du Simplon / Chrétien Des-Loges. [N.p.], 1813.
GB/A.799(4).   v223.

Voyage d'une Française en Suisse et en Franche-Comté depuis la Révolution / [Mme de Gauthier]. En Suisse, 1790. 2v.
GB/A.1314-5; GB/A.690-1.   v224.

Voyage dans l'Oberland bernois / J.R. Wyss; traduit par H. d. C. Berne, 1816-17. 3v; ill., maps. Translated from *Reise in das Berner Oberland*.
GB.476-8; Lloyd.743-5; Lloyd.746-8; Lloyd.748A (v.3 only).   v225.

Voyage dans l'Oberland et les petits cantons / rédigé par les élèves du pensionnat Janin. Genève, 1843.
GB/B.289(19).   v226.

Voyage dans la Suisse d'autrefois / Saint-Georges de Bouhélier. 6e éd. [Avignon, 1940.] [Les grands contemporains.]
GB/A.834.   v227.

Voyage dans la Suisse française et le Chablais / Alfred de Bougy. Les lacs de Genève, de Neuchâtel, de Bienne et de Morat: opuscules posthumes de J.J. Rousseau et lettres inédites de Madame de Warens. Paris, 1860. Map.
GB/A.46.   v228.

Voyage dans la Vendée et dans le Midi de la France, suivi d'un voyage pittoresque en Suisse / Eugène Genoud. Paris, 1821.
GB/A.805(6).   v229.

Voyage dans le Milanais à Plaissance, Parme, Modène, Mantoue, Crémone, et dans plusieurs autres villes de l'ancienne Lombardie / A.L. Millin. Paris, 1817. 2v.
Lloyd.710-1.   v230.

Voyage dans les petits cantons et dans les Alpes rhétiennes / Karl Kasthofer; traduit de l'allemand

par E.J. Fazy-Cazal. Genève, 1827.
GB/A.642.   v232.

Voyage dans les XIII cantons suisses, les Grisons, le Vallais, et autres pays et états alliés, ou sujets des Suisses / M. Robert. Paris, 1789. 2v.
GB.1308(1-2).   v233.

Voyage de deux artistes en Suisse; précédé d'une notice historique sur les révolutions de l'Helvétie / H. de Spinola. Limoges, 1838. Ill.
GB/A.653.   v234.

Voyage de Saussure hors des Alpes / Charles Gos. Neuchâtel, [1935]. Ill., port.
GB.1323(11).   v235.

Voyage de Suisse, d'Italie, et de quelques endroits d'Allemagne & de France, fait és années 1885 [or rather 1685], & 1686: avec des remarques d'une personne de qualité, touchant la Suisse & l'Italie / Gilbert Burnet. Dernière éd. rev., corr. & augm. Rotterdam, 1690. Translated from *Some letters*.
GB.415.   v236.

Voyage en Dauphiné, Savoie et Suisse: voyages et excursions par la photographie / J. Trousset. Paris, [ca 1890]. Ill.
GB/A.58.   v237.

Voyage en Savoie, en Piémont, à Nice, et à Gènes / A.L. Millin. Paris, 1816. 2v.
GB.542-3; Lloyd.668-9.   v238.

Voyage en Savoie et dans le Midi de la France en 1084 [or rather, 1804] et 1805 / A.L. Millin. Paris, 1807.
Lloyd.670.   v239.

Voyage en Suisse / William Coxe; [translated by Michael P. Mandar]. Lausanne, 1790. 3v. Translated from *Travels in Switzerland*.
GB.41-3.   v240.

Voyage en Suisse / Xavier Marmier. Paris, 1862. Ill.
GB/B.276.   v241.

Voyage en Suisse: notes humoristiques au jour le jour / Gallicus [i.e. Xavier Lançon]. Lyon, 1866.
GB/A.800(8).   v242.

Voyage en Suisse en 1777 / E. Rott. Neuchâtel, 1910. Extrait du *Musée neuchâtelois*, mars-avril et mai-juin 1910.
GB/B.288(13).   v243.

Un **voyage** en Suisse en 1819 / Rosalie de Constant; présenté et annoté par Mary Colville et Alice Daulte. Lausanne, 1964. Ill.
GB/A.22.   v244.

Un **voyage** en Suisse en 1849 du peintre Guérard et de ses amis d'après un manuscrit de l'époque / comte Antoine Scitivaux de Greische. Toulouse, 1933. Ill.
GB/B.269.   v245.

Voyage en Suisse, en Lombardie et en Piémont, suivi du tableau résumé des événemens de la Suisse depuis 1830, et d'un itinéraire / comte Théobald Walsh. Paris, 1834. 2v; ill.
Lloyd.848-9.   v246.

Voyage en Suisse, en Lombardie et en Piémont / comte Théobald Walsh. Bruxelles, 1835. 2v (in 1).
Lloyd.175.   v247.

Voyage en Suisse et ascension du Mont Rose, 1860 / F.Th. [i.e. F. Thioly]. [N.p., 1860?]
Lloyd.936.   v248.

Voyage en Suisse, fait dans les années 1817, 1818 et 1819: suivi d'un essai historique sur les moeurs et les coutumes de l'Helvétie ancienne et moderne / Louis Simond. Paris, 1822. 2v; ill.
GB.467-8; GB.551-2.   v249.

Voyage épisodique et anecdotique dans les Alpes / par un Parisien. Paris, 1830.
GB.383.   v250.

Voyage épisodique et pittoresque aux glaciers des Alpes / François Vernes. 2. éd. Paris, 1808.
Lloyd.1617(21).   v251.

Voyage historique et littéraire dans la Suisse occidentale / [Jean R. Sinner]. [Neuchâtel? 1781.] 2v.
Lloyd.771-2.   v252.

Voyage historique et littéraire dans la Suisse occidentale / [Jean R. Sinner]. Nouv. éd. augm. [Neuchâtel?], 1787. 2v.
GB/A.694-5.   v253.

A **voyage** of discovery towards the North Pole, performed in His Majesty's Ships *Dorothea* and *Trent*, under the command of Captain David Buchan, R.N., 1818; to which is added, a summary of all the early attempts to reach the Pacific by way of the Pole / F.W. Beechey. London, 1843. Ill.
GB.846.   v254.

The **voyage** of the *Fox* in the Arctic Seas: a narrative of the discovery of the fate of Sir John Franklin and his companions / F.L. MacClintock. London, 1859. Ill., maps, facsim.
GB.749; GB.964.   v255.

The **voyage** of the schooner *Polar Bear*: whaling and trading in the North Pacific and Arctic, 1913-1914 / Bernard Kilian; with an appendix by Dunbar Lockwood; edited by John Bockstoce. New Bedford, Mass., [1983]. Ill., maps.
GB/B.619.   v256.

The **voyage** of the *Vega* round Asia and Europe / A.E. Nordenskiöld; translated by Alexander Leslie. London, 1881. 2v; ill., maps, ports.
GB.1055-6.   v257.

Voyage pitoresque aux glacières de Savoye, fait en 1772 / par Mr. B. [i.e. A.C. Bordier]. Genève, 1773.
GB.53; GB.263; Lloyd.159; Lloyd.159A.   v258.

Voyage pittoresque à la Grande Chartreuse: suivi de quelques vues prises dans les environs de ce monastère / Constant Bourgeois. Paris, 1821.
Lloyd.1566(1).   v259.

Voyage pittoresque au cap Nord / A.F. Skjöldebrand. Stockholm, 1801-02. 4v (in 1); ill., maps.
GB/C.98.   v260.

Voyage pittoresque au lac de Genève ou Léman. Genève, 1978. Ill. Facsimile reprint of the Zurich, 1820 ed.
GB/C.84.   v261.

Voyage pittoresque au lac des Waldstettes ou des IV cantons. Genève, 1978. Ill. Facsimile reprint of the Zurich, 1820 ed.
GB/C.86.   v262.

Voyage pittoresque aux Alpes norwegiennes / V.M. Carpelan. Stockholm, 1821-23. 2v; ill.
GB/C.16-7.   v263.

Voyage pittoresque aux lacs de Zurich, Zoug, Lowerz, Egeri et Wallenstadt. Genève, 1978. Ill. Facsimile reprint of the Zurich, 1819 ed.
GB/C.85.   v264.

Voyage pittoresque dans la vallée de Chamouni et autour du Mont-Blanc / Désiré Raoul-Rochette. Paris, 1826.
Lloyd.1487.   v265.

Voyage pittoresque dans le canton des Grisons vers le Lac Majeur et le lac de Come à travers les cols de Splugen et de St. Bernardin / J.G. Ebel. Zurich, 1827. Ill., map.
Lloyd.961; Lloyd.1607(1).   v266.

Voyage pittoresque dans le Tyrol, aux salines de Salzbourg et de Reichenhall, et dans une partie de la Bavière / M. le comte de B*** [i.e. F.G. de Bray]. 3e éd. rev. & augm. Paris, 1825. Ill.
GB/C.43.   v267.

Voyage pittoresque en Suisse en Savoie et sur les Alpes / Emile Bégin. Paris, 1852. Ill.
GB.1234.   v268.

Voyage pittoresque en Suisse et en Italie / Jacques de Cambry. Paris, [1801]. 2v.
GB/A.643-4.   v269.

Voyage sur le Mont-Blanc entrepris le 15 septembre 1816 / comte de Lusi. Vienne, 1816.
Lloyd.1615(1).   v270.

Voyage to the Pacific Ocean in 1793 / Alexander Mackenzie; historical introduction and footnotes by Milo Milton Quaife. New York, 1967. Originally published as *Voyages from Montreal*.
GB/A.1890.   v271.

A **voyage** to the Pacific Ocean: undertaken for making discoveries in the Northern hemisphere: to determine the position and extent of the west side of North America: its distance from Asia: and the practicability of a northern passage to Europe. Vol.1-2 / James Cook; vol.3 / James King; [edited by John Douglas]; with additions from the journal of William Anderson]. London, 1784. 3v; ill., maps, ports.
GB.1265-7.   v272.

Voyages au Mont-Perdu et dans la partie adjacente des Hautes-Pyrénées / L. Ramond. Paris, 1801. Ill.
GB/A.59.   v273.

Voyages aux Alpes et en Italie / Albert Montémont. 2e éd., rev., corr. et considérablement augm. Paris, 1827. 3v; ill., map.
GB/A.935-7.   v274.

Voyages dans les Alpes: partie pittoresque des ouvrages de H.B. de Saussure. 2e éd., augmentée des voyages en Valais, au Mont-Cervin et autour du Mont-Rose. Paris, 1852.
GB.224.   v275.

Voyages dans les Alpes: partie pittoresque des ouvrages de H.B. de Saussure. 3e éd., augmentée

des voyages en Valais, au Mont-Cervin et autour du Mont-Rose. Paris, 1855.
GB.287; Lloyd.297.   v276.

Voyages dans les Alpes, précédés d'un essai sur l'histoire naturelle des environs de Genève / Horace Bénédict de Saussure. Neuchâtel, 1779-96. 4v; ill., maps.
GB.1201-4; Lloyd.1386-9.   v276.1.

Voyages dans les Alpes, précédés d'un essai sur l'histoire naturelle des environs de Genève / [Horace Bénédict de Saussure]. Genève, 1786-87. 8v; ill., maps.
GB.590-3 (wanting v.5-8).   v277.

Voyages de Guibert, dans diverses parties de la France et en Suisse, faits en 1775, 1778, 1784 et 1785: ouvrage posthume / publié par sa veuve [i.e. Louise A. de Guibert]. Paris, 1806.
GB.495.   v278.

Voyages en Amérique, en Italie, au Mont-Blanc: mélanges littéraires / René de Chateaubriand. Nouv. éd. rev. Paris, 1860. Ill.
Lloyd.1266.   v279.

Voyages en différens pays de l'Europe, en 1774 et 1776, ou Lettres écrites de l'Allemagne, de la Suisse, de l'Italie, de Sicile, & de Paris / [Carlo Antonio Pilati di Tassulo]. En Suisse, 1778. 2v.
GB/A.688-9.   v280.

Voyages en Suisse: description des curiosités naturelles, détails sur les moeurs et coutûmes, sur la division politique de chaque canton / Clara Filleul de Pétigny. Limoges, 1851. Ill. [Librairie des bons livres.]
GB/A.1402.   v281.

Voyages en Suisse 1643 et 1646 / Elias Bracken-hoffer; traduit par Henry Lehr. Lausanne, 1930. Port., facsim.
GB/A.804(1).   v282.

Voyages en zigzag, ou Excursions d'un pension-nat en vacances dans les cantons suisses et sur le revers italien des Alpes / Rodolphe Töpffer. Paris, 1844.
Lloyd.1392.   v283.

Voyages en zigzag, ou Excursions d'un pension-nat en vacances dans les cantons suisses et sur le revers italien des Alpes / Rodolphe Töpffer. 2e éd. Paris, 1846. Ill.
GB.1243.   v284.

Voyages et découvertes faites par les Russes le long des côtes de la mer glaciale & sur l'Océan oriental, tant vers le Japon que vers l'Amérique: on y a joint l'histoire du fleuve Amur et des pays adjacens depuis la conquête des Russes / ouvrage traduit de l'allemand de Mr. G.P. Müller [i.e. Gerhard F. Müller], par C.G.F. Dumas. Amsterdam, 1766. 2v. Translated from *Sammlung russischer Geschichte*, Bd.3.
GB/A.2199.   v285.

Voyages from Asia to America / Gerhard F. Müller. Amsterdam, 1967. Maps. [Bibliotheca Australiana; 26.] Facsimile reprint of the London, 1761 ed.
GB/A.1863.   v286.

Voyages from Asia to America, for completing the discoveries of the north west coast of America: to which is prefixed, A summary of the voyages made by the Rusians [sic] on the frozen sea, in search of the North East Passage / translated from the High Dutch of S. Muller [i.e. Gerhard F. Müller]. 2nd ed. London, 1764. Maps.
GB/A.1687.   v287.

Voyages, travels and remarkable adventures: principally in Europe / Paul Preston. London, [1843?]. Ill.
GB.14.   v288.

Voyages, travels, and remarkable adventures: principally in Europe / Paul Preston. 2nd ed. London, [1843?]. Ill.
Lloyd.38.   v289.

Un **voyageur** des pays d'en haut / G. Ducas. Montréal, 1824. Ill.
GB/B.528(7).   v290.

Vraye description de trois voyages de mer très admirables / Girard Le Ver. Amsterdam, 1598. Ill., map. Translated from *Waerachtige beschryvinghe van drie seylagien*.
GB/B.644.   v291.

Vue de la source de l'Arveron. [N.p., ca 1780.] A hand-coloured engraving.
GB/C.106.   v292.

Vue de la vallée de Chamouny prise près d'Argentière. [N.p., ca 1780.] A hand-coloured engraving.
GB/C.107.   v293.

Vue des Alpes prise au-dessus du Weissenstein près Soleure / X. Amiet. [Solothurn, ca 1888.] A folding lithograph.
GB/A.1085.   v294.

Vue des Alpes prise au-dessus du Weissenstein près Soleure / X. Amiet. [Solothurn, ca 1888.] A folding lithograph; a different view from that at v294.
GB/A.1050(12).   v295.

Vue prise du Couvercle / G. Lory. Paris, [1826]. From *Voyage pittoresque dans la vallée de Chamouni et autour du Mt-Blanc*.
GB.1334(10).   v296.

Vues de Suisse: Giessbach et Brienz / dessinés d'après nature et lithographiés par J. Jacottet. Vévey, [ca 1850].
GB/A.1209.   v297.

Vues remarquables des montagnes de la Suisse. Amsterdam, 1785. Ill.
GB/C.23.   v298.

Vulcani e tettonica: dal vulcanismo alla deriva dei continenti / Haroun Tazieff; [traduzione di Nevia Ricci Lucchi]. Bologna, 1979. Ill. [Biblioteca di monografie scientifiche; 41.] Translated from *Les volcans*.
GB/A.1965(4).   v299.

Vulkaner i det nordöstlige Island / Th. Thoroddsen. Stockholm, 1888. Ill. [Bihang till K. Svenska vet.-akad. handlingar; bd.4 afd.2 no.5.]
GB/B.635(10).   v300.

-W-

W. Cecil Slingsby: from *The hills of peace* / Lawrence Pilkington. [Leeds, 1932.] P.144 of the *Yorkshire Ramblers' Club Journal*, vol.6 no.20.
GB.1881(24).   w001.

W.A.B. Coolidge, 1850-1926 / René Godefroy. Lyon, 1926. Ports. Pp.[129]-43 of the *Revue alpine*, vol.27 no.3.
GB.1881(38[1]).   w002.

Die Wädensweil-Einsiedeln-Bahn / J. J. Binder. Zürich, [1895?]. [Swiss scenes.]
GB/A.1817(3).   w003.

Waifs and strays, or The pilgrimage of a Bohemian abroad / Lady Florence Dixie. London, [1884].
Lloyd.1616(15).   w004.

The Waldenses, or Protestant valleys of Piedmont, Dauphiny and the Ban de la Roche / William Beattie; illustrated by W.H. Bartlett and W. Brockedon. London, 1838. Ill., map, port.
Lloyd.1429.   w005.

Waldensian researches during a second visit to the Vaudois of Piemont / William Stephen Gilly. London, 1831.
Lloyd.1192.   w006.

Das Walenseetal: Exkursionsbericht / Arnold Albert Heim. [N.p., 1907.] Ill. Sonderabdruck aus dem Bericht über die 40. Versammlung des Oberrheinischen Geologischen Vereins zu Lindau 1907.
GB/A.1052(5).   w007.

A walk in the Grisons, being a third month in Switzerland / F. Barham Zincke. London, 1875.
Lloyd.389.   w007.1.

A walk in the sky: climbing Hidden Peak / Nicholas Clinch. Seattle, 1982. Ill.
GB/A.2067.   w008.

A walk round Mont Blanc / Francis Trench. London, 1847.
GB.445; Lloyd.705; Lloyd.705A,B,C.   w009.

A walk through Switzerland in September 1816. London, 1818. Map. Attributed to Thomas Hookham.
GB.146; Lloyd.215.   w010.

Walking in the Alps / J. Hubert Walker. [Edinburgh, 1951.] A prospectus.
GB.1329(34). w011.

Walking softly in the wilderness: the Sierra Club guide to backpacking / John Hart. [2nd ed.] completely rev. and updated. San Francisco, 1984. Ill., maps.
GB/A.2165(13). w012.

Walks and climbs in the Zillerthal / Lionel W. Clarke. [London, 1897.] Pp.[62]-73 of the *Badminton Magazine*, vol.5 no.24.
GB.1880(1). w013.

Walks and excursions in the valley of Grindelwald / W.A.B. Coolidge. Grindelwald, 1900. Ill., map.
Lloyd.343; Lloyd.343A. w014.

Wall and roof climbing / by the author of *The roof-climbers guide to Trinity* [i.e. Geoffrey Winthrop Young]. [London], 1905.
Lloyd.1624(2). w015.

Walser: gli uomini della montagna. Walser: die Besiedler des Gebirges / Enrico Rizzi; traduzione in tedesco di Elena Wetzel e Marco Bauen. [Milan?], 1981. Ill., maps.
GB/B.554. w016.

Walter Leaf, 1852-1927: some chapters of autobiography / with a memoir by Charlotte M. Leaf. London, 1932. Ill., ports.
GB.763. w017.

Die **Wand**: Tagebuch eines jungen Bergsteigers / Erika Jemelin. Zürich, [1936].
GB.337. w018.

Wander-, Kletter- und Ski-Touren-Führer durch die zentralschweizerischen Voralpen / für die Sektion Pilatus des Schweizer Alpen-Club bearbeitet von Oscar Allgäuer. Bd.2: Die Voralpen zwischen Vierwaldstättersee und Brünigpass (Unterwaldner Voralpen). Luzern, 1930.
GB/A.1570. w019.

Wanderbuch des Unterbarmer Alpen-Clubs: 1901-1905. Barmen, 1906.
GB/A.475. w020.

The *Wanderer*, of Liverpool / John Masefield. London, 1930. Ill., ports.
GB.1209. w021.

The **wanderer** of Switzerland, and other poems / James Montgomery. 7th ed. Edinburgh, 1815.
GB.112; Lloyd.170. w022.

The **wanderer** of Switzerland, and other poems / James Montgomery. 11th ed. London, 1832.
Lloyd.393. w023.

Wanderings among the High Alps / Alfred Wills. London, 1856. Ill.
GB.466; Lloyd.537; Lloyd.695; Lloyd.695A,B,C,D. w024.

Wanderings among the High Alps / Alfred Wills. 2nd ed. London, 1858.
Lloyd.205. w025.

Wanderings among the High Alps / Alfred Wills. 2nd ed., rev. London, 1858.
GB.250; Lloyd.321; Lloyd.321A,B. w026.

Wanderings and musings in the valleys of the Waldenses / James A. Wylie. London, 1858.
Lloyd.229. w027.

Wanderings in the Tyrol and Bavaria / Henry David Inglis. 3rd ed. London, [ca 1865]. Ill.
GB/A.1009. w028.

Wanderings of a pilgrim in the shadow of Mont Blanc and the Jungfrau Alp / George Barrell Cheever. Glasgow, [1847].
GB.899; Lloyd.397; Lloyd.515. w029.

Wanderings of a pilgrim in the shadow of Mont Blanc and the Jungfrau Alp / George Barrell Cheever. New ed. Glasgow, [1847]. Ill.
Lloyd.872; Lloyd.872A. w030.

Wanderings of a pilgrim in the shadow of Mont Blanc / George Barrell Cheever. London, 1848. [Wiley and Putnam's library of American books.]
GB.325. w031.

Wanderings through the ruins of Heidelberg Castle and its environs / edited by Richard-Janillon; from the German by H.J. Grainger. Heidelberg, 1858.
GB/A.382. w032.

Wandern und Bergsteigen in Oberösterreich / Hannes Loderbauer. 3., verb. Aufl. Linz, [1967]. Ill.
GB/A.150. w033.

Wandern und Bergsteigen um Gmunden: das Gmundner Wanderabzeichen / Hannes Loderbauer. 3. Aufl. Linz, [1967]. Ill. [Gmundner

Buchreihe; 2.]
GB/A.181(6). w034.

Wandern und Erleben im deutschen Hochgebirge. Berlin, [1935?]. Ill.
GB/A.2048(10). w035.

Wandern-bergab: 100 schöne Abstiegswege in der
Alpen / Walter Pause. 9., überarb. Aufl. München,
1969. Ill., maps.
GB/B.228. w036.

Wanderstudien aus der Schweiz / Eduard Osenbrüggen. Schaffhausen, 1867-76. 5v.
GB/A.11-5. w037.

Wanderungen durch die rhätischen Alpen: ein
Beytrag zur Charakteristik dieses Theils des
schweizerischen Hochlandes und seiner Be-
wohner / [Peter C. von Tscharner]. Zürich, 1829-
31. 2v.
GB.1328(2) (wanting v.2). w038.

Wanderungen durch die Schweiz / Carl Spazier.
Gotha, 1790.
GB/A.723. w039.

Wanderungen im Zürichgau: Plauderei / Julius
Schwyzer. Zürich, [ca 1940]. 3v; ill.
GB/A.1086-8. w040.

Wanderungen in den Alpen: von Brieg auf das
Eggishorn, den Aletschgletscher und Umgebung
/ Daniel Baud-Bovy. Basel, 1899. Ill.
GB/B.412. w041.

Wanderungen in den Ampezzaner Dolomiten /
Theodor Wundt. [Berlin, n.d.] A prospectus.
GB.1329(22). w042.

Wanderungen in der Gletscherwelt / G.H. [i.e.
Georg Hofman]. Zürich, 1843. Ill.
GB.1326(37). w043.

Wanderungen in weniger besuchte Alpen-
gegenden der Schweiz und ihrer nächsten
Umgebungen / Hirzel-Escher. Zürich, 1829.
GB.111; GB.147(5). w044.

Wanderungen und Feiertage / Georg Finsler.
Bern, [ca 1900].
GB/A.915(3). w045.

Wanderungen und Wandlungen / Henry Hoek.
München, 1924.
GB/A.83. w046.

War discovers Alaska / Joseph Driscoll.
Philadelphia, 1943. Ill., maps, ports.
GB/A.1665. w047.

Was bist du mir, Berg? Schriften und Reden /
Heinrich Pfannl. Wien, 1929. Ill., ports., plan.
GB.1129. w048.

Was ist eine 'erste Besteigung'? / W.A.B. Coolidge. [Vienna, 1893.] Separat-Abdruck aus Nr.375
vom 26. Mai 1893 der *Oesterr. Alpen-Zeitung*.
GB.1340(2). w049.

[A **watercolour** of an Alpine glacier scene] / E.T.
Compton. [N.p., n.d.]
GB.1912(6). w050.

The **way** of war / Hew Scot. London, [1907].
GB.381. w051.

The **way** to Hudson Bay: the life and times of Jens
Munk / Thorkild Hansen; translated and edited
by James McFarlane and John Lynch. New York,
1970. Ill., maps, ports. Translated from *Jens Munk*.
GB/A.1886. w052.

Wayfarers' journal. No.3-4, 6-9, 12-14, 1933-68.
Liverpool, 1933-68. Published by the Wayfarers'
Club.
GB/B.542; GB.1305(1). w053.

We are Alaskans / Mary Lee Davis. Boston, 1931.
Ill., ports.
GB/A.1697. w054.

A **week** in Switzerland: how I reached the hospice
of the Great St. Bernard: a midnight's adventure
among the mountains: nineteen hours on foot and
alone / James A. Monk. Pendleton, [1887].
GB.1335(57). w055.

Der **Weg** nach dem Pol / R. Samoilovitch.
Bielefeld, 1931. [Monographien zur Erdkunde;
46.]
GB/A.2203. w056.

Ein **Weg** zum Nanga Parbat: Leben, Vorträge und
nachgelassene Schriften / Willy Merkl; heraus-
gegben von Karl Herrligkoffer, unter Mitarbeit
von Fritz Schmitt. München, 1936. Ill., port.,
facsims.
GB.1143. w057.

Wege zum Nordpol: Forscher und Abenteurer im
ewigen Eis / Ernst Herrmann. Braunschweig,
[1940]. Ill.
GB/A.413. w058.

Wegweiser durch das Mittelland, Oberland und den Jura des Kantons Bern, begleitet von statistischen Notizen, nützlichen Nachweisungen und Reiserouten. Bern, 1857. Ill., map.
GB/A.1351(8). w059.

Der weisse Berg: meine Erlebnisse am Mont Blanc / Ludwig Steinauer. 4. Aufl. München, 1962. Ill., map.
GB.268. w060.

Die weisse Kordillere / Philipp Borchers; unter Mitarbeit von Wilhelm Bernard, Hans Biersack [et al.]. Berlin, [1935]. Ill., maps.
GB.1054 (impf.). w061.

Der weisse Magnet: Polarfahrten in fünf Jahrhunderten / Ernst Züchner. Berlin, 1932.
GB/A.1630. w062.

Die weisse Spinne: die Geschichte der Eiger-Nordwand / Heinrich Harrer. Wien, 1959. Ill., maps.
GB.1065. w063.

Welsh mountaineering: a practical guide to the ascent of all the principal mountains in Wales / Alexander W. Perry. London, 1896. Maps.
Lloyd.260; Lloyd.260A. w064.

Welsh rarebits / Baldwin Shaw. [London, 1939.] Pp.22-7 of the Climbers' Club Journal, N.S. vol.6 no.1.
GB.1313(12). w065.

Die Welt der Alpen farbig: Mineralien, Pflanzen, Tiere von der Urzeit bis heute / J. Ladurner [et al.]. Innsbruck, 1970. Ill.
GB/B.303. w066.

Wer die Berge liebt: kleine alpine Trilogie. Die Schonheit der Berge. Die Liebe zu den Bergen. Die Macht der Berge / gesammelt und herausgegeben von Walter Schmid. 4. Aufl. Bern, [n.d.].
GB/A.366. w067.

Werden und Wandlungen des Bergsteigens / R.L.G. Irving; die Ubersetzung besorgte Paul Kaltenegger. Wien, 1949. Ill. Translated from The romance of mountaineering.
GB/B.246. w068.

The west buttress of Clogwyn du'r Arddu / A.S. Piggott. [Manchester, 1929.] Ill. Pp.257-60 of the Rucksack Club Journal, vol.6, 1929.
GB.1880(36). w069.

The west buttress of Clogwyn du'r Arddu / Frank S. Smythe. [Edinburgh, 1929.] Ill. Chapter 9 of his Climbs and ski runs.
GB.1335(35). w070.

The west buttress of Clogwyn du'r Arddu / Frank S. Smythe. Leeds, 1929. Ill. Pp.270-81 of the Yorkshire Ramblers' Club Journal, vol.5 no.18.
GB.1880(30); GB.1881(47[1]). w071.

The Western Alps / John Ball. New ed., reconstructed and revised on behalf of the Alpine Club by W.A.B. Coolidge. London, 1898. Ill., maps. [The Alpine guide.]
GB.288; Lloyd.381; Lloyd.381A. w072.

Western Himalaya and Tibet: a narrative of a journey through the mountains of northern India during the years 1847-8 / Thomas Thomson. London, 1852. Ill., maps.
GB.967. w073.

Western Tibet and the British borderland: the sacred country of Hindus and Buddhists: with an account of the government, religion and customs of its peoples / Charles A. Sherring; with a chapter by T.G. Longstaff describing an attempt to climb Gurla Mandhata. London, 1906. Ill., maps.
GB.1165; GB/A.2097. w074.

Die westlichen Ortler-Alpen (Trafoier Gebiet) nach den Forschungen und Aufnahmen / Julius Payer. Gotha, 1868. Ill., maps. [Petermann's Geographische Mittheilungen. Ergänzungsheft; 23.]
GB/B.523(1). w075.

Das Wetterstein Gebirge / M. von Prielmayer. Die Mieminger Kette / Ferdinand Kilger. [Berlin, 1893.] Ill. Pp.[120]-86 of Erschliessung der Ostalpen, Bd.1.
GB.1369. w076.

What may be done in two months: a summer's tour, through Belgium, up the Rhine, and to the lakes of Switzerland / G.T. [i.e. James Michael]. London, 1834. Map. Also attributed to Mrs Bateman.
GB.237; Lloyd.305; Lloyd.305A; Lloyd.311.
w077.

What we did in North Wales: journal / [K.M.W., E.R.H. et al.]. [London, 1875.]
Lloyd.385. w078.

When men & mountains meet / H.W. Tilman. Cambridge, 1947. Ill., maps.
Lloyd.942.   w079.

Where the clouds can go / Conrad Kain; edited with additional chapters by J. Monroe Thorington. Repr. Boston, 1954. Ill., ports.
GB.1048.   w080.

Where the clouds can go / Conrad Kain; edited with additional chapters by J. Monroe Thorington. 3rd ed. New York, 1979. Ill., ports.
GB/A.1907.   w081.

Where the high winds blow / Bruce D. Campbell. New York, 1946. Ill.
GB/A.1703.   w082.

Where the world ends: a description of Arosa as a centre for summer holidays or winter sport and as a health resort for convalescents and invalids / A.A.H. Arosa, 1911. Ill.
GB/A.761.   w083.

Where there's a will there's a way: an ascent of Mont Blanc, (made in August, 1855), by a new route and without guides / Charles Hudson, Edward Shirley Kennedy. London, 1856. Map.
GB.436; GB.437; Lloyd.499; Lloyd.499A,B.   w084.

Where there's a will there's a way: an ascent of Mont Blanc by a new route and without guides / Charles Hudson, Edward Shirley Kennedy. 2nd ed., with two ascents of Monte Rosa. London, 1856.
GB.293.   w085.

Where three empires meet: a narrative of recent travel in Kashmir, western Tibet, Gilgit, and the adjoining countries / E.F. Knight. New ed. London, 1894. Ill., map.
GB.372.   w086.

White battleground: the conquest of the Arctic / Edward F. Dolan. New York, 1961. Maps.
GB/A.1661.   w087.

The **White** Hills: their legends, landscape, and poetry / Thomas Starr King. Boston, 1887. Ill.
GB/A.1766.   w088.

The **White** Mountains. Pt.1. [New York], 1881. Ill., map. Pp.[1]-23 of *Harper's New Monthly Magazine*, vol.63 no.373, June 1881.
GB.1329(33).   w089.

The **White** Tower / James Ramsey Ullman. London, 1946.
GB.518.   w090.

Wierchy: rocznik poswiecony gorom. Rocz.43, 1974. Warszawa, 1975. Ill.
GB/B.403(37).   w091.

Wild flowers of Mount Olympus / Arne Strid. Kifissia, 1980. Ill., maps.
GB/B.518.   w092.

Wild flowers of Switzerland, or A year amongst the flowers of the Alps / H.C.W. [i.e. H.C. Ward]. London, 1883. Ill.
Lloyd.1538.   w093.

A **wild** intrigue / Hew Scot. London, [1910].
GB.433.   w094.

Wild voice of the North / Sally Carrighar. Garden City, N.Y., 1959. Ill.
GB/A.1720.   w095.

Wilde Gesellen vom Sturmwind umweht: ein Berg fahrten buch /Karl Lukan. Umgearb. und erw. Aufl. Salzburg, 1968. Ill.
GB/A.210.   w096.

Wilder Hindukusch: Erlebnisse in Afghanistan und dem zweithöchsten Gebirge der Erde / Max Eiselin. Zürich, 1963. Map. At head of title: Erste schweizerische Hindukusch-Expedition.
GB/A.2064.   w097.

The **wilderness** of Denali: explorations of a hunter-naturalist in northern Alaska / Charles Sheldon; [edited by C. Hart Merriam and E.W. Nelson]. New York, 1930. Ill., map, port.
GB.1100.   w098.

The **wilderness** of the upper Yukon: a hunter's explorations for wild sheep in sub-Arctic mountains / Charles Sheldon. New York, 1913. Ill., maps.
GB/A.1668.   w099.

The **wilderness** trapper: a practical handbook by a practical trapper with extensive experience in the wilds of western Canada / Raymond Thompson. 4th ed. Columbus, Ohio, 1924. Ill.
GB/A.1958.   w100.

William Tell: the hero of Switzerland: a poem. London, [ca 1851]. [Stories for summer days and winter nights; 5.]
GB.1335(29).   w101.

William Tell, or The patriot of Switzerland / Florian. And Hofer, the Tyrolese / by the author of *Claudine*, &c. New ed. London, [1823]. Ill.
GB/A.16.   w102.

William Windham et Pierre Martel: relations de leurs deux voyages aux glaciers de Chamonix, 1741-1742 / texte original français publié avec une introduction et des notes par Théophile Dufour. Genève, 1879.
GB.1138.   w103.

William Windham et Pierre Martel: relations de leurs deux voyages aux glaciers de Chamonix, 1741-1742 / texte original français publié pour la première fois avec une introduction et des notes par Théophile Dufour. Genève, 1879. Extrait de l'*Echo des Alpes*, 1879.
GB.1329(15) (impf.).   w104.

Willo Welzenbachs Bergfahrten / unter Mitwirkung von Eugen Allwein [et al.]; herausgegeben vom Akademischen Alpenverein München. Berlin, [1935]. Ill., ports.
GB.582.   w105.

Wind and hill: poems / Geoffrey Winthrop Young. London, 1909.
Lloyd.372.   w106.

Winter at the hospice. [London, 1895.] Pp.29-39 of the *Cornhill Magazine*, Jan.1895.
GB.1881(53).   w107.

The **winter** book of Switzerland / Doré Ogrizek, J.G. Rufenacht; text and arrangement by Hans Kasser [et al.]; responsible for English version: Stanley Mason. Berne, 1949. Ill., maps.
GB/A.1267.   w108.

Winter in the Arctic regions / Charles Tomlinson. London, 1846. Ill., map.
GB.35.   w109.

Winter sketches in Lapland, or Illustrations of a journey from Alten through Lapland, to Torneå / Arthur de Capell Brooke. London, 1826. Ill.
GB/C.15.   w110.

Winter sports in Chamonix / W.J. Dawson. [London, 1898.] Ill. Pp.[324]-8 of *Travel*, 1898.
GB.1336(7).   w111.

Das **Winzerfest** in Vevey 1955: ein Erinnerungsbuch / Guy Burnand; übertragen von Helen Henrich. Bern, [1956]. Ill. Translated from *La fête des vignerons 1955*.
GB/B.119(6).   w112.

The **witch** knife and how to use it / J. Monroe Thorington. [Baltimore, 1950.] Reprinted from the *Bulletin of the History of Medicine*, vol.24 no.1, January-February 1950.
GB.1339(6); GB.1339(7).   w113.

With a camera in tiger-land / F.W. Champion. London, 1927. Ill.
Lloyd.1315.   w114.

With axe and rope in the New Zealand Alps / George Edward Mannering. London, 1891. Ill., map, port.
GB.1107; Lloyd.1248.   w115.

With Captain Scott, R.N., to the South Pole: the proprietors of the Imperial Picture Palace, 53/55, Queen Street request the pleasure of your company for a private view at the above theatre, on Saturday next the 25th of November, at 2.30 p.m. [Cardiff? 1912?]
GB/A.2165(12).   w116.

With mystics and magicians in Tibet / Alexandra David-Neel. London, 1931. Ill.
GB.780.   w117.

With sack and stock in Alaska / George Broke. London, 1891.
Lloyd.546.   w118.

Wonderland Range / John McMahon, Peter Lindorff. Melbourne, 1975. Ill., maps. [V.C.C. rock climbing guides.] Published by the Victoria Climbing Club.
GB/A.2076(10).   w119.

The **wonders** of Alaska / Alexander Badlam. San Francisco, 1890. Ill., maps, ports.
GB/A.1709.   w120.

Wonders of the physical world: the glacier, the iceberg, the ice-field and the avalanche. London, 1875. Ill.
GB.231.   w121.

Wonders of the world, in nature and art: comprising the most remarkable curiosities and phenomena in the universe / compiled from the best and latest authorities by T.C. Thornton. New ed. London, 1844.
Lloyd.6.   w122.

The **words**, in German and English, of the Tyrolese melodies as sung by the Tyrolese minstrels, the Rainer family before the King and Court at Windsor. London, [1830?].
Lloyd.1572(1). w123.

The **words** of the Tyrolese melodies, sung by the Tyrolese family, Rainer, before the King, at Windsor; to which is added, a memoir of the Tyrolese minstrels / [William Ball]. London, [1830?].
Lloyd.1572(4). w124.

[The **Workman** collection. A collection of negatives, prints and slides taken by Fanny Bullock Workman and William Hunter Workman mainly in the Himalayas, with some other material. ca 1890-ca 1920. With a MS inventory.]
GB/A.2520. w124.1.

The **world** at their feet: the story of New Zealand mountaineers in the great ranges of the world / Philip Temple. Christchurch, 1969. Ill., maps.
GB/A.1000. w125.

The **world** guide to mountains and mountaineering / John Cleare. New York, 1979. Ill. [A Webb and Bower book.]
GB/B.553. w126.

The **world** in miniature / edited by Frederic Shoberl. London, [1821?]. 2v; ill.
Lloyd.77-8. w127.

The **world** in miniature / edited by Frederic Shoberl. Switzerland. London, [n.d.]. Ill.
Lloyd.62; Lloyd.62A. w128.

The **world** surveyed in the 19th century, or Recent narratives of scientific and exploratory expeditions / translated and, where necessary, abridged by W.D. Cooley. 1: Journey to Ararat / Friedrich Parrot. London, 1845. Translated from *Reise zum Ararat*.
Lloyd.1006. w129.

The **worst** journey in the world / Apsley Cherry-Garrard. [London], 1923.
GB/B.528(16). w130.

The **worst** journey in the world: Antarctic, 1910-1913 / Apsley Cherry-Garrard. 4th impression. London, 1938. 2v. [Penguin books; 99.]
GB.1326(38) (wanting v.2). w131.

Wörterbuch für Bergsteiger. Lexique des termes alpins. Vocabolario per alpinisti. Glossary for mountaineering. [Bern, 1966.] Published by the Schweizer Alpenclub.
GB/A.1034(7). w132.

Wudalianchi volcanoes in China / [Feng Mao-seng, Guo Ke-yi, Wang Fu-quan]. Shanghai, 1979. Ill., map. Text in Chinese.
GB/A.1929. w133.

-Y-

Ye mountains of Gilboa! / Cecil Power. [London, 1884.] Pp.426-34 of the *Gentleman's Magazine*, vol.256 no.1841.
GB.1881(30).   y001.

Year book / Ladies' Alpine Club. 1936. [London, 1936.]
GB.1341(9).   y002.

Year book / Public Schools Alpine Sports Club. 1911. London, 1911.
GB/A.2065.   y003.

Year Book / Ski Club. Vol.1 no.2,4-5. London, 1906-09.
Lloyd.1618(54-6).   y004.

A year with a whaler / Walter Noble Burns. New York, 1913. Ill.
GB/A.1908.   y005.

The Yellowstone Park and Alaska / Charles J. Gillis. New York, 1893.
GB/A.1724.   y006.

The Yorkshire Ramblers' Club Journal. Vol.1 no.1-4, vol.2 no.5-7, vol.7 no.25-6. Leeds, 1899-1952.
Lloyd.1607(2-5) (v.1 no.1-4); GB.1647(9-15) (v.1 no.1,4, v.2 no.5-7, v.7 no.25-6).   y007.

Yosemite and its high sierra / John H. Williams. 2nd ed., rev. and greatly enl. San Francisco, 1921. Ill., maps.
GB/A.2139(1).   y008.

Yosemite and the Sierra Nevada / selections from the works of John Muir; edited by Charlotte E. Mauk. Boston, 1948. Ill.
GB/A.1650.   y009.

Yosemite climber / George Meyers [et al.]. London, 1979.
GB/B.593.   y010.

Yosemite National Park: a natural-history guide to Yosemite and its trails / Jeffrey P. Schaffer. Berkeley, 1978. Ill.
GB/A.1974(9).   y011.

You're standing on my fingers! / H. Warren Lewis. Berkeley, [1969]. Ill., maps, ports.
GB/A.1938.   y012.

The young step-mother, or A chronicle of mistakes / by the author of *The heir of Redclyffe* [i.e. Charlotte M. Yonge]. Copyright ed. Leipzig, 1861. 2v. [Collection of British authors; 578-9.]
GB/A.913.   y013.

The young whaler, or Adventures of Archibald Hughson / William H.G. Kingston. Boston, [1860?].
GB/A.2110.   y014.

The Yukon Territory: a brief description of its administration, resources and development. Ottawa, 1944. Published by the Bureau of Northwest Territories and Yukon Affairs.
GB/B.478(3).   y015.

Yuraq Janka: guide to the Peruvian Andes / John F. Ricker. Pt.1: Cordilleras Blanca and Rosko. Banff, Alta., 1977. Ill., maps. Published by the Alpine Club of Canada and the American Alpine Club.
GB/B.528(13).   y016.

-Z-

Zehn grosse Wände: zweite Heimat / Radovan Kuchar: aus dem Tschechischen übersetzt von Erich Mach und Herta Vanikova. Zürich, 1968. Ill. Translated from *Deset velkych sten*.
GB/A.451.   z001.

Zeitschrift des Deutschen Alpenvereins. Bd.1-73, 1869/70-1942. München, 1870-1942. Also known as *Zeitschrift des Deutschen und Osterreichischen Alpenvereins*.
GB/B.21-108; GB.1318(13) (impf. copy for 1930).
                                                        z002.

Zeitschrift für Gletscherkunde und Glazial-geologie. Bd.1-5, 1949/50-1964/68. Innsbruck, 1949-68.
GB/A.154.   z003.

Zénith / Pierre Dalloz. Paris, 1951. [Bibliophiles de la montagne.]
GB/A.1199(10).   z004.

Zermatt: Souvenir-Album mit 38 Ansichten. Zürich, [ca 1905].
GB/A.2048(6).   z005.

Zermatt and its valley / François Gos; recast in English by F.F. Roget. Geneva, [1926]. Ill. Translated from *Zermatt et sa vallée*.
GB/A.2134.   z006.

Zermatt and its valley / François Gos; translated by F.F. Roget. London, 1926. Ill., map. Translated from *Zermatt et sa vallée*.
GB.1132.   z007.

Zermatt and the Matterhorn / W.B. [i.e. William Bellows]. [Gloucester], 1925. Ill.
GB.1326(18).   z008.

Zermatt and the valley of the Viège / Emile Yung; translated by Mrs Wharton Robinson. Geneva, 1894. Ill., ports., facsims. Translated from *Zermatt et la vallée de Viège*.
Lloyd.1507; Lloyd.1507A.   z009.

Zermatt churchyard / Arthur Gray Butler. [Cambridge, 1909.]
GB.1335(26).   z010.

Zermatt et l'ascension du Mont-Rose / F.T. [i.e. F. Thioly]. Genève, 1860. Ill.
Lloyd.1042; Lloyd.1583(2); Lloyd.1624(10).
                                                        z011.

Zermatt et sa vallée / François Gos. Genève, 1925. Ill.
GB/A.1577.   z012.

Zermatt im Sommer und Winter: ein Führer für Spaziergänger, Wanderer, Bergsteiger und Skifahrer / Walter Schmid. 5. Aufl. Bern, 1968. Ill.
GB/A.391.   z013.

The **Zermatt** pocket-book: a guide-book to the Pennine Alps, from the Simplon to Arolla: intended for the use of mountaineers / William Martin Conway. London, 1881.
GB.1324(8).   z014.

Zermatt und seine Berge / Theodor Wundt. Neue, endgultige Aufl. Zürich, 1930. Ill., map.
GB/A.2142.   z015.

Zermatt, with the Cols d'Erin and de Collon: and an ascent to the summit of Mont Blanc: two letters addressed to the editor of the *Liverpool Times* / W. Winter Raffles. [N.p.], 1854.
Lloyd.309.   z016.

Zigzagging amongst Dolomites / Elizabeth Tuckett. London, 1871. Ill.
Lloyd.1530; Lloyd.1530A.   z017.

Die **Zillerthaler** Gruppe / Karl Diener. [Berlin, 1894.] Ill. Pp.[3]-128 of *Erschliessung der Ostalpen*, Bd.3.
GB.1376.   z018.

Zimnie voskhozdeniia / Boris Vasil'evich Minenkov. Moskva, 1967. Ill.
GB/A.152.   z019.

Zivot a smrt na vrcholech sveta / Milan Daniel. Praha, 1977. Ill. [Edice Kolumbus; 78.]
GB/A.1975.   z020.

Zona del Prefouns, Alpi Marittime: guida alpinistica / Alessandro Gogna, Gianni Pastine. Bologna, 1974. Ill., map. [Itinerari alpini; 19.]
GB/A.1351(10).   z021.

Zoology. I: Mammals / Magnus Degerbøl, Peter Freuchen. New York, 1976. Ill. [Thule expedition, 5th, 1921-1924. Report; vol.2 no.4-5.]
GB/A.1824.   z022.

Zoology. II: Birds / R. Herring. Fishes / J.R. Pfaff. Insects / K.L. Henriksen. Crustacea / K. Stephenson. New York, 1976. Ill. [Thule expedition, 5th, 1921-1924. Report; vol.2 no.6-9.]
GB/A.1825(1-4).   z023.

Zum Berg des Himmels: Hindukuschexpedition 1968 / Christian v. d. Hecken. Wien, 1970. Ill. GB/A.470.   z024.

Zur Entwicklungsgeschichte des Alpinismus / Ludwig Purtscheller. [Munich?], 1894. Ill. Pp.[145]-76 of an unidentified periodical. GB.1880(29) (impf.).   z025.

Zur Erinnerung an Edward Whymper, 1840-1911 / Heinrich Dübi. Bern, 1912. Ill., ports. Pp.[183]-216 of the *Jahrbuch des Schweizer Alpenclub*, Jahrg. 47. GB.1331(54).   z026.

Zur Erinnerung an Melchior Anderegg, 1827- 1914 / Heinrich Dübi. Zürich, [1915]. Ill. Lloyd.1609(5).   z027.

Zur Erinnerung an Walther Flender: ein Lebensabriss / Karl Blodig. Leipzig, [n.d.]. Ill., port. Lloyd.1175.   z028.

Zur ersten Besteigung des Finsteraarhorns, 4275m. / C. Montandon. [Bern, 1892.] Ill. Pp.384-6 of the *Jahrbuch des Schweizer Alpenclub*, Jahrg. 27. GB.1881(50).   z029.

Zur Frage des alten Passes zwischen Grindelwald und Wallis / Adolf Wäber. [Bern, 1892.] Pp.[253]-74 of the *Jahrbuch des Schweizer Alpenclub*, Jahrg. 27. GB.1881(61).   z030.

Zur Geologie der Schweizeralpen / Karl Schmidt. Basel, 1889. Ill. GB/A.514(4).   z031.

Zur Geologie des Gebietes zwischen Engelberg und Meiringen / Paul Arbenz. [Zurich, 1907.] Ill. Separatabdruck aus *Eclogae geologicae Helvetiae*, vol.9 no.4. GB/A.1052(3).   z032.

Zur Geschichte der frühesten Wetterhornbesteigungen / Heinrich Dübi. [Bern, 1904.] Pp.375-82 of the *Jahrbuch des Schweizer Alpenclub*, Jahrg. 39. GB.1881(80).   z033.

Zur Geschichte der österreichischen Alpenkunst / Robert Stiassny; Vortrag, gehalten auf dem Internationalen kunsthistorischen Kongresse zu Budapest 1896. Nürnberg, 1898. GB/B.119(1).   z034.

Zur Geschichte des Fremdenverkehrs im engeren Berner Oberlande, 1763-1835 / Adolf Wäber. [Bern, 1904.] Ill. Pp.[212]-61 of the *Jahrbuch des Schweizer Alpenclub*, Jahrg. 39. GB.1881(49).   z035.

Zur topographischen Geschichte des Belalp- und des Aletschgletschergebiets, der Eggishornkette und des Märjelensees / W.A.B. Coolidge. [N.p., 1915.] From *Blättern aus der Walliser-Geschichte*, Bd.4, 1915. GB.1340(47).   z036.

Zürcher Hausberge / Walter Pause, Hanns Schlüter. Bern, 1968. Ill., maps. GB/A.387.   z037.

Der **Zürichsee** / Max Pfister. 2., textlich überarb. und erg. sowie bildlich neu gestaltete Aufl. Bern, 1970. Ill. [Die grossen Heimatbücher; 2.] GB/B.307.   z038.

Zusammengestellt aus den Untersuchungen über die physicalische Geographie der Alpen / Hermann Schlagintweit, Adolph Schlagintweit. Leipzig, 1850. Ill. GB/B.621.   z039.

Zwei Kiesgruben / Aug. Aeppli. [N.p., 1900?] Pp.113-20 of an unidentified publication. GB/A.1052(8).   z040.

Zwei Winter am Weissen Berg: Peter Hardegg zum Andenken / Erwin Schneider. [Vienna], 1930. Pp.[1]-7 of the *Osterreichische Alpenzeitung*, no.1093, Jänner 1930. GB.1880(58).   z041.

Zwei Wochen in der Umgebung des Grand Combin, 4317m., Wallis / W.A.B. Coolidge. Wien, [1891]. Separat-Abdruck aus Nr.324 und 325 der *Osterreichischen Alpen-Zeitung* vom 12 und 27. Juni 1891. Lloyd.1395.   z042.

Zweitausend Meter Fels: ein Watzmann Ostwand-Buch / Hellmut Schoener. 3. Aufl. Salzburg, 1953. Ill. GB/A.416.   z043.

Ein **zweiter** Winter am Mont Blanc / Hermann Hoerlin. [N.p., 1929?] Pp.21-31 of an unidentified periodical. GB.1306(19).   z044.

Zwischen Himmel und Hölle: aus dem Leben eines Bergsteigers / Toni Hiebeler. Frankfurt am Main, [1965]. Ill.
GB/A.994.   z045.

Zwischen Kantsch und Tibet: Erstbesteigung des Tent-Peak, 7363m.: Bildertagebuch einer neuen Sikkim-Kundfahrt 1939 der 'Drei im Himalaja' / Ernst Grob, Ludwig Schmaderer, Herbert Paidar. München, [1940].
GB/A.1075.   z046.

Zwitserland / Paul Guiton; vertaling van W.J.M. Linden. Dl.1: Fransch-Zwitserland. Amsterdam, 1929.
GB/B.403(16).   z047.

Zwitserland / naar het Fransch van Xavier Marmier door S.J. van den Bergh. Haarlem, [1870?]. Ill. Translated from *Voyage en Suisse*.
GB/B.411.   z048.

Zwitsersche berggidsen vertellen / [vertaling: Herman Felderhof]. 3de druk. Amsterdam, 1948. Ill. Originally published as *Schweizer Bergführer erzählen*.
GB/A.1494.   z049.

NAME INDEX

A., G.D.
j019.

A., P.
h100.

A.C. See Alpine Club.

A.S.P.T.T. de Toulouse. Groupes 'Ski et montagne'
n172.

Abadie, A.
i177.

Abalakow, W.
g202.

Abba, Giuseppe Cesare
a284-286.

Abbate, Enrico
g212; g253.

Abbatt, Richard
a713.

Abbot, Ellen
p065.

Abdou, Edmond
a680.

Abdullah ben Kori
m416.

Abel, O.
o097.

Abelein, Manfred
s198.

Abell, H.F.
a165.

Abercrombie, W.R.
a127.

Abildhauge Thomsen, Helge. See Thomsen, Helge Abildhauge.

Abney, W. de. See De Abney, W.

Abney, *Sir* William de Wyveleslie
f003.

Abraham, Ashley Perry
r219.

Abraham, George Dixon
c349; m232; o042; r034; r219; s525.

Abrahamsson, Tore
k040.

Abruzzi, duca degli. See Luigi Amedeo, duca degli Abruzzi.

Academia Sinica
p286.

Académie de Béarn
p331.

Académie de Genève
a040.

Académie delphinale
i170.

Accademia Reale delle Scienze
r169.

Achard, Paul
s277.

Acland, Hugh Dyke
i023.

Acutis, Pensiero
d006.

Adam, Bénédicte
r232.

Adam, Jean Michel
r232.

Adam Smith, Janet
a537; m428; m435.

Adametz, Marie
d181.

Adams, Samuel Drake
h055.

Adams, William H. Davenport
a296; a309-310; m496.

Adams-Reilly, A.
l142.

Addington Symonds, John. See Symonds, John Addington.

Addison, Joseph
r112-114.

Adelman, M.A.
a135.

Adrados, Miguel Angel
s211.

Adrian, W.
a204.

Aeby, Christoph
h189.

Aeppli, Aug.
a790; z040.

Affentranger, Irene
p133; s423.

Afsprung, Johann Michael
r078.

Agassiz, Lewis
j084.

Agassiz, Louis
a097; b129; e176; e204-205; j044; n227; n254-255; u043.

Agassiz, *family*
a093.

Agnolotti, Giuseppe
c399.

Agostini, Alberto M. de. See De Agostini, Alberto M.

Agostini, Enrico de. See De Agostini, Enrico.

Agostini, Ranieri
g283.

Agresti, Henri
m352.

Ahlman, Axel
i147; k013.

Ahluwalia, Hari Pal Singh
e165.

Ahrens, Conrad Meyer. See Meyer-Ahrens, Conrad.

Air India
l007.

Aite, Silvana
t254.

Aitken, Samuel
a490.

Akademiia nauk SSSR
o085.

Akademiia nauk SSSR. Institut istorii. Leningradskoe otdelenie
o020.

Akademiia nauk SSSR. Sibirskoe otdelenie. Institut istorii, filologii i filosofii
s205.

Akademischer Alpen-Club Zürich
f143; j017; s255.

Akademischer Alpenclub Bern
j016.

Akademischer Alpen Verein Innsbruck
b104.

Akademischer Alpen-Verein Berlin
j018.

Akademischer Alpenverein München
b096; w105.

Alaska Agricultural College and School of Mines
b149.

Alaska Railroad Commission
r008.

Albani, G.
a394.

Albanis Beaumont, Jean F. See Beaumont, Jean François Albanis.

Albany Institute, N.Y.
o074.

Albert
d029.

Albertas, Sylvia d'
d071.

Albertini, Renzo
c050.

*Aldalur, José Maria Azpiazu. **See** Azpiazu Aldalur, José Maria.*

Aldebert, Max
a254.

Aldrovandi, Mario
g260.

Alert (Ship)
b246.

Alessi Anghini, Alberto
a003.

Alexander, *Sir* Henry
c010.

Alexander, William S.
l072.

Alexander III, *King of Macedonia*
o041.

*Alfeld, Theodor Müller. **See** Müller-Alfeld, Theodor.*

*Alisma. **See** Stephenson, George Skelton.*

Allain, Pierre
a387; a651.

Allan, Iain
g343.

*Allardice, Robert Barclay. **See** Barclay, Captain.*

Allbut, Robert
t160.

Allemand, F.
d143.

Allen, Everett S.
a625.

Alley, R.
t212.

Allgäuer, Oscar
w019.

Allgemeine Schweizerische Gesellschaft für die gesammten Naturwissenschaften
d059.

Allix, André
o030; v189.

Allom, Thomas
v168.

Allwein, Eugen
b075; w105.

*Almeida, Pierre Camena d'. **See** Camena d'Almeida, Pierre.*

Almen, Kaspar von
u004.

Almer, Christian
c199; f003.

*Alpen-Club Osterreich. **See** Osterreichischer Alpenklub.*

Alpenclub Gerliswil
f149.

*Alpenverein, Munich. Bücherei. **See** Deutscher Alpenverein. Bücherei.*

Alpine Bioscope Expedition
l050.

Alpine Club
a067; a077; a299-300; a311-319; a328-332; c062; c073; c078; c098; c103.3-103.4; e083; e211-213; f049; f055; g097; g182; h087; h129.1; h220; h227; h248-249; i070; k049; l085; l162-163; m105; m174; m415; n222; o054; p069-73; p184; p315-317; r040-41; r262; s018; s294; s450; s542; t250-251; w072.

Alpine Club. Committee
t112.

Alpine Club. Finance Sub-committee
r122.

Alpine Club. Gallery
c077.

Alpine Club. Library
c063; c068-70; e302.

Alpine Club. Special Committee on Equipment for Mountaineers
e089; p322.

Alpine Club. Special Committee on Ropes, Axes and Alpenstock
r131-132.

Alpine Club of Canada
c027; c233; r229; s163; y016.

Alpinistengilde
p116.

Alpinus
a427.

Alstine, T. van.   See Van Alstine, T.

Alt de Tieffenthal, *baron d'*
h136.

Altamira G., Armando
a413.

Altamura, Vincenzo
r150.

Altenberger, Ernst
b084.

Altmann, Johann Georg
e161-164; v127.

Altmeyer, Heinz Weibel.   See Weibel-Altmeyer, Heinz.

Alverà, Pietro
c438.

Alvey Richards, Eva.   See Richards, Eva Alvey.

Alviella, Goblet d', comte.   See Goblet d'Alviella, comte.

Amadesi, Eraldo
c003.

Amaria, P.J.
a632.

American Alpine Club
a483-485; c233; p329; r229; s509; y016.

American Association for the Advancement of Science
r145.

American Geographical Society
a488; b257; c299; g036.

American Karakoram Expedition, 1st, 1938
f066.

American Karakoram Expedition, 3rd, 1953
k004.

American Museum of Natural History
n053.

Amery, Leopold Stennett
a083.

Amicis, Edmondo de.   See De Amicis, Edmondo.

Amicis, Ugo de.   See De Amicis, Ugo.

Amidei, Ademaro Barbiellini.   See Barbiellini Amidei, Ademaro.

Amiet, X.
v294-295.

Amonn, Walther
i043.

Ampferer, Otto
b097; e047.

Amstutz, Walter
e063; t290; u015.

Amthor, Ed.
a209.; s005

Amundsen, Roald
a501; g079; n137; r213.

Amy, Bernard
a397; m340; t038.

Anderegg, Melchior
p170; z027.

Andersen, Hans Christian
r014.

Andersen, Ole G. Norden.   See Norden Andersen, Ole G.

Anderson, Eustace
c170.

Anderson, James
a063.

Anderson, Roger
m465.

Anderson, Warwick
t115.

Anderson, William
t021; v272.

Anderton Brigg, William.   See Brigg, William Anderton.

Andlovic, Joze
k021.

Andrea, Silvia
v179.

Andreae, Johann Gerhard Reinhard
b228.

Andrée, Salomon August
a511; d213; h183.

Andrée expedition
u027.

Andreev, A.I.
o020.

Andreis, E.
g133.

Andreoletti, Arturo
m064.

Andreolli, Marcello
s106; s109.

Andrews, Arthur Westlake
c278.

Andrews, William P.
v135.

Angelini, Giovanni
b193; c223; g216; p242; s021; s189; t024.

Angelis, Gilberto de. See De Angelis, Gilberto.

Angell James, John. See James, John Angell.

Angeville, Henriette d'
a708; e197; m005.

Angerer, Hermann
h095.

Anghini, Alberto Alessi. See Alessi Anghini, Alberto.

Angulo, Miguel
g317.

Annighito Peary, Marie. See Peary, Marie Annighito.

Antonini, Giacomo
n068.

Antonioli, F.
h061.

Antonioli, Paola Ornella
s017.

Antonioli Cerruti, Marina
a397.

Appalachian Mountain Club
a585; a587-591; m477.

Appia, Remo
r052; u057.

Appleton, Daniel, & Co. See Daniel Appleton & Co.

Aquitania (Ship)
c445; l171.

Arbanère, Etienne
t003.

Arbenz, Paul
b024; z032.

Arber, Agnes
p288.

Archer, Edward Caulfield
t161.

Archer Thomson, James Merriman. See Thomson, James Merriman Archer.

Archives des Hautes-Alpes
a532-533.

Archivio di Stato, Turin
p282.

Arcis, C. Egmond d'
e052; n066.

Arctic Institute of North America
a607; b152; c080.1; e222; p203; s579.

Ardito, Stefano
h061; m011.

Arentz, F.
d130.

Argentier, Auguste
c420.

Ariz Martinez, Gregorio
e215.

Armani, Giorgio
a456; g230.

Armengaud, André
p227.

Armour Richards, Joanna. See Richards, Joanna Armour.

Armstrong, *Sir* Alex
p103.

Arnaud, H.
a229.

Arnesen, Odd
r213.

Arnold, Georg
b229.

Arnould, Joseph
h232.

Arrecgros, J.
p109.

Arrighetti, Attilio
s310.

Artaria, Epimaco
n273.

Artaria, Ferdinando
g243.

Artaria, Pasquale
n273.

Arth-Rigi Bahn
a662.

Artoni, Carlo
c091; s278.

Arve, Stéphen d'
f021; m296.

Arzani, Carlo
b169; c357; g005; r003; r185; r189; t023.

Ashenden. See Nowill, Sidney.

Aspin, Jehoshaphat
c410.

Association of British Members of the Swiss Alpine Club
a649; i097; m473; r140; t041.

Association suisse des propriétaires d'auto-camions. See Gesellschaftswagengruppe.

Associazione Glicerio Longa
v190.

Associazione Italiana Insegnanti di Geografia. Sezione Lombarda
i191.

Associazione Nazionale Italiana per il Movimento dei Forestieri
m397.

Astley-Cooper, C.J.
g164.

Astrup, P.
a373.

Atkins, Barton
m230.

Atkins, Henry Martin
a677; a721.

Atkinson, Edwin T.
h115.

Atkinson, George M.W.
s240.

Atwater, Montgomery M.
a819.

Atwood, Mae
i082.

Atwood Henderson, Kenneth. See Henderson, Kenneth Atwood.

Aubert, Edouard
v052.

Aubigné, Robert Merle d'. See Merle d'Aubigné, Robert.

Auerswald, Fabian von
r199.

Augerd, Victor
e197.

Augerd, Victor, *fils*
e197.

Augustin, F., *Freiherr von*
s431.

Auldjo, John
n033-36; s247.

Austin, Cecil Kent
o050.

Austral. See Wilson, Annie.

Australasian Antarctic Expedition, 1911-14
s116-118.

Austrian Alpine Club. See Osterreichischer Alpenverein.

Automobile Club of Switzerland
s544.

Avebury, John Lubbock, Baron. See Lubbock, John, Baron Avebury.

Avout, Jules Pierre A. d', *baron*
n217.

Ayres, Harry
h041.

Azienda Autonoma di Soggiorno e Turismo della città Bolzano
g276.

Azienda Autonoma di Soggiorno e Turismo di Aosta
i049.

Azienda Autonoma di Soggiorno Madonna di Campiglio e Pinzolo
b207.

Azpiazu Aldalur, José Maria
a409.

B., Mr. See Bordier, André César.

B., D.W.
t068.

B., E.
d015.

B., Geo.
l148.

B., J.D.H. See Browne, J.D.H.

B., M.E.
c227-228; h203.

B., T. See Brightwell, Thomas.

B., W. See Bellows, William.

*B***, comte de. See Bray, comte F.G. de.*

*B*****, Mr. See Bridel, Philippe S.*

Babcock, F. Lawrence
s342.

Bach, J.J.
m087-88; m091-92; m095-96; m102-103.

Bachelin, Auguste
a803; j034; n078; t279.

Bächler, Emil
i024.

Bachmair, Heinrich F.S.
b113.

Bachmann, Robert C.
g089.

Back, *Sir* George
h145; n046.

Backer, Andreas
h239; t103.

Bacon, Edward
v089.

Baddeley, Mountford J.B.
i140.

Baden Pritchard, Henry. See Pritchard, Henry Baden.

Badlam, Alexander
w120.

Baedeker, Karl
e016-18; i158; n164; r167; s317; s471-472; s544; s553-561.

Baedeker, Otto
s544.

Baehler, A.
s512.

Baggesen, Jens
p040-41.

Bagnara, Mario
a288.

Bagolini, Bernardino
t268.

Bahadoor, Jung
j083.

Bailey, Jean
a568.

Baillie, Marianne
f060.

Baillie Fraser, James. See Fraser, James Baillie.

Baillie-Grohmann, William Adolphus
g002; s360; t310-311.

Baillods, Jules
i017; p309; r205.

Bailly de Lalonde
l082.

Bainbridge, William
a336.

Baines, Jack
h228.

Baker, Edmund G.
n106.

Baker, Ernest Albert
b239; v195.

Baker, George Percival
m486.

Bakewell, R.
t207.

Bakker, E.M. van Zinderen.   See Zinderen Bakker, E.M. van.

Balavoine, Hippolyte
d020.

Balch, Thomas Willing
a129.

Balchen, Bernt
b115.

Bale, Shelby G.
u033.

Balestra, Antonio
m208.

Balke, Bruno
n017.

Ball, John
b106.1-106.2; c103-103.4; e015.1; g350-350.2; g356-356.2; h129.1; i130.1; n150.1; o069; p069-71; p088; s317.1; w072.

Ball, *Sir* Robert S.
c092.

Ball, William
w124.

Balla, Ignazio
q003.

Ballantyne, R.M.
r203.

Ballarino, Francesco
f028.

Ballerini, Michel
r233.

Balletto, Giovanni
k044.

Balliano, Adolfo
a137; f042; m202; p133; r002; s249; s423.

Ballingall, William
s055.

Ballou, Maturin M.
n098.

Balmat, Jacques
b011; e307; e320; h241; j005-6; m282; n214; p002.

Baltard, Louis Pierre
j045.

Baltardive, M.
m101.

Baltardive, Ph.
m101.

Bancroft, Mary
s533.

Band, George
e230.

Bandlin, J.B.
s064.

Bang, H.O.
l159.

Bangs Morgan, Bernice. See Morgan, Bernice Bangs.

Banks, Mike
c342; m404.

Banovec, Tomaz
p188.

Barace, Alexandre de Lamotte, vicomte de Senonnes.
See Senonnes, Alexandre de Lamotte Barace, vicomte
de.

Barattieri, Dino
g287.

Barbano, Enzo
s398.

Barbarin, Georges
a019.

Barberis, Giancarlo
m312.

Barbero, Franco
o040.

Barbetta, Roberto
a287.

Barbey, Frédéric
r249.

Barbiellini Amidei, Ademaro
g239.

Barbier, V.
m284.

Barbieri, Giuseppe
c050; t127.

Barbone, Donato
c372.

Barclay, *Captain*
p080.

Barclay, George Lippard
g173.

Barcroft, Joseph
m030.

Barford, John Edward Quintus
c254; c281-282; i073.

Bargelesi, Alberto
s400-401.

Bargeton, Roger
a752.

Barham Zincke, F.   See Zincke, F. Barham.

Barkas, Geoffrey
f061.

Barker, Edward
t083.

Barker, Henry Ashton
d088; d102.

Barlow, Guy
i144.

Barnard, George
d210.

Barnes, Malcolm
f092; m454.

Baron
n196.

Barr, William
e222.

Barrell Cheever, George.   See Cheever, George Barrell.

Barrett, Frank
h241.

Barrie, J.M.
c417.

Barrington, *Hon.* Daines
p228.

Barrow, C.L.
c273-274.

Barrow, Henry D.
p026.

Barrow, *Sir* John
d093; e223; m426-427; s488; t133; t146.

Barruel, Paul
m351.

Barry (Dog)
b018.

Barry, Martin
a722-725.1; l037; t293.

Bartels, A.
v208.

Barth, Hanns
h200.

Barth, Hermann von
g051.

Bartholdy, Carl Mendelssohn. **See** *Mendelssohn Bartholdy, Carl.*

Bartholdy, Felix Mendelssohn. **See** *Mendelssohn Bartholdy, Felix.*

Bartholdy, Paul Mendelssohn. **See** *Mendelssohn Bartholdy, Paul.*

Bartholomew, Orland
h090.

Bartle, Jim
t179.

Bartlett, Bob
m061.

Bartlett, W.H.
s068; s535-537; w005.

Barton, William E.
m416.

Basaglia, P.
e027.

Bassetti, P.
a272.

Bastanzi, Giambattista
s497.

Basterfield, George
c431.1; m440; s301-302.

Bates, Henry Walter
t206.

Bates, Robert Hicks
f066; k004.

Bateson, Richard
t105.

Bateson, Sölvi
t105.

Battagel, Arthur
p337.

Battisti, Gino
c090; g206.

Battye, Aubin Trevor. **See** *Trevor-Battye, Aubin.*

Baud, Henri
b020; v053.

Baud-Bovy, Daniel
a653; m015; m303; p075; w041.

Baudino, Carlo
m042.

Bauen, Marco
w016.

Bauer, Paul
a004; a767; d117; d119; h120; i040; k011-12; r198; u020.

Baumann, Peter
m523.

Baumeister, Hans
j090; m173.

Baumgartner, Hans
d015; d132.1.

Bauriedl, Otto
e047.

Bauron, Pierre
m209.

Baxter, George
a707; f104.

Baxter, Wynne E.
q016-17.

Bayberger, Emmeran
g020.

Bazzi, R.
s106.

Bazzini, Maria Paola Ferraguti. **See** *Ferraguti Bazzini, Maria Paola.*

Beaco, Bianca di. **See** *Di Beaco, Bianca.*

Bear (Ship)
g004; r128.

Bearzi, Franca
d152.

Beattie, William
s068; s535-537; w005.

Beaufoix, *chevalier*
l111-112.

Beaufoy, *Colonel*
p228.

Beaufoy, Mark
a047; n024-25.

Beaumont, Jean François Albanis
f086; t208; t247.

Beaumont, L. Elie de
f009; m142.

Beaumont, R.L.
i076; t294.

Beauvais, *commandant*
e235.

Becher, Gianni Pais.   See Pais Becher, Gianni.

Béchervaise, John
a569; a802; s113.

Bechtold, Fritz
d114-115; f096; n017-18.

Beck, Ed.
c048.

Becker, Ethel Anderson
h070.

Becker, Fridolin
i196; u032.

Becker, Ludwig
v206.

Beckford, William
t152.

Beckwith, Charles
r014.

Bede, Cuthbert
m276.

Bedeschi, Giulio
c102; p104.

Beecher Stowe, Harriet.   See Stowe, Harriet Beecher.

Beechey, F.W.
v254.

Beer, Sir Gavin de.   See De Beer, Sir Gavin.

Bégin, Emile
v268.

Behrens, Rudolf
f029.

Behrmann, Hermann
r164.

Belgica (Ship)
a761.

Belica, Marcel
n063.

Belin, J.L.
s220.

Bell, A. Craig
t220.

Bell, *Sir* Charles
p225; t098.

Bell, Florence, *Lady*
l107.

Bell, Gertrude
l107.

Bell, Henry G.
s165.

Bell, J.H.
o098.

Bell, James Horst Brunnerman
b240; p297-298.

Bell, Robert
h250; m059.

Bellefon, Patrice de
p333.

Belli, Mario Ferrucio.   See Ferrucio Belli, Mario.

Belloc, Hilaire
h097.

Belloni, Severino
g061.

Bellot, J.R.
v219.

Bellows, William
z008.

Belluschi, Franco
c111; l036.

Belomorskaia biologicheskaia stantsiia MGU
b163.

Belsham, W.
t234.

Belville, John Henry
m036.

Benda, C.
a218.

Benedetto, Vito di.   See Di Benedetto, Vito.

Bénédite, Léonce
c082.

Benesch, Fritz
b077; d181.

Bengal. Government Secretariat
g011.

Bennett, Alfred W.
f074.

Benoist, Charles René Albert
m302.

Benson, Claude Ernest
b242; c267; o061.

Bent, Allen H.
e008.

Benuzzi, Felice
f135; n125.

Benzenberg, J.F.
b234.

Benziger, Wna Emma
d092.

Beraldi, Henri
r275.

Beran, Felix
m221.

Berchem, Jacob Pierre Berthoud van.   See Berthoud van Berchem, Jacob Pierre.

Berchtold, Leopold von, *Graf*
e156.

Berg, L.S.
g055.

Berg-Osterrieth, Martine van
c179.

Bergamaschi, Arturo
n075.

Bergen, W. von
b156.

Berger, A.
i085.

Bergführerverein Pontresina
h254.

Bergh, S.J. van den
z048.

Berghold, Franz
k056.

Bergier, Jean François
h135.

Berglund Nielsen, Jørn
a027.

Bergman, Sten
k018.

Bering, Vitus
v187.

Berker, Michael
b101.

Berlepsch, Hermann Alexander von
a192; a223; a449-449.1; g128; l200; n234.

Bernard, *Saint, of Clairvaux*
s011.

Bernard, Richard Boyle
t153.

Bernard, Wilhelm
w061.

Bernardi, Alfonso
d004; g132; g144; m373.

Bernardi, Marziano
c119.

Bernardini, Enzo
m368.

Bernasconi, Claudio
b036.

Bernasconi, Mario
g213.

Berndt, Gustav
a208; v015.

Berneck, Max Koch von. **See** *Koch von Berneck, Max.*

Berner Alpenbahn-Gesellschaft
i025.

Bernhard, Oscar
f045; i117.

Bernier, J.E.
c040; m104.

Bernoulli, Johann
s028.

Bernstein, Jeremy
m444.

Bernt, Ernst
e002.

Bertarelli, L.V.
t257.

Berthoud, Fritz
s502.

Berthoud van Berchem, Jacob Pierre
e202; i166-167.

Berti, Antonio
d196; p034; p094.

Berti, Camillo
d196; p094; s307.

Berti, Tito
d196; p094.

Bertino, Serge
g266.

Bertoglio, Giovanni
a412.

Bertoldi, M. de. **See** *De Bertoldi, M.*

Bertoldin, E.
a276-277.

Bertolina, Elio
l007.

Bertolini, Amilcare
g217.

Bertolotti, Davide
v144.

Berton, Robert
a005; c005; p268.

Bertrand, Elie
e152; t066.

Bertrand, Kenneth J.
a488.

Berutto, Giulio
a281; p029; v082.

Berwick Sayers, W.C. **See** *Sayers, W.C. Berwick.*

Bescapè, Carlo
n261.

Besozzi, Manlio
d011-12.

Besse, Eugène
v216.

Bessière, Paul
a381.

Besson, H.
m057.

Bessone, Severino
m401; v026.

Bessuges, J.
e146.

Best, Robert
o121.

Best, S. Payne
v113.

Besta, Beatrice
v079.

Besta, Enrico
b191; s399; v079.

Bettex, Gustave
a258.

Bevilacqua, Eugenia
c046; c108; v036.

Beyer, Hannes
h184.

Biancardi, Armando
v192.

Bianchetti, Enrico
o094.

Bianchi, Alberto
m365.

Bianchi, Luigi
m321.

Bianchi, Vendramino
a053.

Bianco, Piero
s533.

Bianco, Vincenzo dal.   See Dal Bianco, Vincenzo.

Biancotti, Angiolo
a580.

Bible. O.T. Ruth
c443.

Bibliographisches Institut, Leipzig
h197.

Bibliothèque municipale de Grenoble
m337; p267.

Bibliothèque nationale, Paris
i047.

Bibliothèque publique de Genève
h142.

Bickel, Benoit
j025.

Biddulph, John
t270.

Bidou, Henry
c366.

Bieberstein, Marshal.   See Marschall von Bieberstein, Friedrich August.

Biedenkapp, Georg
n135.

Biederman, Dave
s253.

Bierman, Jean Louis
s029.

Biermann, A.
o003.

Biersack, Hans
w061.

Bigarella, Rino
r200.

Bigelow, Mab
e227.

Bigon, Mario
g226; n126.

Bille, Edmond
h076.

Bille, René Pierre
a007.

Billing, Graham
s313.

Billings, Joseph
p330.

Binder, J.J.
w003.

Binet-Hentsch, J.L.
a233.

Bingley, William
b159.

Bini, Gianfranco
d202.

Biolley, A.
t279.

Bird, J. Brian
p130.

Birkbeck, Morris
n197-198.

Birket-Smith, Kaj
a575; c043; c391; e167.

Birmingham University Mountaineering Club
j035.

Birtt, W. Bridges
b273.

Bisaccia, Mario
a391; s207.

Bischoff, E.
t074.

Bishop, Graham
m408.

Bittebierre, Monique
c335; e035.

Biucchi, Basilio
s029.

Bjelke, Rolf
a640.

Bjerregaard, Beth
d156.

Bjerregaard, Peter
d156.

Björck, Svante
l043.

Blache, Jules
h223; m093.

Blackburn, Henry
p334-335.

Blackstone, F.E.
c075.

Blackwood, Frederick Temple Hamilton-Temple, Marquess of Dufferin and Ava. **See** *Dufferin and Ava, Frederick Temple Hamilton-Temple-Blackwood, Marquess of.*

Blakeborough, J. Fairfax
b240.

Blakeney, Edward Henry
a353; p074.

Blanc, Charles
d039.

Blanc, Pierre
b112.

Blanchard, Raoul
a251.

Blanchet, Emile Robert
a451; a748-749; f154; h231; j024; m460.

Blanchet, G.H.
g170; p248.

Blandford Edwards, Amelia. **See** *Edwards, Amelia Blandford.*

Blaxland, Gregory
b173.

Blessington, Marguerite, *Countess of*
h056.

Bloch, Olaf
a349; m460.

Blodig, Karl
a780; a788-789; m281; q010; v155-156; z028.

Bloesch, Hans
a204; c110.

Blond, Elizabeth Le. **See** *Le Blond, Elizabeth.*

Bloomfield, Paul
e157.

Blotzheim, Robert Glutz. **See** *Glutz-Blotzheim, Robert.*

Blum, Christoph
b155.1-155.2.

Blumer, Ed. Naef. **See** *Naef-Blumer, Ed.*

Blumer, S.
a357; v157.

Boada, J.M.
m003.

Bobba, Giovanni
a283; c088; g188; g267; i190; m287; p097; s137.

Boccaccio, Giovanni
d165.

Boccia, Antonio
v141.

Böcher, Tyge W.
a159.

Bockstoce, John R.
a487; v256.

Boddington, Mary
s263.

Bode, Wilhelm
g116; s081.

Bodmer, Daniel
b155.1-155.2; p107.1.

Boeck, Kurt
i112-113.

Boell, Jacques
c210; h085.

Boffa, Felice
m039; m381; v009.

Boghossian, Georges
c116.

Böhm, August von
e068; h195; h205; k033; s024.

Bohn, Dave
g083.

Bohy, J.
l067.

Bois-Melly, Charles du. See Du Bois-Melly, Charles.

Boisbaudran, Lecoq de. See Lecoq de Boisbaudran.

Boles, Glen W.
r229.

Boleso, Carlo
g275.

Bollea, Giacinto
i136.

Bollinger, Josef
i074; p123.1.

Bollman, Louis de
s073.

Bologna, Paolo
b175.

Bölsche, Carl Eduard Wilhelm
s209.

Bolton, Alfred M.
o123.

Bommen, Bror W.
n141.

Bompadre, Guglielmo
e316.

Bonacossa, Aldo
g245.2; r054; r056-57.

Bonapace, Benedetto
d218; f025.

Bonatti, Walter
a009; g010; g069; m201.

Bonavia, Loris
s101.

Bondier, A.C.
p192.

Boner, Charles
c144-145; g328.

Bonetti, Paolo
a519.

Boniforti, Luigi
l013.

Bonington, Chris
a539.

Bonnefous, Eugène
a158.

Bonnefoy, A.   See Bonnefoy, J.A..

Bonnefoy, J.A.
p273.

Bonnet, Charles
e045.

Bonney, Thomas George
a356; a535; a714; b110; c176; c246; c273-274; d166;
f080; f128; g092; h078; h093; m160; m190; n205;
o053; o057; o116; p068; r180; t206; v174-175.

Bonomelli, Geremia
t255.

Bonomini, Giuseppe
c188.

Bonstetten, Ch. Victor de
s042.

Bonvalot, Gabriel
t088.

Bonzi, Leonardo
d105.

Bookwalter, John W.
s204.

Boon, J.M.
d205.

Bootle Wilbraham, Edward. **See** *Wilbraham, Edward Bootle.*

Borchers, Philipp
b075; w061.

Bordeaux, Henry
a821; p060.

Borden, John
l188.

Borden-Field Museum Alaska-Arctic Expedition, 1927
l188.

Bordier, André César
h074; v258.

Borelli, Louis
a680.

Borgognoni, A.
s040.

Borioli, Ermes
a293.

Boroli, Achille
i179.

Boroli, Adolfo
i179.

Bortoli, G. de. **See** *De Bortoli, G.*

Bortolotti, Giovanni
g250; g254-256.

Borzaga, Giovanna
l076; n072.

Boscacci, Antonio
a648; s030; v020.

Bose, S.C.
g035.

Bosio, Piergiorgio
u063.

Bosman, C.A.W.
o015.

Bosshard, Carl
b073.

Bossoli, E.F.
n272.

Bosson, Pierre
r064.

Bossus, Pierre
a116; g316; p245.

Boswell, James
a048; j062-64.

Bottega dell'Alpinista e dello Sciatore
l175.

Botterill, Matthew
g007; o114.

Botti, Renata Pescanti. **See** *Pescanti Botti, Renata.*

Bouché, Henri
t156.

Bouchet, Paul du. **See** *Du Bouchet, Paul.*

Boufflers, *chevalier de*
o022.

Bougy, Alfred de
t128; v228.

Bouhélier, Saint-Georges de. **See** *Saint-Georges de Bouhélier.*

Bouille, Fernand de, *comte*
a675.

Bouillet, J.B.
c416.

Boulenger, G.A.
a064.

Bourgeois, Constant
v165; v259.

Bourleaux, Claude
r050.

Bourne, Samuel
i106.

Bourrit, Charles
n215.

Bourrit, Marc Théodore
a058; b120; c403.1; d079-82; e330; h074; i162-164; l111-112; n215; n249-251; p259; r102-104.

Bourrit, O.
m242.

Boutonnet, Charles
n172.

Bouvet, Jean
d072.

Bouvier, Auguste
a040.

Bouvier, Louis
d045.

Bovier, Léon
s462.

Bovy, Daniel Baud.   See Baud-Bovy, Daniel.

Bowdoin (Ship)
l189.

Bower, George S.
d168.1.

Bowling Mozley, James.   See Mozley, James Bowling.

Boyd, Louise A.
c299.

Boyd Dawkins, W.   See Dawkins, W. Boyd.

Boyé, Marc
g080.

Boyer, Roland
n129.

Boyle Bernard, Richard.   See Bernard, Richard Boyle.

Bozano, Lorenzo
g264.

Bozman, Ernest Franklin
b240.

Brackenhoffer, Elias
v282.

Bradbury, John
t079-80.

Bradley, Paul G.
a135.

Bradshaw, George
b198-201; n181.

Bradt, Hilary
b003.

Brainard, David L.
o117.

Bramanti, Vanni
n262.

Bramley-Moore, William
s227.

Brand, Charles
j065.

Brandt, Maurice
g301.

Brannan, Robert Louis
u025.

Brasca, Luigi
a292; c401; g245.1.

Braunstein, Josef
l055; r170.

Bravais, Auguste
m270.

Brawand, Samuel
g185; h255.

Braxton, Dorothy
a036.

Bray, Anna Eliza
m493.

Bray, F.G. de, *comte*
v267.

Brchel, Lubos
s389.

Bredenbrücker, Richard
d200.

Bredt, E.W.
a197.

Bregani, Giancarlo
c002.

Bregeault, Henry
c086; c128.

Bréhier, Julie Delaye.   See Delaye-Bréhier, Julie.

Brentari, Ottone
g252; g278; g292-295; i192; s402.

Bressy, M.
i188.

Breval, J.
r111.

Brevini, Franco
g135; m322.

Brevoort, Margaret Claudia
f030.

Brewster Emmons, Arthur.   See Emmons, Arthur Brewster.

Brian, Alessandro
g259.

Brickell Kerr, Mark.   See Kerr, Mark Brickell.

Bridel, Jean Louis Philippe
p192.

Bridel, Philippe Sirice
c422; c424; e148-149; p192; s148.

Bridges, George Wilson
a363.

Briet, Lucien
s322.

Brigg, William Anderton
i159.

Brightwell, Thomas
j057.

Briquet, Moise
a693; g332.

British Antarctic Expedition, 1907-1909
h054.

British Association
e216.

British Association. Section E Geography and Ethnology
a079.

British Columbia Mountaineering Club
h257.

British Mount Everest Expedition, 1921
c078; m215; m412.

British Mount Everest Expedition, 1922
a730; a732; k049; m411.

British Mount Everest Expedition, 1924
f039.

British Mount Everest Expedition, 1933
c021-022.

British Mount Everest Expedition, 1953
a710; n115.

British Mount Everest Expedition, 1975
p119.

British Mount Kongur Expedition to China
k065.

British Mountaineering Council
a313; g101; m439; m464; n095.

British Ski Association
s256.

Brizio, Guido
g218.

Broadrick, Richard Wilfred
i077.

Broc, Numa
m359.

Brockedon, William
i021-22; j075-76; w005.

Brockett, Eleanor
b133.

Brockmann-Jerosch, Heinrich
a467; a507.

Brodie, John C.
p042.

Brogi, Paolo
p277.

Broke, George
c103.4; w118.

Brook Northey, W.   See Northey, W. Brook.

Brooke, *Sir* Arthur de Capell
w110.

Brooke, T.
c340.

Brooke George, Hereford.   See George, Hereford Brooke.

Brooks, Bryn
b204.

Brooks, Charles Kent
g047; m207; p114; p117.

Brooks, John Graham
h253.

Brooks, Leonard
a704-705.

Brooks, Vincent
s052.

Brough, Louisa
a429.

Brovelli, Mario
a460-461; d178.

Brower, David R.
e117; g083; r155; s212.

Brower, Kenneth
e015.

Brown, Son, and Ferguson
b248.

Brown, Crum
p289.

Brown, Frederick Augustus Yates
f016.

Brown, George Francis Graham
a095; b168; h246.

Brown, Horatio F.
j027.

Brown, J.J. Graham
j003-4; l087.

Brown, J. Wood
b256; d198.

Brown, John
j029.

Brown, R.N. Rudmose.   See Rudmose-Brown, R.N.

Brown, Thomas Graham
a299-300; a311; b127; b208-214; c112; c285; c311;
c353; d208; e009; e112-113; e278; e297; e306; f040;
f048-50; f058; j066; m068; m260-261; m415; n093;
n100; p118; p124; p254; p275; s197; t299; t301.

Browne, Belmore
c364.

Browne, George Forest
i008; o027; p216; r032.

Browne, J.D.H.
t051.

Browne, Mary Ann
m265.

Bruce, *Hon.* Charles Granville
a730; a732; h121-122; k069; l022; m411.

Bruce, James
i128.

Bruce, William S.
n201; p279.

Brückner, Edouard
s580.

Bruckner, F.
o097.

Bruemmer, Fred
a606; a638; s145.

Brügger, Fr.
e061.

Bruhl, Etienne
v092.

Brun, Carl
s095.

Brun, Friederike
e082; p319; t012.

Bruneau, A.A.
a632.

Brunner, Giorgio
u059.

Brunner, Hans
s252.

Brunner, Joseph
h031.

Brunner, S.
f157.

Bruno, Silvio
g134.

Brushfield, Thomas N.
a344.

Brusoni, Edmondo
g235.

Bruun-Neergaard, Tønnes Christian
j046.

Bryan Owen, Ruth.   See Owen, Ruth Bryan.

Bryce, James, *Viscount Bryce*
t183.

Brydges, *Sir* Samuel Egerton
l018; r038.

Brydone, Patrick
t152.

Bryn, Alf B.
t104.

Buchan, David
v254.

Buchan, John
j028.

Buchanan, John Young
i004.

Buchenauer, Liselotte
a524.

Buchheister, J.
a530.

Buchwald, Vagn Fabritius
m193.

Buckingham, James Silk
b035.

Buckland, William
n221.

Bucknall, B.
m257.

Buddulph, M.S.
n166.

Büdel, Julius
s355.

Bugbee, Willis N.
e023.

Buhl, Hermann
a069.

Bühler, Fritz
g123.

Bühnau, Ludwig
e103.

Bullock Workman, Fanny. See Workman, Fanny Bullock.

Bülow, Otto v.
j012.

Bulwer, James Redford
e249.

Bündner-Oberländer-Verkehrsverein
i027.

Bunnell, J.F.
r218.

Bunny
h212.

Bünsch, Carl
g051.

Bunyan, John
j029.

Burbank, Rachel
f088.

Burch, Ernest S.
a638.

Burckhardt, J. Rudolf
u042.

Burdino, Felice
m401.

Burdsall, Richard Lloyd
f066; m163-164.

Bureau régional du tourisme de la Vallée d'Aoste
v017.

Burford, John
d102.

Burford, Robert
d089-91; d102.

Burgener, Alexander
a150.

Burla, Constantino
l075.

Burlingham, Frederick
h242.

Burman, José
p063.

Burnaby, Mrs Fred. **See** *Le Blond, Elizabeth.*

Burnand, F.C.
t174.

Burnand, Guy
w112.

Burnet, Gilbert
a523; c389; d047; d229; r047; r105; s289-292; t075;
t239; v236.

Burney Yeo, I. **See** *Yeo, I. Burney.*

Burnham, William A.
b164.

Burnley Literary and Scientific Society
m263.

Burns, R., Ltd. **See** *R. Burns Ltd.*

Burns, Walter Noble
y005.

Burpee, Lawrence J.
j073.

Burr, Malcolm
m507.

Burrard, *Sir* Sidney Gerald
s238.

Burroughs, John
i081.

Burton, John Hill
c009.

Bury, Charles Kenneth Howard. **See** *Howard-Bury,*
Charles Kenneth.

Bury, H. Hofer. **See** *Hofer-Bury, H.*

Bury, P. Hofer. **See** *Hofer-Bury, P.*

Buscaini, Gino
a278; a289; g150.1.

Bush, W.M.
a571.

Businger, Joseph Maria
i171; s374.

Busk, *Sir* Douglas
d048.

Busk, Rachel Harriette
v076.

Buss, Ernst
e115.

Bussoli, Nino
e145.

Butler, Arthur Gray
c246; z010.

Butler, Samuel
a436-438.

Butler Cheadle, Walter. **See** *Cheadle, Walter Butler.*

Buxton, Edward North
g097; s201-202.

Buzzati, Dino
b013; s111.

Byrd, Richard E.
a164; a729; m221.

Byron, George Gordon Byron, *Baron*
c190-192; m033; p283.

C., A.
m529.

C., G.D.   **See** *Gaudard de Chavannes.*

C., H. d.
v225.

C., J.
t018.

C., P.L.C.L.D.   **See** *Curti, Leopolde, comte.*

C., R.   **See** *Chambers, Robert.*

C.A. Parsons & Co
h057.

C***.   **See** *Crozet, Felix.*

Caballo, Ernesto
c121.

Cabane Britannia
i097.

Cabaud, Charles
p110.

Cadell, Thomas
o011-12.

Cadell, W.A.
j081.

Cadier, *frères*
a760.

Cadier, Georges
a759.

Cadier, J.
m098-99.

Cadisch, Joos
b023.

Cadore. Comunità
f070.

Caduff, Christian
a365.

Cagna, A.G.
a426.

CAI-UGET. **See** *Club Alpino Italiano. Sezione CAI-UGET.*

Caillat, Bernard
m247.

Caine, Nel
m499.

Cainer, Scipione
g295.

Cairngorm Club
c008.

Calanchi, Natale
m314.

Calder, E.H.S.
a072.

Calegari, G.B.
r184.

Calgari, Carlo
m306.

Cali, François
a240.

Calleri, Giacomo
a172.

Callin, Gino
o036-37.

Calosso, Achille
c140.

Calvert, W.E.
a133; a575; a603; c043; c391; i016; i126; n077; s231.

Calvin, Jean
a040.

Calzini, Raffaele
s156.

Camanni, Enrico
g154; l089.

Cambry, Jacques de
v269.

Camena d'Almeida, Pierre
p336.

Camenisch, Carl
g115; g158.

Camera Club
c062.

Cameron, Verney Lovett. **See** *Lovett-Cameron, Verney.*

Caminiti, Marcello
a474; g245.

Campanile, Vincent
c014.

Campbell, Bruce D.
w082.

Campbell, John Francis
f130.

Campbell, R.
g340.

Campbell, William
a627.

Campbell Gordon, Arthur. **See** *Gordon, Arthur Campbell.*

Campbell Shairp, John.   *See Shairp, John Campbell.*

Campiotti, Fulvio
a504; c337; d164; k001; s103.

Camsell, Charles
s299.

Camus, Théodore
o023.

Canac, Roger
m331.

Canada. Bureau of Northwest Territories and Yukon Affairs
n162; y015.

Canada. Bureau of Northwest Territories and Yukon Affairs. Lands, Parks and Forests Branch
o115.

Canada. Department of Indian and Northern Affairs
c040.

Canada. Department of Indian Affairs and Northern Development. Northern Economic Development Branch
c026.

Canada. Department of Marine and Fisheries
r130.

Canada. Department of Railways and Canals
r138.

Canada. Department of the Interior. Northwest Territories and Yukon Branch
g170; p248.

Canada. Department of the Interior. Railway Lands Branch
u030.

Canadian Archives
j073.

Canadian Arctic Expedition, 1913-1918
f065; m106.

Canadian Institute, Toronto
m059.

Canadian Pacific Railway News Service
t086.

Canault, Jean
r162.

Canavese, Sergio
v178.

Candido, Italo de.   See De Candido, Italo.

Candler, Edmund
u049.

Canetta, Nemo
s104-5.

Cannan, Joanna
h234.

Canoe Club
d094.

Canstein, Philipp von, *Baron*
b174.

Canterbury Mountaineering and Tramping Club
c034-35.

Cantù, Cesare
g228.

Canziani, Giovanni
e137.

Canzio, Ettore
a107; a110; i093-94; v120.

Capis, Giovanni
m156.

Capitaine, L.
s499.

Cappeller, Moritz Anton
p156.

Cappon, Massimo
a151; a396.

Capuis, Emmeli
l131.

*Carbonnières, Louis F. E. Ramond de.
See Ramond, Louis*

Cardellina, Osvaldo
g251; o100.

Cardiff and County Club
r266.

Carelli de Rocca Castello, Jacques
a672.

Carlesi, Piero
a472.

Carne, John
l105; r075.

Carnot, Maurus
l153; p055.

Carpelan, V.M.
v263.

Carr, Alfred
a092.

Carr, Glyn
i005.

Carr, Glyn.   See also Styles, Showell.

Carr, *Sir* John
c012; n159.

Carrara, Gino
v188.

Carraro, Giuseppe
m152.

Carrel, Georges
a252; a692; l102; v055.

Carrel, Jean Antoine
j022.

Carrier, Michel
e320; n214.

Carrighar, Sally
w095.

Carslaw, R.B.
l052.

Carson Roberts, A.   See Roberts, A. Carson.

Carteret, John Grand.   See Grand-Carteret, John.

Casanova, Oscar
e138.

Casara, Severino
a120; a655; f082; m348; p269; v117.

Casaubon, Isaac
h152.

Casiraghi, J.
s106; s109.

Caspari, Theodor
a816.

Caspari, W.
h207.

Cassarà, Emanuele
q009; t291.

Cassarini, Alessandro
c057.

Cassin, Riccardo
g010; m342; s446.

Castelli, Lina
m324.

Castello, Jacques Carelli de Rocca.   See Carelli de Rocca Castello, Jacques.

Castelnuovo, Antonio
e316.

Casteret, Norbert
c093.

Castiglioni, Ettore
c207; d188; g291.

Catelin, Camille de, vicomte.   See Arve, Stéphen d'.

Catholic Church
f028.

Catlin, George
n144.

Catlow, Agnes
s248.

Catlow, Maria E.
s248.

Caulfield Archer, Edward.   See Archer, Edward Caulfield.

Cavadini, Fernando
v049.

Cavagna, Paolo
a465; p135; u056.

Cavazzani, Francesco
l198; u050; v039.

Cavendish, Georgiana, Duchess of Devonshire.   See Devonshire, Georgiana Cavendish, Duchess of.

Caviézel, Michael
o004.

Cazal, E.J. Fazy. See Fazy-Cazal, E.J.

Cazin, Jeanne
e059.

Ceard, Robert
s335.

Ceccopieri, Fiory
d004.

Cecioni, Enrico
u068.

Cei, José Miguel
a505.

Cellerier, J.E.
a040.

Cellini, Benvenuto
l150; m146.

Cenise, Charles Rochat. See Rochat-Cenise, Charles.

Centre national de la recherche scientifique.
h103.

Centro Alpinistico Italiano. See Club Alpino Italiano.

Centro Camuno di Studi Preistorici
c179.

Centro Documentazione Alpina
g148; r209.

Centro Italiano Studio Documentazione Alpinismo Extraeuropeo
m341.

Centro Italiano Studio Documentazione Alpinismo Extraeuropeo. Archivio
a410.

Centro Studi Biellesi
a172.

Centro Studi per la Val del Sole
c334; v013.

Cérésole, Alfred
a008; f145; l066; m399; s057.

Cerlini, Aldo
s406.

Cermenati, Mario
a149.

Cernuschi, Francesco Lurani, conte. See Lurani Cernuschi, Francesco, conte.

Ceron, Nico
v031.

Cerretelli, Paolo
s347.

Cerutti, Marina Antonioli. See Antonioli Cerutti, Marina.

Cervi, Giuliano
c049.

Cessole, Victor de
c139; c402; p036; p321.

Ch., S.
d015.

Chabert, C.
e001.

Chabod, Renato
c017; c206; g133; m370.

Chaillu, Paul du. See Du Chaillu, Paul.

Chaley
p215.

Chambers, Ernest J.
u030.

Chambers, John R.
a614.

Chambers, Robert
t173.

Chambers, William
t135-136; t143.

Champin, Jean Jacques
n218.

Champion, F.W.
w114.

Chapin, Frederick H.
l021; m477-478.

Chapman, Frederick Spencer
m147-148.

Chappaz, Maurice
h047.

Chapuys Montlaville, Louis Alceste de
l128.

Charcot, Jean
a807.

Chardon, *sénateur*
s149.

Charlebois, O.
c186.

Charlemagne, *Emperor*
c177.

Charlet, Armand
v191.

Charnock, Richard Stephen
g354.

Charpentier, Jean de
e150.

Chase, Charles H.
a308.

Chasseur, Michel Joseph
l102.

Chastagnol, Robert
g313.

Château, Jean
c183.

Chateaubriand, François René de
a735; v217; v279.

Chateauvieux, *marquis de*
a253.

Chatelain, Clara de
m509.

Chatellus, Alain de
a424; d035.

Chatterton, Georgiana. *See Chatterton, Henrietta Georgiana, Lady.*

Chatterton, Henrietta Georgiana, *Lady*
p345.

Chaube, S.K.
h125.

Chavannes, Gaudard de. See Gaudard de Chavannes, Mr.

Chavannes, Herminie
l116.

Cheadle, Walter Butler
e216.

Chearful, Charles
c338.

Cheatham Churchill, George. See Churchill, George Cheatham.

Cheever, George Barrell
t201; w029-31.

Cheever Shattuck, George. See Shattuck, George Cheever.

Chemin de Fer de Paris à Lyon et à la Méditerranée
g285.

Cherry-Garrard, Apsley
w130-131.

Chersi, Carlo
i180.

Chesson, W.H.
a340.

Chetwode Eustace, John. See Eustace, John Chetwode.

Chevalier, Pierre
s445.

Chevalley, Gabriel
a820; f092.

Chevalley, Theo
p244.

Chevallier, Jean Jacques
g177.

Chevallier, Raymond
a762.

Chezy, Helmina von
n139.

Chi, Jian-mei
g091.

Chiappini, Vincenzo
m367.

Chicago Mountaineering Club
n112.

Chiesa, Angela Ottino della. *See Della Chiesa,
Angela Ottino.*

Chiggiato, Giovanni
a399.

Chinese Mountaineering Association
h089.

Chorier, Nicolas
h178.

Chouinard, Yvon
s017.

Christen, Ernest
m116.

Christian, Edgar
d046.

Christie, E.W. Hunter
a567.

Christillin, J.J.
l068.

Christoffel, Ulrich
b048; m319.

Christomannos, Theodor
d181.

Church, Earlyn
a485.

Churchill, George Cheatham
d172.

Cicognara, R. Petrali. *See Petrali Cicognara, R.*

Cigolla, Arturo
r179.

Cillia, Manlio de. *See De Cillia, Manlio.*

Cima, Claudio
g180; s038.

Cingria, Alexandre
c378; i178.

Cingria, Charles Albert
p032.

Cipriani, Eugenio
v154.

Ciraolo, Clara
a522.

Cita, Alessandro
c437.

Citizen (Ship)
a634.

Civiale, A.
a230.

Claes, Astrid Gehlhoff. *See Gehlhoff-Claes, Astrid.*

Claparède, Arthur de
c172.

Claris de Florian, Jean Pierre. *See Florian, Jean
Pierre Claris de.*

Clark, Edmund J.
a682; a699; n043.

Clark, Henry W.
h170.

Clark, Ronald William
d030; e007; g165; p138; q002; s225; s357; v149.

Clarke, Edward Daniel
t219.

Clarke, Lionel W.
w013.

Claude, Robert
l201.

Claut, S.
a276-277.

Clavarino, Luigi di, *marchese*
s009.

Cleare, John
w126.

Clerici, Ildefonso
i060.

Clifton Paris, T. *See Paris, T. Clifton.*

Climbers' Club. *See also Series Index (Climbers' Club guides to Wales)*
b257.1; c238-240; c250; c278; r262.1; r265.1.

Clinch, Nicholas B.
c226; w008.

Clinker, Charles
u023.

Clissold, Frederick
n031.

Clive, I.H.
m118.

Clos, Bernard
p227.

Clowes, George
f100; p149.

Club alpí català. Centre excursionista de Catalunya
p227.

Club alpin académique de Genève
h051.

Club alpin belge
r160.

Club alpin catalan. See Club alpí català.

Club alpin de Londres. See Alpine Club.

Club alpin français
a541; a544; c044; e001; g314; m189; m333; m346; r048; t281.

Club alpin français. Groupe de haute montagne
a380; a531; a542; i168; l174; m044; m346; s382.

Club alpin français. Réunion générale, 1934
o071.

Club alpin français. Section de Chamonix
p014; s153.

Club alpin français. Section de Paris-Chamonix
b258.

Club alpin français. Section de Pau
d040.

Club alpin français. Section de Provence
c106-107.

Club alpin français. Section de Savoie
r017-18.

Club alpin français. Section des Alpes-Maritimes
a383; p321.

Club alpin français. Section des Pyrénées centrales
o071.

Club alpin français. Section du Caroux
r016.

Club alpin français. Section Léman
g300.

Club alpin français. Section lyonnaise
r159.

Club alpin française. Spéléo-club de Paris. See Spéléo-club de Paris.

Club alpin italien. See Club Alpino Italiano.

Club alpin suisse. See Schweizer Alpen-Club.

Club Alpino Accademico Italiano
a551.

Club Alpino di Torino. See Club Alpino Italiano.

Club Alpino Español
a579.

Club Alpino Italiano
a107; a267; a292; a746; b177-178; b269; d070; d195; g010; g062; g256; g288; i111; i190; m040; m043; m381; o076; p005; p048; p098; p323; r063; r109; r181; r185-186; r207-208; r210; s180; t056; t267; v120; v143.

Club Alpino Italiano. Biblioteca nazionale
c061.

Club Alpino Italiano. Centro Alpinistico.
a265-266; m040.

Club Alpino Italiano. Comitato Coordinamento Trentino-Alto Adige
g246; s173.

Club Alpino Italiano. Comitato Nazionale per le Onoranze ad Emilio Comici
a408.

Club Alpino Italiano. Comitato Scientifico
a411.

Club Alpino Italiano. Comitato Scientifico. Commissione Medico-Fisiologica
n264.

Club Alpino Italiano. Comitato Scientifico. Commissione Toponomastica
d162.

Club Alpino Italiano. Commissione Centrale delle Pubblicazioni
t271.

Club Alpino Italiano. Commissione Centrale per lo Sci-Alpinismo
s179.

Club Alpino Italiano. Commissione Glaciologica
b180.

Club Alpino Italiano. Commissione Nazionale Scuole di Alpinismo
g032.

Club Alpino Italiano. Congresso Nazionale, 70th
a744.

Club Alpino Italiano. Consiglio Direttivo
o076.

Club Alpino Italiano. Corpo Soccorso Alpino
s150.

Club Alpino Italiano. Gruppo Sci Alpinistico di Torino
r006.

Club Alpino Italiano. Sede Centrale
m040; p048.

Club Alpino Italiano. Sezione Agordina
s189.

Club Alpino Italiano. Sezione Alpi Liguri
c433.

Club Alpino Italiano. Sezione Alto Adige
g225.

Club Alpino Italiano. Sezione Antonio Locatelli
a552.

Club Alpino Italiano. Sezione Cadorina
c208.

Club Alpino Italiano. Sezione CAI-UGET
p005; r006.

Club Alpino Italiano. Sezione Calabrese
g076.

Club Alpino Italiano. Sezione di Aosta
a582.

Club Alpino Italiano. Sezione di Bassano del Grappa
c288.

Club Alpino Italiano. Sezione di Belluno
b193; d187.

Club Alpino Italiano. Sezione di Belluno e Val Zoldana
t024.

Club Alpino Italiano. Sezione di Bergamo
d135-135.4; g296; p265; r188.

Club Alpino Italiano. Sezione di Biella
a553.

Club Alpino Italiano. Sezione di Bologna
a593-594; i181; l014.

Club Alpino Italiano. Sezione di Bolzano
b184.

Club Alpino Italiano. Sezione di Brescia
g244.

Club Alpino Italiano. Sezione di Busto Arsizio
c287.

Club Alpino Italiano. Sezione di Como
a554; g235.

Club Alpino Italiano. Sezione di Conegliano
c286.

Club Alpino Italiano. Sezione di Feltre
a276.

Club Alpino Italiano. Sezione di Fiume
p222.

Club Alpino Italiano. Sezione di Imola
g280.

Club Alpino Italiano. Sezione di Jesi
g270.

Club Alpino Italiano. Sezione di Lecco
a555.

Club Alpino Italiano. Sezione di Lecco. Sottosezione di Belledo
r021.

Club Alpino Italiano. Sezione di Lucca
g255.

Club Alpino Italiano. Sezione di Macugnana
r193.

Club Alpino Italiano. Sezione di Milano
a266; a556; c216; c289; e044; g213; i182; m071;
m365; n272; r054; r187; s137.

Club Alpino Italiano. Sezione di Modena
g255.

Club Alpino Italiano. Sezione di Padova
a647; c326; p094; s207.

Club Alpino Italiano. Sezione di Pavia
i189.

Club Alpino Italiano. Sezione di Piacenza
a557.

Club Alpino Italiano. Sezione di Pisa
t267.

Club Alpino Italiano. Sezione di Roma
g218; g232; n260; t168.

Club Alpino Italiano. Sezione di Sassari
a117.

Club Alpino Italiano. Sezione di Thiene
t248.

Club Alpino Italiano. Sezione di Torino
a393.1; a402; a521; c047; c088; e189; g267; n232.1;
p097; r062; r215; s041; v046; v081.

Club Alpino Italiano. Sezione di Torino. Gruppo
Studentesco S.A.R.I.
d008.1.

Club Alpino Italiano. Sezione di Torino. Sottosezione G.E.A.T.
n263.

Club Alpino Italiano. Sezione di Trieste
a516; m339.

Club Alpino Italiano. Sezione di Valdagno
v031.

Club Alpino Italiano. Sezione di Varallo
i095-96; p155; v136.

Club Alpino Italiano. Sezione di Varese. Gruppo
Roccia
a687.

Club Alpino Italiano. Sezione di Venezia
d196.

Club Alpino Italiano. Sezione di Vicenza
a099; c437.

Club Alpino Italiano. Sezione di Vigevano
a167; a171; a578.

Club Alpino Italiano. Sezione Fiorentina
b179; c001.

Club Alpino Italiano. Sezione Ligure
a558; b181; n232.

Club Alpino Italiano. Sezione Napoletana
s190.

Club Alpino Italiano. Sezione Trivenete
s021.

Club Alpino Italiano. Sezione Universitaria
a394; g217; m037; p091; r181; s099.

Club Alpino Italiano. Sezione Valle Spluga
v040.

Club Alpino Italiano. Sezione Valtellinese
s030.

Club Alpino Italiano. Sezione Valtrompia (Brescia)
c188.

Club Alpino Italiano. Sottosezione di Dongo
t263.

Club Alpino Italiano. Stazione Universitaria
p091-91.1; v008.

Club du jeune ami des animaux de la vallée du Gier
s507.

Club Excursionista de Gracia
e214.

*Club suisse de femmes alpinistes. See Schweizer-
ischer Frauen-Alpen-Club.*

Cluverius, Philippus
i131.

Coaz, J.W.
h201; l045.

Cobbett, James P.
j054.

Coche, Raymond
a427.

Cochrane, John Crawford
t178.

Cochrane, John Dundas
n158.

Cockburn, Henry
c069-70; l088.

Cockburn, James
s529; v171-172.

Coghlan, Francis
h008.

Cojazzi, D.A.
v186.

Col, Umberto de.   See De Col, Umberto.

Colby, Merle
a122.

Coldevin, Thorolf
i003.

Colding, Jon Jensen
d017.

Cole, *Mrs* Henry Warwick
l012.

Coleman, Edmund Thomas
s052.

Colladon, D.
n210; s149.

Collège de Genève
e024.

Collet, Léon W.
m228; s433.

Colli, Dante
a476; c090; g206; l044.

Collie, John Norman
c259; c265; s225; s270.

Collings, Henry
s564.

Collingwood, William Gershom
d111; l145.

Collins, Francis Arnold
c071.

Collins, Henry B.
a611.

Colnago, Carlo
e137.

Colomb, Eugène
p043.

Colton, C.C.
t071.

Colville, Mary
v244.

Combe, Edouard
a232; e022.

Combe, G.A.
t100.

Comer, George
a635.

Comici, Emilio
a408; a655; v117.

Comino, Sandro
g211.

Comitato Glaciologico Italiano
b180; r196.

Comité des travaux historiques et scientifiques.
Section de géographie
m359.

Comité himalayen de Genève
e188.

Comité national français des recherches antarctiques
e146.

Commissione Sentieri e Segnavia Alpini
g248.

Compagnie Air-Union Aéronavale
t156.

Compagnie des guides de Chamonix.   See Syndicat des guides Chamonix-Mont Blanc.

Compagnoni, Achille
u054.

Compton, Edward T.
e002; w050.

Compton, Thomas
n156.

Conci, Giuliano
c213.

Condamine, Charles Marie de la.   See La Condamine, Charles Marie de.

Confederazione Nazionale Sindacati Fascisti dell'Agricoltura
a743.

Conference on United States Polar Exploration, Washington, 1967
u033.

Congrès des Clubs Alpins, Annecy, 1876
t280.

Congrès géologique international, 11th, Stockholm, 1910
e198; k066.

Congrès international d'alpinisme, 3rd, Chamonix, 1932
t281.

Congrès international de l'alpinisme, Turin, 1885
g277.

Congrès international de l'alpinisme, Paris, 1900
c359.

Congrès international de l'alpinisme, Monaco, 1920
b250-251; c358.

Congrès médical de Genève, 1877
d045.

Congresso Alpino Nazionale, 17th, Turin, 1885
g277.

Congresso Alpino Nazionale, 26th, 1894
g208.

Congresso degli Alpinisti Italiani, 32nd, Brescia, 1901
o038.

Congresso degli Alpinisti Italiani, 39th, Florence, 1908
m396.

Congresso degli Alpinisti Italiani, 42nd, Turin, 1913
i190.

Congresso Nazionale della Montagna, 1st, Sondrio, 1931
a743.

Conighi, Elio
o036-37.

Conly, Maurice
i007.
Conradt, Krieger
b003.

Consiglio, Paolo
p027; p031.

Consiglio Nazionale delle Ricerche
m398.

Consociazione Turistica Italiana
a266; s452; s455.

Constance (Ship)
i066.

Constant, François M.S.
l046.

Constant, Rosalie de
v244.

Constantin, A.
d148.

Constantin Marie, *brother*
t269.

Conty, Henry A. de
s468.

Conway, Derwent
s573; t020.

Conway, William Martin, *Baron Conway.   See also Series Index (Conway and Coolidge's climbers' guides).*
a070; a073; a333; a431; a441-442; a706; b176; c242-246; c257-258; c273-274; d129; d215; e228; f057; l084; m441; m454.1; m455-456; m462; t308; z014.

Cook, B.H. Kemball.   See Kemball-Cook, B.H.

Cook, Charles
t081.

Cook, Eliza
t107.

Cook, Elsie Thornton
q011; v184.

Cook, Emily Constance
m447.

Cook, Frederick Albert
c054; r154; t108; t114.

Cook, James
n049; v198; v272.

Cook, Thomas, & Son.   See Thomas Cook Ltd.

Cooke, Alan
e231.

Cooke, George
t306.

Cooley, W.D.
w129.

Coolidge, William Augustus Brevoort.   *See also Series index (Conway and Coolidge's climbers' guides).*
a082; a109; a166; a232; a306; a366; a442; a468; a804; b107-108; b155.1-156; b250-251; c087-088; c104-105; c122-123; c137-138; c177; c199; c215; c270-271; c303-304; c307-308; c310; c314-316; c325; c331-332; d022; d060; d122; d128; d132.1; d215; e071-073; e075; f111-112; g157; g209-210; g319; g345; h129.1; h179; h182; h188; i168; j026; j033; l065; l074; l084; l170; l196; m074-76; m079; m187; m248; m286; m288; m383; m498; m523; n007; n128; n235; o031; o083-84; p046; p051; p107-107.1; p115; p166; p252; p256; r019; r268; s285; s393; s531; t122; t246; t276; t303; u017; w002; w014; w049; w072; z036; z042.

Cooper, C.J. Astley.   See Astley-Cooper, C.J.

Cooper, James Fenimore
e209; r148; s244.

Copeland, Fanny S.
b031.

Copland, Dudley
l184.

Corbellini, Giancarlo
s104-105.

Corbinian, Pater.   See Steinberger, Stephan.

Cordes, Aug.
h186.

Cordier, Patrick
p243.

Corin, Joseph
e132.

Cornaz-Vulliet, Charles
e053.

Corner, George W.
d168.
Corner, Julia
h171.

Corona, Giuseppe
c059; p134.

Corpo Nazionale di Soccorso Alpino
b169; r185; s272.

Corso Nazionale Istruttori, 2nd, Col d'Olen, 1958
s150.

Correvon, Henry
a259; a736; f076.

Corti, Alfredo
a271; p179; r054.

Cortiana, Marcello
t248.

Corwin (Ship)
r126-127.

Coryate, Thomas
c408.

Cossard, Italo
h144.

Cossard, Rino
t058.

Cosson, César
s359.

Cotelli, Franco
s102.

Cotelli, Mario
s102.

Cotta, Bernhard von
a180; g042.

Coupé, Serge
e131.

Coupland, Reginald
l185.

Courthion, Pierre
m330.

Courval, M. de
e001.

Couttet, James
s250.

Coutts, Walter
s365.

Couturier, Marcel
g067.

Couvert du Crest, Roger
v056.

Covino, Andrea
d002.

Cowell, J.J.
o054.

Cowles, Elizabeth S.
a304.

Cox, James R.
c226.

Cox, Samuel S.
a631.

Coxe, Henry
p140; t192; t194.

Coxe, William
a066; g021; l115; l177; s245-246; t224-227; v240.

Cozzani, Ettore
g064; m320; q003; v130.

Cozzani, Matelda
f154.

Cracroft, Sophia.   See Franklin, Sophia.

Cramer, John A.
d158-159.

Crane, Jane Miriam
s522-523.

Craufurd Grove, Florence.   See Grove, Florence Craufurd.

Craven, *Miss*
l111-112.

Crawford Cochrane, John.   See Cochrane, John Crawford.

Creasey, C.H.
j030; l146.

Crest, J.B. Micheli du.   See Micheli du Crest, J.B.

Crest, Roger Couvert du.   See Couvert du Crest, Roger.
Crétier, Nerina
s479.

Crettez, Maurice
m116.

Creux, René
b036.

Crichton Somerville, D.M.M.
s257.

Cristofolini, Mario
n091.

Crockett, S.R.
r007.

Croly, George
t022.

Crombie Ramsay, Andrew.   See Ramsay, Andrew Crombie.

Crousaz, Henry de
i171.

Crouse, Nellis M.
s144.

Crowley, Aleister
g161.

Crowther, B.M.
i073.

Crozet, Félix
n218.

Cruikshank, George
l025.

Cucagna, Alessandro
c051.

Cucchetti, Gino
n071.

Cuenod, Elizabeth A.
m519.

Cuénot, Henry
a805.

Culbert, Dick
a326.

Cumming, Constance F. Gordon. **See** *Gordon-Cumming, Constance F.*

Cumming, James
n048.

Cummings Johnson, Anna. **See** *Johnson, Anna Cummings.*

Cunningham, Allan
e229.

Cunningham, Carus Dunlop
f003; p168-169.

Cunninghame Graham, R.B.
e157; n202.

Curchod, Pierre
g313.

Curonici, Giuseppe
m319.

Curti, Léopolde, *comte*
l124.

Curti, Riccardo
i117.

Custine, Astolphe de, *marquis*
m145.

Cvetisic, Vjekoslav
s003.

Cyriax, Richard J.
s222.

Cysarz, Herbert
b068.

Cysat, Johann Leopold
b125.

D., A.   **See** *Douglas, Andrew.*

D., J.   **See** *Dornford, Joseph.*

D., J.M.
g114.

D., M.   *See Douglas, M.*

D., W.
t019.

D., Monsieur.   **See** *Dentand, Pierre Gédéon.*

D., Monsieur.   **See also** *Luc, Jean André de.*
D*******
v193.

D'Aurora, Elio
t032.

D'Ivernois, *Sir* Francis
t004-5.

Daffern, Gillean
k019.

Daffern, Tony
k019.

Dahinden, Josef
m278.

Dainelli, Giotto
a262; b255; g008; m243; m371; r055; s396.

Dal Bianco, Vincenzo
c223; m376.

Dal Mas, Giuliano
p030.

Dalbono, Paul
m229.

Dalla Porta Xidias, Spiro
a041; d152; e037; m317; m360; p093; s458; t166; t169; t254; t258; v025.

Dallago, Armando
p299.

Dallago, Franz
r192.

Dalloz, Pierre
g199-200; h046; p195; z004.

Dalton Hooker, Sir Joseph.   **See** *Hooker, Sir Joseph Dalton.*

Damen, Christianus Henricus
d157.

Dandolo, Tullio
s515; s517.

Daniel, Milan
z020.

Daniel Appleton & Co
g023.

Daniels, F.J.A.
v109.

Danish Peary Land Expeditions
m182.

Danmark-ekspeditionen til Grønlands nordøst-kyst, 1906-1908
s511.

Dansk Nordøstgrønlands ekspedition, 1938-39
u024.

Dapponte, Corrado
m034.

Darío, Rubén
e049.

Darmon, Eric
a094.

Darmstädter, Ludwig
g189.

Daudet, Alphonse
a089; p220; t029-32.

Daulte, Alice
v244.

Daunt, Achilles
c430.

Dauzat, Albert
m238; t163.

Dauzère, Camille
o017.

Davenport Adams, William H.   See Adams, William H. Davenport.

David-Neel, Alexandra
m533; t099; w117.

Davidson, C.J.C.
d141.

Davidson, Mavis M.
m409.

Davies, John
f059.

Davies, Joseph Sanger
d173-174.

Davies, Raymond Arthur
a617.

Davis, Mary Lee
a125; u022; w054.

Davy, Cha.
r102; r104.

Davy, Fred.
r102; r104.

Dawes, P.R.
n020.1.

Dawkins, W. Boyd
c225.

Dawson, Alastair G.
g086.

Dawson, Muir
c226.

Dawson, W.J.
w111.

Day, Beth
g085.

De Abney, W.
p168-169.

De Agostini, Alberto M.
m203; t266.

De Agostini, Enrico
r024.

De Amicis, Edmondo
a152.

De Amicis, H.   See De Amicis, Ugo.

De Amicis, Ugo
a137; c214; p111.

De Angelis, Gilberto
i183.

De Beer, *Sir* Gavin
a434; c110; d208; e014; f048-50; h177; m260; p275; s473; t197.

De Bertoldi, M.
a268.

De Bortoli, G.
a276-277.

De Candido, Italo
a512-515; a517-518; h208.

De Cillia, Manlio
a458.

De Col, Umberto
p299.

De Eccher, Anita Terragni. **See** *Terragni De Eccher, Anita.*

De Ferrari, Angelo
a458.

De Filippi, Filippo
a711; r278; s396; v050.

De Florian, Giulio
s103.

De Gemini, F.
g063.

De Infanti, Sergio
p093.

De Long, *Lieutenant*
o109.

De Long, Emma Wotton
e236.

De Peyster, J. Watts
d231.

De Pollenghi, Andrea Pollitzer. **See** *Pollitzer de Pollenghi, Andrea.*

De Riso, D.
p031.

De Santi, Marinella
i183.

De Simoni, Giovanni
v040.

De-Maurizi, Giovanni
o093.

De-Vit, Vincenzo
m158.

DeArmond, R.N.
l010.

Dease, Peter Warren
m180.

Debelmas, J.
a229.

Debraine, Yves
d019.

Debriges, E.
a237; a448.

Dechy, W.
m277.

Decurtins, A.
c037.

Deer, W.A.
s577.

Deflorian, Tarcisio
g247.

Degerbøl, Magnus
z022.

Degiampietro, Candido
s404.

Degregorio, Bepi
c406.

Dehansy, Charles
s465.

Dejaco, Valerio
b215.

Deketelaere, Caroline
n096.

Del Zotto, Giancarlo
a391.

Delacampagne, Christian
l006.

Delachaux, L.
c229.

Delafaye-Bréhier, Julie
a248.

Delaye, Théophile Jean
m086.

Delcros, François Joseph
n225.

Delebecque, André
s501.

Delétra, D.
m259.

Delkeskamp, Friedrich Wilhelm
m025.

Della Chiesa, Angela Ottino
a657.

Dellenbach, Marguerite E.
c367.

Delmard, Sophia Duberly
v177.

Dematteis, Luigi
c053.

*Denham Smith, Joseph.   **See** Smith, Joseph Denham.*

Denina, Ch.
t006.

Denkinger-Rod, H.
h147.

Dennis, Andy
a372.

Dent, Clinton Thomas
a037; a321; f156; m231; m455-456; p131.

Dent, Edward J.
t261.

Dentand, Pierre Gédéon
r100.

Denton, J.W.
c250.

Depoli, Aldo
a153; s422.

Depping, Georg Bernhard
s464.

Depraz, Charles
c084.

Derville, Henri
m282.

*Des Landres, Jean R. Frey.   **See** Frey des Landres, Jean R.*

Des-Loges, Chrétien
v223.

Desbarrolles, Adolphe
m239; v222.

Descostes, François
t280.

Desfayes, Jean Bernard
d055.

Desimoni, Giovanni
m394.

Desio, Ardito
c371; g061; v152.

Desmaison, René
m312; m335; t277.

Desor, Edouard
a097; a679; b129; d036; d066; e204-205; g013; j034;
j044; l154; m405; n256; p059.

Désormaux, J.
d148.

Dessauer, Alfred
b099.

Deutsch, Karl
a477; l056.

Deutsch-Schweizerische Nepal Himalaya Expedition, 1962
p327.

Deutsche Antarktische Expedition, 1938-39
d116.

Deutsche Himalaja Expedition, 1938
n017.

Deutsche Himalaja-Stiftung
n017.

Deutsche Himalaya Expedition, 1934
f096.

Deutsche Himalaya Expedition, 1973
d118.

Deutsche Hochschule für Leibesübungen
b087.

Deutsche Naturwissenschaftliche Gesellschaft
a182.

Deutsche Nordpolar Expedition, 1868
e111.

Deutscher Alpenverein
a216; a736; b090-91; m225-226; z002.

Deutscher Alpenverein. Bücherei
k037-38.

Deutscher Alpenverein. Sektion Bayerland
j014; m173.

Deutscher Alpenverein. Sektion Berchtesgaden
g181.

Deutscher Alpenverein. Sektion Berlin
m114.

Deutscher Alpenverein. Sektion Gröden
g190.

Deutscher und Osterreichischer Alpenverein
a376; a469; a528-530; a737; c434; d031; d175; d177;
e091; e108; g059; g125; h194; h200; m224; v204;
z002.

Deutscher und Osterreichischer Alpenverein.
Hauptausschuss
s066-67.

Deutscher und Osterreichischer Alpenverein.
Section Ampezzo
s381.

Deutscher und Osterreichischer Alpenverein.
Sektion Bayerland
m173.

Deutscher und Osterreichischer Alpenverein.
Sektion Berlin
f034.

Deutscher und Osterreichischer Alpenverein.
Sektion Bonn
f151.

Deutscher und Osterreichischer Alpenverein.
Sektion Bozen
r257.

Deutscher und Osterreichischer Alpenverein.
Sektion Halle
v159.

Deutscher und Osterreichischer Alpenverein.
Sektion Mark Brandenburg
b103.

Deutscher und Osterreichischer Alpenverein.
Zentral-Bibliothek
b254.

Devers, Sylvie
a639.

Devescovi, Guido
r202.

Devies, Lucien
a106-106.1; a114-115.2; g150.1; g199; g320-321;
j031; m080-81; m272-275.

Devonshire, Georgiana Cavendish, *Duchess of*
p044-45; s232.

Dhaulagiri-Expedition, 1958
l129.

Di Beaco, Bianca
s458.

Di Benedetto, Vito
c435; c447.

Di Evaldo, Cinzio
g077.

*Di Montilera, Lorenzo Rossi. See Rossi di Montilera,
Lorenzo.*

Di Pascale, G. Paolo
b012.

Di Pietro, Pericle
v139.

*Di Tassulo, Carlo Antonio Pilati. See Pilati Di
Tassulo, Carlo Antonio.*

Di Tella, G.
b192.

Di Vallepiana, Ugo
n173; r176; s099.

Diana (Ship)
r129.

Dickens, Charles
p142; u025.

Dickerson, Mahlon
e238.

Dickinson, Mary Lowe
e029.

Diebitsch Peary, Josephine. **See** *Peary, Josephine Diebitsch.*

Diehl, W.
g019.1.

Diemberger, Kurt
t170.

Diener, Carl
a498; g014; k034; v202; z018.

Dieterlen, Jacques
c185.

Diggelmann, A.W.
j097.

Dikenmann, R.
p020.

Dingle, Graeme
f044.

Direction générale des postes suisses. **See** *Switzerland. Post-, Telegraphen- und Telephonverwaltung.*

Discovery (Ship)
b246.

Dittert, René
a820; f092; p050.

Diubaldo, Richard J.
s385.

Dixie, *Lady* Florence
w004.

Dixon, William Hepworth
s575-576.

Dock, W.
o055.

Dodd, H. Martyn
g337.

Dodderidge, M.
m032.

Doglio, Ettore
o105.

Doig, Desmond
h086; s215.

Dolan, Edward F.
m115; w087.

Dolin, H.
r250.

Dollé, Frédéric
h132.

Dolomieu, Déodat Guy S.T. de Gratet de
j046.

Donaldson, Florence
l083.

Donati, Elio
c373.

Dondio, Willy
d185; d194; i104; r182-183; r201; v022; v151.

Donegani, Giovanni
g238.

Donkin, William F.
c083; e287.

Donnet, André
s011.

Donovan, E.
d087.

Donvito Gossi, Rosalba
a290; c117; g065; m072-73.

Doolard, A. den
f106; v012.

Dore, Robert.
a227.

Doren Honeyman, A. van. **See** *Honeyman, A. van Doren.*

Dorion-Robitaille, Yolande
c040.

Dorje Zödba. **See** *Sherap, Paul.*

Dornford, Joseph
m253.

Dorothea (Ship)
v254.

Dortous de Mairan, Jean Jacques
d160.

Dübi, Heinrich. *See also Series Index (Hochgebirgsführer)*.
a231; b107; b155.1-156; d132.1; d215; e013; e116; p002; p107-107.1; s004; u011; v199; v201; z026-27; z033.

Dubochet,
a253.

Dubois, Auguste
r053.

Dubois, Lucien
p212.

Ducas, G.
v290.

Ducati, Silvio
d218; f025.

Duchaussois, Pierre
a584; a814; c344; f031.

Ducis, C.A.
q014.

Ducommun, Jules César
e199-200.

Dufferin and Ava, Frederick Temple Hamilton-Temple-Blackwood, *Marquess of*
l097-98.

Dufour, Ch.
r028.

Dufour, El.
g182.

Dufour, Théophile
w103-104.

Dufour-Vernes, Louis
a503.

Dufranc, Michel
m077; s013.

Dufrenoy, Pierre Armand
m142.

Dufresne, Frank
m539.

Duhamel, Henry
a757; b016; c104-105; c304; c307; g319; h188; i168.

Duloum, Joseph
a520.

Dumas, Alexandre
g084; i053-58; s479; s530; t220.

Dumas, C.G.F.
v285.

Dumler, Helmut
g178; p099; q010; t254.

Dummett, G.A.
m480.

Dumollet, *Monsieur, de Saint-Malo*
m002; m246.

Dumont d'Urville, Jules. *See Urville, Jules Dumont d'*.

Dunant, Edouard Wyss. *See Wyss-Dunant, Edouard.*

Duncan, W.O.
e003.

Dundas, Lawrence John Lumley, Earl of Ronaldshay. *See Ronaldshay, Lawrence John Lumley Dundas, Earl of.*

Dundas Cochrane, John. *See Cochrane, John Dundas.*

Dunlop Cunningham, Carus. *See Cunningham, Carus Dunlop.*

Dunmore, Charles Murray, *Earl of*
p012.

Dunn, J.K.W.
i145.

Dunn, Robert
s191.

Dunn Gardner, John. *See Gardner, John Dunn.*

Dupaigne, Albert
m350.

Duparc, Louis
s501.

Duppa, Richard
m216.

Durandi, Iacopo
a280; d052.

Durham, William Edward
s482.

Durier, Charles
h139; m290-293.

Durio, Alberto
b144.

Dürst, Arthur
n259.

Dutton, Mary
f124.

Duverney, Jacques
t131-132.

Dyer, R.A.
m062.

Dyerberg, Jørn
l159.

Dyhrenfurth, Günter Oskar
h111.

Dyhrenfurth, Hettie
m162.

Dyhrenfurth, Norman G.
a489; d056.

E.U.M.C. *See Edinburgh University Mountaineering Club.*

Eaton, Charlotte Anne
c385.

Eaton, J.E.C.
c276-277; m108; m110; p067; t303.

Ebel, Eug.
p255.

Ebel, Johann Gottfried
a525-527; a739-741; g326; i123; m048-55; n246; s060; t193-194; v266.

Eberli, Henry
e066.

Ebersold, Friedrich
d227.

Ebner, Oswald
k015.

Eccher, Anita Terragni de. See Terragni de Eccher, Anita.

Echegaray, José
m151.

Eckenstein, Oscar
a354; k032.

Eckert, Max
g125.

Eckerth, W.
g015.

Ecole Albert-le-Grand
p255.

Ecole pratique des hautes études (VIe section). Centre d'études économiques
e025.

Economical Family
a090.

Edgcumbe, Richard J.F.
f047; m219.

Edinburgh University Mountaineering Club
c380; e030; e031; g340; j036.

Edwards, Amelia Blandford
m199; u047-48.

Edwards, John Menlove
c281-282; g163.

Egede, Hans
a799; g006.

Egerton Brydges, Sir Samuel. See Brydges, Sir Samuel Egerton.

Egerton-Warburton, R.E.
m217.

Egger, Carl
a108; i042; m197; p137; p170.

Egger, Rudolf
a187.

Eggers, C.U.D. von
b041.

Eggler, Albert
g071.

Eggstein, Otto
s158.

Egli, Emil
t185.

Egli, Johann Jakob
s070.

Egloff, Carl
i024.

Egmond d'Arcis, C.   See Arcis, C. Egmond d'.

Egyptian Hall, Piccadilly
d103; e034; h023-29; m510-511; n117; s567.

Ehrenberg, Fritz
a021.

Ehrenreich von Fichtel, Johann
m206.

Eidenschink, Otto
r171-172.

Eiselin, Max
w097.

Eisenlohr, Louis H.
m159.

Elander, Magnus
o086.

Elias, E.L.
e235.

Elie de Beaumont, L.   See Beaumont, L. Elie de.

Elizabeth, *Queen consort of George VI, King of Great Britain*
r274.

Elliot, George
m406.

Elliott, Henry W.
l086; o106.

Elliott, J.H.
g344.

Ellis, Edward S.
a491.

Ellis, Robert
e069; t260.

Ellis, Sarah
s481.

Elton, Charles Isaac
a051.

Elvin, Axel
t070.

Emery, M.S.
m256.

Emery, Mabel Sarah
s574.

Emery Verrill, Addison.   See Verrill, Addison Emery.

Emmer, Johannes E.
a530; g059.

Emmons, Arthur Brewster
m163-164; n053.

Encyclopaedia Britannica
h182.

End, G.
c293.

End, Willi
a422; g194.

Endicott, Wendell
a084.

Engel, Claire Eliane
b019; d161; e010; h173; l179; m279; m299-300; s473; t007; t067.

Engelhard, Georgia
p106.

Engelhardt, Christian Moritz
m388; n061.

Engelmann, *Dr.*
a800.

Engelmann, Gustav
l123.

Ente Provinciale del Turismo di Bologna
g280.

Ente Provinciale del Turismo di Ravenna
g280.

Ente Provinciale per il Turismo, Bergamo
b056.

Ente Provinciale per il Turismo, Bolzano
f017; g246; g289; p092; r183.

Ente Provinciale per il Turismo, Piedmont
i110.

Ente Provinciale per il Turismo, Trieste
i180.

Ente Provinciale per il Turismo, Vicenza
p318.

Enzberg, Eugen von
n136.

Enzensperger, Ernst
b087; v205.

Enzensperger, J. Josef
b096; h202.

Erbach, Albrecht
b042.

Erebus (Ship)
r254.

Erler, Heinrich
a451; b055; d056; h099; j024.

Ermel, Elisabeth
i045.

Erngaard, Erik
g175.

Erskine Murray, James.   See Murray, James Erskine.

Ertl, Hans
b098.

Escarra, Jean
j007.

Escher, G. von
a527.

Escher, Hans Caspar Hirzel.   See Hirzel-Escher, Hans Caspar.

Escher von der Linth, Hans Conrad
a562-563; b124; j023.

Escuyer, Pierre
a738.

Eskeland, Øystein Orre
v010.

Espinasse-Mongenet, L.
m285.

Espouy, Raymond d'
p339.

Etoile.   See Mitchell, Edward.

Etter, Paul
g074.

Etterlin, Peterman
k067.

Euringer, Gustav
p007.

Eustace, John Chetwode
c224.

Evaldo, Cinzio di.   See Di Evaldo, Cinzio.

Evans, Allen Roy
r067.

Evans, Charles.   See Evans, Sir Robert Charles.

Evans, Edward Ratcliffe Garth Russell, Baron Mountevans.   See Mountevans, Edward Ratcliffe Garth Russell Evans, Baron.

Evans, *Sir* Robert Charles
e331; k022; k048; o043.

Eve, A.S.
j030; l146.

Everett, William
c324.

Everyman's Encyclopaedia
h110.

Expedición Alpamayo 72
e214.

Expédition antarctique belge
a761.

Expédition française à l'Himalaya, 1936
h112.

Eyre, Vincent
m204.

F., W.
g181.

Faa, John
r007.

Fabbiani, Giovanni
p278; s008.

Fabre, Saturnin
c184.

Fabrikant, Michel
g314-315.

Faè, Gianni
i069; m323.

Fagel, *greffier*
b153.

Faillot, Marcel
b266.

Fain, Piero
a466.

Fairbanks Montagnier, Henry.   See Montagnier, Henry Fairbanks.

Fairfax Blakeborough, J.   See Blakeborough, J. Fairfax.

Falck, Rob.
a654.

Falcon (Ship)
f011.

Falcon Scott, Robert.   See Scott, Robert Falcon.

Falconnet, Jean
a676.

Faletto Landi, Lucienne
v178.

Falke, Konrad
i030.

Falkner, C.
s448.

Falsan, Albert
a249-250.

Family Eight
n190.

Fankhauser, E.F.L.
d062.

Fantin, Mario
a022-23; a025; a410; a412; a457; c118; i155; m341; q008; s196; s348-349; s457; t271.

Faoro, Giulio
g269.

Fappani, A.
c188.

Farquhar, Francis Peloubet
c226; m419.

Farrar, John Percy
f054; h155-156; i075; n203; o052; r041; s293.

Farrar Smellie, Thomas.   See Smellie, Thomas Farrar.

Fasana, Eugenio
c217.

Fäsi, Johann Conrad
s370-371.

Fasolo, Ugo
c003.

Fasso, Carlo
n068.

Fasso, Luigi
n068.

Fassola, G.B.
n068.

Fatio, Guillaume
g027.

Faure, Gabriel
v217.

Favre, Alphonse
c377; n227; r027.

Favre, Ernest
r161.

Favre, Henri
p341.

Fazy, Henri
g029.

Fazy-Cazal, E.J.
v232.

Fearnley, Dave
c060.

Feather, A.G.
k050.

Featherstone, B.K.
u031.

Fédération des sociétés pyrénéistes
b268.

Fédération française de la montagne
g314; p338; p341; s151-152.

Fédération française de la randonnée pédestre. Comité national des sentiers de la grande randonnée
c405.

Federazione Italiana Escursionismo
m378.

Federer, Heinrich
m107; p157.

Federici, Federico
i111.

Federspiel, Bruno
c205.

Fee, A.L.A.
p303; p306.

Feierabend, August
r195; s089.

Feilberg, Jon
p132.

Feilden, H.W.
s440.

Fejes, Claire
p090.

Felderhof, Herman
z049.

Fell and Rock Climbing Club of the English Lake District
a550; c277.1; c280.1; c431.1; d168.1; d203; e019; g164; j070; l167; p162-163; p314; s035.

Fell and Rock Climbing Club of the English Lake District. Library
l160-161.

Fell and Rock Climbing Club of the English Lake District. London Section
s301.

Fellenberg, Edmund von
d170-171; g044; h189; i194; r259.

Fellowes, Peregrine Forbes Morant
f061.

Fellows, *Sir* Charles
n032-32.2; n047.

Fels, Theodor Gsell.   See Gsell-Fels, Theodor.

Feng, Mao-seng
w133.

Fenimore Cooper, James. See Cooper, James Fenimore.

Fenn, Geo. Manville
c441-442.

Fennell Robson, George.   See Robson, George Fennell.

Fenzi, Sebastiano
m262.

Ferber, Aug. C.F.
e097.

Ferber, Johann Jacob
b123; p129.

Ferguson, Robert
s524.

Ferland, Léonie
v215.

Ferraguti Bazzini, Maria Paola
u063.

Ferrand, Henri
e172; h138; i170; n177; p258; r049; r245-247; t045.

Ferrandi, Mario
a475.

Ferrari, Agostino
i190; m289; n070; r181; r186; t122.

Ferrari, Angelo de.   See De Ferrari, Angelo.

Ferrari, Casimiro
c055.

Ferrari, Mario
v044.

Ferraris, Franco
o093.

Ferreri, Eugenio
a269-270.

Ferrero, Felice
v060.

Ferrucci, Antonio
t175.

Ferrucio Belli, Mario
s403.

Fetridge, W. Pembroke
h040.

Feyfar, Zdenko
l002.

Fiala, Ivan
p270.

Fichtel, Johann Ehrenreich von.   See Ehrenreich von Fichtel, Johann.

Field, Alfred Ernest
p073.

Field, Henry M.
o110.

Field Museum
l188.

Fient, G.
s366.

Fierli, Mario
u053.

Figari, Bartolomeo
a416; g264; m308.

Filippi, Filippo de.   See De Filippi, Filippo.

Filleul de Petigny, Clara
v281.

Fillol, André
p341.

Fincato, Lucio Alberto
m395.

Finch, George Ingle
c343; m021; m386.

Finden, Edward
i023.

Fine, Oronce
e193.

Fini, Franco
c003; g134; m380.

Fink, Christian
m070.

Finnie, Richard
l207; n053.

Finsler, Georg
w045.

Finsterwalder, Richard
f096.

Fiorio, Cesare
d005; p098.

Fischer, Andreas
a510; h192-193.

Fischer, Burkheld
r064.

Fischer, Christian August
b086; u014.

Fischer, Wilhelm
a160.

Fischer-Møller, K.
s231.

Fissont, P.
g331.

Fitzgerald, Edward Arthur
c273-274; h093.

Fitzgerald, Walter, Viscount Milton.   See Milton, Walter Fitzgerald, Viscount.

Fitzroy, Robert
b014.

Fitzroy Somerset, Lady.   See Somerset, Lady Fitzroy.

Flahault, Ch.
n252.

Flaig, Walther
a641; g107; h185; h191; i041; v200.

Fleiner, Albert
u032.

Fleming, Robert
c067.

Fleming, *Mrs* Robert
c067.

Flemwell, George
f079; s499.

Flender, Walther
z028.

Fletcher, Theodora C. Stanwell. See Stanwell-Fletcher, Theodora C.

Fletcher Kirkus, Colin.   See Kirkus, Colin Fletcher.

Flint, Richard Foster
c299.

Floreancigh, R.
g244.

Flori, Ezio
p173.

Florian, Giulio de.   See De Florian, Giulio.

Florian, Jean Pierre Claris de
g363; w102.

Florstedt, Alexander
i063.

Flückiger, A.
a386.

Flückiger, Otto
s079.

Foa, Eugénie
a248.

Foam (Ship)
l098.

Focolaccia
s110.

Foddanu, Piero
a172.

Foglietti, Raffaele
d053.

Foighel, Isi
h221.

Fondation suisse pour explorations alpines.   See Schweizerische Stiftung für Alpine Forschungen.

Fondazione Svizzera per Esplorazioni Alpine.   See Schweizerische Stiftung für Alpine Forschungen.

Fondazione Antonio Berti
d196; p094.

Fondragon, Mengin, baron de. See Mengin-Fondragon, baron de.

Fontaine, Emile
a102; a389; a694; c006; d073; n207; t253.

Fontanet, Jean Claude
m334.

Fonvielle, W. de
g098.

Forbes, George
t065.

Forbes, James David
l142; n163; n170; o018; o063; p081; p280; p290; r090; r121; t125; t145; t243-246.

Forbes, *Sir* John
p126-128; s213.

Forbes, Murray
d139.

Forbes Morant Fellowes, Peregrine. See Fellowes, Peregrine Forbes Morant.

Forcher-Mayr, H.
r257.

Förderreuther, Max
a156.

Fordyce Mavor, William. See Mavor, William Fordyce.

Forel, F.A.
e174; g131; o039; r028; s508; v094-104.

Forest Browne, George. See Browne, George Forest.

Forester, Thomas
n166.

Forestier, Alcide de, *vicomte*
a253.

Fornelli, Lino
a281.

Forster, Edmund
e068.

Förster, Hans Albert
b140; b166.

Forster, Thomas
a536; e064; e155; f004; i020; r147.

Forsyth, Joseph
r110.

Fort, Gaudy Le. *See Le Fort, Gaudy.*

Fortescue, Michael
c346.

Foster, Michael G.
f045.

Foster, W. Bert
f133.

Fowler, William
m508.

Fox (Ship)
v255.

Fox, Joseph Holroyd
h210.

Fox, Lorene K.
a566.

Fox Tuckett, Francis. *See Tuckett, Francis Fox.*

Fraas, Eberhard
s045.

Fraccaro, Plinio
g240.

Fradeloni, Sergio
g204.

Fraenkel, Knut
a511.

Fraipont, Gustave
j099; v211.

Fram (Ship)
f020; f110.

Francé, R.H.
a182.

France. Army. Réserve
r076.

France. Ministère de l'agriculture. Direction générale des eaux et forêts. Eaux et génie rural
r149.

France. Ministère du travail et de la prévoyance sociale
s377.

Franceschini, Gabriele
a464; c085; p009.

Francese, Gianfranco
v027.

Franchetti, Carlo
m037.

Franchetto, Ermanno
c403.

Franck, Harry A.
l204-205; v011.

Franck, Harry A., *jr*
l204-205.

Franco, Jean
m018.

François Simond *& fils*
s016.

Franke, Hermann
m389.

Frankland, C.D.
a068.

Franklin, *Sir* John
a620-622; a629; e179; f113-114; h145; l152; n026; n158; p326; s142; s222; s429; t068; t110; v219; v255.

Franklin, Sophia, *Lady*
l010.

Franklin Bozman, Ernest. *See Bozman, Ernest Franklin.*

Franz, Hans
m168.

Fraser, David
m060.

Fraser, Esther
c029.

Fraser, James Baillie
j058.

Frass, Hermann
b183; d185; f017; i104.

Frass, Hilde
v151.

Frassy, P.J.
n247.

Fredskild, Bent
h216-217.

Freeman, Andrew A.
c054.

Freeman, Roger D.
e239.

Freeston, Charles L.
g345; h092.

Frenademez, Albino
a452.

French Himalayan Expedition, 1936. **See** *Expédition française à l'Himalaya, 1936.*

Frendo, Edouard
f002; t039.

Freshfield, Douglas William
a071; a345; b037; e232; f156; h037; i152-153; l151; m455-456; n025; r243; t230; u045.

Freshfield, Henry Douglas
m154.

Freshfield, *Mrs* Henry
a305; s487.

Fresia, Camillo
c446.

Freuchen, Dagmar
p105.

Freuchen, Peter
a609; p105; z022.

Freudenberger, S.
a801.

Frey, Karl
a781.

Frey des Landres, Jean R.
i123.

Frey-Fürst, F.
e061.

Friedlander, Herman
v164.

Friedrich, Max
n121.

Fries, Th. M.
u067.

Friis, Herman R.
a616; u033.

Frischauf, Johannes
a423.

Frisia, Emilio
c336.

Frislid, Ragnar
f068.

Frison-Roche, Roger
c045; c219; g146; m278; m326; m332; m338; m353; n005; p249-250; r020; r118; r152-153; v091.

Frith, Henry
a727; t029.

Fröbel, Julius
r083.

Frobisher, Martin
l152.

Frosini, Vittorio
t258.

Frossard, Emilien B.D.
t009.

Fründen hut
c269.

Fryxell, Fritiof
i102.

Fuchs, Wilhelm
v111.

Fuessli, J.H.
e093.

Führerverein Grindelwald
g185.

Fukada, Kyuya
h123.

Fuller, Sir Francis
v090.

Fullerton, Arthur Grey
s495.

Fumagalli, Alberto
m037.

Fürst, F. Frey. See Frey-Fürst, F.

Furter, Willy
e100.

Fury (Ship)
j050.

Fusco, Vincenzo
c289.

Füssli, Johann Conrad
s372.

Fux, Adolf
a150; b018; k043.

G., *Freiherr von Saar*
d025.

G., *Armando Altamira. See Altamira G., Armando.*

G., C. *See Clowes, George.*

G., G.F. *See Gugliermina, Giuseppe F.*

G., H.
s571.

G., L., *of Geneva*
a030.

G., R. *See Gwynne, Robert.*

G.A.B. *See Gruppo Amici di Bismantova.*

Gaberell, Jean
s084.

Gaberscik, Rino
g279.

Gabert, Pierre
a245.

Gabrielli, Giuseppe
c334.

Gabrisse
g001.

Gachot, Edouard
a016.

Gadler, Achille
g225; g241-242.

Gaillard, Emile
a001; a101; a235-236; a238; a384; a732; c343; d067; j041; l118; m100; m303.1; p111; r031; v147.

Gaillarde, Raphaël
l006.

Gaisberg, Erwin von
a088.

Gaisberg, Pleasaunce von
a088.

Galasso, Carlo
b183.

Galignani
t194.

Galitzin, Emmanuel, *prince*
n131.

Gallais, A. Le. See Le Gallais, A.

Gallenga, Antonio
c413.

Gallet, Julien
d018; d068.

Gallhuber, Julius
b059; d176.

Galli, Mario
m395.

Galli-Valerio, B.
c333.

Gallicus. See Lançon, Xavier.

Gallo, Emilio
i018.

Gallois, Lucien
a508.

Galloni, P.
s006.

Galton, Francis
a652; v005-7.

Gamba, Angelo
i184; p265; r188.

Gandini, Carlo
d196.

Gandola, Sandro
d063; t263; v080.

Ganpat. See Gompertz, M.L.A.

García Viel, Emilio
s211.

Garden, J.F.
s167.

Gardiner, Frederick
a306.

Gardini, Galdino
r197.

Gardner, Arthur
a650.

Gardner, John Dunn
a696.

Garelli, Franco
c355.

Garello Guarisco, Carla
m305.

Garibaldi, L.A.
a521.

Garimoldi, Giuseppe
v046.

Garnier, E. Henri
n241.

Garobbio, Aurelio
a273-275; a392; d003; l079; m034; m344; p033; r151; s122.

Garrard, Apsley Cherry. See Cherry-Garrard, Apsley.

Gartok expedition, 1904-1905
g169.

Garwood, E.J.
a076; c392; f057.

Gastaldi, Bartolomeo
e193; s019; s503.

Gaston. See Series Index (Gaston's Alpine books)

Gaudard de Chavannes, *Mr*
j042.

Gaudin, A.
s567.

Gaudin, Charles Th.
f078.

Gaudin, Jean
m048-51.

Gaullieur, Eusèbe Henri
h142; s075-76; s474.

Gaussen, Henri
m351.

Gaussot, Philippe
s250.

Gautenon, Louis F.
e170.

Gauthier, *Mme de*
v224.

Gautier, E.F.
s010.

Gautrat, Jacques
d144.

Gavin, J.M.L.
t048.

Gayet-Tancrède, Paul. See Samivel.

Gaze, Henry
s539.

Geck, Heinz
g017.

Geer, Gerard de
c298; e198; g037; k066; n146; r046.

Gehlhoff-Claes, Astrid
b226.

Geiger, Hermann
d019; g018.

Geikie, Archibald
t060.

Geistbeck, Alois
s155.

Gelba, K.
h091.

Gelpke, R.
e061.

Gelzer, Heinrich
d211.

Gemini, F. de.   See De Gemini, F.

General Post Office, Switzerland.   See Switzerland.
Post-, Telegraphen- und Telephonverwaltung.

Genoud, Eugène
v229.

Gentil, H.
a806; b221.

Geographical Club
a098; l166; t259.

Geographische Gesellschaft, Hannover
f096.

Geological Society
a039; c392; e158; n221; r124.1.

Geologists Association
a549; l164.

Geophysical Year, 1957-58
r196.

George, Hereford Brooke
m518; o006.

George, Pierre
g034.

George V, King of Great Britain
n103.

George VI, King of Great Britain
r274.

Gepp, Hubert Majendie
f056.

Gerard, Alexander
a049; n021-22.

Gerard, P.J.
i160.

Gerber
i129.

Gerig, E. Redelsberger. See Redelsberger-Gerig, E.

Germain, Félix
a009; a391; a539; d064; d132; e086; e190; g145;
s298.

Germain, Jeanne
a539; e086; e190; g145.

German-Austrian Alpine Club.   See Deutscher und
österreichischer Alpenclub.

Gersdorf, Adolf Traugott von, Baron
j066.

Gershom Collingwood, William.   See Collingwood,
William Gershom.

Gervasutti, Giusto
m356; s036.

Gerwer, R.
h189.

Geschichtsforschender Verein von Oberwallis
l070.

Gesellschaft Alpiner Bücherfreunde
b113; d013; d032; g052.

Gesellschaftswagengruppe, Switzerland
a768.

Gesner, Conrad
o055.

Gex, F.
d021.

Geyer, Georg
h205.

Gherardi, Guido
s384.

Ghezzi, M.
v020.

Ghielmetti, Giuseppe
c111; l036.

Ghiglione, Piero
d008; d010; e106; h101; i052; m369.

Ghiringhelli, Paolo
a642.

Giacosa, Giuseppe
c058; g031; n262.

Giæver, John
l181; l209; r001.

Giani, Emilio
n264.

Giersing, Mona
g175.

Giglio, Pietro
s107.

Gigon, Fernand
h150.

Gigord, Edouard de
a112; c128.

Gilbert, Josiah
c004; d172.

Gilbert, Linney
b030.

Gilic, Stanislav
e139; m026.

Gilkerson, William
a487; a636.

Gillies, M.
i066.

Gillies Ross, W.   **See** *Ross, W. Gillies.*

Gillis, Charles J.
y006.

Gillis, Elsie McCall
n150.

Gilly, William Stephen
m140; n039-42; w006.

Gilpin, William
o013.

Giorcelli, Augusto
g061.

Giordani, Giovanni
c328.

Giordano, Felice
a684.

Giordano, Scipione
t047.

Giovane Montagna, Verona
q004.

Girard, C.F.
a243.

Girdlestone, Arthur Gilbert
h082.

Girier, Alain
e026.

Giudiceandrea, Giuseppe
b215.

Giussani, Camillo
a266; c187.

Giusta, Giovanni Antonio
g224.

Glaisher, James
o058; o060; o066-67.

Glareanus, Henricus
d076.

Glasgow University Mountaineering Club
m008.

Glenz, Marian
b001.

Glover, Samuel
d096.

Glutz-Blotzheim, Robert
h035; m056.

Gnifetti, Giovanni
n265-266.

Gnudi, Maurizio
d007.

Gobbi, Toni
s108; s179-180.

Gobessi, Iginio
s221.

Gobetti, Andrea
f129.

Goblet d'Alviella, *comte*
d024.

Godeffroy, Ch.
n226-227.

Godefroy, René
n056; w002.

Godsell, Philip H.
a633.

Goethe, Johann Wolfgang von
g115-116; s081.

Goetzmann, William H.
l193.

Gogarten, Emil
u001.

Gogna, Alessandro
a404; c101; e134; e136; g151; g205; v048; v084;
z021.

Gohl, Colin
t001.

Goja-ekspeditionen, 1903-1907
n137.

Golay, Charles
h254.

Golay, H.C.
g298.

Golbéry, Marie Philippe de
h143; s518.

Gold, F.
t232.

Goldwin, *Mr*
b222.

Golfströmsexpedition, 1936
i142.

Golliez, H.
t040.

Gompertz, M.L.A.
m009; r212.

Gonella, F.
a686.

Gonthier, François A.A.
e170.

Goodwin, C. Ross
b028.

Gordon, A.R.
r130.

Gordon, Arthur Campbell
c263.

Gordon, George, Lord Byron. **See** *Byron, George Gordon Byron, Baron.*

Gordon, *Sir* Thomas Edward
r240.

Gordon-Cumming, Constance F.
i091.

Gorfer, Adolfo
a118.

Gorfer, Aldo
s279; v038; v078.

Gorman, Jack
p095.

Gorret, Amé
a028; v148.

Gorse, André
p343.

Gos, Charles
a385; c115; c436; e085; h137; h233; m450; n267;
p262; p313; t177; v235.

Gos, François
z006-7; z012.

Gossi, Rosalba Donvito. **See** *Donvito Gossi, Rosalba.*

Goswami, S.M.
e182.

Gotch, M.S.
o049.

Gothic Hall, Pall Mall
c081.

Gothofredus, Jacobus
h178.

Gotta, Salvator
a453.

Götz, J.
t037.

Gould, Laurence McKinley
c313.

Gourdault, Jules
a015; e219; s461.

Graber, Alfred
m520.

Gradenigo, Sergio
p232.

Graefe, H.
s075.

Graf, J.H.
o080.

Graffigna, Carlo
h036.

Graffigny, H. de
m066.

Graham, J.C.
r256.

Graham, R.B. Cunninghame.   See Cunninghame Graham, R.B.

Graham, William Woodman
c450; e291; t189; u062.

Graham Brown, Thomas.   See Brown, Thomas Graham.

Graham Irving, Robert Lock.   See Irving, Robert Lock Graham.

Grainger, H.J.
w032.

Gramer, Kurt
g196.

Grancey, Edmond de Mandet, baron.   See Mandet-Grancey, Edmond de, baron.

Grand Hôtel Couttet et du Parc, Chamonix
g138.

Grand Hôtel Royal Bertolini
c419.

Grand Trunk Pacific Railway. General Passenger Department.
c032; m423.

Grand-Carteret, John
m336.

Grande, Julian
b111.

Grande Chartreuse
n122; n218; n239-240; p160; v182; v259.

Grande Traversata delle Alpi. Comitato Promotore
g148.

Grandjean, Maurice
a017.

Grandvoinet, R.
s570.

Grant, James
r042.

Granville Bruce, Hon. Charles.   See Bruce, Hon. Charles Granville.

Grass, Carl
f107.

Grasserus, Johannes Jacobus
i198.

Grassi, Gian Carlo
v051.

Grassler, Franz
b166.

Grasso, Paolo
v178.

Gratacap, L.P.
n105.

Gratet de Dolomieu, Déodat Guy S.T. de.   See Dolomieu, Déodat Guy S.T. de Gratet de.

Gratzl, Karl
h129.

Gray, David
r134.

Gray, Robert
l095.

Gray, Thomas
p190.

Gray Butler, Arthur.   See Butler, Arthur Gray.

Great Britain. Air Ministry
l182.

Great Britain. Board of Trade
b014.

Great Britain. Parliament
m069.

Great Britain. Royal Navy
s222.

Great North Atlantic Telegraph
g167.

Grebauval, Armand
a756.

Greely, A.W.
a501; g173.

Greely Relief Expedition
g173; r133.

Green, William Spotswood
a496; e234; h081.

Greene, Raymond
o129.

Greenman, David
b003.

Greenwood, A.M.
m017.

Greg, Edward Hyde
n051.

Gregory, Alexander Tighe
p235-238.

Gregory, Alfred
p139.

Gregory, C.J.
t109.

Gregory, John Walter
c392; f057; t109.

Greinz, Rudolf
b057.

Greische, Antoine Scitivaux de, comte.   **See** *Scitivaux de Greische, Antoine, comte.*

Grellet, Pierre
g153.

Greloz, R.
u061.

Gremli, August
f073.

Gresham Club
r264.

Grey Fullerton, Arthur.   **See** *Fullerton, Arthur Grey.*

Gribble, Francis Henry
e011; l011; l017; m466; s410.

Grierson, Thomas
a812.

Griffin, Arthur Harold
i122.

Griffiths, Ellis
s427.

Griffiths, William Nelson
l110.

Grill, *Family*
g181.

Grill, Johann
g181.

Grimm, *Brothers*
f153.

Grinnell, Elizabeth
g120.

Grinnell, Henry
a620-622.

Grinnell, Joseph
g120.

Grinnell Expedition, 2nd
a620-622.

Gritstone Club
j037; r263.

Grob, Ernst
z046.

Groff, Lionello
d133.

Grohmann, Paul
m227; s121.

Grohmann, William Adolphus Baillie.   **See** *Baillie-Grohmann, William Adolphus.*

Grønnow, Bjarne
a027.

Grøntved, Johs.
b194.

Gros, R.H.
m098-99.

Grosjean, G.
f137.

Gross, Aldo
l044.

Gross, H.S.
c277.1.

Grosse, Carl, *Marquis von Pharmusa*
g056.

Grosspietsch, Walter
f007.

Grote, George
s184.

Groupe pyrénéiste de haute montagne
p338.

Grove, Florence Craufurd
f131.

Grube, A.W.
a217-218; u005.

Gruchy, A. de
a732.

Gruner, Gottlieb Sigmund
e039; h146; n058.

Gruner, J.R.
d051.

Gruppi Universitari Fascisti
a394.

Gruppo Alpinisti Rocciatori Sciatori
a516.

Gruppo Alpinisti Sciatori Lucchesi
s110.

Gruppo Alpinistico Corvacci
g237.

Gruppo Amici di Bismantova
p154.

Gruppo Condor di Lecco
p180.

Gruppo Italiano Scrittori di Montagna
m309.

Gsell-Fels, Theodor
s071.

Gualandris, Alverio
p219.

Guaraldo, Carlo
a393.

Guarisco, Carla Garella. **See** *Garella Guarisco, Carla.*

Gudme, Iver
p208.

Gueca, Catherine
s491.

Guérard, Eugène
v245.

Guernsey, A.H.
p198.

Guggenbühl, *Dr.*
a030.

Gugliermina, G.B.
a107; a746; v120; v136.

Gugliermina, Giuseppe F.
a107; a746; c318; g217; m298; m374; v120; v136.

Guibert, Jacques Antoine de, *comte*
v278.

Guibert, Louise A. de, *comtesse*
v278.

Guichonnet, Paul
a245; h159.

Guidetti, Etienne
h225.

Guillarmod, J. Jacot. **See** *Jacot-Guillarmod, J.*

Guillaume, *dr.*
a803; j034; t279.

Guillaume, A.
q015.

Guillimannus, Franciscus
d042.

Guillon, Edouard
a258.

Guise Tyndale, Henry Edmund. **See** *Tyndale, Henry Edmund Guise.*

Guiton, Paul
r245; s460; z047.

Guler, R.
o005.

Guler von Weineck, Johann
r004.

Gümbel, C.W.
a528.

Gumuchian, O.
m089-90; m094; m097.

Gunn, Wade W.
b152.

Gunneng, Asbjørn
c272.

Guo, Ke-yi
w133.

Gupta, R.K.
b151.

Gurney, A.
d028.

Gurtner, Othmar
s061.

Gusset, H.
a219.

Güssfeldt, Paul
i062; m259; m362.

Gustav III, *King of Sweden*
k064.

Guthrie Tait, Peter. **See** *Tait, Peter Guthrie.*

Guttridge, Leonard F.
i010.

Gwynne, Robert
b026.

Gyatso, Sonan. **See** *Sonan Gyatso.*

Gygax, Georges
d019.

Gyger, W.J.
g338.

H., A.A.
w083.

H., A.M.
o004.

H., E.R.
w078.

H., G. **See** *Hofman, Georg.*

H., J.
m284.

H., K. **See** *Hevat, Kirkwood.*

H., R.A. **See** *Hodgkin, Robert A.*

H. Perkins & Co.
m137.

Haag, Peter
e035.

Haas, Rudolf
l133.

Hackaert, Jan
s082.

Haek, D.
e104.

Haenicke, Alexandrine
u021.

Haensel, Carl
k017; l208.

Hager, Hannsjörg
p092.

Hager, Karl
p055.

Hahn, Carl von
k039.

Halas, Alojz
h128.

Halder, Arnold
b085.

Hall, A.S. Marshall. See Marshall-Hall, A.S.

Hall, A. Wilford
s443.

Hall, Anna Gertrude
n019.

Hall, Basil
p054.

Hall, Charles Francis
a629; l152; m149.

Hall, Charles Henry
m150.

Hall, Charles W.
a081.

Hall, Charlotte
t089.

Hall, E.G.
h120.

Hall, Ludwig
m278.

Hall, *Mrs* S.C.
b197.

Hall-Jones, Gerald
m237.

Hallberg, F.
s249.

Haller, Adolf
a139.

Haller, Albrecht von
a139; a179; a185; v128-129.

Haller, Gottlieb Emanuel von
v126.

Halliburton, Richard
r255.

Hamel, Joseph von
e240-241; r088; r099.

Hamer, Samuel Hield
d180.

Hamilton, *Sir* William
a052; o011-12.

Hamilton-Temple-Blackwood, Frederick Temple, Marquess of Dufferin and Ava. See Dufferin and Ava, Frederick Temple Hamilton-Temple-Blackwood, Marquess of.

Hamsa, *Bhagwan*
h219.

Hannibal
b253; c204; c302; c425; d158-159; e069; h037-39; h140-141; t260; t286.

Hanning Speke, John. See Speke, John Hanning.

Hanoteau, Guillaume
a254.

Hansen, Eric Steen
l141.

Hansen, Godfred
n137.

Hansen, Hagmund
p208.

Hansen, Jens C.
c356; s510.

Hansen, Thorkild
w052.

Hansen Høyer, Liv. See Høyer, Liv Hansen.

Hanssen, Helmer
g079.

Hantzsch, Bernhard
m534.

Harcourt, A.F.P.
h113.

Hardegg, Peter
z041.

Harding, Warren 'Batso'
d206.

Hardmeyer, J.
l187; m514.

Hardwick, Charles
o119.

Hardy, Alfred
r039.

Hardy, Joseph
p146.

Hardy Peacocke, Thomas Arthur.   See Peacocke, Thomas Arthur Hardy.

Harewood, Brian
p100.

Harewood, Quintin
p100.

Hargreaves, A.B.
c283; c432; i071.

Hargreaves, A.T.
d203; s035.

Harlin, John
d152; s426.

Harmon, Byron
g162.

Harmon, Carol
g162.

Harpe, Eugène de la.   See La Harpe, Eugène de.

Harpe, Jean François de la.   See La Harpe, Jean François de.

Harpe, Ph. de la.   See La Harpe, Ph. de.

Harper, Arthur Paul
p167.

Harrer, Heinrich
s187; w063.

Harriman. See Series Index (Harriman Alaska Series).

Harriman Alaska Expedition, 1899
l193.

Harris, A.C.
a128.

Harris, P. Wyn
c018.

Harrison, Frederic
m522.

Harrisson, Frances
a495; a809.

Harrowfield, David L.
s262.

Hart, John
w012.

Hart Merriam, C.   See Merriam, C. Hart.

Hartmann, G.
a373.

Hartmann, Georg Leonhard
v125.

Hartmann, Otto
i046.

Hartwig, G.
p198.

Harvard Mountaineering Club
c381; h042-43.

Harvard Travellers Club
h029.1.

Harvey, D.W.
s350.

Harvey, Edmund George
h247.

Harvey Williams, John.   See Williams, John Harvey.

Hasenclever, Eleonore Noll.   See Noll-Hasenclever, Eleonore.

Haskett Smith, Walter Parry.   See Smith, Walter Parry Haskett.

Hasler, G.
b107; n152.

Hasse, Dietrich
m192.

Hasselbrink, F.
f144.

Hastings, Warren
i107.

Haston, Dougal
v124.

Hatt, E.M.
s445.

Haug, Emile
o082.

Haughton, Henry Lawrence
s358.

Hauri, J.
l027.

Hauser, Michael
k005.

Hauser, Otto
m112.

Haushofer, Max
s023.

Haussez, Charles Le Mercher de Longpré d', *baron*
a241; a242; e171; s340.

Havergal, Frances Ridley
s522-523.

Hawes, *Sir* Benjamin
n032-32.2.

Hawes, William
n032-32.2.

Hawkwood, *Sir* John
s223.

Hayden, *Sir* Henry Hubert
n200; s238; s359.

Hayden, John
s234.

Haydn, Alois
f142.

Hayes, Isaac I.
a612; a613; h145; l020.

Hayes, J.J.
m149; m175; o019.

Hayman Wilson, Horace. *See Wilson, Horace Hayman.*

Hayward, Abraham
j078; s280-281.

Hazlitt, William
i081; i146.

Headley, Joel Tyler
a440; l099; t201; t216.

Healy, M.A.
r126-127.

Heathman, W.G.
s566.

Heckel, Vilém
g073.

Hecken, Christian v. d.
z024.

Heckmair, Anderl
d212.

Hecla (Ship)
j050; n037; r213.1.

Hedin, Sven
a086; d226; t182.

Hedlund, S.A.
s078.

Heer, Gottlieb Heinrich
b083.

Heer, J.C.
g342; s069.

Heering, P.
i114.

Heger, Thomas
t149.

Hegetschweiler, Johann
r089.

Hegner, Ulrich
b050.

Heid, Maurice
p331.

Heigelin, J.F.
b236.

Heilmann, Luigi
p035.

Heim, Albert
f006; g012; h032; r270; s448; u001; u041.

Heim, Arnold Albert
w007.

Heissel, Werner
a216.

Helbronner, Paul
s170.

Heller, Frank
s097.

Helm, A.S.
a570.

Helmholtz, Hermann
p291.

Hemann, H.N.
b029.

Henderson, Ebenezer
i011.

Henderson, Kenneth Atwood
a483.

Henderson, Yandell
m030.

Hendrik, Hans
m149.

Henrich, Helen
w112.

Henriksen, K.L.
z023.

Henry, *abbé*
h148; p257.

Henry, D.M.J.
r026.

Henry, Pierre
a106; a106.1; a115.2; g198-200; m272-275.

Henson, Matthew
m115.

Hentsch, J.L. Binet. *See Binet-Hentsch, J.L.*

Hepworth Dixon, William. *See Dixon, William Hepworth.*

Herbert, Agnes
t295.

Herbert, Henry
f098-99.

Herbig, Friedrich August
p047.

Hergesheimer, Joseph
b237.

Hering, George E.
m494.

Herring, R.
z023.

Herrliberger, David
n086; r058; v210.

Herrlich, Albert
l019.

Herrligkoffer, Karl Maria
i034; w057.

Herrmann, Ernst
d116; w058.

Herzog, Gérard
l197.

Herzog, Maurice
a254; a537; a540; m330; r051; u055.

Herzog, Theodor
k016.

Hess, Adolfo
a105; i110; m372; n271; s007; t265.

Hess, David
b005.

Hess, Hans
u012.

Hess, Heinrich
e068; h197-200; o021.

Hesse-Wartegg, Ernst von
t113.

Hesselbo, A.
b194.

Hevat, Kirkwood
m528.

Hewitt, L. Rodney
m409.

Heyerdahl, Thor
g168.

Heylyn, Peter
c409.

Heywood, B.A.
v003.

Hibbert, Edward
n023.

Hibbert Taylor, R.   *See Taylor, R. Hibbert.*

Hicks Bates, Robert.   *See Bates, Robert Hicks.*

Hiebeler, Toni
a031; a032; b071; c222; c335; d152; d225; e037; i032; n147; t166; z045.

Hield Hamer, Samuel.   *See Hamer, Samuel Hield.*

Hiély, Ph.
e127-130.

Hilber, Paul
h164.

Hildreth, Brian
t043.

Hillary, *Sir* Edmund
a710; c372; h086.

Hillary, Peter
f044.

Hilscher, Herb
a131.

Hilscher, Miriam
a131.

Hiltbrunner, Hermann
e062; h204; r166; v057.

Himalayan Club
h117; i105.

Hinchliff, Thomas Woodbine
c113; o125; s314; s486.

Hindukuschexpedition, 1968.
z024.

Hinrich, Helen
m135.

Hipp, Engelbert
s088.

Hirschfeld, C.C.L.
b230; l026; n081.

Hirst, John
s304.

Hirzel-Escher, Hans Caspar
w044.

Historic Society of Lancashire and Cheshire
n269.

Historical and Scientific Society of Manitoba
p241.

Hjort, Christian
o086.

Hodgkin, Robin A.
h104; i076; m067; m442; m512; p164; t294.

Hoek, Henry
b076; d058; s058; w046.

Hoerlin, Hermann
z044.

Hofer, Andreas
h203; m150; w102.

Hofer, Ernst
a630.

Hofer-Bury, H.
v012.

Hofer-Bury, P.
v012.

Hoffmann, Georg
b051; p018.

Hoffmann, Hans
a791; s305.

Hofmann, Karl
g050.

Hofmann-Montanus, Hans
b066.

Hoffmeister, Werner
t211.

Hofman, Georg
w043.

Hog, Roger
t147.

Hogard, Henri
r030.

Holcroft, Thomas
t241.

Hölder, C.H.
m132; m134.

Holder, H.W.
f156.

Holdsworth Lunn, W. See Lunn, W. Holdsworth.

Holl, Peter
o088.

Holland, C.F.
c280.1.

Holland, Clive
e231; m058.

Holland, Peter
r039.

Holmes, Lewis
a634.

Holmes, William Henry
p205.

Holroyd Fox, Joseph. See Fox, Joseph Holroyd.

Holtved, E.
a133.

Höltzl, Sepp
s174.

Hölzhuber, Franz
a561.

Home, David Milne. See Milne-Home, David.

Homespun, John Timothy
a089.

Hommerberg, Sigge
b115.

Hone, J.F.
s551.

Honeyman, A. van Doren
r068.

Hong Kong Mountaineering Club
h228.

Hood, Robert
t110.

Hooft, Jenny Visser. See Visser-Hooft, Jenny.

Hooker, *Sir* Joseph Dalton
h118; r254.

Hooker, William Jackson
j053.

Hookham, Thomas
w010.

Hookins, Philip
n148.

Hope, Ascot Robert
r237.

Hope, Robert Philip
a320.

Hoper, M.W.
f105.

Hoppus, John
c384.

Hopwood, Victor G.
t233.

Hormayr, Joseph, *Freiherr von Hortenburg*
m150.

Horn, Johann von
s068.

Hornby, Emily
m487; t144.

Horneck, Karl
a766.

Hornung, Moise
e054.

Horr, A.R.
l189.

Horstig, C.G.
t011.

Hortenburg, Joseph Hormayr von, Freiherr. See Hormayr, Joseph, Freiherr von Hortenburg.

Hosel, Jutta
a564.

Hösli, Jost
a562.

Hospice du Grand St. Bernard
h232; m241; p102; p310; s011; w055; w107.

Hottinger, J.J.
j023.

Houben, H.H.
r260; s438.

Houghton, D.
a368.

Houston, C. Stuart
t110.

Houston, Charles Sneed
c252-253; d057; f061; g119; k004; n008.

Houston-Mount Everest Expedition, 1933
f061.

Houtt, William
b197.

Howard, E.
p166.

Howard, Lynda M.
b028.

Howard, William
n027; n050.

Howard Tutton, Alfred Edwin.   See Tutton, Alfred Edwin Howard.

Howard-Bury, Charles Kenneth
a006; m412.

Howell, George D.
d138.

Howell, George Rogers
o074.

Høyer, Liv Hansen
f117.

Høygaard, Arne
i045.

Hoyte, John
t286.

Hübel, Paul
f146.

Huc, Evariste Régis
r035.

Hudson, Charles
w084-85.

Hudson Bay Railway
r138.

Hudson's Bay Company
a633; c404; h251.

Hudson's Bay Record Society
c404.

Hug, Lina
s534.

Hug, Oscar A.
p107-107.1.

Hugi, Franz Joseph
g106; n059; u003.

Hugo, Victor
a435.

Huish, Robert
l041; t236.

Hulme Hall
h252.

Humble, Benjamin Hutchison
s303; s320.

Humboldt, Alexander, *Freiherr von*
k054; t293.

Hunt, John, *Baron Hunt*
a703; a704; a705; a710; c372; o077; o107; s225; v146.

Hunt, William R.
a626; t108.

Hunter Christie, E.W.   See Christie, E.W. Hunter.

Hunter Murray, Alexander.   See Murray, Alexander Hunter.

Hunter Workman, William.   See Workman, William Hunter.

Huntsman, A.G.
f065.

Huot-Sordot, Leon
e050.

Hurdle, Jonathan
a347.

Hurlbert, William H.
p144.

Hürlimann, Martin
s077.

Hutchison Humble, Benjamin.   See Humble, Benjamin Hutchison.

Hutchison Murray, William. **See** *Murray, William Hutchison.*

Hutter, Franz Karl
u018.

Hyde Greg, Edward. **See** *Greg, Edward Hyde.*

Hydle, Halvdan
s392.

Hymans, Louis
m283.

Ichac, Marcel
a731; g198; g200; r051.

Ilhurst, J.C.
c019.

Illmersdorf, Hans Meyer. **See** *Meyer-Illmersdorf, Hans.*

Imber, Walter
s355.

Imendörffer, Benno
m129.

Imfeld, Xavier
s300.

Imhof, Eduard
g195; i197; m025; r270.

Imperial Picture Palace, Cardiff
w116.

Imperial Transarctic Expedition
i051.

Imperial Transarctic Expedition. Ross Sea Party
s115.

Imseng, Ferdinand
h155.

Ineichen, Fritz
a364.

Infanti, Sergio de. **See** *De Infanti, Sergio.*

Ingle Finch, George. **See** *Finch, George Ingle.*

Ingleton, Geoffrey C.
c074.

Inglis, Alex
n160.

Inglis, Henry David
s572; t309; w028.

Innerkofler, *family*
b079.

Innerkofler, Sepp
k015.

Innstädten, Karl Sonklar, Edler von. **See** *Sonklar, Karl, Edler von Innstädten.*

Insel-Verlag
i121.

Institut géographique national, France
i047.

Institut national genevois
b258.1.

Institute for Northern Studies
m534.

Instituto Nacional de Glaciología
r158.

Instituto Panamericano de Geografía e Historia
a611.

International Exhibition, Paris, 1867
p239.

International Geological Congress, 1910
g037.

International Polar Year, 1st, 1882-83
e222.

International Prehistoric Congress
m177.

International Tin Research and Development Council
h154.

Internationaler Kunsthistorischer Kongress, Budapest, 1896
z034.

Investigator (Ship)
d155.

Iozawa, Tomoya
t264.

Irish Mountaineering Club
i141; r226-227.

Irving, Robert Lock Graham
c093; c209; d161; e262; m111; m452; r235; t049-50; w068.

Isselin, Henri
a111; b015; d217; m125.

Issler, Richard
n082.

Istituto Geografico Centrale
p029; v082.

Istituto Geografico De Agostini
a418; a474; b143; d011; h101; i139; m369.

Istituto Geografico De Agostini. Sezione Calcocromia
g357.

Istituto Geografico Militare
b219.

Istituto Italiano d'Arti Grafiche
a284– a286.

Istituzione Nazionale Alpina Universitaria SUCAI
s099.

Istria, Dora d', *comtesse*
s466; s571.

Italia (Ship)
t117.

Italy. Ministero della Difesa. Stato Maggiore. Esercito
e141; g203; m244.

Italy. Ministero della Difesa. Stato Maggiore. Esercito. Alpini
a378; c355.

Italy. Ministero della Difesa. Stato Maggiore. Esercito. Ufficio Storico
g222.

Ittlinger, Josef
e194; h034; v207.

Ivakovick, Arlette
h102.

Ivanov, S.V.
o085.

Ives, Jack D.
i125.

Izzard, Ralph
i118.

J., E. Ll.
n123.

J., R. M'K.
j004.

Jackman, S.W.
m165.

Jackson, A.Y.
a608.

Jackson, H.H.
n030.

Jackson, James
s176.

Jackson Hooker, William. *See Hooker, William Jackson.*

Jacob, *son of Aaron, High Priest of the Samaritans*
m416.

Jacob, Louis
f094.

Jacot-Guillarmod, J.
s226.

Jacottet, J.
p017; v297.

Jaeggli, Mario
c097.

James, Bessie Rowland
o117.

James, Edward John
l156.

James, John Angell
p181.

James, W. Powell
l206.

Jameson, Robert
e070.

Jamieson, Robert
e196.

Janillon, Richard.   See Richard-Janillon.

Janssen, Jules
c350-351; n175-176; n178; o016; q006; s504; s506.

Jardine, Matheson *& Co. Ltd.*
k065.

Jarvik, Erik
d131.

Javelle, Emile
a340; g064; r174; s328.

Jayal, Narendra Dhar
c376; n016.

Jean (Ship)
n048.

Jeannette (Ship)
i010; o109; p285.

Jeannel, Maurice
h075.

Jeffery, Frederick J.
h153; n269.

Jegerlehner, Johannes
h255; s512.

Jelinek, Otto
g073.

Jemelin, Erika
w018.

Jena, Ruth Michaelis.   See Michaelis-Jena, Ruth.

Jenkins, Thomas
m031.

Jenness, D.
m106.

Jenni, Mathias
c291.

Jenni-Züblin, Mathias
c291.

Jennings, H.H.
l038.

Jenny, Ernst
e096; h192-193; r259.

Jensen, E. Omholt.   See Omholt-Jensen, E.

Jerin, Zoran
h098.

Jerosch, Heinrich Brockmann.   See Brockmann-Jerosch, Heinrich.

Jest, C.
h103.

Joanne, Adolphe
i169; i176; s459.

Joanne, Paul
i165; i175; p332; s463; s467.

Johansen, Fredrik Hjalmar
f020.

Johansen, Margaret Alison
o072.

Johnson, A.M.
c404.

Johnson, Anna Cummings
c411.

Johnson, James
c174; c175.

Johnson, John Willes
j059.

Johnson, Samuel
h175; j062; j087-88.

Johnstone, C.E.
g172.

Joint Services Mountaineering Association
c251.

Jolis, Agustín
p227.

Jonas, Rudolf
h184.

Jones, C.A.
f089.

Jones, Dora M.
h209.

Jones, E.D. Wynne
g022.

Kelemina, Oscar
c221.

Kellas, A.M.
r139.

Keller, Ferdinand
l015-16.

Keller, Heinrich
c345; d085; p022.

Keller, Paul
e036.

Keller, Ronald
c125.

Kelly, Harry M.
h096; p162; p163.

Kelsey, Michael R.
c237.

Kemball-Cook, B.H.
p196.

Kemble, Fanny
a089.

Kempe, D.R.C.
s577.

Kempe, John
e230.

Kempf, Bertrand
g333.

Kempf, H.
a206.

Kennedy, *Sir* Alexander B.W.
a443-444; e058.

Kennedy, Benjamin E.
m536.

Kennedy, Edward Shirley
p072; w084-85.

Kennedy, Lawrence D.
m237.

Kent Brooks, Charles.   See Brooks, Charles Kent.

Kent Kane, Elisha.   See Kane, Elisha Kent.

Keralio, Louis Félix de
h146.

Kerr, J.W.
n020.1.

Kerr, Mark Brickell
m424.

Keysler, Johann Georg
t240.

Kiesewetter, Fr.
f114.

Kilger, Ferdinand
w076.

Kilian, Bernard
v256.

Killias, Ed.
c301; k072.

King, Clarence
m481-483.

King, Edward J.
r244.

King, James
v272.

King, Samuel William
i154.

King, Thomas Starr
w088.

Kingdon-Ward, Francis
m540.

Kingsley, M.H.
a698.

Kingston, William H.G.
y014.

Kipling, Rudyard
k046.

Kippis, Andrew
n049.

Kircheiss, Carl
p209.

Kirkaldy, J.F.
f101.

Kirkpatrick, William Trench
a320.

Kirkus, Colin Fletcher
i071.

Kirwan, L.P.
p208.

Klæbo, Arthur
f019.

Kleppe, Peter
h004.

Klier, Heinrich E.
o101; s435.

Klinterberg, Robert af
m205.

Klipstein, A.
s062.

Klopfenstein, Jacques
a502.

Klucker, Christian
a088; e096.

Knight, Edward Frederick
f011; w086.

Knight, Lorne
p078.

Knight, Max
r155.

Knight, William Henry
d136.

Knobel, J.
i026.

Knonau, Gerold Meyer von.   *See Meyer von Knonau,*
Gerold.

Knorr, Otto
g197.

Knox, Ray
t072.

Knubel, Peter
h156.

Knuth, Eigil
m182; u024.

Kober, Leopold
b025.

Koch, I.P.
s511.

Koch, Karl D.
a195; a196.

Koch, Lauge
s428.

Koch, Palle
d065; s261.

Koch von Berneck, Max
g334.

Koenig, F.N.
f001.

Koenig, N.
d078.1.

Kohl, Johann Georg
a213.

Kolb, Fritz
p116.

Koldewey, K.
e111.

Koll, Lois
f140.

Kollbach, Karl
d121.

Komitee 'Hilfe für deutsche Forscher im Polareis'
e220.

Kondrat'ev, R. Ya.
u069.

Kongliga Svenska Vetenskaps-Akademien
r045-46.

König, Erich
e047.

König, Franz Nikolaus
a801; r082.

König, L. Fr.
h163.

Königer, Franz
m364.

Korte, J. de
o015.

Kranz, C.A.
a201; a202.

Krassin (Ship)
t117.

Kraus, Karl
b226.

Krawczyk, Chess
m463.

Kretschmer, H.E.
h001; m438; n268.

Kristoffersen, Finn
j008.

Kristensen, Thomas K.
b165.

Kropf, Ferdinand Aloizovich ·
s343.

Kruszyna, Robert
c234; r229.

Kübeck, Max von
a798.

Kubin, Andreas
d175.

Kuchar, Radovan
z001.

Küchler, Hans Lorenz
a147.
Kuenlin, Franz
h162.

Kugy, Julius
a279; a350; a577; a774; j093; k006; k034; m196; r156; r177.

Kuhn, Bernhard Friedrich
r082.

Kumar, Narinder
n124; t275.

Kunelius, Rick
s253.

Kunstmuseum, Bern
a800; a801.

Kurverein Arosa
a645.

Kurz, Louis
c126; g302-305; p043.

Kurz, Marcel
a390; b114; d214; d216; e109; g304-305; g310-311.3; h105-108; m454.

Küttner, G.B.
b233.

Kutzner, J.
c293.

L., M.
a644.

L., P.B.   *See Bosson, Pierre.*

L., W.   *See Longman, William.*

*L.S.E.M.C.   **See** London School of Economics Mountaineering Club.*

L'Evêque, Henry
p137.

La Bédoyère, Henri de
j043.

La Condamine, Charles Marie de
j060-61.

La Harpe, Eugène de
a231; a259.

La Harpe, Jean François de
c347.

La Harpe, Ph. de
f078.

La Martinière, Pierre Martin de
n237.

*La Platière, J.M. Roland de.   **See** Roland de la Platière, J.M.*

La Roche, *Monsieur de*
v221.

La Roche, Sophie de
e095; t013.

Labande, François
m080-81.

Labhard, Toni
b155.1; b155.2.

Labiche, E.
m255.

Laborde, Jean Benjamin de
t010.

Labroue, Emile
a020.

Lachenal, Louis
l197.

Lacombe, Geraldine Doux.   *See Doux-Lacombe, Geraldine.*

Lactantius, L.C.F.
r105.

Ladies' Alpine Club
l008; y002.

Ladies' Edinburgh Debating Society
l009.

Ladner, Johann Baptist
l031.

Ladoucette, Jean C.F. de, *baron*
h131; h149.

Ladurner, J.
w066.

Laeng, Walther
a271; c303; c308; l074; o084; s393.

Laffi, Franco
k002.

Lagarde, Jacques
c201; g201; m272-273; n209.

Lagerheim, G.
u027.

Lalaubie, Henry de
v214.

Lalonde, Bailly de.   See Bailly de Lalonde.

Laloue, Maurice
g320-321; m080-81.

Lambert, Gustave
e218.

Lambert, Raymond
a820; f092.

Lambton Surtees, R.   See Surtees, R. Lambton.

Lammer, Eugen Guido
a374; f087; j094.

Lamotte Barace, Alexandre de, vicomte de Senonnes. See Senonnes, Alexandre de Lamotte Barace, vicomte de.

Lampugnani, Giovanni
g329.

Lampugnani, Giuseppe
a107; i096; p155; t167; v136.

Lampugnani, Pinin
c086.

Lana, Girolamo
g223.

Lançon, Xavier
v242.

Lancrenon, P.
d038.

Lander, John
t236.

Lander, Richard
t236.

Landi, Lucienne Faletto.   See Faletto Landi, Lucienne.

Landi Vittorj, Carlo
g136-137.

Landon, Perceval
l135-136; n073.

Landor, A. Henry Savage.   See Savage-Landor, A. Henry.

Landquart-Davos Railway
l027.

Landres, Jean R. Frey des.   See Frey des Landres, Jean R.

Landseer, Edwin
s282.

Landseer, John
s282.

Lane, Ferdinand C.
s400-401.

Lang, Georg
o001.

Lange, Franz
g048.

Langes, Gunther
d179; n133; r241; s168.

Langle, *marquis de*
p148; t008.

Langone, John
l147.

Languepin, Jean Jacques
n012.

Lanoye, Ferdinand de
m175.

Lantier, E.F. de
t196.

Lanza, Benedetto
i068.

Lanzara, P.
i183.

Laplace
n241.

Laporte, Albert
e055.

Lapp, P.A.
a632.

Lapworth, Charles
t060.

Larden, Walter
g355; i120; r037.

Largaiolli, Tullio
d218.

Larichev, V.E.
s205.

Larsen, Fridtjov Barth
h260.

Larsen, Henry
n153.

Larsen, Hj. Riiser. *See Riiser-Larsen, Hj.*

Lascelles, Rowley
g025; s232.

Lasker-Schüler, Else
b226.

Latrobe, Charles Joseph
a214; a215; p079.

Lauder, Toofie
l071.

Laughlin, Mary T.
t063.

Lauridsen, Peter
v187.

Laursen, Dan
q005.

Lavaggi, Carolina Palazzi. See Palazzi-Lavaggi, Carolina.

Lavis-Trafford, Marc A. de
b253; c204; c302; d222; e193; m343.

Law, William John
a446; s295.

Lawes Long, Henry. See Long, Henry Lawes.

Lawrence, T.E.
m210; s185.

Lawrie, Robert, Ltd. See Robert Lawrie, Ltd.

Lawson, William
b173.

Lazzarin, Paolo
a519; g233.

Lazzarino, Antonio
c120.

Le Blond, Elizabeth
c173; h080; h088; m200; m532; t249; t284-285; t298.

Le Fort, Gaudy
p308.

Le Gallais, A.
c202.

Le Mercher de Longpré d'Haussez, Charles, baron. See Haussez, Charles Le Mercher de Longpré d', baron.

Le Mesurier, W.H.
i059.

Le Queux, William
c016.

Le Sage, George Louis
n216.

Le Ver, Girard
v291.

Leader, John Temple.   See Temple-Leader, John.

Leaf, Charlotte M.
w017.

Leaf, Walter
w017.

Leahy, Arthur
a643.

Lebenwald, Adam Lebwald von und zu.   See Lebwald von und zu Lebenwald, Adam.

Lebwald von und zu Lebenwald, Adam
d013.

Lechner, Ernst
p177-178; t062; t094-95.

Lechner, Sigi
a461; d178.

Lecky, Elisabeth
v182.

Leclerc, Bernard
g308.

Leclerc, Jeanne
g308.

Leclercq, Jules
a602; t312.

Lecointe, Georges
a761.

Lecoq, Henri
c416.

Lecoq de Boisbaudran
s346.

Lee, G.W.
n201.

Lee, John Edward
l015-16.

Lee, Katherine
i087.

Lee Davis, Mary.   See Davis, Mary Lee.

Lee Newcomb, Raymond.   See Newcomb, Raymond Lee.

Leeds University Climbing Club
l060-61.

Lefebure, Charles
m189.

Lefroy, John Henry
i084.

Lega Montagna ARCI-UISP
g237.

Leggett, Benjamin F.
t180.

Legione Trentina
r206.

Legobbe, Bruno
s029.

Lehmann, H.L.
r142.

Lehne, Jorg
e035.

Lehner, Wilhelm
b074; e102.

Lehr, Henry
v282.

Leifhelm, Hans
m172.

Leigh-Mallory, George.   See Mallory, George Leigh.

Leising, William A.
a637.

Leitmeier, Hans
o097.

Lejean
h145.

Lemercier, Abel
d014.

Lemoine, Bernard
b212; h045; m186; n253.

Lendenfeld, Robert von
a779.

Lengemann, Werner
a509.

Linden, W.J.M.
z047.

Lindorff, Peter
w119.

Link, Ulrich
g122.

Linnaeus, Carl
l035.

Linth, Hans Conrad Escher von der.   See Escher von der Linth, Hans Conrad.

Linton, David
f102.

Liotier, Max
c096; k007; s157.

Lioy, Paolo
s405.

Lisibach, L.
c293.

Lisker, Tom
f064.

Lisle Strutt, Edward.   See Strutt, Edward Lisle.

Lister, H.
h057.

Livanos, Georges
a753; u004.

Liverpool Geographical Society
a698.

Liverpool Literary and Philosophical Society
h153; p102.

Livingstone, Charles
n044.

Livingstone, David
l185; m220; n044.

Livingstone, Leslie
l184.

Livingstone Wilson, Edward.   See Wilson, Edward Livingstone.

Livraghi, Tito
m311.

Lloyd, George
a049; n021.

Lloyd, Robert Wylie
c309; d061; d075; e083; f055; m269; n116; t250-251; v105.

Lloyd, *Sir* William
n021-22.

Lloyd Burdsall, Richard.   See Burdsall, Richard Lloyd.

Löbl, Robert
g231.

Lochaber Mountaineering Club. Mountaineering and Mountain Rescue Course
p293.

Lochmatter, Franz Joseph
i075; p123; p170.

Lockington Vial, A.E.   See Vial, A.E. Lockington.

Lockwood, Dunbar
v256.

Loderbauer, Hannes
w033-34.

Loetscher, Hans
h030.

Loewe, Fritz
s115.

Loewy, A.
h207.

Logan, Hugh
m410.

Loges, Chrétien des.   See Des-Loges, Chrétien.

Löhlein, Georg
a203.

Lohmüller, Wilhelm
m363.

Loisirs Animazione Culturale
l007.

Lombardy. Province
r060.

London Museum, Fleet Street
d087.

London School of Economics Mountaineering Club
l001.

London School of Economics Mountaineering Club Himalayan Expedition, 1956
p247; r136.

Long, Lieutenant de. **See** *De Long, Lieutenant.*

Long, Emma Wotton de. **See** *De Long, Emma Wotton.*

Long, Henry Lawes
h039.

Longa, Glicero
v190.

Longland, J.L.
o129.

Longman, C.J.
f056.

Longman, William
e259; j069; l058; s228; s450.

Longmore, John
p087.

Longpré d'Haussez, Charles Le Mercher de, baron. **See** *Haussez, Charles Le Mercher de Longpré d', baron.*

Longstaff, Tom George
a314; m472; n015; n199; t069; w074.

Lopez, Jerónimo
s211.

Lopez, Maria Savi. **See** *Savi-Lopez, Maria.*

Lorentz, Gunnar
b115.

Lorentzen, Finn Schultz. **See** *Schultz-Lorentzen, Finn.*

Lorenz, Hans
u006.

Lorria, August
a354.

Lortet, Louis
d124.

Lory, Gabriel, *fils*
d127; s096; v296.

Lory, Gabriel, *père*
d127; s096; v296.

Losana, Pietro
a269.

Losito, Carlo
a405.

Loudon, Jane
f005.

Louise A. Boyd Arctic Expeditions, 1937, 1938
c299.

Lovejoy, Celia
t116.

Lovering, J.F.
l039.

Lovett-Cameron, Verney
h145.

Lovey-Troillet, Ernest
v021.

Lovie, Jacques
s034.

Lovins, Amory
e117.

Lovisato, D.
a117.

Lowe, Emily
u037.

Lowe, Jeff
i006.

Lowell Putnam, William. **See** *Putnam, William Lowell.*

Lowenberg, Julius
s085.

Lubbock, John, *Baron Avebury*
s047.

Lublink Weddik, Bartholomaeus T. **See** *Weddik, Bartholomaeus T. Lublink.*

Luc, Jean André de
g038; h140-141; l120-121; o009; r091; r100.

Lucangeli, Charles
m229.

Lucchesi, Alexis
e121-125.

Lucchi, Nevia Ricci.   *See Ricci-Lucchi, Nevia.*

Lückhoff, C.A.
t001.

Ludwig, A.
a785.

Luigi Amedeo, *Duca degli Abruzzi*
a686; a711; e315; n069; v143.

Lukan, Karl
a198; a422; a822; b089; g194; w096.

Lumley Dundas, Lawrence John, Earl of Ronaldshay.
See Ronaldshay, Lawrence John Lumley Dundas, Earl
of.

Lumsden, Thomas
j080.

Lundborg, Einar
s391.

Lunn, *Sir* Arnold
a428; c109; e067; f015; g166; m437-438; m503; o130;
s164; s568; t299.

Lunn, Henry S.
h245.

Lunn, W. Holdsworth
h245.

Lurani Cernuschi, Francesco, *conte*
n272.

Lusi, *comte de*
v270.

Lusser, Karl Franz
k028.

Lütgen, Kurt
n002.

Lüthi, Gottlieb
i024.

Lutz, Markus
d146.

Luzzi, Gion
c443.

Lynch, John
w052.

Lynge, B.
b194.

M., Helen
r115.

M., J.E.   See Muddock, J.E.

M., T.   See Martyn, Thomas.

Macaree, David
h257.

McArthur, Alex.
p241.

Maccá, Gaetano
s394.

McCall Gillis, Elsie.   See Gillis, Elsie McCall.

MacCauley, Clay
j020.

MacClintock, F.L.
v255.

McClintock, *Sir* Leopold
f114.

McClure, *Sir* Robert
d155; f114.

McCorkle, Ruth
a136.

MacCormick, Arthur David
a668.

McCrackan, William D.
r238.

McCurdy, *Major*
t077.

Macdonald, David
l023; t292.

McDonald, Edwin A.
p203.

MacDougall, George Frederick
e179.

McFarlane, James
w052.

McGill, Jean
n154.

Macgregor, John
a707; d094; m535.

McGuire, J.A.
i086.

Mach, Erich
z001.

Machetto, Guido
s178; t102.

MacInnes, Hamish
i130.

Macintyre, Donald
h126-127.

Macintyre, Neil
a742.

Mackenzie, *Sir* Alexander
i050; v271.

Mackenzie, *Sir* George Steuart
t215.

Mackenzie, William M.
i145.

McKinley Gould, Laurence.   See Gould, Laurence McKinley.

Mackintosh, A.J.
m471.

Maclagan Wedderburn, Ernest Alexander.   See Wedderburn, Ernest Alexander Maclagan.

McLintock, W.F.P.
g348.

McMahon, John
w119.

MacMillan, Donald B.
a625; l189.

Macmillan, Hugh
h215.

Macmorland, *Mrs*
d026.

McNab, Robert
o035.

Macneven, William James
r009.

McNevin, W.J.   See Macneven, William James.

M'Nicol, Donald
j088.

McNish, K.T.
e166.

MacNiven, N.
g340.

Macor, Celso
r177.

MacPhee, G. Graham
c241.

Macpherson, W.D.
c269.

Macrobert, Harry
b045; i144.

Maduschka, Leo
j095.

Madutz, Johann
j026.

Maeder, Herbert
b064; i083.

Maestri, Cesare
a010; a011; a646; d224; k058.

Maestri, Fernanda
d224.

Maestri, Walter
d201; p171.

Maestrini, Franco
i187.

Magellan, Ferdinand
n241.

Magistretti, Mario
p275.

Magni, Fermo
g281.

Magnusson, Finnur
g192.

Mahoney, Michael
h041.

Maillart, H.
p251.

Main, Elizabeth.   See Le Blond, Elizabeth.

Mair, Kurt
a200; h196.

Mairan, Jean Jacques Dortous de.   See Dortous de Mairan, Jean Jacques.

Maison des jeunes et de la culture de Bourg-Argental
e051.

Maiuri, Amedeo
a656.

Maix, Kurt
b060; i029; m168.

Malartic, Yves
c365.

Malaurie, Jean
a639.

Malcolm, Howard
t213; t229.

Malherbe, R. de
c343.

Malkin, Arthur Thomas
l053-54.

Mallaret, Chantal
m303.2.

Mallaret, Jean-Jacques
m303.2.

Malleson, G.B.
c041.

Mallet, George
l122; t130.

Mallet, H.
d077.

Mallet, J.P. Pictet.   See Pictet-Mallet, J.P.

Mallet, P.H.
d147.

Mallet Du Pan, Jacques
e147.

Mallory, George Leigh
m027; s225.

Malnati, Franco
a687; d007.

Malo, Charles
s219.

Malusardi, Alberto
i185.

Malvezzi, Piero
v140.

Maly, Charles
m078.

Manaresi, Angelo
p038.

Manchester Corporation Central Library. Special Collections
c071.

Manchester University Mountaineering Club
j038.

Mandach, Conrad von
a800; d127; f001; s096.

Mandar, Michael P.
v240.

Mandat-Grancey, Edmond de, *baron*
d023.

Mandelli, Gian Maria
v083.

Mandrot, A. de
a803.

Manent, M.
e087.

Manera, Ugo
n263.

Manget, Jacques Louis
c165; c171; d086; v054.

Manley, Seon
p202.

Mannent, René
a224.

Mannering, George Edward
e038; f115; s229; w115.

Manni, Graziano
i135.

Mannin, Ethel
s316.

Manning, Harvey
m422; n145.

Manning, Samuel
s527-528.

Manson, John
a435.

Mantegazza, Paolo
s497.

Mantl, Norbert
c451.

Manton Smith, J. **See** *Smith, J. Manton.*

Mantovi, Franco
i135.

Manville Fenn, Geo. **See** *Fenn, Geo. Manville.*

Manzoni, Marcello
a573.

Maquelin, L.
a685; a693.

Maraini, Fosco
g010; p039.

Marchal, Michel
v173.

Marchelli, M.G. Moneta. **See** *Moneta Marchelli, M.G.*

Marcilhacy, Gilbert
s154.

Marcotti, Giuseppe
s223.

Marester, Guy
q012.

Margarita, *Queen Consort of Umberto I, King of Italy*
q011.

Margollé, Elie
a689; a690; a691; g087-88; m425.

Marguerettaz, Pietro
f024.

Mariétan, Ignace
a480; v016.

Marignié, Jean Etienne François
h222.

Marimonti, Lorenzo
v084.

Marine Historical Association
p205.

Marinelli, Olinto
g271.

Mariner, Ernst
v024.

Marion, Macé
b224.

Markham, *Sir* Clements R.
l028.

Marks, C.
t078.

Marmier, Xavier
v241; z048.

Marmontel, Jean François
s194-195.

Marrack, Richard
h247.

Marret, L.
s499.

Marsay, *comte de*
l113-114.

Marschall von Bieberstein, Friedrich August
g024.

Marsden, A.D.
c251.

Marsh, Herbert
t304.

Marshall-Hall, A.S.
a808.

Marsigli, Maurizio
g237.

Martegani, Ugo
t057.

Martel, Aline
l157.

Martel, Edouard Alfred
c198; d125; e001.

Martel, Pierre
a060; p258; w103-104.

Martelli, A.E.
g267.

Martignon, Andrée
m327.

Martin, Alexandre
h072; s475; s516.

Martin, E.
m255.

Martin, Lawrence
a134; m089-92; m094; m097.

Martin, Martin
d097.

Martin, Victor
a815.

Martin, Wilhelm
d056; f139.

Martin, William
c195.

Martinelli, Mario
a818; b184.

Martinelli, Vittorio
a075.

Martinez, Gregorio Ariz. See Ariz Martinez, Gregorio.

Martinière, Pierre Martin de la. See La Martinière, Pierre Martin de.

Martiniori, *ing.*
s020.

Martins, Charles
d123; d126; d220; v208.

Martyn, Thomas
a592; g325; s236-237; t150.

Marzatico, Ulisse
n091.

Marzio, Simone
r050.

Mas, Giuliano dal. See Dal Mas, Giuliano.

Masefield, John
w021.

Mason, Alfred Edward Woodley
a497; r271-272.

Mason, Kenneth
a034; h117.

Mason, Stanley
w108.

Massajoli, Pierleone
c444.

Massie, J.W.
r036.

Massillon, Jean Baptiste
p108.

Masson, Alexandre Frédéric Jacques de, marquis de Pezay. See Pezay, Alexandre Frédéric Jacques de Masson, marquis de.

Mathews, Charles Edward
a535; a718; j009; m518; n038; r117; s420.

Mathews, William
s018.

Mathiassen, Therkel
a603; r135.

Mattana, Gigi
g134.

Matthès, François E.
i102.

Matthews, Henry
d140.

Matthey, André
b008.

Matthisson, Friedrich von
b225; e093.

Mattox, William G.
b164.

Mauk, Charlotte E.
y009.

Maurer, Hans Rudolf
k052.

Maurer, Jul.
f006.

Mauretania (Ship)
c445; l172.

Mauri, Carlo
a573.

Mauri, Giancarlo
e140.

Maurizi, Giovanni de.   See De-Maurizi, Giovanni.

Mauro, Francesco
c216; s137.

Maury, Léon
n130.

Mavor, William Fordyce
m118.

Mawson, *Sir* Douglas
s116-118.

May, Daniel
p259.

May, W.G.
m449.

Mayer, Eduard
h195.

Mayer, Guido
i036.

Mayer, Theodor
a187.

Mayhew, Athol
m255.

Mayhew, Henry
m255.

Mayr, H. Forcher.   See Forcher-Mayr, H.

Mayr, Willi
u007.

Maza, Michele
a263.

Mazeaud, Pierre
g313; m317; m349.

Mazuchelli, Nina Elizabeth
i108.

Mazzenga, Gianni
s154; s207.

Mazzolini, Giordano
a033.

Mazzotti, Giuseppe
a001; a406; d067; g155-156; i132; i134; m318; m358; v147.

Mazzuchi, Maria
a104.

Meade, Charles Francis
a600; e081.

Mecatti, Giuseppe Maria
d153.

Mechel, Chrétien de
i173; p137.

Mechini, Pietro
c372.

Meciani, Pietro
a506; e183.

Mecking, Ludwig
g036.

Medici, Berthe
c116.

Medicus.   See Watson, G.C.

Meiners, Christoph
b235.

Meisner, Friedrich
r082.
Meissner, Hans Otto
i050.

Meister, Leonard
n085; s098.

Melchiori, Giacomo
c437.

Meldgaard, Morton
a027.

Mele, Pietro Francesco
s215.

Mélesville
v032.

Mélèze, Josette
d151.

Melland Robinson, Anthony. **See** *Robinson, Anthony Melland.*

Mellano, Andrea
t042.

Mellet, Bernard
k003.

Melly, Charles du Bois. **See** *Du Bois-Melly, Charles.*

Melmoth, William
l115; s245-246; t224.

Mélon, Pierre
g143; m325.

Melou, Max
p271.

Meltofte, Hans
o015; o086; p218.

Melucci, Paolo
b218.

Melville, Herman
c125.

Menapace, Luigi
l077.

Menara, Hanspaul
p092.

Mendelssohn Bartholdy, Carl
b227.

Mendelssohn Bartholdy, Felix
b226.1; b227.

Mendelssohn Bartholdy, Paul
b226.1; b227.

Menegus Tamburin, Vincenzo. **See** *Tamburin, Vincenzo Menegus.*

Meneguz, Giovanni
c213.

Mengin-Fondragon, *baron de*
s333.

Menlove Edwards, John. **See** *Edwards, John Menlove.*

Menu von Minutole, H.C.
r077.

Menzies, Alexander
l090.

Menzies, William John
l090.

Mercanti, Andrea
a745; m038; t184.

Mercey, F.B. de
s339.

Merci, Lucillo
b184; p175.

Merian, Matthaeus
t123.

Merisio, Pepi
v188.

Merizzi, J.
v020.

Merkl, Willy
w057.

Merle-d'Aubigné, Robert
s151.

Merriam, C. Hart
w098.

Merrick, Hugh
n147; p161.

Merriman Archer Thomson, James. **See** *Thomson, James Merriman Archer.*

Merry, *Old*
o034.

Merryfellow, Martin
c338.

Merzbacher, Gottfried
a782.

Messerli, Bruno
i125.

Messner, Reinhold
d194; q009; r201; s177; s181.

Mesurier, W.H., Le. **See** *Le Mesurier, W.H.*

Metcalfe, A.E.
s411.

Methner, Wilhelm
b131.

Meunier, Stanislas
c042; g090.

Meurer, Julius
b130; h033.

Meyer, C.F.
g115.

Meyer, G.I.
m484.

Meyer, Hans
a072; o095.

Meyer, Hieronymus
r071.

Meyer, J.
g043.

Meyer, J.J.
m014.

Meyer, Johann Rudolf
r071; r073.

Meyer, Oskar Erich
b049; t036.

Meyer-Ahrens, Conrad
h058-59.

Meyer-Illmersdorf, Hans
i085.

Meyer von Knonau, Gerold
e090; e094.

Meyers, George
y010.

Meynieu, Jacques
r050.

Miansarov, M.M.
b146.

Michael, James
w077.

Michaelis-Jena, Ruth
s022.

Michel, Aimé
m355.

Michelet, Jules
m328-329.

Micheletti, Paolo
r208.

Micheli du Crest, J.B.
o080.

Midland Association of Mountaineers
b259; d150; h006; j071; r124.

Mieille, Paul
r275.

Miethe, A.
e220.

Mieville, Gabriel Antoine
e170.

Migliorini, Elio
c051; v014.

Migliorini, Veneto
v112.

Migot, André
a112.

Mikkelsen, A.
q005.

Mila, Massimo
e105.

Milan. Comune
m365.

Milan. Consiglio Provinciale
q019.

Milburn, Geoff
g118.

Milesi, Carlo
d167; m379.

Miller, J.H.
a570.

Miller Waring, Samuel.   See Waring, Samuel Miller.

Millin, A.L.
v230; v238-239.

Monnier, Paul
p032.

Monod, Jules
p253.

Monro, Donald
d098.

Monroe Thorington, James. See Thorington, James Monroe.

Monson, Frederick John, *Baron Monson*
j052.

Montagna, Euro
a282; p010.

Montagnier, Henry Fairbanks
b150; d207; e012; e084; f155; i072; j041; l118; l151; m303.1; n050; n177; t055.

Montague, Charles Edward
f036.

Montagu, Lady Mary Wortley. See Wortley Montagu, Lady Mary.

Montaigne, Michel de
j047.

Montaldo, Lorenzo
a282.

Montandon, C.
z029.

Montandon, Paul
e109; h106.

Montanus, Hans Hofmann. See Hofmann-Montanus, Hans.

Montcel, Robert Tézenas du. See Tézenas du Montcel, Robert.

Monteith, James
m179.

Montémont, Albert
t148; v274.

Montet, Albert de
d142.

Montgomerie, T.G.
r251.

Montgomery, James
w022-23.

Montgomery, Richard G.
a085; p078.

Monti, Virgilio
m310.

Montilera, Lorenzo Rossi di. See Rossi di Montilera, Lorenzo.

Montipò, Gino
p154.

Montlaville, Louis Alceste de Chapuys. See Chapuys Montlaville, Louis Alceste de.

Monzino, Guido
g152; i150; s347-349.

Moorcroft, William
t231.

Moore, William Bramley. See Bramley-Moore, William.

Moore, Adolphus Warburton
a443; a444; a445; e066.

Moore, John
v160-161.

Moore, Terris
m163-164; m513.

Morant Fellowes, Peregrine Forbes. See Fellowes, Peregrine Forbes Morant.

Morassutti, Lalla
a464.

Mordecai, David
h124.

Moreau, G.
a006.

Morell, J.R.
b201; s114.

Morf, C.
p172.

Morgan, Bernice Bangs
v133.

Morgensen, Gert S.
i019.

Morice, Adrian G.
t063.

Moriggl, Josef
a529; v204.

Morin, Micheline
e056; t176.

Morin, Nea E.
a537; h112; m428.

Moriondo, Carlo
m010.

Morisset, Jean Marie
a239.

Morland, *Sir* Samuel
h180.

Morlot, A. von
e098.

Morne, Håkan
v010.

Moroder, Edgard
v022.

Moroder, Franz
g190.

Morris, C.J.   See Morris, John.

Morris, John
g364; l183.

Morris, John J.
a121.

Morris, Maurice O'Connor
r013.

Morrow Lindbergh, Anne.   See Lindbergh, Anne Morrow.

Morse, George H.
c178.

Mortillet, Gabriel de
s503.

Morton, Friedrich
a792.

Moryson, Fines
i199.

Mosdal, Gert
m193.

Mosso, Angelo
m169; u058.

Mottarella, G.
s476.

Motti, Gian Piero
e134; g205; r215.

Mottinelli, D.
c061.

Motwani, Mohan
c376.

Mougin, P.
r149; t126.

Moulam, Anthony J.J.
n095.

Moulinié, C.E.F.
p310-312.

Moulton, Robert D.
l202.

Mount Everest Committee
t112.

Mount Everest Reconnaissance Expedition, 1951
m414; n115.

Mount Everest Reconnaissance Expedition, 1952
n115.

Mount Jolmo Lungma Scientific Expedition
p120.

Mount Shishma Pangma Scientific Expedition
p121.

Mountain Club of East Africa
i124.

Mountain Club of South Africa
a548; j072; m430; p063.

Mountaineering Association
l191; m433.

Mountevans, Edward Ratcliffe Garth Russell
Evans, *Baron*
d106; m029.

Mousson, Albert
g104.

Mowat, Farley
d107; g017; o079; p089; p201; t287.

Moyle Sherer, Joseph. **See** *Sherer, Joseph Moyle.*

Mozley, James Bowling
m508.

Mückenbrunn, H.
s249.

Muddock, Joyce E.
j002; n122; s419.

Mügge, Theodore
s565.

Mugna, Piero
d054.

Muir, John
t210; y009.

Muirhead, Findlay
f116; s548.

Muirhead, Lockhart
j077.

Muleur, G.
p255.

Müller, Alfred
s092.

Muller, August
a014.

Muller, Chr.
a708.

Müller, Ernst
h036.

Müller, Frans
h207.

Müller, Fred
g019.1

Müller, G.P. **See** *Müller, Gerhard F.*

Müller, Gerhard F.
v285-287.

Müller, Johann Georg
r079.

Müller, S. **See** *Müller, Gerhard F.*

Müller-Alfeld, Theodor
e177.

Mullik, B.N.
s260.

Mumm, Arnold Louis
a319; f067.

Mummery, Albert Frederick
f156; m188; m202; m525-527; s225.

Munchausen, *Baron*
m517-518.

Munck, Ebbe
s430; u024.

Munk, Jens
w052.

Munro, *Sir* Hugh
g046.

Münster, Sebastian
d041.

Muoth, Giachen Caspar
i027; o128.

Muratori, Giuseppe
m157.

Murphy, *Lady* Blanche
s127.

Murray, Alexander Hunter
j073.

Murray, Athol
p095.

Murray, Charles, Earl of Dunmore. **See** *Dunmore, Charles Murray, Earl of.*

Murray, Hugh
e070; s519-520.

Murray, James Erskine
s485.

Murray, John
g099.

Murray, John, *Publisher*
h017.

Murray, John A.
i109.

Murray, William Hutchison
m479-480; r220; s123-124; s413-414; u028-29.

Musafir, *Captain*
c041.

Musée National du Luxembourg, Paris
c082.

Museo di Palazzo Braschi, Rome
g232.

Museum, Piccadilly
s200.

Museum of Practical Geology, London
g348.

Musgrave, George M.
p160.

Musset-Pathay, Victor Donatien de
r076.

Muston, Alexis
i146.

Mutuelle Sports, Loisir, Culture. Section alpinisme et escalade
e126.

Muyden, *Madame van*
f091.

Myconius, Oswaldus
d076.

Myles, Eugénie
n150.

N., Y.S.   *See Dutton, Mary*

Naef, Albert
c194.

Naef-Blumer, Ed.
c290-c292.

Nagayama, Mokuo
s265.

Nanda, V.S.
t275.

Nangeroni, G.
g032.

Nansen, Fridtjof
f020; f056; f110; f117-119; f122; n019-20; n136; t164; v119.

Naples, *Kingdom of*
r060.

Napoleon I, *Emperor of the French*
p141; v213.

Narborough, John
a050.

Nares, *Sir* George
m149.

Nash, T.A.
d027.

Nater, Emma
e063.

Nathorst, A.G.
a026; b155; f110; h183; k071; n004; r046; u027.

National Archives Conference
u033.

National Geographic Society
a134; g112; t296.

Naval Arctic Research Laboratory, Point Barrow, Alaska
a623; b152.

Naysmith, John K.
c026.

Nazaroff, Pavel Stepanovich
m507.

Neatby, Leslie H.
m534.

Nebbia, Alessio
g357.

Necker de Saussure, Albertine
f108.

Nederlandsche Pool-expeditie, 1882-83
n064.

Needham, John T.
o008.

Neel, Alexandra David.   See David-Neel, Alexandra.

Neergaard, Tønnes Christian Bruun.   See Bruun-Neergaard, Tønnes Christian.

Neff, Felix
m140.

Negrelli, L. de
a797.

Negri, Carlo
a398; r216.

Negri, G.
f070.

Neider, Charles
b135.

Nelson, E.W.
w098.

Nelson Griffiths, William.   *See Griffiths, William Nelson.*

Neri, Italo
t057.

Nerli, Angelo
a267; a268.

Neruda, Louis Norman.   *See Norman-Neruda, Louis.*

Neruda, May Norman.   *See Norman-Neruda, May.*

Nesbit, Paul W.
l192.

Nesheim, Asbjorn
s027.

Ness, Bertha
h167.

Neureuther, Gottfried
n213.

Neve, Arthur
t159.

Neve, Ernest F.
b136; t159.

New York Historical Society
d231.

New Zealand Alpine Club
b260; c060; m237; m408; m410; n109; r261.

New Zealand Antarctic Society
l194.

Newcomb, Raymond Lee
o109.

Nga-Wang Lop-Sang Tup-Den Gya-Tso, *13th Dalai Lama*
p225.

Nice, Bruno
m398.

Nichol, J.R.
s387.

Nicholas, *Saint*
b249.

Nichols, R.C.
e207-208; e210; m504.

Nickul, Kalle
s027.

Nicolas, R.
s062.

Nicoli, Ezio
m402.

Nicolle, Henri
c427.

Nicolson, *M.*
a673.

Nieberl, Franz
e101; k057.

Niedermann, Erwin
h256.

Nielsen, Jørn Berglund.   *See Berglund Nielsen, Jørn.*

Nielsen, Niels
v108.

Nielsen, Troels F.D.
p114; p117; p246.

Nigay, Gilbert
b148.

Nil, Martin
h255.

Nilo, Mario
i179.

Nimlin, J.B.
s320.

Nimrod (Ship)
a750.

Nineteenth [XIXth] Century Art Gallery, London
a315.

Nisson, Claude
c368.

Nouvelle société helvétique
s029.

Novarese, Vittorio
m112; m375.

Nowill, Sidney
a358.

Noyce, Wilfrid
d109; e190; m280 s268; s315.

Nugent, Thomas
l150.

Nunziata, Felice
m176.

Nyka, Józef
g072; i064.

O.A.V. See Osterreichischer Alpenverein

O'Connor, *Sir* Frederick
o062.

O'Connor Morris, Maurice. See Morris, Maurice O'Connor.

O'Conor, Matthew
p147.

O'Malley, Martin
p052.

O'Reilly, Bernard
g174.

Oakley, E. Sherman
h218.

Ober, P.
o007.

Oberhummer, Eugen
a469; e078.

Obersteiner, Ludwig
h195.

Oberwalder, Louis
o099.

Oddo, Guido
a418.

Odelberg, Carl Eric
i142.

Odell, Noel Ewart
n010-11; n013.

Odorico da Pardenone
v142.

Oechslin, Max
a377; g075.

Oggioni, Andrea
h036.

Ogier Ward, R. See Ward, R. Ogier.

Ogrizek, Doré
s533; w108.

Ohio State University. Institute of Polar Studies
s115.

Oitzinger, Anton
a577.

Okonomische Gesellschaft, Chur
n084.

Oliphant, Laurence
j083.

Oliver, F.W.
p288.

Ollivier, Robert
p338; p341; p344.

Olrog, Claes Chr.
i142.

Olsen, Jack
c231.

Oltmann, C. Ruth
k020.

Omholt-Jensen, E.
b115.

Ongari, Dante
p263.

Onraet, Tony
s230.

Operation Deep-Freeze, 1954-58
c203.

Oppenheim, Edwin Camillo
n097.

Ordinaire, *Monsieur*
a673.

Orell, H. von
n080.

Origlia, C.
g063.

Origlia, Gian
g287.

Orlando, Massimo
k002.

Ormes, Robert M.
g349.

Orsieres, J.M.F.
h161.

Ortelli, Toni
a412.

Osborn, Sherard
d155; s429.

Osenbrüggen, Eduard
a243; g127; h187; w037.

Osers, Ewald
s319.

Ostermann, H.
a132-133; m004.

Osterreichische-ungarische Nordpol-Expedition
e219.

Osterreichischer Alpenclub
b088; h188.

Osterreichischer Alpenverein
a216; a323; b093; b247; f035; h095; m227; n111; o096;
t035.

Osterreichischer Alpenverein. Museum
e002.

Osterreichischer Alpenverein. Sektion Salzburg
h256.

Osterreichischer Touristen-Club
a307.

Osterreichischer und Deutscher Alpenverein. **See**
Deutscher und Osterreichischer Alpenverein.

Osterrieth, Martine van Berg. **See** *Berg-Osterrieth,*
Martine van.

Osterwald, S.F.
d083.

Ottin Pecchio, Cesare. **See** *Pecchio, Cesare Ottin.*

Otto, Emil
g048.

Ottolenghi di Vallepiana, Ugo. See Di Vallepiana, Ugo.

Outram, *Sir* James, *Bart.*
i089.

Overseas Education League
v181.

Owen, Dilys
h085.

Owen, John
t234.

Owen, Ruth Bryan
l051.

Oxley, T. Louis
j005.

P., *Graf von*
r084.

Paccard, Michel Gabriel
b011; d207-208; e248; e307; m197; n177; p002-3;
p251.

Packe, Charles
g353; p223; s354.

Paczkowski, Andrzej
g072.

Padovani, Pia
i018.

Page Rives, Judith. **See** *Rives, Judith Page.*

Paidar, Herbert
z046.

Paillon, Mary
f030; m005; p011.

Paillon, Maurice
m188.

Pais Becher, Gianni
e135.

Paitson, Leonard W.
f073.

Palace Theatre, London
l050.

Palau, Carlo
f101.

Palazzi-Lavaggi, Carolina
r173.

Palazzo, Pasquale
s190.

Palazzo Vescovile, Aosta
i049.

Palla, Eduard
a737.

Palliser, Arthur
p075.

Palmer, F.
r138.

Palmer, J.C.
t091.

Palmer Putnam, George. *See Putnam, George Palmer.*

Palmieri, Arturo
m313.

Pampanini, Renato
f070.

Pan, Jacques Mallet du. *See Mallet du Pan, Jacques.*

Pankotsch, Hans
k055.

Panorama, Leicester Square
d088-90; d102.

Panorama, Strand
d091; d102.

Pantanelli, Dante
a595.

Paoli, Pasquale
a048.

Papon, Jakob
e060.

Paragot, Robert
m020.

Parc national de la Vanoise. Conseil d'administration
p028.

Pardo, Manuel
m151.

Paris, T. Clifton
l106.

Parisi, Francesco M.
e028.

Park, Mungo
l143.

Parker, Alfred Traill
s293.

Parker, Charles Stuart
s293.

Parker, Herschel C.
c364.

Parker, John P.
c038.

Parker, Samuel
j079; s293.

Parker, Theodor
a147.

Parker Smith, J. *See Smith, J. Parker.*

Parkes, Joseph
p181.

Parley, Peter
s175; t014-15.

Parnell, Thomas
p191.

Parona, Carlo Fabrizio
v085.

Parrot, Friedrich
u009; w129.

Parry, C.H.
s530.

Parry, William Edward
h145; j050; n037; n158.

Parsons, C.A., & Co. *See C.A. Parsons & Co.*

Pascal, Cesar
d034.

Pascale, G. Paolo di. See Di Pascale, G. Paolo.

Paschetta, Vincent. *See also Series Index (Guide Paschetta des Alpes Maritimes).*
a234; a383; c327; h049; m184-185; n119; s013-14; v029.

Pascoe, John
h002; s318.

Pasquale, Carlo
l062.

Pasquier, Léon du. See Du Pasquier, Léon.

Pasteur, H.
l053.

Pastine, Gianni
z021.

Paterfamilias. See Tupper, Martin.

Paterson, M.
m470.

Paterson, Sam.
b153.

Paterson, William
g346.

Pathay, Victor Donatien de Musset. See Musset-Pathay, Victor Donatien.

Patin, Charles
r108; t238.

Patrucco, Giuseppe
u063.

Patton, Brian
c031.

Paulcke, Wilhelm
b062; p099.

Pauli, Ludwig
a191.

Paulus, Eduard
i156.

Pauly, Hans
g003.

Pause, Walter
a038; a193; a207; g196; i035; i038; i044; i065; m222; s022; s063; s254; v203; w036; z037.

Pavesi, Ezio
v023.

Payan, Louis
n012.

Payer, Julius
b074; e219; s447; u067; w075.

Paynter, James A.
m406.

Payot, Jean
b161.

Payot, Paul
a763; a764; c164; c360; r274.

Payot, Venance
c064; g358-359; o091.

Peacocke, Thomas Arthur Hardy
m461.

Peale, Titian Ramsay
t106.

Pearce, Stephen
c429.

Peary, Josephine Diebitsch
c193.

Peary, Marie Annighito
c193.

Peary, Robert E.
a073; f064; n149; t108.

Peary Arctic Club
n149.

Peat, Neville
i007; l194; s266.

Peattie, Roderick
g171; s212.

Pecchio, Cesare Ottin
l203; s026.

Pecher, R.
s319.

Peck, Annie Smith
s143.

Pedersen, Einar Sverre
p207.

Pedrotti, Egidio
c056.

Pedrotti, Mauro
c089.

Pedrotti, Remo
b117; b204; d186; f017; s424.

Péguy, Charles Pierre
c124.

Péguy, Suzy
g312.

Peirce, Benjamin Mills
r137.

Peissel, Michel
b141.

Pellegatta, Piero
c287.

Pellegrinon, Bepi
a414; c207; f010; m063-64; p008-9.

Pelletier, Alexandre
a682.

Pelloux, Albert
t122.

Pelosi, Carlo
a012.

Peloubet Farquhar, Francis. See Farquhar, Francis Peloubet.

Pembroke Fetridge, W. See Fetridge, W. Pembroke.

Penck, Albrecht
s580; v115.

Pennant, Thomas
t137-140.

Pennell, Elizabeth Robins
o120; p183.

Pennell, Joseph
p183.

Penney, Scott Moncrieff
h009.

Pennington, Thomas
c386; j082.

Pensionnat Janin
v226.

People's Physical Culture Publishing House,
Beijing
m476.

Perco, G.A.
p232.

Pereira, George
p084.

Pérès, Jean Louis
m357.

Perkins, H., & Co.   See H.Perkins & Co.

Perla, Ronald I.
a818.

Perna, Giuliano
p174.

Pernisch, J.
u066.

Perren, Peter Anton
k029-30.

Perret, Robert
p024.

Perrig, Alexander
m135.

Perrin, André
p273.

Perrin, Charles Louis
g028.

Perrin, Felix
b017; c104; c105; g319; h188; i168.

Perrin, Jean
s215.

Perrucca, Mario
c403; o078.

Perry, Alexander W.
w064.

Persson, Thomas
l043.

Pertsov, N.A.
b163.

Perzalghi, Rolando
a400.

Pescanti Botti, Renata
d001.

Pescio, Lorenzo
l073.

*Pesme de St Saphorin, François Louis de. See St
Saphorin, François Louis de Pesme de.*

Pestalozzi, *Mrs* Conrad
m538.

Peter, Marc Ernest
g030.

Peter Whyte Foundation
g162.

Peterlana, A.
s271.

Petermann, August Heinrich
a208; d092; e111; g128; r074; s447; v015; w075.

Peters, Ed.
m465.

Petersen, H.C.
k005.

Petersen, Peter Milan
v093.

*Petigny, Clara Filleul de. See Filleul de Petigny,
Clara.*

Petit, Victor
b007; s334.

Petrali Cicognara, R.
b056.

Petterssen, Sverre
k068.

Pettersson, Carl Anton
l034.

Pettigiani, Giorgio
c399.

Peyer, Gustav
g060.

Peyré, Joseph
m027; m113.

Peyronel, Enrico
u055.

Peyrot, Ada
i049; v037.

Peyster, J. Watts de.   See De Peyster, J. Watts.

Pezay, Alexandre Frédéric Jacques de Masson,
marquis de
s276.

Pezolt, Gg.
a148.

Pezzl, Johann
i200.

Pfaff, Friedrich
n060.

Pfaff, J.R.
z023.

Pfann, Hans
a794; f147; m001; m173; m252.

Pfannl, Heinrich
w048.

Pfeiffer, G.
a671.

Pfister, Max
z038.

Pfister, Otto von
s218.

Pfyffer von Wyher, Ludwig
p022.

Philips, Francis
r022.

Phillips, Walter J.
c329.

Phillipps-Wolley, *Sir* Clive
s361.

Phoutrides, Aristides Evangelos
m419.

Piacenza, Mario
p274.

Piachaud, *Dr*
a674.

Piaget, Emile
p019.

Piana Regis, Renza
g265.

Pianetti, Danilo
c435; c447.

Piani, Gianguido
q010.

Piantanida, Erminio
a403.

Piaz, Tita
a024; d132; m195.

Pichot, Michel
g312.

Picot, Jean
s375-376.

Pictet, Adolphe
c421.

Pictet, M.A.
r097.

Pictet-Mallet, J.P.
i161; n243-245.

Pidoux, Edmond
a574; v196.

Piehler, H.A.
s544.

Pieropan, Gianni
d223; m377; p136.

Pierre, Bernard
b006; m428; v146.

Pieth, Friedrich
p055.

Pietro, Pericle di. *See Di Pietro, Pericle.*

Pietrollini, G.
h061.

Pietrostefani, Stanislao
g136-137.

Pigeon, Anna
p065.

Piggott, A.S.
w069.

Pighini, G.
g258.

Pilati di Tassulo, Carlo Antonio
v280.

Pilgrim
n196.

Pilkington, Charles
m489.

Pilkington, John
b003.

Pilkington, Lawrence
a369; w001.

Pilkington White, T. *See White, T. Pilkington.*

Pilley, Dorothy E.
c249.

Pim, Bedford
c341.

Pingret, Edouard
p305.

Pinkerton, John
a057; g021.

Pitman, C.B.
t088.

Pitschmann, Hans
f071.

Pitschner, Wilhelm
m295-296.

Pius XI, *Pope*
c276-277; s137.

Pizzi, Giovanni
a395.

Planché, J.R.
l048.

Planinska Zveza Slovenije
t272.

Planta, A. von
g130.

Planta, Joseph
h181.

Plantamour, E.
m191.

Plantin, Jean Baptiste
h062-63.

Plattner, Placidus A.
g058.

Platts, John
b186.

Platz, Ernst
a339.

Plessis, J. du, comte.   *See Du Plessis, J., comte.*

Ploucquet, Wilhelm Gottfried
v132.

Plummer, R.W.
t220.

Plunket, Frederica
h068.

Pocar, Ervino
a279; m196.

Pock, Julius
s436.

Poesch, Jessie
t106.

Pogliaghi, Lino
e133.

Pohl, Frederick J.
r154.

Poisson, Bernard
e120.

Polar Bear (Ship)
v256.

Polaris (Ship)
g098.

Polidori, G.
p045.

Pollenghi, Andrea Pollitzer de.   *See Pollitzer de Pollenghi, Andrea.*

Pollino, Piero
g272-274.

Pollitzer de Pollenghi, Andrea
m339.

Pöllnitz, *baron de*
n238.

Pollock, *Sir* Frederick
c068.

Polybius
h152.

Pomarici, Ugo
c435; c447.

Poncins, Gontran de
p025.

Pontet, R.L.A. du.   *See Du Pontet, R.L.A.*

Pontoppidan, Carl
h259.

Pope, Alexander
p191.

Porta Xidias, Spiro dalla.   *See Dalla Porta Xidias, Spiro.*

Porter, Horace D.
v145.

Porter, Russell Williams
a616; r276.

Potton, Craig
a372.

Pouilly, Jean Simon Lévesque de.   *See Lévesque de Pouilly, Jean Simon.*

Pourchier, Marcel
t039.

Pourquoi Pas? (Ship)
a807.

Powell James, W.   *See James, W. Powell.*

Power, Cecil
y001.

Praag, S. van
t117.

Pracchi, Roberto
l190.

Pracht, Egon
d177.

Prada, Sandro
a415; b220; g362; m178; r005; s172; u052.

Pranzelores, Antonio
p221.

Prati, Pino
d189.

Prati, Raffaello
f087.

Prescott, J.R.V.
l039.

Presnova, V.A.
v131.

Preston, Paul
v288-289.

Preston-Thomas, Herbert
m485.

Pretyman, Herbert Edward
j067.

Preuss, G. Paul
a119; p269.

Previdoli, Mauro
s101.

Prévost, Pierre
n216.

Price, Robert
a060.

Prielmayer, M. von
w076.

Prieur de Sombreuil, D.
p113.

Prieuré de Chamonix
p273.

Pringle, *Sir* John
d154.

Prior, Herman
a728.

Prior, Samuel
u034-35.

Pritchard, Henry Baden
b032; t181.

Priuli, Ausilio
i101.

Privat, Edouard
p331.

Prochaska, Edouard
o101.

Pryde, George S.
t262.

Public House Trust
s284.

Public Schools Alpine Sports Club
p324-325; y003.

Puerari, Giuseppe
v024.

Puiseux, Pierre
o102.

Pulle, Giorgio
v142.

Pullen, H.F.
p326.

Pullen, W.J.S.
p326.

Pullen Expedition
p326.

Pullinger, F.A.
h001.

Purohit, *Swami*
h219.

Purtscheller, Ludwig
a780; h197-200; s024; s436; u012; z025.

Putnam, George Palmer
m061.

Putnam, William Lowell
c233; c234.

Puttrell, James W.
j019.

Pyatt, Edward Charles
n204.

Quadrini Schir, Wanda
d218.

Quagliotto, Renzo
s039.

Quaife, Milo Milton
v271.

Quam, Louis O.
r145.

Quartermain, L.B.
a572; n110; t297.

Quattrini, Antonio G.
c312.

Queensberry, John Sholto Douglas, *Marquis of*
s353.

Queling, Hans
s146.

Querlon, Anne Gabriel Meusnier de.
j047.

Questa, Emilio.
g264.

Queux, William Le.   See Le Queux, William.

R., R.
s494.

R., W. v.   See Rhetz, Wilhelm von.

R. Burns, *Ltd*
b132; m490.

Rabensteiner, Wolfgang.
s435.

Rabinovitch, W.
s363.

Rabot, Charles
a750; e233; p213; s356; v119.

Raden, Woldemar.   See Kaden, Woldemar.

Radio-Radiis, Alfred
f138.

Radloff, Wilhelm
a795.

Rae, John
a610; c404.

Rae, Lettice Milne
l009.

Raeburn, Harold
m468.

Raechl, Walter
f096.

Ræstad, Arnold
s356.

Raffaella, Maria
d004.

Raffles, Thomas
l093-94.

Raffles, W. Winter
z016.

Rafn, C.C.
g192.

Ragni, F.
g244.

Ragozza, Erminio
n067.

Raikes, H.
f059.

Rainer, *family*
w123-124.

Rainoldi, Luciano
a167; a171; a578; v034; v047.

Raitmayr, Erich
k053.

Rákosi, Viktor
q003.

Rambaud, Placide
e025.

Rambert, Eugène
a244; a255; a256; a257; a783; e173; m400; m520; s328.

Ramella, Carlo
s401.

Ramond, Louis
l115; t227; t232; v273.

Rampini, A. Luigi
a538.

Rampini, Arturo
e118.

Rampold, Josef
b079; s449.

Ramsauer, Franz
a211.

Ramsay, Andrew Crombie
o032-33.

Ramsay, George C.
d031.

Ramsay, J.A.
c020.

Ramsay Peale, Titian. See Peale, Titian Ramsay.

Ramsey Ullman, James. See Ullman, James Ramsey.

Ramuz, C.F.
p058.

Randhawa, M.S.
k070.

Raoul-Rochette, Désiré
l126-127; v265.

Rasero, Aldo
a378.

Rasky, Frank
e237.

Rasmussen, Knud
a132-133; i016; i126-127; m004; n077; o014; s261; s392.

Raspe, R.E.
a052.

Ratcliff, Arthur
s022.

Ratti, Achille. See Pius XI, Pope.

Ratti, Carlo
p098.

Ravelli, Luigi
v086.

Ravizza, Giuseppe
n261.

Rawling, C.G.
g169.

Ray, Dorothy Jean
e143.

Raymann, Arthur
e192.

Read Wilkinson, Thomas. See Wilkinson, Thomas Read.

Reade, Herbert Vincent
s294.

Reale Società Geografica Italiana. See Società Geografica Italiana.
r024.

Rebitsch, Mathias
s216.

Rébuffat, Françoise
t264.

Rébuffat, Frédérique
t264.

Rébuffat, Gaston
a599; b133; c011; c117; c168; d219; e074; e168; g065; m072-73; m297; n065.

Reclus, Élisée
h167.

Reday, Ladislaw
b003.

Redelsberger-Gerig, E.
h060.

Redford Bulwer, James. See Bulwer, James Redford.

Redi, Francesco
e144; e227.

Reed, John C.
a623.

Regazzoni, Guido
g226; n126.

Regionalassessorat für Fremdenverkehr der Region Trentino-Tiroler Etschland
b117.

Regis, Giancarlo
g265.

Regis, Renza Piana. See Piana Regis, Renza.

Reichard, Heinrich August Ottaker
g318; h074; i200; m022-23; p047.

Reichert, Federico
e049.

Reid, James
t142.

Reid Young, James. See Young, James Reid

Reifsnyder, William E.
f088; h258.

Reilly, A. Adams. **See** *Adams-Reilly, A.*

Reineggs, Jacob
g024.

Reinhard, Raphael
p049.

Reinhardt, Johann Christian
c322.

Reisigl, Herbert
f071.

Reiss, Ernest
r217.

Reiss, G. Fr.
s075-76.

Reist, Dölf
b063; t185.

Relave, Pierre Maxime
r230.

Rémy, Claude
s367.

Rémy, Yves
s367.

Ren, Bing-hui
g091.

Rendu, Louis
n227; r120-121; t064-65.

Renevier, Eugene
n228; s001.

Renker, Gustav Friedrich
b082; m136.

Renner, Georg
b171.

Rensselaer, Jeremiah van. **See** *Van Rensselaer, Jeremiah.*

Renzi, Renzo
m314.

Resolute (Ship)
e179.

Restelli, Carlo
n132.

Reuschel, Paul
f139.

Rey, *fl. 1835*
q007; s311.

Rey, Gérard
r016.

Rey, Guido
a137; a384; a401; a402; b055; c317; f013; f042; m108-112; m285; m375; p067; p328; r031; t046.

Rey, Louis
g191.

Rey, William
g186.

Reynold, Gonzague de
p061.

Reynolds, J.N.
e238.

Reynolds, Robert
a121.

Rhätische Bahn
r164.

Rhetz, Wilhelm von
r080.

Rho, Franco
c039.

Ricci, Vincenzo
c047.

Ricci Lucchi, Nevia
v299.

Rich, E.E.
c404.

Richard
g324; m055.

Richard-Janillon
w032.

Richards, Alfred Valentine Valentine. **See** *Valentine-Richards, Alfred Valentine.*

Richards, Eva Alvey
a624.

Robertson, Alexander
t087.

Robertson, Douglas S.
t111.

Robertson, *Mrs* Wharton
z009.

Robilant, Esprit Benoît de
d037.

Robino, Gilbert
g179; m127; m301; s308.

Robins Pennell, Elizabeth. **See** *Pennell, Elizabeth Robins.*

Robinson, Anthony Melland
a361.

Robinson, Bart
c031; g162.

Robinson, J. Lewis
o115.

Robinson, William
a322.

Robischung, F.A.
c300.

Robitaille, Yolande Dorion. **See** *Dorion-Robitaille, Yolande.*

Robson, George Fennell
s048.

Roby, John
s186.

Rocca Castello, Jacques Carelli de. **See** *Carelli de Rocca Castello, Jacques.*

Roccati, Alessandro
n069; r169.

Roch, André
c370; e188; g009; g075; h050; k031; m240; o051; s521.

Rochat-Cenise, Charles
j006.

Roche, Monsieur de la. **See** *La Roche, Monsieur de.*

Roche, Roger Frison. **See** *Frison-Roche, Roger.*

Roche, Sophie von La. **See** *La Roche, Sophie von.*

Rochette, Désiré Raoul. **See** *Raoul-Rochette, Désiré.*

Rochford, comte de. **See** *Rumford, Benjamin Thompson, Count.*

Rock, Joseph F.
g112.

Rod, H. Denkinger. **See** *Denkinger-Rod, H.*

Röder, G.W.
k026.

Rodgers (Ship)
o109.

Roeckl, Eugen
b087.

Roemer
b128.

Røer, Hans H.
n140.

Rogers, Nigel
n094.

Rogers Howell, George. **See** *Howell, George Rogers.*

Roget, F.F.
z006-7.

Rohan, Henri, *duc de*
m144.

Rohrer, Max
a370; g051; l131.

Roland de la Platière, J.M.
l119.

Rolando, A.
b038.

Rolfsen, N.
n136.

Romano, Giorgio
a576.

Romiti, Cesare
g286.

Ronaldshay, Lawrence John Lumley Dundas, *Earl of*
l029.

Roney, *Sir* Cusack Patrick
a439.

Ronhovde, Andreas G.
a623.

Rook, Clarence
s545.

Roper, Ian
n094.

Roper, Steve
a695; c235; f037.

Rosa, G. Titta. *See Titta Rosa, G.*

Roscoe, Thomas
l030; m146; r010.

Rose, Eugene A.
h090.

Rose, Lisle A.
a729.

Rosenthal, Philipp Wilhelm
k034.

Ross Sea Party. *See Imperial Transarctic Expedition.*

Ross, Francis Edward
v195.

Ross, *Sir* John
h145; l041; r094.

Ross, W. Gillies
a635.

Ross Goodwin, C. *See Goodwin, C. Ross.*

Rossaro, Enrico
d190.

Rosset, David
m013.

Rosset, Georges A.
m016.

Rossi, Amilcare
d009.

Rossi, Giovanni
r057.

Rossi, Marcello
m345.

Rossi, Piero
a459; c100; d187; e139; g216; g261-262; m064; s059; s111; s120.

Rossi di Montilera, Lorenzo
v045.

Rota, Annibale
m342.

Roth, Abraham
d170-171; f043; g108.

Rothpletz, August
a339.

Rototaev, P.S.
p197.

Rott, E.
v243.

Rottauscher, Alfred
s174.

Rottmann, Leop.
a148.

Rouff, Marcel
h224.

Roulin, Désiré Célestin. *See Constantin Marie, brother.*

Rousseau, Jean Jacques
l117; v228.

Roux, G.
a783.

Roux, Xavier
a226.

Rovereto, Gaetano
g264.

Rowan (Ship)
l052.

Rowe, Peter Trimble
m031.

Rowell, Galen A.
e154; m501; o059.

Royal Air Force Mountaineering Association
a078; c220; m211; n113.

Royal Canadian Mounted Police
a627.

Royal Forth Yacht Club
l165; o028.

Royal Geographical Society
a481; b010; c180; g033; k049; l169; n224; p295; r125; r252-253; s187.

Royal Geographical Society. Mount Everest Committee
c078; s480.

Royal Institution of Great Britain
a610; n186.

Royal Institution of South Wales
r254.

Royal Navy and Royal Marines Mountaineering Club
l202.

Royal Observatory, Greenwich
o058; o066.

Royal Scottish Geographical Society
p320.

Royal Society
c112; d154; o009; o011-12; r106.

Royal United Service Institution
a643; b022.

Rubenson, C.W.
n140.

Ruchat, Abraham
d049-50.

Rucklidge, John C.
p114.

Rucksack Club
h007; h096; n230; r258; t251.

Rucksack Club. Library
c071.

Rudatis, Domenico A.
l131; s177.

Rudbeck, Olof
h172.

Ruden, Joseph
f014.

Rudmose-Brown, R.N.
b245; f072.

Ruesch, Hans
p001.

Rufenacht, J.G.
s533; w108.

Rumford, Benjamin Thompson, *Count*
o008.

Runge, Friedrich
g073.

Ruong, Israel
s027.

Rusconi, Giovanni
a392; p033.

Ruskin, John
d110-111; i079; l059; l145; m233-234; p240; r274; s183; s390; s437; t065; v018.

Russell, Henry, *comte*
f097; g150; p342; r275; s329-330.

Russell, Israel C.
t296.

Russell, R. Scott
m446.

Russell Institution
s142.

Russell-Killough, Henri, comte. **See Russell, Henry, *comte*.**

Russo, Cesare
a169.

Ruthner, Anton von
a776; a796; b054; e114; m028; u016.

Ruttledge, Hugh
e185-187; n015.

Ruud, Bjorn
h239.

Ryan, V.J.E.
e256.

Ryerson, John
h251.

S., A.
f108.

S., Edward
p082.

S., J.A.
b002.

S.P.C.K. *See* *Society for Promoting Christian Knowledge.*

S.U.C.A.I. *See* *Club Alpino Italiano. Sezione Universitaria*

S.U.M.C. *See* *Sheffield University Mountaineering Club.*

Saba Sardi, Francesco
a822.

Sabaini, Giordano
s425.

Sabatier
r275.

Sabbadini, Attilio
a267.

Sack, John
a720.

Sage, George Louis Le. *See* *Le Sage, George Louis.*

Sagliani, Ermanno
l007.

Saglio, Silvio
a294; d070; m381.

Saibene, C.
g032.

Saint Andrews University. Students' Representative Council
c323.

Saint John, Bayle
s441.

Saint Loup, A. de
m320.

Saint Loup, Stanislas de
v130.

Saint Séverin, Hector de Tredecini de, marquis. *See* *Tredecini de Saint Séverin, Hector de, marquis.*

Saint-Georges de Bouhélier
v227.

Sainte-Maure, Charles de
n104.

Sajnoha, Marian
d134.

Sakünlünski, Hermann Schlagintweit. *See* *Schlagintweit-Sakünlünski, Hermann.*

Salesi, Bruno
c007; c094; c433; d209.

Salesi, Francesco
c007; c094; c433; d209.

Salis, Renzo Sertoli. *See* *Sertoli Salis, Renzo.*

Salisbury, Charlotte Y.
m506.

Salisbury, F.S.
r015.

Salome, Giulio
s179.

Salone di Trecento, Treviso. Mostra internazionale, 1967
m318.

Salvaneschi, Nino
s364.

Salvatore, Ada
f106.

Samivel
a479; c211; c383; f103; g147; g198; h226; m002; m246; r002; s312.

Samoggia, Anna Luisa
c003.

Samoilovitch, R.
w056.

Sanger Davies, Joseph. *See* *Davies, Joseph Sanger.*

Sangtoft, Johannes
b217.

Sanmarchi, Giuseppina
s121.

Sanmarchi, Toni
a455; a462; a463; a466; c208; s121.

Sansom, Joseph
t209.

Sanson, George S.
c247.

Santa Maria Novella, Florence
d198.

Santi, M.C.
g133.

Santi, Marinella de.   **See** *De Santi, Marinella.*

Santi, Venceslao
a595.

Santini, Vincenzo
g234.

Sapori, Francesco
d192.

Saporta, G. de
a249.

Sapper, Karl
n057.

Saragat, Giovanni
a401; f013.

Sardi, Francesco Saba.   **See** *Saba Sardi, Francesco.*

Sarenne, Jean
t278.

Sarperi, V.
a268.

Sarthou, Sylvain
m087-88.

Sartorius von Waltershausen, Wolfgang
r029.

Sarychev, Gavriil
p330.

Saudan, Sylvain
s578.

Saunders, T.J.
n196.

Saussure, Albertine Necker de.   **See** *Necker de Saussure, Albertine.*

Saussure, César de
f091.

Saussure, Horace Bénédict de
a057; a670; c209; d045; d077; e024; e251; f021; g021; g025; h222; j041; j068; l111-112; l118; l151; m141;

m303.1; o010; o026; p137; p259; p277; r095-96; r101; s033; s237; v235; v275-276.1; v277.

Saussure, René de
a670.

Savage-Landor, A. Henry
i088; j085; t097.

Savary, Claude Etienne
i128.

Savi-Lopez, Maria
l078.

Savoisien, G.C.
a673.

Savonitto, Andrea
c197.

Savoy, *princes of*
p282.

Saxe-Coburg-Gotha, Leopold, Duke of.   **See** *Leopold, Duke of Saxe-Coburg-Gotha.*

Say, J.B.
n236.

Sayers, W.C. Berwick
o118.

Sazerac, Hilaire Léon
l123.

Scalet, Samuele
g269.

Scandellari, Armando
v030-30.1; v176.

Scarpa, Dario
d182.

Schachmann, Carl A. von
b046.

Schaden, Adolph von
v197.

Schaer, J.P.
g322.

Schaffer, Jeffrey P.
y011.

Schardt, Hans
c415; r161; s001; s500.

Schätz, Josef Julius
a189; a190; a371; b092; l132.

Schatz, Ruedi
r217.

Schaub, Charles
d099; g332; s076; s474.

Schaub, *chevalier*
e160.

Schaubach, Adolph
d120.

Schaumann, Walther
d167; g236; m379.

Scheffel, P.H.
v116.

Scheffel, Joseph Viktor von
g115.

Scheffer, John
h172.

Scheuchzer, Johann Jacob
b119; h064; n052; n259; o111-112.

Scheuermann, E.
p210.

Schidlowsky, A. Th.   See Shidlovsky, A.F.

Schimper, A.F.W.
a222.

Schiner, Hildebrand
d084.

Schinz, Hs. Rudolf
b139.

Schir, Wanda Quadrini.   See Quadrini Schir, Wanda.

Schivardi, Plinio
m316.

Schlagintweit, Adolph
l154; n087; u008; z039.

Schlagintweit-Sakünlünski, Hermann
n087; z039.

Schley, Winfield S.
r133.

Schlüter, Hanns
z037.

Schlytter, Boye
c272.

Schmaderer, Ludwig
z046.

Schmid, Toni
j090.

Schmid, Walter
c116; g113; k063; m171; r119; s161; w067; z013.

Schmidkunz, Walter
b055; b069; b070; b098; b102; b113; e063; m131.

Schmidt, Angelika
c434.

Schmidt, C.W.
s072.

Schmidt, Carl
b157; g039; z031.

Schmidt, Jürgen
c434.

Schmidt, Theodor
a793.

Schmied, Ernst
b072.

Schmiemann, Siegmund
s319.

Schmilinsky, Michael
h051.

Schmithals, Hans
a181.

Schmitt, Fritz
a323; b094; w057.

Schneider, Adolf
g229.

Schneider, Erwin
b075; h111; z041.

Schneider, Siegmund
m129.

Schoberl, Frederic.   See Shoberl, Frederic.

Schoch, C.   See Schoch, J.C.

Schoch, J.C.
h035.

Schomberg, Reginald Charles Francis
b134.

Schöner, Hellmut
g202; j092; z043.

Schönhuth, Ottmar Fr. H.
n088.

Schøyen, Carl
f136; v150.

Schrader, Franz
p331; v104.

Schroder-Stranz, Herbert
e220.

Schröter, Carl
c330; f077.

Schröter, L.
c330; f077.

Schüler, Else Lasker. **See** *Lasker-Schüler, Else.*

Schultes, G. von
s259.

Schultes, J.A.
r069.

Schulthess, Emil
t120.

Schultz-Lorentzen, Finn
a605.

Schulz, Karl
a074; a374; a777; b205; e107; g189; i037.

Schuster, Claud, *Baron Schuster*
j030; l146; m167; p066; p231.

Schuster, Oskar
f148.

Schütz, *Herr*
h044.

Schütz, Karl von
r085.

Schütz Wilson, Henry. **See** *Wilson, Henry Schütz.*

Schwaiger, Heinrich
k035.

Schwartz, Myrtil
e159; v118.

Schwarz, Th.
u013.

Schwatka, Frederick
s483; t296.

Schweiger-Lerchenfeld, Amand von, *Freiherr*
a210.

Schweizer, J.J.
f022.

Schweizer Alpen-Club.
a173-178; a293; a343; a364; a365; b048; b114; b157;
b270; c065; c285; c291; c292; c293; c294; c295; c296;
d214; d216; e022; e115-116; f143; g105; g301; g310;
g311.1-3; i193-197; j010-12; k059-60; m045; m319;
p043; p172; p245; r165; r189; r270; s001; s306; s379;
s383; t034; t059; u044; v134; v199; v201; w132.

Schweizer Alpen-Club. Basler Sektion
p018.

Schweizer Alpen-Club. Centralcomité
c290; g026; g306; g309; r217.

Schweizer Alpen-Club. Centralcomité Glarus
v134.

Schweizer Alpen-Club. Section genevoise. **See infra,**
Sektion Geneva.

Schweizer Alpen-Club. Sections romandes
e021.

Schweizer Alpen-Club. Sektion Bern
b155.1; b155.2; b156; c289.1; d132.1; g019.1; g183.1-
2; j015; m223; p107-107.1; p217; s160; s380; t155;
t302.

Schweizer Alpen-Club. Sektion Blümlisalp
j089.

Schweizer Alpen-Club. Sektion Diablerets
a244.

Schweizer Alpen-Club. Sektion Geneva
b261; e021; g306; g316; n219; p294.

Schweizer Alpen-Club. Sektion Grindelwald
a468.

Schweizer Alpen-Club. Sektion Leventina
g268.

Schweizer Alpen-Club. Sektion Moléson
g309.

Schweizer Alpen-Club. Sektion Monte Rosa
m382.

Schweizer Alpen-Club. Sektion Pilatus
w019.

Schweizer Alpen-Club. Sektion UTO
t041; u032.

Schweizer Alpen-Club. Sektion Zimmerberg
f152.

Schweizer Alpen-Club. Sektion Zofingen
g183.1-2.

Schweizer Alpen-Club. Zentralbibliothek
k036.

Schweizer Bibliophilen-Gesellschaft
h076.

Schweizer Historikertag, 1979
h135.

Schweizerische Hindukusch-Expedition, 1st
w097.

Schweizerische Historische Gesellschaft
s076.

Schweizerische Landesausstellung, Bern, 1914
s090.

Schweizerische Oberpostdirektion. *See Switzerland. Post-, Telegraphen- und Telephonverwaltung.*

Schweizerische Postverwaltung. *See Switzerland. Post-, Telegraphen- und Telephonverwaltung.*

Schweizerische Stiftung für Alpine Forschungen
a373; b065; c109; e181; e183; e188; f063; g009; g071; g195; k031; m116; m354; m454; s091.

Schweizerische Verkehrszentrale
b036.

Schweizerische Zentrale für Handelsförderung
s570.

Schweizerische Zentrale für Verkehrsförderung. *See Schweizerische Verkehrszentrale.*

Schweizerischer Institut für Kunstwissenschaft
s082.

Schweizerischer Kunstverein
s095.

Schweizerisches Alpines Museum, Bern
f137.

Schwingshackl, Anton
f141.

Schymik, Hans
b100.

Schwyzer, Julius
w040.

Sci Club Milano
g213; g291.

Scidmore, E. Ruhamah
a124.

Scitivaux de Greische, Antoine, *comte*
v245.

Scize, Pierre
e048.

Scoresby, William
a056; f113.

Scot, Hew
w051; w094.

Scott, Barbara H.
k047.

Scott, J.M.
g068; p224.

Scott, John
s242.

Scott, Leader
s223.

Scott, Robert Falcon
c320; l130; p213; w116.

Scott, *Mrs* W.L.L.
v167.

Scott, *Sir* Walter
m117; n188; p193.

Scott of Buccleuch, *family of*
a145.

Scott Polar Research Institute
m058.

Scott Polar Research Institute. Library
l138-139.

Scotti, G.
a394.

Scottish Himalayan Expedition
s123-124.

Scottish Mountaineering Club. *See also* Series Index
(*Scottish Mountaineering Club guide*).
a765; b045; b262-263; c241; g046; i144-145; l168;
m174; m212; n114; n220; n223; n229; n231; r267;
s125; s320.

Scottish Mountaineering Club. Library
:072.

Scottish Mountaineering Trust
c379.

Scottish National Antarctic Expedition
l149.

Scottish National Antarctic Expedition. Committee
a598.

Scottish Spitsbergen Syndicate
s126.

Scottish Youth Hostels Association
g341.

Scribe, Eugène
v032.

Scrinzi, Gino
i103; v044.

Scuola Alpina della Guardia di Finanza di
Predazzo
s103.

Scuola Militare Alpina di Aosta
t291.

Scuola Nazionale di Alpinismo 'Agostino
Pallavicini'
m365.

Seatree, George
s176.

Sebastiani, Eugenio
p222.

Sebesta, C.
s271.

*Sedgwick Whalley, Thomas.   See Whalley, Thomas
Sedgwick.*

Ségogne, Henry de
c127; h112; m085.

Seibert, Dieter
a029.

Seidenfaden, Gunnar
m235.

Seidlitz, Wilfried von
e076.

Seigne, Jean Maurice
h051.

Seigneur, Yannick
m020.

Seive, Fleury
a251; m302.

Seligman, Gerald
r146.

Sella, Corradino
s020.

Sella, Quintino
s019.

Sella, Vittorio
d004; m105; m384-385; s357; v166.

Selous, Henry C.
d090.

Senden, G.H. van
a194.

Senebier, Jean
m141.

Senonnes, Alexandre de Lamotte Barace, *vicomte de*
p305.

Seringe, Nicolas Charles
r082.

Serra, Luciano
v124.

Sertoli Salis, Renzo
p281; v079.

Service, Robert
r168.

Serviss, Garrett P.
c256.

Sestini, Aldo
p004.

Seton Karr, Heywood W.
s199.

Sewell, Elizabeth M.
j049.

Sexby, Edward
k045.

Seylaz, Louis
a261.

Sforza, Gian Galeazzo
a003.

Shackleton, *Sir* Ernest Henry
a750; a771; h054.

Shackleton, Kathleen
p118.

Shairp, John Campbell
l142.

Shapiro, Deborah
a640.

Shapley, Deborah
s188.

Sharma, Man Mohan
o024.

Sharp, Alec
g117.

Sharp, Samuel
l101.

Shattuck, George Cheever
h029.1.

Shaw, Baldwin
w065.

Shaw, Morton
a612; i128.

Sheffield Library
c076.

Sheffield University Mountaineering Club
s002.

Sheldon, Charles
w098-99.

Shelley, Mary
h168-169.

Shelley, Percy Bysshe
a051; h168-169.

Sheppard, John
l092.

Sherap, Paul
t100.

Sherer, Joseph Moyle
n180.

Sherman, Paddy
c284; e224.

Sherring, Charles A.
w074.

Sherrington, *Sir* Charles
g184; s197.

Sherwill, Markham
a682; a699; b223; n043; t071; v183.

Shidlovsky, A.F.
b147; s203.

Shillinglaw, John J.
n045.

Shipton, Eric
n009; n014; t283; u064-65.

Shirahata, Shiro
a264; a430; e178.

Shirakawa, Yoshikazu
h123; m016.

Shirley
a359.

Shluwalia, R.S.
s196.

Shoberl, Frederic
p150; t196; w127-128.

Shuckburgh, *Sir* George
o009.

Shuttleworth, R.J.
a044.

Sibbald, *Sir* Robert
a061.

Siegen, Johan
l067.

Sieger, Robert
a183.

Siegfried, J.J.
g105.

Siegrist, A.
s569.

Sierra Club
c235; f088; g083; h258; s210; w012.

Sigismondi, Vittorio
v186.

Signot, Jacques
p046.

Sigrist, Georg
b249.

Siliprandi, O.
g258.

Silk Buckingham, James.   *See Buckingham, James Silk.*

Simko, J.
h091.

Simler, Josias
d032; d043-44; j033; r143-144; v058-59.

Simler, Rudolf Theodor
t119.

Simmel, Eugen
s344.

Simmons, George
t026.

Simmons, Herman G.
f075.

Simon, Charles
e099.

Simond, François, & fils.   *See François Simond & fils.*

Simond, Louis
s549-550; v249.

Simoni, Giovanni de.   *See De Simoni, Giovanni.*

Simony, Friedrich
p122.

Simpson, Alexander
l144.

Simpson, Thomas
l144; m180; p241.

Sinclair, J.D.
a810.

Singh, J.S.
e080.

Singh, Nagendra
b142.

Singh, Tej Vir
i125.

Sinigaglia, Leone
c261.

Sinner, Jean R.
v252-253.

Sinnett, *Mrs* Percy
r035; s565.

Sinton, James
j056.

Siple, Paul
m221.

Sironi, M.A.
t056.

Sismonda, Angelo
o092.

Skar, Alfred
f018.

Skelton Stephenson, George.   *See Stephenson, George Skelton.*

Sketchley, Arthur
o113.

Ski Club. Biblioteca sezionale
e044.

Ski Club of Great Britain
s251; y004.

Ski Club Torino
g287.

Skjöldebrand, A.F.
v260.

Skuhra, Rudolf
s439.

Slaatelid, Aasmund
m120.

Sleen, W.G.N. van der
f105.

Slingsby, William Cecil
i078; m263; n168; w001.

Sloan, K.
l193.

Smedal, Gustav
e092; n169; s341.

Smellie, Thomas Farrar
a615.

Smid, Jan
l002.

Smida, Vlastimil
k009.

Smidt, Erik L.B.
a547.

Smith, Albert
b195; b196; e034; f104; h023-29; m218; m249-251; m271; m276; m509-511; n117; p145; p296; s415-418; s421; s434.

Smith, Alexander
s484.

Smith, Hubert
t054.

Smith, J. Manton
l057.

Smith, J. Parker
a042.

Smith, James Edward
s235.

*Smith, Janet Adam.   **See** Adam Smith, Janet.*

Smith, John
m390.

Smith, Joseph Denham
v194.

*Smith, Kaj Birket.   **See** Birket-Smith, Kaj.*

Smith, Philip M.
f132.

Smith, Walter Parry Haskett
c255; h220.

Smith, William
a091.

*Smith Peck, Annie.   **See** Peck, Annie Smith.*

Smithsonian Institution
m245.

Smollett, Tobias
p264.

Smythe, Frank S.
a087; a334; a335; b004; b170; b244; b272; c021; c022; c266; c267; e033; e260; e317; f051-52; i002; k008; k023-24; m448; m451; m474; m512; m531; n062; n107; n174; n184; o124; o126; r044; s352; s408-409; p176; t299; w070-71.

Snaith, Stanley
a298; a733.

*Sneed Houston, Charles.   **See** Houston, Charles Sneed.*

Sneedorf
b232.

Snellen, Maurits
n064.

Snellgrove, David
h119.

Snijders, Henri
t044.

Snoeck, C.A.
p301.

Snow, Robert
m153.

*Snow baby.   **See** Peary, Marie Ahnighito.*

Società Alpina delle Giulie
a516; i180.

Società Alpina Meridionale
b182.

Società Alpinisti Vicentini
v114.

Società degli Alpinisti Tridentini
a456; d189; g241-242; g247; p323.

Società delle Guide
t028.

Società Escursionisti Milanesi
c217.

Società Geografica Italiana
m155; r024.

Società Speleologica Italiana
m041.

Società Valsesiana di Cultura
c390; n068; s398.

Société d'Archangel
b147.

Société d'études des Hautes Alpes
b264-266.

Société d'histoire de la Suisse Romande
h003.

Société d'histoire du Haut-Valais. **See** *Geschichts-*
forschender Verein von Oberwallis..

Société d'histoire et d'archéologie de Maurienne,
Savoie
c204; c302.

Société d'histoire naturelle de Savoie
t126.

Société d'utilité publique de Montreux
m399.

Société de géographie de Genève
e175.

Société de la flore valdôtaine
e073.

Société de statistique des sciences naturelles et des
arts industriels du département de l'Isère
h138.

Société des eaux d'Evian
g300.

Société des guides Pol
p019.

Société des touristes du Dauphiné
a543; e172.

Société florimontane
d148.

Société pour le développement de la connaissance

des Alpes
g306.

Société royale académique de Savoie
m143.

Société scientifique et littéraire des instituteurs de
France
m266.

Société vaudoise d'utilité publique
g360.

Société vaudoise des sciences naturelles
c352; c415.

Society for Promoting Christian Knowledge
h073.

Society of Friends
a772.

Soeurs grises canadiennes
f031.

Solandieu
l069.

Solar, Gustav
a562; s082.

Solberg, Thorfinn
m138.

Solina, Franco
i187.

Solinas, Giovanni
s386.

Solly, Godfrey Allan
g114; n051.

Sombreuil, D. Prieur de. **See** *Prieur de Sombreuil, D.*

Somerset, *Lady* Fitzroy
f032.

Somervell, Theodore Howard
a096.

Somerville, D.M.M. Crichton. **See** *Crichton Somer-*
ville, D.M.M.

Somis, Ignazio
h157; t282.

Sommaruga, Pietro
e316.

Somme, Lauritz
s296.

Sonan Gyatso
s260.

Sonklar, Karl, *Edler von Innstädten*
a528; r092.

Sonnier, Georges
m121; m126; m347; o103.

Sonntag, Wolfgang
f117.

Sopwith, T.
m392.

Sora, Gennaro
c354.

Sordot, Leon Huot. **See** *Huot-Sordot, Leon.*

Sørensen, Jon
f119.

Sorgmann, Antoni
h165.

Soubiron, Pierre
p339.

Souci, Antoine
a161; a162; a163.

Soulé, H.B.D.
o055.

South African Biological and Geological Expedition, 1965-66
m062.

South Sea Surveying and Exploring Expedition
e238.

Southern Railway Company
n103.

Southwell, Thomas
n206.

Sowerby, J.
f093.

Spallanzani, Lazzaro
v139.

Spänhauer, Fritz
r058.

Spazier, Karl
w039.

Spedizione 'Città di Lecco', Alaska, 1961
s446.

Spedizione Italiana all'Everest, 1973
s347.

Spedizione Italiana alle Ande Patagoniche, 1957-58
i150.

Spedizione Mares-G.R.S.T.S. in Kenya e Tanzania, 1968.
i068.

Spedizione Scientifica Italiana nel Himàlaia, Caracorùm e Turchestàn cinese, 1913-14
s396.

Spedizioni G.M.
s348-349.

Speer, Stanhope Templeman
e196.1; o065.

Speke, John Hanning
h145.

Spelterini, Eduard
f006.

Spéléo-Club de Paris
e001.

Spencer, Sydney
c279; m460; p073.

Spencer Chapman, Frederick. **See** *Chapman, Frederick Spencer.*

Spender, Harold
e057; i080.

Spescha, Placidus A.
p055.

Spezia, Giorgio
p284.

Spiehler, Anton
a154; l056.

Spillmann, Charles
g066.

Spindler, Robert
a186.

Stefansson, Evelyn
h071.

Stefansson, Vilhjálmur
s385; u039.

Stefenelli, Fausto
g062.

Steger, Friedrich
b053.

Steidle, Robert
a207.

Stein, *Sir* Marc Aurel
m443; o041.

Steinauer, Ludwig
w060.

Steinberger, Stephan
l055.

Steiner, André
g258.

Steiner, Johann Casper
g049.

Steinheil, Oskar
s544.

Steinitzer, Alfred
a420; a421; d032.

Steinitzer, Wilhelm
j021.

Steinkötter, Heinz
g215.

Steinmüller, Johann Rudolf
b121; n079.

Steinwachs, Hans
b154.

Stenico, Scipio
s272.

Stennett Amery, Leopold. *See Amery, Leopold Stennett.*

Stephen, *Sir* Leslie
a449-449.1; b188; m166; p184-187; s444; s496; u060.

Stephens, George
m149.

Stephens, John L.
i098-100.

Stephenson, George Skelton
r116.

Stephenson, K.
z023.

Stettler, Michael
a534.

Steuart Mackenzie, Sir George. *See Mackenzie, Sir George Steuart.*

Stevens, Ernest H.
a445; e248.

Stevenson, Seth William
t134.

Stewart, Alexander
c348.

Stewart, Balfour
u038.

Stewart, R.N.
r204.

Stewarton
p141.

Stiassny, Robert
z034.

Stick, Allen
a695.

Stieler, Karl
b058; i156.

Stifter, Herbert
v209.

Stillingfleet, Benjamin
a060; l177.

Stockman Tarr, Ralph. *See Tarr, Ralph Stockman.*

Stoesser, Walter
f008.

Stolberg, Friedrich Leopold zu, *Graf*
t241.

Stolp, Gertrude Nobile. *See Nobile Stolp, Gertrude.*

Stone, S.J.
i061.

Storr, G.K. Ch.
a212.

Stowe, Harriet Beecher
s492-493.

Strabo
s295.

Straka, B.
h091.

*Stranz, Herbert Schroder. **See** Schroder-Stranz, Herbert.*

Strauss, Wilhelm
r163; s218.

Strickland, F. de Beauchamp
s368.

Strid, Arne
w092.

Strigini, Pietro
p155.

Strindberg, Nils
a511.

Strobele, Giovanni
i153; v138.

Strohmeier, Peter
k027.

Strutt, Edward Lisle
a447.

Strutt, Elizabeth
d197.

Strutt, *family*
a145.

Strzelecki, *Sir* Paul E.
s224.

*Stuart Houston, C. **See** Houston, C. Stuart.*

Stubbendorff, Knut
s391.

Stuck, Hudson
a701-702; t052-53.

Studer, Bernhard
g054; j044; o081; r082.

Studer, Gottlieb
a097; b051-052; p023; p217; p252; t124; u010-11.

Stüdl, Johann
g050.

Sturm, Günter
e091; s206.

Stutfield, Hugh Edward Millington
c265.

Stutte, Heinz Lothar
m192.

*Styles, Showell. **See also** Carr, Glyn.*

Styles, Showell
m491.

Suchanow, Valentin
t117.

Suffling, Ernst R.
c440.

Sughi, Marisa
q002.

Sugliani, L.B.
g290.

Sulzer, Johann Georg
b047; b118; n052.

Summers, Roger
v089.

Surface, Matthew
p125.

Surtees, R. Lambton
j055.

Süss, Eduard
e077.

Sutermeister, O.
a773.

Sutherland, Halliday
l033.

Sutton, Geoffrey
s268.

Sutton, Shelagh
s412.

Tassulo, Carlo Antonio Pilati di.   See Pilati di Tassulo, Carlo Antonio.

Tastu, Sabine Amable
a248.

Täuber, Carl
a784; b105.

Tauernkraftwerke Aktiengesellschaft. Tauernkraftwerk Glockner-Kaprun
t037.

Taufer, Enrico
c213.

Taugwald, Johann zum
b162.

Taut, Bruno
a301.

Taylor, Joseph
m213.

Taylor, R. Hibbert
p102.

Taylor, Sedley
s443.

Taylor, William C.
s270.

Taylor, William E.
a638.

Tazieff, Haroun
v299.

Tedeschi, Mario
a266.

Tedeschi, Renato
a407.

Tell, Wilhelm
g363; h182; w101-102.

Tella, G. di.   See Di Tella, G.

Telmann, Konrad
u040.

Temple, Philip
m035; w125.

Temple Hamilton-Temple-Blackwood, Frederick, Marquess of Dufferin and Ava.   See Dufferin and

Ava, Frederick Temple Hamilton-Temple-Blackwood, Marquess of.

Temple Stanyan, Abraham.   See Stanyan, Abraham Temple.

Temple-Leader, John
s223.

Templeman Speer, Stanhope.   See Speer, Stanhope Templeman.

Ten-Hamme, Joë Diericx de
g323.

Tennant, Charles
t151.

Tenzing Norgay
c365; e105; i001.

Terragni de Eccher, Anita
g231.

Terray, Lionel
c361-362; j031; v209.

Terror (Ship)
r254.

Tessadri, Elena
v137.

Tessari, Giorgio
v083.

Testoni, Alfredo
s478.

Tézenas du Montcel, Robert
c095.

Tgetgel, Heinrich
s087.

Th., F.   See Thioly, François.

Tharp, Louise
a093.

Theobald, Gottfried
b271; g040-41; n054-55.

Theuerdank
o055.

Thiébault, Jacques
g313.

Thierry, Maurice de
m294.

Thioly, François
a678; a681; a683-684; c423; d033; e201; p307; v248;
z011.

Thomas, Emmanuel
c066.

Thomas, Eustace
m530.

*Thomas, Herbert Preston. See Preston-Thomas,
Herbert.*

Thomas, P.W.
h240; n118.

Thomas, Tay
f085.
Thomas Cook *Ltd.*
c398; g339; g352; o113.

Thompson, Alfred
l155.

*Thompson, Benjamin, Count Rumford. See
Rumford, Benjamin Thompson, Count.*

Thompson, David
e239; t233.

Thompson, Raymond
w100.

Thomsen, Helge Abildhauge
p182.

Thomson, A.R.
c277.1; c431.1.

Thomson, James Merriman Archer
c255.1;c278.

Thomson, Thomas
w073.

Thorbeke, Franz
a193.

Thoreau, Henry David
i081.

Thorington, James Monroe
a433; a486; c232; f026; f046; g111; h077;m271;
m497; m502; o055; o070; p329; s509; w080-81;
w113.

Thornhill, Henry B.
r242.

Thornton, Cyril
r010.

Thornton, T.C.
w122.

Thornton Cook, Elsie. See Cook, Elsie Thornton.

Thoroddsen, Th.
v300.

Thourel, Albin
h133.

Thule Expedition, 5th, 1921-1924
a133; a575; a603; b194; c043; c391; e167; i126-127;
m004; n077; o014; q005; r135; s231; z022-23.

Thurmann, J.
e151.

Ticconi, Mario
i157.

*Tieffenthal, Alt de, baron d'. See Alt de Tieffenthal,
baron d'.*

*Tighe Gregory, Alexander. See Gregory, Alexander
Tighe.*

Tigri, Giuseppe
s169.

Tillier, Jean Baptiste de
h160.

Tilly, Henri de, *comte*
a688; m521.

Tilman, Harold William
a712; c196; m413; n076; s267; t300; w079.

Tindal, Marcus
c173.

Tirindelli, Lionello
g269.

Tissot, Roger
a755; m254.

Titian
c004.

Titta Rosa, G.
s040.

Titus, Silius
k045.

Trier, Hermann
d056.

Trimble Rowe, Peter.   See Rowe, Peter Trimble.

Triner, F.
b156.

Trinity College, Cambridge
c324.

Troillet, Ernest Lovey.   See Lovey-Troillet, Ernest.

Trolle, Alf
u024.

Trollope, Anthony
s012; t198.

Trombe, Félix
e020.

Trompeo, Pietro Paolo
p006.

Trousset, J.
v237.

Trower, Henry
j069.

Troye, J.
s200.

Troyon, Frédéric
h003.

Tschabuschnigg, Adolf Ignaz von
b252.

Tscharner, Hans Fritz von
a769.

Tscharner, Johann Baptist von
b113.

Tscharner, J.K. von
k025.

Tscharner, K.L.
r082.

Tscharner, Peter Conradin von
k026; w038.

Tscharner, Vincent Bernhard von
a185; d145; d147.

Tschudi, Aegidius
d041.

Tschudi, Friedrich von
a222; m242; s243.

Tschudi, Iwan von
g159; t289.

Tschudi, Johann Heinrich
b122.

Tschudi, J.J. von
r074.

Tschudi, P.
c291.
Tuckett, Elizabeth
b027; h248-249; p143; z017.

Tuckett, Francis Fox
f111-112; h186; n101; p166.

Tudsbery, M.T.
s138.

Tupper, Martin
p056.

Turletti, Vittorio
a747.

Turner, Joseph Mallord William
t290.

Turner, Samuel
m524.

Turri, Eugenio
m366.

Tuscany, *Grand Duchy of*
r060.

Tutton, Alfred Edwin Howard
h079.

Tyler, J.E.
a348.

Tyler Headley, Joel.   See Headley, Joel Tyler.

Tyndale, Henry Edmund Guise
a088; a350; m445; n018; s133.

Tyndall, John
g093-96; g103; h045; h235-238; j030; l146; m475;
m508; n102; n186; o056; p280; p291-292; r120-121;
t308; v004.

Tyndall, Louisa Charlotte
h238.

Tyrrell, J.B.
n160.

Tyson, George Emory
g098.

U., A.
o127.

U.I.A.A. **See** *Union internationale des associations d'alpinisme.*
U.S. Commission of Fish and Fisheries
i119.

U.S. Congress. House of Representatives. Committee on Merchant Marine and Fisheries
i133.

U.S. Department of Agriculture Forest Service
a818.

U.S. Department of the Interior
a126.

U.S. Department of the Treasury
l086; r141.

U.S. Geological Survey
t296.

U.S. National Park Service
m418.

U.S. Naval Support Force, Antarctica. Public Information Office
c203.

U.S. Navy Department
p285.

U.S. State Department
r137.

Ubiergo, Jean
m357.

Uferschützverband, Thuner- und Brienzersee
j013.

Ufficio Nazionale Svizzero del Turismo. **See** *Schweizerische Verkehrszentrale.*

Ufficio Nazionale del Turismo Indiano, Milan
l007.

Ufficio Provinciale per il Turismo di Bolzano. **See** *Ente Provinciale per il Turismo, Bolzano.*
p092.

Ujfalvy, Károly Jenö
a778.

Uibrig, Holm
f029.

Ullman, James Ramsey
a489; g145; h084; k051; w090.

Ullmann, S.O.A.
m166.

Ullrich, Titus
r087.

Ulrich, J.H.F.
u002.

Ulrich, Martin
g124.

Ulrich, Melchior
b051; b052; g019; s159; v185.

Ulrich, Rolf
g055.

Umlauft, Friedrich
a184; a429.

Underhill, Miriam
g078.

Undrell, J.
a045; a046.

Unicorn (Ship)
l042.

Union internationale des associations d'alpinisme
d070; r061.

Union internationale des associations d'alpinisme. Assemblée générale
d070.

Union touristique 'Les Amis de la nature'
a382.

United Kingdom. **See** *Great Britain.*

Università degli Studi di Bologna. Facoltà di Lettere e Filosofia
p035.

Università di Padova. Facoltà di Lettere e Filosofia
a288;c046.

Università di Roma. Istituto di Geografia
v014.

Università Popolare di Venezia
a399.

Université de Toulouse
o017.

University College, London
c176.
University College of North Wales Mountaineering Club
j039.

University of Cambridge Mountaineering Club
c018; c019; c020.

University of Edinburgh
u036.

University of Edinburgh. Department of the Practice of Medicine
l087.

University of Edinburgh Expedition to Arctic Norway, 1953
u036.

University of Glasgow
g100; i115.

University of Groningen. Arctic Centre
p287.

University of Oxford
l059; v018.

University of Oxford Mountaineering Club
o129.

Unterbarmer Alpen-Club
w020.

Unwin, David J.
m453.

Uriarte, Felipe
v106.

USSR/USA Bering Sea Experiment
u069.

Ursella, Angelo
m345.

Urville, Jules Dumont d'
n241.

Ussel, Jean d'
e206.

Usteri, John Martin
l195.

V.C.C. *See Victoria Climbing Club.*

Vaccari, Lino
a028.
Vaccarone, Luigi
b178; g267; i111; p282; v153.

Vacchelli, S.
s362.

Vacchino, Rosella
i137.

Vagand, Jo
j025.

Vailati, Dante
s351.

Vaillant, Pierre
p267.

Valbusa, Ubaldo
p276; v123.

Valcanover, Adolfo
g247.

Valentine-Richards, Alfred Valentine
c103.3.

Valentini, Gianfranco
f084.

Valenza, Gianni
r231.

Valerio, B. Galli. *See Galli-Valerio, B.*

Valéry, Paul
i048.

Valin, William B. van. See Van Valin, William B.

Vallepiana, Ugo di. See Di Vallepiana, Ugo.

Vallino, Domenico
m384-385.

Vallino, Filippo
s477.

Vallot. See also Series Index (entries starting Guide Vallot).

Vial, A.E. Lockington
a324.

Vialls, Mary Alice
c261; f127.

Vianelli, Athos
i181.

Viazzi, Luciano
o089; v019.

Victor, Paul Emile
g080; p057.

Victor Emmanuel II, *King of Italy*
v148.

Victor Emmanuel II, King of Sardinia. *See Victor Emmanuel II, King of Italy.*

Victoria Climbing Club
w119.

Viel, Emilio García. *See García Viel, Emilio.*

Vierthaler, Franz Michael
r070.

Vigna, N.
i093-94.

Villani, Ariberto
g284.

Villari, Linda
a711; c418; h069.

Villars, Dominique
h131.

Vines, Stuart
h093.

Viollet-le-Duc, Eugène
m082;m257.

Viriglio, Attilio
a002; j022; m516; p053; t025.

Vischi, Antonino
o036-37.

Visentini, Luca
d191; d193; g207; g214; s031.

Visser, Philips Christiaan
a494; d199; n001; o073.

Visser-Hooft, Jenny
a494.

Vit, Vincenzo de. *See De-Vit, Vincenzo.*

Vittorj, Carlo Landi. *See Landi-Vittorj, Carlo.*

Vittoz, Ed.
m183.

Vittoz, Pierre
r217.

Vitu, Auguste
g331.

Vogel, J.
s064.

Vogt, Arthur
e225.

Vogt, Carl
a097; b129.

Voiart, Elise
r214.

Volck, B.J.G.
n064.

Volmar, J.
r166.

Volpe, Riccardo
v035.

Volta, Alessandro
a149.

Vouga, Albert
a222.

Vuarnet, Jean
s112.

Vulliet, Charles Cornaz. *See Cornaz-Vulliet, Charles.*

Vulliez, Hyacinthe
m303.2.

W., C.
c236.

W., D. *See Wilson, Daniel.*

W., G.B.
l063.

W., H.C. **See** *Ward, H.C.*

W., J. **See** *Waller, James.*

W., K.M.
w078.

W., S. v.
s373.

Wäber, Adolf
d101; e110; f157; u011; z030; z035.

Waddell, L. Austine
a492; a493; l137.

Wager, L.R.
c018.

Wagner. **See** *Series Index (Wagner's Alpine Spezialführer).*

Wagner, Johann Jacob
h151; m181.

Wagner, Richard
r170.

Wagnon, Auguste
e203; g307.

Wahlenberg, Göran
r157.

Wahnschaffe, Felix
e041.

Wakefield, Arthur W.
a663.

Wakefield, Gilbert
p190.

Wakefield, Priscilla
j100.

Wakeham, William
r129.

Walcher, Joseph
n003.

Walcher, Samuel
t033.

Walcheren-Wien, S.
b088.

Waldburger, U.
r058.

Waldensian Church
h158; h180; i146; n039-42; p272; w006.

Waldie, Jane
s239.

Walker, *Colonel*
b022.

Walker, *Miss*
t298.

Walker, Donald
b241.

Walker, James Hubert
w011.

Walker, Mary Adelaide
u046.

Wall, Daniel
t193.

Wall, David
r239.

Wallace, James
a061.

Wallau, Heinrich
s058.

Waller, James
e191; h083.

Wallis, Eliot
o129.

Wallroth, F.A.
a330.

Walser, Gabriel
k073.

Walsh, Théobald, *comte*
n208; v246-247.

Walter, Hans
b061.

Walters
c113.

Waltershausen, Wolfgang Sartorius von. **See** *Sartorius von Waltershausen, Wolfgang.*

Walthard, Rod.
n248.

Walton, Elijah
f080; p068; v174-175.

Walton, W. Kevin
t307.

Walton, W.L.
t077.

Wanderer (Ship)
w021.

Wang, Fu-quan
w133.

Wanner, Martin
g053; g057.

Warburton, R.E. Egerton. *See Egerton-Warburton, R.E.*

Warburton Moore, Adolphus. *See Moore, Adolphus Warburton.*

Ward, C.S.
i140.

Ward, F. Kingdon. *See Kingdon-Ward, Francis.*

Ward, H.C.
w093.

Ward, R. Ogier
c306.

Ward, Lock, *& Co.*
g347.

Wardman, George
t273.

Warens, Louise de
v228.

Waring, Samuel Miller
t191.

Warren, C.B.M.
u065.

Wartegg, Ernst von Hesse. *See Hesse-Wartegg, Ernst von.*

Warth, Dietlinde
m019.

Warth, Hermann
m019.

Warwick Cole, Mrs Henry. *See Cole, Mrs Henry Warwick.*

Washburn, Bradford
m417; t157.

Watkins, Gino
g068.

Watkins, Pennoyre
t242.

Watkins, Thomas
t242.

Watson, G.C.
h130.

Watson, *Sir* Norman
r244.

Watson, W.G.
l091.

Watts, Alaric A.
l178.

Watts, William Lord
s264.

Watts de Peyster, J. *See De Peyster, J. Watts.*

Wayfarers' Club
b267; w053.

Wead, Frank
g004.

Webb, Clint
f133.

Weber, Franz S.
l047.

Weber, J.C.
a201-202.

Weber, Julius
k059.

Weber, P.X.
p158.

Wedderburn, Ernest Alexander Maclagan
m017.

Weddik, Bartholomaeus T. Lublink
a194.

Weeks, Edwin Lord
m429; s286-287.

Wegener, K.
e220.

Wehrli, Leo
g045.

Weibel-Altmeyer, Heinz
a205.

Weigl, Joseph
h044.

Weilenmann, Johann Jacob
a786-787; b051-52.

Weineck, Johann Guler von. See Guler von Weineck, Johann.

Weir, Thomas
c024; h094; u019.

Weiss, Jurg
m519.

Weitzenbock, Richard
f139.

Weld, Charles Richard
a813; s142.

Welden, Ludwig von, *Freiherr*
m387.

Weller, Siegfried
n213.

Wellesley, Arthur, Duke of Wellington. See Wellington, Arthur Wellesley, Duke of.

Wellington, Arthur Wellesley, *Duke of*
e064.

Welponer, P. Victor
d185.

Wels, Horst
b206.

Welsh Mountaineering Club
c382.

Welzenbach, Willo
b087; d056; w105.

Wentworth, W.C.
b173.

Wepf, Johannes
a199.

Wernerian Natural History Society
a473.

West, Thomas
g351.

West Col Productions, *associates of*
d064.

Westmacott, M.H.
e230.

Weston, Stephen
s044.

Weston, Walter
m467.

Wet, C.R. de
s432.

Wethered, F.T.
a367.

Wetterfors, Paul
f118.

Wetzel, Elena
w016.

Wey, Francis
h048.

Wey, Max Sigmund
e079.

Whalley, George
d046.

Whalley, Thomas Sedgwick
m258.

Wheeler, Arthur Oliver
s166.

Wherry, George
a342; n182.

Whistler, Hugh
i090.

Whitaker, John
c425.

White, George Francis
v162-163.

White, John Claude
s214.

White, T.H.
f109.

White, T. Pilkington
r236.

White, Walter
h214; o044; t107.

White Pass and Yukon Railway
o068.

Whitehouse, Ian
c060.

Whitman, Walt
i081.

Whitney, Ernest
l072.

Whymper, Edward
a064; a716; b053; b161-162; c147-163;e033; e119;
e221; e319; h244; j029; l085; m032; m488; n205;
p253; s037; s040; s127-134; s225; t202; t204-205.1;
t206; t303; v061-75; z026.

Whymper, Frederick
h073; t187-188.

Whyte, Joh.
g162.

Wichmann, Franz
a425.

Wickersham, James
b149.

Wickham, Henry L.
d158-159.

Wickham, Hill D.
h158.

Widmann, Joseph Viktor
s345.

Widmer, Joh.
e062; v057.

Wieland, *Oberst*
m130.

Wien, Karl
b075.

Wien, S. Walcheren. **See** *Walcheren-Wien, S.*

Wilberforce, Edward
s273.

Wilbraham, Edward Bootle
n028-29.

Wilcox, Walter Dwight
c023.

Wild, Roland
a615.

Wilde, *Mrs* W.R.
g084.

Wilford Hall, A. **See** *Hall, A. Wilford.*

Wilhelmi, Karl
i143.

Wilkerson, James A.
m123-124.

Wilkes, Benjamin
e065.

Wilkes, Charles
t106.

Wilkes Expedition
t106.

Wilkey, Edward
n188.

Wilkinson, Charles
g024.

Wilkinson, Spenser
h038.

Wilkinson, Thomas
t162.

Wilkinson, Thomas Read
h211.

Willard, Berton C.
r276.

Willem Barents (Ship)
v122.

Willes Johnson, John. **See** *Johnson, John Willes.*

Williams, Charles
a450.

Williams, Helen Maria
n236; t141.

Williams, John Harvey
y008.

Williams, William
m537.

Williams, William Matthieu
t084-85.

Williams Porter, Russell.   See Porter, Russell Williams.

Willien, Renato
m010; n270.

Willink, Henry George
a362.

Willoughby, Barrett
a130.

Wills, *Sir* Alfred
a709; e005-6; t065; w024-26.

Willy, Anton
s258.

Willy-Merkl-Gedächtnisexpedition, 1953
i034.

Wilson, Andrew
a035.

Wilson, Annie
l049.

Wilson, Claude
c268; c305; c400; e084; m457-459.

Wilson, Daniel
l096.

Wilson, Edward Livingstone
m429.

Wilson, Henry Schütz
a302-303; a717; e040; e195; s563.

Wilson, Horace Hayman
t231.

Wilson, J.D.B.
s320.

Wilson, Joseph
h174.

Wilson, R.C.
n015.

Wilson, Riley
m159.

Wilson, T.
t014.

Wilson, W. Rae
n179.

Wilson, Woodrow
r008.

Wilton, Andrew
t290.

Windham, William
a060; p258; w103-104.

Winkelried, Arnold von
h182.

Winkler, Georg
e047.

Winkler, Jürgen
i035.

Winnett, Thomas
m515.

Winter Raffles, W.   See Raffles, W. Winter.

Winterbottom, J.M.
m062.

Winterhalter, Kaspar
l129.

Winther, Chr.
m006.

Winthrop Young, Geoffrey.   See Young, Geoffrey Winthrop.

Wistaz, A.
d221.

Withers, Percy
f120.

Witkamp, P.H.
a194.

Witmer, Urs
m194.

Witte, Karl
a379.

Wocher, Marquard
l195.

Wödl, Hans
h205.

Woerl, Leo
s086.

Wohnlich, A.
d215.

Wolf, Ferdinand Otto
m065; v077.

Wolff, Henry W.
c414.

Wolff, Karl Felix
a522.

Wolforth, John
n161.

Wolley, Sir Clive Phillipps.   See Phillipps-Wolley, Sir Clive.

Wood, Alexander
j086.

Wood, James
e043.

Wood, John
j086; p101.

Wood Brown, J.   See Brown, J. Wood.

Woodbine Hinchliff, Thomas.   See Hinchliff, Thomas Woodbine.

Woodford, James
v180.

Woodley Mason, Alfred Edward.   See Mason, Alfred Edward Woodley.

Woodman Graham, William.   See Graham, William Woodman.

Wooster, David
a351; a352.

Wordsworth, William
d095.

Workman, Fanny Bullock
c363; i092; p064; t305; w124.1.

Workman, William Hunter
f027; i092; p064; t305; w124.1.

World Book Encyclopaedia
h086.

Worster, W.
i016.

Wortley Montagu, *Lady* Mary
l108.

Wrangell, Ferdinand Petrovich
n131.

Wright, Jeremiah Ernest Benjamin
c262.

Wulff, Thorild
t070.

Wundt, Theodor
c120; i012; m114; w042; z015.

Wurmbrand, Irmgard
o087.

Wyatt, Colin
c015.

Wyher, Ludwig Pfyffer von.   See Pfyffer von Wyher, Ludwig.

Wylie, James A.
w027.

Wylie Lloyd, Robert.   See Lloyd, Robert Wylie.

Wynne Jones, E.D.   See Jones, E.D. Wynne.

Wyss, Johann David
r214.

Wyss, Johann Rudolf
i013; r081; s119; t061; v225.

Wyss, Max Albert
m013; m016.

Wyss, Rudolf
a510; g183.1-2.

Wyss-Dunant, Edouard
a754.

Wyttenbach, Jacob Samuel
b126; b138; d147; m057.

Wyttenbach, T.S.
h163.

Wyveleslie Abney, Sir William de.   See Abney, Sir William de Wyveleslie.

Xidias, Spiro dalla Porta.   See Dalla Porta Xidias, Spiro.

Yakushi, Yoshimi
c079-080; h109.

Yamada, Keiichi
h109.

Yates, *Mrs* Ashton
l109; s562.

Yates, Edmund
m251.

Yates Brown, Frederick Augustus.   See Brown, Frederick Augustus Yates.

Yeld, George
c088; m498; s135.

Yeo, I. Burney
n189.

Yokohama Literary Society
j020.

Yonge, Charlotte M.
k042; y013.

Yorkshire Ramblers' Club
m489; y007.

Yosy, Ann
s540; t017.

Young, Delbert A.
l042.

Young, Geoffrey Winthrop
e261; i115; m135; m161; m186; m431-432; m505; n253; o046-49; s065; s225; s268; w015; w106.

Young, Jack Theodore
m163-164.

Young, James Reid
g046.

Young, Peter
h116.

Young Buchanan, John.   See Buchanan, John Young.

Younghusband, *Sir* Francis
e086-87; e184; h052-53; h099; i107; p084.

Yule, Henry
j086.

Yung, Emile
z009.

Zahn, Ernst
a138.

Zaltroni, Cesco
t248.

Zampedri, L.
c188.

Zandonella, Beppe
m345.

Zandonella, Italo
a454; c218; m345.

Zanelli, C.F.
s362.

Zangheri, P.
f070.

Zangrandi, Giovanna
l080.

Zanolli, Renato
r191-192.

Zanone, M.
p096.

Zanotto, André
a583; h134.

Zapparoli, Ettore
s217.

Zappelli, Cosimo
a470; a471; g227.

Zaslow, Morris
o075.

Zavatti, Silvio
i148.

Zawada, Amdrzej
g072.

Zay, Karl
g121.

Zechinelli, Mariuccia
r174.

Zechmann, Heinz
g070.

Zedtwitz, Franz, *Graf*
i031.

Zehender, Marquard
r064.

Zeidler, Paul Gerhard
p206.

Zeller, H.
b052.

Zeller, Willy
r194.

Zentralbibliothek, Zurich
s082.

Zeppezauer, Moriz
a530.

Zermatten, Maurice
m306; s015.

Zettler, Ernst
a155.

Zhang, Rongzu
m421.

Ziak, Karl
b011; m170.

Zieger, Antonio
s395.

Ziegler, Anton
b087.

Zincke, F. Barham
m391;s518.1;w007.1.

Zinderen Bakker, E.M. van
m062.

Zintl, Fritz
s206.

Zolfanelli, Cesare
g234.

Zoppi, Giuseppe
l140; p058; q001.

Zorell, Franz
i041.

Zotto, Giancarlo del.   **See** *Del Zotto, Giancarlo.*

Zovetti, Violante
o087.

Zschokke, Heinrich
d074; r073; s080.

Zsigmondy, Emil
d014; g016; i037.

Zsigmondy, Otto
a498.

Zuccarelli, G.C.
m315.

Züblin, Mathias Jenni.   **See** *Jenni-Züblin, Mathias.*

Züchner, Ernst
w062.

Zuchold, Ernst A.
n170.

Zumaglino, Vittorio
c119.

Zuntz, N.
h207.

Zur-Lauben, *baron de*
m144.

Zurbriggen, Matthias
f127.

Zurcher, Frédéric
a689; a690; a691; g087-88; m425.

Zürcher, Otto
b106.

Züsli, Fridolin
f149.

Zwahlen, Otto
k014.

SERIES INDEX

Actualités scientifiques et industrielles. Expéditions polaires françaises. Missions Paul-Emile Victor.
g080.

Alpenklub-Ausgabe.
h188.

Alpenvereinsführer. Reihe: Nordliche Kalkalpen.
h194.

Alpenvereinsführer. Reihe: Südliche Kalkalpen.
c434; d175; d177.

Alpenvereinsführer. Reihe: Zentralalpen.
a524; o088; o101; s435.

Les Alpes et les hommes.
a387; a424; m356.

Alpes et Midi-ski.
a806.

Le Alpi.
a522; d201; f084; g362; j022; l079; m195; m344; m516; r002; t057; u052; v023; v192.

Le Alpi venete.
b193; p242; t024.

American mountain series.
s212.

Andar per monti.
m063.

Appel des sommets.
a754.

Archaeografia e storia in valle d'Aosta.
v041; v043; v088.

Arctic Institute of North America. Technical papers.
b152; e222.

The Backpacking guide series.
b003.

Ball's Alpine guides.
b106.1-106.2; c103-103.2; e015.1; g350-350.2; g356-356.2; n150.1; p043.1; p088; s3171.1; w072.

Bestimmung der Höhen der bekanntern Berge des Canton Bern.
b137.

Bibliophiles de la montagne.
m126; z004.

Biblioteca alpina.
a406; i132; m358; r174.

Biblioteca della montagna.
c140; d007; e138; r006.

Bibliothèque de l'alpinisme.
a651; v146.

Blackwell's mountaineering library.
a445.

Brescia.
c188.

Canadian Arctic Expedition, 1913–1918. Report.
f065; m106.

Cartes et guides de Corse.
g315.

Cartes et guides de Savoie.
m089-90; m095-96; m102-103.

Cartes et guides du Dauphiné.
m087; m094; m097-99.

Cartes et guides du Dauphiné et de Savoie.
m091-92.

Les cent plus belles courses et randonnées.
a239; m078; p243; p333.

Centro Studi Biellesi. Pubblicazioni.
a172.

Climbers' Club guides to Wales.
g117-118.

Climbers' guides to the English Lake District.
c277.1; c280.1; c431.1; d168.1; p163.

Climbing guides to the English Lake District.
d203; e019; g164; p162; s035.

Club Alpino Italiano. Sezione Universitaria. Manuali.
See Manuali SUCAI.

Club Alpino Italiano. Stazione Universitaria. Manualetti. *See Manuali SUCAI.*

*Clubführer des Schweizer Alpen-Club. **See also** Guide del Club Alpino Svizzero; Guides du Club Alpin Suisse.*
f143.

Clubführer durch die Bündner Alpen.
b114.

Clubführer durch die Walliseralpen.
v199; v201.

Collana di piccole guide locali dell'Alto Adige.
m176.

Collana di studi alpini.
b218.

Collection alpine.
a480; m240; p050.

Conosci l'Italia.
a656-661; f023; f069; f083; i149; i151; p004.

Conway and Coolidge's climbers' guides.
a082; a447; b107-108; c104-105; c126; c242-243; l084; m498; r019.

Da rifugio a rifugio.
d195.

Danmark-ekspeditionen til Grønlands nordøstkyst 1906–1908.
s511.

Die deutschen Bergbücher.
m172.

Dolomiten-Kletterführer.
b206; c222; n133; r241; s168.

Dolomiti di Fassa.
c089.

Dolomiti orientali.
c221.

Eclogae geologicae helveticae.
b116; r161.

Escursioni e gite nelle Alpi Giulie orientali, Slovenia, Jugoslavia.
t272.

Gaston's Alpine books.
c163.

Gemälde der Schweiz.
k026-28.

Geographica bernensia.
m194.

Gmundner Buchreihe.
w034.

Le grandi montagne.
h101; m369.

Les Grisons.
e062; r166; v057.

Grosse Bergsteiger.
a787; v202.

Guida alpina delle Dolomiti.
r191-192.

Guida alpinistica.
s039.

Guida d'Italia del Touring Club Italiano.
t257.

Guida dei monti d'Italia.
a267; a269-270; a278; a281-283; a289; a292; a294; d188; d196; g133; g136-137; m370; p136; p263; r054; r056-57; s059.

Guida delle valli di Susa.
o105.

Guida sci alpinistica.
c447.

Guide alpin de la montagne marocaine.
m086.

*Guide del Club Alpino Svizzero. **See also** Clubführer des Schweizer Alpen-Club; Guides du Club Alpin Suisse.*
a293.

Guide dell'Appennino settentrionale.
g250; g254-256.

Guide des Alpes valaisannes.
d214-216.

Guide I.G.C.
p029; v082.

Guide Paschetta des Alpes-Maritimes.
a234; h049; n120.

Guide Paschetta des Alpes-Maritimes. Alpinisme.
m077.

Guide Paschetta des Alpes-Maritimes. 2: Randonnées et alpinisme.
m184-185; s013; v029.

Guide Paschetta des Alpes-Maritimes. 2: Randonnées et ascensions. Circuits automobiles.
s014.

Guide Paschetta des Alpes-Maritimes. 3: Nice, Riviera, Côte d'Azur.
c327.

Guide skieur.
a806.

Guide Vallot. La chaîne du Mont Blanc.
a106-106.1; a114-115.2; g150.1;m272-275.

Guide Vallot. Description de la haute montagne dans le massif du Mont-Blanc.
a112-113; c127; g198-201.

Guide Vallot. Description de la moyenne montagne dans le massif du Mont-Blanc.
c167.

Guide Vallot. Tourisme en montagne dans le massif du Mont-Blanc.
c169.

Guides du Caroux.
r016.

*Guides du Club Alpin Suisse. **See also** Clubführer des Schweizer Alpen-Club; Guide del Club Alpino Svizzero.*
p245.

Harriman Alaska series.
m245.

Hochgebirgsführer durch die Berner Alpen.
b155.1-156; d132.1; g019.1; g183.1-183.2; p107-107.1.

Hudson's Bay Record Society. Publications.
c404.

Idee di alpinismo.
l089.

Itinera montium.
m394.

Itinerari alpini.
a268; a454-455; a458-459; a461-463; a466; a470-472; a476; a512-515; a517-519;c090; c205; c218; c223; d007;d008.1; e133-137; e139-140; g180; g205-206; g216; h208; i184; l044; m401; p008-9; p093; p154;

s038; s104-106; s108-109; v020; v027; v030;v030.1; v045; v048; v051; v084; v151; v154; v176; z021.

Jahresgabe der Gesellschaft alpiner Bücherfreunde.
b113; d013; g052.

Kleine Dolomiten-Wanderführer.
f142.

Lehrschriften für die Jugendgruppen und Jungmannschaften des O.A.V.
a323.

Lumière de l'Arctique.
r020.

Manuali SUCAI.
a394;m037;p091;r181; s099.

Meddelelser om Grønland. Bioscience.
a159; a499; a545-547; b164-165; i019; l141; m182; o015; o086; p132; p182; p218; v093; v109.

Meddelelser om Grønland. Geoscience.
d131; g003; g047; g086; h216-217; k047; l043; m207; n020.1;p114; p117; p246; s577.

Meddelelser om Grønland. Man & society.
a027; c346; c356; d156; h221; k005; l159; m193; s510.

Minima turistica Piemonte: il Novarese, lago d'Orta.
o040.

Monographien aus den Schweizeralpen. Beilage zum Jahrbuch des S.A.C.
s306.

Montagna.
d149; f087; f154; g064; g155-156; m320; n127; o087; p058; q001; q003; s043; s182; v130.

Montagne (French series).
a385; a749; a821; c115; d067; e056; e119; g009; h045; k031; m186;m300; m519; n253; r156.

Montagne (Italian series).
c206; g065; g132; g144; m373; q008; t170.

Montagne celebri.
d190; s278; v022.

Les montagnes de France.
j099; v211.

Montes.
a137.

Montes mundi.
g195.

Mountain guides to the Pyrenees.
p340.

Murray's handbook.
h009-022.

New Alpine library.
m445; m505; p231.

Per l'alpinismo.
v008.

La piccozza e la penna.
a002; a402; a521; d010; f042; m202; s037; t046.

Il Piemonte e le sue valli.
g272-274.

Quaderni alpini.
m322.

Quaderni della Società Valsesiana di Cultura.
n068.

Quaderni di cultura alpina.
c053; g154; i101; m012.

Raccolta di studi storici sulla Valtellina.
b191; c056; p281; s399.

Le regioni d'Italia.
e046; f123; l190; t127; v112.

*Rock-climbing guides to the English Lake District. **See** Climbing guides to the English Lake District.*

Schweizerführer.
g159.

Sci alpinismo.
c435.

Sci Club Milano. Guide sciistiche.
g213.

Scottish Mountaineering Club guide.
b045; g046; i144-145; r220; s320.

Sempervivum.
a009; a111; a391; a539-540; a753; a820; c096; c124; c183; c335; c369; c383; d132; d217; e168; g018; g067; m020; m122; m125; m349; p271; r233; s157; s578; v092.

Sierra Club exhibit format series.
g083.

Sierra Club totebooks.
c235; f088; h258.

Storia della Valtellina e del contado di Chiavenna.
v079.

Studi sul 'Maso Chiuso' alto-atesino.
m398.

La Suisse romande en zig-zag.
e053.

Swiss scenes.
a662; c301; i129; k072; l027; l200; m514; t092; u066; w003.

Thule expedition, 5th, 1921–1924. Report.
a132-133; a575; a603; b194; c043; c391; e167; i016; i126-127; m004; n077; o014; q005; r135; s231; z022-23.

Travaux scientifiques du Spéléo-club de Paris, C.A.F.
e001.

L'uomo e le Dolomiti.
a465.

V.C.C. rock climbing guides.
w119

Valais and Chamounix.
m065; v077.

Valli dell'Alto Vicentino.
a099.

La vie en montagne.
a427; b019; c185; c210.

Voci dai monti.
a041; a414-415; c002; c039; d152; d223; e037; f082; f135; g151; m317; m348; r176; s309; s422; t023; t166; t169; t254.

La vostra via sportiva.
b021; p269; q002; s102-103; s112; s177; t291.

Wagner's Alpine Spezialführer.
a641.

Wander- und Kletterführer.
m192.

West Col Alpine guides.
d064.

Wissenschaftliche Ergänzungshefte zur Zeitschrift des D. und O. Alpenvereins.
g125.

INDEX OF MISCELLANEOUS ITEMS

These collections, and in particular the Graham Brown collection, contain a number of items which may be of interest to readers, but are not easy to locate in the present Catalogue. These include press cuttings on various aspects of alpinism; photographs (prints, negatives and slides), engravings, and other pictorial items; and ephemera, such as certificates, notices of club meetings, etc., which have been classed under the heading **Miscellaneous**. In almost all cases the relevant entry in the Library's General Catalogue consists of a description in square brackets, which has been included in its correct alphabetical position in the main sequence of this catalogue; but, since these are invented titles and may therefore be difficult to find, a short finding list of them has been compiled, under the headings **Press cuttings**, **Photographs and illustrative material**, and **Miscellaneous**.

Press cuttings
a068; a664–666; c450; e242–248; e250–329; m261; n115–118; n183; p266.

Photographs and illustrative material
a140–148; a343; c083; d102; f040; f104; g219; i106; l050; p015; p021; p118-124; s046; s056–56.1; s388; t073; t077-078; t306; v292–298; w050; w124.1.

Miscellaneous
a098; a344; a473; b185; b189; c112–113; c320; f032; l102; m174; m215; n220; n222–224; n229–231; p013; p123–123.1; r123.1; r140; r157; r253; r263; s136; t302-303; v198.